WITHDRAWN

A HANDBOOK
OF
HUMAN SERVICE
ORGANIZATIONS

by

Harold W. Demone, Jr., Ph.D.

Dwight Harshbarger, Ph.D.

Behavioral Publications
New York
1974

Library of Congress Catalog Number 73–12280
ISBN: 0-87705-120-8
Copyright © 1974 by Behavioral Publications

BEHAVIORAL PUBLICATIONS
72 Fifth Ave.
New York, New York 10011

Printed in the United States of America

987654   123456789

Library of Congress Cataloging in Publication Data

Demone, Harold W   comp.
    A handbook of human service organizations.

    1. Social service—Addresses, essays lectures.
2. Social work administration—Addresses, essays, lectures.
I. Harshbarger, Dwight, joint comp.
II. Title
HV37.D43   361   73–12280

To Peg and Emily

CONTENTS

PART III. SOME CENTRAL CONCERNS OF HUMAN SERVICE ORGANIZATIONS

PART IV. ROLES AND ROLE PROBLEMS

PART VII. PERSPECTIVES FOR THE FUTURE

A. FUTURISM

B. INNOVATION

C. AN EXAMPLE IN FUTURE PLANNING: HEALTH

Preface

Do-gooding is a major growth industry. From simple organizations supported principally by voluntary sources, the human services have become big business; large, complex, and diverse. In order, recreation is the largest, education second, defense is the third, and health, the fourth. And health is now the fastest growing of the nation's major economic forces. Collectively, the human services constitute millions of consumers and employees, and billions of dollars.

Our organizational frame for this volume is the human services, which we view as a broad spectrum encompassing the entire health, welfare, recreation, and rehabilitation field. If pressed we would also include education as well, for it too deals with the problems arising from being human. Moreover, we are inclined to question the artificiality of the boundaries that have been placed between the various human-serving sub-systems. In the same vein, we would challenge the continuing functional value of boundaries which separate professions and professionals.

If we cast our conceptual net to begin with the client or patient —the consumer of services—and follow him through the maze of service networks, it becomes clear that the caregiving system is rarely designed for his benefit. In addition, the roles played and problems encountered are surprisingly similar for both consumer and provider, independent of the form of the delivery system. Thus, the readings in this handbook are generally applicable to persons in such diverse, but similar, roles as school superintendent, hospital administrator, social agency executive, community mental health planner, or city recreation director. If the commonality of their problems can be realized, then the artificiality of their boundaries can be identified.

Written for the administrator, embryonic or experienced, these readings have been selected from a wide range of fields for their application to human service organizations, both governmental and voluntary. Most of the readings have been tested at the Laboratory of Community Psychiatry, Dept. of Psychiatry, Harvard Medical

School, in seminars made up of multi-disciplinary groups of post-graduate Fellows. In this teaching situation the readings have been used as the basis for class discussions. They could also be used to accompany various texts on administration or complex organizations.

This set of readings was developed because the typical text in business and public administration seldom focuses on the human services, an area which we believe has its own distinct problems. Consequently, the readings are aimed at problems which business-management texts do not ordinarily consider.

The focus is not on human relations in management. Our assumption, probably erroneous in some cases, is that administrators in human service organizations are, by definition, concerned about human relations or they would not have elected to pursue careers in the fields of human service.

Instead we have chosen the perspective of organizations attempting to remain viable and constructive in an increasingly complex, turbulent, technological, and depersonalized society. The readings, and our discussions which precede them, deal with the many issues of rapid social change, the environmental forces interacting with human service organizations, roles and role problems, management and planning tactics and strategies, administrative outcomes, and the future of human service organizations. We assume that in such a complex environment, managerial functions assume progressively important roles in ensuring the delivery of effective human services.

Although not all management goals are discussed or even identified, an effort is made to be reasonably inclusive. For example, there is some discussion regarding goal setting and goal changes, comprehensiveness, continuity of care, program quality and quantity, flexibility (the capacity to experiment with alternative solutions), systems analysis, planning, decision-making, efficiency (maximum utilization of resources), innovation, and prevention.

We believe that administrators can and must be developed, and that management tools and generic principles can be identified and transmitted. At the same time variation in administrative style must be acknowledged. Each administrator must develop procedures with which he is comfortable, and which he can accommodate to a democratic ethos and still achieve organizational goals. No blueprint is available, but guidelines and principles can be developed and applied.

In the article which follows we suggest that a variety of management tools are available to the human service organization manager. For example, we discuss: (1) automated data systems, (2) simulation,

(3) information systems, (4) systems analysis, (5) operational research, (6) program planning budgeting systems, (7) demonstrations, (8) personnel practices, (9) boards and committees, and (10) planning.

The articles in this volume were not chosen to specifically illuminate each of these tools, for texts are readily available to cover all of them. Instead we would remind each human service administrator that he ignores those mundane technologies at his peril. Even if he hires specialists competent in their management it is incumbent on him to understand their general workings, if for no other reason than to protect himself from his own specialists. Most of our readers will know of large-scale organizations essentially controlled by their business managers or limited in flexibility by their personnel directors. Sufficient knowledge to be able to ask intelligent questions is the required minimum. Even more important is that all managers and organizations, to be successful, need certain capacities: (1) to collect data about needs and resources, (2) to establish objectives (3) to evaluate the effectiveness of various programs, (4) to promote cooperation and collaboration, (5) to understand the nature of systemic relationships, (6) to have a knowledge of social change tools, (7) to develop a problem-solving orientation, and (8) to maintain an awareness and sensitivity to policy and policy decisions.

Conclusion

The readings in this volume have been chosen for administrators and students of management and intra- and interorganizational relationships in the fields of the human services. Hopefully they will raise significant questions and suggest new directions of thought to the reader. To highlight the significant issues and to bridge the various substantive components, we have accompanied each chapter, section, and article with a brief introductory essay.

Contributors*

Frank Baker, Ph.D.
Head, Program Research Unit, Laboratory of Community Psychiatry and Assistant Professor of Psychology Department of Psychiatry, Harvard Medical School, Boston, Mass.

Robert J. Bazell
The New York Post

Warren G. Bennis, Ph.D.
President, Univ. of Cincinnati, Cincinnati, Ohio

N. H. Berkowitz

Gerald Caplan, M.D., D.P.M.
Professor of Psychiatry; Director, Laboratory of Community Psychiatry, Harvard Medical School, Boston, Mass.

Marion Clawson, Ph.D.
Director of Research in Land Use and Management Resources for the Future

Alan M. Cohen
President of Social Planning Councils of Ontario and Vice-President of the Ontario Welfare Council

William J. Curran, LL.M., S.M. Hyg.
Frances Glessner Lee Professor of Legal Medicine Faculties of Public Health and Medicine Harvard University, Boston, Mass.

Harold W. Demone, Jr., Ph.D.
Executive Director, The United Community Services of Metropolitan Boston; Associate Clinical Professor of Social Welfare, Laboratory of Community Psychiatry, Dept. of Psychiatry Harvard Medical School; Lecturer on Social Medicine, Division of

*Most recent known affiliation.

Psychiatry, Boston University School of Medicine and Boston University Law-Medicine Institute

James P. Dixon, M.D.
President, Antioch College, Yellow Springs, Ohio

Elizabeth Brenner Drew
Washington Editor, The Atlantic Monthly

Leonard J. Duhl, M.D., F.A.P.H.A.
Professor of Urban Planning, Dept. of City and Regional Planning Univ. of California, Berkeley

Ray H. Elling, Ph.D.
Professor of Sociology, Univ. Connecticut Health Center, Univ. of Connecticut

Franklin Fogelson, LL.B., Ph.D.
Director of Planning, Jewish Federation of Metropolitan Chicago

Harvey M. Freed, M.D.
Assistant Director of Education, Illinois State Psychiatric Institute

Melvin A. Glasser, LLD
Director, Social Security Department, United Auto Workers Union; Detroit, Michigan

Dwight Harshbarger, Ph.D.
Associate Professor of Psychology, Dept. of Psychology, West Virginia University

Howard W. Johnson
Chairman of Corporation, Massachusetts Institute of Technology

David Kantor, Ph.D.
Chief Psychologist, Boston State Hospital, Mass. State Dept. of Mental Health, Director of Center for Training in Family Therapy, Director of Institute for Study of Family and Youth

James A. Kent, M.A.
Director, Behavioral Science Section Division of Public Health

and Preventive Medicine Department of Health and Hospitals
Denver, Colorado

M. W. Klein

Irving Kristol
Editor, The Public Interest

Sol Levine, Ph.D.
Professor of Sociology in Community Medicine, Boston University School of Medicine; Executive Officer of University Professor's Program

David F. Long, M.S.W.
United Central Services, Toledo, Ohio

M. F. Malone

Carl Martin
Director, Dane County Social Planning Agency, Madison, Wisconsin

Walter J. McNerney, F.A.P.H.A.
President, Blue Cross Association, Chicago, Illinois

Harold B. Meyers
Fortune Magazine

Robert Morris, D.S.W.
Professor of Social Planning; Director of Levinson Gerontological Policy Institute, Florence Heller Graduate School of Social Welfare Brandeis University, Walham, Mass.

Edward Newman, Ph.D.
Linton, Mields, and Coston, Inc., Washington, D.C.

Edward J. O'Donnell, Ph.D.
Social Science Analyst Division of Intramural Research Social Rehabilitation Service, U.S. Dept. of Health, Education and Welfare

Don K. Price
Dean, John F. Kennedy School of Government, Harvard University

Herbert C. Schulberg, Ph.D.
Associate Executive Director, United Community Services of Metropolitan Boston, Associate Clinical Professor, Laboratory of Community Psychiatry, Harvard Medical School, Boston, Mass.

Alan P. Sheldon, M.B., B. Chir., D.P.M., S.M. Hyg.
Associate Professor of Business Administration, Harvard Business School, Boston, Mass.

C. Harvey Smith, M.P.H.
Director, Health Education Service, Division of Public Health and Preventive Medicine, Department of Health and Hospitals Denver, Colorado

Mayer Spivack, M.C.P.
Principal Associate of Psychiatry, Medical Laboratory of Community Psychiatry, Harvard School, Boston, Mass.

Marilyn M. Sullivan
Research Associate, Health and Welfare Association of Allegheny County, Pa.

Henry Wechsler, Ph.D.
Research Director, The Medical Foundation, Inc. Boston, Massachusetts

Robert S. Weiss, Ph.D.
Associate Professor of Psychology Laboratory of Community Psychiatry, Harvard Medical School, Boston, Mass.

Acknowledgments

Part I

Demone, Harold W., Jr., and Dwight Harshbarger, "Issues in the Management and Planning of Human Service Organizations," original article.

Harshbarger, Dwight, "The Human Service Organization," original article.

Part II

Spivack, Mayer, "Statement on Human Behavior and the Environment to United States Senate Select Committee on Health and Housing" *91st Congress*, Oct. 1, 1970, 1766-1776.

Spivack, Mayer, and Robert S. Weiss, Gerald Caplan, Alan P. Sheldon, and Herbert C. Schulberg, "Mental Health Implications of the Organization of the Large Scale Physical Environment," original article.

Duhl, Leonard J., "Environmental Health: Politics, Planning, and Money," *American Journal of Public Health*, Vol. 58, No. 2, Feb. 1968.

Schulberg, Herbert C., and Harold W. Demone, Jr., "Regional Human Services Delivery Systems," original article.

Meyers, Harold B., "The Medical-Industrial Complex," *Fortune*, Jan. 1970, 90-91, 126-128, 130.

Harshbarger, Dwight, "Turbulence and Resources: The Bases for a Predictive Model of Interorganizational Communication in the Human Services," original article.

Elling, Ray H., "The Shifting Power Structure in Health," *The Milbank Memorial Fund Quarterly, Dimensions and Determinants of Health Policy*, Vol. XLVI, No. 1, Jan. 1968, Part 2.

Demone, Harold W., Jr., and David F. Long, "Information-Referral—The Nucleus of a Human-Needs Program," *Community*, Sept.-Oct. 1969, 9-11.

O'Donnell, Edward J., and Marilyn M. Sullivan, "Service Delivery and Social Action Through the Neighborhood Center: A Review of Research," *Welfare Review*, Nov.-Dec. 1969, 1-12.

Part III

Glasser, Melvin A., "The Approaching Struggle to Provide Adequate Health Care for All Americans," *Social Work*, Vol. 15, No. 4, Oct. 1970, 5-14.

Bazell, Robert J., "Health Care: What the Poor People Didn't Get from Kentucky Project," *Science*, Vol. 172, April 30, 1971, 458-460.

Demone, Harold W., Jr., "Experiments in Referral to Alcoholism Clinics," *Quarterly Journal of Studies on Alcohol*, Vol. 24, No. 3, Sept. 1963, 495-502.

Kantor, David, and Harold W. Demone, Jr., "The Concept of Coordination by a State-Sponsored Alcoholism Program," *Proceedings of the Northeast States Conference on Alcoholism*, New Haven, Conn., May 1959.

Kristol, Irving, "Decentralization for What," *The Public Interest*, Spring, 1968, No. 11.

Part IV

Harshbarger, Dwight, "High Priests of Hospitaldom," *Hospital & Community Psychiatry*, Vol. 21, No. 5, May 1970, 156-159.

Morris, Robert, "Overcoming Cultural and Professional Myopia in Education for Human Service," *Journal of Education for Social Work*, Vol. 6, No. 1, Spring, 1970, 41-51.

Price, Don K., "Purists and Politicians," *Science*, Vol. 163, Jan. 3, 1969, 25-31.

Freed, Harvey M., "The Community Psychiatrist and Political Action," *Archives of General Psychiatry*, Vol. 17, Aug. 1967, 129-134.

Kent, James A., and Harvey Smith, "Involving the Urban Poor in Health Services Through Accommodation—The Employment of Neighborhood Representatives," *American Journal of Public Health*, Vol. 57, No. 6, June 1967, 997-1003.

Part V

Newman, Edward, and Harold W. Demone, Jr., "Policy Paper: A New Look at Public Planning for Human Services," *Journal of Health and Social Behavior*, Vol. 10, No. 2, June 1969, 142-149.

Demone, Harold W., Jr., "The Limits of Rationality in Planning," *Community Mental Health Journal,* Vol. 1, No. 4, Winter, 1965, 375-381.

Fogelson, Franklin B., and Harold W. Demone, Jr., "Program Change Through Mental Health Planning," *Community Mental Health Journal,* Vol. 5, No. 1, 1969, 3-13.

Curran, William J., and Harold W. Demone, Jr., "Implementing Mental Health Planning Recommendations Into Statutes: The Legislative Process in Massachusetts," original article.

Drew, Elizabeth Brenner, "The Health Syndicate: Washington's Noble Conspirators," *The Atlantic Monthly,* Sept. 1968, 75-82.

Levine, Sol, "Organizational and Professional Barriers to Interagency Planning," *Proceedings of a Conference, Planning Responsibilities of State Departments of Public Welfare,* Brandeis University, Waltham, Mass., 1966, 54-60.

Martin, Carl, "PPB Or Not To Be?," *Community,* Vol. 44, No. 1, Nov.-Dec., 1968, 8-11.

Cohen, Alan B., "Best Resources Allocation and Best Program Selection," *Community,* Vol. 44, No. 4, May-June, 1969, 13-15.

Part VI

Bennis, W.G., M.F. Malone, N.H. Berkowitz, and M.W. Klein, "Can the Behavioral Sciences Contribute to Organizational Effectiveness: A Case Study," Paper read at the Annual Meeting of the American Public Health Association, Oct. 22, 1959.

McNerney, Walter J., "Health Care Reforms—The Myths and Realities," *American Journal of Public Health,* Vol. 61, No. 2, Feb. 1971, 222-232.

Schulberg, Herbert C., and Henry Wechsler, "The Uses and Misuses of Data in Assessing Mental Health Needs," *Community Mental Health Journal,* Vol. 3, No. 4, Winter, 1967, 389-395.

Baker, Frank, "The Living Human Service Organization: Applications of General Systems Theory and Research," original article.

Part VII

Bennis, Warren G., "A Funny Thing Happened on the Way to the Future," *American Psychologist,* Vol. 25, No. 7, 1970, 595-608.

Clawson, Marion, "Urban Renewal in 2000," *American Institute of Planners Journal,* Vol. 34, No. 3, May 1968, 173-179.

Johnson, Howard W., "Education for Management and Technology in the 1970's," *Science*, Vol. 160, May 10, 1968, 620-627.

Demone, Harold W., Jr., and Herbert C. Schulberg, "Planning for Human Services: The Role of the Community Council," original article.

Dixon, James P., "The Health Agenda for the Future," *Milbank Memorial Fund Quarterly*, Vol. XLVI, No. 1, Part 2, Jan. 1968, 259-264.

Demone, Harold W., Jr., Louisa P. Howe, and Bernard W. Kramer, "Principles and Criteria for National Health Insurance," *Committee on Public Policy, Medical Sociology Section, American Sociological Association*, 1971, original article.

Part I

Introduction

1. Issues in the Management and Planning of Human Service Organizations

Harold W. Demone, Jr., and Dwight Harshbarger

It is seldom that human service professionals are trained in the theory and practice of management. Rather, they are usually trained in their substantive fields and, through processes of quasi-natural selection, find themselves with growing administrative responsibilities. Unfortunately, the process of natural selection is limited in its effectiveness because it is seriously constrained at important and vital points in the selection process. For example, women serve as a major professional manpower resource in human service fields, but seldom are given major responsibilities in accordance with their abilities in the field.

Similarly, in the health fields, a most unusual phenomenon is at work. Most major administrative roles are restricted to physicians who make up only two percent of the manpower pool. Thus, artificial selection processes essentially exempt 98% of the available personnel. And within the two percent remaining, the selection process probably operates at a rather low level of effectiveness, for, in general, American medicine reveres the manager in all fields except its own. Strangely, the medical professional requires physician managers, then disparages them. This process is hardly designed to bring out the best of men, or the best in men.

As in other fields, racial factors also enter into the selection process. Although few blacks are to be found in medicine or dentistry, they are found in relatively substantial numbers in the general social welfare field. Blacks were actively engaged in social work long before they entered other professional fields. Nevertheless, few black administrators are to be found in social welfare, except in inner city agencies, and even this is a relatively recent phenomenon.

Thus, although natural selection of administrators is at work in the human service field, it tends to select from a relatively small

3

pool of available manpower, with certain important countervailing factors at work in health organizations.

Not surprisingly, administrators in the human services are under increasing attack for their management failures. The responsibility now rests with human service organizations and executives to move in new directions. Prejudicial discrimination of all types must be stopped. Management tools and skills must be taught. The administrator must be competent not only in his substantive field, but also prepared to deal with the complexities of personnel administration, budgeting, operational research, planning, boards and committees, interorganizational relationships, politics, and organized labor. To one degree or another he needs to be an applied social and behavioral scientist, educator, lawyer, and advocate. Effective administration is desperately needed and increasingly dependent upon the skilled use of modern management methods.

Nor is it sufficient to train selected human service professionals in administrative skills if most of their professional peers disdain management concerns as significant to goal achievement. They too must have some competence, at best, or sympathy, at least, for issues in management. Considerations about administration should be integrated into all specialized training programs. It is seldom that a human service professional, even a solo practitioner, can avoid administrative concerns.

The belief-value systems of professional disciplines also provide difficult problems for the effective development of human service organizations. For example, when physicians are contrasted with other human service professionals on nine organizational criteria, differentiation occurs on five of these criteria. Organized medicine looks adversely upon the following five essential management components for complex organizations; to the contrary, these components are generally accepted by other human service disciplines: (1) working under a policy-making board, (2) working for an annual salary, (3) high status for administrator, (4) stress on the important role of government, and (5) belief that all are equally entitled to services independent of other factors. The various human service professional disciplines, including medicine, generally agree on four organizational criteria, all of which can be viewed as adverse to long-term problem solving: (1) all are oriented to direct services, (2) none focus on primary prevention, (3) all have an individual rather than systemic view of their enterprise and its environment, and (4) planning has low status.

In summary, while the ideology of organized medicine is particularly antithetical to the rational operation of complex organizations, the other human service disciplines also show certain incongruities. None of these have the effect of enhancing organizational success. We are suggesting that our professional disciplines, which are effective in promoting higher standards among their members, as well as professional-organizational advancement of those disciplines, are, in important respects, dysfunctional for the modern complex human service organization in contemporary America.

The Setting

Today no characteristic of American life is more pervasive than the extraordinary rate of major social change. Although social change, historically, has always been a notable feature of America, such as in de Tocqueville's commentary, its present rate and pervasiveness is unparalleled. No sector of the United States—urban, suburban, rural—is removed from direct confrontation with the dramatic, and sometimes destructive, consequences of these change processes.

Few of the present operating models for human service organizations in health and welfare are products of contemporary America. Rather, they were designed for and developed in the midst of populations, problems, and perspectives of earlier eras of American life. The modern, and often dysfunctional, state mental hospital, a product of the early and mid-nineteenth century, is but one of many examples. Adapting those institutions and organizations which define themselves as providing human services, to the populations, problems, and perspectives of the United States of the 1970s promises to be *the* major problem for the immediate future within human service organizations. This may also be the primary problem faced by politicians, social planners, and consumers as they experience the pressures generated by organizations which are out of phase with the problems they were allegedly designed to solve.

In generating strategies for organizational change and development, decision makers in human service organizations must be able to generate perspectives regarding the organizational identities and roles their organizations have assumed in the past; those identities and roles which their organizations are assuming now; and those identities and roles which their organizations intend to assume in the future. Doing this successfully means knowing a great deal about the goals, teams, players, opposition, and the environmental conditions under which the ecological games of human service organizations are played. Too often, these perspectives and this knowledge have been lacking.

Strategies of administration, planning, and organizational change become most critical when examined against both the rates of social change and the inequities in American life and its social systems. As Americans become increasingly aware of their ethnic and reference group pluralism, they are simultaneously becoming aware of the inequities in income, health care, education, and social welfare which characterize these groups.

Strangely, in a time of affluence, social systems in America seem to be simultaneously moving closer to, and further away from, the goals of equity and quality in American life. That is, the relative quality of human welfare is improving for most, though not all, segments of America, but at differing rates. Thus many groups find themselves relatively further from quality education, health, or housing today than ever before.

Disturbing questions are beginning to be asked of human service organizations in health and welfare, regarding their participation in both the creation and maintenance of these inequities. Critics are pointing to the well intentioned, but often unwitting, processes through which certain problems have not been answered, important questions not asked, and dangerous consequences not anticipated.

At the heart of these problems may lie some basic assumptive postures which have been adopted by human service organizations. Historically these organizational postures and the consequent kinds of qualitative responsiveness have been of a reactive, rather than a proactive, nature. The kind of preparedness developed in many, perhaps most, human service organizations and service systems has been to be ready to react to a series of qualitatively different kinds of human problems. Only rarely have resources been systematically used to predict and act in an anticipatory or proactive manner.

This seems to have been due to two primary factors. First, there is the extent to which hierarchical, often medical-like models of administration and service have permeated and been adopted by these organizations, without a critical examination of the functions and dysfunctions of these models. This has led to organizational strategies and policies in which these organizations have adopted relatively narrow conceptions of their missions and goals. Further, the major thrusts of the operations of these organizations have been framed within an ideology that advocates secondary and tertiary, not primary, prevention. That is, the problems of people who have been labeled diseased, disabled, and often disenfranchised have been dealt with only after these people have become or have been labeled diseased, disabled, or disenfranchised. Organizational strategies aimed at prevention and active social change programs have not gained widespread acceptance.

A second factor is perhaps more important in understanding why human service organizations have been, and are, less proactive than we would like them to be. It seems a fact of organizational life, particularly in the human services, that organizations will, over time, experience entropy. A gradual movement toward stability occurs, usually through over-bureaucratization and the development of relatively rigid intraorganizational traditions. Too often organizations lack a means of self-renewal. The cutting edge of the new human service organization often becomes dull with age, and far too few sharpening mechanisms have been developed.

Because of these factors, human service organizations have found themselves out of phase with social change. One of the more frequent and obvious desynchronizing processes in urban areas has been the movement of an agency's target population away from geographic areas served by that agency. Simultaneously, incoming populations have brought with them problems which have been poorly understood and ineffectively dealt with by the agencies of that area. The outcomes of this process have been many: a mutual anger felt by consumers and agency staff; sit-ins; resignations; poor quality of services; and political pressures.

Two modes of action have generally been adopted to deal with these situations. The first, and perhaps the most common, has been the development of new agencies or human service organizations and institutions. This has structurally assumed the form of a pyramiding of social agencies and institutions. It has seemed to result from solution-minded problem solving by a combination of traditional human service professionals and politicians. No doubt it has often seemed the only way to confront problems without long bureaucratic delays and without threatening in any substantive way the interinstitutional political and economic equilibrium of a region.

The liabilities of this approach are only beginning to become evident. Not only is it a very expensive means of addressing problems, but it also tends to avoid, or severely limit, attacks on causal factors. The new organizations which are established to deal with particular problems tend to work in specific problem areas. Limited funds usually prevent a larger exploration of causal and contributory factors in human ecosystems. Most important, new organizations become "old" organizations quite quickly. Within a very few years, they too are accused of bureaucracy and institutional hardening of the arteries.

In addition, this approach does not deal with the possibility that other human service organizations may be working at cross purposes to the new organization and/or its clients. Often the unanticipated consequences of one organization's acts adversely affects the aims and outcomes of the new organization. Or, in a more active sense, one or more organizations in the public sector might be playing important roles in the *creation* of problems which the new agency will address. They will continue to do so, largely unchecked, when a new and separately funded organization is established, for normally no cross checking, feedback, or other influence processes are deliberately built into the design of organizations and their interorganizational relationships.

Perhaps the most blatant and long-term examples of these problems have been the architectural atrocities which have been built for low cost public housing—and the intense and costly needs for human services that have resulted from the dysfunctional living patterns these institutions have created.

It would appear from present economic indicators that the levels of resources available to attack health and welfare problems in the 1970's will not increase dramatically, or immediately, even though the frequency and intensity of problems will increase. Decision makers in human service organizations will probably find themselves solving problems within what will be, relatively, increasingly restrictive economic parameters. The need for new and more effective strategies of administration, planning, and organizational change will become critical. It seems fairly obvious that the potential for addressing these needs lies in the development of new linkages and networks among previously unrelated human service systems, and concomitantly, the shaping of new internal organizational structures.

The movement from a reactive to a proactive posture in human service organizations promises to be a shift which will be difficult, problematical, and probably of limited success. Its roots will have to reach into educational and training institutions, legislatures, boards of trustees, and consumer groups, as well as the organizations themselves. The traditions of organizations, professions, and professionalisms are deeply socialized into both those of us who would advocate and resist change.

This volume is aimed at speeding up this shift from reaction to proaction—for the the time available to human service organizations to become organizationally conscious of themselves, and to act on that knowledge, may be only too brief before the problems become truly overwhelming. If there is a long lag time from (a) a limited awareness of organizational problems to a fuller awareness of those problems, and (b) problem awareness to proactive responses based on that awareness, then the possibility for human service organizations to grow more irrelevant, and to deal with ever smaller segments of ever larger problems, will increase exponentially. The need for vigorous administrative decisions, and reflective organizational awareness, has never been greater.

ORGANIZATIONAL ISSUES

At least four fundamental and far-reaching program-oriented issues must be dealt with by every human service organization. Both the manner in which these issues are resolved and the resulting decisions themselves are crucial determinants of what is possible for these organizations.

Program Control

If any single organizational issue is likely to underlie a host of other organizational issues and problems, it is that of program control. It is here that multiple and sometimes overlapping constituencies and their representatives interact around the direction, intensity, and structure of human service programs. Ultimately, of course, the resolution of this problem acts as a major determinant in the "personality" of the organization itself.

At least four vested political interest groups and their respective constituencies can be indentified: 1) the human service professionals and their supporters; 2) middle-class volunteers, a constituency long interested and fairly heavily invested in the voluntary health and welfare system; 3) advocates of community control of programs; and 4) advocates of consumer control of programs.

Although major control of resources in most human service organizations typically rests with professionals and the community power structure, consumers and community representatives have increasingly become part of the political mix which makes decisions about organizational programs. Changes in the nature of the decision makers are often couched in terms of community control, decentralization, or local decision-making, but essentially these changes reflect our increasing population, its complexity, and our accelerated technology, industrialization, and subsequent depersonalization.

This problem of the alienation of service consumers represents one of the pressing problems of the human service industry, one which often arises because some of industry's own stereotyped solutions are not viable. "Community control" is often recommended as an alternative, but unfortunately it is not likely that "communities" represent a realistic description of or conceptual model for urban America. Peattie (1968) for example, suggests that the term "neighborhood" is essentially valueless in American urbia. She notes that even locality-rooted people are unable to agree on geographic boundaries nor do they have a clear sense of belonging to a distinct neighborhood. Similarily Gans (1965) notes that outsiders may view a locality as a neighborhood but not the inhabitants.

In working in and around Boston's South End for more than a decade, the senior author of this volume was impressed by the dedication of those who were anxious to protect the lower-middle-class mixed ethnic and racial family composition of their neighborhood-community, but none spoke for the substantial numbers of socially isolated homeless men (aged, infirm, retarded and/or mentally ill), the prostitutes and drug dependents who also called the South End home and who were very dependent on its capacity to absorb varying personality and social types. To force them out, as the community-developed plan implied, meant that a series of associated institutions also had to move (flophouses, low-cost restaurants, second-hand clothing stores, package stores featuring inexpensive wines, employment agencies for the unskilled, and pawnshops). This was truly a neighborhood for the displaced and a series of symbiotic institutions developed around them. Yet "community" planning excluded them. The city renewal agency supported but the "community" opposed an alcoholism rehabilitation program in the South End for South End residents. It seems that the urban and suburban American is neighborly in direct proportion to crisis and threats from the outside. Neighborhood associations are born in crisis and die in stability.

The naivete about "community" is paralleled in many references to community "power structures." Although social science has long since discarded the notion as an accurate reflection of urban decision making, it remains a powerful tract in the rhetoric of today's activists. In our pluralistic society a variety of interest groups have developed depending on the issue under discussion. Their influence is essentially a negative one in that they may exercise veto power with respect to direct threats to their existence. Few groups have the power to bring about major change in the face of opposition, and their influence is usually quite limited. The conversion of massive social power into effective large-scale social influence by any single organization is too costly, and requires too many trade-offs and commitments, to be a viable strategy for social change in a complex social system.

Program Auspice

Historically we have tended to dichotomize our human services into relatively simple public-private categories; however, intervention by different levels of government in providing for human services has rendered these categories obsolete. Moreover, while various mixes of tax revenues still act as the basis for exclusively governmental service delivery systems (e.g., city hospitals, mental hospitals, public welfare), other organizational models are being developed which provide greater flexibility for administrators. Some examples: a client advocacy system might be developed which purchases services for clients (e.g., vocational rehabilitation); a credit card voucher system might allow a client to purchase whatever services he needs, within certain defined areas of need; contractual arrangements between human service organizations might allow for one organization to meet the needs of the other's clients (e.g., comprehensive community mental health programs); a tax-based human service organization might subcontract its program to certain private-sector human service organizations.

As these and many other options become operational, human service administrators are finding that their program options are increasing, sometimes dramatically.

Building or Program Emphasis

Historically our human service planning has been building, or bricks and mortar, oriented. We have tended to view our human service programs as requiring, first, walls to contain them; then later we have worried about how to extend them beyond the walls.

While there are far too many examples of such planning, not the least of which is our formal educational system, a most recent example is that of the funding of comprehensive community mental health centers. Congressional timing made construction funds available a year before program plans had been fully developed, and this has given a strong bricks and mortar flavor to the community mental health movement.

Although it may be argued whether such an arrangement is or is not an appropriate one, the issue is the extent to which an organization must devote resources to construction vs. program planning early in the phasing of program development.

Core Service

A human service organization's core services, or those supportive activities which might be applied to a number of programs, must be defined and their potential links to programs developed. In order to do this an organization should have a reasonably firm idea of where its middle-range program planning will take it, and when. Core services which have certain components which are generalizable to a number of programs can only be developed if those programs are known.

Demone and Long (1969) have indicated a number of factors which should be given consideration in the development of core services: 1) developing a well-trained staff; 2) developing an effective, trained volunteer staff; 3) the program and delivery system must be economical; many, such as store front programs, have tended not to be economical; 4) an awareness of the complexities involved in receiving, counselling, diagnosing, and referring; 5) providing a system of program monitoring and evaluation; 6) developing and maintaining up to date resource files; in urban areas this may take from 3 to 6 months; 7) an annual reporting system, with critical evaluations included, which is available to the public and related service organizations; 8) using the information and referral component to serve as an indicator of community problems and community coping potential; 9) developing programs to train staff of individual agencies to serve as their own staff; 10) compiling and distributing directories of community services; and 11) serving as an aggressive advocate for clients.

In general, core service models seem to reflect the bias of their sponsors, be it health, rehabilitation, social service, or education.

Source of Authority

An analysis of the issues of organizational viability and capacity necessarily brings into focus the organizations' sources of authority. The American caregiving network increasingly receives its sanctions and resources (financial and volunteer) from multiple sources. Such a broadening of the authority and financial base can be a mixed blessing. To the degree that an organization is financially supported primarily by a single source it can be relatively independent, either aggressively pursuing desirable but unpopular ends or, contrariwise, ignoring the forces of social change and increasing its isolation. To the degree that consumers or many supporters are necessary, flexibility may be limited, but so too is the potential for agency irresponsibility and irrelevance.

The broader the financial base the more the organization is constrained. In general, the government, organized religion, and the United Fund have the largest bases of financial support of the U. S. A. Because of this, all are seriously constrained, especially organized religion and the United Fund. If they advocate too many unpopular causes they will alienate their base of voluntary support.

By definition, all organizations are limited and constrained. On an operating basis, the executive and legislative branches of government, Boards, Advisory Councils, Community Councils, and United Funds all serve as sanctioning, constraining, and boundary maintenance groups. In defined circumstances they may also serve open-system roles, examining ecological relationships between multiple organizations.

ORGANIZATIONAL MODELS

As organizational issues are resolved, and a human service organization develops a sense of identity and mission, the organization is likely to begin to deal with the concrete problems of how it might accomplish certain specific goals. These might include, for example, how resources are to be deployed and the administrative structuring of both service delivery and supportive activities. While there are numerous alternatives, the following four models have emerged as widely adopted human service organizational models: 1) the advice and referral center; 2) the diagnostic center; 3) the one-step multi-purpose center; and 4) a linked comprehensive network.

Information and Referral

An information and referral service is an option which has proved valuable and useful over the past 40 years. The basic notion is quite simple: a small group of persons with knowledge about available services in a community make this information known to community residents and agencies. In urban areas this is typically assuming the form of a centralized health and welfare council, one which makes perhaps 5,000-10,000 referrals per year, plus small information and referral centers located in neighborhoods throughout the community.

Some advantages: 1) it is relatively inexpensive to operate; 2) assuming agency cooperation, referral is likely to be simple and effective; and 3) it requires minimal organizational change, hence the probability of agency cooperation is maximized.

Some problems: 1) information and referral *alone* can be counter-productive if actual services are not available; 2) such a system does not change or remove inequities, inefficiencies, and gaps in the service delivery systems; and 3) the interpersonal and interorganizational demands which are created if the model is to effectively operate are rarely anticipated. For a researcher's perspective of some of the problems involved in such a model, see William Ryan's *Distress in the City* (1967).

The Diagnostic Center

This organizational model is a somewhat more medically-oriented version of the information and referral center. Here the referral model is supplemented by a staff capable of problem diagnosis, and the outcome is that more individually tailored, specific referrals can be made on the basis of the diagnostic information.

From the point of view of agencies, such a model has the advantage of requiring that all clients enter the care-giving system through certain sanctioned gates, or diagnostic centers. However, from the point of view of the client, this structuring of entry into a caregiving system is likely to be seen as an unnecessary delay in reaching needed services; rather, why not go, initially, directly to the service itself.

Following Ryan's findings, it is likely that the greater the number of layers or boundaries a client must pass through in a service system, the greater the probability that clients will drop out of the caregiving network. The result? At one level there will be increasing selectiveness in the client populations reached, and decreasing comprehensiveness and effectiveness of the service organizations. At another, more fundamental, level there will occur rising frustration and anger in the client population.

One-Stop Multi-Service Centers

During the middle and late 1960's, federal funding programs made it attractive to develop this model of human service organization, one in which characteristics of the preceding models were present, but one which also incorporated the internal capacity to follow through on client problems. There are currently about 200 of these health and service centers; however, the number is decreasing as it becomes more and more difficult to obtain federal funds for this purpose.

Although the basic concept of the multi-service center remains attractive, at least two important problems have been observed. First, cost analyses have failed to justify the level of expenditures required to maintain these centers, or their repetition on a nation-wide scale. Second, the continued development of these centers is likely to lead to improved, but still segregated, "ghetto" programs.

Some long-range benefits have accrued, however, as many professional groups and agencies developed cooperative patterns for perhaps the first time. Also, the inner city began to receive some quality services, and began to gain some control over programs. Finally, agency advocacy for clients was tested in a service organization.

Network

An integrated network of human service organizations has been suggested by numerous authors and planners, among them March (1968), OSTI (1969), and Baker and Schulberg (1970). Such a model rests upon the concept of interorganizational linkages which are likely to maximize service to the client, and prevent unnecessary duplication across human service organizations.

Within this model, generic information and referral organizations would continue to exist, but the major thrust of federal funds, formerly used to develop new, perhaps unreplicable organizations, would be to facilitate availability of services and effective service delivery. The problems involved in developing and maintaining continuity of care for different kinds of problems would be examined in terms of systemic inadequacies and discontinuities. Accountability and advocacy for clients is integral to the effective functioning of such a system. For example, accountability might be assumed by the organization of first contact with a client. Further, this organization would be compensated at a level which allows it to maintain accountability at an effective level.

Perlman and Jones (1967) have suggested some alternative strategies which might enable communities to move towards comprehensive service networks. Where there is a generally adequate level of human services, the primary focus might be on information and referral; where there are gaps in the human service delivery system, organizations might take on the selective responsibilities for filling selective gaps; where services are virtually absent, or totally inadequate, some form of a comprehensive center might be developed to provide services.

Generally, any attempt to move towards a comprehensive network of services must recognize the realities of organizational pluralism, market-place decisions, and the probable unavailability of outside funds. A comprehensive network that is effective must emerge from within existing organizational relationships, and deal with the bonds and antagonisms that have historically characterized interorganizational relationships in that community. Formal feedback arrangements and effective planning are critical components if the network is to be successful.

ADMINISTRATIVE ISSUES

Involved in day-by-day issues, the administrator often laments the complexity of his role and the lack of awareness of its many component parts. He focuses on fire control, not fire prevention. Seldom can he plan ahead. He complains about overlapping jurisdiction, gaps in responsibility, organizational parochialism, domain protection, boundary maintenance, and an overly specialized division of labor. On reflection it becomes clear to him that even if the organization has retained its viability, it has also found itself increasingly involved in the complexities and existential problems of intra- and inter-organizational life.

Certain requirements, such as organizational comprehensiveness and identification of component functions and problems, must be met. What are the organization's superordinate, medium-, and short-range goals? What is its function? Why does it exist?

Formal organizations, based on statutes, charters, constitutions, and bylaws, all have specified goals. They represent objectives; end points in action. They reflect a belief that goals can be identified, problems delimited, and means secured. Collectively they reflect a belief in rational action by rational men. Individuals and families have problems, for example, with alcohol, in family relations, and heart disease. Organizations can be established to confront these problems; symptoms can be treated, etiology uncovered, and mechanisms for primary, secondary, and tertiary prevention can be developed. At first, preventive mechanisms are nonspecific,

reflecting the underdeveloped stage of knowledge. Later, as a consequence of study and experience, more specific preventive tools
are developed.

Another common organizational model is based upon belief or
faith. Organized religion, formal education, and character-building
organizations (Boy Scouts, Boys' Clubs, Four-H Clubs, etc.) serve
as a philosophical or educational base on which individuals can
build their lives. Certain types of potential problems, it is posited,
will be prevented. In varying degrees, process and participation
is seen as an end in itself.

Thus the superordinate goals of organizations may be concrete
and specific or encompassing and diffuse. The more delimited
the goals, the more the results can be measured. In either case,
organizations—their policy makers and administrators— must consciously reflect upon their goals and separate them into specific
program objectives. Will the programs now being used truly contribute to the superordinate goal? What are the relative priorities
of alternative programs with respect to goal achievement?

An important leadership function is to instill an understanding
of and belief in the agency's goals. The people—staff, supporters,
constituents, and consumers—must share certain common understandings.

Most administrators profess, perhaps even believe, that if only
their organization was given more money they could effectively
cope with their assigned area of responsibility. Since this is ordinarily
not an accurate diagnosis of the state of the problem or the agency's
capacity to cope with it, the administrator and his organization
are viewed as puffing their wares—perhaps even "empire building."

If an organization's policy makers and administrators view their
future in time-limited terms such a tactic may be justified. On any
long-term basis it tends to erode their credibility in the eyes of
allocations and budget committees. The latter tend to be wary of
unrealistic claimants, especially in an era where problems are more
and more complex, and simplistic solutions are unlikely to succeed.

The agency decision-making mechanism, always a critical variable
in program success, is not only increasingly important and complex
but operates under more intense challenges than ever before. A
basic problem is to somehow combine adequate substantive understanding of the field in question on the one hand with a fresh,
stimulating perspective on the other; to stimultaneously build-in
technology and citizen participation; and to balance some sort of
order, stability, and predictability with rapid social and organizational change.

As population size increases and shifts its concentration, urbanization expands, rates of technological innovation escalate, pluralism
in politics and planning booms, and general system changes in
organizational relationships are reflected in major social change
processes. Simultaneously, the citizen tends to feel increasingly
alienated from decision-making centers.

Such value premises as humanism, participation, ecology, civil
rights, justice, and opportunity are, under these conditions, in conflict with other beliefs: free enterprise, efficiency, social Darwinism,
caveat emptor, and law and order. Long-standing and cherished
beliefs are being challenged, and human service administrators
may long for "the good old days." The future promises only that
their organizations will almost inevitably be both a participant in
and focus of conflict and confrontation.

Technological and socio-technical innovations have brought
along with them major and unanticipated side effects, as enzymes
have been added to detergents, color to TV, STOL aircraft per-
fected, milieu therapy introduced to general hospitals, welfare
recipients organized, and maximum feasible participation of the
poor introduced into human service organizations.

Specialists in the human services may be convinced of the values
of technology and specialization, but they remain in disagreement
about the relative values of their disciplinary specialties, the respective balance of basic and applied research, or priorities of social
problems.

The human service administrator must deal not only with these
problems, but the more general one of somehow including scientific
technology in his organizational decision making, without allowing
it to dominate that decision making. Uses of computers, simulation,
games, information systems, systems analysis, and operational
research are but a few of these problematical technologies.

This dilemma is seldom resolved by simple inclusion of technology within financial constraints, for these technologies rarely
make alternative decisions more objective. For example, there are
many stereotypes about the causes of welfare recipiency, but little
systematic hard data which factors out the many subgroups and
gives clear directions to programs designed to reverse the causes
of low income. A simple and direct solution may be to provide
an adequate income, but this decision can only be facilitated, not
made, by technological tools.

Boffey (1967) illustrates other decision-making dilemmas. "civil
governments can't just throw out old subway systems and antiquated
school buildings the way the Defense Department junks an obsolete

weapons system. They generally have to incorporate existing systems into any new systems, and this lessens the opportunity for radically new approaches. Further constraints arise because civil government can't order their constituents to use a new system (say, a mass transit system) the way the Defense Department can—thus the system must have market capability [p. 1029]."

Two simultaneous but divergent trends, scientific management technologies on the one hand and citizen participation on the other, clearly must be accommodated if we are not to have a new wave of antiscientific and countervailing behind-the-scene maneuverings by highly specialized technocrats-bureaucrats. This unreal war fought with different weapons in different locations could be extraordinarily disruptive in our society since neither science nor a desire to belong and participate can be halted. The accommodation is at the level of policy-making in which all persons are equal. Democracy was not designed to assign policy-making to technocrats.

In all of this the organization must be flexible and responsive. What is often called bureaucracy—the protection of organizational self-interest and status quo—promises to have a troubled and uncomfortable future. Kurt Lewin (1947) described the network of social and organizational forces as creating a condition of "quasi-stationary equilibrium." But as the forces of social change press on organizations, organizations may respond by closing in on themselves, thus securing their domains, boundaries, and internal quasi-stationary equilibrium. They will also become isolated from significant social problems.

From the perspective of the authors, the trends of increasing sophistication about structure and function and the new management and planning technologies, as opposed to the citizen participation movement, are collectively destined to confront directly all the historical tendencies to protect institutions. The type of organization notwithstanding, the critical issue is the capacity to change, to be responsive to the environment, and not to respond merely in additive ways. Most human service organizations are quite willing to add new programs, often substantially different from their present programs, if new funds are made available. Being committed to job descriptions, people, sites, and facilities, they find internal adjustment of priorities difficult and threatening. Given these conditions the manager has to be knowledgeable about why people resist change, how to deal with this resistance, and how to build-in structural mechanisms which produce change, innovation, and experimentation on an ongoing basis. He must recognize that contemporary solutions are based on present knowledge which may soon be obsolete, and that organizational truths are generally relative, not absolute.

The essential factor is accountability to sanctioning agents, to authorizing and funding sources, to the client system, to the organization's policy board, and to oneself.

Although the focus thus far has been on intraorganizational concerns and on the organization's capacity to relate and respond to its constituents and to the forces of social change, a modest literature on interorganizational relationships has been developing in recent years. The extraordinary point, as noted in some of the articles which follow, is that many agencies are unaware of and disinterested in the essential symbiosis which overlays the entire human service network. This awareness, when manifested, occurs frequently in the forms of competition, prejudice, and distrust. Boundary maintenance and domain protection are more common than collaboration and cooperation.

A pluralistic society that fosters the invention of new organizations as the problem-solving strategy of choice, precludes the effective management of interorganizational relationships. Yet the Federal government has been particularly active in fostering the strategy of encouraging the development of new organizations, rather than making it attractive for existing groups to modify policies and programs (e.g., O.E.O., Juvenile Delinquency, Neighborhood Services Center, etc.) to meet newly emergent social needs. That a certain naivete underlies this approach—groups can always be found to establish new organizations if funds are made available, and they too very quickly become "old" organizations—still does not deny its popularity. Elected officials in office for two, four, or six years work on a limited time schedule. Results must be immediate. The advantage of the new organization formula is that it allows for constant experimentation, initiative, and competition. The disadvantages are that it is wasteful of limited resources, has limited success, and may conflict with the goal of comprehensiveness and continuity.

Clearly the administrative role does not stop at organizational boundaries. Interorganizational and intersystem demands have become very complex, demanding, and divergent. With respect to these problems in the health industry, Becker (1966) notes that "every hospital, every public health official, and every insurance executive recognizes the interdependence of all pieces in the health care puzzle. No one segment of the health industry can stand alone and be isolated from the mainstream of community organization and still hope to remain vital [p. 1099]."

Unfortunately, our research base on which to teach interorganizational theory and practice is limited, for it depends on the objective development of complex and subtle interrelationships between roles, status, personality, culture and social systems, and complex organizations. That is no small order. But even with a limited research base, interorganizational experience grows. As interagency coordination and linkage is increasingly stressed, each agency administrator is compelled to improve old skills and develop new ones. As the present patterns of service delivery and decision-making are increasingly challenged, they must be modified and new ones developed. If for no other reason than organizational self-interest, an investment in goal setting and organizational roles is essential. Alternative planning strategies may range from complete independence from other formal organizations to a role of dependence upon other organizations; from cooperation to conflict and intense competition.

REFERENCES

Baker, F., & Schulberg, H.C. Community health caregiving systems: Integration of interorganizational networks. Chapter 8 in Sheldon, A., Baker, F., and McLaughlin, C., (Eds.) *Systems and medical care*, Cambridge, Mass.: MIT Press, 1970.

Becker, H. New problems in public-private relationships. *Bulletin of The New York Academy of Medicine*, 1966, 42, 1099-1108.

Boffey, P.M. Systems analysis: No panacea for the nation's domestic problems. *Science*, 1967, 158, 1028-1030.

Demone, H.W., Jr. Human services at state and local levels and the integration of mental health. *The American handbook of psychiatry*, Vol. II, G. Caplan, Editor, Basic Books, New York, forthcoming 1973.

Demone, H.W., Jr., and Long, D.F. Information-referral—The nucleus of a human-needs program. *Community*, 1969, 44, 9-11.

Gans, H. *The urban villagers: Group and class in life of Italian Americans.* Glencoe, Ill.: The Free Press, 1965.

Lewin, K. Frontiers in group dynamics. *Human Relations*, 1947, 1, 5-41.

March, M. The neighborhood center concept. *Public Welfare*, 1968, 26, 97-111.

Organization for Social & Technological Innovation. *Neighborhood centers draft manual*, Office of Economic Opportunity, April, 1969.

Peattie, L.R. Reflections on advocacy planning. *AIP Journal*, 1968, 34, 80-88.

Perlman, R., and Jones, D. *Neighborhood service centers.* Office of Juvenile Delinquency, Dept. of Health, Education and Welfare, 1967.

Ryan, W. *Distress in the city.* New York: Russell Sage Foundation, 1967.

2. The Human Service Organization

Dwight Harshbarger

Despite the tendency to treat organizational theory as an illegitimate child of an illicit coupling between the College of Commerce and the Sociology Department, and hence relegated to accepting academic hand-me-downs, there has been, over the past 10 years, a rapid acceleration of information, conceptual models, and theories of complex organizations.

The 1930's saw the development of such work as Barnard's *The Function of the Executive* (1938); the 1940's, Whyte's *Human Relations in the Restaurant Industry* (1948); the 1950's, March and Simon's *Organizations* (1958) and Haire's *Modern Organization Theory* (1959).

The 1960's, by contrast, have been years of vigorously accelerated increases in the amounts of new information and conceptual models produced by students of complex organizations. McGregor (1960), Etzioni (1961a, 1961b), Likert (1961, 1967), Blau and Scott (1962, Rice (1963), Trist *et al.,* (1963), Argyris (1964), Balke and Mouton (1964), Kahn *et al.,* (1964), and Katz and Kahn (1966) are but a sampling of the major works that typify a most productive decade.

Both historically and currently, however, a rather substantial proportion of the work in this field shares the thematic commonality of its major thrusts being based upon, and relevant to, complex organizations in the private sector. Business organizations have provided the natural environment for the majority of field research which has served as the foundation for model and theory development. Although there have been many notable exceptions to this statement, such as Selzick's *TVA and the Grass Roots* (1949), Stanton and Schwartz' *The Mental Hospital* (1954), and more recently Etzioni's *The Semi-Professionals* (1969), the vast majority of inquiry into the nature and dynamics of complex organizations has fallen into the domain of business organizations. Whether or not this is an adequate base for theories of complex organizations is an open question.

It may be, as Blau and Scott (1962) and Etzioni (1961) have suggested, that the type of organization being dealt with is a rather critical variable in generating organizational theory. And, although Blau and Scott have developed a conceptual framework for examining different taxonomic forms of organizations, there has been relatively little systematic use of the taxonomic approach in most organizational research. There has been little differentiation among types, or species, of organizations in terms of either the assumptions involved in the research, or the consequences of the findings. Thus data and conceptual models generated in research in business organizations have been integrated into organizational theory in a manner that implies that they are appropriate to most species of organizations.

The purposes of this paper are to suggest that taxonomic, species difference-oriented considerations should play a more prominent role in organizational theory and research; to develop a model of important taxonomic dimensions of complex organizations (or species characteristics); and to suggest a number of definitive characteristics of one species of complex organization, the human service organization.

A Taxonomic Model

In their four-way classification of complex organizations, Blau and Scott proposed the following primary forms of organizations: 1) *business concerns,* which benefit owners; e.g., General Motors, department stores, banks; 2) *commonweal organizations,* which, theoretically, benefit the general public; e.g., Internal Revenue Service, police departments; 3) *mutual benefit associations,* which benefit the members of the organizations; e.g., unions, professional societies; and 4) *service organizations,* which benefit their clients; e.g., hospitals, social welfare agencies, schools.

While Blau and Scott's focus on the goals and beneficiaries of organizations as a means of classification is certainly workable, their schema tends to neglect the more systemic properties of complex organizations. That is, their classifications are largely output oriented, and, consequently, do not take into account other important sets of organizational variables, such as input and throughput factors, which may create important similarities and differences among organizations. For example, commonweal and service organizations share a number of important commonalities, such as their service and nonprofit orientation, and their professionally-based value systems. The fact that they are aiming themselves at different client populations may be an artifact which does not adequately reflect their organizational similarities.

An approach more grounded in systems theory, such as that proposed by Katz and Kahn (1966), might more effectively delineate important components of organizational resources, structure and throughput, output, and beneficiaries. Such an approach is indicated in Figure 1. This schema attempts to integrate Blau and Scott's approach with that of Etzioni and Katz and Kahn.

Fig. 1.   Dimensions for a Taxonomy of Complex Organizations

Resource Base-----Organization---------Output----------Beneficiaries

A. Private resources —profits, investments, returns.	A. Structure 1. Positions: degree hierarchical 2. Roles: degree formalized 3. Actors: degree professionalized	A. Technical B. Socio-technical C. Social (services)	A. Primary 1. Staff 2. Member 3. Owner 4. Client
B. Public resources —taxes, bonds, endowments.	B. Type of power (Etzioni) 1. Coercive 2. Utilitarian 3. Normative 4. Mixed C. Individual member's involvement (Etzioni) 1. alientative 2. calculative 3. moral		B. Secondary 1. Staff 2. Member 3. Owner 4. Client

Within this framework, and within any particular organization, or group of organizations, a number of dimensions would seem to naturally relate to each other, or cluster together, in such a way that suggests their relative independence, or uniqueness, as complex organizations. For example, private, structured-utilitarian-calculative, technical, owner-beneficiary would provide one such cluster of dimensions. It refers, of course, to a business organization, and is generally congruent with Blau and Scott's earlier description of a business concern. However, such a multi-factor systems approach to describing organizational differences would seem to have the potential for and the advantage of easily and simply referring to different forms of business organizations without having to develop new descriptive indices.

Similarly, service and commonweal organizations may differ *only* in the nature of their primary and secondary beneficiaries and be largely the same along the other systematic dimensions. They might be more accurately described as two forms of the same general type of organization, the human service organization.

In terms of their systemic properties, human service organizations might generally be described as based upon public resources, relatively structured, normatively based and morally involving, social or socio-technical service oriented, and aimed at clients, residents, or members as primary beneficiaries, and staff members as secondary beneficiaries. Organizationally, the nature of their efforts is to deal with those bio-social problems which arise from the vagaries and complexities of being human. Organizations which define themselves as in the fields of health, education, and social welfare would, generally, fit this definition.

Forcing such conceptual distinctions as these, *a priori,* upon organizational researchers should result in a movement away from the pronounced tendency to glibly refer to and do research upon "complex organizations." Rather, certain taxonomic characteristics might, when elaborated, suggest principles, properties, and practices which are unique to, say, organizations whose resources are based in the private sector, as contrasted with organizations whose resources are based in the public sector.

Such distinctions would seem to be of considerable importance if an understanding is to be developed of the world of human service organizations, and their directors of development. To blithely assume, as has often seemed to be the case in the past, that the properties and dynamics of, for example, an IBM or a division of General Dynamics, are generally and easily comparable to the organization of a state department of welfare or mental health, or a United Community Services, is to overlook some major species differences between these forms of organizations.[1]

CHARACTERISTICS OF THE HUMAN SERVICE ORGANIZATION

The public sector human service organization differs, substantively and significantly, from other organizations. Although, by definition, no organization can claim sufficient uniqueness to remove it from comparisons with other organizations, the relative uniqueness of public sector human service organizations, *vis-a-vis* private sector business organizations, is large enough to suggest the value of different taxonomic categories, and perhaps, the operation of differing principles of both organizational change and human behavior in organizations.

More specifically, public sector human service organizations differ from private sector, technical production-oriented organizations, along the dimensions indicated in Table 1.

TABLE 1
Contrasting Dimensions of Production and Service Organizations

Private sector, technical production organizations	*Public sector, human service organizations*
Resource Base	
1. Resources obtained from private, individual, or corporate sources.	1. Resources obtained from public, tax, or bond-based resources, or private monies donated to the public sector.
2. Resource stability is directly affected by economic market fluctuations.	2. Resource stability is affected only by relatively long-term economic fluctuations.
3. The potential for risk and loss is relatively high.	3. The potential for risk and loss is relatively low.

[1]While realizing, of course, that there are many structural similarities in the problems of these organizations, such as role definition, role conflict, resource acquisition, etc.

Private sector, technical production organizations	*Public sector, human service organizations*

The Organization

1. The organization is structured and organized in accordance with production cycles-systems.	1. The organization is structured and organized in accordance with professional values and membership subgroupings.
2. Type of power is primarily utilitarian.	2. Type of power is primarily normative.
3. Organizationally defined tasks provide the primary bases of social segregation and inter-action.	3. Professional membership groups provide the primary bases of social segregation and interaction. Task definition is usually developed by these groups.
4. Social hierarchies and social power are based in the formal organizational distribution of power.	4. Social hierarchies and social power are based in professional hierarchies, and their relative possession of power.
5. Intraorganizational norms and behaviors are largely based in production standards of desired efficiency (in both formal and informal organizational sub-systems).	5. Intraorganizational norms and behaviors are largely based in the values of professional and organizational membership groups.
6. The individual member's involvement is primarily calculative.	6. The individual member's involvement is primarily moral.
7. The first allegiance of an individual is to his organizational membership group.	7. The first allegiance of an individual is to his professional membership group.
8. The allegiance of the individual to the organization tion is assumed, and is not an area of major conflict.	8. The allegiance of the individual to the organization is problematical, and may be an area of major conflict.
9. No (or very limited) use of job tenure.	9. Widespread use of job tenure.

Private sector, technical Production organizations	*Public sector, human service organizations*
10. Organizational and role performance of the individual is assessed by a profit criterion.	10. Organizational performance of the individual is assessed by criteria based in professional values.
11. Personnel are hired and retained largely in terms of their effectiveness in organizational production.	11. Personnel are hired and retained largely in terms of professional value judgments.
12. The consumption of materials is end-product oriented.	12. The consumption of materials is means, or process, oriented.

Output

1. Relatively clear definition of end product.	1. Relatively unclear definition of the end product.
2. Cost-effectiveness indices are relatively easily developed.	2. Cost-effectiveness indices are difficult or impossible to develop; the major problem is the measurement of effectiveness.
3. There is an end-product orientation; the end product is given high organizational salience.	3. There is a quasi-end-product orientation; the salience of means is often higher than the salience of ends.
4. The over-all mission or purpose of the organization is established by a small group (e.g., board of directors) which acts in the best interests of the organization and its ownership.	4. The over-all mission or purpose of the organization is established by a relatively large group (e.g., legislators) which acts in the best interests of the public.
5. The primary criterion for the development of new purposes for the organization is that of organizational survival.	5. The primary criterion for the development of new purposes for the organization is the public interest. It is assumed that meeting public needs will give certainty to organizational survival.

Private sector, technical production organizations	Public sector, human service organizations

Beneficiaries

1. Primary beneficiaries are owners.

2. Secondary beneficiaries are staff and clients or consumers.

1. Primary beneficiaries are usually clients, but sometimes are staff.

2. Secondary beneficiaries are usually staff, and the general public; sometimes they are the clients.

Organizational Ecology

1. Economic indicators (profit-loss) are indices of effectiveness of an organization's adaptive strategies.

2. Involvement in political decision-making in the surrounding environment is legitimate and seen in the interest of the organization.

3. The nature of political involvement will be structured by organizational norms.

1. Degree of judged adherence to professional and social values, through derived behavioral and ideological criteria, are indicators of effectiveness of an organization's adaptive strategies.

2. Involvement in political decision-making in the surrounding environment is seen as questionable and probably not in the interests of the organization.

3. The lack of political involvement will be maintained by organizational norms.

A number of important factors other than those indicated in Table 1 serve as both foundations for organizational stability, and as sources of resistance to major organizational change efforts in human service organizations. For example, equilibrated, mutually supportive relationships between physicians and hospital administrators, or social workers and nursing home administrators, give a sense of stability to the parent organizations of these persons. This stability is further strengthened and its base broadened through both relationships with Boards of Trustees, and symbiotic, mutually beneficial relationships with other human service organizations.

Consequently, human service organizations which have some organizational longevity are usually found to have developed a broad-based, consensually validated complex of organizational purposes and goals. Changing these purposes is a difficult task, for the roots of these organizations go deep into the fabric of society. Ostensibly, these organizations serve as living testimony to a society's social concerns.

Because of this, it might be suggested that theoretically, conceptually, and practically, human service organizations deserve more thoughtful treatment than they have historically received. As organizations they have been continuously subjected to principles and criteria derived from the study of other species of organizations. As an environment for natural observation, research, and theory building they have been utilized too little. It terms of benefiting, practically, from advances in complex organizational theory, they are far behind other species of organizations.

The consequences of this neglect have been economically expensive, socially dysfunctional, and individually demeaning and deleterious. Schools, mental hospitals, and welfare agencies have not been the most distinguished forms of complex organizations that our society has produced, although they may be among the most important.

Health, education, and welfare organizations in both the private and public sectors currently comprise nearly one-third of our gross national product. As organizations, and social systems, they are radically in need of repairs and changes. Health services in the United States are grossly inadequate; welfare agencies may often be doing no more than serving as social accounting and check dispensing organizations; and as Charles Silberman (1970) has recently indicated, we are facing a serious and pervasive crisis in the classroom.

As students of complex organizations, and as persons concerned with the relatively healthy, adaptive development of social systems, we could do worse than devoting a greater effort to the study of human service organizations. In terms of the social utility of our efforts, perhaps we could not do much better.

REFERENCES

Argyris, C. *Integrating the individual and the organization.* New York: Wiley, 1964.

Barnard, C. *The functions of the executive.* Cambridge, Mass.: Harvard University Press, 1938.

Blake, R. R., & Mouton, J. S. *The managerial grid.* Houston, Texas: Gulf, 1964.

Blau, P., & Scott, W. *Formal organizations.* San Francisco: Chandler, 1962.

Etzioni, A. *A comparative analysis of complex organizations.* New York: Free Press, 1961. (a)

Etzioni, A. (Ed.) *Complex organizations: A sociological reader.* New York: Holt, Rinehart, and Winston, 1961. (b)

Etzioni, A. *The semi-professionals and their organization: Teachers, nurses, social workers.* New York: Free Press, 1969.

Haire, M. (Ed.) *Modern organization theory.* New York: Wiley, 1959.

Kahn, R. L., Wolfe, D. M., Quinn, R. P., Snook, J. D., & Rosenthal, R. A. *Organizational stress: Studies in role conflict and ambiguity.* New York: Wiley, 1966.

Likert, R. *New patterns of management.* New York: McGraw-Hill, 1961.

Likert, R. *The human organization.* New York: McGraw-Hill, 1967.

March, J. G., & Simon, H. A. *Organizations.* New York: Wiley, 1958.

McGregor, D. *The human side of enterprise.* New York: McGraw-Hill, 1960.

Rice, A. K. *The enterprise and its environment.* London: Tavistock Publications, 1958.

Selznick, P. *TVA and the grass roots.* Berkeley: University of California Press, 1949.

Silberman, C. *Crisis in the classroom.* New York: Random House, 1970.

Stanton, A. H., & Schwartz, M. S. *The mental hospital: A Study of institutional participation in psychiatric illness and treatment.* New York: Basic Books, 1954.

Trist, E. L., Higgin, G. W., Murray, H., & Pollack, A. B. *Organizational choice.* London: Tavistock Publications, 1963.

Whyte, W. F. *Human relations in the restaurant industry.* New York: McGraw-Hill, 1948.

Part II

Environmental Forces
Acting on and Reacting to
Human Service Organizations

Introduction

Human service organizations are, perforce, becoming increasingly aware of the environment within which they operate. To some extent this awareness is a byproduct of normal interorganizational relationships. However, given the conflicted and often turbulent nature of contemporary society, this awareness may be produced in large part by an increasing schism between human service organizations and the socio-cultural environments and constituencies these organizations have been designed to serve.

In this section a number of central questions are raised regarding the effects of environmental conditions on organizational functions. These questions are representative of those that will confront persons involved in the planning and administration of human service organizations. For example, what are the significant sources of human and organizational crises which can be identified in community environments? What are the traditional and nontraditional approaches through which human service organizations have attempted to deal with these problems? What have been some of the functional and dysfunctional consequences of these approaches? Might these consequences have been predicted? What are viable alternatives in the design of the intervention strategies of the future?

Although to the human service organization administrator and planner the latter question is perhaps the most important, it can only be intelligently dealt with if the earlier questions have at least been partially answered. And, attaining these answers is contingent upon the development of a perspective on the dynamics of human service organizations' external environment and the organizational exchanges and transactions in that environment.

Because we are all so much a part of our personal environments, it is often difficult to grasp and understand the effects of environmental factors on our personal relationships. And, although this is a difficult problem for individuals, it is even more complex and difficult for organizations. What kinds of mechanisms are necessary to give feedback to organizations so that they, as organizational entities, might reflect on the transactional nature of their existence? How might these mechanisms be designed so as to increase the effective, functional adaptation and productivity of human service organizations and their client communities?

Section A

Environmental Forces:
In the Surrounding Environment

As overcrowding and overuse of the physical environment force an increasing awareness of environmental limitations, we are simultaneously beginning to gain some insights into the adaptive and maladaptive effects of both controllable and, as yet, uncontrollable environmental factors in human ecosystems.

Human service organizations will be called upon to deal with many of these environmentally-produced problems, and will be required to become aware not only of environmental factors per se, but also of the dynamics and consequences of environmental flux and change. The latter will place increasingly difficult stresses and limitations upon both the internal stability and adaptive problem-solving potential of human service organizations.

Given current rates of technological changes, population shifts, increasing population density, and the social consequences of these interacting factors, human service organizations are finding it necessary to alter many of their traditional organizational structures. More, and perhaps more radical, organizational changes may be required in the immediate future.

It is in this turbulent environment, with its often temporary modes of organization and adaptation, that human service organizations find themselves.

3. Statement on Human Behavior and the Environment to United States Senate Select Committee on Health and Housing

Mayer Spivack

What does it mean when someone says "there's no place to go"? What does it mean to residents when the interior environment of, say, a housing development, or the external environment of a neighborhood do not provide places for meaningful human functions and relationships?

What are the behavior settings that neighborhood and community environments should provide for residents and users? What are the responsibilities of human service agencies in ensuring that: 1) we do not repeat our architectural and community design atrocities of the past; and 2) the quality of community life might be enhanced through appropriate environmental design?

As is indicated in the following Senate testimony, the answers to these questions have serious and far-reaching implications for human service organizations.

STATEMENT OF HON. CHARLES H. PERCY, A U.S. SENATOR FROM THE STATE OF ILLINOIS

Senator Percy: The Chairman, I understand, is on his way, but suppose I read an opening statement to get us underway, and we will just presume he will be along in a few moments.

The Select Committee on Health and Housing will continue this morning. Our focus today will be on planning and action for better health through better housing.

I have asked Dr. Mayer Spivack of the Laboratory of Community Psychiatry at Harvard to discuss with us his recent studies on human behavior and the environment. His work provides new tools for planning man's residential environment. We need new tools to make that environment work to expand man's horizons and opportunities instead of limiting his growth.

In order to gain first-hand information about what it means to operate housing programs in a major U.S. city, we have asked Mr. Bailus Walker of Cleveland to be our second witness this morning.

We look forward to hearing recommendations for solving these problems and also some of the achievements Cleveland has made.

Dr. Spencer Parratt of the Maxwell School has been asked to give his testimony as the next witness.

Dr. Robert Knittel of the Department of Community Development, Southern Illinois University, will advise us on how we can improve better community organization.

As our last witness, we have invited Mr. Eric Mood of Yale University to formulate a comprehensive program of action to improve housing and health, a program that will deal with both the physical things and the social activities that constitute our residential environment.

For our first witness, we are pleased to call Dr. Mayer Spivack.

STATEMENT OF DR. MAYER SPIVACK, DIRECTOR, LABORATORY OF COMMUNITY PSYCHIATRY, HARVARD MEDICAL SCHOOL

Senator Percy: Dr. Spivack, we have copies of your testimony. If you would like, you may read the entire content of it. If you would prefer to summarize it, we will, of course, put the entire testimony in the record. I will leave it entirely to you.

We have 2 hours now and five witnesses. We can proportion our time accordingly.

Dr. Spivack: I think, with your permission, I would prefer to present the testimony in full, and I hope to move as quickly as possible without obscuring it.

I thank you for allowing me to come and participate in this process, and I hope that my discussion can be of some relevance to the topic.

Any discussion on the environment, even the narrowed field of the residential environment, is fairly complex, and in order to deal with the subject, I felt that I should attack it as broadly as possible without getting diffuse. I shall provide rather specific problem definitions, if I can.

This means I am going to have to cover a good deal of ground, and I think in order to make my testimony easier to follow, I would like to give you an index ahead of time of what I will talk about.

First, I expect to deal with the education of architects, how to educate architects in evaluation procedures so that the buildings they produce will work, instead of just look good.

Then, what happens when a few people have a great deal of design responsibility, and many other people must live in the results of their work?

Following that, how to avoid multiplying our mistakes all over the country when we have public building projects on what I would call genotype buildings, such as schools, or mental hospitals, or offices. The term genotypic buildings describes a kind of building that tends to be completed without imagination and only minor variations wherever you find it.

I will also talk about crises in local communities. This is a crisis that I hope to be able to define in terms of setting deprivation and blandness, the "no place to go" kind of syndrome that we feel in our suburbs and gray areas.

What are the necessary components of a whole human community? This is a difficult subject, and it isn't often addressed, and I think it should be considered at this level.

I would like to talk about walking communities, face-to-face communities, and what happens when you don't have them, why people feel isolated, and what we can do about making a remedy.

I would like to talk about recreation, especially for children, and discuss the possibility that playgrounds have proved inadequate, no matter what you call them, and that what we need is the different concept of play and play space allocation, and I suggest play routes instead, which is a continuous web of play space throughout communities.

I would like to discuss mass-produced or industrialized housing, or shelter of any kind. I shall describe ways to prevent a dangerous condition which results in this kind of building when we tend to reproduce our mistakes again and again, because we don't analyze ahead of time what we are going to do, and don't evaluate it afterwards.

Our existence as city building and city dwelling men is marked by a tragic paradox. While we aspire to build a world which is the realization of our dreams, we struggle to contend with an urban environment which is both our reality and our nightmare.

The architects and planners of our physical environment have seen their task, as if schooled in noblesse oblige, as that of designing environments within which other men should be content to live. Their buildings and cities have evolved most often from idiosyncratic, intuitive fantasies in which spaces and forms are moulded by aesthetic principles. Architects are encouraged to conceive individual buildings in terms of their visual qualities—almost as sculptures.

Buildings which meet sculptural criteria are good—and necessary—if the environment is not to become even uglier than it is.

But they are not good enough. Architects must learn to attend to human behavior, and to design to human needs.

It is now clear that while our behavior can obviously modify the environment, the environment can also modify our behavior, at all temporal and physical scales, for individuals and for societies. This is a kind of feedback loop which in good circumstances is responsible for the evolution of the behavior of the species and its physical environment, as well.

The loop can be interrupted at several points. If individuals are under stress or in a condition of poverty or illness, it will be much harder for them to change their environment because they will lack access to suitable political power and authority, to actual tools, money and time.

Under just such conditions, lives are most vulnerable to being distorted by outside forces—the inconvenient arrangement of the city or house, the impoverished sensory and social sterility of public housing or hospital, the imposition of limited housing opportunities by political or economic forces.

If we are to live in full health in whole, life-supporting environments, we must radically reorient our goals. We must concern ourselves with the quality of life and the quality of life's settings.

Our architecture and city planning schools are as backward as is our building industry. Architectural education is directed towards producing famous idiosyncratic architects, and formal, monumental buildings. We must instead train architects to ask questions, solve problems, and study the results of their work.

Architects are responsible for guiding the evolution of our society by their control over the evolution and design of buildings which are the containers and shapers of our culture. There is no tradition in the practice of architecture in which architects are expected to evaluate publicly their own or other architects' work.

Only careful scrutiny of working buildings in use can hope to produce an evolution in quality of building types. There has never been a necessary steady progression of design quality or appropriateness in our public projects—housing, hospitals, schools, or our private offices, factories, et cetera.

We must institute and sponsor, from the Federal level, innovations in architectural education which focus upon research and evaluation. We must require that all federally and State-sponsored construction be preceded by detailed analysis of program requirements for each building. Therein, design solutions should be related as hypothesis to the eventual behavior of the population to be housed.

Every building must also have a follow-up evaluation study performed by the architect or other capable analyst, which is directed toward identifying and solving malfunctions in the design as well as noting where the structure successfully supports the use and behavior of its inhabitants.

Our environments are for the most part designed and built by a few for use by the many. Rarely do people ever have the opportunity to significantly influence, or even modify the form of their shelter. This practice guarantees that in the absence of evaluation procedures, whatever omissions or mistakes are made by the designer will be repeated, and will become the burden of all to live in.

This magnification of error has for many years continued unquestioned and unchecked. Our contemporary urban crises, social and physical, are in part the legacy of this practice.

Federally sponsored building or rebuilding projects should require a maximum of user participation and control in the design and later administration of all building efforts.

Such projects should also be required to distribute architectural contracts over as large a group of individual design firms as possible. These designers must be bound by contract to work with local potential or present users.

The more designers, the less monotony and the less multiplication of errors. Having more designers per large project also facilitates working in small groups with neighborhood groups or user committees.

Youth, especially, should be involved in design and planning decisionmaking. Where other age groups have been consulted in past experience, youth has been traditionally ignored. Young people are experimenting with the shape of their own new environment, with life styles and social structure. Give them the tools to implement their experiments and discoveries, and they will put down weaponry.

The problems of our central cities receive national attention (but not much support). We must remember that a city is not an isolated patch of civilization, but is enmeshed in a larger web of population centers. Many of the greatest contemporary social problems are rooted in the inadequacy, barrenness and environmentally deprived and narrow local communities and neighborhoods, both inside and outside of major cities.

We must reevaluate the viability of our neighborhoods. While we focus on the problems of the decaying central city, we must not lose sight of the function of neighborhoods and houses, wherever they exist in the metropolitan area.

The details of day-to-day experience in houses and neighborhoods determine the quality of life for all people in all the extensions of urban life, from downtown to suburb. While the obvious and violent crises of our cities are being attended—or ignored—we must be aware of a growing mute crisis in our towns and neighborhoods.

Wherever people in America live today, they are plagued by the symptoms of social dysfunction. Social problems arise in neighborhoods and remain there to poison the overall quality of life. We worry about drug addiction, rising divorce rates and incidence of mental illness, increases in school dropouts, rising juvenile delinquency, rising crime rates, and we experience anomie, the lack of community life which marked the early years of American life.

Some, if not many, of these ills can be traced to the inadequacy of the physical—and, therefore, the social—environments of our local communities. Our communities, towns and neighborhoods have grown cold, barren and inhospitable. In simple language, "there is no place to go" in most suburbs and in many cities. This constitutes what I call setting deprivation.

Setting deprivation can be said to exist when some or all of the range of social settings, and their physical facilities, necessary to the support of healthy community and individual life, are missing.

Communities in a state of setting deprivation are bound to produce people who are in some sense rootless. Where the environment deprives us of opportunities to meet together under a variety of conditions, either indoors or out, in both planned and spontaneous gatherings, the cohesive bonds of society dissolve.

Living overlong in an environment composed of too few or improperly organized environmental possibilities drains the meaning, the social context, and the stimulation from our lives. Established traditions, the desirable behavior patterns of communication, mutual government, peace-keeping and child care, recreation, courtship and other elements disintegrate or disappear without the support of appropriate environmental settings.

Mutation of social behavior, not always in negative evolution, will result as old behavior patterns disappear. Populations adapt to even the most barren of surroundings. They may also maladapt.

As the physical environment becomes less functional, it fails to support, as it did in the past, the context for the social behavior that the society is built upon, and when the physical context disappears, in the words of Dr. Roger Barker, the "behavior settings" disappear.

Then, lacking the support of the context, some of the social behavior begins to disintegrate, and I think we can analyze many of the problems we see around us now in that context.

If we neglect to provide the complete range of settings in our communities, to compensate for those we no longer can contain within our homes, and to maintain adequate access to those which never were within the home, we may expect new behavior patterns to arise suddenly. These will, lacking stable environments and the support of a strong physical and social setting, change rapidly according to fad or to demogoguery.

In other words, I suggest that lacking the proper supports and proper kinds of settings in the physical environment, behavior fluctuates, becomes labile, and will attach itself to the strongest kind of stimulus that is available, and that might not be a physical environment. It could be demogoguery.

Every neighborhood in this country either urgently needs or could significantly benefit from, an increased variety and density of settings. Viable neighborhoods cannot be achieved without a greater range of behavior settings than we presently find in most communities, and all must be within easy, rapid transportation—or, preferably, walking distance—of every resident.

This is a crisis-oriented country. We have heard this said many times. I think that when I said our neighborhoods are in mute crisis, it pointed to a danger, because this is a crisis that isn't going to scream at us, maybe not for a long time, and I think that now is the time to address it, when there is still a possibility of making major changes, major solutions, major provisions, so that we don't end up with a crisis later.

We are in the middle of a good deal of rebuilding, and I think that if we successfully emerge from the international crisis that we are in now, we will be able to put more funds into our cities, and, we should do it with that kind of mute crisis in mind, and attempt to enrich the environment.

What follows is an attempt to describe a whole community. If you go over your own neighborhood, or the neighborhoods where you used to live, you may find on a Sunday when you were looking for outside stimulus, there was nothing to do there, no place to go. Many community settings which are so commonplace as to be out of awareness when they are present, can be keenly missed in their absence in an environmentally deprived area.

At the minimum, every neighborhood requires extra beds for transients and visitors, in the form of rentable rooms or hotels; there must be eating and drinking places where people can meet and talk; we must provide facilities for youth to carry on courtship rituals under conditions appropriate to the rapidly changing youth culture.

There must be jobs available, now almost non-existence, close to most suburbs. The zoning of our suburbs tends to be so tight that men, women and children are artificially separated for a good quantity of their lifetimes by zoning. They are zoned out of each other's areas of responsibility and out of each other's life experiences.

People need to meet in formal, ritualized competition, as in sports; everyone, especially children, needs several kinds of nearby recreation resources. Shopping must be close by and within the time/distance range of the aged and of those women who are heads of households, who must take children along.

Healthy community and political life can only continue so long as men can meet privately or publicly, and discuss anything, in any size group, without the possibility of permission denied; we need meeting places. Obviously, all need shelter, bathing and toilet facilities. Not all have them.

We all need to get above it all and contemplate the activity around us from the vantage of a safe meditative lookout—we need a window on the world. Our individual territories connected by daily routes and paths tie it all together to form the network of each human community. A whole community contains no less—and perhaps much more.

Access to the whole community is especially important as we grow old, and participation in community life shifts to less active involvement.

The aged need the opportunity to meet with their peers, to communicate their world view and experience to the young, and to enjoy the youngest. They have to be able to shop, vote, and walk safely in the streets.

While housing for the aged requires special attention to detail, it must not be isolated in ghettos for the aged or "projects." Such housing should be mixed into the community in order to remove stigma and provide a variety of housing and life styles for people to choose from as they age.

Our routes and paths, our roads, are choked and lethal and must be relieved by massive public investment in individualized public transportation systems which are not tied to fixed routes. Roads and automobiles are killing us at a rate which competes with war.

If it seems that occasionally I strayed from the residential environment to talk about things like roads, I would like to mention that when the environment is considered, no part of it can be left unanalyzed, because it is an interconnected interdependent system. In any human community, even the smallest town, the quality of its residential life, even the indoor experience, is dependent upon the design of roads, the placement of the roads, the density of traffic, and whether or not a road which was originally a human walking footpath can still be used for that purpose.

Walking has many ramifications in our social life, which I hope to get into, and if the path has become a super highway, then the small-scale face-to-face human activities are eclipsed by the speed, the noise and the danger of the automobile.

As major functional places in our man-made habitat—the public or community-centered ones—were removed to more and more distant shopping and other specialized "centers," the notion of what distance is a reasonable walking distance proceeded to shrink. Now, with no place to go, we simply don't walk if we can drive.

Thus, we often don't know all the streets in our immediate neighborhood, nor do we recognize more than a small number of our neighbors by sight. We certainly don't find long walks through the monotonously repetitive housing developments rewarding enough for any but desperate measures on a dreary, housebound weekend.

An experience—walking, and its legitimate setting—the path—have fallen away. Probably our physical health has suffered by its absence. Certainly, because our neighbors are unrecognized, our neighborhoods have become anonymous and, perhaps partly because of this, dangerous.

Circularly, we retreat to our cars and ignore the environment, covert our neighborhoods to freeways, our meeting houses and parks to parking lots. We learn that we must drive with our windows closed and our doors locked.

Women with children to care for are often terribly, dangerously isolated and lonely. They need places to walk to in cities and suburbs, eating places, meeting and working places. Contemporary zoning practices militate against an interesting walking community by excluding interesting destinations. When people don't walk, they don't meet, and remain isolated.

Play Space

It is the growing concern of playground designers and observers that conventional playgrounds, vestpocket parks and tot lots are only marginally effective as play resources. I think they don't work at all. Play space must reflect the nature of the play experience. It must be fluid, changing, full of variety, challenge, mystery, opportunity, fantasy and exploration. It must permeate the environment.

New towns and urban renewal projects must require all future designs to incorporate a continuous web of play routes on publicly owned and maintained land to be ubiquitous in the plan. Playgrounds I have observed favor athletic boys, ignore girls, and do not provide for the much more frequent nonathletic play activities.

Youth

A rich, varied community environment will have activity foci which are especially attractive to, and preferably operated by young people. As long as suburban "bedroom communities" become more restrictive in their zoning, and police harassment of active young people in quiet suburban neighborhoods continues, kids will leave their homes and hometowns in search of action elsewhere.

This deprives the local communities of the stimulus and growth of young energy and imagination. It also puts unreasonable pressure on the host communities in metropolitan areas, often leading to trouble for all.

We should be building and supporting programs in every community, using rented quarters, in which young people run and regulate their own social, political, medical and recreational activities. This cannot be accomplished easily in many neighborhoods because land-use zoning has become too restrictive. Federally-aided projects should encourage relaxation of zoning regulations where social and recreational uses are involved.

Schools

Last, our public schools will be under the greatest pressure in the next few years to reorient their spaces and curricula in an effort to become more competent institutions. Some communities have already begun to replace obsolete school buildings with mass-produced industrialized buildings.

Industrialized architecture is a welcome experimental alternative to both the high cost of construction and the shelter shortage.

However, there is, again, the probable danger that we will be multiplying our mistakes.

Such projects should always be preceded by the most careful predesign programing, analysis of activities, behavior patterns, traffic flow within the building, acoustic qualities, lighting, airflow and temperature requirements. Most important, we need to predict how well a good teacher will be able to relate to students, and how well the children can work.

We must become more sophisticated about specifying the performance of the architecture in behavioral and psychological terms.

Each building project where industrialized housing is tried should be preceded by a pilot building, and that pilot building must be evaluated and tested in actual use, where its mistakes and inappropriate configurations may be inspected and corrected before similar structures are built elsewhere.

We made a mistake on a large scale, in about 1830, when the Kirkbride mental hospitals were being built all over the country, and even now we are suffering from that error.

Up until recently, there weren't any normal analyses of how poorly the Kirkbride buildings were designed, and we were building them up to a few years ago.

I think we are in danger of duplicating that process again with every kind of building program, that the Federal Government has influence over.

The Federal Government should consider establishing a clearing-house for educational facilities, making design information public. This agency should be responsible for the disbursement of any Federal funds for the construction of educational buildings in local communities.

Such construction should be required to adhere to a design pro-tocol of preprograming, pilot testing, and postconstruction evalua-tion and report of findings. If we fail to institute such procedures, we run the danger of replacing outmoded schools all over the country with look-alike structures made from the same cookie-cutter molds, none of which work more effectively than the ones they replace.

If we put legislative and budgetary emphasis anywhere in the hometown environment, we must reserve for the schools the highest priority.

THE CHAIRMAN: Thank you very much, Mr. Spivack.

On the point you make on educational buildings, I have a number of building contractors and architects coming to see me, and I know they have other Senators, complaining about the lack of imagination and the use of some of the best information about how the buildings ought to be constructed, and expressing the same kind of dissatisfaction that you do here about the lack of use of the best designs and the most viable type of construction.

Is that a general feeling on the part of better informed architects and building contractors?

DR. SPIVACK: Well, if I can answer your question, there seem to be three kinds of architects. There are lots of bad ones. There are some very good ones, and then there are some architects who seem to be intimately familiar with procedures for analyzing behavior, for designing appropriately for behavior, for making buildings that function well.

It isn't always true that architects who have a lot of imagination, who are well-known and have a good reputation, are in this latter category.

There are so few architects in the latter category that I think it places us in jeopardy. There are really two groups pleading for better architecture, not to mention the consumers. There are the architects who want to see better monumental, more aesthetic constructions, more lavish constructions, and then there are those architects who feel that buildings of that sort, while not necessarily malfunctioning, often do, and that more attention ought to be spent on really analyzing what is needed there before the building is built.

In fact, more attention should be spent on whether the building is really necessary at all.

THE CHAIRMAN: What I understand you are recommending in your closing paragraph here is that there ought to be somewhere in the Government a clearinghouse where these factors that you have been suggesting here, together with other considerations, could be evaluated and various model designs suggested for the construction of buildings, at least those that involve Federal funds. Is that correct?

DR. SPIVACK: Partially. I don't mean to indicate that a model design is an appropriate way to handle the problem, because I really feel that model designs tend to be copied. The implication is that they are there to be copied. Every community is going to have rather special needs, and special requirements. There will be different ethnic groups there, different customs, different educational and different other kinds of philosophies.

What is needed instead is a storehouse of information about the way things work in buildings, what happens if you organize the layout of a building one way as opposed to another, how does the traffic flow work, what happens if you use one type of airflow system or another, perhaps the effects of facing the windows to the east or west, what happens to the perception of people when the walls are painted one color and not another?

THE CHAIRMAN: That would involve, would it not, some of the system analysis that has been used in defense contracting and the space program, where you have to look at the total environment and not just the design of the building without reference to the surrounding needs. Is that correct?

DR. SPIVACK: Well, I think the systems approach may eventually be the appropriate one, but I am afraid we are going to wait some years before the information in the field is of sufficient density and precision to constitute a system.

I think that instead we are going to have to store information in terms of patterns, essentially.[1]

THE CHAIRMAN: Where, in either this country or elsewhere in the world, would you say that urban planning is best informed on the demands of behavior and space needs? Can you point to some areas that you are familiar with where you think the problem is being handled properly.

DR. SPIVACK: That is a hard one. It really is a hard one. I can't think of an area. I tend to look at social indicators when I am asked a question like that, and I can't think of an urban environment anywhere in the world where social indicators don't tell me that there is something wrong.

I think if one wanted to look for a model of a community that was successfully handled, one would have to look back in time, not, I think, look at the present.

I may be wrong. My experience isn't that vast, and I suspect that a successful model could be found by looking back to country towns, where the decisions were made not unilaterally, but by a great many people over a long period of time.

THE CHAIRMAN: People are moving out of the country towns.

[1]For an explanation of patterns read: *A Pattern Language Which Generates Multiservice Centers,* Christopher Alexander, Center for Environmental Structure, 2701 Shasta Rd., Berkeley, Calif. (1968), pages 15–16.

DR. SPIVACK: It no longer serves the function that we need to serve. In other words, economic forces and other forces tend to make environments like that obsolete, but for their time they were appropriate. They were less hazardous, less noxious, than our environments are now, because I think the decisionmaking was spread out over time, and it was spread out over people.

THE CHAIRMAN: We live in a highly mobile society, as you know.

Who really ought to make the decisions about neighborhood functions? I mean, should every neighborhood serve the same function? If not, there are variations. Who ought to have the chief voice in restructuring those neighborhoods, the residents, the people who really live in the communities, not Government experts or design experts, but primarily the people who live in those communities?

DR. SPIVACK: The neighbors.

The role of the Government expert, of the city planner, I think, is in for change. I think it is changing now. I think it is certainly changing among the students in the city planning schools.

It is changing to the role of consultant, where I, personally, think it belongs.

No one, no agency, no man, has enough information, or even can gain access to enough information, or can understand the complexity of the network of a human community, and I think to structure it right, your input has to be diversified enough to cover all the needs, styles and all interest groups in a community.

Now, I know that is hard to get. We have to develop techniques and competance for consulting to neighborhoods.

We have to find ways of getting around our professional training in which professionals talk mostly to other professionals. We have to get down to the issues of what is needed, what the people need, what do they want, and then be able to tell them how best to get what they need and want, how best to design the environment.

THE CHAIRMAN: If you were given the responsibility to rebuild or revitalize a rundown neighborhood near the Capitol here, or any place else, if you had the responsibility of making it a more pleasant and viable place for people to live, how would you go about it? Would you begin with the experts, or would you begin by talking to the people who live in the neighborhood? How would you crank up a program of rebuilding?

DR. SPIVACK: I guess I would attempt to hire the people in the neighborhood to run the program. I probably would attempt to hire a range of people from the neighborhood, not only people who have a reputation for competence in that neighborhood, people who have been successful in business and in public programs, who have spent a life of competence, but I would also want to hire, and this may sound a little contradictory, I would want to hire people who don't have a reputation for making it, because those people know where the problems are. Those people are always bumping their heads, and it may have nothing to do with incompetence. That is a poor word, anyway.

What we need is people who have been suffering with the problems that we are trying to redress, to come and redress the problems themselves.

I think there is competence in neighborhoods stored among people who have to battle every day with the same kind of details that make their lives miserable. There is a lot of competence that could be shared and brought out, shared across communities from one community to another, and could be shared within the community, which would make the community more viable.

THE CHAIRMAN: Do you think it is feasible to develop neighborhood codes, like some of our building codes, setting minimum standards that would have to be met, or does that result too much in a community form of development?

DR. SPIVACK: I think that is an interesting idea. It is not one that I previously had thought of, of breaking the zoning and coding down to the neighborhood level; in other words, to make it that finegrained.

But it is an attractive idea. There is a possibility that you could develop quite specific, quite distinctly appropriate kinds of environments, environments which were subculturally specific, that were socially specific with respect to kinds of economic possibilities that the residents have. Yes; I think that is interesting.

THE CHAIRMAN: Thank you very much, Dr. Spivack. We appreciate your testimony.

4. Mental Health Implications of the Organization of the Large Scale Physical Environment*

Mayer Spivack, M.C.P. (City Planner)
Robert S. Weiss, Ph.D. (Sociologist)
Gerald Caplan, M.D., D.P.M. (Psychiatrist)
Alan P. Sheldon, M.B., B.Chir., D.P.M., S.M.Hyg. (Psychiatrist)
Herbert C. Schulberg, Ph.D., S.M.Hyg. (Psychologist)

It is imperative that human service organizations pose serious questions regarding the psycho-social consequences of environmental characteristics, including the rates at which those characteristics are changing. The probabilities and potential for human adaptation or maladaptation to unprecedented stresses must be systematically examined.

Human service organizations have what are perhaps their most serious trials ahead of them. They must develop organizational structures and intervention programs for facilitating the productive adaptation of individuals and social networks to increasing environmental stresses. A first step might be to develop criteria and dimensions which could be used to assess the characteristics of the large scale physical environment; Spivack and his colleagues outline a beginning.

In December of 1966, a team of investigators in the Laboratory of Community Psychiatry at Harvard Medical School were asked to present testimony to the Department of Health, Education and Welfare on what they termed "environmental hazards" to be considered in the planning of programs for that federal agency over the next fifty years. Headed by a city planner, the team focused on mental health issues that intersect with the structure and

*Research supported in part by a grant from The Permanent Charities, Inc., to the Medical Foundation, Inc., and from a National Institute of Mental Health contract, PH43-66-1150, to the Laboratory of Community Psychiatry, Harvard Medical School.

organization of the physical environment. This very timely series of multi-disciplinary discussions, focusing so directly on problems especially relevant to our field, provided the context for a useful forum in which to evaluate ideas which this planner had long felt were crucial issues for urban planning.

The large scale physical environment affects the lives of men chiefly at the points where individuals or groups of individuals meet together and interact. Both the large and small scale physical environments of the city constitute organized sets of subsystems, which aside from the organizing principles of economics, transportation, and other physical-ecological patterns, are formed around, and in turn give supporting structure to, the social and personal lives of their inhabitants.

The physical environment may therefore be seen as propitious and supportive when it "works" properly and "agrees" with the living patterns and needs of its inhabitants. It is inhibiting when its structure interferes with, distorts, or prevents the performance processes and movements associated with basic life-space needs.

Incongruities result when the structure, form, or plan of the physical world isolates individuals from one another, or thrusts them into constant conflict. Further problems arise when the environment unequally supports the activities of one group over another by virtue of space allocations or rights to territory or by cutting a group off from the mainstream of life as is often the case in housing projects and mental hospitals. Social disorganization may occur in environments which inappropriately match the needs and living patterns of the user population. Critical areas for planning include not only the interaction of man with man, machine, building and transportation system, but also at earlier points, where the necessity for control over the environment is manifested, man's communications, which act upon others who in turn control an environment which in turn acts to modify or limit his own further behavior.

Generally, then, it may be said that the political status of men and their communities, the delicate balance of freedom from excessive control, and the freedom to control their own lives, environments, and their communications or efforts at the control or adjustment of the environment, are among the most critical issues in circular, mutually regulating relationships, which link behavior and the physical environment.

Incongruity is produced wherever one's voice in the control over environmental issues is lost. Such a loss of vote and veto over large and small issues can in itself constitute a considerable danger to the mental and social and political health of the individual and society. As a result of this kind of frequently accidental disenfranchisement, the individual may suffer serious losses and deprivations in still other areas, and come to view himself, not without reason, as a victim of social forces and physical circumstances beyond his control. Thus, a defect in control occurs when the information flow or feedback from the user fails to reach its mark, and the communication path is seriously interrupted. Here the environment itself may be at fault, for a major positive attribute of a well organized environment is that it provides wide access to decision-making processes and power centers where control actions are taken.

When deprived of opportunity to participate in the dialogue concerning these issues, individuals in the community run the risk of inheriting a man-made environment which is out of control, and highly unrelated to their needs. The structure and organization of the man-made environment may present distinct and far-reaching personal, social, and cultural obstacles by the following routes:

1. Individuals and groups may be forced to operate within a *too limited* environment. The world may "close in" on them as in a ghetto or urban slum. To some extent new towns and suburbs are prone to this problem when too few opportunities for diversion or change of activity patterns are presented.

2. When the environment is *insufficiently structured* and fails to provide a clear set of instructions to the users suggesting how they might use it, people often find themselves at a loss for something to do or somewhere to go. Many public institutions, such as mental hospitals, housing projects, and schools, are so designed.

Thus, a criterion for a successful environment may be one which contains a wide spectrum of clear alternative frameworks for social and personal behavior (behavior settings).

3. Behavior-supporting environmental structure may be culturally *inappropriate* to the life patterns of the subculture using it. However rigid or loosely structured, it is essential that the structure be well matched to the variety of social and personal needs common to the lives of the users. Brand new renewal housing and vertical housing projects often are disruptive to the network of interdependent social relationships common to the former "slum" dwellers who often must move into them.

4. The environment must be *plastic,* it must be able to change over time in order that it may be adapted to newly-emerging needs of its users. Buildings, both interior and exterior, as well as the

city within which they are set, have an extremely long life when compared with the rapidly changing populations and their constantly changing demand patterns.

4a. A stable population group will pass through sequential and predictable life cycle stages, each having its characteristic way of altering the patterns of individuals and social behaviors, and their correspondingly appropriate physical settings.

As individuals pass from one stage of the life cycle to the next they frequently move to a community better fitted to their new social and personal needs. Such moves are typically from shared rented quarters or a furnished room to newer rented apartment space in the city at the point of marriage, followed by a move, for the middle class, to owner-occupied housing in a suburb when children arrive, back to rented or condominium quarters in the city as children mature and move away, and later, sadly, into nursing homes or housing for the elderly. Each of these changes marks the end of one living pattern and radical adjustment to a whole new life style. It is notable that here also are the common points at which personal and family crises occur. Some of these crises are borne of the changes in living patterns *per se*—such as the birth of a first child or the marriage of the last offspring, leaving the parents alone and comparatively lonely. These, in turn, may produce increased anxiety: for example, parents whose children have moved away may find themselves alone and "rattling around" in too large a house in the suburbs. If they move to a smaller apartment closer to the city, they will have somewhat severed those extrafamilial and community ties which enriched their lives previously. In the new situation, they must go about energetically establishing a new set of friends and relationships with the community. Their efforts will be somewhat frustrated and certainly complicated by the fact that, in their new niche, neighborhood patterns and the conventions governing the boundaries between privacy and intimacy are changed. They have moved from a suburban setting where neighbors are far enough away and can therefore afford to be friendly and visit or exchange favors often. In the new apartment they may find it more difficult to meet their neighbors across the hall who wish to remain nearly anonymous. They will have to establish their new acquaintanceships through their employment if they are not already retired, or resort to other formal and institutionalized supports for their sense of community. This can be a difficult period for many people. Some may fail to successfully negotiate the change and retire into loneliness, TV-itis, depression, anomie, alcoholism, or perpetual nomadism.

In addition to the standing patterns of individuals who pass through the various life cycle phases there is the strong possibility that the life cycle phases themselves are changing in length both relatively and absolutely, e.g., childhood is growing shorter, adolescence correspondingly earlier and also longer, adulthood and childbearing earlier and longer, old age later and longer. These changes will both exacerbate and complicate the need for appropriate settings.

4b. Certain areas of the city may be subject to periodic shifts in population groups. The so-called grey areas and slums have historically been host to a succession of ethnic and racial groups. Each of these shifts in population type will bring with it a changed demand pattern for the environment based upon its traditions, its subculture, relative social position, and degree of acculturation. Even in the unlikely event that such areas are kept in good repair, problems will arise which focus about the use of space. Most eastern cities have areas which give evidence of the inapplicability of spaces designed for the 19th century upper and upper middle class living standards and social patterns to the current needs of poverty-stricken Negro families.

4c. Further changes may be imposed upon a stubborn, inflexible and therefore (in our terms) incongruous environment by general changes in the structure of the societies' living patterns as a whole, as for example from a society of busy, skilled interdependent craftsmen to an automated, anonymous, and leisured society.

4d. Continuing difficulties are produced, as is well known, from the dual problem of absolute and relative obsolescence of the man-made world. Absolute obsolescence is just another way of euphemizing the plain old age and decay of physical structures which cannot be or are not removed; and relative obsolescence is what happens to brand new hospitals before they are built. They are rarely designed according to the best and latest trends in medical practice and technology, may require years in planning and construction, and therefore have a high potential replacement rate and cost. As building technology accelerates, as is surely bound to happen, a greater variety of building types will suffer the same fate. It is important to remember here that technological innovations have reverberating social and cultural effects, and that a building obsolete for these reasons is not only obsolete relative to the newest construction techniques but is also not well adapted to the new needs of a society whose basic structure has been changed by other technologies.

5. An increase in *crowding* is a somewhat predictable condition

for the city dweller of the future, if it is not already with us to an undesirable degree. Every culture reacts to crowding or increased population density in a unique style and pattern of compensation. New interpersonal and individual adjustments may arise based upon the previous, less crowded history. These new social styles and adjustment patterns will exhibit varying degrees of individual and social pathology, which derive from the original and also the changing values of the culture, which are relatively different from other cultures in similar states of population concentration and explosion. It is hard to differentiate the pathologies of crowding from those attributable to the often associated conditions of poverty, relative political disenfranchisement, low social status and consequent exposure to persecution and prejudice, and physical confinement irrespective of human density. However, it is almost certainly true that the dynamics of behavior under overcrowded conditions—so far only studied in dense animal populations—are to some extent operating in our own human social systems.

The various units within which individuals live—the marriage, the family, the neighborhood—each require some protection against undesired invasion. Crowding interferes with their boundaries, e.g., when families are squeezed into too few rooms, the relationship of the married couple cannot be bounded from the children; when many families are squeezed together, the children become the wards of the neighborhood, rather than members of a family, and traditional control of children by their parents is disturbed. It would be well to learn what we can from new studies of what happens to Americans under conditions of simple crowding as experienced on military ships.

6. *Isolation.* When the organization of the environment is incomplete and discontinuous—when areas of the city or parts of buildings are functionally isolated from the main body of the city or from its subunits—an inequity is created. The isolation of man from man, and of men from their resources, constitutes a threat to the economic strength and social and mental health of whole populations.

6a. *Isolation and the Individual.* Individuals are rarely singled out for isolation, but the experiences of accident victims, explorers, and the research results from sensory deprivation studies point to the basic need for continuous and organizable sensory experience without which men suffer from acute personality disorganization and hallucinations. Such experiences, of course, cannot happen in a social context.

6b. *Group Isolation.* When groups are isolated en masse from the mainstream of society, unreasonable hardships are produced in the most minute areas of their daily lives. The Columbia Point Housing Project in Boston is an example of such physical isolation of a lower income group. This large complex of public housing buildings is situated at the end of a point of land which extends into Boston Harbor, near a foul dump, and connected to the city by a long, unpopulated, dreary road. The populations of this and other similarly situated areas cannot move out of their island-like situation without an automobile which they are often unable to afford. Public transportation is either not available or infrequent and may involve long travel times and many change-overs before a work destination in the city may be reached. Deprived of access to the more common services and resources, such a community must often do without what they cannot themselves supply. Even such basic resources as emergency hospital care may be dangerously far removed. Further disadvantages are incurred as social isolation and the stigma of unfamiliarity brands the children of such communities as outlanders in their schools. The additional factors of a high concentration of large, poor, ill-educated, and ill-housed families with few members employable or employed provides little in the way of opportunities for mutual assistance in any but the morally supportive sense, and may increase the "contagion" of maladaptive or undesirable modes of social behavior among the inhabitants, especially the children.

6c. *Social Isolation within the City.* Rooming house areas, often the large sprawling skid-row sections of the city, and apartment hotel districts which are the "homes" of countless thousands in every large city, are filled with individuals who constitutionally lack either the physical strength and ability or the social skills necessary for the establishment of viable relationships with any but the most primitive and fundamental resources in the immediate neighborhoods. These same people frequently lack for the same reasons a supportive and psycho-socially necessary circle of friends and acquaintances. If they are without immediate family located nearby, or, as is sometimes the case, are estranged from family, then they may be truly isolated within the most populous urban areas. The lack of facilities which could enrich the lives of such people in our cities is a significant addition to their burdens.

6d. A major hazard in a metropolitan area is an inadequate transportation system. For instance, lack of transportation between suburbs and central city may maroon many women, especially newcomers, in bedroom communities where they may be far from

7. *Dispossession.* Many individuals and families in downtown areas
friends and may spend their days in soul-destroying idleness and
boredom.
of nearly all American cities now face the sometimes severe
psychological and social stresses created when they are forced to
give up their homes to a renewal or highway program. Such programs usually fail to adequately deal with relocation problems of
the displaced, let alone provide the necessary connections to emergency services for the kinds of trauma associated with these moves.

People tend to grow "roots," in other words they appear to invest
themselves emotionally in the safety and security of an enduring
home-place. This need to establish territory may be one basic
attribute of all higher forms of living things, man included.
8. Danger, in its more commonly recognized forms, seems to lurk
in particular kinds of *unregulated public spaces.* Central Park in New
York City and other similar public areas have recently received
an unusual amount of bad publicity due to their high incidence
of violence of various sorts. Public spaces, the roadways, parks,
parking lots, vacant lots, and alleys are often legally nearly a no-
man's-land. Responsibility for the upkeep and quality of such environments is often either unclear or divided in an irrational fashion
among a multiplicity of city and state departments. Most public
agencies pay far too little attention to the details of good design
and maintenance of such areas, and it is not surprising, therefore,
that in their neglect, these spaces are really nonsettings in which
anything can, and often does, happen. Most parklands are an indispensable boon to any urban area. However, the more intensely
used or travelled parts of these places need some degree of structure
and control over their use. Responsibility in all its ramifications,
legal, physical, and social, is a key issue in the preservation of
safe public spaces. Neighborhood involvement in the responsibilities of administration, maintenance, and control of public
spaces in their areas, perhaps under changed legal conditions, can
do much to make these areas more useful.
9. *Complexity.* Urban areas, as they continue to spread and grow,
are becoming more complex in their organization as well as physically larger. Connections between points are often invisibly linked
by underground transportation systems. Subway travellers often
have unclear conceptions of their path between points, or the relationships of discrete geographic entities within the city whole.
Associated with this cognitive inability to grasp the order of the
environment there may be indications of psychic stress appearing
in the forms of disorientation and restricted movement patterns.

10. Active government-sponsored programs which seek to extensively alter the physical environment are multiple, such as demonstration cities and urban renewal and highway programs. Centralized master planning of the urban ecology has dangerous limitations based on the limited comprehensiveness of our knowledge of urban ecological and city-building and community-building dynamics. The notion that the range of experience, aesthetic tastes, and ideas of a handful of designers, developers, and planners is sufficient to satisfy the life-space requirements of communities of 500,000 individuals is a questionable one, and may diminish the ecological, social, and economic viability and diversity of these communities. It almost certainly increases the experiential monotony. Even the best of phased master plans may suffer from these stubborn shortcomings. New planning policies, techniques, and requirements could more finely distribute economic planning and design responsibility among the professionals and the future users of these areas. There is a need for phased information feedback to the planners of these projects with seriously expanded evaluation follow-up studies.

11. *An Unstable Environment.* Paradoxically, in the future we may be exposed increasingly to a hazard emerging from improvements in transportation. Supersonic plane travel, which suddenly transports us to new cultural surroundings and upsets our biophysical rhythms by rapid traversal of time and date lines, may result in disorientation and lowered efficiency for hours or days. Judgment during that period is likely to be defective, and unless arrangements are institutionalized for a moratorium to provide an opportunity to recover from the crisis before serious work is undertaken, we will be exposed to major stress.

This discussion of cause and effect relationships which links the large scale urban physical environment to the mental health of populations, while neither exhaustive or prescriptive, suggests a range of concerns within which urban planners and policy makers and social scientists and mental health specialists may usefully collaborate.

5. Environmental Health: Politics, Planning, and Money

Leonard J. Duhl, M.D., F.A.P.H.A.*

The following article is a thoughtful, provocative treatment of environmental planning problems. The human dimensions of planning environmental change, and their inherent problems are brought into focus. Central to this process is the problem of how we, collectively, both maintain the symbolic codes which characterize our society, and at the same time alter those codes to meet dynamics and pressures of contemporary problems in living.

Human service organizations will, in large part, be called upon to provide both the long-range dreams and the immediately practical models for confronting and dealing with these problems. How effectively they respond may well depend upon their ability to respect and revise their own internal organizational and interorganizational symbolic codes.

The problem of comprehensiveness in the field of health planning is as old as the Greeks, and yet as modern as the day-by-day problems confronting any community in America. There are times when those who would rise to the challenge presented then, as now, would desire nothing more than to play God in their suggestions of solutions to the problems of planning for the environmental health of a nation, or for a community within.

For, in fact, throughout man's history of time, most planners (or philosophers) who have attempted to create communities of the future—models of what could be—have assumed that responsibility more in theory of an optimum, of what might be, rather than in practical concept of what has been and what is. They have

*Dr. Duhl was special assistant to the Secretary, Department of Housing and Urban Development, Washington, D.C. 20410, when this paper was written.

This paper was presented before the First General Session of the American Public Health Association at the 94th Annual Meeting, San Francisco, Calif., October 31, 1966.

substantiated their theorizing with fine reports and studies and in the beauty of their persuasive maps and charts; utilizing their very ability, salesmanship, and charismatic qualities of leadership, they have thus presented their ideas—duly supported with the backing and power of the most legitimate forces in the community or nation—asking for acceptance and a mandate to effect these ideal goals.

Such goals of an environmentally healthy world, nation, or even community, sadly, are elusive goals. For the problems and their solutions are neither as neat and defined as the work of Ebenezer Howard whose Garden City concepts have affected city planning for years, nor as precise as the society created by Robert Owen in New Harmony, Ind. If the goal were to create a "thing"—a physical project, isolated, uncontaminated by people, perhaps it could be realized. We would require only funds, resources brought to bear upon the problem and we could reach the moon, the stars, Utopia.

I am certain that most of us would be willing, if not delighted, to sit down and design the prototype of a healthy community—to determine how land and space and minerals and air should be combined, add water, transportation, buildings, facilities, the endless array of all that would produce an ideal life in our society. Yet, I am not truly certain that, with all of our combined efforts and energies, we could design that situation which would anticipate all of the contingencies, and the ebb and flow of what is termed the political process. For panaceas are not responsive to environmental changes. Optimal environments can, at times, be created in the study of rats—but rats do not read *Time Magazine,* are not aware of being studied, and are not given to emitting constant feedback as we muddle through in our attempts to provide more—and more comprehensive—programs and activities.

The problems of health, alone, are complicated ones, for they reach far beyond the confines of the medical profession into the total fabric of community life. And the community is no longer local in nature, for it is intimately tied to the community of the nation as a whole. Inherently, this is a demand for integration and comprehensiveness.

The Task Forces of the National Commission of Community Health Services were designed with the notion that the end product of their work would not be a report—for reports do not, in themselves, make planning. Reports, though they may be comprehensive in nature, do neither guarantee comprehensiveness, nor integration. For reports are ofttimes much like coordinating commit-

tees—they have a title and good purpose, but, by themselves, they
are no more than a decorative set of covers within which can be
found the latest wisdom. They can be nicely filed away with all
the others each of us has on our desks or bookshelves in our
offices—unless. . . .

Being perceptive of that "unless," the Task Force on Environmental Health expressed their concern to participate in that endless
process of trying to improve our community, indicating that their
report is a foundation upon which to build. It is that concern with
action, with the here and now, with the realization that decisions
made today set the stage for the programs of the future, and that
those decisions have more import for planning that all the reports
ever to be written, that makes all of this significant.

Planning and Financing

I wish to concentrate the major portion of my remaining comments on some of the Task Force's thoughts on planning and financing—perhaps extending and modifying a bit here and paraphrasing
there.

"Planning" is not a product, but a process—an evolutionary continuum. If planning is to have pertinence to decision-making, to
resources allocations, expenditures of funds and utilizations of personnel energies, then planning—the process of planning—becomes
part and parcel of the total structure of politics. We would go
further to suggest—to firmly state—that it is in the political arena
that basic decisions to meet needs and demands are made, where
negotiations between competing programs and activities are
resolved, where all, geared from differing vantage points toward
helping somebody, something, or the total community, meet and
are met.

At this point in time—within our body politic—we are a society
where the importance of selling cigarettes and automobiles to ado-
lescents outweighs the import of understanding that adolescent's
needs relative to the process of his becoming a responsible adult
in our community. Not until our society is willing to concern itself
primarily with what kind of people we would like to have in our
communities, not until we are willing to place human needs above
economic values, above profit and even above selfish interests, not
until we have achieved this will we be able to have that kind of
healthy environment about which we are all concerned.

In the establishment of priorities for health, it is obvious in today's world that no one, under the current system of resources allocation, no one in his right mind would meet our Utopian-considered goals. For the process of resources allocation is such that priority values are given to such matters as land speculation, to profit, so that the construction of things and building is really much more important in the hierarchy of values than many of the issues which are of concern to us.

What Is Important in a Community?

I am, therefore, primarily questioning the values of our society. I am questioning what is really important to the people in our communities, and for what they are willing and anxious to spend their money. For these reasons, any planning for environmental health must be planning for programs and activities—and loud voices and screams when necessary—to educate, to activate, and to fight for these values which are basic to each of us from the moment of birth throughout our life. Planning for environmental health, then, is much more than a step-by-step, carefully thought out program of where and what and how much. It is also how and when and why, and which. Planning is a process of education; it is the process of redefining the goals and the objectives of our society and of the communities within.

In 1954, during a period of self-soul-searching, IBM realized that its primary concern as a business was not punch cards, but information retrieval. By realizing this, the total objectives and thus the activities of the organization were altered. It grew, it expanded; new devices, new tools were created, and new programs directed toward objectives heretofore considered outside the ken of the corporation were established. But the process of change from one view of a business to another is a long and arduous one.

The job of the planner in environmental health is the job of assuming the role of a Socrates—a questioner, advocate, and provocateur. It is asking the questions which promote a sort of soul-searching as to what objectives are achieved through designing a project, a program, or community in such and such a manner. He must constantly ask questions about the relationship between sewage lines and the ultimate development of the community. He must speak to questions which people do not realize are related to the problems of health—point out that the health of the city may very well be related to the political participation of its people, related to the attitudes of the total community toward minority groups, the poor, the people living in housing projects. He must raise questions, be the provocateur, the conscience of the community, asking whether they would like a healthy community; if so, how could they best achieve that end. It may mean raising questions about whether we allocate our limited resources primarily on the basis of giving-more-to-those-who-shout-the-loudest, or whether we should allocate them on the basis of need, thus, perhaps, giving higher priority to the communities of the poor—even to those who cannot marshal their forces to rebel, to riot.

He must raise questions about the values of all decisions of a long-range nature. He must not permit expediency or availability of "ear-marked" funds to cloud the issue of values. For, as we have noted, even the very little decisions of today, indeed, are the decisions which affect the future much more importantly than any long-range planning of planners.

Confrontation and criticism are inextricably part of the planning process, as is public, democratic airing of issues which involve the very people who are affected. It is also the process of negotiation and change, of learning and education, not only for the people of the community, but for the planner himself. For a plan to be effective, the plan must change, and for a planner to be effective, the planner must change.

Thus, planning is a broad, political process; any subdivision of planning for the total community, such as environmental health planning, must be cognizant of all the peripheral programs, activities, and other planning in effect which may have pertinence thereto. Thus, if we are to be concerned with environmental health planning, we are also to be concerned with all the factors in the environment with which the doctor, or, indeed, the medical profession has neither felt at home nor has his prior involvement been welcomed. Generally, the physician does not understand the process of planning housing; in fact, he has usually been a self-contained unit in a nice, neat container labeled "Health Programs," working on activities and issues which impinge upon many other compact containers within the community labeled "housing," "urban renewal," "sewage," or "transportation"—never does he come in contact with other planners. The structure of planning has been such that planners from one area can only talk to and communicate with other planners from the same area.

The Demonstration Cities and Metropolitan Development Act of 1966 marks the first governmental attempt to bring together new city, central city, or metropolitan (area-wide) planning with social and physical and environmental planning. It is this weaving together of specialized organs—of housing, educational, health, welfare operations—the woof with the warp—that carries great potential for creating comprehensive and over-all structures which will, in turn, permit the real processes of planning to take place. This has great implications for all whose primary concern is environmental health planning, for the planners of health facilities and programs will here be asked to meet on the same sacred ground as those who are involved in physical and economic development —to coordinate, correlate, and cooperate.

Establishment of New State Agencies

The Surgeon General has said "health is so interwoven into the fabric of the American culture that its utlimate design can only be determined by the people themselves." This year (1966) Congress passed legislation which will further facilitate this involvement, while at the same time providing for health planning involvement in new HUD programs—including the push toward more comprehensive one-stop facilities and services. This, the "Partnership for Health Bill," provides for the establishment of a State Planning Agency and a State Health Planning Council. The State Health Planning Agency will have as its concern planning for *all* health facilities and programs in the state. The State Health Planning Council will have representation from all local and state agencies—both governmental and voluntary—and from the ranks of the health consumers.

The Comprehensive Health Planning aspects provide grants for manpower, services, and facilities, for area-wide planning, and for training of personnel, studies, and demonstrations in the health planning field. Though regional functions, Hill-Burton agencies, and State Public Health Departments will maintain their responsibilities, the emphasis is definitely now on linking, strengthening, developing interrelationships, opening channels of communication between these and other programs extant. For perhaps one of the first times, rather than taking earmarked dollars and looking for an appropriate problem site, the emphasis is placed on local and state determination of goals, and problems, with a newly gained ability to package resources into programs to meet these needs.

The question of finance is one which becomes deeply related to our penchant for allocating resources in particular ways. So long as crises and emergencies continue to draw our attention to issues far from the immediate environmental concerns of our communities, it will be extremely difficult to find sufficient funds, or resources, for the development of healthy and competent cities. However, in addition to the two above-mentioned planning-centered or planning-oriented programs, HUD has several other planning assistance programs. Briefly, HUD 701 Urban Planning Assistance funds can be used to support virtually all planning and programing activities, including capital improvement programing, preparation of zoning codes and subdivision regulations, and coordination and liaison function between local and area-wide planning agencies. The design of most types of public facilities can be assisted under the HUD Section 702 Public Works Planning Program—it can carry planning through the project design stage, after the 701 program leaves off. The more willing health-concerned people become to climb out of their neat little containers, to become involved with and in other programs and activities, the more plausible is a climate in which additional resources will become available.

Here, our concerns become integrally tied to the concerns of the nation—even the world. For health planning must be part and parcel of the total planning in every community, every city, and in every metropolitan area. The health officials, in fact the entire health profession, must become part of the forum in which such decisions are made. Leadership in the health field must make itself known. One can expect neither comprehension nor leadership to arise from outside our profession.

Leadership must come from people who know; "knowing" means more than knowing about health, it means knowing the relationship of health to all other areas; it means understanding the broad, ecological model of our total environment; it means understanding the behavior of people and how they react; it means understanding resistance to change and the fantastic inertia of bureaucratic structures in government and in public and private institutions; it means starting a process and understanding that it is a rocky one.

It may mean muddling through; it may mean the making of alliances, of negotiations, and battles. It requires live—what I call "swingers" in the system—people who are ready and willing to modify, innovate, and change. It means breaking the bureaucratic molds when necessary, being willing and able to change one's own organization and institution so that it constantly renews itself, so that it can face the problems of the present and deal with the problems of the future.

The recent Ribicoff hearings reflect a mushrooming concern for the total environment of our cities; they also reflect a growing awareness of the inextricable ties between physical environment and social environment—an often discordant interdependency which cries out for a rejuggling of past planning mechanisms and creation of new models and communities of solutions for every problem. This cry extends to a call for new mechanisms in the federal government, in the regions and metropolitan areas, as well as new mechanisms in the cities—all of which are then able to pull together the many separate operations into meaningful wholes. This must take place, for planning for organizational change is as important as planning for change itself. This must take place if we are to ask for additional planning-for-the-future money.

Our society must be educated so that it comprehends this need to plan for the future. This, in itself, is an effort because we are a here-and-now culture, a respond-to-crisis society, concerned more with the immediate that with the long-range. We find it difficult, if not impossible, to concern ourselves too geatly with the very real prospect that the atmosphere will be totally polluted in 100 years.

The word used in one of the Task Force reports was to "listen." I think those of us concerned with environmental health planning must listen and participate. Listening requires hearing the voices not just of ourselves, but of others—the voices of the consumers and those who feel pertinence to our planning.

I do not believe that we are capable of creating an environment, at least not by our minds, that would be perfect for years to come —even for tomorrow. For plans and institutions which effect them, like people, tend to get old; even with the best of intentions, they bureaucratize and become sclerotic. Sometimes they must be markedly changed; sometimes they need to be excised and operated upon; and sometimes they must be replaced.

Plans and institutions, like people, must always be self-renewing; and unless this continued process of renewal takes place within our planning, our institutions and our people, we will neither have healthy communities nor healthy people. Thus, even though permanent Utopian construction should be left to the dreamers, we can and must create a structure for planning, for active participation in the political arena, which will permit us to modify and change and deal with problems as they evolve, and hopefully, will permit us to anticipate some of them.

6. Regional Human Services Delivery Systems

Herbert C. Schulberg, Ph.D., and Harold W. Demone, Jr., Ph.D.

In an attempt to demythologize such concepts as regionalization, centralization, and decentralization, the authors of the following article examine the process of regionalization as a planning tool. Like any other strategy or tactic, it has certain functional and dysfunctional properties, and is likely to be best used under certain specifiable conditions. Further, it is likely to pay highest dividends to organizations with particular taxonomic characteristics.

It would appear that regional planning throughout the human services is to become much more prevalent in the immediate future. Without giving careful and differentiated consideration to regionalization as a planning strategy, and in particular to differential outcomes which will vary as a function of organizational goals and population problems, we may be generating unrealistic expectations regarding the relative merits of this planning tool.

There can be little doubt in the minds of even ardent skeptics that the rationale for, and the manner in which, human services are provided in 1973 differs significantly from the patterns of a decade ago. For example, the psychoanalytic precepts which guided the clinician's definition of problems and his assessment of treatment alternatives continue to be well-regarded, but no longer as the fundamental cornerstone upon which a mental health program is built. Social psychiatric concepts which recognize environmental influences as well as the principles of learning theory have become equally relevant for structuring clinical services and guiding personnel utilization. Along with the changes in conceptual rationales, we have witnessed related shifts in the professionals' armamentarium; for example, outpatient community care rather than inpatient hospitalization is now the treatment of choice for both acutely as well as chronically disturbed individuals. Furthermore, clinicians have come to accept the fact that they alone cannot resolve all behavioral problems and that the participation of other community caregivers, with varying degrees of sophistication, is essential to their mission. In addition, many practitioners now are willing to acknowledge that the problems of the designated client often are as much rooted in his community's tumultuous social structure and fragmented caregiving system as in his personal psyche. Inevitably then, our contributions as individual practitioners will always be severely limited if they do not fit into a broader context.

THE CONCEPT OF HUMAN SERVICES SYSTEMS

It is the definition of this broader context which we contend is undergoing change. In the past decade our perspective and activities have expanded from the isolated clinic to the neighborhood health center and now to prepaid comprehensive health services. During the 1970's we will be challenged to evolve our scope even further by designing far-flung human service systems which seek to provide comprehensive and coordinated assistance to clients. March (1968) has described these new caregiving systems as incorporating the following features: comprehensiveness of services; decentralized facilities located in areas of high population density; and integrated program administration which permits continuity of care from one service element to the next with a minimum of wasted time and duplication.

The increasing tendency to designate a community's variety of health and social welfare services as human service organizations reflects not only the desire to provide services more efficiently but also a growing societal as well as professional recognition of the common denominator inherent in the varied problems presented to us by clients. It also indicates an appreciation for the generic quality integral to the helping actions of professional and non-professional caregivers despite the multiple technologies utilized by them. The long adhered to distinctions between the problems germane to a psychiatric clinic and an alcoholism clinic, for example, or the traditional distinctions between the functions of different health and social welfare professionals have become increasingly artificial, and many agencies have drastically revised their intake policies and clinical practices accordingly.

As these developments have unfolded, it has become clear that genuine, effective, comprehensive services can be rendered only through the forging of systemic linkages which bring together the various caregiving agencies needed to provide a complex array of resources, technologies, and skills. At the heart of these efforts is an implicit, if not explicit, conceptual framework for helping people which recognizes that human service programs operate as a system of organizations whose participants are interdependent and must be appropriately linked (Baker and Schulberg, 1970; Holder and Dixon, 1971). Systems concepts increasingly are being applied to the analysis and operation of human service programs, and they are expected to be particularly relevant in defining the problems of management, of changing human service organizations, of interorganizational relations, and of organizational-environmental interaction.

In seeking to apply human services systems concepts to a wide range of programmatic concerns, planners and administrators repeatedly are being challenged to explicate the size and pertinent characteristics of the geographic domain within which human services delivery systems should be organized and operated. The past choices have ranged, indeed even vacillated, from rigidly defined territorial entities geared to organizational rather than client needs to fluid community bases seeking to maximize client accessibility but foregoing fundamental organizational requirements. In recent years, human services delivery systems based upon a "regionalized" geographic definition have gained increased prominence as a contemporary environmental locus within which to structure caregiving efforts. The regional approach assumes that all citizens are entitled to a variety of human services and that government has the responsibility for ensuring that citizen needs are met. The remainder of this paper will review the history of regional strategies as a political and administrative option for meeting community needs, and the significant issues confronting human services programs seeking to adapt this approach to their particular needs.

THE REGIONAL APPROACH

Interest in the regional solution of community problems goes back more than 80 years, during which time it has been the subject of an extensive literature (Hodge, 1969). For example, as long ago as 1889 a Metropolitan District Commission (MDC) was created in Massachusetts to solve Boston's water, sewage, and transportation needs. Despite being in the vanguard of the regionalization movement, Metropolitan Boston in the 1970's still is struggling to develop organizational structures and functional patterns for managing and coordinating its governmental and voluntary services. This problem is national in scope and Friedmann (1963) observed a decade ago that regional planning has usually involved much research but little implementation in a rather ill-defined combination of physical, economic, human resource, and natural resource concerns.

Over the years, a wide number of regionalization strategies have been developed where by the state authorizes local communities to share certain programs or to contract with a larger governmental unit (usually a county) to manage specified activities. Following the Massachusetts MDC model, special districts have been legislatively established in other states to deal with special services, water, and sewage control. The New York Port Authority is a prominent example of such an agency, and it is involved with transportation programs for Metropolitan New York City.

The urban county is a further model for regionalization whereby the county unit assumes responsibility for such services as libraries and fire and police protection. Florida's Dade County is often cited as an example of an effectively operating county structure. The annexation and consolidation of suburban areas by central cities was once very popular, and metropolitan centers like Houston grew in such a manner. Annexation is no longer commonplace, and in most states such an arrangement now requires the approval of the affected citizens and sometimes even the legislature so that it is an infrequently used regionalization strategy.

Federated government is often considered to be a model for contemporary regional arrangements. In Metropolitan Toronto, 13 municipalities assigned jurisdiction for selected services and planning to a Metropolitan Council representing all member communities (Farre, 1969). Although not originally intended as such, the Councils of Government, which were stimulated by federal aid to cities, have developed as metropolitan planning agencies. Recent federal acts and guidelines require that the Councils review the many applications for federally-aided projects which impact upon a metropolitan area. In a number of areas, the Council of Government is now viewed as a base from which some form of metropolitan government can grow. Generally then, the regionalization problem has become increasingly complex as specialized geographic structures are established for selected purposes. Every metropolitan area now has interlocking combinations of federal, state, and city districts, plus regionalization patterns established by individual profit and voluntary nonprofit organizations.

In many parts of the country, the pressure for regionalization of human service programs has come primarily from the federal rather than local government. There has not been any concurrent effective local pressure to consolidate small governmental units into larger ones, or even for state-supported services to follow similar geographic boundaries. As a result, the consumer, administrator, planner, and delivery specialist are all harassed by the increased complexity of the service system. We have also been faced with an apparent paradox. The steady growth of metropolitan areas has stimulated regional problem-solving strategies, while increased recent concern with the needs of the inner city has simultaneously directed attention and effort in the opposite direction. As we will note later, the seemingly contradictory pressures toward centralization and decentralization may not be as incompatible as they first appear.

Despite the cautiousness with which regionalization is being adopted in the health and, particularly, the social welfare field, it is, nevertheless, clear that the complexity of urban living patterns leaves few meaningful alternatives. (The major alternative is a massive new mass transportation system.) There has been a general incapacity to formulate comprehensive solutions which would provide total coverage to given populations. Costs are rising, and inefficiency is being created by duplicate and overlapping services and small agencies.

Efforts to rationalize the human services caregiving system are taking many forms. The Federal Community Mental Health and Mental Retardation Acts of 1963, as well as the comprehensive health planning and regional medical program legislation of 1966 and 1967, have provided a major impetus for relating public, private, and voluntary programs under a regional umbrella. In Cleveland, for example, multicounty health planning had been in progress for some time, but Public Law 89-749 became a major force in assuring the implementation of earlier recommendations.

U. S. Bureau of the Budget Circulars A-80 in 1967 and A-95 in 1969 represent other significant federal influences in that they attempt to impose orderly guidelines upon a state's disbursal of federal funds within congruent regional settings. By encouraging states to exercise leadership in delineating and establishing a system of planning and development regions, the Bureau of the Budget hopes that a consistent geographic base would emerge for federal, state, and local programs. The Allied Services Bill introduced by President Nixon in 1972 is another comparable thrust. Local community health and welfare councils for more that a decade have been similarly urging the merger of voluntary agencies so as to produce broader geographic coverage.

Purposes of Regionalization

It is important to be explicit about the specific purposes of a regional human services program since misconceptions about expected attainments can lead to failure. The range of possible purposes is indeed varied; it includes conceptual, abstract aims as well as practical, logistical goals. Regional community mental health programs are based upon the principle of ensuring that at least five essential services are available to all persons residing within the area covered. Regional community retardation programs are based on a similar strategy emphasizing service delivery. Comprehensive health planning, on the other hand, has not defined a minimal array of essential services as the cornerstone for regionalization, and instead, it is utilizing regionalization as the vehicle for ensuring representative citizen participation, particularly by consumers, in program planning and development.

Programs most commonly are regionalized to provide a comprehensive solution to a pressing problem. This is done by linking or merging various programs which have common or overlapping functions and contiguous or coterminous geographic boundaries. It is our impression that the combining of public and private resources has been more effectively achieved thus far in newer suburbs than in the core cities where long-standing prejudices, practices, and rigidities create significant constraints. Furthermore, rationalization has been more easily achieved when directed toward the solution of specific problems than when attempting to integrate total networks of services. Thus, an agency performing a single function can be organized to cover a county-wide or metropolitan area, particularly if it utilizes few professionals and many volunteers, e.g., Big Brothers and Big Sisters. If the bulk of the services are provided in the client's home, as in Homemaker programs, central administration is also eased. Conversely, multifunction agencies with a high volume of services usually find it necessary to limit their programs to smaller geographic bases.

The regionalized program can encompass planning, administration, and service. It can enhance the client's opportunity to receive quality care, permit specialization where needed, and increase agency accountability for program effectiveness, service delivery, and fiscal allocations. An example of such a motive for regionalization is seen among local Visiting Nurse Associations, many of which could not meet Medicare standards for specialist services without merging or developing formal contractual interorganizational agreements to exchange staff. When formally linked, however, they possessed the capacity to negotiate governmental contracts which permit them to offer a broad array of services. Some regional programs currently are being designed with the additional aim of assuring the broadest possible geographic base for citizen participation in policy setting.

An often overlooked consideration is that regionalization can simultaneously be a means for administratively centralizing a disparate group of programs while also decentralizing services within a centralized system. Such functions as purchasing, construction, research, or data processing could be performed more efficiently on a larger scale and, hence, should be centralized. On the other hand, many decisions about who is to be served and the nature of service programs could best be dealt with at the local level. The key question is not, "Do we centralize or decentralize?" but rather, "How can we best organize human services to guarantee the highest quality to all who use them?" Functional analysis should become the necessary study tool for accepting or rejecting regionalization. It should be stressed that regionalization has little merit when it is arbitrarily undertaken as an approach with inherent magical values. Rather, it should be viewed as an alternative administrative strategy permitting a contemporary approach to problems which cannot be resolved without coordinated effort on a larger territorial base.

In addition to its benefits, regionalization also creates a variety of complications, some rational and some nonrational. Any change, whether towards centralization or decentralization, implies an alteration in the present balance of power. Domains are affected and statuses changed. For example, minority groups view metropolitan government as a constraint upon their growing political power and, therefore, urge decentralization. The teachers' union in New York City, on the other hand, viewed decentralization as weakening its city-wide professional identity and political strength and resisted such efforts in the late 1960's with a bitter work stoppage.

A further constraint upon regionalization, rationally devised, emanates from the fact that home rule and local autonomy often are barriers to functional program analysis. The hostility of suburbs to municipal politics and politicians is long-standing, and their distrust is often so profound as to even preclude initial discussions. Also, whether the size of regions should be similar in each state (or nationwide), or be dominated by metropolitan areas is still ambiguous. Would it be possible, for example, to accommodate the natural megalopolises from Boston to Washington, D.C., or San Francisco to Los Angeles, within a regional framework?

The community mental health movement with its goals of prevention and treatment has raised particular problems for human services systems by specifying geographic service areas. Does assignment as a Center imply ownership of turf and clients? Does mental health center responsibility imply that other psychiatric and non-psychiatric organizations are precluded from offering human services in the same catchment area or region? Intra- or interregional organizational rivalries are still possible, and may even be accentuated on the interregional level as they develop and grow. Who does the overall planning and coordination? How do other parts of the state not in major metropolitan areas defend their interests, for the customary strategy of drawing concentric circles usually excludes major sections, especially when developed exclusively on an intrastate level?

A final complication of regionalization for human services is evident on the interstate level. Few state boundaries are still viable for service delivery systems, particularly when they divide metropolitan areas. Regionalization, to be effective at this level, would require the combining of several sovereign political entities but to date the resulting problems have been overwhelming and few effective interstate human services programs exist although interstate compacts are commonplace.

DEVELOPING REGIONS

A major problem in developing regional programs is the definition of the program's geographic scope. Levin (1968) has noted that the entire Southeast of the United States has been defined as a region for some purposes, while miniscular regions with populations less than 10,000 have been organized and funded for other purposes. The "urban regions" of the 1950's were in most cases roughly equivalent to standard metropolitan statistical areas and had populations well under a million. The redevelopment areas of the early 1960's were even smaller; a number of rural areas had populations of only a few thousand. By the late 1960's, however, we had witnessed the creation of at least nine mammoth economic development regions covering over a third of the nation's land area and a quarter of its population. These new regional agencies which resulted from the Appalachian legislation and the 1965 Public Works and Development Act began by spending the bulk of available funds on costly physical development programs. Subsequently, though, it was expected that an increasing share of their concern and funds will be devoted to human resource development.

As we strive to establish regional human services delivery systems, decisions about their appropriate community and territorial bases assume vital importance (Demone and Schulberg, 1971). In some parts of the country, the principles for defining geographic regions are well thought out, but in most cases guidelines have emerged primarily in response to the pressures of federal requirements and other such mandates. When all of a state's human service programs adhere to the same geographic territory, e.g., in Pennsylvania and Massachusetts, voluntary agencies have found it convenient to adopt the same regional boundaries. Later adjustment and modification of the boundaries tend to create a new set of problems.

It is clear that the purposes of the human services program must be considered so that its unique requirements can help determine its specific boundaries. Zusman (1969) pointed out that in designing catchment areas for community mental health services, it is necessary to consider such criteria as the sources of community interest and support, the location of existing and future state mental hospital districts, and the availability of general hospital facilities. Pertinent to most human service programs are such factors as natural geographic boundaries and barriers, political jurisdictions, economic and marketing areas, population density, population trends, population heterogeneity, transportation networks, expected service demands, existing utilization patterns, and complexity of financing.

A minimal population base is essential for a regional human services program so that fiscal support can be obtained, and programming can be undertaken with adequate staff support. The National Institute of Mental Health requires a population range of 75,000 to 200,000 as the base for community mental health programs. Whittington (1970), however, has pointed to the balkanization of the public mental health enterprise which has resulted from arbitrary adherence to the policy of a catchment area restricting its upper limit to 200,000 people. Many geographic areas, urban metropolitan ones in particular, cannot be meaningfully divided within this restriction, and Whittington contends the National Institute of Mental Health has created a series of independent duchies unresponsive to local government even though NIMH is often dependent upon this lower governmental level for program support and monitoring. Thus, in complex urban settings the mental health program goals of accessibility, comprehensiveness, and continuity of care may not be attainable through rigid adherence to a geographic catchment area model containing arbitrary population limits.

Despite these problematic considerations, other federally-supported human service programs are guided by similar catchment area requirements. In some states, comprehensive health planning agencies have adopted the regions previously developed for mental health and retardation with minor modifications even though the history of their origin has led to controversy over the relevance of these geographic entities to personal health services. Nevertheless, these efforts together with other federally-directed regionalization patterns, e.g., regional medical programs, OEO, Model Cities, and air pollution control districts, in many ways have been beneficial; but they also have led some communities to complain that the federal schemes have little relation to local needs. A recurring problem is that publicly and voluntarily supported human services within the same regional boundaries function independently of each other since these two systems often define their program responsibilities along differing geographical lines. By utilizing the concept of a comprehensive "delivery system," the planner at least approaches the problem with a framework recognizing the complementary contributions of each program component and the need to integrate them. Comprehensive health planning, in particular, has sought to utilize all potential resources of both a public and voluntary nature; and necessary geographic changes are resulting.

The Standard Metropolitan Statistical Area (SMSA) is another traditional federal pattern for defining regional boundaries. Because of the wealth of data analyzed and reported according to these sprawling areas, local planners have been subtly pressured to conform to SMSA's in the face of more pressing programmatic considerations. However, the Census Bureau's move to localized geo-coding in 1970 has provided planners and administrators with more flexibility. Despite the constraints and reservations created by these varied federal requirements, they, nevertheless, have produced a major thrust toward expanded geographic coverage.

One of the variations developed in moving from smaller to larger regional arrangements is the use of geographic building blocks. The "community of solution" will differ according to the purpose of the program; in certain instances, e.g., air-water pollution, a much larger geographic base is necessary than in others, e.g., local health centers. Instead of designing a new region unrelated to existing boundaries, it generally is possible to create a fresh "community of solution" by combining several smaller areas into a larger region. The integrity of the existing local community base is thus preserved while allowing the locality, simultaneously, to become an integral component of a broader strategy. This tactic has the additional advantage of permitting easier change in boundary lines as goals and functions are modified.

In the voluntary human services delivery system sector, United Funds and Community Councils are increasingly being challenged to reexamine the geographic regions which they serve. Most Councils have viewed their appropriate planning and service-delivery regions as being identical to those within which United Funds conduct money-raising campaigns. This was a reasonable premise as long as the major orientation of the Council was toward working primarily with human service agencies receiving fiscal support from the United Fund campaigns. As Councils move toward a policy oriented and problem-solving focus, however, the congruence of their planning and service-delivery regions with those of United Funds may vary according to the problem under study. The primary criterion becomes that of the natural "community of solution," including privately- and publicly-supported resources, rather than the artificial regions which have historical precedent but no contemporary rationality. In turn, United Funds also have been forced to modify their geographic coverage. As industry moves to the suburbs, their "community of solution" for fund raising is also undergoing change.

SUMMARY

The finer features of human services programs during the 1970's can only be dimly perceived at present; and yet enough of the general outline is evident to recognize that the major characteristics of these programs will include less segmented and more comprehensive approaches to client problems, decentralized facilities closer to population centers, and integrated program administration permitting continuity of care. The increased complexity of urban living patterns has reached the point, however, where comprehensive human services can only be provided through regional arrangements. Previous failures to implement this approach have produced inequalities of service, overlapping territorial bases, duplicate administrative authorities, increased costs, and inefficiency. Progress in overcoming the obstacles to regional solutions undoubtedly will be dependent on the willingness and ability of large funding sources like the federal and state governments and United Funds to use both the carrot and the stick. Since each of these systems is constrained by its own set of sanctions, progress will be piecemeal, segmental, and possessed of its own nonrational components. Yet, the overwhelming logic of new service designs and the force of the regional social movement will lead inevitably to a plethora of efforts. Regionalization will be scattered and difficult—but inevitable.

REFERENCES

1. Baker, F., & Schulberg, H. Community health caregiving systems. In A. Sheldon, F. Baker, & C. McLoughlin (Eds.), *Systems and medical care*, Cambridge, Mass.: MIT Press, 1970, pp. 182-206.
2. Demone, H., & Schulberg, H. Regionalization of health and welfare services. In R. Morris (Ed.), *Encyclopedia of Social Work* (Sixteenth Issue). New York: National Association of Social Workers, 1971, pp. 1083-1088.
3. Farre, G. H. Can megalopolis govern itself? *The Christian Science Monitor*, Saturday-Monday, November 8-10, 1969, p. 9.
4. Friedmann, J. Regional planning as a field of study. *Journal of the American Institute of Planners*, 1963, 29, 168-175.
5. Hodge, G. Urbanization in regional development: A selected bibliography. Monticello, Illinois: *Council of Planning Librarians*. Exchange Bibliography 96. September 1969.
6. Holder, H., & Dixon, R. Delivery of mental health services in the city of the future. *American Behavioral Scientist*, 1971, 14, 893-908.
7. Levin, M. The big regions. *Journal of the American Institute of Planners*, 1968, 34, 66-79.
8. March, M. The neighborhood center concept. *Public Welfare*, 1968, 26, 79-111.
9. Whittington, H. Balkanization of the city—An unresolved consequence of the community mental health center. *American Journal of Orthopsychiatry*, 1970, 40, 230.
10. Zusman, J. Design of catchment areas for community mental health areas. *Archives of General Psychiatry*, 1969, 21, 568-573.

7. The Medical-Industrial Complex

Harold B. Meyers

Health and welfare are no longer merely honorable enterprises. They may be quite profitable. Writing in Fortune Magazine, Meyers describes the major growth industries serving the health market. The expansion of the drug houses is well known; less publicized are the thousands of different products now used by the health industry. Hundreds of companies, including many industrial giants, have now entered the health hardware field.

The underlying theme is, again, rapid change, and increasing complexity and technological advances combined with increasing costs and rapid obsolescence.

Looked upon as a product, medical care in many respects eludes the grasp of market forces. Price, choice, measurable performance, channels of expression for consumer discontent—all these elements are either missing or distorted because of the product's peculiar nature. But the market economy is very much present and at work in what is coming to be known as the "medical-industrial complex," the business of manufacturing and selling the varied equipment, from bandages to two-million-volt cobalt machines, that doctors and hospitals use. The demand for such products is so strong that many new companies, some of them giants in other fields, have joined the old-line manufacturers in a bid for new profits.

Fortune estimates that outlays for health care totaled $63 billion last year. An impressive share of those expenditures went for manufactured goods of all kinds. In 1967, the last year for which official figures are available, the value of medical-related items *alone* totaled more than $6 billion at the time of shipment by the manufacturers. Since then the market has been growing at a compound rate of 10 to 15 percent a year. Submarkets have reached some surprising totals: $185 million for all types of surgical dressings, about $100 million for hypodermic needles and syringes (see table opposite).

A big part of this business goes to companies that have been

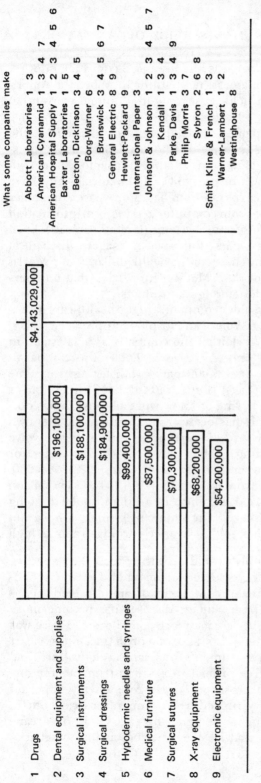

What some companies make						
Abbott Laboratories	1	3				
American Cyanamid	1	3	4	7		
American Hospital Supply	1	2	3	4	5	6
Baxter Laboratories	1	5				
Becton, Dickinson	3	4	5			
Borg-Warner	6					
Brunswick	3	4	5	6	7	
General Electric	8					
Hewlett-Packard	9					
International Paper	3					
Johnson & Johnson	1	2	3	4	5	7
Kendall	1	3	4			
Parke, Davis	1	3	4	9		
Philip Morris	3	7				
Sybron	2	6	8			
Smith Kline & French	1	3				
Warner-Lambert	1	2				
Westinghouse	8					

1 Drugs — $4,143,029,000

2 Dental equipment and supplies — $196,100,000

3 Surgical instruments — $188,100,000

4 Surgical dressings — $184,900,000

5 Hypodermic needles and syringes — $99,400,000

6 Medical furniture — $87,500,000

7 Surgical sutures — $70,300,000

8 X-ray equipment — $68,200,000

9 Electronic equipment — $54,200,000

Components of a Growing Market

Thousands of different products, supplied by hundreds of companies of all kinds and sizes, make up the total medical market for manufactured goods. This list shows the variety of companies being drawn to health products, and the way companies that were long in only one major market, like Abbott in drugs, are beginning to branch out. In some cases, medical products are handled by divisions of a large corporate entity, which have well-established identities of their own. Davol had long been a well-known manufacturer of surgical products before it was acquired by International Paper in 1968.

This sampler of medical markets is based on Census Bureau figures for 1967, the most recent available. The values given are as of the time of shipment by the manufacturer, and are regarded in the industry as understating the actual totals. Many of the listed companies are active in categories not included here—e.g., General Electric makes a new type of permeable membrane, and International Paper manufactures disposable gowns for surgeons.

Drugs still rank as the largest single medical submarket. But the growth of technical devices reflects the changes in medical care. According to Arthur D. Little Inc., the total market for medical technology, including electronic devices, probably exceeds $450 million a year.

in the field for a long time, such as Eli Lilly and Baxter Laboratories. But an array of other companies is now cutting in. When the American Hospital Association held its seventy-first annual convention in Chicago last summer, 495 commercial exhibitors took booths. Among them were companies rarely thought of as active in the health business, including Zenith and Motorola, I.B.M. and Addressograph Multigraph, Bigelow-Sanford and Monsanto. Many conglomerates—from Litton Industries to C.I.T. Financial—now have medical groups in their corporate families. Aerospace companies are involved in everything from computerized medical information systems (Lockheed) to life-support systems (United Aircraft). Even tobacco companies, for years the special target of medical researchers, are joining the chase for the health dollar. Philip Morris has formed a new division, ASR Medical Industries, that numbers sutures and surgical blades among its products.

One of the fast-growing older companies in the health-care industry is its largest distributor, American Hospital Supply Corp. When President Harry K. DeWitt joined the company as a salesman in 1941, its catalogue had only 100 pages. Today the company's catalogues contain more than 3,000 pages with listings for some 60,000 items, and DeWitt says: "I am grateful that I am no longer a salesman charged with having to know what all these things do." American Hospital Supply has been gradually increasing its own manufacturing capability, and 45 percent of its sales now involve its own products, including rubber gloves, laboratory cages for animals, and an organ-preservation machine that sells for $15,300. The company's sales rose from $219 million in 1964 to $387 million in 1968. In the same period, earnings more than doubled, going from 33 to 67 cents a share. The company's stock, long a hot favorite of Wall Street, has sold at a price-earnings ratio as high as 50.

American Hospital Supply's rapid growth reflects the impact of two concurrent trends—increased government and private spending on health, and the greater complexity of modern medical science. Says DeWitt: "As treatment of diseases has become more complex, so has equipment become more complicated. There was no thought ten or fifteen years ago of cobalt machines, heart pacemakers, cryosurgical instruments for cataract removal, artificial hearts, artificial heart valves, or microsurgical instruments for surgery performed under a microscope." In one recent five-year period the number of laboratory procedures commonly carried out in hospitals tripled, creating a demand for all kinds of arcane instrumentation in fields that DeWitt describes as the "ometries," "ologies," and "ographies" (e.g., chromatography, the separation of closely related compounds).

Johnson & Johnson, probably the world's largest maker of surgical dressings, is another old company that has changed and grown with its industry. In the 1959–68 decade, Johnson & Johnson's domestic sales went from $298 million to $580 million. Earnings more than tripled, rising from $15 million in 1959 to $50 million in 1968. Besides surgical dressings, the company makes a wide variety of well-known consumer products—baby powder, baby oil, and Band-Aids—as well as medical equipment and drugs. One of its new products, RhoGAM, is a vaccine against Rh disease, which has killed as many as 10,000 babies a year in the U.S. alone.

A Turn to Leasing

Not long ago an x-ray machine was likely to be a hospital's single most complex piece of equipment. The medical market for such machines, dominated by General Electric, continues to be lively: an estimated $68 million a year. But today the range of electronic equipment required by a fully equipped hospital covers a broad spectrum, from patient monitoring to kidney machines and blood analysis—with computers doing the paper work.

Best known as a maker of propellers for aircraft engines, Hamilton Standard, a division of United Aircraft, came to medical electronics by way of the space industry. The company won a research contract from NASA in the early 1960's to develop and build a telemetry-type cardiac monitor for use by astronauts. Out of that research grew a variety of products for commercial sale, including a telephone monitoring system for cardiac patients. By using that $660 unit, a post-coronary patient can relay electrocardiogram data from his home to his doctor's office by telephone. A more complex version of the system enables a single nurse to keep watch over as many as four hospital patients without leaving her station.

Another outgrowth of Hamilton Standard's work with life-support systems for astronauts was the Simas pump, a computer-controlled heart pump. When a patient in the throes of a heart attack is put on the pump, the machine takes over much of the work of the heart. It was first used two years ago in Montreal on a forty-seven-year-old sales executive named Samuel London. At the time he was put on the pump—which had been under experimental study for two years by a heart specialist at the Jewish General Hospital—London's doctor gave him "less than a 5 percent chance of recovery." London was able to go home seven weeks later. Thirty-seven of the machines, which cost $9,900 each, are now in use by hospitals, and Hamilton Standard is at work, under a National Heart Institute contract, on a more advanced "circulatory assist device." This one will employ a special pressure suit, not unlike those used by the astronauts, which ambulance drivers or other relatively untrained personnel could put on a heart patient. The suit would help maintain heart action through a sequence of carefully timed pulsations.

The electronic equipment being offered to hospitals is expensive—a single x-ray unit can cost $100,000—and is subject to rapid obsolescence. To conserve their capital, some hospitals are leasing rather than buying the equipment. The chief advantage, as Milton H. Sisselman, vice president for coordination and planning at New York's Mount Sinai Medical Center, explains, is that dollars spent on leasing come out of operating funds, rather than capital funds. In addition, all costs are known in advance. When General Electric leases x-ray equipment to hospitals, G.E. provides total maintenance. Borg-Warner—which became interested in hospital furnishings after one of its executives, convalescing from an operation, studied the shortcomings of his hospital bed—recently leased furniture for 142 patients' rooms to LaGuardia Hospital in New York.

93 Percent Disposable

The greatest change in health-care products in recent years has been the emphasis on items that are discarded after a single use. Becton, Dickinson & Co. (1969 sales: $206 million) does 79 percent of its business in health products—and about 70 percent of that segment is represented by "disposable" items such as hypodermic needles, syringes, scalpels, and gloves. The percentage is even higher for Sherwood Medical Industries Inc., which is 85 percent owned by Brunswick Corp. About 93 percent of Sherwood's annual sales, which totaled $41 million in 1968, comes from disposable products. Most of the remainder of Sherwood's business represents sales of medical equipment and furniture, including examining tables.

Behind the demand for disposables lie two inescapable facts of medical life today. One is that a re-usable instrument or product carries a hidden, but unavoidable, risk of infection; no matter how careful the sterilization process may be, some obdurate germ may be lurking out of its purifying reach. Another circumstance, just as compelling, is of economic rather than biological importance.

More than 60 percent of the typical hospital's budget goes for labor costs. To make a medical item ready for re-use is a demanding, time-consuming task—one that requires a considerable investment of labor.

In a talk before security analysts, DeWitt of American Hospital Supply detailed the steps that a "simple surgical drape" must go through before it can be re-used: "After the used cloth leaves the operating room, it often is pre-soaked to help remove any blood stains. Then it has to be washed. (And if contaminated, it must be washed separately.) Next it has to be inspected on a large lighted table where every hole found must be circled and patched. The towel clips used so frequently in surgery can make eight to ten holes per clip. Each of these holes must be patched. Next, the sheeting must be inspected for lint. To remove the lint, hospital employees use either a special roller or tapes of sticky paper wrapped around the hand and moved over both sides of the entire sheet." Even after all that laborious process is completed, the surgical drape must still be folded, packed, sterilized, and stored. So hospitals buy sterile, pre-packaged surgical drapes and discard them after use.

The demand for disposable fabric products has drawn many paper companies into the health-care industry. International Paper, Scott Paper, and Kimberly-Clark manufacture items like surgical drapes and surgeons' gowns out of nonwoven fabrics. Kimberly-Clark recently doubled its manufacturing capacity for the medical-disposable market.

But disposables, whether hypodermic needles or surgeons' gowns, can also create difficulties of their own. Suppliers must maintain large, conveniently located stocks of everything they offer, thus tying up capital in inventory. American Hospital Supply has installed an intricate computer-based ordering system to link its customers with its warehouses, and in the last few years has doubled its warehouse capacity. Further, as Borg-Warner's President James F. Beré says, "disposing of the disposables" presents difficulties. A product like International Paper's Confil fabric remains strong when wet, which is important in medical use. Burning is about the only way to get rid of a Confil garment—particularly one that has been contaminated. But that adds to air pollution.

Section B

Environmental Forces:
In Social Systems

A significant number of social-environmental factors play important roles in the organizational lives of human service organizations. These factors might be generally placed under the rubrics of intra- and interorganizational relationships. Together they comprise what might be considered focal points in human service organizations' perceptions of themselves *vis à vis* their organizational environments.

The articles in this section have been selected in part to provide some points of view which might help develop an awareness of those organizational characteristics and relationships which are relevant considerations in the ecology of human service organizations. In addition it is hoped that these articles will help the reader to consider the mechanisms by which individual organizations might become aware of these characteristics.

8. Turbulence and Resources: The Bases for a Predictive Model of Interorganizational Communication in the Human Services*

Dwight Harshbarger

Expanding on his article in Part I, Harshbarger stresses the symbiotic and interorganizational nature of the human services industry as it operates in an increasingly turbulent environment. As a consequence of these factors, an increasing investment in organizational maintenance is required, reducing either or both the quality or quantity of service. Yet simultaneously, expanded services are required as people find it increasingly difficult to cope with their rapidly changing environment.

Somehow organizational and boundary maintenance must be transferred into proactive planning which both focuses on increasing the quality, availability, accessibility, and continuity of services and at the same time increases the resources directed at primary prevention.

In recent years I have found myself becoming more frequently and more deeply concerned with human service organizations, both in a theoretical and a very pragmatic sense. Theoretically it is an arena rich in the lore of human behavior within organizations, as well as in interorganizational relationships. Pragmatically, these organizations are concrete expressions of our human value systems, and are major instruments of both maintenance and change in systems of human ecology.

The consequences of the actions of human service organizations are felt by all of us to a greater or lesser degree, for they deal with basic social problems in the areas of health, education, and welfare. Beyond certain theoretical interests, for most persons read-

*An earlier version of this paper was presented at an APA Symposium on "Systems Approaches to Community Problems," Washington, D.C., September, 1971.

ing this article the direct effects of changes in human service organizational patterns are likely to be felt in terms of exercising options in the areas of health and education. Generally, our concern will be with which options might be selected to best meet needs, or perhaps the quality of those options selected.

To many outside this readership, the direct effects of changes in human service organization patterns are likely to be felt in terms of whether or not there will be any options at all to be exercised. For perhaps one-third of the population of the United States, human service organizations of various kinds are slender ecological threads; threads which delicately hold a family above a bare subsistence level of living, or a child in school, or an unhealthy wage-earner in a job.

Upon occasion, these organizations have been major agents of social change; effective means of addressing the problems involved in a redistribution of wealth and human resources in the United States. Unfortunately, they have too often represented systems of welfare which are disabling, systems of education which are demeaning, and systems of health services which disappear upon demand.

The Human Service Organization

Organizationally, the public or quasi-public sector human service organization possesses certain characteristics which render it different from other kinds of organizations, particularly those which might be placed in the private sector and generally regarded as production-type organizations; i.e., profit making, product producing organizations. (I should add that as I examine the literature on organizational theory and research, by far the greatest portion of this literature seems to have been generated in production-type organizations. How much of this theory and research can be easily generalized to human service organizations is an open question.)

In another paper (Harshbarger, 1973) I have suggested that human service organizations might be generally described "as based upon public resources, relatively structured, normatively based and morally involving [in Etzioni's (1961) framework], social or socio-technical service oriented, and aimed at clients, residents, or members as primary beneficiaries. Organizationally, the nature of their efforts is to deal with those bio-social problems which arise from the vagaries and complexities of being human."

More specifically, the following are but a few of the many dimensions which differentiate production from human service organizations, and give rise to the relative uniqueness of human service organizations:

1. With respect to their base of economic resources:
    a. The production organization obtains resources from monies allocated to the private sector, while the human service organization obtains resources from monies allocated to the public sector.
    b. The relative potential for economic loss is considerably higher in production organizations than in human service organizations.
2. With respect to the nature of these organizations' internal processes:
    a. The production organization is structured and organized in accordance with production cycles-systems, while human service organizations are more likely to be structured in accordance with professional values and membership subgroupings.
    b. Power in production organizations is primarily utilitarian, while in human service organizations it is primarily normative.
    c. In production organizations functions or tasks provide the primary bases of social segregation and interaction, while in human service organizations professional membership groups provide the bases for segregation.
    d. Formal organizational power is likely to have its roots in the formal organizational structure in production organizations, while in human service organizations social hierarchies and social power are more likely to be based in professional hierarchies and their relative possession of power.
    e. Individual members are more likely to identify with the production organization, while members of human service organizations are more likely to identify with their professional membership groups.
    f. Human service organizations use job tenure in a widespread manner; production organizations rarely use job tenure.
    g. In production organizations persons are retained largely in terms of their productivity, while in human service organizations persons are retained largely on the basis of professional value judgements.
3. With respect to output:
    a. Production organizations have a relatively clear definition of output or outcome, while human service organizations only rarely can clearly define output.
    b. In production organizations there is an end-product orientation, and cost-effectiveness indices are relatively easily developed; in human service organizations the salience of the means is often higher than that of ends, and cost effectiveness indices are relatively difficult to develop.
    c. The over-all mission of the production organization is determined by a small group (e.g., board of directors) acting in the

best interests of the organization; the over-all mission of the
human service organization is determined by a relatively large
group (e.g., legislators) acting in the best interests of the public.

These and a number of other dimensions of human service
organizations which I have developed more fully elsewhere (Harshbarger, 1973) operate, collectively, to give rise to a rather unique
species of organization; one that is replete with value-based decisions, multiple political constituencies, and considerable disagreement over who (what person or profession) has the political-moral
right to define the reality on which intraorganizational feedback
will be based.

Interorganizationally, human service organizations have not been
a happy lot. Their organizational relationships have rarely approached canons of professional ethics so often referred to by their
resident staff. In a recent review of some literature on interorganizational relationships, Harold Demone and I indicated that "the extraordinary point is that many agencies are unaware of and disinterested in the essential symbiosis which overlays the entire human
service network. This awareness, when manifested, occurs frequently in the forms of competition, prejudice, and distrust. Boundary maintenance and domain protection are more common than
collaboration and cooperation." (Demone and Harshbarger, 1973).

Turbulence and Resources

Recent social history has pointed to many problems, and few
solutions. In the years of post-World War II United States, we
have experienced major and profound shifts in the ecological texture of our environment. While many factors have been a part
of this change process, not the least of which has been our pronounced tendency to avoid a society which is not experiencing
war or a war economy, certainly the factors of population growth
and migration and the processes of technological change have been
central in these changes in human ecosystems.

In their very fine paper on the causal texture of the environment,
Emery and Trist (1965) have suggested that certain social change
processes set in motion changes in the environment itself. They
referred to this as a condition of environmental turbulence. Under
the condition of a turbulent field, as Emery and Trist refer to
it, there is among organizations in this environment both a competition for resources and, simultaneously, changes in the environments
which surround these organizations. These changes occur indepen-

dently of the relationships between the actors in the field, and are likely to exceed the capacities of organizations to predict change.

There arises, Emery and Trist suggest, a condition of relevant uncertainty, in which organizations are no longer able to predict the immediate or long-range future with any sense of confidence. Not only will these organizations lose control over certain segments of their environment, but they are also likely to lose control over their own destiny.

Environmental turbulence in organizational relationships is not limited to urban America, although we usually think of it in this context. A loss in human service organizations' ability to predict socio-environmental change, and hence, find themselves considerably lowered in their adaptive abilities, can be as easily seen in the Appalachian Region as in Boston's urban problems. While relevant uncertainty might arise in an urban area from rapid population increases, industrial expansion, and technological increases and changes, this same condition might be generated in rural areas as a function of rapid population decreases, industrial contraction or closings, or a relative decrease in technological services and changes.

In short, both urban and rural human service organizations have found themselves in turbulent environments for related, but different, reasons. One consequence of this condition has been the need for these organizations to commit increased levels of resources to the function of reducing relevant uncertainty, and attempting to gain some predictive handle on their respective environments.

However, at the same time that it has been necessary for organizations to commit more resources to this ecologically important function, the levels of surrounding human service problems have increased, sometimes quite dramatically. This has led to increased demands upon human service organizations to provide ever larger amounts of both direct and preventive services. Demands for effective intervention programs in the areas of human welfare and comprehensive health services, not to mention demands for changes in educational practices, have never been higher.

Unfortunately, our increase in resources for the human services, while steadily growing, has not matched the virtually exponential growth of problems and demands for those services. The sad fact of life is that while one dollar may buy a dollar's worth of human services, one problem is likely to generate another problem; while dollars may be increased in a linear fashion, problems are likely to multiply exponentially, with crisis-ridden families, neighborhoods, or regions requiring vast and complex arrays of comprehensive health and welfare services in order to survive.

If we add to this composite the ingredient of a sluggish economy, one which may or may not be moving out of an economic recession, and its relative impotence in generating major new revenues for the human services without increases in taxation, the picture is, indeed, bleak.

Some General Consequences of an Interorganizational Environment Which is Turbulent and Limited in Resources

1. The Emergence of Value Concerns.   In their 1965 paper, Emery and Trist make the point that under the conditions of environmental turbulence, and the resulting relevant uncertainty for that environment's organizations, there will be an emergence of concerns with values that have overriding significance for all members of the field. They state it as follows:

> "Unable to trace out the consequences of their actions as these are amplified and resonated through their extended social fields, men in all societies have sought rules, and sometimes categorical imperatives, such as the ten commandments, to provide them with a guide and ready calculus.... The relevance of large classes of events no longer has to be sought in an intricate mesh of diverging causal strands, but is given directly in the ethical code. By this transformation a field is created which is no longer richly joined and turbulent but simplified and relatively static. Such a transformation will be regressive, or constructively adaptive, according to how far the emergent values adequately represent the new environmental requirements [1965, p. 8]."

2. A Strain Towards Irrelevance.   In their examination of the widespread phenomenon of goal displacement and goal intangibility in organizations, Warner and Havens (1968) have suggested that underlying this problem was a rationale which went as follows: "what is sanctioned tends to be what can be evaluated, and what can be evaluated tends to be what is visible, tangible, and measurable [p. 550]."

In a later paper (Harshbarger, 1972), I have suggested that the problems associated with goal displacement are particularly acute in human service organizations, primarily because of the tendency of these organizations to be deficient in outcome criteria which work in favor of the consumer, rather than the provider of services. In addition, organizational life is infused with professional values and value judgments.

Consequently, while agreeing with Warner and Havens that what was likely to be sanctioned would be what could be evaluated, and what would be evaluated would be that which was visible, tangible, and measurable, I suggested that, unfortunately, given the nature of the state of the art of evaluation, and given the nature of human service organizations, what is most visible, tangible, and measurable may not reflect important concerns and primary purposes of human service organizations. For example, we tend to measure a public school or mental hospital's program effectiveness in terms of their being quiet, orderly environments; welfare agencies by the nature of the case records; and health services by the number of hospital beds available.

I went on to suggest that as the conditions of environmental turbulence occurred, and there were corresponding problems in maintaining levels of resources which were adequate to the demands placed on human service organizations under these conditions, there would occur a strain towards irrelevance. That is, the activities which human service organizations were likely to sanction would be those activities which worked towards the purposes of visibility, tangibility, and measurement. Given the fact that the sense organs and evaluative instruments in question are generally in the province of agency professionals, not the consumer, it is predictable that substantial organizational efforts might be viewed as irrelevant from the point of view of the consumer of services. (My own view is that the consumer's charge of irrelevance will be accurate far more often than it is inaccurate.)

3. The Emergence of Topological Concerns. Extending the probable consequences of these conditions a step further, it seems likely that there will be an increased concern with Lewinian (1951) factors which have to do with the topology of the organization; that is, with issues concerning interorganizational valences, tensions, forces, vectors, locomotion, and most particularly, with organizational boundaries.

In the conceptual framework of Lewin's field theory, human service organizations will, under the conditons of environmental turbulence, become increasingly concerned with mapping their own means-ends structure of the environment, or mapping the environment's "hodological space."

In terms of the survival of the organization, little else makes better sense. Survival cannot be insured, even minimally, unless the organization develops a relatively accurate map of the field of forces which affect its political and economic base of resources.

4. A Shift in the Nature of the Game.   In recent years game theory has provided a rich conceptual framework within which some important dimensions of social behavior have been examined. While this area of research has often been short on "hard" data derived from the realities of everyday life, it has produced a number of economic game models which have been helpful in conceptualizing bargaining and other forms of interpersonal and interorganizational behavior.

In terms of the behaviors of human service organizations in their interorganizational relationships, it seems likely that under the conditions of a relatively placid environment, particularly an environment in which there is not a critical shortage of resources, interorganizational relationships might be characterized by nonzero sum games. That is, these relationships will be characterized by economic games in which all of the players can make economic gains, or a game in which players can mutually enhance each other's gains.

Under conditions of environmental turbulence, and particularly under the conditions of both turbulence and limited resources, it might be predicted that the game strategies will shift from those of a nonzero sum to a zero sum game. The probability will increase that each human service organization will see any gains on the part of its competitors as subtracting directly from its potential pool of resources. Hence, each organization is likely to increase its level of competition in the political arena, and further, these levels of competition are likely to be noncomplimentary. That is, they will be aimed at the exclusive benefit of only one organization, and depart from coalitional or coalignment relations even between organizations with mutual interests. These strategies of gaming will have the cumulative effect of increasing the over-all turbulence of the interorganizational environment.

SOME SPECIFIC CONSEQUENCES OF TURBULENCE AND LIMITED RESOURCES IN TERMS OF COMMUNICATION PATTERNS WITHIN AND AMONG HUMAN SERVICE ORGANIZATIONS

The Emergence of Value Concerns

1. There will be an increase in communications which suggest that an organization has the right to be doing what it is doing

simply because "it is right." This has been, and will probably continue to be, relatively characteristic of many poverty organizations, particularly those which have obscured or in one way or another failed to clarify just what it is they are about, and some of the ends they hope to accomplish.

Similarly, there will be an increase in communications which attempt to justify increased resources for certain organizations because they share and perhaps speak to the value systems of the consumer. Whether these value systems are relevant to the bio-social needs of these consumer groups may still be an open question.

2. There will be an increase in professional rivalries, and perhaps petty professional jealousies among professionals within any given organization. Intraorganizational behavior will reflect many of the surrounding interorganizational pressures and dynamics, and moral or value based attempts will be made to legitimize the paramount position of given professions, with the hope of increasing one profession's relative possession of power and resources, *vis à vis* other professions, within an organization.

A Strain Towards Irrelevance

1. Interorganizational communications will increasingly reflect a perception of human service organization behavior as irrelevant from the point of view of various consumer groups. This is, of course, contingent upon the existence of viable consumer groups. In their absence it is likely that human service organizations will levy these charges against each other.

2. Intraorganizational communications will suggest, particularly in large organizations, that various professions (never one's own) are involved in irrelevant activities.

3. There will be an increase in defensive communication, generally as a reaction to the preceding. Here, both offensive and counteroffensive communications will be aimed at maintaining existing levels of resources and of possibly gaining at the expense of one immediate competitor.

The Emergence of Topological Concerns

1. There will be a distinct increase in communication having to do with the definition of functional boundaries of human service organizations and of their respective delivery systems. Of primary concern will be the definition of boundaries of service respon-

sibilities and authority *vis à vis* human service organizations in the same community environment.

2. Following from the preceding, there will be an increase in interorganizational communications defining boundary crossing; i.e., who is eligible to enter a system, under what conditions, and most importantly, who is to be kept out or extruded from an organization or human service system. Similar communication patterns will occur intraorganizationally, generally around the themes of maintaining professional integrity and identity.

3. Substantial communication efforts will be devoted to the process of checking out or mapping the political valences and vectors in the interorganizational environment.

CONCLUSION

My observations represent distillations of my own experiences; while these have not been rigorously systematic, neither have they been entirely casual. I am deeply concerned that the patterns of intra- and interorganizational relationships, as reflected in their communication patterns, represent human service functions which only occasionally deal with the problems these organizations have been mandated to confront. If, as Philip Slater (1970) suggests, American culture is at the breaking point, it may be paradoxical that human service organizations, with their often inappropriate, irrelevant, or infrequent intervention strategies, may be facilitating the dysfunctional social processes that they would hope to prevent.

In a paper this brief I think I can justify presenting some recommendations which are painted in rather broad strokes. Hence, some unoriginal, but important recommendations for changes in the immediate future:

1. The current routinized practices of welfare systems should be abolished. A system of income maintenance, perhaps through negative income tax, should be adopted, and operated at the federal level. Major state and local revenues in the welfare sector should be used to employ people in effective case management, not as good detectives. It is likely that this will only occur if the parameters surrounding state and local welfare systems, e.g., the production of revenue, are radically altered.

2. Comprehensive health planning should be intensified and given interorganizational clout. This clout might extend, for example, even into the prevention of classes of professionals from practicing in certain geographic areas, such as some of our affluent suburbs, which are already disproportionately overserviced. This

clout should also make economically attractive those models of service delivery which depart from historical models of cottage industries, or patterns of institutional giantism. Further, it should generate models of comprehensive health delivery which are truly comprehensive, a word to which we give lip service, but a practice in which we rarely engage.

3. We should move towards the development and use of systematic change models in education. Presently, only one state, North Dakota, is systematically and systemically attempting to generate internal change at the level of its state system of education.

Recently, I wondered if many of our human service organizations were not unlike the deacon's famed, wonderful, one-hoss shay, a machine which was built in such a logical way, and ran a hundred years to the day; then, all of a sudden, it went to pieces.

It is not difficult to trace the developmental pattern-setting of too many of our large and most expensive human service organizations to the 19th century. It is more difficult, however, in those same organizations, to discern changes which have paralleled the social changes of the 20th century.

References

Demone, H. W., Jr., & Harshbarger, D. The planning and administration of human services. In H. C. Schulberg, F. Baker, & S. Roen (Eds.), *Developments in human services*. New York: Behavioral Publications, 1973.

Emery, F. E., & Trist, E. L. The causal texture of organizational environments. *Human Relations*, 1965, 18, 1–10.

Etzioni, A. *A comparative analysis of organizations*. New York: Free Press, 1961.

Harshbarger, D. The strain towards irrelevance. *Human Relations*, 1972.

Harshbarger, D. The human service organization. In H. W. Demone, Jr., & D. Harshbarger (Eds.), *A handbook of human service organizations*. New York: Behavioral Publications, 1974.

Lewin, K. *Field theory in social science*. New York: Harper and Brothers, 1951.

Slater, P. *The pursuit of loneliness: American culture at the breaking point*. Boston: Beacon Press, 1970.

Warner, W. K., & Havens, W. E. Goal displacement and the intangibility of organizational goals. *Administrative Science Quarterly*, 1968, *12*, 539–55.

9. *The Shifting Power Structure in Health*

Ray H. Elling

The functioning of health systems, like any other set of structured organizational relationships, is based in large part upon the operation of power and influence. Sometimes this takes the form of directives and mandates, and at other times assumes the form of bargaining and exchange of resources to attain mutually desirable ends. Over time, and in relatively placid environments, these relationships assume patterns which become normative, often attaining the status of tradition.

Problems arise when organizational environments become less placid than expected. This can occur through basic changes in the composition of client communities, or, as noted in the following article, when the structure of the system itself undergoes changes, often at different levels of system operation.

Delimiting the bases and systemic organization of power can have important implications for the design and functioning of human service organizations. It is these factors that are addressed in the article which follows.

This paper deals with a complex, difficult topic about which little is known. The paper considers social power in a general way; makes some observations on power changes internal to the health establishment, including observations on "the" physician's role and the university health center; examines the increasing role of government, particularly at the federal level; the changing role of lay community leaders; and the awakening, but as yet relatively inactive, consumer public. Following these considerations, the conclusion will present some thoughts on the central problem of the paper: the implications of power analysis for structuring the planning and administration of regionalized health services and facilities and the preparation of persons for this endeavor. To grasp these problems, a brief examination will first be made of social power and certain broad changes in the health systems of complex, technological societies.[1]

SOCIAL POWER

Social power is here defined as the ability to influence the orientation and behavior of others. How does an individual or group obtain social power in a social system? Individual and group power is given through the consent of others in the social system.[2] That consent is dependent upon certain recognized bases or sources of power that are described below. An individual may "hold" power or "exercise" influence, but he can do so only if others do his bidding. The power structure in health (or any other sphere) changes, as does the control of different individuals and groups over the bases of power.

Some authors differentiate between power and influence on the basis of resistance versus acquiescence in the relationship. For example, friends are said to influence each other, while opponents wield power.[3] Since social interaction is always redefining some situation or reducing some ambiguity from a situation,[4] the above distinction between power and influence is rejected. For no matter how much in accord two persons or groups may be, if they engage in symbolic exchange, the resistance of prior definitions must be overcome. Thus the category of no resistance is essentially a null category in human intercourse and the problem of a substantive basis for distinguishing between power and influence is not a useful one.

If it is not important to make a distinction between power and influence on the basis of resistance being present or not (since it is always present to some degree), it may be more valid and useful to make a distinction on a temporal basis. Thus, one might suggest that power applies only to potential, or undemonstrated realization of an actor's influence.[5] Influence then is actualized power. Instances of influence are evidence that power existed and has been employed. Power is always present in a situation and will show itself as influence before a particular "scene" or other bit of interaction is completed.[6]

To more fully understand social power and have some way of assessing or "toting up" what Norton Long calls "the power budget"[7] of the health administrator or other persons and interest groups in the health system, the bases on which power rests must be studied. Some or all of the following bases of power may be involved in a given interaction between a staff physician and the hospital administrator, between a hospital and a planning agency and so on:

1. The interpretation of traditions, philosophies, and history is one important tool by which men may be moved. The administrator who can remind board members of past traditions of delivering maternity care, when some members of the board were themselves born in the hospital, has considerable power in opposing a planning agency's moves to consolidate maternity services in another hospital.

2. The ability to generate believable myths, whether intentionally mythical or not, is another idea tool of some importance. Simply mentioning the Orson Wells-directed radio broadcast of the Invasion from Mars, during which some people jumped into the Hudson River to save themselves, validates W. I. Thomas' aphorism, "When men define things as real, they are real in their consequences." The same phenomenon is seen in the health field (usually with less frightening results) when justification is sought in "magic numbers"—one public health nurse per 5,000 population, 4.5 general hospital beds per thousand population, and so on. Often such figures are justified very little in terms of function and need; yet plans are drawn, budgets passed, and building programs launched in response to such calculations.

3. Reasoning ability or the power of logic seems clear enough not to need illustration.[8] However, it differs from "force of presentation" in the sense of personal style or other valued social characteristics. One can illustrate that distinction by "the brains of the outfit" (a person with knowledge as well as reasoning ability), who may act from a relatively hidden position of the state health department where some abrasive personal characteristics cannot do much harm, while his influence is felt through the actions and programs he suggests to others.

4. In most community (and other) power structures the expert who controls technical knowledge or skills fills an essential place. He may or may not constitute an initiating and perpetuating force, but he is essential at some point to certify the soundness of a program.

5. Control of economic resources is a major base of power. To Marx, this factor was important enough to base a theory of history on control over the means of economic production. Indeed, it may be that regional health services planning structures can have their major impact on coordination of services through control over the channeling of both operating and capital funds. But at least four conditions limit the power of the person or group who controls resources: those to be influenced may have resources the controller badly desires; they may obtain the same resources elsewhere; they

may have power on other grounds to force relinquishment; they may resign themselves to do without.[9] Some of these limiting conditions reflect the operation of other bases of power.

6. The authority one has as a function of his office in a formal organization may be a source of far-reaching influence. This source of power has increased in importance and to some extent changed hands as the administrative function in hospitals, health departments, and other organizations has emerged as a special endeavor.

7. Apart from holding an office, control over an organization of men through formal or informal means is a familiar, but nonetheless important part of accomplishing tasks, especially large-scale ones. One or more nonelected power figures may control a political party, a government bureaucracy, even a health services planning agency from "behind the scenes." Such control may involve a formal office, as in the case of a large employer who is asked to head the United Fund drive; or it may not involve formal office, as in the case of the racketeer who moves into the nursing home field.

8. Position in the social structure (aside from prestige as discussed below) can be an important determinant of power. It is not impossible, but very much less likely, that the "lower-class" patient will have as great access to or control over any of the sources of power as will the health professional who seeks to influence his behavior. The health organization that is primarily "plugged in" to the "lower class" will be similarly short in its power budget.[10]

9. Prestige can be thought of as the combined impression of a person or organization due to valued social characteristics. Whatever causal role these characteristics play in the generation of power, considerable evidence may be found of their association with those identified as powerful. This has been regularly noted among community leaders.[11] It has also been noted for high-prestige occupational roles such as that of the physician. Outwardly, given some native intelligence, training makes the physician. But this is not all, for he is expected to have certain of what Everett Hughes terms "auxiliary characteristics."[12] In the United States, these expectations operate to exclude many women, Negroes, and others from these roles.[13] That condition may change, however, in the face of manpower shortages and public demands.

10. Direct popular or political support is an important power base to which public health professionals have given inadequate attention while attempting to justify their programs to political figures on economic grounds. Within certain limits, the costs do not matter if the people in general are sophisticated enough about health

problems and services to vigorously demand adequate care as a basic human right.

11. The "miraculous cure" lends charisma to the one seen by the patient as responsible, for the event breaks all expectations of disaster. Charisma is not a mystical source of power. It can be empirically indexed by behavior that violates rules or expectations with good results. Some community health leaders acquire charisma as they demonstrate ability to ignore various bureaucratic labyrinths while achieving results for their followers.

12. The power of violence is gone as soon as it is unleashed. Only in the potential of its use are men moved out of fear to do the bidding of its wielder. To a considerable degree, the potential of violence on the mental patient's part structures the whole mental hospital, even to some of the fine points of architecture. In some institutions this is seen as the ultimate problem. Even if the threat of violence achieves negative results, it can influence the behavior of others.

13. But even violence, to have its effect, requires, as Simmel pointed out, the reciprocity of the threatened person.[14] The narcotized patient has no ability to influence the surgeon, but we could not say that social power is involved in this relationship. The matter of hypnosis is an interesting and problematic relationship from this point of view.

To distinguish these several foundations upon which social power rests may be arbitrary and no doubt overlaps occur, which a better categorization might eliminate. Nevertheless, an inventory of these sources of power for a given health administrator or planner and his organization, as compared with the same assessment for those to be influenced, would yield a reasonably adequate estimate of the "power budget" available to develop and institute plans.

Plans, of course, have their own definitional power when developed throughout the system to be affected. Further, the various sources of power may be differentially weighted and these weightings may vary with the context of opposition or encouragement faced by the planning organization. Clearly, the power budget is no static entity granted within some fiscal period. The total budget may increase or decrease and its component parts shift depending on changing definitions, new enthusiasms, crises, and other events.

The Changing Health System

The relevance of the size and complexity of a social system will be seen if certain broad shifts in the health system are considered that have altered access to and control over the bases of power and have thus changed its power relationships.

First, in recent years a vast proliferation of new health specialties has taken place. By way of illustration, Dochez examined the records of two cases of heart disease in the same hospital, one in 1908 and the second in 1938. The first case developed a written record of two and one-half pages reflecting the observations of three professionals—an attending physician and a house officer, with consultation from a pathologist-bacteriologist. In the later case, the record occupied 29 pages reflecting the contributions of 32 professionals, more than ten times the number involved in the first case. These included three attending men, two residents, three interns, ten specialists, and 14 technicians.[15]

New groups continue to enter the field. "The trend toward new careers is yet to be fully appreciated. Among the 200 plus careers listed by title in the *Health Careers Guide Book,* the majority represented but a small segment of total health manpower prior to World War II. Many careers, e.g., inhalation therapist, nuclear medical technologist, radiologic health technician, cytotechnologist and medical engineering technician, did not exist."[16]

Within the once relatively unified, single profession of medicine, numerous specialities now operate in effect as independent occupational groups.[17] Whereas, in 1931, five general practitioners were found for every full-time specialist in active private practice, 30 years later one-half were specialists. "Between 1931 and 1959 the number of full-time specialists more than tripled, increasing from 22,158 to 78,635. On the other hand, the number of general practitioners (including part-time specialists) decreased from 112,116 to 81,957."[18]

Increased complexity is also evident for health organizations. In his book, published in 1945, covering 95 national health agencies of the nongovernmental, promotional type (National Tuberculosis Association, American Child Health Association, etc.), Cavins noted that no attempt was made to deal with all national voluntary health organizations. Further, none of the organizations dealt with was formed before 1904. In the following two decades they sprang up "mushroom-like."[19]

In 1961, a report for the Rockefeller Foundation by an ad hoc citizen's committee counted, aside from hospitals, over 100,000 national, regional, and local voluntary health and welfare agencies that solicit contributions from the general public.[20] The growing complexity of governmental organizations in the health field is not much, if any, less striking. For example, in recent federal legislation granting 256 million dollars in addition to matching state and local monies for activities in the field of mental retardation, Congress provided for no less than 12 federal agencies to disburse these funds.[21]

In 1950, Roemer and Wilson examined this problem from a new perspective. In the words of Joseph W. Mountin, they "Attempted to set down systematically the structure and function of all organized health services having an impact on the people of one county."[22] In this semi-rural county of what is now identified as "Appalachia," they found no less than 604 agencies involved in organized health service that had some impact on health care in that county. Locally based health-relevant organizations numbered 155.[23]

In addition to increasing complexity, the health system shows striking evidence of increased size, change in relative size of different components and change in position in society generally. As regards occupational groups, "It is estimated that the health professions requiring college education or professional preparation accounted for approximately 200,000 persons in 1900. The number of individuals in these same categories increased to 409,000 in 1920; 692,000 in 1940; and 1,140,000 in 1960... Individuals in the health occupations accounted for 1.2 per cent of the experienced civilian labor force at the turn of the century. This proportion increased to 2.1 per cent by 1940; 2.4 per cent by 1950; and 3.0 per cent by 1960."[24] Relative to other groups, physicians have lost dominance simply in terms of numbers. "Whereas at the turn of the century, three out of five health professionals were physicians, by 1960 rapid growth in other disciplines reduced the proportion of physicians to one out of five professional health workers. A continued decline is to be anticipated as other disciplines experience more rapid rates of growth and new categories of personnel emerge."[24] According to another estimate, the present ratio of physicians to all health personnel is less than one to ten.[25]

From fear-inspiring, segmental units serving only the displaced and disinherited of society, some of the most essential health organizations, such as clinics and hospitals, following the development of scientific secular medicine, became more effective, highly desired, and generally used.[26] The rate of admissions to general hospitals, for example, rose from about one in every 18 persons in 1931, to approximately one in seven in 1962. Modern health

care has come to be regarded as a basic human right.[27] Health
institutions have moved squarely into the community. They have
become community institutions.

CHANGING POWER RELATIONS

General

It is not possible to detail the impacts on power relations in
the health system of the increased complexity, size, change in relative size of certain components (e.g., physicians relative to other
health workers), and overall shift in the place of the health services
industry in society. Yet several observations seem evident. First,
with the rate of technological and social change in this field the
power structure is certainly very fluid. That is not news. But perhaps
it is this very fluidity throughout modern society that seems to
accentuate the striving of occupational groups and organizations
to protect or increase their autonomy, gain greater support and
generally hold or improve their "place in the sun." Perhaps, too,
this complexity and fluidity of power relations is what makes the
problem of planning health services so important, yet at once frustrating and fascinating. In any case, it is not anything that could
be characterized as a stable structure; the power budget is fluid.
Thus, rather than carrying the assigned title, this paper should
have "power relations" in its title.

Second, some growth has taken place in the power of the total
health system. In these perilous, warring times, health has not
achieved, and may never approach, the concentration of power
C. Wright Mills found combined in the "defense" establishment
as it serves the interests of "Big Business," "Big Labor," Government, and The Military.[28] But with the generally high regard
in which health services have come to be held, increased utilization
and greater proportions of personnel and funds, health now
occupies a more substantial place in society. For this, and other
reasons to follow, health affairs have become matters of important
public concern and political action. For example, see the conflicts
between groups of elderly voters, the American Medical
Association, and other interest groups as detailed in Richard Harris'
series on the legislative process involved in the development of
Medicare.[29]

Third, although the system overall may be more powerful (at
least when overwhelming budgets for international conflict do not
intervene), power is more dispersed, shared as it is among a myriad

Table I. Professional Rank and 1964 Incomes of Selected Occupational Groups in Public Health, by Self Identity, Degree and Self-identified Basic Discipline*

Work Group	Professional Rank**	Under $5,000 N	%	5,000–9,995 N	%	10,000–14,999 N	%	15,000 and Over N	%	Total N	%	No Resp.	Not Appl.	Median Income	Income Ranking
Physicians†	1	37	8.0	40	8.6	80	17.2	308	66.2	465	100	39	10	17,850	1
Public health dentists	2	4	6.8	22	37.3	25	42.3	8	13.6	59	100	3	3	10,700	4
Veterinarians	3	2	2.8	28	37.8	28	37.8	16	21.6	74	100	5	4	11,250	3
Laboratory scientists	4	47	13.0	207	57.3	84	23.3	23	6.4	361	100	14	24	8,200	9
Health officers	5	9	3.7	52	21.5	104	43.0	77	31.8	242	100	14	18	12,850	2
Public health engineers	6	6	2.0	154	52.1	111	37.5	25	8.4	296	100	10	15	9,550	6
Biostatisticians	7	36	28.6	63	50.0	21	16.7	6	4.7	126	100	4	14	7,100	11–13
Public health nurses	8	760	58.9	513	39.7	18	1.4			1,291	100	59	174	4,200	16
Other Nurses	9	77	56.7	55	40.4	4	2.9			136	100	4	15	4,400	15
Hospital administrators	10	27	6.1	181	40.8	133	30.1	102	23.0	443	100	26	37	10,500	5
Other public health administrators	11	69	13.4	240	46.4	109	21.1	99	19.1	517	100	25	13	8,900	8
Health educators	12	42	21.8	128	66.7	18	9.4	4	2.1	192	100	7	19	7,100	11–13
Nutritionists	13	23	20.5	77	68.8	9	8.0	3	2.7	112	100	4	12	7,100	11–13
Public health social workers	14	12	10.7	84	75.0	14	12.5	2	1.8	112	100	1	3	7,600	10
Sanitarians	15	273	48.8	279	49.8	7	1.2	1	.2	560	100	25	29	5,100	14
Occupational hygienists	16	5	2.4	121	57.3	65	30.8	20	9.5	211	100	6	3	9,150	7
Other††	unranked	964	27.6	1,194	34.2	595	17.0	741	21.2	3,494	100	184	363	8,250	unranked
Total		2,393	27.6	3,438	34.2	1,425	17.0	1,435	21.2	8,691	100	430	756		

* Exact means of delimiting groups furnished on request.
** See reference 32 for derivation of this ranking.
† There are largely clinical physicians in public health, epidemiologists, specialists in preventive medicine and occupational health physicians. Excludes M.D.s who identified themselves in other categories, such as health officer, hospital administrator, etc.
†† Includes a number of "professional" categories with only a few members as well as secretaries, clerks and certain other "nonprofessional" categories plus those unemployed or not in the labor force.

of health occupations and organizations in different public and private jurisdictions. That entails unnecessary inefficiency, expense, and suspected lower effectiveness. Certain reactions have occurred to the dispersal of power within the health system. Government has begun to play a larger part as have various quasi-governmental health bodies. Consumers too, particularly in poverty areas, have begun to insist on a role in determining the character of health services delivered to them.

In The Health System

Although the position of "the" physician in society may have remained relatively constant and high in the view of the general public,[30] insiders are beginning to realize that "the" physician is a myth. Not only do medical schools differ in their emphases in the two, four, or five years their programs run, but differentiation within specialties has progressed to such an extent that when someone collapses in a gathering it no longer makes sense to shout, "Is there a doctor in the house?" Doctors in a range of specialties who really treat patients might answer the call (if they are not afraid of a malpractice suit as a consequence of treating someone outside their usual, well-equipped work setting). But what of the administrator, the researcher, specialists in "thing-oriented" fields such as radiology. What of epidemiologists? Or psychiatrists who have only *talked* to patients for years? Could they do much more for the victim than the nurse or even the lay person trained in first-aid?

The specialization and development of new health occupations in not limited to physicians.

What are the consequences of specialization for the power of a given occupational group or representative thereof? On the one hand is a tremendous increase in esoteric, technical knowledge and, in situations whe   it is relevant, it affords tremendous power. On the other hand, the monopoly the physician once had in the health field is gone.[31] Not only is his own house often divided against itself, with different specialties having different associations and making different representations, but many newcomers are on the scene. Often the newcomers are as vital as any particular type of physician in the provision of care. For example, a radiologist recently complained that he was leaving his practice in a community hospital in part because he was no longer in complete control of therapy—a physicist now determines the use of the cobalt unit. It is this "functional equality" that is beginning to make one member of the health team as vital as another.

Although the colleague rather than leader-follower relationship among health workers has not been given wide recognition, to some extent it is a fact and it makes some health workers uneasy. After imperialistically referring to "sub-professionals" for years and recently modifying this to "ancillary professionals," the vogue among physicians now is to speak of "allied professionals."

Of course, prestige and income differentials suggest that the label may only be a sop. The left-hand column of Table 1 shows a ranking of several listed groups according to "how professional" their members are judged to be by a general sample of public health workers (members of the American Public Health Association or one of its state or regional affiliates).[32] In the right-hand column are the median incomes determined from reports by members of these occupational groups in the same mailed questionnaire. Although new words like "allied professionals" may only be a cover for continued exploitation, they probably reflect change in power relations.

In the struggle for position, now with particular reference to occupational groups, various strategies and means are employed.[33] But one that comes under myth-making should be examined briefly as it is so pervasive, ubiquitous, and consequential for the question of health manpower. That is the master myth of "professionalization." If a group can become known as "professional," as seen in Table 1, it is more likely (though the rank-order correlation is only .57) to enjoy a better income. Other conditions lending prestige and power to the group are also correlated with this appellation. Indeed, after a careful analysis of available studies and theoretical discussions, Becker has concluded that "professional" is only a term of approbation, and does not clearly distinguish one work group from another except possibly in terms of power and prestige.[34] Yet, a great deal is made of the term with extensive ideologies and much effort is invested in "becoming professional." Aside from a certain assurance of quality to the public, the net result may be a narrowness of outlook, special jargon, restricted supply, higher costs, sloughing off of necessary but "dirty" tasks, divorce from those most in need of service (such as poverty, "lower-class," and certain ethnic groups)[35] and expensive machinery to license, accredit, lobby, and otherwise protect secrets and domains. In short, as has been seen in various parts of the world, "when the chips are down," doctors and nurses are not so different from other work groups; they make use of the ultimate labor weapon like anyone else; that is, the strike, though it may be called "mass sick leave" or "a professional holiday."[36]

Control of the health organization, too, is changing. In the hospital, particularly, a new breed of nonmedical administrators has entered upon the scene in the past 30 years.

Sharply prepared in quantitative aspects of management, personnel relations and organization theory and other aspects of the social sciences, they are in a better position to respond to the problems of the complex health organization than is the case-oriented, biologically prepared physician, however much he enjoyed (or did not) his preventive medicine and public health courses. Over the years, the administrator has also learned the value of having the board in his corner. Through his board, if it has the right composition, the administrator has access to the community leadership—the industrial, financial, legal people. Physicians and other health professionals listen when and if these men become interested in "a new wing," "a new professorship in surgery," "a hospital planning agency," and so on.

Public health organizations are also showing signs of change, even at the very top of the structure. A blue-ribbon committee composed largely of public health physicians conclude the following:[37]

> "To say, however, that the departments of health are the logical agencies to take on major responsibility for the planning and coordination of the delivery of these (personal health) services is not to say that they are now ideally equipped for the job. A responsibility of this breadth will of course require special personnel to meet it, and this brings us back again to the problems of education for public health, especially in the schools of public health. The simple fact is that very few people are being prepared in schools of public health today, or anywhere else, who could justifiably be presented to a community as qualified for this task. . . .
> The schools of public health should give immediate attention to establishing a doctoral curriculum which would blend the contributions of economics, political science, sociology, the health sciences, certain of the physical sciences and other fields of study."

Although the power of formal position and control over an organization have accrued to the administrator's balance to an ever increasing degree as the hospital has taken on greater central importance in the health system, important counter trends have appeared. With the increasing size of the health system (in terms of overall budget, personnel, and other matters) and complexity of modern care and consequent rising costs, no health organization is an island unto itself. If, as Martin Cherkasky has indicated, the hospital must become "a sharpened instrument" used in the right way for the right case at the right time, it must be integrally tied in to preventive services, ambulatory care, domiciliary care and diagnostic services, home care, nursing homes and other extended care and rehabilitation units. That means a sharing of power and the likelihood of numerous interorganizational problems.[38] In any case, it is no longer fruitful to look at the hospital as an autonomous unit with definite boundaries outlined by its walls. Instead, it has become a kind of point of intersection for several functions that must be carried out by the community or regional health system as a whole.

The development of organizational networks, as well as other conditions that will be discussed presently, has turned the organization outward. The Surgeon General, William Stewart, has reflected on this trend as it affects medical schools by pointing out that after developing two faculties, the so-called "basic" science faculty and the clinical faculty, medical schools have begun to develop a third faculty—a community medicine faculty. Growing community awareness is in no way limited to or particularly characteristic of medical faculties. Other patient care professionals, the administrators and board members of the university-based health center are becoming community conscious. Since the Flexner report, the medical school particularly, but other schools of the health professions as well, have served increasingly as the establishers of new knowledge and legitimators of values in the health system. In addition, the university-based health center has gathered, in most cases, the most elaborate and effective armamentarium of personnel, equipment, and facilities of any organization in the immediate vicinity. To the extent of these occurrences, the university health center has become the power center of the local health system. Now, in addition, the Regional Medical Care Program, even if it is interpreted as primarily educational in character, may add major impetus to the abilities of the centers to reach into the surrounding networks of health organizations and occupational groups.

Changes in the Environment

Four general developments seem noteworthy: the efforts of organized occupation groups; the increasing political nature of health issues; the increasing interest of lay community leadership in health planning; and a slowly awakening desire of consumers of health services to determine policy with regard to local service institutions.

As mentioned in the previous section, occupational groups, the number of which are increasing in the health field, are on the move toward "establishment." Their efforts are sometimes carried out within the health organization and could have been treated as part of the internal analysis, as one examination of the "negotiated order" suggests.[39] But many of these efforts are frank moves in the larger body politic to gain legislative support for higher salaries, a different, more advantageous system of payment, higher stipends to aid recruitment, and stricter licensure to maintain better control over a domain of work.

That health issues have achieved political status indicates a reaction to rising costs, fractionation, inefficiency, impersonality, suspected ineffectiveness, and the dispersal of power among the units of the complex health system. The engagement of political power in the determination of health policy has of necessity held in view the action of government, particularly the federal government.[40] The state, after all, is, at any level of government, the only institution of society that covers or intends to cover all elements of the society no matter how disparate and diverse. The larger part that government plays in health policy is not only a matter of payment and decisions as to criteria and standards for these expenditures. Government is also an adjudicator, a guardian of the public interest as regards licensure of individual practitioners and health organizations. The hearings conducted by Commissioner Smith of Pennsylvania on Blue Cross rates demonstrated that even where a private insurance organization is concerned, the state may inquire into the public interest.

As effective and desirable as modern health care has become, the public has an ambivalent attitude. On the one hand is the possibility of saving life, preventing disability, even realizing and enhancing human potential. On the other hand are fantastically rising cost,[41] and impersonality and disjointedness in a family's care which is difficult for even the most sophisticated to tolerate.[42] Thus, health services have become matters of public concern, particularly to large, so-called "third-party" payers (government, labor, industry, insurance organizations), but also to community leaders, philanthropic interests, and consumers. As a result, health issues have become key political issues with government at all levels entering the health care picture to an increasing degree.

Since Bismarck's time, politicians have seen that they can protect their power or obtain election in part by making adequate health services more available. Although the determination of health policy has always been to some degree external to the health system because the actions of health agencies and professionals require the support and acceptance of the surrounding society. Such determination is currently moving into the conscious scrutiny of mass politics and could easily mean the setting of goals and priorities that "professionals" would not choose. The bulk of the voters are not health professionals, although the sizable interest group, particularly the large "third-party" is likely to have the expertise of health workers at its command.

Sometimes a lack of correspondence is noted between the general public mandate for action to improve health services as expressed in the election of officials and legislators and the specifics of health legislation and administration of such legislation. No exact correspondence exists, for example, between the DeBakey Report, representing an expression of broad public interest in the receipt of "the latest" medical care, and the Regional Medical Program Legislation. On the one hand, the pressures of public demand and political promise build up relevant to very general health goals. On the other, the expertise of health officials is applied to specific measures in a context of what is possible in Congress and the political arena generally.

Political parties as such have not as yet engaged themselves in the health sphere to any great degree at any level. True, the major parties have included health concerns in their platforms and presidential candidates have included issues such as Medicare in their campaigns. But good health care is an amazingly nonpartisan issue and detailed questions of financing and organizing are generally too complex to make good public issues. Although it is difficult for political parties as such to develop and take positions on health questions, they can be expected to do so increasingly as good health care is more and more regarded as a fundamental human right. Furthermore, politicians, as individual campaigners and as policy makers, can be expected to take greater interest in the details of health issues in the future. Men like Hill and Fogarty have already become expert guides to their congressional colleagues on health policy.

At the local level, health questions—especially when they involve the determination of the location for a new hospital or other facility; or the expenditure of public funds for programs and improvements—often become points for political action; sometimes this is rather acrimonious, as Banfield's analysis of the Cook County Hospital expansion plans indicates.[43] But, again, these are seldom developed into party issues with one party vigorously supporting one side and so on. Instead the local party leader is called upon to meet the demands of various organized interests that do not fall along strict party lines. Of course, when a hosiptal rests under the control of the party in power, a continuing struggle occurs between patronage and appointment and promotion for merit. But, again, the Cook County case is instructive. Although the hospital administrator, Meyer, had built up "an organization" it was not for party politics.[44]

On occasion a local party will adopt a program of economy, perhaps even focusing on welfare and indigent care. The mayoral candidate may run on that issue with success (the case of Newburg, New York, comes to mind). Or the issue may be improvement of services in city or county health institutions, a situation that may be developing now in New York, where state legislators and others have made tours of Bellevue and other public hospitals and found appalling conditions. These developments obviously have important implications for retaining personnel and for general ability to deliver services. Usually the issues depend less on party competition than on other organized interest groups (welfare association, medical or dental society, trade unions) or civic leadership. By common consent political parties tend to avoid "stirring up fights" on religion, schools, and hospitals.

Another reaction in the environment of the health system has been the establishment of new, sometimes quasi-governmental systems of planning and control that cut across health occupations, organizations, and even communities where "area-wide" or regional planning is envisioned. Lay community leaders have begun to assume an increasing role in these endeavors. One official of a powerful planning agency, composed of nonelected financial and industrial leaders (and two ministers to lend a sense of contact with the populace), was asked from where his board derived its authority. His answer: "They asserted it."

With the colossal capital and operating expenses required by the modern hospital in an urban region, the men who control the large economic and organizational resources that are likely to be financially bled to death, have begun to band together to seek economies. So far the emphasis of community leaders has been on the costs of bricks and mortar rather than on sophistication about people and service programs. They have also concentrated their interests on those organizations requiring the most private capital (hospitals) with little awareness of the total community health system.[45] But one can expect community leaders to expand their interests to other organizations, supply of manpower, and concern for services, including their quality and controls, in a continuing and expanding search for an answer to the question, "Are we getting our money's worth?"

With the activities of the Office of Economic Opportunity, particularly the Community Action Programs that arose in response to the poverty-civil rights revolution now in progress, a larger voice is demanded by consumer groups. These are mainly "lower-class," neighborhood-based groups with social structural characteristics similar to those Gans described for the once-vibrant West End of Boston.[46] It is evident that on the local scene where a direct confrontation can take place between health professionals and those they serve, or should serve (a confrontation even the political system or some vast and distant bureaucracy of the state does not provide), "the forgotten" may develop a contribution to determine the policy for operating a given network of health service agencies. New forms of nonbureaucratic organization may evolve in which these populations will exercise control and learn to seek health care before it is too late. The present wilderness of outpatient clinics may be particularly anachronistic in this context.[47]

In summary, thus far, to assess the power budget available to the health planner, one must realize how the bases of power have come to be distributed through complex changes, internal and external, to the health system. These have entailed fluidity in power relations; a more prominent place for health concerns generally in society, but dispersal of power among occupational groups and organizations in the system, including a less exclusive and dominant role for "the" physician and a more prominent role for administrators and planners; the development of organizational networks in which hospitals and university health centers play key roles; and certain public reactions including a vast politicalization of health policy issues, sometimes with political party involvement and greater involvement of "third-party" payers, community leaders, and the consumer generally.

IMPLICATIONS

Research

From this brief and necessarily abstract overview of a complex topic, one thing is clear; knowledge, even an adequate framework, is lacking in the field. This is not the place to specify a long list of research opportunities and needs, but a few examples are called for.

What is the relative contribution of each of the bases of power to the outcome of various issues in the health field? Is "professional magic" (myth-making), scientific knowledge, tradition, economic and organizational resources, official authority, charisma, or some other source of power the dominant factor in resolving various issues?

How do power relationships alter with changes in organizational complexity, size, and arrangement?

What is the relative contribution of various types of health experts and lay leaders to decisions at the policy-planning level in the local community and at regional, state, and national levels?

How do lay leaders' connections with and understandings of the health system and its component organizations differ according to the socioeconomic composition of the community and the structure of the leadership itself? What places do health and particular health endeavors hold in the value hierarchies of lay leaders such that the position of health in the priorities of public policy is affected?

Must the "value" of health be expressed in economic terms or is a potent political force that is desirous of better and more health services enough to assure health a high priority in public policy?

If the health system is to be regionalized, how does "community power structure" relate to "regional power structure" (if such exists) and what effect does crossing local and state jurisdictions have on regionalization?

The Organization of Regional Health Planning

The accomplishment of efficient, effective delivery of health services to all segments of the population within a specific geographical region will require special personnel and special organization to accomplish the task. The concluding section will discuss the preparation of community-wide health services administrators and planners. All aspects of the organizational question will not be considered, for that involves a determination of 1) the potential of the population, given adequate health care; 2) the relative place of health in the overall endeavors of the region and the investment that can be made in health; 3) sociocultural variations in the population; 4) the available resources including manpower; 5) the setting of priorities among health activities; 6) delegation of responsibility and authority for assigned, functionally interrelated tasks; 7) two-way (center—periphery—center) flow of communication, patients, staff; 8) evaluation, and so forth. Here, interest is limited to power relationships.

Much discussion has centered around the "locus" of the health planning effort in the future. Will it be the hospital? Will it be the Health and Welfare Association? Will it be the Health Department? Will it be the university-based health center? Will it be public or private? These questions cannot be answered in any final sense at this time. In fact, the problems should be treated in experimental fashion across different regions. Nevertheless, if the foregoing analysis is at all accurate, and since the effective power is now dispersed throughout many organizations and occupational groups in the local system, no present single component will be adequate to carry out planning.

Some new organization will be required that, above all, will have to bring to bear the effective power structure of the region. The "power budget" must be adequate to the task. Where the power structure is fractionated and uninformed as to the overall health system, planning will be little more than several unheeded staff functions located where they cannot become an embarrassment. Where the power structure is united in the achievement of well-understood specific goals, the planning process will be integral to the total endeavor of the system. Under these ideal conditions, planning would not be exclusively assigned to a given unit. Instead, the development and institution of plans would go on throughout the system to be affected.

Major contributors to the power structure as regards health are: 1) government and legal authority; 2) lay community leaders, particularly financial and industrial figures, depending somewhat on the composition of the community;[48] 3) increasingly, consumer groups who may have an impact through local government, health organization boards, or neighborhood groups; 4) the university-based health center; 5) large "third-party" payers; 6) particular organizations, such as dominant hospitals that are well connected with lay community leaders; 7) particularly well-organized occupational groups.

Although the pattern of regional health planning for the future cannot be envisioned, it is possible to suggest that this become a problem for the design and evaluation of planned change. With a legal mandate and the engagement of the effective power system, along with health planners, health service personnel, social scientists and other researchers to aid in the design and evaluation, various health planning systems can be tried out in different regions. Careful research methods involving before-after and cross-regional comparisons will be necessary. In some settings, nothing should be undertaken other than the before-after measurement of the efficiency and effectiveness of the local health system. The most sophisticated theory will be required to develop the design, with deliberate variation on key points to "test" the impact of crucial factors on the operation of various regional health planning structures. Under this plan the region will become a laboratory for the design, institution, and evaluation of planned change.

Preparation of Regional Health Administrators and Planners

It was of major concern to the Joint Committee on Education for Public Health that nowhere in this country today is an adequate effort consciously being put forth to provide the kind of persons required for the above task.[37] What would such preparation involve?

Several components of the university would be required to carry out a program at the doctoral level in regional health services administration and planning. It would be necessary for the student to become acquainted with the subculture of the health world, its occupations, its organizations, its traditions and patterns generally. That could be done in part through reading and class work, but more through varied field experiences. The student would need to have social science theories and methods at his command, the tools of quantitative management, an understanding of the place of science in society, knowledge of political and economic systems and an understanding of, if not expertise in, epidemiological research. He would give special attention to the planning process and to the design and evaluation of planned change.

For the student to develop ability in practice, teaching, and research, the school or health center that prepares him would ideally have responsibility for the planning and delivery of health services in the surrounding region. As suggested above, community leaders and consumers might play determining policy-making roles to assure that the health center carry out its responsibilities to the public. Through this means, students could be assigned in such a manner that the teaching would be beneficially focussed, and in turn the teaching would be altered to confront realities seldom imagined in the insulated classroom.

It is not necessary that students in such a program be of any particular health discipline or profession. Excellence in a liberal arts and sciences background should be adequate. Nor should a certain amount of experience be required, since practice in regional health services administration and planning would be gained in the program itself. It should be clear that persons of any health discipline or profession and any amount of experience would also be admitted on grounds of ability and interest in pursuing such a program.

References and Notes

[1]By a system is meant a collection of identifiable units inter-related in their effects on some outcome. The many health agencies, occupational groups and individuals involved in them make up the health system of a community or region (some geographically bounded place containing a human population) for these units act to affect for good or ill the level of disability in the population.

[2]Bierstedt, Robert, An Analysis of Social Power, *American Sociological Review*, 15, 730-738, December, 1959.

[3]Weber, Max, *The Theory of Social and Economic Organization* (Trans. A.M. Henderson and T. Parsons), New York, Oxford University Press, 1947, p. 152. Most modern sociologists accept the essentials of Weber's definition and have only slightly qualified it—e.g. Schermerhorn, R.A., *Society and Power,* New York, Random House, Inc., 1961, pp. 9-10. Blau also excludes power from "intrinsically rewarding" relationships and re-serves its applicability to relationships that are unilateral (as opposed to reciprocal) and involve extrinsic elements, i.e., those which can be de-tached from the persons supplying them. Blau, Peter M., *Exchange and Power in Social Life,* New York, John Wiley & Sons, Inc., 1964, pp. 312-313. But this seems unnecessarily complicated. It implies (as the author recog-nizes) a static theory of social life and structure, and good theoretical grounds in the symbolic interaction school of thought indicate that some ambiguity or "resistance" must be overcome in any human interaction. Thus, some "extrinsic" or general social element is always in the relation-ship, almost by definition, so long as one remains at the human, social level and is not concerned simply with any unsymbolized biological aspects that probably are involved in the most ideal reciprocal, love relationship.

[4]A classic experiment identifying the element of ambiguity and some factors associated with its removal in one direction or another is given in Sherif, Muzafer, Group Influences Upon the Formation of Norms and Attitudes, *in* Maccoby, E., Newcomb, T., and Hartley, E. (Editors), *Readings In Social Psychology,* Third edition, New York, Henry Holt and Company, 1960, pp. 219–232.

[5]To Bierstedt, power is always potential, Bierstedt, *op. cit.* Weber's use of the term "probabilities" suggests the same. A different kind of distinction that may be useful reserves power for intentional effects on another's behavior while influence is broader, including unintended effects. Van

Houten, Donald R., Opportunity and Influence: A Study of Medical Leadership in Community Hospitals, Ph.D. thesis, University of Pittsburgh, 1967.

[6]It may be on this basis that a basic unit of social interaction could be identified; something comparable to the atom, various subparticles, or "quanta" (whatever is current in physics these days). Various frameworks have been suggested for the social sciences with the recognition of this problem in view. For example, Foote, Nelson N., Anachronism and Synchronism in Sociology, *Sociometry*, 21, 17-29, March, 1958.

[7]"The lifeblood of administration is power. Its attainment, maintenance, increase, dissipation, and loss are subjects the practitioner and student can ill afford to neglect. Loss of realism and failure are almost certain consequences... Power is only one of the considerations that must be weighed in administration, but of all it is the most overlooked in theory and the most dangerous to overlook in practice... Analysis of the sources from which power is derived and the limitations they impose is as much a dictate of prudent administration as sound budgetary procedure. The bankruptcy that comes from an unbalanced power budget has consequences far more disastrous than the necessity of seeking a deficiency appropriation." Long, Norton E., Power and Administration, *in The Polity*, Chicago, Rand McNally & Co., 1962, pp. 51-52.

[8]These may be the formal rules of logic recognized in disciplined intercourse or the "folk logic" of everyday interchange. *See* Rose, Arnold M., Popular Logic in the Study of Covert Culture, *in Theory and Method in the Social Sciences*, Minneapolis, University of Minnesota Press, 1954, pp. 320-326.

[9]Blau, *op. cit.*, pp. 118-119.

[10]The author and co-workers suggested that different relations to the class structure would explain the lower support received by local governmental hospitals as compared with voluntary hospitals. Elling, R., and Halebsky, S., Organizational Differentiation and Support, A Conceptual Framework, *in* Scott, W. R., and Volkart, E. (Editors), *Medical Care— Readings in the Sociology of Medical Institutions*, New York, John Wiley & Sons, Inc., 1966, 543-557. The paper by Robb Burlage included in this volume analyzes the working of a program in New York City designed to upgrade the public hospitals by affiliating them with voluntary hospitals.

[11]For example, Freeman, Linton, *et al.*, *Local Community Leadership*, Syracuse, University College, 1960. A recent study in Pittsburgh also found a great predominance of male, white, Anglo-Saxon, Protestants among those reputed to be leaders of the community. Elling, R.H., and Lee, O.J., Formal Connections of Community Leadership to the Health System, *Milbank Memorial Fund Quarterly*, 44, 294-306, July, 1966.

[12]Hughes, Everett C., Dilemmas and Contradictions of Status, *The American Journal of Sociology*, 50, 353-59, March, 1945.

[13]These trends seem particularly marked among industrial physicians. Shepard, W.P., Elling, R.H., and Grimes, W.F., Study of Public Health

Careers: Some Characteristics of Industrial Physicians, *Journal of Occupational Medicine*, 8, 108-119, March, 1966.

[14]Simmel, George, *The Sociology of George Simmel*, Glencoe, The Free Press, 1950.

[15]As cited by Rosen, George, The Hospital: Historical Sociology of a Community Institution, *in* Freidson, Eliot (Editor), *The Hospital in Modern Society*, New York, the Macmillan Company, 1964, p. 27.

[16]Kissick, William L., Health Manpower in Transition, *Millbank Memorial Fund Quarterly*, No. 1, Jan. 1968, Part 2.

[17]Bucher, R., and Strauss, A., Professions in Process, *American Journal of Sociology*, 66, 325-334, January, 1961.

[18]Stewart, W.H., and Pennell, M.Y., Physicians' Age, Type of Practice, and Location, *in Health Manpower Source Book No. 10*, Washington, Public Health Service Publication No. 263, section 10, 1960, p. 4.

[19]Cavins, H.M., *National Health Agencies*, Washington, Public Affairs Press, 1945.

[20]Hamlin, R.H., *Voluntary Health and Welfare Agencies in the United States*, New York, Schoolmasters' Press, 1961.

[21]These funds and organizational arrangements were provided by the Mills-Ribicoff Act (Public Law 88-156) and the Mental Retardation and Community Health Centers Construction Act (Public Law 88-164). A study of coordination resulting from planning for mental retardation activities in several states has been funded and carried out by Conrad Seipp, Edward Suchman, Ray H. Elling, and research associates Edmund Ricci and Malcolm MacNair.

[22]From the preface of Roemer, M.I., and Wilson, E.A., *Organized Health Services in a County of the United States*, Public Health Service Publication No. 197, 1952.

[23]*Ibid.*, p. 77 and Table I, p. 78.

[24]Kissick, *op. cit.*, p. 4.

[25]Somers, Anne R., Some Basic Determinants of Medical Care and Health Policy: An Overview of Trends and Issues, in this volume.

[26]Sigerist, H.E., An Outline of the Development of the Hospital, *in* Roemer, M.I. (Editor), *Henry E. Sigerist on the Sociology of Medicine*, New York, M.D. Publications, 1960.

[27]"Health care, like education, should be available to everyone in the United States, and it can be. Whether looked at from the standpoint of a good life for the individual or the excellence of the society, its absence causes a large, measurable loss—one an affluent, civilized nation cannot, morally or economically, afford." *The New Republic*, Supplement: "Health: Are We the People Getting Our Money's Worth?" November 9, 1963, p. 37. Also, Roemer, M.I., Changing Patterns of Health Service: Their Dependence on a Changing World, *The Annals*, 346, 53, March, 1963.

[28]Mills, C. Wright, *The Power Elite*, New York, Oxford University Press, 1959. For a sharpened, even if disturbing version of Mills' analysis, see *The Causes of World War III*, New York, Simon and Schuster, Inc.,

1958. In this connection, recall also President Eisenhower's parting speech in which he identified the combination of business and military as almost overwhelming of civilian control in government. Senator Fulbright has recently issued similar warnings.

[29]See *The New Yorker:* Annual of Legislation, Medicare, Part I: All Very Hegelian, July 2, 1966, pp. 29-62; Part II: More Than a Lot of Statistics, July 9, 1966, pp. 39-77; Part III: We Do Not Compromise, July 16, 1966, pp. 35-91; Part IV: A Sacred Trust, July 23, 1966.

[30]Hodge, Robert W., Siegel, Paul M., and Rossi, Peter H., Occupational Prestige in the United States, 1925-1963, *American Journal of Sociology,* 70, 286-302, November, 1964.

[31]Wilson, R.N., The Physician's Changing Hospital Role, *Human Organization,* 18, 117-183. Winter, 1959-60.

[32]The prestige ranking in Table 1 is based on useable replies to the question: "People differ in their opinion with regard to the professional status of various occupational groups. In your own judgment, how professional is each of the following groups?" The number of responses to this question varied by occupational group. The useable replies from the general sample ranged from 4879 to 4769, or an average of 4624 useable responses. A rank was obtained for each group by scoring responses as follows and obtaining an average: "highly professional," 4; "professional," 3; "somewhat professional," 2; "not professional at all," 1; "Don't know" responses were fairly evenly distributed and were not scored. On the average, 234 cases responded "don't know" to the question of professional ranking. Since other ways of manipulating the scoring system are possible and since different samples might give different results, this ranking cannot be viewed as final. Further, it is supposed here that change may occur in the position of any of these groups over time.

For other methodological details of the study *see* Shepard, Elling, and Grimes, *op. cit.*

[33]These strategies and means have been discussed elsewhere: Elling, R.H., Occupational Group Striving and Administration in Public Health, to appear *in* Arnold, M., Blankenship, L.V., and Hess, J. (Editors), *Health Services Administration,* Atherton Press, forthcoming.

[35]Walsh, James L., Professional Group Striving and the Orientations of Public Health Professionals Toward Lower Class Clients, Ph.D. Thesis, University of Pittsburgh, 1966.

[34]Becker, Howard S., The Nature of a Profession, *in Education for the Professions,* Sixty-first Yearbook, Chicago, The National Society for the Study of Education, 1962, Chapter 2.

[36]Badgley, Robin F., and Wolfe, Samuel, *Doctor's Strike,* New York, Atherton Press, 1967.

[37]Fry, H.G., Shepard, W.P., and Elling, R.H., *Education and Manpower for Community Health,* based on the Report of the Joint Committee on the Study of Education for Public Health, Pittsburgh, University of Pittsburgh Press, 1967.

[38]Not the least interesting of these is the question, "With more than

one hospital in town, which one becomes the center of the health center?" Of course they might all be if specialization and division of labor were shared among hospitals, but that assumes a degree of personal and institutional selflessness yet to be achieved. At present, competition for support is too acute to permit such functional specialization and integration. *See* Elling, R.H., The Hospital Support Game in Urban Center, *in* Freidson, Eliot, *The Hospital in Modern Society,* the Macmillan Company, 1963, pp. 73-111.

[39] Strauss, A., *et al.,* The Hospital and its Negotiated Order, *in* Freidson, *op. cit.,* pp. 147-169.

[40]"Not every political power as such is state power, but in the eyes of its incumbents at least, every political power is potentially state power." Heller, H., Power, Political, *Encyclopedia of the Social Sciences,* New York, the Macmillan Company, 1933, Vol. 12, p. 301.

[41]"In 1929 total expenditures for health and medical care, including health-facility construction and medical research amounted to $3.6 billion and accounted for 3.6 per cent of the gross national product. By 1963 such expenditures came to over nine times this amount—some $33.8 billion—and represented 6.0 per cent of the gross national product." Folsom, M.B., *Responsibility of the Board Member of Voluntary Health Agencies,* second Michael M. Davis Lecture, University of Chicago, Graduate School of Business, 1964 (pamphlet). At present, health is a $40 billion enterprise with the Social Security Administration's projections for the next fiscal year at $44 billion. And indications are that it will probably increase by 7.5 per cent per year within the next decade. Experts do not doubt that the ratio of health expenditures to GNP "will eventually move to 8-10 per cent." Somers, *op. cit.*

[42]For a humorous, but still tragi-comic account of an "upper-class" person's, experience, *see* Franken, Rose, *You're Well out of a Hospital,* New York, Doubleday & Company, Inc., 1966. For a less humorous account of "lower-class" experiences, *see* Strauss, A., Medical Ghettos, *Transactions,* 4, 7-15, May, 1967.

[43]Banfield, E.C., *Political Influence,* New York, the Macmillan Company, 1961.

[44]*Ibid.,* p. 26

[45]Elling and Lee, *op. cit.*

[46]Gans, Herbert, *The Urban Villagers: Group and Class in the Life of Italian-Americans,* New York, The Free Press, 1962.

[47]By comparing the known characteristics of "middle-class" bureaucracies and "lower-class" neighborhood residents, the appearance of an effective organization has been theorized elsewhere: Elling, R.H., The Design and Evaluation of Planned Change in Health Organization, *in* Shostak, A. (Editor), *Sociology in Action,* Chicago, Dorsey Press, 1966. 1966.

[48]Walton, John, Substance and Artifact: The Current Status of Research on Community Power, *The American Journal of Sociology,* 71, 430-38, January, 1966.

Section C

Environmental Forces:
In Changing Subsystems

Every organization is required to adapt to a changing environment. When the environmental changes become radical, this often necessitates equally radical changes in those organizations which are attempting to survive in that environment. Thus, what emerges is a situation in which both organizations, and their environments, are simultaneously undergoing considerable change. Emery and Trist have described this as a "turbulent environment."

The articles in this section deal with both environmental change and organizational responses to those changes in turbulent environment. Too often, unfortunately, human service organizations have responded to environmental changes through increasing what have already proven to be maladaptive programs, or, at best, maintaining programs and organizations which have been of very limited value in dealing with pressing social problems.

While these articles deal with social welfare organizations and programs, the problems of adaptiveness and flexibility in organizational development, and the development of programs which promise improvement in chronic social problems, are factors of concern to all human service organizations. Similarly, the characteristics and potential processes which the authors suggest building into social welfare organizations are applicable to most, if not all, human service organizations.

10. Information-Referral: The Nucleus of a Human-Needs Program*

Harold W. Demone, Ph.D. and David F. Long, M.S.W.

If human service systems are to move beyond their present specialized views of themselves and their communities, then an information technology which facilitates this movement will have to be developed and implemented. Such a technology will have to offer benefits which surpass organizational investments in maintaining the status quo.

Human service organizations have not distinguished themselves in their zeal to develop common funds of information which might be used in interorganizational planning and program development. To the contrary, organizational secrecy and competitiveness have seemed to be much more typical of these organizations. Too often, attempts to develop mutually shared funds of information have been seen as potential sources of embarrassment to organizations, as well as providing data which might be used to reallocate public resources away from one's own organization.

Although the following article does not deal with the socio-political problems in developing information systems in the human services, it does indicate some of the benefits which will accrue to the public through the uses of such a system.

Established in 1936, the Information and Referral Service of the United Community Services of Metropolitan Boston formally covers a wide area, including 64 towns and cities with a population of two and a half million people. However, our Service is in contact with many public and private agencies and private practitioners located outside our own area.

*This article is an abridgement of a paper presented by Dr. Demone at the 1968 Annual Convention of the National Easter Seal Society for Crippled Children and Adults.

Its present purpose is to provide information on and referral to community resources, for the most expedient handling of social problems. Our task is divided into four parts: information and direction, referral, short-term counseling, and consultation with referral sources and resource agencies. Requests are received from individuals, social agencies, business firms, labor unions, civic organizations, churches, other professional workers, hospitals and businessmen.

Such inquiries—thousands each year—provide an accurate test of felt needs and trends. To the degree that the needs are not effectively met, the inquiries offer information about program gaps. Finally, they give important information about the response of the care-giving system.

Our experience in Boston has led us to conclude, as many others have done, that traditional patterns for delivering service are not sufficiently comprehensive to cope with the multi-problem situations so often presented by clients and their families. The intersecting of many diverse factors requires an expeditious intervention capacity. This should include competency in health, social service, economics, rehabilitation and housing.

Some agencies take a parochial view of comprehensive human needs. A child guidance clinic sees the problem as emotional; an employment agency, as vocational; the public welfare office, as financial. But someone must view issues, needs and resources broadly. Clearly, a panoramic assessment is needed, in which the clients' needs are seen in toto.

Many consider that the time has come to expand information-referral services—but is this evidence of an information gap? Or is it really a disguised demand for more services?

Referral of clients from one agency to another is a function shared by many health, mental health, and welfare professionals and para-professionals. Because of its importance and the time allotted to it, one might expect of find considerable research devoted to referral and referral techniques, but these remain relatively unexplored areas of social casework. Therefore, assuming that expansion is desirable, we are faced with a number of unresolved issues and unanswered questions:

• Should the expanded service be generalized, serving a metropolitan population?
• What are the long-range effects of maintaining the present specialized information-referral services?
• There has been a rapidly mounting variety of categorical services, many established by federal initiative; will their complex eligibility

standards necessitate further specialized information-referral services?

• Most professionals recognize that referrals can be meaningless without follow-up and guaranteed delivery of service; to what extent are agencies prepared to cooperate with information-referral staff in following the referred client through the care-giving maze?

• Has adequate emphasis been placed on meeting a community's human needs, or are we still responding to the needs of agencies and institutions?

• Information-referral should be the connecting link in the care-giving chain, but who links the existing plethora of information-referral operations in the large metropolitan areas?

Recently, new emphasis has been placed on the development of additional comprehensive services. This trend will require a new level (or levels) of collaborative planning and evaluation around such issues as traditional referral procedures, the ability of agencies to locate potential clientele, and the further development of in-depth resource information.

Information-referral is conducted largely by telephone. How effective is this? What are the losses and slippages, compared with face-to-face interviews? If it should be learned that telephone interviewing does not affect outcome, additional centralized services can be developed, but if large numbers of telephone contacts are not resulting in appropriate referrals, decentralized drop-in offices having sufficient opportunity for face-to-face contact will be the pattern to employ.

However, although much more research is needed, and new patterns of service will require adjustments in established methods, certain basic principles are unlikely to change. From our own experience, we are prepared to put forward for discussion the following fundamentals, as the basis for an expanded and integrated information-referral network:

1. Information-referral should be under a variety of auspices, both public and private. While constantly pressing for rationality, we also must acknowledge the pluralism of our health, welfare and mental health systems.

2. Information-referral should have a paid, well-trained core staff, although volunteers—*properly selected, trained and supervised* —can play a significant role. Each operation must have sufficient size and funding to develop expertise and experience. Although store-front neighborhood centers have had initial emotional appeal, experience is showing that small operations lack staying power.

3. Referrals take many forms, depending upon agency policy,

the motivation of client, referring agency and care-giver, the urgency of the problem and the ability of the care-giver to cope with it. The referral process ranges from the minimum of suggesting a specific agency by telephone, to the maximum of taking the client there. The entire procedure, which includes accurate diagnosis of the problem and the frequently difficult process of linking the client to the network, often is viewed simplistically, but it can be highly complex. If done badly, it is damaging to the client and the care-giving system, and may be expensive.

4. Evaluation and monitoring are indispensable. An information-referral operation needs an up-to-date resource file. For a generic service to a metropolitan community such as Boston, we estimate that from three to six months lead time is necessary to establish such a file. Staff should have sufficient time to visit the major providers of service. Much is still to be learned; therefore, the program should be considered experimental and kept open to change.

5. The service should report its experiences at least annually; facts, opinions, criticisms and recommendations should be documented and made available to the public and appropriate organizations. An information retrieval system should be developed for use in planning, evaluation and administrative decision-making. This will allow rapid, accurate and inexpensive analysis of the data and will answer, among others, these key questions:
* What kinds of problems are presented?
* Who is being served?
* Who made the referral?
* To what agencies are people being referred?
* What are the gaps in services?
Information-referral should be able to measure the incidence and distribution of community problems as well as the community's readiness and capacity to cope with them. Accurate knowledge of waiting lists is a basis for developing new or additional resources, or reallocating existing ones.

6. Information-referral should be prepared to train and consult with agencies on the use of community resources, and to help inform new agency staff members about the nature, availability and extent of these resources. Agencies should be encouraged and helped to make direct, effective referrals. Our own aim is to place as few intermediaries as possible between care-giver and client, while always functioning as the back-up resource.

7. Directories of community services should be compiled and made widely available to all interested care-givers.

8. The service should be an aggressive advocate for its con-

stituents, and serve as a central bureau to process suggestions or complaints about community services and agencies.

9. We must place in perspective the theory that information-referral merely adds to the load on already overtaxed services. Although the heavy demands upon health and welfare services are cause for legitimate concern, should we perpetuate ignorance of their existence in order to reduce the pressure? Many problems, if detected early, are resolved expeditiously. A generic, comprehensive information-referral system is the nexus and core fo a multi-human-service delivery system, which gives the client the option of going directly to a particular agency or using the information-referral service for guidance when the problem-resource arrangement is not clear.

10. The information-referral service must never be considered as competing with other organizations. If it is funded by a "line" agency, it should be administered separately. The sponsoring agency must remain objective and neutral, to enable the service to cut across the network of agencies and meet client needs as effectively as possible.

When the now fragmented information-referral network becomes integrated, correct referrals will be facilitated; data will be accessible for planning, management decisions and research; and the helping agent at last will be able to see *the whole person*. When properly conceived, information-referral is the nucleus of a human-needs program. Underlying this entire discussion are suggested organizational changes, which when implemented will improve the referral system.

There exists in our communities a dynamic interrelated series of agencies and people. A comprehensive view should encompass all available resources and procedures—those directed toward the client, those directed toward the environment, and those directed toward the care-giver and the referral agent—for they are systematically linked, inevitably and intimately.

11. Service Delivery and Social Action Through the Neighborhood Center: A Review of Research*

Edward J. O'Donnell and Marilyn M. Sullivan

Although the following article could as easily have been placed in the section on outcome assessment as in the present one, it was located here because of the rise of the neighborhood service center as an increasingly popular organizational model for both providing better service and effecting social change in communities. Whether this kind of organization is capable of achieving either or both of these goals is the question raised in the article.

The authors not only point to a number of evaluative dimensions through which neighborhood service centers might be assessed, but they introduce a number of difficult, yet critical, administrative choices which virtually every neighborhood service center staff must make. The resolution of these choices is likely to determine the nature and character of any particular neighborhood service organization.

From an internal administrative point of view it may be helpful to know that these are choices which seem of major importance in most neighborhood human service organizations.

From the point of view of an outside observer, it might be speculated that it is in making these directional choices that neighborhood service centers will experience their greatest number and degree of organizational tensions and problems. Consequently, these might be seen as key issues around which both administrators and organizational consultants might focus their efforts to effect organizational decision-making and organizational change.

---

*This is the third article in *Welfare in Review* about the neighborhood service center. The first, "An Organizational Twiggy: A Review of Neighborhood Service Centers," was published in the October 1967 issue; the second, "The Neighborhood Service Center: A Place To Go and A Place To Be From," was published in the January-February 1968 issue. Oliver Moles, author of the next article in this issue of *Welfare in Review,* also contributed to the ideas developed in this article.

The star of the "income strategy" is ascending.[1] And it is high time. Poor people need money; ours is a money economy and "money talks." Poor people need power, too; they must organize and act. Some want to; a few will. People need money and people need power. Service is a poor substitute.[2] A "service strategy" is not at all fashionable; some say not at all relevant. Kravitz, for one, argues: "To talk about new forms of delivery of service ... is to offer smelling salts when the patient is strangling, band-aids when the patient is bleeding to death ... Building ... new neighborhood centers amid slum squalor is immoral."[3] Perhaps so. But Specht reminds us of the "many needy people who may only want more and better service—who may not want to organize or protest, but simply to find alternatives to fighting City Hall and Bureaucracy."[4] The neighborhood service center holds promise of doing both—of providing better service and effecting social change. This article examines that promise.

The traditional organizations and institutions designed to provide services have, increasingly, come under fire. They have been swept along by social currents to the point of their being too big, too distant, and too self-serving. The traditional agency has been criticized as formal, fragmented, impersonal, officious, and timid; as alienating and intimidating people; as insuring long delays and expecting those it serves to accept its policy without question. But the neighborhood center has been championed as informal, integrated, personal, courteous, and courageous; as making people feel they belong; as offering instant service and promoting the active participation of the neighborhood in its program. Such, at any rate, is the rhetoric of the advocates of neighborhood centers.

The Impetus Behind It

The development of the neighborhood center owes much to a number of forces and movements—not the least significant of which has been the long-term migration of low-income Negroes and members of other minority groups to the cities, the out-migration of the more affluent white people to the suburbs, the increasing irrelevance of community agencies to the problems of poor people,[5] and the gradual decline of machine-dominated city politics. All but gone is the neighborhood ward "healer" and his patronage system for obtaining jobs, welfare, and legal advice for the poor.

The neighborhood center is an attempt to institutionalize many of the services performed by local political bosses. The neighborhood service system has become the functional equivalent of the old political ward system. The ward man has become the neighborhood worker; the political club, the neighborhood center. "People came to ... [the ward man] to inquire about welfare payments, to get their relatives into public institutions, to get something done about neighborhood nuisances. ... and to make complaints about the police or other city departments."[6]"He had to know his neighborhood thoroughly ... catering to local interests and problems. He found jobs for needy families, or loaned them money. ... For businessmen and saloon-keepers, he granted relief from some law or city ordinance; for gamblers, prostitutes, and gangsters in trouble, he found bail, or ... he could arrange for the 'right' lawyer and the 'right' judge, who would arrange for the 'right' sentence."[7]

"If the ward leader was shrewd, he made his ward clubhouse into a pleasant place where a tired Manure Inspector or an Assistant Health Warden could find relaxation at the billiard table or at the bar where he could chew over the latest political gossip. If he was particularly canny, he would create a neighborhood esprit de corps ... by having his club sponsor clambakes, picnics, summer outings ... at least two 'balls' a year ... torchlight parades and rallies. ... Deeply political as it was ... it served as a social institution as well. The clubhouse, like the saloon, was a haven for recreation and good fellowship, and a refuge from wives. And the club itself provided a means by which the native poor, or an immigrant Irishman or German, could advance to some social standing."[8]

Obviously, the comparison between the neighborhood service center and the old political club stops far short of many of the wardhealer's "services"; and though there are no more "tired" manure inspectors and neighborhood centers do not typically offer billiards and bars, the idea of a center's being a "pleasant place" and the effort to "create neighborhood esprit de corps" are not unalike. And though the center is no longer a "refuge from wives" (indeed, more likely a refuge from children), it can be "a haven for recreation and good fellowship." And, finally, though the "social standing and status" of "an immigrant Irishman or German" is no longer relevant, the advancement of the Appalachian, the Negro, the Puerto Rican, and the Mexican-American most certainly is. Just as the political club replaced the saloon as *the* grassroots center for neighboorhood activity, so perhaps the neighborhood service center will eventually assume this role and responsibility.

But understanding the impetus behind the rise of the neighborhood center does not clarify all questions about its goals.

These questions particularly stand out: Is the neighborhood service center primarily a means for making the best use of services by overcoming geographic and psychological distances? Can it successfully promote social action and institutional change? Is it merely a fact-gathering operation concerned with the identification of inadequacies in the welfare system and other traditional agencies? Can the center change services for the better? Can it provide better services itself? What is the best mix of service and action efforts?[9]

By examining some research evidence we can perhaps shed some light on these questions and raise still other issues.

Its Organizational Structure

Potentially, the settings of neighborhood service centers are as diversified as the programs they offer and the people they serve. "Such centers could be located in a variety of places, including public housing projects . . . settlement houses, neighborhood stores and shopping centers. They would be pleasant places to come to, open weekends and some evenings, with . . . overriding courtesy."[10] The continuing involvement of residents in the planning and staffing of programs is one of the center's innovations. Typically, area residents participate in center activities both as members of boards and committee and as staff workers. "Except for the very poor, the most militant, and the established political leadership, the boards represent a reasonable cross-section of the neighborhood."[11] Neighborhood center staffs vary greatly in size—from one-man operations to those employing over a hundred. The median size of the 20 centers Perlman and Jones studied was 14;[12] a Brandeis University study of 54 centers found a median size staff of 15.[13] The proportion of workers from the neighborhood varies from center to center; however, virtually all try to employ some neighborhood people.

The neighborhood service center study by Kirschner Associates, and the studies of community action programs by Brandeis University and Hallman, indicate that more women than men were involved as staff employees and that, except in small towns and rural areas, more Negro than white women.[14]

Though the evidence on the employment of neighborhood workers indicates reasonable success, that on the participation of residents on boards and committees is less than compelling.[15] Kirschner Associates found that "the participation of the poor as employees . . .

seems to be well advanced and largely successful. . . . Participation of the poor as policymakers and administrators seems to have been achieved on a quantitative basis but there appears to be little effective involvement due to a lack of training in some cases and a lack of authority in others."[16] Similarly, in reporting on the findings of a study of 12 community action programs, Clark writes that "the poor were involved as staff in all effective programs and as participants in voter registration drives, rent strikes and the like, but the degree of their participation was guided and to a large extent controlled by leaders not themselves poor . . . In no case of an effective program were elected poor influential in major decisions, though several programs envisioned gradual involvement of neighborhood boards at policy-making levels."[17]

The Services It Offers

First and foremost, neighborhood service centers provide social services. Many combine services and social action, but all of them provide service in some form.

Kirschner Associates found wide variations in the kinds of services offered, ranging from centers concentrating on one service such as employment counseling to centers offering many different kinds of services to many different kinds of people. Almost all offered employment counseling and job placement services. Next came welfare, primarily through the aid to families with dependent children (AFDC) program. At least half provided educational and health services. Housing, recreational, consumer education, and legal aid services were offered in decreasing order with decreasing frequency.[18]

A study of neighborhood service programs undertaken by Abt Associates noted that "family life, welfare assistance, health, legal aid, and education programs" were generally offered to residents of the areas served.[19]

A sample of cases studied by Perlman and Jones at the Roxbury center in Boston found that the problems people presented, in order of frequency, were employment, legal, economic, housing, family, and health[20]—all consistent with services that centers generally make available.

Requisites for Good Service

Though the neighborhood service center has the obvious potential of being all things to all men, a reasonable list of requisites would include the following:[21]

Accessible. The center should be easy to get to. It should be open evenings and weekends and should provide emergency telephone service 24 hours a day.

Acceptable. The center should be clean, comfortable, and informal; its operation should be consistent with the neighborhood's way of life. Neither its employees nor its services should be foreign or alien. Faces should be familiar, and workers should be friendly and courteous.

Immediate. The center should provide prompt, efficient, immediate service. It should be able to respond to day-to-day problems without long hours of waiting and many rounds of appointments.

Comprehensive. The center should offer a full range of usable, on-the-spot services or easy access to other resources by available transportation. It should gear itself to the needs that people have—especially poor people—and provide for the simultaneous handling of problems where possible.

Integrated. The center should insure the coordination and integration of services so that they might be more effectively brought to bear on all the problems that people present.

Responsive. The center should reflect the needs and desires of the neighborhood. It should provide ways in which residents can shape the program and continue to contribute to its course and development. It should be relevent and ready to respond to changing needs.

These categories are neither mutually exclusive nor exhaustive. Several overlap. And though still others could be used, these seem to provide an analytically useful way to approach the literature.[22]

Research Findings and Performance Criteria

These characteristics are criteria against which the achievements of the center can be measured. Together they are one basis for assessing centers and for organizing the findings of a variety of studies.[23]

Are centers accessible? Centers are located in low-income areas and, by virtue of their physical location, are at least more accessible than traditional agencies. Kirschner Associates note that the center is a way of introducing conventional community services to people for whom they have been previously unavailable.[24] Perlman and

Jones report that, "in general, neighborhood centers serve people who live within walking distance or on transportation lines."[25] Data from their centers indicated that most clients were "walk-ins." In only one did the number referred from other agencies exceed that of those who came in on their own or who were referred by family, friends, or neighbors.[26] A number of centers have set up outreach operations. But some have had to cut back such efforts because of heavy demands on resources.[27] Most have found no shortage of persons to serve.

Nevertheless, the proportion of residents served varies greatly. Perlman and Jones' estimates suggest that their centers contacted from less than 2 percent of the area population of the Mobilization for Youth program in New York City to as many as 20 percent of the service population of Community Progress, Inc., in New Haven.[28] Based on figures from 10 of 20 sample centers, Kirschner Associates estimate that some 18 percent of the people in their neighborhood areas were reached.[29]

The number reached, however, may not reflect the actual number served. One neighborhood program, for example, contacted about 10,000 people but served fewer than 500.[30]

Great effort is going into reducing the psychological distance between client and service unit by employing neighborhood people and making them visible and accessible in and out of the center. They typically provide outreach service and otherwise encourage agency-shy persons to use the center. Though it may be argued that centers are doing all they can to make their services accessible, it is clear that there are many more clients who need to be served and that clients will continue to overrun as many centers as are established.

Are services immediate?   There is little evidence that centers as yet offer "instant" service. However, to the extent that they are at convenient locations, are open evenings and weekends, provide transportation, employ generalist receptionists and intake workers, have a range of on-the-spot services or access to such services through links to community agencies, the centers probably can rather promptly attend to client problems, particularly the day-to-day critical problems of poor people. Perlman and Jones describe the prospect for immediate service this way: "A receptionist, most often a woman who handled incoming calls and some clerical work, greeted the client, took her name and address, and arranged an appointment with one of the workers within a matter of minutes; rarely was there a wait of more than fifteen or twenty minutes.

If an answer could be given ... the receptionist would give the information; otherwise she would refer the client to another worker."[31] "In Roxbury, 74% of the clients were seen immediately by one of the services, 14% were seen by appointment, and 12% were not recorded."[32]

Centers are usually inundated with demands on their scarce resources and find themselves having to make the same hard choices as traditional agencies. Perlman and Jones note that "going beyond" instant service "requires the investment of a substantial amount of staff time with clients who require intensive and extended service" and raise this issue: "Should quick service to ten clients take precedence over intensive service to one?"[33] Given the great demand and the relatively few resources at their disposal, their centers soon responded in either of two ways. They continued to do what they could to serve individual clients and families by stretching or expanding resources and by cutting back on client recruitment, or they played down individual services and organized neighborhood groups to demand more and better services from other agencies.[34]

The second recourse—community action—becomes problematic, however, when the client's perception of the neighborhood center is taken into account. "In their view the purpose of the center is to help people by providing them with the services they need ... the idea of organizing the poor to help themselves is not very prominent in the client's perceptions."[35]

The question of whether neighborhood centers have the ability to respond promptly to resident needs remains open. They may be able to serve a few and to cut redtape for a few others but for the rest—a prompt reception may stop far short of much-needed service. A client cutback is no solution. Is an invitation to "come, let us organize together" any better?

Are services acceptable? Services should be in keeping with neighborhood life styles. Perlman and Jones observed an "easy and friendly atmosphere" in the centers they visited,[36] and Kirschner Associates refer to the "modest size and relatively simple organization" of most of their sample centers. "There is every indication that people ... found them warm and welcoming."[37]

Though most centers have the kind of casual and informal atmosphere that appeals to poor people, Kirschner Associates observed that in some cities, the very large centers have assumed an unattractive institutional quality.[38] Abt Associates found that in nine of the 13 programs they studied, core service facilities were inadequate due to cramped space and lack of privacy. Large meeting rooms within the center itself were not generally available but were provided by schools and churches; in any event, poor facilites apparently had not hindered program effectiveness.[39] Generally, the facilities available for neighborhood centers have been more or less adequate and relatively acceptable to residents.

As we have indicated, the presence in the program of workers from the neighborhood, people with whom the residents can readily identify, also makes the center more acceptable. In commenting on the phenomenon that a few residents came from considerable distances to the center, Perlman Jones allude to psychological proximity. "Some find the centers less formidable than large, impersonal offices of agencies that may actually be closer to them; some Negroes or Puerto Ricans feel more at home in an agency where they find people of their own ethnic group on the staff."[40] In the Kirschner Associates study, the characteristics of both the people served and the center staffs were similar. In fact, the only differences between the two were that the residents had larger families and the staffs more education.[41] The characteristics of the nonprofessional staff members of the community action program reported in the Brandeis study were also similar.[42] To the extent that such similar characteristics contribute to the client's ability to identify with workers and feel more "at home," neighborhood centers seem to be acceptable to the people served.

Are services comprehensive?   One sign of a comprehensive center is the variety of its programs and activities. The 54 centers in the Brandeis study offered from four to 10 services. Half were locally developed, direct services, 25 percent were "national emphasis" and other programs, and the rest were neighborhood organization and self-help activities.[43] The specific services most often provided focused on health, recreation, counseling, employment, and education; the economic programs on buyers' clubs and tenant unions; and the special projects on neighborhood clean-up campaigns and voter registration drives. Four of every five centers promoted these programs and projects,[44] and most provided some combination. The neighborhood service programs reported on by Abt Associates were heavily weighed toward service. Few programs had developed community action to the point where neighborhoods were able to manage their own affairs and develop their own areas.[45] Among the component programs of the neighborhood service programs, about 60 percent emphasized social service; some 35 percent "opportunity enhancement;" and 10 percent community mobilization.[46]

Kirschner Associates found a very broad range of social services in their centers. Though programs in the smaller communites and rural areas were more diversified, most provided several different services. A highly specialized center was unusual.[47] The method of providing service varied greatly—from information and referral to on-the-spot service. "The bulk of their service functions involve . . . traditional services . . . very few . . . are 'new inventions'."[48] What is novel is the neighborhood package of public and private services.

In examining the extent to which center services approach comprehensiveness, the relative mix of services becomes crucial. Kirschner Associates' findings are relevant here: 60 percent of their centers offered employment and welfare services *or* employment and health services, and 40 percent linked four services together—education, employment, welfare, and health.[49]

But the fact that centers offer a range of services does little to insure their use. In fact, data from the Roxbury center raise serious questions about the comprehensiveness of service—from the client's view. The service outcome of a 15 percent sample of clients served in 1965 was as follows: of 92 cases presented at intake, 36 were referred to social service, 33 to employment, and 19 to the legal unit. The receptionist handled one case; the fate of three others is not clear. Of those referred fully 69 had contact with one unit only. Of the 23 recipients who had subsequent contact with another unit, 16 had direct contact with two and seven with three.[50] Thus, it appears that fewer than three of 10 clients were able to use more than one service. The Roxbury data seem consistent with those of the Kirschner Associates study, which found that clients are oriented to a single service and "often do not even know that it is a neighborhood service center as such."[51]

If the neighborhood center merely provides increased accessibility to selected services, it is possible that single-service agencies decentralized into a neighborhood center would accomplish the same purpose. At any rate, the case for comprehensive, one-stop service in the neighborhood center is less than persuasive. It is not enough for services to be accessible, even immediately available, if they cannot meet the different needs that people have. Moreover, they are only potentially comprehensive unless the different services can be effectively coordinated and made meaningful and usable.

Are services integrated?   Proximity of itself may facilitate but cannot insure coordinated services,[52] a point Perlman and Jones make about the presence of staff representatives of other agencies in neighborhood centers, holds for center staffs, too. Abt Associates note that, though core service activity was relatively successful in coordinating the movement of clients through the system of the neighborhood service programs, in four the core service unit was separate from other service units and that this separation contributed greatly to service fragmentation and lack of coordination.[53] Even where staff members are present together, problems of communication and coordination exist and are exacerbated when the center director has no effective administrative control over workers from other agencies. In eight of the 13 neighborhood service programs, the directors had no control over other agency workers.[54] When center workers are responsible to other agencies, problems in communication and effective service coordination are more likely to occur. But, just as physical proximity does not guarantee integrated services, neither does administrative control.

Perlman and Jones found that, in the Roxbury center, "barriers to interdisciplinary cooperation were serious within . . . core staff . . . under the same administration."[55] Such a problem is fairly widespread. The Kirschner Associates study suggests that linked services do not automatically insure coordination. They found little evidence of "carefully planned efforts to present well coordinated service programs. This is something often talked about but rarely achieved."[56] Abt Associates also found that the integration and coordination of services was a major problem.[57] Few formal coordinating mechanisms had been set up, and workers mostly relied on informal relations and communications.[58] Kirschner Associates found some successful "case" coordination, but at a cost of considerable time and effort.[59] Perlman and Jones note that "commitment to the goals of marshalling resources for the benefit of clients seems to be most crucial in these arrangemetns" and that such commitment must be shared by both agency and worker.[60] Though centers have devised some means for coordination—the rotation of intake, the anchor worker, the case conference, the central file system, the case coordinator—none of them have been wholly effective.

As pointed out, most center contacts are with one service only. Of the 23 cases provided with two or more services in the Roxbury sample, only four were the subject of a "review conference." The service coordinator was often pressed into providing direct service and could not spend enough time in interservice coordination.[61] Abt Associates found a similar situation.[62] The Roxbury center concentrated multiservice activity on proportionately few cases. In one month's period, 5 percent of the recipients had 30 percent of the contacts.[63] Thus, even when multiservice activity takes place, only a few recipients can be served. It is clear that neighborhood centers suffer from some of the traditional problems of specialization and fragmentation. Just as different agencies strive to maintain autonomy and independence, so do different center services. Organizational sovereignity and professional ideology both contribute to this condition, as does the need for organizational survival and professional status. "Each service tends to perceive problems in its own terms and is reluctant to 'surrender' its clients or share them with another service."[64] Because services are "different," they are likely to draw on different resources, use different people, perform different functions, and serve different needs in different groups of people.

In the Kirschner Associates centers, though education and employment services were linked in some 60 percent of the centers, there was no evidence of their coordination. "To the contrary, the two services deal with different clientele."[65]

The attempt to coordinate and rationalize services is at many levels: within the center's service units, between the center and participating agencies, and between the center and all other agencies serving the neighborhood. As one of their tasks, centers try to coordinate and improve community services. The Brandeis study found, in fact, that some 14 percent of their centers saw coordination as a primary objective—taking precedence over the provision of direct service, community organization, and case finding and referral.[66] Kirschner Associates found, however, little marked success in this regard.[67] Because few centers provide "new" services, they are left trying to use, coordinate, and improve traditional community services. The Abt Associates study reports that, at first, residents in many communities did not want to work with traditional agencies, which had neglected them for years, and were reluctant to share their few resources with the community.[68] The strain between neighborhood centers and community agencies is an obvious obstacle to effective coordination.

But still other functions of the center may also block the coordination of services: "Some centers concentrate on developing an informal atmosphere that is inviting to the poor people of the neighborhood. These centers are less concerned with service integration or refinements. Other centers encourage attitudes and organizational arrangements associated with aggressive community action and these appear antithetical to close collaboration with traditional agencies."[69] Either stance militates against effective integration. Coordination of services remains an elusive objective, if not the major challenge.

Are services responsive?   One way to judge the responsiveness of centers to neighborhood needs is to look at the response of the residents to the centers. Such response has far exceeded expectations.[70] Moreover, the services provided seem to be more or less consistent with the problems. Abt Associates report that residents were generally consulted about their most pressing problems and that these problems were those the programs attempted to handle.[71] Though some centers have shifted programs to meet resident needs and demands, others have done so for want of funds and resources. In all neighborhoods service programs, activity has been limited by lack of money, staff, and proficiency. They have not been fully responsive to resident needs for employment, job training, and housing. But, in general, they "have addressed themselves to the most salient needs of the community, where they had the resources to do so."[72]

Perlman and Jones report that their centers apparently served people who both racially and ethnically represented the neighborhood. Moreover, by and large, these centers attracted the kinds of people who could best be helped, given the kinds of service offered.[73]

Though few centers are set up for formal, systematic review and followup, recipients can take part in center programs and policymaking in several ways—principally through board, committee, staff, and volunteer work. Abt Associates found an overriding desire in residents for a larger voice in neighborhood service programs. But, of 13 programs, "only in five of the cities have the residents really had a voice in setting policy."[74] Here the staff positions open to neighborhood people promised rapid advancement and opportunity to effect key decisions; participation on boards, committees, and neighborhood corporations was rewarding and residents could influence program activities.[75] The opportunity for rewarding involvement in the other eight centers, however, apparently left much to be desired. As we have seen, the evidence for effective resident participation on center boards and committees is hardly persuasive; the obstacles are many and hard to overcome; and, though there is reason for optimism about participation by neighborhood workers, the limits of their role circumscribe their contribution.

To the extent that the center's responsiveness is assessed by the opportunity neighborhood people have for shaping policies and programs, most centers could be much more "responsive." But to the extent that centers have moved at all to facilitate resident expression and to make programs accessible and acceptable, they have made a beginning.

But are they effective?   Assuming that services are accessible and acceptable—which they are—and assuming that they are responsive and comprehensive—which they may well be—and even assuming that they are immediately available and well integrated—which they are not—the question remains: Are they effective?

The evidence for the effectiveness of neighborhood centers is based at this point on gross impressions and guesswork. Until data are available on the ways in which centers help solve the problems people have or strengthen their capacity for dealing with them and until we learn whether and how centers improve the quality of neighborhood life and influence community agencies and institutions, there is really little to say. Nevertheless, we can review and summarize the prevailing impressions.

Abt Associates report that in most of the cities they studied, programs have been reasonably effective. In the few cities where they have not been, the neighborhood service program "has proved to be yet another program that promises many benefits and produces few results."[76]

In general these centers have provided an impressive array of services and, though quality varies greatly, service is now available, and all within a short time.[77] Specifically, eight of the neighborhood programs had improved neighborhood services and had begun to meet resident needs. They had introduced new resources and had begun to coordinate and integrate others. Traditional agencies had become more responsive and were modifying hiring policies to the advantage of poor people. These centers have gained the confidence of the people they serve and have demonstrated that neighborhood people can develop and operate their own programs.[78]

Kirschner Associates interviewed some 189 clients and neighborhood residents. The responses of those interviewed to two questions are especially pertinent in assessing how helpful the centers were. When asked what the centers had done for them and their families, three out of 10 said "nothing." Though 70 percent mentioned receiving one or another service, the fact that nearly a third of those presumably served replied "nothing" rules out any great enthusiasm for the centers.[79] Yet a question tapping whether residents felt better off because of the center yielded less equivocal findings. Some 60 percent of the respondents in medium-sized and large cities and fully 95 percent in small towns and rural areas felt "much better off" because of the centers.[80] These centers were mostly service oriented and were, by virtue of their small size, less forbidding than large, bureaucratic urban organizations.[81]

In summing up, Kirschner Associates say that neighborhood centers have undoubtedly contributed to change: several public and private agencies have become more flexible and have modified practices to make them more relevant; political institutions have become more alert and, in some instances, more sensitive. But economic institutions and the neighborhood environment appear to be little affected. The poor people employed by the centers appear to have changed the most, and many seem to have acquired confidence and a sense of having made worthwhile contributions. Some board members share this enthusiasm, but others are disillusioned. Of the persons served in general, they note "that most have not yet been reached in a meaningful way at all; that some have become clients for services and perceive the centers as givers of services and themselves as recipients of services; and that a still smaller number regard themselves as active members of society with the right and ability to influence it. To the extent that these feelings represent shifts from apathetic, helpless attitudes they are significant and appear to relate to some involvement with the center."[82]

Perlman and Jones found that neighborhood centers were able to identify pressing needs and were moving toward meeting them. They also observed that centers were instrumental in stimulating traditional service agencies to change and had found rather creative ways to make full use of their scarce resources.[83] Given their relative youthfulness and the many constraints under which they function, even small successes are impressive.

Social Action

Neighborhood service centers always include a service component—it is their reason for being. However, the "package deal" offered may or may not include a social action component. Implicit in describing social action efforts in centers are these questions: What type of social action can be promoted? and What is its relative weight in the program? Data from the Brandeis study indicate that, though community organization projects absorbed only about 25 percent of the center's activities, 43 percent of the centers saw the organization of residents as their primary objective.[84]

Social action is difficult to define; its methods may run from complete cooperation with other groups to all-out conflict. "Social action . . . means and demands the stimulation of concern among individuals who share a common predicament; who are victims of long standing community problems and injustices, who can be induced not only to identify their problems but to seek to determine the methods by which they can be resolved, and who are able to develop and sustain the initiative for the type of collective action, which, in fact, does resolve or ameliorate these problems."[85]

Perlman and Jones explicate four goals for social action: delivering social services more effectively; fostering concrete self-help efforts; providing for the poor the social and pyschological benefits of taking part in organizational life; and changing policies and practices among relevant agencies and institutions.[86]

The Kischner Associates study found no clear evidence of the effectiveness of social action. Attempts were made to develop new service programs and activities such as tutoring programs, day-care centers, thrift shops, and recreation programs. And half of their centers had conducted cleanup campaigns, but these were invariably started by community action officials. "This type of community action is not a spontaneous thing for poverty area residents. Rather it is a middle-class concern . . ."[87]

Clark suggests "that the threshold of tolerability for significant changes in the predicament of the poor is rather low for politicians and may be somewhat higher but not particularly high for middle-class professionals and even those staff members who are charged with the responsibility for directing community action and other programs in behalf of the poor. . . . This . . . tends to result either in the maintenance of the status quo or in the restriction of community action programs to techniques and methods acceptable to the middle class, thereby limiting the rate or the amount of change permitted the poor."[88]

The problems inherent in the development of citizen organizations are how to stimulate and how to sustain interest. Research shows that poor people are physical, visual, problem-centered, and action-oriented rather than verbal. Committee meetings, written reports, and abstract discussions may not accomplish specific goals.[89]

Perlman and Jones, say: "Neighborhood groups find it difficult to move from a situation of shared individual interests to a common concern for larger social issues."[90] Bread-and-butter issues are necessary. Unless there are immediate rewards, rank-and-file participants quickly lose interest.

Abt Associates found less resident interest in community mobilization than in some of the more concrete social services, and few of their centers tried to foster community organization.[91]

Organizing for more effective delivery of social services and stimulating self-help are directed toward amelioration and not change. For this reason, residents may see such goals as demeaning and palliative and as "put-offs." Nevertheless, they can offer invaluable educational benefits and a point of departure for residents.

Another rationale for social action is the social and psychological benefits derived from participating in organizational life. Ideally, participation in collective social action may "reduce alienation and anomie; provide opportunities for self-fulfillment; overcome feelings of powerlessness; improve the individual and group self-image of those who participate; and generally increase community integration and control."[93] But we have little evidence to suggest that it does all or any of these.

Institutional change is usually only a small aspect of a center's program. We have little data on the success of efforts in this direction. Wharf's recent study of the Roxbury Multi-Service Center found that the center had minimal effect on its "targe agencies" and could not achieve significant organizational change.[94] This objective is sometimes directed at other than service institutions and is often put into operation with conflict-oriented social action methods. Here, the keys are money and power; the kinds of technique range from nonviolent protest marches and economic boycott of merchants and public transportation to more violent demonstrations such as "sit-ins," work stoppages, and riots. Explicit goals are usually "against" rather than "for" something—mobilizing voter registration to defeat a racist candidate, for instance.

Perlman and Jones identify two central issues in promoting social action:

- The centers cannot create and hope to control autonomous and independent groups.
- The groups may threaten the sponsor or other relevant reference groups in the community.[95]

Such problems inhibit the widespread development of neighborhood and community action efforts.

Is it any wonder that few if any neighborhood service centers engage in conflict-oriented social action? Hallman says: "Except for a very small number of communities, the Community Action Program does not involve a predominant commitment to the strategy of giving power to the poor, of deliberate confrontation with established power, of purposefully created conflict."[96]

Similarly, Kirschner Associates found conflict-oriented social action against the political power structure in few of the rural centers and in only about 25 percent of the urban centers partly because of the relationship to the sponsor.[97] Marris and Rein, in commenting on this dilemma, say: "If the sponsors cannot disdain responsibility for the organization they create, and if . . . they defeat their own purpose in seeking to control it, only a sponsor free from other commitments can afford to support his organization in whatever course it chooses. . . . It is not unlikely that participants who are encouraged to take action . . . may challenge the sponsor's basis of allocating resources; and the 'citizens' organization may want to utilize tactics and develop strategies which the sponsor may find incompatible with its own principles."[98]

Realize, though, that the question of what type of social action to be implemented is not merely a this-or-that position; even highly cooperative community development efforts can have undesirable consequences for the center. Clearly, however, conflict-oriented social action methods are not usually followed under the guise of the neighborhood service center, and collaborative and cooperative efforts for change only operate successfully within a defined sphere of influence. Cohen suggests: "I think of these service type operations as a range within which there can be certain levels of social action, but I don't think it is a mechanism through which we can get at the larger question."[99]

Thus, the social action component in the neighborhood service center tends to be a self-help, community development effort based on cooperation and collaboration and the use of mild protest and peaceful demonstration only in certain circumscribed situations to obtain immediate and concrete goals.

Services or Action?

What exactly is at issue in weighing social services against social action?

Rainwater says: "In the services business it is easy to forget about . . . the things that people need and want that aren't provided by services. . . . The minute you adopt a service strategy . . . for dealing with the problem of poverty . . . you're setting priorities for the families involved. . . . Poor people would rather make these decisions themselves."[100] Social service and social action programs often aim at different goals: the first at having "the professional" decide what the poor person needs and administering the right measure; the second at giving the poor enough power and leverage to decide and to act to get what they want and need.

Overlying both goals are the organizational problems raised by a neighborhood service center. The limitation of resources, both of staff time and program funds, almost intrinsically demands a choice of service or action as the major program goal. All too often "agencies try to cover too much ground; . . . they are good neither in service nor in . . . social action."[101]

Perlman and Jones found that in five programs they studied, three deemphaiszed social services and stressed community organization. The others continued to emphasize services but had to cut back programs by either stretching resources or providing special services or closing intake at several points until the caseload became manageable.[102]

Grosser, in a study of community organization in six youth programs, found that "social action and service components may exist either as part of a comprehensive project, or more desirably, as separate cooperative entities. The separation of the services and action functions into discrete organizations is suggested because the two functions are frequently in disharmony . . . and because the dispensers of public agency services are congenitally and organizationally unable to distinguish between the protest and service function when practiced by the same organization."[103]

Findings from the Brandeis study further suggest "that it is not possible to give equal attention to both of the objectives . . . in a single unit and that most frequently service delivery requirements take precedence over . . . action."[104] Kirschner Associates make a similar point: "The evidence indicates that is is extremely rare to find both aggressive community action and well executed service programs within the same center."[105]

Perlman and Jones further suggest that the form of the services-action relationship in a center depends both on the activities involved in each and on what the community is willing to accept.[106] To ease tension between the two, they suggest that a center become primarily an instrument of social action, that its services act only to attract participants and to help them with their problems.

The Kirschner Associates study supports the method of attracting the poor to the center with the offer of services. They found that "the idea of community action in which the poor organize to deal with their problems themselves is not very prominent in their thoughts about the neighborhood centers. The poor, however, do understand the idea of services."[107]

Combining services and action in one center, as we have seen, is not without its problems, however, because of the difficulty of coordinating center programs and those of other community agencies. The autonomy of the center, its interest in community

action, and the participation of residents are, as noted, key
influences contributing to lack of service coordination between the
neighborhood center and the "downtown" agency.

Hallman reminds us, however, that the "variation found among
the communities does not reflect a choice between services and
citizen organization. Those who follow the most activist approach
to resident participation also provide services, and many but not
all of those with effective service programs pursue certain forms
of resident participation. The crucial difference is the approach
to institutional change and to planning and coordination."[108]

Although Hallman is undoubtedly correct in suggesting that a
broad overlap exists between services and action and in specifying
that the choice in the world of the neighborhood service center
is usually one of method rather than policy, nevertheless, methods
do ultimately contribute to program emphasis and action.

Thus, the durable services-action issue is one that each center
must inevitably confront.

Issues Without Answers

In this section we will attempt to indicate some of the more
salient issues to be confronted—if not completely resolved. The
main issues revolve around questions of organizational sponsorship;
the specification of goals; the kinds of interventions developed;
the types of workers employed; and the implications of any or
all of these for the survival and success of the neighborhood center.
Though some of these questions can be cast as either-or-dilemmas,
it is not necessary that one preclude the other. In fact, both will
be present in some form; it is a question of relative emphasis and
of possible trade-offs between the two. These options are, of course,
unduly simplified, even arbitrary, not necessarily contradictory, certainly not exhaustive, and in many ways artificial.

A center may emphasize professional direction and administration
or resident participation and neighborhood control. If *administration*,
programs and services may be run more smoothly and efficiently—but
may not be entirely relevant to the needs and desires of residents;
if *participation*, the center may be more responsive to neighborhood
wants—but lack the administrative sophistication and organizational
skill to operate effective programs.

A center may emphasize the provision of service *or* social action.
If *service*, individual needs may be better satisfied—but some of the
larger community issues may be neglected; if *action*, collective needs

may be fully addressed—but the particular problems that people have may not be solved.

A center may emphasize special functions *or* general activities. If *special*, unusual and particular functions may be carried out with dispatch—but the effective integration of activities will be weak; if *general*, the center may be better coordinated—but no one aspect will receive the kind of attention required to make a real contribution.

A center may emphasize professional service *or* nonprofessional services. If *professional*, a relatively few clients may be competently served—but many potential clients may not be reached; if *nonprofessional*, many more neighborhood residents will be attracted to the center—but deeply personal problems will not be presented and complicated problems may not be adequately handled.

A center may emphasize information and referral *or* client advocacy and followup. If *information*, existing agencies may become more widely known and used—but questions of service modification and agency practice will not be sufficiently dealt with; if *advocacy*, traditional services may be challenged and different patterns of relationships hammered out—but fewer clients may be actually served and other problems may be created in the process.

A center may emphasize collaborative and cooperative methods *or* contest and conflict tactics. If *cooperative*, the good will and resources of other agencies and institutions may be more readily available—but the center may become preoccupied with the process to the neglect of hard results; if *conflict*, the center may be able to force some issues and achieve some action—but may have to go it alone and run the risk of diminishing resources and community support.

A center may emphasize neighborhood development and resident self-help *or* community change and political action. If *development*, residents may gain a sense of satisfaction, pride, and confidence—but the broader institutions that impinge on the neighborhood may remain untouched; if *change*, important political issues may be confronted—but the immediate effect on the neighborhood and its residents may be less than obvious.

A center may emphasize the problems and prospects of one particular group or institution *or* many different groups or institutions. If *one*, the group or institution may become better known and more surely helped or influenced—but others may remain unaffected if not disaffected by the center's work; if *many*, a number of different groups or institutions may be touched but perhaps no one in particular will become sufficiently well identified and changed by the center.

Again, these alternatives are not so much choices to be made as they are chances to be taken and risks to be run. In practice, both may be pursued simultaneously; indeed, the pursuit of one may lead to the other. But, at some point, the fact that they often require different resources, point in different directions, and have different costs and consequences may mean, to the extent these alternatives are attempted in the same center, that one or the other emphasis will eventually be given primacy.

In describing the experience of one of the early neighborhood service centers sponsored by Mobilization for Youth, Cloward and Elman sum up their impression this way: "The storefront on Stanton Street has been in existence a little less than four years and its work has increased tenfold . . . . It is still too early to evaluate its permanent contributions to life in the community. Its powers have been limited. It has not yet been able to change substantially the terms of economic dependency when it still seems to be the consensus among most legislators and their constituents that such dependency is to be discouraged, abhored, and punished. Many more people from Stanton street are on welfare than before. The storefront's clients are better clothed, better housed, and better fed than they were four years ago. Many now have telephones, quite a few have washing machines and television sets. Are they better people? Are they worse? Such questions seem like the supreme irrelevancy. For if they are not better for their improved economic circumstances, the society is better for their actions against it." And so it is.

This is the bottom line: the extent to which we help people is the ultimate test. We must ask—as a result of the center—are people better off? And we must, sooner or later, be able to answer—yes—or stand to abandon the idea.

REFERENCES AND NOTES

[1]President Nixon's proposed family assistance plan is one indication of this, as is the interest in the negative income tax, children's allowances, and the income supplementation plan of the President's Commission on Income Maintenance Programs. See *Poverty Amid Plenty: The American Paradox*, Report of the President's Commission on Income Maintenance Programs, Nov. 12, 1969.

[2]See *Special Report: Sick Cities—and the Search for a Cure*, especially Daniel P. Moynihan, "The Urban Negro *Is* the 'Urban Problem'," pp. 36–38, and Lee Rainwater, "The Services Strategy vs. the Income Strategy, pp. 40–41, *Trans-action*, Oct. 1967.

[3]Sanford Kravitz, "Issues and Opportunities Facing Public Welfare," *Public Welfare*, vol. XXVI, No. 1, Jan. 1968, pp. 5–6.

[4]Harry Specht, "Community Development in Low-Income Negro Areas," *Social Work*, Oct. 1966, p. 78. It is interesting to note that the Heineman Commission sees the neighborhood center as a worthy vehicle

for service delivery at the local level: "We recommend that the basic services provided through Federally-aided programs be included in multi-purpose urban neighborhood service centers which would provide a single location from which social services could be dispensed. These neighborhood service centers also could provide information and referral services, have outlets for manpower programs, and provide space for clinical services." See *Poverty Amid Plenty: The American Paradox*, p. 162.

[5]See, for example, Albert Rose, "The Social Services in the Modern Metropolis," *Social Service Review*, Dec. 1963, pp. 375–389.

[6]Edward Banfield, *City Politics* (Cambridge Mass.: Harvard University Press, 1963), as quoted in Robert Perlman and David Jones, *Neighborhood Service Centers*, Office of Juvenile Delinquency, Welfare Administration, U. S. Department of Health, Education, and Welfare, 1967, p. 8.

[7]Alexander B. Callow, Jr., *The Tweed Ring* (New York: Oxford University Press, 1966) pp. 104–105.

[8]Callow, pp. 105–106.

[9]See, for example, Perlman and Jones, p. 37.

[10]"The Advisory Committee on HEW Relationships with State Health Agencies," Report to the Secretary, U. S. Department of Health, Education, and Welfare, December 30, 1966, p. 53.

[11]"OSTI Revised Decentralized Training Paper," *Organization for Social and Technological Innovation*, Apr. 30, 1969, p. 53.

[12]Perlman and Jones, p. 82.

[13]"Neighborhood Organizational Units of the Community Action Agency," *Community Representation in Community Action Programs*, Report No. 4, Florence Heller Graduate School for Advanced Studies in Social Welfare, Brandeis University, Nov. 1968, p. 8.

[14]Kirschner Associates, *A Description and Evaluation of Neighborhood Centers, A Report for the Office of Economic Opportunity*, Dec. 1966, p. 69; "Community Representation in Community Action Programs," Report No. 5, Final Report, The Florence Heller Graduate School for Advanced Studies in Social Welfare, Brandeis University, Mar. 1969, pp. 74–75; Howard W. Hallman, *The Community Action Program—An Interpretive Analysis of 35 Communities, Examination of the War on Poverty*, vol. IV, U. S. Senate Committee on Labor and Public Welfare, September, 1967, p. 908.

[15]Edward J. O'Donnell and Catherine S. Chilman, "Poor People on Public Welfare Boards and Committees," *Welfare in Review*, May-June 1969, pp. 1–9.

[16]Kirschner Associates, p. 47.

[17]Kenneth B. Clark, "Urban Crises—Gimmicks vs. Serious Programs," paper presented at the Annual Forum of the National Conference on Social Welfare, New York City, May 26, 1969, pp. 6–7.

[18]Kirschner Associates, p. 32.

[19]"Summary and Recommendations," *A Study of the Neighborhood Center Pilot Program*, prepared for the Executive Office of the President, Bureau of the Budget, Abt Associates Incorporated, vol. 1, Apr. 30, 1969, p. 11.

[20]Perlman and Jones, p. 27.

[21]See Hobart A. Burch and Edward Newman, "A Federal Program for Neighborhood Services," paper presented at the national conference on social welfare, San Francisco, May 27, 1968; Thomas H. Walz "The Emergence of the Neighborhood Service Center," *Public Welfare*, Apr. 1969, pp. 147–156; and Michael S. March, "The Neighborhood Center Concept," *Public Welfare*, Apr. 1968, pp. 97–11.

[22]See also Kirschner Associates, pp. 41–42, and "An Approach to Measuring the Impact of Existing Service Systems on Problems of Urban Poverty," Greenleigh Associates, Inc., New York, Chicago, pp. 1–8, for still other schemes for evaluation.

[23]Obviously, the major studies reviewed here vary considerably: for example, Perlman and Jones studied 20 centers operating six major programs; Kirschner Associates studied 20 OEO centers; Abt Associates studied 13 centers sponsored jointly by five Federal Departments; and Brandeis University studied 54 OEO centers as part of its study of resident participation in community action programs. Thus, these preliminary findings reflect the experience of neighborhood centers supported through Federal programs—primarily OEO. They do not necessarily speak to the long experience of traditional settlement houses, for example, and should be regarded as tentative pending the outcome of such further systematic research as is underway in the Social and Rehabilitation Service, U. S. Department of Health, Education, and Welfare, and the Office of Economic Opportunity.

[24]Kirschner Associates, p. 15.

[25]Perlman and Jones, p. 30.

[26]Perlman and Jones, p. 30.

[27]Perlman and Jones, p. 41.

[28]Perlman and Jones, p. 81.

[29]Kirschner Associates, p. 24.

[30]"An Evaluation of the Thirteen Neighborhood Service Programs," *A Study of the Neighborhood Center Pilot Program*, prepared for the Executive Office of the President, Bureau of the Budget, Abt Associates Incorporated, vol. 2, part 2, Apr. 30, 1969, p. 41.

[31]Perlman and Jones, p. 26.

[32]Perlman and Jones, p. 26.

[33]Perlman and Jones, p. 33.

[34]Perlman and Jones, p. 40.

[35]Kirschner Associates, p. 17 See also, Charles F. Grosser, "Helping Youth—A Study of Six Community Organization Programs," Office of Juvenile Delinquency and Youth Development, Social and Rehabilitation Service, U. S. Department of Health, Education, and Welfare, 1968, p. 57.

[36]Perlman and Jones, p. 31.

[37]Kirschner Associates, p. 26.

[38]Perlman and Jones, p. 26.

[39]Abt Associates, vol. 2, part 2, pp. 52, 110.

[40]Perlman and Jones, p. 30.
[41]Kirschner Associates, pp. 24, 27.
[42]Brandeis University, Report No. 5, pp. 74–75.
[43]Brandeis University, Report No. 4, p. 9.
[44]Brandeis University, Report No. 4, Appendix C.
[45]Abt Associates, vol. 2, part 2, p. 22.
[46]Abt Associates, vol. 2, part 2, p. 101.
[47]Kirschner Associates, p. 14.
[48]Kirsnhner Associates, p. 15.
[49]Kirschner Associates, p. 33.
[50]Perlman and Jones, p. 34.
[51]Kirschner Associates, p. 45.
[52]Perlman and Jones, p. 37.
[53]Abt Associates, pp. 52–54.
[54]Abt Associates, p. 144.
[55]Perlman and Jones, p. 37.
[56]Kirschner Associates, p. 34.
[57]Abt Associates, vol. 2, part 2, p. 40.
[58]Abt Associates, vol. 2, part 2, p. 145.
[59]Kirschner Associates, p. 44.
[60]Perlman and Jones, p. 37.
[61]Perlman and Jones, p. 34.
[62]Abt Associates, vol. 2, part 2, p. 90.
[63]Perlman and Jones, p. 40.
[64]Perlman and Jones, p. 34.
[65]Kirschner Associates, p. 34.
[66]Brandeis University, Report No. 4, p. 12.
[67]Kirschner Associates, p. 44.
[68]Abt Associates, vol. 1, p. 14.
[69]Kirschner Associates, p. 53.
[70]Perlman and Jones, p. 75.
[71]Abt Associates, vol. 2, part 2, p. 22.
[72]Abt Associates, vol. 2, part 2, pp. 76, 79.
[73]Perlman and Jones, p. 29.
[74]Abt Associates, vol. 2, part 2, p. 126.
[75]Abt Associates, vol. 2, part 2, p. 127.
[76]Abt Associates, vol. 2, part 2, p. 43.
[77]Abt Associates, vol. 2, part 2, p. 6.
[78]Abt Associates, Vol. 2, part 2, p. 42.
[79]Kirschner Associates, p. 25.
[80]Kirschner Associates, Appendix V, table 7.
[81]Kirschner Associates, p. 26.
[82]Kirschner Associates, p. 50.
[83]Perlman and Jones, p. 78.
[84]Brandeis University, Report No. 4, p. 12.
[85]HARYOU-ACT, quoted in Perlman and Jones, p. 53.

[86]Perlman and Jones, pp. 49–51.

[87]Kirschner Associates, p. 17.

[88]Clark, p. 15.

[89]Catherine S. Chilman, *Growing Up Poor,* Welfare Administration Publication No. 13, U. S. Department of Health, Education, and Welfare, May, 1966.

[90]Perlman and Jones, p. 51.

[91]Abt Associates, p. 91.

[92]Perlman and Jones, p. 51.

[93]For a recent attempt to measure changes in participants, see Louis A. Zurcher, Jr., "Social-Psychological Changes Among OEO Indigenous Leaders as a Result of 'Maximum Feasible Participation'," paper presented to the Society for the Study of Social Problems, American Sociological Association Meetings, Boston, Aug. 25, 1968.

[94]Brian W. H. Wharf, "Boundary Personnel: An Exploratory Study of their Role Responsibilities in the Interorganizational Relationships of a Mult-Service Center," unpublished doctoral dissertation, Brandeis University, June 1969.

[95]Perlman and Jones, p. 61.

[96]Hallman, p. 900.

[97]Kirschner Associates, p. 97.

[98]Peter Marris and Martin Rein, *Dilemmas of Social Reform* (New York: Atherton Press, 1967), p. 168.

[99]Nathan E. Cohen, "Building a Social Movement Among the Poor," (discussion) in John B. Turner, ed., *Neighborhood Organization for Community Action,* National Association of Social Workers, New York, 1968, p. 71.

[100]Lee Rainwater, "Neighborhood Action and Lower-class Life-styles" (discussion) in Turner, p. 72.

[101]Cohen in Turner, p. 71

[102]Perlman and Jones, p. 40.

[103]Grosser, p. 58.

[104]Brandeis University, Report No. 4, p. 5.

[105]Kirschner Associates, p. 22.

[106]Perlman and Jones, p. 72.

[107]Kirschner Associates, p. 25.

[108]Hallman, p. 900.

[109]Richard A. Cloward and Richard M. Elman, "Advocacy in the Ghetto," *Trans-Action,* Dec. 1966, p. 109.

Part III

**Some Central Concerns
of Human Service Organizations**

Introduction

There are virtually as many important concerns of human service organizations as there are definable bio-social problems. Through legislative acts, and failures to act, we have, by design and default, established certain priorities for intervention. Whether these are or were appropriate priorities has frequently remained unknown until opportunities for effective action have passed. Too often we have found ourselves with the wrong programs, in the wrong places, at the wrong times.

The major domestic social problems of the immediate future loom with a menacing importance. In all probability they possess a larger and more destructive potential than any set of domestic problems since those of the 1930's. Environmental pollutants threaten the existence of the ecological foundation of life itself; public educational systems are conflict-laden and often internally decaying; unrenewed and unrestored inner cities are becoming increasingly inhabited by affluent corporations and impoverished minorities; cities are becoming characterized by unrest and disorder; the facilities and programs for physical and mental health are too often inadequate or outmoded. These represent only a few of the problems and concerns which are immediately relevant to human service organizations.

The concerns that are highlighted in this section, health care, agency organization, and alcoholism, were selected to represent the more generic problems of comprehensive health, the organization of intervention, and programmatic intervention. Hopefully it will be possible to generalize to the larger problems from these selected starting points.

The readings in this section have, obviously, been chosen from among a population of problems about which something has been written. We find it disconcerting that those concerns and problems about which nothing has yet been written will compose the most critical, but still invisible, problems of our times.

Section A

Some Central Concerns
of Human Service Organizations:
In Health

The citizen's right to health and adequate health care may be the number one national domestic priority in the immediate and forseeable future. And, while the basic knowledge necessary for effective treatment has expanded rapidly, service delivery systems continue to funnel that knowledge into the implementation strategies of marginally effective human service organizations.

A comparative examination of rates of death from various major illnesses for the years 1919 and 1969 indicates that, with the exception of infectious diseases, rates have been decreased for only a few types of illnesses. The rates for major killers, cancer and cardiovascular disorders, have worsened. (Of course, since death is inevitable, if some rates improve, others must necessarily worsen.) Despite this caveat it is less than encouraging to realize that in this same 50-year period the mortality rate for males at age 65 has gone virtually unchanged for whites, and worsened for blacks. Among females, blacks have a mortality rate at age 65 that is equivalent to that of white males in 1919 (about 35 per 100,000 population), while the rate for white females has dropped, significantly, from 32 to 17 per 100,000 population in this span of time.

Statistics such as these serve as dramatic testimony to the pressing need for a critical examination of our health delivery systems. If these systems are to be effective agents of intervention in human ecology, it is imperative that there be an active exploration of new organizational models of service delivery, including research concerning the problems of implementing new organizational models. Although it is unlikely that the costs of these systems will decrease, it is essential that the benefit side of cost-benefit ratios be increased.

163

12. The Approaching Struggle to Provide Adequate Health Care for All Americans

Melvin A. Glasser

If, as is suggested in the following article, the word "system" is a very incorrect one to describe present patterns of health care, the problems of restructuring health care may involve, as a first priority, the creation of health care systems. And, it is possible that by working toward the creation of these systems, the problem of restructuring existing patterns of health services will be solved; i.e., health care systems will be attained only when there has been a significant restructuring of the organization of health services.

The health consequences of the present "nonsystem" of service delivery organizations is documented in the paper to follow, as are proposals and criteria for future health care systems. Most importantly, research is cited which suggests possible benefits for a population from differing organizational approaches to delivery systems.

It is almost two decades since social work, joined with other progressive forces, lost the fight to provide federally financed comprehensive health insurance to all through the Wagner-Murray-Dingell Bill. In the meantime Medicare—the "half-loaf" measure to care for the aged—was passed. Along with it, Title XIX of the Social Security Act—Medicaid—was enacted to provide a somewhat expanded hodgepodge of "welfare medicine" to a portion of those Americans too poor to pay for services in the wildly escalating health care marketplace. These piecemeal approaches have helped meet some of the health needs of some of the people. They have also proved harmful, for they have contributed in major ways to the skyrocketing of costs, fragmentation of services, lack of effective controls on quality of care, and shortage of health personnel owing to inappropriate and wasteful use of scarce talents.

This situation has brought the nation to the point where our

164

health care services are deteriorating and many of the programs are on the verge of collapse. New forces are at work to provide constructive solutions to this crisis. Concurrently, the organized medical profession—which is gaining most from America's chaotic medical programs—is preparing massive new efforts to thwart meaningful social change.

For years the social work profession, in the platform statements of the National Association of Social Workers and resolutions passed by NASW's biennial Delegate Assemblies, has called for comprehensive health services to all through federal national health insurance.[1] The gap has been wide, however, between the statements of objectives and meaningful social action to achieve them. The present crisis presents an important opportunity for social workers to inform themselves of the issues and to determine whether the profession will take a vigorous role in finding constructive solutions in the struggle for health care as a right.

Nonsystem of Health Care

The dictionary defines system as "an assemblage or combination of things or parts forming a complex or unitary whole."[2] America's existing health care pattern does not conform to this definition. Rather it is a nonsystem that can most appropriately be characterized as disjointed, inefficient, ineffective, and wasteful in organizing and providing health care services. Illustrative of the health care nonsystem are the following:

Inflation. By fiscal 1968–69, the total outlay for health ($60.3 billion) represented 6.6 percent of the gross national product, a fivefold increase from the 1949–50 expenditure of $12.1 billion (4.6 percent of the GNP). In the current fiscal year it is estimated that expenditures will reach $73 billion.

Health care expenditures for individuals rose 94 percent during the sixties—from $151.59 in fiscal 1960–61 to $293.78 in fiscal 1968–69.[3] Although the consumer price index for all items rose 29 percent from January 1960 to January 1970, overall medical care prices rose nearly 50 percent during this same period.[4]

Waste. Reuther estimated that some 22 percent of the money spent for health services in the United States is wasted.[5] In a time of critical shortages of funds and personnel the nonproductive expenditure of approximately $14 billion should be an issue of grave national concern. Included in Reuther's catalogue of waste is the duplication and competing sales and administrative costs of hundreds of private insurance carriers, hospitals built in the wrong places and for the wrong purposes, patients admitted to hospitals for procedures not requiring hospitalization, inadequate and inappropriate use of extended care facilities and home care programs, tens of thousands of needless surgical procedures, inadequate use of the ancillary health professions, and inappropriate use of scarce medical personnel.

For years it has been recognized that hospital boards, with an eye toward enhancing the prestige of their institutions, insist on funding costly, underutilized, and sophisticated medical techniques that may already be available and underutilized at other facilities in the same community. For example, in some large cities as many as four hospitals perform open-heart surgery when the patient caseload is sufficient to justify only one such facility. Similarly, consumers and taxpayers are asked to support duplicate and wasteful obstetrical, pediatric, and cardiac care units because hospitals have in the main resisted efforts to centralize such programs in a few key community facilities.

Maldistribution of personnel. Egeberg, assistant secretary of the Department of Health, Education, and Welfare, estimates that this country requires fifty thousand new physicians and tens of thousands of social workers, nurses, and other allied health personnel to meet the nation's minimum needs.[6] Manpower experts, however, point out that much of the shortage is relative, rather than absolute. It is a reflection both of inappropriate use of personnel and of maldistribution. For example, in Dyersville, Iowa, a new ninety-bed hospital built to attract physicians to this area of eighteen thousand is staffed by a single overworked doctor.[7] Rural Deckerville, Michigan, where four veterinarians serve the cattle and pets, is in danger of losing its only physician and having its modern twenty-five-bed hospital stand empty.[8] These examples are by no means unique.[9]

> Despite their greater need, the urban poor have fewer health services than the more well-to-do. Health professionals have fled to the suburbs along with the middle-class whites. Not uncommonly, the physician-population ratio in the ghetto is one-half to one-fifth that of the city as a whole.[10]

Failure of Private Insurance

Although at the end of 1968 the private health insurance industry covered over 169 million Americans by one or more forms of private health insurance,[11] this extensive coverage met only 35.7 percent of all consumer expenditures for private health care. Thus nearly two-thirds (64.3 percent) of consumer health expenditures were paid by the individual.[12] Moreover, the lower the family income, the less likely a family was to have private health insurance; only 35 percent of families with annual incomes under $3,000, but 90 percent of families with incomes over $10,000, had some health insurance coverage. The U.S. Public Health Service estimated that 24–34 million Americans under age 65 had no private health insurance coverage.[13]

Even among the insured in 1968, coverage was uneven by type of service. While 76.5 percent of the population was covered for hospital care expenses, the percentage of people covered for other expenses descended from surgical care (73.6 percent) through X-ray and lab tests (about 50 percent) to 9.6 percent for nursing care and only 2.9 percent for dental care.[14]

Thus private health insurance has provided partial and largely inadequate coverage of the costs of illness. Of equal concern is the view that in its twenty-five years of operation, the private insurance system has not demonstrated the capacity to provide preventive health protection, to control costs or quality, or to effect constructive change in outmoded methods of delivering health care services.

Solo-Practice Medicine

The majority of America's physicians function today in a "cottage-type industry" organizational pattern that is a major cause of the present health care crisis and is a roadblock to change. It is widely recognized that the advances in medical-scientific knowledge call for closely integrated functioning teams of medical specialists in conjunction with the allied health professions of nursing, social work, psychology, and other disciplines. Recent developments in technology call for the use of expensive medical equipment manned by specially trained technicians. Yet most Americans continue to receive their medical care by the cumbersome fee-for-service method with individual visits to general practitioners, separate visits to physicians practicing more than thirty medical specialties, and additional trips and bills for X-rays, laboratory tests, surgery, hospital care, nursing home care, and so forth.

The general practitioner attempts to function at the center of this nonsystem, where he is expected to be a trained diagnostician and therapist, wise counselor, psychologist, social worker, laboratory technician, businessman, and committed community worker.

Last year he put in an average of fifty-eight hours a week at these tasks. It is small wonder that he has not been able to succeed in most of them. It is less surprising that the isolated way in which he practices medicine, except when he relates to a hospital, is proving to be grossly inefficient, wasteful of highly trained and scarce manpower, and costly to his patients and society.

An essential prerequisite to change in the health care system is the replacement of individual practice with organized health care teams that are linked to other health care providers and facilities. Hospital-based comprehensive programs that provide in- and outpatient care, neighborhood health centers related to the entire range of health facilities, prepaid group practice programs, and regional medical programs are but a few of the newer types of organization that are required to replace today's "piecework medicine."

Inadequacies of Public Programs

Public expenditures for personal health services rose dramatically with the inauguration of Medicare and Medicaid. The Medicare program has provided important protection and needed services to millions of older men and women, but there is grave question whether the expenditure of some $11 billion in public funds for the combined programs in fiscal 1969 resulted in an appropriate return for the dollars spent.[15] By the end of 1968 Medicare met only 45 percent of the personal health expenses of the elderly. One-fourth of the Medicaid expenditures were used to supplement Medicare. Despite this, some 30 percent of the health care expenses were paid by the aged themselves or by their children.[16]

In essence, Medicare features that costly characteristic of the private health insurance world—the major medical approach. This means that the patient must make substantial payments (called deductibles) before Medicare payments begin and then shares the cost of a percentage of expenses after Medicare payments start (coinsurance). To this "major Medicare" deficiency must be added the fact that Medicare offers benefits of only limited duration and excludes important areas of expense, such as prescription drugs.

More important, however, the program's design prohibits it from dealing effectively with the problems of organization of services that underlie the escalation of costs and inadequate quality controls. The law states specifically:

> Nothing in this title shall be construed to authorize any Federal officer
> or employee to exercise any supervision or control over the practice

of medicine or the manner in which medical services are provided. . . .[17]

It is this problem and the inability to change the delivery system
through Medicare that led the advisory committee to the Senate
committee studying health aspects of the economics of aging to
conclude: "Deficiencies in the delivery system for health care services play a direct role in creating dollars and cents problems for
the elderly."[18]

Medicaid has proved to be a costly and increasingly ineffective
approach to the health care needs of the medically indigent, including those on public assistance. Its deficiencies are lucidly summarized by Dr. John H. Knowles, nationally known public health
authority:

> Medicaid has degenerated into merely a financing mechanism for
> the existing system of welfare medicine which is not adequate and
> must be changed. The present law and the present implementation
> guarantee that it will not be changed. It perpetuates the very costly,
> highly inefficient, inhuman, and undignified means test in the stale
> atmosphere of charity medicine carried out in many instances by
> marginal practitioners in marginal facilities, largely municipal facilities
> in most of the urban locations of our country.
>
> Nearly $5 billion total annually [1968] is poured into this same
> old inadequate system with no improvement sought or gained. The
> leverage of $5 billion is not being used to alter the system as it should
> be.[19]

Health Status of Americans

It is generally acknowledged that this country has made tremendous gains in advancing the frontiers of medical-scientific knowledge. We know far more today about how to prevent disease and
handicaps, treat illness, and rehabilitate the disabled than ever
before. But the gap between what the nation is capable of doing
and what is being made available in personal health services appears
to be widening. The wealthiest nation in the world—with a GNP
approaching $1 trillion—is not providing anything approaching
the best health care. We lag far behind most industrial nations
in four of the key measures of a nation's health status:

1. While we ranked eighth in infant mortality among a select
group of industrial nations in 1953–54,[20] by 1968 we had slipped
to thirteenth place.[21]

2. While the United States had the fewest number of maternal deaths associated with childbirth in 1951–53 (in comparison with twenty-nine other nations), the World Health Organization reports that by 1966 the United States had dropped to seventh place in this vital health index. Thirteen of the fifteen European nations listed had a greater percentage of decline in maternal mortality between 1951–53 and 1966 than we did.[22]

3. In 1965 the United States ranked eighteenth in life expectancy of males and eleventh for females in comparison to other industrial nations.[23]

4. The 1966 death rate for middle-aged males is higher than any nation of Western Europe and many other countries.[24]

While these indices are startling and tragic, geographic and racial comparisons within the United States are even more appalling:

1. In 1967 nonwhite babies were almost *twice* as likely to die in the first year of life as white babies.

2. In 1967 nonwhite mothers were more than *three times* as likely to die in childbirth as white mothers.

3. Both infant and maternal deaths are *lowest* in the most prosperous region of the country (Washington, Oregon, and California), while they are *highest* in the poorest region (Kentucky, Tennessee, Alabama, and Mississippi).[25]

4. The crisis afflicting our cities is aptly demonstrated by the fact that the maternal mortality rate for Detroit in general is *twice* as high as the Michigan-wide rate. However, in the inner city of Detroit, the rate is over 3½ *times* that of the city at large.[26]

Illness Versus Health

In addition to the maladies already listed, a fundamental problem in the approach to providing health services and insuring against health contingencies is that we concentrate almost exclusively on the episode of illness or injury. In ancient China physicians were paid to keep patients well and payments were withheld during sickness. Today there is an almost total reversal of this philosophy. Federal government and private insurance reports for 1969 do not even indicate the ımber of Americans with insurance coverage for periodic physical or screening examinations since the total is almost too infinitesimal to measure. Those Americans who *have* health insurance (an estimated 25–34 million have *no* health insurance) are covered by what can best be defined as sickness insurance: provision of hospital, surgical, or medical care only when they are ill or injured.

There is a better way of providing health coverage, but only about three or four million persons are benefiting from it—that is, organized prepaid group practice plans that offer a near-total range of health care to subscribers who pay monthly premiums, regardless of the number of services they require or use.[27] The services range from diagnostic and preventive care, through the more traditionally covered hospital, surgical, or medical care, to rehabilitation services. Services are received from salaried groups of physicians who rely on the concept of a health team of physicians and other health professionals to provide care.

Measurements of the performance of such plans indicate clear advantages over other health insurance plans. For example, some eight million federal employees are offered the choice of five types of health insurance coverage including Blue Cross-Blue Shield, Aetna Life and Casualty Company, employee-sponsored plans, individual practice, and group practice. The most recent report of the federal employees' play reveals that subscribers enrolled under group practice plans use approximately one-half as many hospital days as those enrolled in other plans. Of equal importance is the evidence that members of prepaid group practice plans had almost half as many appendectomies as those in the fee-for-service system, one-third as many tonsillectomies and adenoidectomies, and half as many operations for gynecological co plaints.[28] The dramatic differences in surgical rates result not from differences in the population served or because group practice plans neglect their patients but because such plans have professional and economic incentives to keep people well. Because in-hospital care represents the most costly component of health care, efforts to reduce utilization by offering preventive care and alternatives to costly hospitalization help to introduce meaningful health care economies.

The comprehensiveness of services provided under group plans is demonstrated by the fact that the Kaiser-Permanente Health Plan meets about 76 percent of the cost of medical services (compared to 50–60 percent under the best Blue Cross or private health insurance policies) and that the costs of providing care under the Kaiser plan have risen about one-half as fast as for the nation as a whole. Despite these achievements, seventeen states prohibit consumer-owned-and-operated prepaid group practices.[29]

It seems obvious from a review of the data that organized prepaid group practice plans offer a practical method for controlling costs, rationally organizing a health team, and guaranteeing total care to the patient.[30] In 1966 and 1967 a number of government reports, conferences, and committees recommended group practice.[31] In April 1970 President Nixon proposed an amendment to Medicare that would permit the elderly to enroll in health maintenance organizations, either groups of physicians paid on a fee-for-service basis or organized prepaid group practice plans, with payment by the federal government for the whole range of in-and outpatient services made on a per capita basis (that is, a fixed annual amount per enrollee). This is an important and constructive modification of the Medicare system. Such a program, combined with financial incentives to groups to practice "team medicine," when built into a comprehensive and universal national health insurance program, can begin to make needed changes in the way medical care is delivered in this country.

The Debate Begins: Universal Health Insurance

Within the past year America's health care crisis has been brought home to the American people by such diverse magazines as *The New Republic, Business Week, Fortune,* and *Look.*[32] CBS-TV recently presented a two-part exposé titled "Health in America." President Richard M. Nixon has expressed deep concern about the problem and a year ago stated: "We face a massive crisis ... and unless action is taken both administratively and legislatively, ... we will have a breakdown in our medical care system."[33] Major changes are imminent. Federal Administration priorities for military and other expenditures and exphasis on balanced budgets have delayed the fundamental restructuring of health care many believe is essential. It appears likely, however, that restructuring will take place in the near future.

The past 1½ years have witnessed the introduction of some seven major proposals for various forms of national health insurance. These proposals run the spectrum of political philosophy from the American Medical Association-sponsored "Medi-credit" to the Committee for National Health Insurance's "Health Security."

Of the several legislative proposals, Medi-credit (the Health Insurance Assistance Act of 1970) would provide the fewest changes, simply permitting a tax credit against individual income taxes to offset the cost of private health insurance. The poor with little or no tax liability would be issued a federal "medical care insurance certificate" to purchase private health coverage, an approach dubbed by the late Walter Reuther as "health food stamps." A further deficiency is that coverage would be voluntary.

Private health insurers would only be required to offer a limited scope of benefits. The sponsors of Medicredit state it is designed to make no changes in methods of offering or delivering health services. State medical societies would establish peer review organizations essentially to "selfpolice" utilization, charges, and quality of services.

The Pettengill plan of the Aetna Life and Casualty Company proposes special health insurance for the poor and related groups through a government-subsidized insurance pool administered by private carriers. It requires employers providing health insurance to meet certain standards of coverage in order to obtain full tax deduction for their employees' health premium payments. The plan provides for state supervision of the insurance pool, a rather limited range of benefits, and reimbursement to providers of care in the traditional manner; it fails to provide incentives for reorganizing the existing health structure.

COMPREHENSIVE PLANS

The National Health Insurance Bill, introduced by Senator Jacob Javits of New York, would, in essence, extend the benefits of Medicare to all Americans, add coverage for critically needed maintenance drugs for chronic illnesses, and provide annual physical checkups for all and dental care for children under age 8. This program would be financed by an increase in the social security earnings base. General revenue financing would underwrite benefits for those on public assistance and the unemployed.

The principal merit of this proposal is that the secretary of health, education, and welfare can enter into agreements with comprehensive health service systems (group practices, health insurers, hospitals, clinics, medical school staffs, or combinations thereof) that would receive incentive payments for achieving costs less than the average cost of providing services to the general population in their area.

The health insurance bill offered by Representative Martha Griffiths of Michigan would provide a comprehensive range of hospital, medical, and dental services for all with a minimal deductible and patient copayment feature designed principally to discourage overutilization of services. It would be social security financed. The plan would have national administration through boards and councils representing health professionals and consumers. It offers a wide range of incentives to promote comprehensive and better organized health delivery systems. A unique feature is that patients could choose a physician annually for primary health services. Since this approach is essentially similar to the health security program, it is likely that the two proposals will be merged in the coming months.

The health security program sponsored by the Committee for National Health Insurance is the first major proposal to have had Senate hearings in September 1970.[34] Its criteria for a viable health insurance program are as follows: (1) universal coverage as a right; (2) an organized and cohesive system of health care; (3) comprehensive benefits, including prevention through diagnosis and early detection and treatment and rehabilitation when needed; (4) control over the inflation of health care costs; (5) quality control; and (6) built-in democratic controls—full consumer participation at all levels of policy-making.

The health security program would be an integral part of the nation's social insurance system and be financed by contributions from employers, employees, and federal general tax revenues. (The employers would be permitted to assume all or part of the employee's contributions.) The medically indigent would be blanketed in through general tax revenue contributions. Present public progr ıs for personal health services (including Medicare and most of Medicaid) would be absorbed into the national health insurance system.

Payment to providers of services is designed to assure full financial protection for consumers and be fair to the professionals delivering care. Whenever possible, the plan would emphasize ambulatory care, i.e., coverage of out-of-hospital services in preference to hospital or other institutional services.

While the health security program would permit payment to physicians who choose to remain in private practice, financial and other incentives would be given to those practitioners who opt for the team medicine approach to encourage movement away from individual practice. The leverage of financial incentives is thus viewed as the key element in systematizing the existing non-system. It is expected that per capita payments would be selected as the preferred alternative to the existing fee-for-service payment method.

A unique feature of the program would be allocation of a percentage of the trust fund (initially 2 percent or $800 million) to a resources development fund. This fund, controlled by the managing health security governing board, would be used to increase the supply of health personnel and facilities, with priority given to stimulating further development of group practice programs and other innovative and productive health care alternatives. The fund would also help to increase incentives for medical practice in rural and undermanned urban areas. Thus, reconstruction of the entire nonsystem is essential in any national health insurance that should be considered. Providing tax credits or federal funds simply to buy more health benefits will fail; the lesson of Medicare and Medicaid is that more dollars pumped into the present fragmented nonsystem result in administrative failures and costly inflation.

There are some who would counsel that America must deal with the medical manpower shortage before proceeding to comprehensive national health insurance. There are others who argue that there must be funding of a reorganized delivery system before health insurance is legislated. The evidence suggests, however, that piecemeal approaches, regardless of their rationale, are essentially self-defeating.

To counsel delay may well precipitate confrontation between the establishment and the 25–34 million Americans presently denied adequate health care as well as the vast majority of those who have some private insurance coverage but nonetheless find the costs intolerable and the delivery system increasingly unsatisfactory. Long ago, Aristotle wrote that health is so fundamental to the good life that men have an absolute moral right to the measure of good health that society can provide. As with civil rights, it is too late to suggest that if people are content to wait a decade or more for reform, they may eventually receive equal and acceptable treatment.

Today America is in grave trouble abroad and at home. The provision of properly financed and organized health services to all will not solve all our social problems. But it can and will constitute a giant step forward in reordering our national priorities and in meeting a complex of major unmet domestic needs.

REFERENCES AND NOTES

[1] See Goals of Public Social Policy (rev. ed.; New York: National Association of Social Workers, 1967), pp. 22–27.

[2] Random House Dictionary of the English Language (New York: Random House, 1966), p. 1230.

[3] Dorothy P. Rice and Barbara S. Cooper, "National Health Expenditures, 1929–68," Social Security Bulletin, Vol. 33, No. 1 (January 1970), pp. 3–20.

[4] See Prices, A Chartbook, 1953–62, Bulletin No. 1351 (Washington, D.C.: U.S. Department of Labor, Bureau of Labor Statistics, December 1962), pp. 118 and

133; and "Current Labor Statistics," *Monthly Labor Review*, Vol. 93, No. 3 (March 1970), Tables 23 and 24, p. 97.

[5]Walter P. Reuther, "Universal Health Insurance: A Constructive Approach to Meeting America's Health Care Crisis." Address to the New England Hospital Assembly, Boston, Mass., March 23, 1970.

[6]Roger Egeberg, MD, "Our Plan Is to Get Care to Those Who Need It," *American Medical News*, Vol. 13, No. 3 (August 3, 1970), p. 6.

[7]"Gleaming New Iowa Hospital, Built to Attract Doctors, Has 90 Beds and a Staff of One," *New York Times*, April 21, 1970, p. 32.

[8]"Nationwide Plea for Doctor Made by Village in Thumb," *Detroit News*, November 27, 1969, p. 15-B.

[9]In Michigan 200 small towns of 1,000 or more people are searching for physicians. Connecticut, which had the highest per capita income in 1967 ($3,978), had 186 physicians per 100,000 population, while Mississippi, ranking fiftieth in per capita income ($1,900) had just over one-third as many: 76 per 100,000. *See Statistical Abstract of the United States, 1969*, (Washington, D.C.: U.S. Bureau of the Census, 1969), pp. 66 and 320.

[10]*Rx for Action*, Report of the Health Task Force of the Urban Coalition (Washington, D.C.: The Urban Coalition, 1969), p. 9.

[11]*Source Book of Health Insurance Data* (New York: Health Insurance Institute, 1969), p. 11.

[12]Louis S. Reed, "Private Health Insurance, 1968: Enrollment, Coverage, and Financial Experience," *Social Security Bulletin*, Vol. 32, No. 12 (December 1969), pp. 19–35.

[13]Louis S. Reed and Willine Carr, "Private Health Insurance in the United States, 1967," *Social Security Bulletin*, Vol. 32, No. 2 (February 1969), pp. 7–8.

[14]Reed, op. cit.

[15]Barbara S. Cooper, *National Health Expenditures, Fiscal Years 1929–69 and Calendar Years 1929–68*, Research and Statistics Note No. 18 (Washington, D.C.: Social Security Administration, November 7, 1969).

[16]Dorothy P. Rice and Barbara S. Cooper, *Outlays for Medical Care of Aged and Non-aged Persons, Fiscal Years 1966–69*, Research and Statistics Note No. 12 (Washington, D.C.: Social Security Administration, July 16, 1969).

[17]Public Law 89–97, Sec. 1801, p. 6.

[18]Special Committee on Aging—U.S. Senate, "Health Aspects of the Economics of Aging" (Washington, D.C.: U.S. Government Printing Office, July 1969), p. 700.

[19]Special Committee on Aging—U.S. Senate, "Hearings Before the Subcommittee on Health of the Elderly, July 17–18, 1969" (Washington, D.C.: U.S. Government Printing Office, 1969), pp. 582–583.

[20]*Statistical Bulletin of the Metropolitan Life Insurance Company*, Vol. 48, No. 5 (May 1967), p. 3.

[21]*Population and Vital Statistics Report*, United Nations Series A, Vol. 22, No. 1 (January 1, 1970), pp. 12, 16, 22, and 24.

[22]*World Health Statistics Report*, World Health Organization, Vol. 22, No. 6 (March 26, 1970), p. 3.

[23]*Demographic Yearbook, 1966* (New York: United Nations, 1967), pp. 574–582.

[24]Ibid., pp. 415–482.

[25]*Statistical Abstract of the United States, 1969*, pp. 55, 57, and 320

[26]"Pregnancy, Death Are Still Linked in Inner City," *Detroit Free Press*, October 16, 1969, pp. 1-C, 2-C.

[27]Among the better known plans are Kaiser-Permanente, Health Insurance Plan of New York, Community Health Association of Detroit, Group Health Cooperative of Puget Sound, and Group Health Association of Washington, D.C.

[28]George S. Perrott, *The Federal Employees Health Benefits Program: Seventh Term (1967) Coverage and Utilization* (Washington, D.C.: Group Health Association of America, March 21, 1970). A 1969 comparison of in-hospital use under Detroit's Community Health Association and the Michigan Blue Cross confirms the advantages of group plans: 537 days of hospital care per 1,000 under the Community Health Association, 1,093 days per 1,000 under Blue Cross. *See Annual Report, 1969* (Detroit: Community Health Association Research and Planning Division, Michigan Hospital Service, 1969).

[29]Walter J. McNerney, "The Health Administration Establishment: Under-achiever." *Proceedings, 19th Annual Group Health Institute* (New York: Group Health Association of America, June 1969), pp. 24–35.

[30]*See* Avedis Donabedian, "An Evaluation of Group Practice," *Inquiry,* Blue Cross Association, Vol. 6, No. 3 (September 1969), pp. 3–27.

[31]*See Report to the President on Medical Care Prices* (Washington, D.C.: U.S. Department of Health, Education & Welfare, February 1967); *Consumer Issues, 1966,* Report to the President from the Consumer Advisory Council (Washington, D.C.: Committee on Consumer Interests, June 12, 1966); *Promoting the Group Practice of Medicine,* Report of the National Conference on Group Practice (Washington, D.C.: U.S. Department of Health, Education & Welfare, October 1967): *Report of the National Conference on Medical Costs* (Washington, D.C.: U.S. Department of Health, Education & Welfare, June 1967); *Report of the National Conference on Private Health Insurance* (Washington, D.C.: U.S. Department of Health, Education & Welfare, September 1967); *Report of the National Advisory Commission on Health Manpower* (Washington, D.C.: National Advisory Commission on Health Manpower, November 1967); and *Health Is a Community Affair,* Report of the National Commission on Community Health Services (Cambridge, Mass.: Harvard University Press, 1966).

[32]*See* "Our Ailing Medical System," *Fortune,* Vol. 71, No. 1 (January 1970), pp. 79–99; "The $60-Billion Crisis Over Medical Care," *Business Week* (January 17, 1970), pp. 50–64; "The Plight of the U.S. Patient," *Time* (February 21, 1969), pp. 53–58; Fred Anderson, "Growing Pains of Medical Care," *The New Republic,* Part I: "Paying More, Getting Less" (January 17, 1970), pp. 15–18; Part II: "We Can Do It Better Cheaper" (January 24, 1970), pp. 13–16; and Part III: "Paying for Health" (February 7, 1970), pp. 17–19.

[33]"President Warns of 'Massive Crisis' in Health Care," *New York Times,* July 11, 1969, pp. 1 and 40.

[34]The committee's one hundred members include Vice-Chairman Dr. Michael E. DeBakey, the eminent surgeon; Whitney M. Young, Jr., NASW president; and Mrs. Mary Lasker, the prominent philanthropist. Charles I. Schottland, former NASW president; and the author are other social workers on the committee.

13. Health Care: What the Poor People Didn't Get from Kentucky Project

Robert J. Bazell

Does active consumer representation make a difference in restructuring health services? The following article, a description of an OEO pilot project in rural health delivery in the heart of Appalachia, suggests that it is of critical importance if new attempts to alter medical service delivery organizations are to do more than reinforce and enrich the status quo.

We continue to learn the sad story of "how to fail" through the repetition of dramas similar to the one described here. However, our collective misfortune is intensified when human service organizations fail, for, as a result of these failures, patterns of life and even life itself may be pathologically altered or ended.

Floyd County, Kentucky. In 1967, the Office of Economic Opportunity (OEO) funded a "Comprehensive Health Care Program" for the poor people of this coal mining county in Appalachian Kentucky. As in most of eastern Kentucky and other parts of Appalachia, the poor in Floyd County are afflicted by staggering social, environmental, and medical problems. Over half the county's population of 34,000 falls below the poverty line. Most of these people live in small houses or shacks in the rural hollows along creeks filled with garbage and sewage.

Coal no longer provides jobs for everyone, so for years young people have been leaving the hills to find work in the cities to the north. Those who remain tend to be the very young, the middle-aged, and the elderly. Often the men have worked in the mines for years and are unable to work any longer, suffering from such occupational disabilities as pneumoconiosis, the dreaded Black Lung disease that can turn a man of age 50 or 55 into a wheezing, coughing derelict.

After spending more than $5 million, the OEO program has yet to provide anything resembling comprehensive health care. It has, however, been the source of a major political battle involving most of the county's doctors and politicians, a welfare rights organization, and eastern Kentucky's powerful Democratic congressman, Carl D. Perkins. The Floyd County situation in itself is worthy of notice, but it has a more general relevance since it could be repeated time and time again if Congress enacts some form of national health insurance.

The OEO went into the health business during the Johnson Administration because of the realization that poverty and ill health reenforce each other. At the time the health projects were established, OEO planners intended to provide alternatives to existing health services for the poor and, in doing so, to establish models that might influence the direction of American medicine. Indeed, such facets of OEO health care as family-centered preventative medicine, salaried group practice, training of paramedicals, and consumer participation in decision making, have become elements in the debate over national health insurance.

The Floyd County project, however, was a striking exception to OEO policies. Funded as a "research and demonstration" project, it attempted to improve the health care of isolated, rural poor people by working within the existing health care structure.

The medical facilities in the county, while sparse by national standards, are average or better for eastern Kentucky. There are 15 physicians in private practice. The only specialists are surgeons: there are no obstetricians, pediatricians, or internists. The county has 126 beds in three hospitals, and the doctors practice primarily in those towns that have the hospitals. But very little "charity medicine" was offered. People often went without medical care.

Instead of bringing in doctors and establishing clinics, as OEO did elsewhere, the Floyd County project employed a number of aides who transported people to the county's private physicians and hospitals upon the referral of the program's medical staff. Moreover, control of the program was left entirely in the hands of the local board of health, which is composed of three doctors, a dentist, a nurse (the wife of a state assemblyman), the County Attorney, and the County Judge. Under the direction of the Board of Health, the program appeared, at times, to serve the interests of the county's doctors and politicians rather than the interests of the poor. For the doctors, there was increased business; for the politicians, the $1.3 million per year program provided more than 100 new jobs for patronage.

In a 1970 report describing the Floyd County program, an OEO investigator noted that, in violation of OEO regulations, poor people were excluded from decision making and were offered neither jobs nor taining. "There were reports," said the investigator, "that, if a person wanted a job with the program, he had to have political concurrence."

Furthermore, the report noted that "physicians were receiving fees for the care of the program's consumers, while establishing the policy for the program. This resulted in a rule, passed by the Board, that no recipient can be served by a physician who is not a member of the OEO program. Patients often had to travel 25 to 30 miles to visit a Floyd County doctor, when they could have traveled 5 to 10 miles to see a doctor in a neighboring county. Also, program employees were told only to refer patients to the private doctors; thus neither the program's full-time doctor nor its nurses were allowed to treat patients.

Naturally, the program led to increased business for Floyd County doctors. Not only did they derive fees directly from the OEO program (the 15 doctors billed the program for over $175,000 yearly), but the program's vehicles brought them additional Medicare and Medicaid patients as well. According to the OEO investigator, "some physicians in Prestonsburg (the county seat) were seeing as many as 100 patients per day." In 1968, an OEO medical audit team, after surveying the records of several patients treated under the program by those same Prestonsburg doctors, declared that, "The medical content of the patient contacts was extremely poor. There seems to have been little or no effort to provide a complete examination; in fact, the attention paid to the presenting complaint was minimal." Since no records had been kept, the team's report went on to question whether some of the patients had even seen the doctor.

Despite gross violations of regulations and the intent of the grant, OEO continued to fund the Floyd County project. Members of the Eastern Kentucky Welfare Rights Organization (EKWRO), a group of unemployed and wives who have vocally opposed the program, allege that OEO's inaction was influenced by Representative Perkins. They point out that Perkins, as chairman of the House Education and Labor Committee, wields tremendous power over the OEO program. Moreover, some of the people running the project are Perkins' friends and close political allies.

According to many local residents, County Judge Henry Stumbo, who has been the county's chief judicial and administrative officer for over 30 years, is the most powerful man in the county. The welfare rights people claim that the judge controls, through patronage, the votes that are crucial to Perkins' reelection.

Perkins' influence on the program may have been of a subtle nature. As one official in OEO Health Affairs told *Science*, "You have to understand the power that Perkins has over OEO. He might never have asked that a program in his district, run by his political cronies, be left alone. But we would try to anticipate his desires. There could be worse committee chairmen than Perkins, and we would try to do them a favor whenever we could."

Perkins' himself emphatically denies ever having tried to influence the program. "Nobody can say that Carl Perkins has ever interfered with the specific running of the Floyd County Health project," he told *Science*. "If there's anything wrong with that program, OEO should correct it."

On at least one occasion, Perkins did try to change the staff of the program. A Floyd County dentist told *Science* that, while serving as acting project director, he had been telephoned by Perkins and asked to reinstate an employee who had been fired. Also, employees of OEO Health Affairs claim that Perkins telephoned OEO director Frank Carlucci to demand that the project director be fired. Perkins denies making the demand.

In mid-1969, OEO was forced to reevaluate the program when Kentucky's Republican Governor Louis B. Nunn, a political opponent of Perkins, conducted his own investigation of the project and concluded that "$1 million was being spent annually to deliver $383,000 worth of medical care." Soon after Nunn's public announcement, OEO dispatched to Floyd County an investigator who ran the program for several months and instigated several changes.

Control of the program was transferred from the County Board of Health to a new corporation, consisting of representatives of several interest groups in the community as well as consumers. A new project director, Arnold Schechter, a physician from Chicago, was hired. However, few of the program's policies changed under the new board of directors.

The long-standing opposition of the local doctors to anyone else's practicing medicine in the county was upheld by the new board. In fact, the board fired Schechter in short order after he offered a plan that called for nine OEO doctors to come to the county to practice.

Politicians Keep Control

One reason for the lack of change in the program is that most of the powerful politicians in the county found their way onto

the new board. Besides Judge Stumbo, County School Superintendent, Charles Clark, whose position has traditionally had great
influence in eastern Kentucky, sits on the board. Douglas Adams,
a Prestonsburg physician and the county medical association's representative, owns part interest in a drug store and a nursing home,
both of which receive payments from the program; in addition,
he employs two of the other board members through these enterprises.

Perhaps more significant than the local power structure's ability
to have its voice heard on the governing board is the total lack
of input from the ten consumers on the 20-member board. Representation of the poor has been a standard facet of all OEO programs. And now consumer control of health care has become a
rallying cry of radical medical workers. The Kennedy health insurance plan even contains some provision for consumer participation.
Yet in Floyd County, the concept has been virtually meaningless.
For the first several months that the new board met, the low-income
members never once cast a vote against the Establishment members.
Critics of the program ascribe the poor people's acquiescence to
intimidation and fear of reprisal for speaking out.

"The power of the County Judge and the other courthouse politicians reaches more people than you'd ever know," said Ruth James,
a middle-class resident of Prestonsburg and member of the board.
"The poor people are afraid for their jobs, their food stamps, or
whatever means of income they have." Mrs. James believes that,
because she has spoken out during board meetings, her son, now
away at college, will never be allowed to teach in Floyd County.

One group of poor people that has spoken out, however has
been the 400-member EKWRO. "The doctors in that health program treat poor people like they was dirt," said Eula Hall, chairman
of the organization. "All they're interested in is making money.
Usually we don't know what's wrong with a person until after they
die," she said.

The members of EKWRO have written letters to OEO officials
and to Representative Perkins, demanding that the program be
turned over to them. In addition, they have picketed and held
public hearings publicized as exposing the program's "murderous
and corrupt practices." Both the local politicians and Congressman
Perkins dismiss EKWRO as the tool of the young antipoverty workers in Floyd County. Certainly the outsiders, some of them former
VISTA and other OEO employees, had a hand in organizing
EKWRO. But the organization's members are perfectly articulate
in their criticisms of the program. "Judge Stumbo scares the people

into thinking that they will lose all their rights if they don't cooperate," said Mrs. Hall. "So the only way we're going to get decent medical care is to keep fightin' until we have new politicians and the poor people gets control of their own program."

Whether or not EKWRO is given control of the program, another round of changes appears imminent. In a March 1971 memorandum, OEO's Director of Health Affairs Thomas E. Bryant said, "The project continues to utilize as its basic mode of operation a system in which patients are referred in a haphazard fashion to private physicians and dentists. . . . This type of operation makes it substantially impossible to acheive the goals of the OEO grant." Bryant further charged that the reaction of the board to the dissatisfaction of local residents with the "sporadic and inefficient health services" has been "an attempt to suppress and stifle dissent rather than to make meaningful reforms."

As a result of Bryant's charges, OEO director Frank Carlucci sent a letter to the board of directors threatening to stop the program altogether unless major changes are made. Whatever his position might have been before, Representative Perkins has now urged OEO officials both publicly and privately to "clean up the Floyd County program."

The Exception in Floyd County

In describing the reasons that OEO funded the project in Floyd County back in 1967, Elisabeth Schorr, who worked for OEO Health Affairs at the time, told *Science,* "Most people in the agency were convinced that, to help the poor, you had to do something fundamentally different from supporting existing health systems. Some argued, however, that in certain communities such as Floyd County, the Establishment wouldn't ever go along with an innovative program. And any program was better than none at all."

Now, after 3 years of this unsuccessful experiment of putting additional money into the existing health care system to help the poor, OEO is demanding that changes be made. But the question still remains whether the Establishment, Floyd County's doctors and politicians, will block any attempts at reform.

The lessons learned here are of little use to OEO since, under the Nixon Administration, the agency is proceeding on a self-destruct mission and is unlikely to fund many more health projects. But in rural areas throughout the country, where local doctors control all of the health options, particularly for poor people, more money will not necessarily bring better medical care. And if Congress pours more money into the existing health care system on a national scale, the story of Floyd County could be repeated many times over.

Section B

Some Central Concerns
of Human Service Organizations:
in Programmatic Intervention

The humane use of human service organizations may prove to be the paramount problem in the human services in the 1970's. Contradictory pressures may force choices between the most practical, cost-effective uses of these organizations, and less cost-effective approaches which perhaps more humanely meet the broad-based needs of existing and potential clients. And, it is a problem which could become more, not less, intense unless we identify as a primary issue the importance of integrating the increasingly sophisticated management and planning technology and hardware with citizen decision-making.

Essential to the development of relatively rational, reasonably effective means of making these choices, are data which describe existing programs accurately; not in terms of idealized models of what we would like to do or think we should do, but in terms of objective reality. What is actually happening? Who is being served? With what results? It appears increasingly evident that human service organizations are not immune to the constraints of large scale complex bureaucracies. Too often their principal constituency is their own employees. In observing one large state human service agency, a rough ranking of the priorities of constituencies would be: (1) the employees, (2) the Governor's office, (3) the Budget Bureau, (4) the legislative Ways and Means Committees, (5) the organized special interest groups, (6) organized tax-payers groups, (7) the felt needs of tax-payers, and (8) the clients.

Although this analysis may appear to be cynical it is abundantly clear that most large complex organizations can generate enough intraorganizational concerns to keep them busy without the input of many clients. But these are not new discoveries. It is only that new technologies (functional budgets, client information system, etc.) are making more evident the costs of such activities.

The natural tendency upon discovery is first to deny, then to scapegoat, and then to move program units around. Imagery, magic, and simplistic solutions are not the exclusive domain of Madison Avenue.

The following articles document some efforts, ranging from modes of incremental adjustments to change in auspice, to modify programs.

14. Experiments in Referral to Alcoholism Clinics

Harold W. Demone, Jr.[1]

In any intervention, three major subsystems can be identified; the host, the agent, and the environment. All three are subject to influence. In the following article, it is noted that in the treatment of alcoholics the patient (the host) is typically blamed for treatment failures; i.e., described as poorly motivated, in order to explain a low success rate. Further, there is a clinical inclination to classify or label certain patients as "unreachable," and through these definitions exclude them from potentially effective treatment. Instead of altering the environment or the clinical procedure to accommodate individual client variance, the patient is held responsible for what is really a societal and organizational problem.

A human service problem of the 1970's, more effectively delivering services to alcoholics, drug dependents, and other identifiable low income and minority group members, will not easily be accommodated within a framework of "business as usual." Methods of analyzing how and why populations are reached or not reached, and designing new and more flexible intervention strategies are necessary leadership responsibilites. A flexible staff, with goals clearly established and operational research integrated as a component management tool, will be necessary for organizational effectiveness.

Alcoholic patients, of types usually described as "unreachable," were participants in four demonstrations that skyrocketed rates of successful referral to alcoholism clinics from a low of less than 1 per cent to as high as 65 per cent. All the patients in these demonstrations presented a history of serious social problems including criminality, destitution and severe pathology. This dramatic increase in successful referrals came about without the aid of wonder drugs, black magic, threats or police enforcement. The procedures used by the Division of Alcoholism of the Massachusetts State Department of Public Health and its clinics, and their implications, are described in the present paper.

[1]Executive Director, The Medical Foundation, Inc., Boston.

187

In order to achieve these goals a number of techniques were used. The demonstration, in which the staff of the alcoholism agency "demonstrates how to do it" to the staff of another agency, was one. In the four experiments to be described there were a series of alternate subgoals. They were to stir up some discontent in the caretaking community so that it would reexamine its existing program; to develop positive sanctions for those caretakers and administrators who were favorably disposed to a new program but felt that it lacked either support or sufficient priority; and to demonstrate that the situation was not hopeless.

DEMONSTRATION 1

An Emergency Ward

A study (1) of the emergency ward of the Massachusetts General Hospital in 1957 found that over 1,200 alcoholics were admitted yearly. Despite a nominal policy of referring these patients to the hospital's alcoholism clinic, less than 1 per cent actually sought such treatment. As a consequence, in 1959, the state-supported alcoholism clinic at the Massachusetts General Hospital "initiated a program of research designed to assess the effectiveness of a clinical method in establishing treatment relations with the alcoholics admitted to the emergency ward ..." (2). Certain operational assumptions were made by Dr. M. E. Chafetz, Director of the Clinic, and his research staff. They saw the emergency ward visit as a severe crisis for the patient and one in which motivation for treatment would be significantly higher than in a noncrisis period (2).

Following a pilot program, a research design was developed consisting of an experimental group of 100 patients and a control group of 100, subjects being assigned alternately by the chief medical officer of the emergency ward. A period of 10 months was required to complete the study groups. Criteria for selection for the study groups were that the patients *(1)* must be diagnosed as alcoholics, *(2)* must be males, *(3)* must not have been treated in the alcoholism clinic less than 60 days prior to admission, *(4)* must not live more than 20 miles from the hospital, and *(5)* must not have been previously included in the project.

The 200 men in the study group were primarily middle-aged (mean age 48 years), predominantly Roman Catholic, usually single, separated or divorced, and usually unemployed. Over half were brought to the emergency ward by the police. A substantial number were homeless and destitute. Another large group lived alone or in an institution.

The treatment program for the experimental group consisted of two parts. Following assignment to the group an initial contact was made with the patient in the emergency ward by a psychiatrist; simultaneously a psychiatric social worker focused on environmental and interpersonal factors. They became the patient's doctor and social worker and concerned themselves with "utilization of the alcoholic's dependency needs, consideration for his lowered self-esteem, reduction of frustration, continuity of care, and communication through action" (2).

The control patients were handled as usual by the emergency ward physicians who then made the appropriate referral.

At the end of 1 year, follow-up interviews were conducted and an analysis of the success of referral was made. Of the experimental group 65 per cent made an initial visit to the clinic. The corresponding percentage of the control group was 5. Further, 42 per cent of the experimental group, in contrast to 1 per cent of the control group, returned to the clinic 5 or more times (2).

DEMONSTRATIONS 2 AND 3

A Correctional Institution for Women

The second and third demonstrations were conducted at the Massachusetts Correctional Institution in Framingham, a state institution for women offenders. Legislation enacted in 1956 required that all alcoholics at this and another state correctional institution (for men) be referred to one of the 16 State Health Department alcoholism clinics for follow-up care after discharge. A review in 1958, prior to the demonstrations, revealed that less than 1 per cent of the women thus referred had attended a clinic. A study[2] of 122 consecutive admissions[3] to Framingham found that 80 per cent of the women were either currently sentenced for the crime of "drunkenness" or had a history of severe drinking problems. Of the remaining 20 per cent with a mean age of 27, it is likely that some of the younger women who still appear to retain some control over their drinking will show a similar history in the future.

Dr. D. J. Myerson (3), who directed Demonstration No. 2, describes the clinical features of the alcoholic women at Framingham

[2]Cramer, M. J. and Blacker, E. "Early" and "late" problem drinkers among female prisoners. [Unpublished paper, 1961.].

[3]Ten subjects who were hospitalized or were transferred almost immediately to another institution were not interviewed. Ten Negro women are not included in the present profile. Two women refused to be interviewed. These subjects were excluded from the study group.

thus: "Manifestations of the primitive nature of their orally fixed drives were seen in the early onset of their addiction, their sexual perversions and their extreme dependency needs. . . . . Diagnostically these women resemble sociopaths. Judging from their total failure to adapt to society and their ambivalent reactions to slight frustrations, they certainly can be categorized among the most disturbed of the alcoholic group."

Demonstration 2.—Myerson and his associates, at the Peter Bent Brigham Hospital Alcoholism Clinic,[4] in conjunction with the Massachusetts Correctional Institution, Framingham, and the Division of Legal Medicine of the Massachusetts Department of Mental Health, established in 1958 a pilot project for the rehabilitation of alcoholic women prisoners at the Framingham institution. One of the goals of the project was "to determine whether continuous relationship therapy can lead to a successful transfer to the alcoholism clinic" (4).

During a 25-month period from August 1958 to September 1960, 49 women were seen at Framingham by psychiatric social workers from the Peter Bent Brigham Hospital Alcoholism Clinic—the same social workers who would see them following discharge. The sessions, lasting from 10 to 45 minutes, were essentially supportive in nature. Patients were chosen by the staff of the institution and were usually under 45 years of age with former residence in the Greater Boston area. Though some coercive elements may have existed in this referral, since it took place in a prison setting, the program was essentially voluntary. The patients could, and some did, refuse treatment (4).

The women ranged in age from 18 to 55; the majority were in their middle 30's. All described a childhood of severe emotional deprivation. With one exception all were unskilled workers with an unstable work history. Their adult life conformed with their childhood history. Ten were overt homosexuals. Thirty-six were or had been married; the majority of the marriages had been broken. Fifteen out-of-wedlock and 34 legitimate children were recorded, most of whom were supported by the state. Twenty-one of these women had been committed to Framingham on the present occasion for "drunkenness"; the others for crimes such as violation of drug laws, neglect of minor children, idle and disorderly conduct, lewd and lascivious conduct, manslaughter, "stubborn child," forg-

[4]The clinic is supported by the Division of Alcoholism, Massachusetts Department of Public Health.

ery, or assault and battery. Two had committed themselves voluntarily as alcoholics.

In 29 of the 49 cases (59 per cent) a referral to the Alcoholism Clinic at the Peter Bent Brigham Hospital was successful. Of these 29, 18 (37 per cent of the total group) continued in some sort of beneficial therapeutic relationship. Some of the others also continued in treatment but were not able to use the clinic in any "demonstrably advantageous way" (4).

In spite of many unclarified problems, this must be regarded as another example of how a poor record of less than 1 per cent attending a clinic following referral can be improved dramatically by a program of intensive contact with the prospective patients.

Demonstration 3.—A complementary demonstration project was carried out in 1960–1961. The Alcoholism Coordinator of the Massachusetts Division of Alcoholism (a counseling psychologist) met weekly with a small group (8 maximum) of Framingham inmates for sessions usually lasting 1 hour and 15 minutes. A correction officer participated as an observer for training purposes. This differed in two respects from the first Framingham project: the patients were seen in a group rather than in individual sessions, and the group leader did not continue with the patient following discharge from the institution. Instead, a social worker from an alcoholism clinic near the patient's home would attend a group therapy session meeting with the patient just prior to her discharge.

A follow-up of the first 21 discharged patients revealed that 9 (43 per cent) had contacted a clinic at least once, and 6 (26 per cent of the total), 4 or more times.

The population in this demonstration was essentially the same as that described in Demonstration No. 2. Again we see a striking improvement in the rate of follow-up.

DEMONSTRATION 4

A Correctional School for Juveniles

The fourth experiment concerns juvenile delinquent problem drinkers. At the request of members of the Massachusetts Youth Service Board and their staff, the Division of Alcoholism and the Peter Bent Brigham Alcoholism Clinic, in conjunction with the Youth Service Board, began a preliminary investigation of delinquents reported to be alcoholics. A review of 500 consecutive male admissions, aged between 7 and 20, with a mean age of 15, indicated that 10 per cent of the boys could be considered problem drinkers. They drank before or instead of breakfast, drank to drunkenness, "passed out," experienced "blackouts," and engaged in assaultive behavior after drinking.[5]

Prior to this study, referrals had been made from the Youth Service Board institutions to state alcoholism clinics. Few of the boys had reported to the clinic; none remained in treatment. A demonstration project was then established following the procedure of Demonstration No. 2 at the Framingham Institution. A social worker from the outpatient clinic worked with the boys in a casework relationship at the training school. The same social worker saw the boys at the clinic when they returned to the community. The parole officer, working closely with the social worker, assumed a firm paternal role in giving support to the treatment procedure. More than 50 per cent of the boys referred under these conditions continued in treatment.[6]

DISCUSSION

The demonstration projects touched on the role of the patient, the environment, the caretaker, their interrelationship, and the medical care that results. A discussion of these factors will help to explain the increase in successful referrals.

Interrelationship. Irrespective of the particular factor under discussion at any particular moment, it must be remembered that a total program should encompass and give consideration to all available procedures, those directed toward the patient, the environment and the caretaker, for they are linked intimately in a dynamic process.

Referrals take many forms, depending upon the urgency and the patient's problem, the ability of the caretaker to cope with the problem, the motivation of both patient and caretaker, and agency tradition. The process may range from the caretaker leading the patient by the hand to the agency to which referral is made, to merely suggesting that the patient see a physician or a treatment agency about his problem.

The Patient. In discussions about the manipulation of motivation, psychological descriptions of the dynamics of motivation are

[5]MacKay, J. R., Blacker, E., Demone, H. W., Jr. and Kelly, F. J. Deliquency and drinking. [Unpublished paper, 1961].

[6]MacKay, J. R. Problem drinking among juvenile delinquents. [Presented at the conference on "Alcohol, Alcoholism and Crime," Chatham, Mass., 7 June 1962.]

common. Ordinarily they are focused on increasing the threat. Pfeffer and his colleagues (5) have discussed this factor in relation to a clinic utilized by industrial concerns. They note that ordinarily an alcoholic will not seek help until after he has incurred great losses. Alcoholics still employed often do not feel this pressure, but referral by the employer using a probationary status and threat of loss of employment impels acceptance of treatment. Thus an attempt is made to manipulate the alcoholic's denial system.

Motivation is also often discussed in relation to sustained contact with the therapist. Typical is the remark of Strayer (6): "The ability to sustain contact with the clinic may be an expression of the strength of the patient's motivation to get well."

The Environment. Sociologists usually avoid the motivation question entirely by attributing it to the socialization process (7), although Homans (8) has recently subjected motivation to a complex analysis derived from a combination of reinforcement theory and classical economies.

Consideration of the environment has been developed in the "therapeutic community" concept in which a constellation of variables is utilized (9, 10). Can the environment be changed? Can a milieu be created which provides support and impetus in carrying out therapeutic programs?

The Caretaker. The challenge posed by the demonstrations discussed above focuses attention on the referral agent. Is the agent subject to change? Is it an appropriate link in effectuating change in the referral process?

Medical Care. It has been suggested[7] that the quality of medical care can be measured by three variables: The technical skills of the caretaker, the time available for the patient, and continuity of care. In each of the experiments, improvement over existing practices by these three measures was introduced into the institutional setting. Time was given to the patients. Contact was made prior to discharge from the institution. Referrals were made to specific clinics and individuals for a definite time. Follow-through occurred. The caretakers were competent and experienced in working with alcoholics, although their specific training did not appear to be a critical variable. However, these caretakers shared two beliefs—that the patient could be helped, and that the responsibility rested upon them, not upon the patient. Their approach was "aggressive."

[7]Prof. Richard Titmuss. [Lecture, Brandeis University, 23 April 1962.]

SUMMARY

Approximately 200 alcoholic patients, consisting primarily of subjects with serious social problems, criminality, destitution, and severe pathology, were the participants in 4 demonstration projects in 3 different institutions: a general hospital emergency ward, an adult female correctional institution, and a male juvenile correctional institution. Previous experience showed that less than 1 per cent attended alcoholism clinics following referral from these settings. With these patients, usually described as "unreachable," three different types of projects were designed to demonstrate that the referral process could be improved so that existing resources would be utilized more effectively.

Physicians, social workers and other personnel applied a variety of techniques, including intensive individual interviews, active help, and group meetings, as a means of engaging the prereferral patients in an effective relationship. In two of the institutional demonstrations the project personnel came from the clinics to which referral was to be made, and the same therapists continued to work with the patients in the outpatient clinic.

In comparison with the previous record all the experiments were strikingly successful. In the various experiments, from 43 to 66 per cent of these poorly motivated categories of alcoholics were induced to come for repeated visits to clinical settings. Further, from 26 to over 50 per cent of the several groups remained in treatment despite many environmental problems and limited or nonexistent ancillary community resources.

It is concluded that the low utilization rate of therapeutic services by alcoholics can be overcome by techniques which give positive sanction to goals that usually have negative sanctions.

REFERENCES

1. Mendelson, J. H. and Chafetz, M. E. Alcoholism as an emergency ward problem. Quart. J. Stud. Alc. **20:** 270-275, 1959.
2. Chafetz, M. E., Blane, H. T., Abram, H. S., Golner, J., Lacy, E., McCourt, W. F., Clark, E. and Meyers, W. Establishing treatment relations with alcoholics. J. nerv. ment. Dis. **134:** 395-409, 1962.
3. Myerson, D. J. Clinical observation on a group of alcoholic prisoners. With special reference to women. Quart. J. Stud. Alc. **20:** 555-572, 1959.
4. Myerson, D. J., Mackay, J., Wallens, A. and Neiberg, N. A report of

a rehabilitation program for alcoholic women prisoners. Quart. J. Stud. Alc., Suppl. No. 1, pp. 151-157, 1961.

5. Pfeffer, A. Z., Feldman, D. J., Feibel, C., Frank, J. A., Cohen, M., Berger, S., Fleetwood, M. F. and Greenberg, S. S. A treatment program for the alcoholic in industry. J. Amer. Med. Ass. **161:** 827-836, 1956.

6. Strayer, R. A study of the Negro alcoholic. Quart. J. Stud. Alc. **22:** 111-123, 1961.

7. Davis, J. A. Two critiques of Homans in his *Social Behavior: Its Elementary Forms*. A sociologist's view. Amer. J. Sociol. **67:** 454-458, 1962.

8. Homans, G. C. Social Behavior. New York; Harcourt, Brace; 1961.

9. Mechanic, D. Relevance of group atmosphere and attitudes for the rehabilitation of alcoholics. A pilot study. Quart. J. Stud. Alc. **22:** 634-645, 1961.

10. Forizs, L. Therapeutic community and teamwork. Quart. J. Stud. Alc. **20:** 591-595, 1959.

15. The Concept of Coordination by a State-Sponsored Alcoholism Program

David Kantor, M.S.W.[1]
Harold W. Demone, Jr., A.M.[2]

The concept of coordination in the human services has tended to be treated as one might treat a distant relative–politely, but as a peripheral character in the events of one's life. In addition, within human service organizations the task of coordination has often been the function assigned to marginal employees, usually those lacking specialized expertise and power.

Times change, and yesterday's minor concern has become today's major interest. As approaches such as systems theory elaborate the complex nature of human ecology, and as intervention agencies become increasingly aware of how limited are the resources available to attack immense problems, the need for effective coordination has become highly a salient concern; an important strategy for generating effective utilization of human service resources. In the paper which follows the authors describe a consultative, action-oriented approach to coordination which was successfully adopted by one public agency.

INTRODUCTION

Although alcoholism as a focus of concern to society preceded the rise of western civilization, a significantly widespread professional interest in the problem began only about 20 years ago. This surge of professional interest, following the repeal of Prohibition, was inspired by the success of Alcoholics Aynonymous, and was reinforced by the establishment of what is now known as the Yale Center of Alcohol Studies. In turn these latter historical events

---

[1]Formerly Alcoholism Coordinator, Office of the Commissioner on Alcoholism. Now Chief Mental Health Coordinator, Massachusetts Department of Mental Health.

[2]Commissioner on Alcoholism, Commonwealth of Massachusetts

have accelerated the development of specialized treatment education, and research agencies under public and private auspices. One of these specialized agencies is the Massachusetts Office of the Commissioner on Alcoholism.

By law this office has four functions: treatment, education, research and coordination. It is to the fourth function that this paper addresses itself.

Our enabling legislation required that the Commissioner and his staff " . . . seek to coordinate the work of all departments and agencies dealing with the care and treatment of alcoholics [and] receive . . . reports from all such departments and agencies. . . ." In this report we will describe the nature and discuss the goals of coordination as we see them after 28 months of operation.

Rationale for a Coordinating Agency

Today, traditional health agencies in order to promote social and mental health are assigned three functions: treatment, education, and research. These are the "classical" functions of health agencies. The need for a fourth major function, coordination, calls for an explanation.

In most health agencies, when coordination comes into the picture it is not identified as a separate function but occurs in passing in relation to the major procedures or goals. For example, coordination by a treatment agency may be accomplished when the personnel of an alcoholism clinic give a specialized kind of advice and consultation to others—let us say to those people with "caretaking" problems, such as hospital and prison personnel, or to workers in agencies which focus only peripherally on alcoholism, such as social service agencies the parole board and churches. Coordination here extends the alcoholism agency's treatment function by helping other workers to use their own particular skills more effectively with specific alcoholics. This concept of coordination is both valuable and appropriate because it maximizes the effectiveness of other agencies. Such activities should be encouraged. However, the concept and practice of coordination itself, under certain circumstances, needs to be extended.

As we have developed this practice, coordination is an attempt to meet the needs of the many organizations and institutions which deal either specially or incidentally with the problem of alcoholism and to help each one maximize its own effectiveness. Coordination is thus both an independent function of major importance and one that is related to other functions, i.e., treatment, research and education. Implicit in this approach to coordination, is the recognition that organizations and agencies are social systems with needs of their own. They must concern themselves with their own policies, procedures, goals and identities, and with their relationship to other agencies in the field of health as well as with their relationship to clients and patients.

These concerns are in the final analysis the crux of each community's health and welfare plan. Only as each agency contributing to this plan reaches fulfillment in relation to itself and to all other agencies, can the community's over-all program be effective. Must each and every health agency, therefore, develop a separate coordinative function? Not necessarily. Many health agencies can confine themselves to the three traditional functions and at the same time achieve their general purposes. The cancer field is a case in point. Cancer is a clear-cut disease process, a special health problem requiring specialized treatment. The nature of the disease is clear, even if, like alcoholism, the exact cause is not. In other respects, however, it is unlike alcoholism. Except for an occasional reluctance to act because of man's longstanding dread of this disease, there is no confusion about where to go and what needs to be done once the disease is suspected or definitely detected. Everyone would agree that medical attention and intervention is necessary. The course to be taken by the control agency ordinarily is not complicated by the existence of other problems of equal or greater consequence which accompany the original disorder. Cancer is treated by specific methods based on existing knowledge.

Where these conditions obtain, coordination can remain a secondary peripheral function. Interagency relationships are unfettered by diverse opinions and overlapping responsibilities. Where the opposite occurs there are a large number of existing agencies and disciplines whose services are directed toward a common problem and coordination becomes necessary.

An appraisal of alcoholism service patterns throughout the Commonwealth of Massachusetts 3 years ago showed that some agencies were duplicating functions better handled elsewhere; that some programs were ineffectual and clearly archaic while others were doing a splendid job but were lost in obscurity although knowledge of them as public agencies was greatly needed; and that expanded services for alcoholics were needed in some geographical and operational areas. These were but a few of the reasons behind the establishment of the Office of the Commissioner on Alcoholism.

The Office of the Commissioner on Alcoholism, therefore, may be seen as a hub functioning in the center of the vast field of alcoholism activities. During its limited life, it has come into daily contact with numerous individuals, agencies and programs. During the past year, the Office had dealings with over 100 different agencies and institutions in such areas as tuberculosis, education, correction, mental health, and public welfare. This position of centrality within the network of existing social and welfare institutions in the Commonwealth has been an extraordinary advantage for achieving the goals of coordination.

COORDINATION

Goals

Briefly, the goal of coordination in the field of alcoholism is to develop and improve the reciprocal relations between various programs or agencies concerned with alcoholism toward the end of raising the quality, efficiency, balance, and effectiveness of over-all operations.

Two dimensions may be described in order to demonstrate how the Office of the Commissioner on Alcoholism performs. These are the activities themselves and the techniques used in these activities.

Coordination Activities

We are constantly being drawn into, or have ourselves initiated contact with many of the people who are or should be concerned about alcoholism. The specific coordinative activities in which the Office of the Commissioner on Alcoholism participated last year are too numerous to comment on in full. A full listing of the agencies and organizations with whom we have worked is available in the 1958 Annual Report.[3] Extensive activities with many State departments such as Public Health, Correction, Mental Health, and Education, and equally important though fewer activities with other departments, suggest that some headway has been made during the past year in carrying out that aspect of our legislation which requires us to "... coordinate the work of all departments...." In addition, our network of activities includes work with many private and professional agencies and organizations, and cuts across all levels of government, from the smallest local unit to Federal agencies. These coordination efforts are increasing at a continuously accelerating rate.

On close examination of our activities, we find that coordination

[3]Activities Report, January 1957–January 1958. Boston; Office of the Commissioner on Alcoholism; 1958

may operate in different ways. The nature of our working involvement with others seems to fall into one of four categories as follows:

Autonomous Intradepartmental Activities. We may participate with one or more divisions or sub-units of a department or organization. However, the work with each unit is independent and not immediately related to activities going on with other units of the larger organizations. It is possible, however, that they will relate, at a later date, as areas of common concern manifest themselves. For example, a local health officer (from the Department of Public Health) consulted us specifically with respect to problems of alcoholism within his district, while at the same time we were also working separately with other divisions in his department.

Intramural Activities. Here, we participate with and bring to a common focus, activities with more than one unit within a single department. The many joint endeavors with the Department of Correction illustrate this type of coordinative activity. Because that department has a profound desire to improve its rehabilitation programs for the many alcoholics cared for in its institutions, a long series of cooperative enterprises with the Office of the Commissioner on Alcoholism have been instituted, beginning at the administrative level and thereafter entering several phases of their operations. These include, among others, our participation in their correction officer training program, studies of their penal programs, joint planning of pilot programs, and research.

Interdepartmental Activities. Here, two or more State departments are involved in efforts to deal with alcoholism problems which affect all simultaneously. The evolvement of a plan for pilot half-way houses for alcoholics is one example. The Departments of Correction, Education, Public Health, Public Welfare, Mental Health, Public Safety, Parole, Probation, Registry of Motor Vehicles, and Rehabilitation as well as representatives from private agencies, played a part in the study, design, and recommendations for the proposed program for the establishment of State-sponsored half-way houses in the Commonwealth. These rehabilitation facilities will offer relief to agencies in several State departments dealing with alcoholics.

Interorganizational Activities. The scope of certain activities is so broad as to cut across departmental and organizational lines and levels in and out of government. Activities related to tuberculosis and alcoholism, for example, have involved Federal, State, county and city governmental agencies. It has also been necessary to coordinate with the activities of the above agencies, those of private organizations and educational institutions.

The Techniques of Coordination

Every coordinative activity has special characteristics determined by the unique demands of the situation or the specific request of the recipient. Ordinarily the techniques and procedures involved in the activities will fall into one of four categories: consultation, collaboration, follow-up activities and incidental activities.[4] A brief example of each will make clear what we mean.

Consultation.—Because alcoholism is an illness which has drawn attention from almost every possible societal group, large numbers of professional people from different disciplines, with different points of view and with different goals and responsibilities, have demonstrated a legitimate concern. The Office of the Commissioner on Alcoholism is consulted by many of these people. Often we are asked to suggest, to counsel or to prescribe some blueprint of action. Consultation, as we have tried to practice it, may include these things, but it is something more. Briefly, we consider the technique of coordination to be functioning at its best when the consultee, whether an individual or group, is helped to understand the problem presented and to mobilize resources and skills necessary for its solution. The aim is to make each consultee more effective in his own function and within the range of his own set of skills. Characteristically, the contact initiated by the recipient differs from some other coordination methods, in that we rarely participate directly in the action or follow-up.

Many consultations are held with those who are in caretaking roles, for example, those in penal, mental and tuberculosis institutions, and general hospitals, and such community workers as public health nurses, police, probation and parole officers. Others are not. The recently organized North Shore Committee on Alcoholism (a citizens' committee) has consulted us on a continuous basis from its organizational phase to its present development of programs of prevention, education and treatment. We have also served as consultant to the Social Action Committee of the Massachusetts Baptist Conference in which Baptist clergy and laity are reviewing their goals and procedures in alcohol education.

Collaboration—By collaboration, we mean concerted action—planning, programming and research—that is collaterally executed by more than one agency. The Office of the Commissioner on Alcohol-

[4]It is not always possible to narrow down the description of these techniques because one or more procedures may be involved in relation to a single activity. When several activities or several agencies are involved in a complex project the entire range of techniques may be needed.

ism collaborated with the Departments of Education and Mental Health, and the National Institute of Mental Health in planning and executing a 3-day conference on "The Mental Health Aspects of Alcohol Education" attended by 40 teachers from secondary schools, guidance personnel, principals, representatives of teachers colleges and superintendents. In a united effort the Office of the Commissioner on Alcoholism shared with the other departments the responsibility for guiding and presenting the program and editing and publishing the resulting proceedings.[5] The publication has had its own impact; the Federal Government has purchased additional copies, the journal of a national educators organization has reprinted certain sections, and the Yale Summer School of Alcohol Studies has requested additional copies for teaching purposes. Thus, extended developments and effects may result unexpectedly from some initial activity.

Catalytic Action or Follow-Up.—As illustrated above, it is rarely the case that, once completed, a coordination activity becomes a dead issue. Most often the after-effects lead to new activities and additional coordinative functions by the Office of the Commissioner on Alcoholism. For instance, consultation with the North Shore Committee on Alcoholism led to (1) collaborative planning and execution of a program for local educators, and (2) the strengthening of the local family service agency. In still another instance, recommendations from our study at the Massachusetts Correctional Institution, Bridgewater, led to a pilot treatment program in which we serve as consultant. Now after 6 months of experience this program is being doubled in size. In a sense, therefore, every coordinative function may act as an impetus to further activities.

Other Activities.—In addition, there are other activities, pervasive and unplanned, which nevertheless extend the agency function. For example, a chance contact between a member of our staff and a university faculty member led to a lecture on alcoholism in the professor's class; to a special issue on alcoholism of a journal for which the professor served as editor; to consultation on a proposed textbook on social pathology; and to interest on the part of the professor's students in the subject of alcoholism. Following up such chance encounters is a legitimate part of our over-all program.

It is important to note the intimate relationship between research and education functions, on the one hand, and coordination on the other. In the first place, research and education activities can

[5]Mental Health Aspects of Alcohol Education. Boston; Office of the Commissioner on Alcoholism; [1959]

serve as catalytic agents that make for coordination. Secondly, our research and education staffs serve also as research and education coordinators, coordinating the activities of others within these special fields.

There are two other features of coordination that are not properly grouped under consultation, collaboration or follow-up. These are: (1) freeing communication channels, and (2) integrating working relationships. While they are techniques of coordination, they also seem to border on other procedural phenomena—goals and methods of coordination.

Defective or undeveloped lines of communication are a malady that afflicts many organizations. This problem can seriously hamper the accomplishment of an agency's aims. Thus, the importance of this function looms large in our attempt to coordinate a community-wide network of alcoholism activities. We have set our sights on improving communications both within an organizational unit and between agencies. The Office of the Commissioner on Alcoholism is aided in its attempt to improve communications by its central position among alcoholism-focused agencies. We have been handed, as a matter of course, many opportunities for encouraging interaction as others have come to use to utilize our education, research, and coordination services. We have tried to utilize these opportunities and have in addition taken the initiative by reaching out to State and private agencies and to the general public, in order to develop and increase interaction between ourselves and others, but more important between the various community agencies and groups.

The collaboration between several departments in the planning and carrying out of the conference on alcohol education illustrates how interaction can improve communication. Educators attending the conference pointed out that merely getting to know workers from other disciplines in meetings and workshops paved the way for future collaboration. They also noted that participation by and communication between leaders and administrators and front-line personnel increased the chances of improved alcohol education programs in the schools.

Communication between agency personnel and legislators is seriously underdeveloped. There are very few opportunities for legislators to meet workers and leaders in the various health and welfare fields. Legislators can come to a better understanding of the aims of various programs through informal contacts with the people who carry them out, and workers in the field can come to a better understanding of the economic and political realities which legis-

lators face. More equitable allocations and more reasonable requests
are likely to result when communication channels between these
two groups are built. In an informal meeting at the State House,
workers in public and private alcoholism programs in Worcester
County and all Worcester County legislators were brought together.
The excellent turnout of legislators indicated that they were eager
for this sort of experience. The reactions on both sides were so
encouraging as to suggest that this technique for building communication channels should be continued.

Another function of coordination similar to improving communications is to produce more effective working relationships between
groups. There are many factors which keep groups from working
together effectively. Lack of information can deny one agency the
benefits of services that another is willing to offer. Poor communication between various services within an institution frequently results
in a poorly integrated program. Geographical distance often
separates agencies that have identical or similar interests and should
or could work more closely together. Thus, some techniques for
integrating working relationships between groups are information-
giving, planning opportunities for joint participation, and arrang-
ing regularly scheduled meetings.

The Office of the Commissioner on Alcoholism applies these
techniques in various ways. For example, we encourage the development of new Alcoholics Anonymous groups in tuberculosis sana-
toria and at Bridgewater, and recommend more intensive and
extensive use and support of A.A. We circulate among researchers
and others a report of all current research on alcoholism in the
State. We participate with the staff of the Boston City Hospital
Department of Psychiatry in their longrange planning, as a result
of which their program will be tied more closely to the Boston
Tuberculosis Sanatorium (where some residents will work with
tuberculous alcoholics), to the Boston City Hospital's treatment
program for acutely ill alcoholics and to the outpatient alcoholism
clinic.

Problems in Coordination

In a general sense it can be said that coordinative efforts are
most likely to be successful when the agency or discipline either
invites us to help or is already restive and in a self-examining stage.
When the agency or discipline is self-satisfied and complacent it
is extremely unlikely that it will accept our urging to examine its
role in relation to alcoholism. We find for the most part, however,
that agencies are disturbed about the problems they are having

with alcoholics and respond well to the possibility of receiving help with this problem.

CONCLUSION

Our thesis is simple: alcoholism is not a special isolated health problem. No single agency or agent can deal effectively with this problem. It is a general, social, health and community problem. Our coordination program emanated from this belief.

Coordination is the keyword in defining the activities of the Office of the Commisssioner on Alcoholism. Our objectives are to bring together, to integrate, to activate and to help function those agencies concerned directly or indirectly with the care and treatment of alcoholics. In addition, as part of its research and coordinating functions, the Office of the Commissioner on Alcoholism seeks to appraise existing alcoholism services and to insure the careful balancing of treatment facilities.

An indication of the scope of the coordinative activities of the Office of the Commissioner on Alcoholism can be seen in its work with over 100 different agencies and institutions during the past year. Through consultation, collaboration and program planning the Office of the Commissioner on Alcoholism has offered assistance and guidance to those organizations that wish to develop and make more effective the services that they offer to the alcoholic. Thus, through coordination, the Office of the Commissioner on Alcoholism seeks to strengthen the numerous caretaking agencies and disciplines so that they may better help in solving the alcoholism problem.

SUMMARY OF GROUP DISCUSSIONS

Mr. Demone's paper describing the function of his agency revealed a new concept in the field of alcoholism, an attempt at coordination and integration of the various agencies whose services are geared to meeting this common problem. The goal of a coordinating agency is integration of relations between different service agencies, leading to greater effectiveness of the over-all program in the treatment of the alcoholic.

An agency such as Mr. Demone described of necessity operates through competence rather than authority. It must, therefore, communicate effectively with the specific service agencies. The need for the program has to come from within the cooperating agency and cannot be imposed by the coordinating agency. It is the function of the latter, however, to stimulate the former in recognizing this need. This often involves the working through of barriers, a capacity for self-examination, and an ability to give up immediate goals in exchange for the ultimate achievement of long-term objectives.

Removal of Barriers.—In the removal of barriers the coordinating agency must be able to communicate at the level of understanding of the cooperating agency. Barriers can most effectively be removed through the cultivation of individual relationships and the nurturing of existing relationships. Individual employees in the cooperating agency must be reached, stimulated and utilized. This frequently involves supporting a key person so that he can stimulate other staff members. There is a need to get down to the least common denominator, the alcoholic and the person who works directly with him. This of necessity also involves support on the higher administrative levels.

Other Aspects of Coordination.—Barriers to cooperation can also be obviated through research. Through this technique preconceived images of the alcoholic may be revised and a more favorable climate created. There is also a need for the coordinating agency to recognize its limits, otherwise it can reinforce old barriers and perhaps activate new ones. Equally important is the need to relate the program to the community and to stimulate community awareness, thus creating community support and reinforcing the agency's position.

Coordination in Other Settings.—The Massachusetts program can well serve as a model for other State programs interested in coordinating more effectively their alcoholism services and utilizing more constructively facilities for treatment of the alcoholic. Allowance must be made, however for differences within each setting. Basically there must be a reorganization of thinking, an awareness of the implications involved in an isolated attitude on the part of specialized alcoholism treatment services. Although most specialized tre.tment centers attempt to do a certain amount of coordination, particularly as it relates to community agencies, we must ask whether this is the most effective approach and whether the therapist himself feels comfortable in what he is doing. Is there a need for a specialized type of service staffed by consultants functioning in a manner similar to the Massachusetts system? This is something for each program to evaluate in its own setting.

16. Decentralization For What?

Irving Kristol

Recent years have witnessed a growth of concern with decentralization as a philosophical principle and operating practice in public human service systems. In the abstract it has had strong appeal as an attractive, simple alternative to pyramidal, bureaucratized service delivery systems. It is also an ideological principle that, however attractive, has been a source of confusion, conflict, and community tension when put into practice.

One source of the many problems created by attempts to decentralize the human services, Kristol notes in the following article, is the failure to adequately translate a principle of organization into a working reality; i.e., to interpret its meaning in terms of current organizational issues and problems. A related problem is the failure to effectively deal with the realignment of power in complex organizations, including the paradox of decentralizing in order to recentralize power at different levels of the organization.

The major story on page 1 of *The New York Times* for November 17, 1967, reported that the Model Cities Program was getting under way:

"The Administration made public today a list of 63 cities . . . that will take part in the first phase of the model cities program . . .

" . . . The winners will share $11-million in planning money appropriated by Congress last year. The exact amount of each grant will be worked out in negotiations between federal and local officials.

"After the cities have drawn up detailed plans and submitted them to Washington, they will become eligible for $300-million appropriated last month to carry out the rebuilding process."

At first glance, this looks all too familiar—a recipe for bureaucratic nightmare, after the fashion of the older urban renewal program, now generally thought to be something less than a success. You will have a small group of experts in the sixty-three cities—men who will, for the occasion, be presumed to be highly knowledgeable about slum life, slum people, slum buildings, slum real estate, etc.—trying to come up with a blueprint they can sell to their local constituencies and to their Washington overseers. You will have a smaller group of presumed experts in Washington, working desperately to make sense of the detailed plans submitted to them hoping against hope that the plans will actually be carried out as intended, worrying endlessly (and legitimately) about whether the reports they are receiving "from the field" have any connection with what is really happening. Very few of the experts will, of course, be expert enough to avoid major miscalculations. And even if they were, there would still be the delays imposed by bureaucratic red tape to throw their calculations into disarray. In short: a typical social welfare program that threatens to metamorphose into one controversial shambles after another.

Only, in this case, there is something new. The men who devised the Model Cities program were alert to the problems of bureaucratic mismanagement. They therefore wrote into the law a provision for "popular participation" in this bold new venture into city planning. To get its allotted funds, each of these sixty-three cities has to demonstrate to Washington's satisfaction that citizens' governing boards in the affected neighborhoods "participated actively in planning and carrying out" the program. These boards are now being formed via popular election. In Atlanta, a white neighborhood has elected a couple of Ku Klux Klansmen. In Detroit, in a half-Negro, half-white neighborhood, the board is all-Negro. Officials in Washington are reported to be very upset at the way things are going.

Which leads one to comtemplate the possibility that there is more than one kind of bureaucratic nightmare—and that the worst kind may yet turn out to be of the "anti-bureaucratic" variety.

The Right Problem at the Wrong Time

Americans have never taken questions of public administration too seriously. To do so is to suggest that there may be inherent limitations on the execution of the popular will (and our democratic ideology discourages such a notion) or that the natural capacities of the average American may be inadequate to the detailed tasks of government (a national heresy since the days of Andrew Jackson). But the experience of liberals during the Kennedy Administration was a critical one. Whereas they had previously scoffed at criticisms of "bureaucracy"—by conservatives in general, and businessmen in particular—they soon discovered that there really was such a thing and that its power to thwart or distort social programs was never to be underestimated. Just as most intellectuals only get interested in education when their children start going to school, so the liberal intellectuals around John F. Kennedy suddenly found themselves getting interested in public administration when they discovered that their good ideas and fine intentions got mangled on the way to achieving reality.

The simple fact, they learned, is that the number of programs the political and sociological imagination is capable of inventing always exceeds the number of available people who can realize these programs *as intended*. You always end up with programs being carried out by a bureaucratic hierarchy that understands them only imperfectly and possibly may not even be much interested in them at all.

So it became proper for liberals to talk about the problems of "bureaucracy" and of "centralization," and many started doing so. As a matter of fact "decentralization" has in general become a very fashionable idea. Thus, where political scientists used to argue that municipal government was incapable of coping with the problems of the city and that larger, more comprehensive metropolitan governments were needed, this argument has suddenly been reversed. In his recent presidential address to the American Political Science Association, Robert Dahl pointed out that the population of New York City is about the same as that of Sweden, and that New York is "badly in need of being broken up into smaller units for purposes of local government." Indeed, Professor Dahl took a dim view of any unit of local government that encompasses more than 200,000 souls.

So far, so good. We have become keenly aware—and it's about time too—of the deficiencies of overly centralized planning and overly centralized government. We are all decentralists now. But unfortunatley, liberal intellectuals do seem to have an uncanny knack for focusing on the right problem at the wrong time, and in the wrong way. They have opted for decentralization with the same kind of enthusiastic abstractness they once brought to centralization. They have slighted, when they have not entirely ignored, the supreme political consideration—circumstance. For, as Edmund Burke long ago observed, "Circumstances . . . give in reality to every political principle its distinguishing colour and discriminating effect. The circumstances are what render every civil and political scheme beneficial or noxious. . . ."

I shall have something to say later about the most significant "circumstance" that today affects (or should affect) our efforts at decentralization. But, first of all, it is worth taking a look at the way the *idea* of decentralization became the *ideology* of decentralization.

Populism and Neo-populism

We have, during this past decade, witnessed a mounting anxiety about the fate of democracy in a mass, industrialized society. We have simultaneously witnessed a sharp upsurge of populism in American feeling—both on the left and (to a somewhat lesser extent) on the right. A "credibility gap" has emerged which separates the citizen, not merely from any particular administration, but from government itself. As a result, the need for "visible government" (in Mayor Lindsay's phrase) and the importance of "participation" (in just about everyone's phrase) has become widely accepted among social critics and social reformers. The vision of the American people regaining a lost political heritage through a revival of "the town meeting" within our large urban centers has become exceedingly attractive. And, since there is no blinking the fact that ours is a complex and interdependent society, the constituency for such "town meetings" is frequently redefined along "functional" lines, so as to transcend mere locality and encompass all those involved with one governmental program or another. Has not Sargeant Shriver roundly announced that "welfare without representation is tyranny"?

At about the same time, various sociologists, psychologists, anthropologists, and social theorists came to the conclusion that conventional populism was not enough. The people had not merely to be "involved" or "consulted" so as to gain their active consent. The people had to "participate" in their democracy in a very special way—i.e., through "social conflict." What these social critics had in mind was no reconstituted New England town meeting of any kind: *that* was a vehicle for consensus. Rather, they entertained images of mass picketing, rent strikes, organized boycotts of local merchants, harassment of all official bureaucracies, etc. Activities such as these, it was insisted, were necessary to the mental health and spiritual uplift of the people, and especially the poor and dispossessed among them.

Just where this particular ideology came from, and how it achieved its popularity, is an interesting question but, for our purposes, an irrelevant one. (Obviously, it had more to do with an initial animus against the status quo than with any ripe sagacity about the difficulties of public administration in a large democracy.) In any event, it came to be accepted by many eminent authorities and respectable institutions. The Ford Foundation has been a leader in stimulating this novel version of populism. A group of scholars at the Columbia School of Social Work has also played a notable role in sponsoring a neo-populist rebellion against "the welfare establishment." The New Left has made it clear that, in its eyes, "participatory democracy" was essentially connected with the class struggle. And black nationalism in the ghettos has learned to insist that pure democracy is essentially connected with race conflict, and indeed is quite simply Black Power.

The whole business has by now become a thoroughly confusing tragi-comedy of errors. And no group has been more confused than our governing authorities. Congressmen who voted for Community Action Programs and all sorts of "maximum participation" clauses, thinking they were striking a blow against "bureaucrats" and in favor of "the grass roots," are beginning to wonder what they have wrought. In desperation, they resort to the only kind of defensive action they can think of: indiscriminately cutting the budget for social services.

The Schools of New York

Meanwhile, the impulse to decentralization, oblivious to its own ideological muddle and blind to circumstance, gathers momentum. The most sensational venture of the "new decentralization" is the Ford Foundation's program for turning over New York's public schools to locally elected school boards. This is not the occasion to go into a detailed critique of the Ford plan. Suffice it to say that in my opinion—and it is not mine alone—Ford's plan will drive white parents out of integrated (i.e., mixed) neighborhoods, white children out of public schools, and white teachers out of the city altogether. It will have the same effect on many middle-class Negroes. In addition, it will certainly result in inferior education for Negro children in the central city, as experienced white teachers move (or are moved) elsewhere. All this will be accomplished in the name of "decentralization" and "neighborhood self-government"—which, in reality, will mean school boards that polarize and intensify all latent racial and political conflicts in any particular section of the city.

It is conceivable—let us even say it is probable—that, had the Ford program been introduced fifteen or twenty years ago, it would have represented an improvement. At that time, the politics of the Negro community centered around the demand for "integration," and Negro leaders would have had considerable latitude in negotiating with whites over the manner and matter of education. This is no longer true. The dominant political ethos of the Negro community is now black nationalism.[1] So far as one can see, this ethos will become stronger rather than weaker in the troubled years that lie immediately ahead. This being the case, the popularly elected school boards are going to be forums for conflict and hostility rather than cooperation and communality. They are going to be weak and turbulent authorities, not strong and resolute centers of direction. (Indeed, where such school boards already exist, on an advisory basis, this is precisely what is happening.) And if, after the initial turmoil and chaos, they should become strong and resolute, they are very likely to behave in a thoroughly racist way.

Decentralization Confused With Democracy

To criticisms of this kind, which have been directed against its plan for reorganizing public education in New York, the Ford Foundation has only one strong rejoinder: the present system doesn't work. It would be more accurate and more candid to say that the system "works" no less well than it ever did, but that it has not been able to cope with lower-class Negroes as it previously coped with, say, lower-class Italians. (Essentially the same thing can be said about our welfare system.) Still, it is clear enough that New York's public education system, even when and where it works, is very efficient in enforcing petty regulations, extremely inefficient in coping with new problems or new opportunities. There is indeed, then, *in the abstract*, a valid case for decentralization. But, even in the abstract, what kind of decentralization?

It is always a good idea, when reforming an institution or a program, to take guidance, not only from general principles or preconceived opinions, but from comparable institutions and programs that do seem to work. Now, not all of education in New York City is out of popular favor. The affluent private schools, on the whole, are well regarded by parents, students, and teachers. So are the anything-but-affluent parochial schools, which the major-

---

[1] I am not saying that the majority of Negroes are, or ever will be, black nationalists—except perhaps in a highly attenuated and rather passive way. But is seems clear that no Negro group will be able to *oppose* black nationalism without committing political suicide. The anti-nationalists are already in the process of being transformed into "moderate" nationalists.

ity of Negro parents would be delighted to send their children to, were there room for them. What is it that makes these schools acceptable at the least, desirable at the best?

The answer has nothing to do with schools being run on principles of local democracy which they are not. It has everything to do with these schools being run on principles of *delegated authority*. Specifically, the reason these schools "work" better is that they are governed by headmasters who have considerable managerial power, managerial discretion, managerial immunity to outside pressures (*including* parental pressures). From what I have seen of public school principals in New York City, they compare favorably enough to private school headmasters. What they lack is any kind of real power to do a good job.

I am not unaware of the difficulties involved in conceding to them this power. Indeed, the difficulties are just about identical with those the Ford Foundation program is likely to encounter, but with the tumult swirling around the choice of principal instead of the school board. In any case, I am not here interested in arguing the case for one particular kind of educational reform as against another. I wish only to stress a significant, and frequently misconceived, point: decentralization is one thing, democracy is another. The government of Sweden is far more decentralized than the government of New York City, but it is not thereby more democratic. Indeed, the Swedish government is probably *less* democratic than is New York's—and better governed.

Or, to put it another way: *decentralization, if it is to work, must create stronger local authorities, not weaker ones. Effective decentralization does not diffuse authority; it takes the power that is diffused throughout a large bureaucracy and concentrates it into new nuclei of authority.* Before we commit ourselves to any scheme of decentralization, we ought to make certain that this particular reconstitution of authority is what we really want. And I find it instructive to note that many of those who favor radical decentralization of education in our Northern urban regions are simultaneously demanding the extension of federal bureaucratic controls over education in the South.

The Most Important Circumstance

In the United States today, the key "circumstance" that ought to affect one's attitude toward decentralization is the relationship between black and white—the present racial tensions we dare not ignore, the future integration we dare not despair of. Every reforming enterprise must, first of all and above all, take its bearings from this circumstance. It is always useful to inquire to what extent we can decentralize our cumbersome service bureaucracies (in education, welfare, housing, perhaps even policing). But it is even more useful to inquire to what extent we can decentralize our services *without fractioning our heterogeneous political community*. I am not saying that, under present circumstances, such decentralization is always undesirable. I am saying simply that we must always ask *whether* it is, in the light of these circumstances.

Indeed, were it not for the racial heterogeneity of this nation, the organization of our social services would be a relatively superficial problem. Politicians, of course, might kick up a big fuss about one thing or another. But whichever way the issue were resolved, it wouldn't make all that amount of difference. Take education, for instance. To begin with, were it not for the race issue, it might not be widely regarded as a "problem" at all. (In the all-white neighborhoods of Brooklyn, Queens and Staten Island there isn't even as much dissatisfaction with the New York public school system as, in my opinion, there ought to be.) Second, if one wished to experiment with various forms of "decentralization," one easily could—whatever controversies they engendered would not be more damaging than, say, present controversies in smaller communities over local school board issues. (In these controversies, feelings run high—but only temporarily.) Third, one could even contemplate experimenting with quite radical reforms that go beyond "decentralization"—such as extending "consumer sovereignty" to the educational sector by abolishing "free" schools and disbributing educational expenditures (in either cash or vouchers) to parents, who could then shop for schools as they please. The important thing is that, whatéver was tried or not tried, whatever worked or didn't work, would not seriously affect the shape of the American republic or its ultimate destiny.

But we *are* a racially heterogeneous nation. And we *are* committed to creating a racially integrated society[2] this fact and this commitment are—and ought to be—dominant in our minds. It is therefore

[2]One of the arguments of those who propose decentralization along racial lines is that "integration" is turning out to be a will o'-the-wisp, anyway. I think these people have an erroneous and highly utopian notion of integration. Yes, of course the proportion of all-Negro or predominantly Negro schools is increasing in our central cities, as the Negro population of those cities grows. That is inevitable. But I would argue that this is a stage in the process of integration, rather than some kind of contrary tendency. The Irish, the Italians, and the Jews also flooded their local schools, in their time. Integration doesn't mean instant assimilation. It doesn't mean—has never meant in America—that a new ethnic group is going

of great importance that the major impulses toward "decentralization" now come from the white segregationists in the South and the black nationalists (together with their white, radical allies) in the North. Should these impulses prevail, the task of molding this country into one nation will be made infinitely more difficult, and perhaps impossible. The statesman's responsibility is to resist these impulses where he can, to "contain" them where he cannot resist. "Decentralization," in practice, has come too often to mean the hasty "appeasement" of these tendencies.

The School As Scapegoat

There are two further—and not unimportant points—to be made:

1. "Decentralization" is not likely to solve any of the problems of education in our Northern ghettos.

The sociological evidence seems to be conclusive that the schools themselves have only a partial—maybe only marginal—impact on broad educational achievements. What we glibly call the "problem of education in the ghetto" is probably little more than an aspect of the problem of poverty. Though a devoted, imaginative, and inspiring teacher can always make a difference, in any school, any time there's not much point in asserting that what the ghetto needs is masses of such teachers: they just don't exist in the mass. Nor is there any evidence that changes in the curriculum matter much; or new school buildings as against old; or even smaller classes as against larger ones. What does count is the environment, as established by home and community. The basic fact is that middle-class Negroes, living in middle-class neighborhoods (whether integrated or not), do *not* have a "crisis in education." Centering one's attention on the school is an effective way of distracting one's attention from the far more important realities of poverty and discrimination.

One can understand why residents of the slums should be tempted to make the schools scapegoats for all of their frustrations. One can even understand—though with less tolerance—why gov-

to be warmly welcomed into the bosom of the old. It means, to begin with, the establishment of a checkerboard pattern of ethnic neighborhoods—and many Negro "neighborhoods" are now emerging in different sections of New York City, for instance. (We mindlessly persist in calling them all "ghettos," but many people who live there don't think of them as such. After all, even in Bedford-Stuyvesant some 15 per cent of the residents are homeowners.) Every day, and in almost every way, New York City is becoming much more "mixed-up" racially than it used to be. Decentralization can freeze the pattern and reconvert neighborhoods back into ghettos.

ernment officials should join in this witch hunt, denouncing the schools for failing to achieve what no schools can achieve. But it is less easy to understand why social scientists in general should wish to participate in this demagogic campaign. Perhaps they do so for the same reason right-wing groups also tend to make the school a center of controversy: they feel impotent to engender controversy about anything else.

2. It is an accidental fact, but an important one, that *our large and cumbersome bureaucracies, in such fields as education, welfare, and in the civil service generally, happen to play a crucial role in integrating large numbers of middle-class Negroes into American Society.* These bureaucracies are, in truth, the best-integrated sectors of American society. To this end, they "work" exceedingly well. Decentralization of these bureaucracies will almost certainly mean disintegrating them. We shall end up with only Negro teachers in Negro schools, only Negro police in Negro neighborhoods, only Negro social workers handling Negro clients, etc. That, in my view, would be a major step backward. And I take it as a terrible irony that the idea of "separate but equal" should, fourteen years after the Supreme Court's *Brown* decision, become so dear to the progressive heart and mind.

Even among the various racial and ethnic minorities themselves, decentralization is already furthering conflict. In New York City, the anti-poverty program is pitting Negroes against Puerto Ricans in open hostility, with each side claiming that the results of local elections to the governing boards of various agencies are "unrepresentative." And, indeed, since so few people take part in these elections, the consequences are bound to be haphazard. The city is trying to cope with this problem by issuing directives that set "correct" numerical ratios, according to race, creed, and color. Since neighborhoods are always changing their ethnic complexion, these directives are subject to constant, and mathematically refined, revisions.

Nor is that all. If this kind of apportionment is to continue, someone will have to decide *who* is black, white, or in-between. This is less simple than would appear at first sight. A group of Negro employees of New York's Community Development Agency have opposed a Negro candidate for the post of commissioner on the grounds he is "not really black." The group informed both the city authorities and the press that it reserved the right to define blackness.

I began this essay by suggesting that, at this time and this place, bureaucratic nightmares might not be the worst imaginable nightmares. I also believe that, if by some miracle these bureaucracies did not now exist, we should have to invent them, as an undispensable mechanism of racial integration. Come to think of it, if we *did* invent them, and gave them a fancy over-all title (Office for Professional Equality?), we should probably flatter ourselves on having taken a great stride forward to the Great Society.

Decentralizing these bureaucracies remains a valid and important long-term objective. But in these times, under these circumstances, it is precisely the wrong objective.

Part IV

Roles and Role Problems

Introduction

In the past decade Americans have become increasingly concerned about the nation's social problems. The media headline; the clergy preach; legislators enact; and scientists study. A growing body of information continues to detail our increasing awareness of the immensity of such problems as hunger; mental illness; social, emotional, and intellectual deprivation; decaying inner cities, and the decaying inner selves of inner city residents.

In this section we will delineate some of the factors that have influenced and molded contemporary approaches to the problems confronted by human service organizations. As such we will focus on two broad areas: socio-organizational factors and traditional-nontraditional roles and problems.

In surveying current interfaces of human problems and human service organizations, one can gain some sense of where these organizations are, collectively, in meeting human needs. One can also get some idea of where these organizations have been; that is, the programs and participants which have been instrumental in the recent past. In both cases we have been deeply impressed by the frequently nonproductive nature of the institutional and institutionalized influences which have been exerted on the development of human service organizations and programs in general, and on the development of professionals in particular. It might be argued that all things considered, the socialization of professionals, as well as the socio organizational contexts in which they work, have often operated to actively inhibit creative approaches to the solution of human problems.

As professional standards and procedures have become routinized, they have too often appeared to be more focused on protecting their hard-earned domains and extending their boundaries than examining the current value of their disciplines. Unfortunately, professionalized human service organizations share with other organizations the problem of institutional hardening of the arteries.

It has become almost a cliche to state that as more programs are developed and enlarged to meet human needs, the number of persons who are needy will similarly expand to overburden those programs. This has been somewhat humorously expressed in the phrase "mental illness follows the development of mental health programs." In short, we continually find ourselves unable to cope with the immediate present. Or, we are able to only partially deal with what we planned for yesterday.

By definition, all complex societies need certain formal organizations and all formal organizations are constrained by the requirements of accountability. They have been organized, formalized, and supported for specific purposes. Although these purposes may change over time, to survive the organization must retain a base of financial support and constituents. The effective and viable administrator must first be aware of the sources of his constraints and develop the skills to test and later alter them as needs change. These needs may range from the survival of the organization as an organization, to maximizing the potential contribution of the organization.

What seems too often absent, but critically necessary, are system mechanisms which will facilitate flexible and adaptive programs, roles, and approaches to changing human problems. Consequently, in selecting the readings for the present section we have chosen readings which illustrate both the need for flexibility and adaptiveness in the roles which are enacted in human service dramas, and factors which operated to prevent the development of these characteristics. These readings also suggest that flexible, adaptive approaches to roles and problems are possible, although often fraught with difficulty.

Section A

Roles and Role Problems:
In a Socio-Organizational Context

Social and organizational pressures and problems arise in any complex organization in a manner which can be thought of as independent of the personalities of the participants of that organization. These organizational pressures are both internally and externally generated, and have their bases in such factors as the legal mandate of an organization, its sources of funding, the political *qua* political, and political *qua* professional influences on the functioning of a organization.

Operationally, these pressures assume substance and form in the shared expectations and normative behaviors within an organization, and are often referred to as the organizational climate. Collectively these factors compose the medium within which the organization's participants function. Perhaps McLuhan's phrase, "the medium is the message" (or massage) might serve as an apt description of the significance of these factors in the internal dynamics of any organization, and in particular in health and welfare organizations. That is, the socio-organizational medium or environment within which important decisions are made and roles enacted subtly molds and shapes these decisions and role behaviors. The organization and its participants continue to think and act, often without reflective awareness of their acts, within the individual and corporate limits imposed by the existing socio-organizational medium and its traditions.

The following three articles examine the possible sources and potential outcomes of these subtle, but broadly-bases and inordinately powerful factors.

17. High Priests of Hospitaldom

Dwight Harshbarger, Ph.D.

Historically, the hierarchical organization of mental hospitals has not been subject to major changes. Physical structures and structured social systems have acted in collusion to support and maintain this form of social organization. For example, the presence, in the 1970's, of an 1854-designed staff dining room, complete with sterling silver napkin rings, has consequences for the organization's socio-cultural climate, even though the room and its rings remain unused.

The following article focuses, at a descriptive level, on some consequences of mental health planning, and suggests that once activated, systems of positions and roles develop relatively autonomous properties of self-maintenance which may depart substantially from the needs that the positions and roles were originally designed to serve. In addition, these roles develop properties that are strangely impervious to change efforts.

"There is a place outside of time and space, although its influence on people's lives is very great. The name of that place is Expertland, the residents are called Experts, and they speak a language known as Expertise. The inhabitants are multiplying rapidly and spreading far beyond their original borders. It appears that they may eventually occupy all the world. They used to be content to reside in Expertland, talking to others of similar bent and performing obscure rituals in an inscrutable manner. Some people had assumed that experts would gradually become assimilated and come to think, speak, and act like real people. This has not happened and the expert is as much a stranger as when he lived far away."[1]

Like certain other institutions in our society, the traditional mental hospital is a relatively closed subculture, with entrances and exits regulated by highly paid gatekeepers. Within its facilities the deviant, disenfranchised, and disturbed interact, each seeking some

[1]Sommer, Robert, *Expertland,* Doubleday, Garden City, New York, 1963, p. 1.

224

means of coming to grips with existence in this totally involving subculture. For these people, the patients, the institutions of the larger society that specialize in reconciling man to an often incomprehensible fate have not worked; something else has been needed.

The mental hospital offers a possible means of reconciliation through its experts who, because of their specialized professional training, are equipped to help patients return to social reality. Patients accord these formally defined experts considerable deference, status, and almost religious respect.

The institution's experts often respond by viewing themselves in a rather priestly manner. For example, with slight encouragement, an expert may discuss the many patients he has rescued through therapeutic intervention at precisely the right moment. That apparent boasting is of no small importance, for the status system in most professional mental health disciplines is based at least partly on the frequency of successful intervention into patients' lives.

However, his status is also dependent on other and perhaps more significant factors than his professional competence. For example, when he enters the mental hospital subculture, his status is determined by the general socioeconomic ranking of his profession, based primarily on the number of years his education required, his income, and his membership groups.

But those factors serve only as a beginning point for his status in the mental hospital. Perhaps the single most important practice through which a professional can attain status in the hospital is the use of magic, the secret and private rituals about which laymen and experts from other disciplines know little, and allegedly could not really understand if they knew. It is through these unobservable processes, which bring about psychological and behavioral changes in the patients, that the expert asserts himself and ascends the institutional status ladder. It is often incumbent on him to conceal the manner in which he produces the changes, because once it is revealed, one of two equally undesirable events could occur. Either his colleagues might adopt the technique and use it more effectively than he, or the practice might be revealed as very ordinary.

Just as there are many orders of priests, there are many disciplines of experts. I have selected four that I feel represent the problems and opportunities of the expert in the mental hospital:

Social Workers. This group of experts is at an immediate disadvantage upon entry into the hospital culture, for they typically hold only a B.A. degree, although a few may have an M.S.W. As Sommer has noted, it is axiomatic in Expertland that the holders of doctorates are better than the holders of master's degrees, the holders of master's degrees are better than those with bachelor's degrees, and anyone without a bachelor's degree just isn't significant.[2] Consequently the social worker finds that his entering status is far from satisfactory to an upwardly mobile professional.

The social worker's expert status is also weakened because much of his work takes place in public and is open to scrutiny by other professionals as well as patients. Further, his jargon is largely borrowed from the psychologist, tending to relegate him to a status rung beneath that of the psychologist. However, that might be turned to advantage if psychologists manage to reach the top of the status hierarchy. Second place has more prestige than fourth place.

General Physicians. Their entering status is quite high because of their many years of education and generally exalted position in our culture. However, their position is weakened by their public performance of duties and the necessity of their seeing many patients for routine physical problems that nurses and others in the system might handle just as competently.

Perhaps the most significant factor in enhancing the physician's status is his prescription and administration of drugs and electroshock therapy. Only he truly understands the rapid and dramatic alterations in behavior brought about by those magic agents of change. Under certain conditions he will explain these practices—for example, in lectures or seminars—but always using the jargon of the medical profession. That ensures his explanation will be understood only by others like himself, most of whom know it anyway.

Psychologists. Although psychologists may perform many kinds of duties, they look upon individual testing and psychotherapy as their exclusive domains. Behind doors closed for therapy, they and their patients interact in ways that remain secret and unknown to the outside world. The secrecy results from the participants' commitment to a "professional code" that bans disclosure of what actually occurred. Nevertheless, the code is violated by both therapist and patients—for example, when the former describes his effectiveness, or the latter discusses his therapeutic progress.

Although the changes psychologists allegedly bring about in patients' behavior usually occur less rapidly than those wrought by physicians, they are frequently just as dramatic. And, like physi-

2. *Ibid.*, p. 11.

cians, this professional group keeps its magic practices secret from persons outside the profession, except to reveal them in the manner of the true expert, through highly specialized technical jargon. Because social workers' are highly motivated to maintain their knowledge of psychologists' jargon, and psychologists are determined to maintain distance from social workers, psychologists tend to use increasingly specialized terminology.

The esoteric interpretation of mental tests is also carefully guarded by psychologists. While psychologists agree that most mental health professionals are capable of learning to administer most psychological tests, they believe their own unique training equips them alone to interpret test results. Their rigidity and insistence about it usually is directly proportional to the number of social workers who can interpret tests.

Psychiatrists. This group is usually at the top of the status ladder. However, as with other experts, their status is only occasionally related to their actual effectiveness as therapists. They are, in the gamesmanship of experts, double-barreled threats, because they draw upon the secrets and magic of both medicine and psychology. When faced with challenges from experts in either of the two disciplines, they can invoke the jargon of the other. People are thus hesitant about challenging psychiatrists and, furthermore, are worried by the possibility that psychiatrists, with their multiple group memberships, could give privileged professional information to antagonistic groups.

Two additional factors enhance psychiatrists' expert status. First, their organizational positions and roles embody considerable legal power and social prestige. Second, because there are relatively few psychiatrists in any one mental hospital, they are not subject to frequent challenges from within their profession.

An endlessly fascinating process results from the interactions of these participants and others. The games are played with great intensity, and the payoffs are quite high in terms of institutional power and prestige. Perhaps games reach their most sophisticated level when, at various times during the year, that most expert of experts, the organizational consultant, arrives for a visit. Regarded as a high priest, the consultant may belong to any of the professions previously mentioned, although most come from academic psychology or psychiatry.

The consultant usually arrives with the ambiguously defined purpose of "looking at the total institution" and making recommendations on improving its general functioning. His advice is respected by most and seen as ultimate wisdom by many. In the logic of the mental hospital, the wisdom of the consultant is virtually self-defining, for he must truly be a most superior being in order to evaluate a total institution, including its many priesthoods of local experts.

The consultant's visit arouses considerable ambivalence in the local experts. The fact that he may be evaluating any or all of their performances is rather threatening. However, he is one of their own kind and might, through a well-chosen phrase or some other symbolic act of high regard, provide just the right impetus to further their ascent in the status—power hierarchy.

The dramatic and exciting events of the organizational consultant's visit occur in three main phases: the Arrival, the Visit, and the Departure.

The Arrival. The most striking feature about the arrival of the organizational consultant is the mystery surrounding it. With the exception of the Welcoming Committee (whose membership is sometimes secret, and always rumored to be changing), no one is really certain just where or by what form of transportation he will arrive—or even when.

Gaining membership on the Welcoming Committee is a small but worthwhile maneuver. It is often done through a well-planned, though apparently spontaneous, public burst of knowledge related to the consultant's main area of expertise. Usually there are a few local experts who are willing to pursue the often boring and laborious tactics necessary to complete this gambit successfully. This small group gains a substantial, though temporary, advantage in game position.

Although the probability of any major payoff is limited during the early and brief period of interaction with the consultant, there are advantages. The major one seems to lie in the juxtaposition and display of local experts in relation to the consultant. As they return from the airport, the committee will be sitting alone with him, and will be viewed by others as possibly having had access to privileged information. The members of the committee subtly encourage that inference and are often successful. However, the possibility of payoff on this gambit rapidly decreases as other experts maneuver themselves into private conversation with the consultant. Actually the trip from the airport is made up of inconsequential exchanges such as "Where's Jones now?"

The Visit. The first major in-house ploy used by the local experts is to attempt to garner large chunks of the consultant's time. Their rationale is that he can observe their staff meetings and, as it is often put, "get a feel for our problems." What they are really trying to do is place the consultant in routine, large, and highly structured group meetings in which he will be virtually unable to get a word in edgewise. The professionals will then be able to deliver their best routines. The approach is surprisingly successful, even with a veteran consultant who is well aware of what is being perpetrated. Possibly that is due to his allegiance to fellow experts, and a feeling that he should give them an opportunity to display their professional wares.

If the consultant resists the attempt to structure his time, and insists on attending a random selection of meetings, or perhaps just walking around chatting with different staff members, he will find himself facing a wall of resistance. That is due not so much to the staff's fear of his locating real and embarrassing institutional inadequacies as it is to their having prepared to act out their most expert, professional roles for him. They are understandably upset if denied that opportunity.

Generally the local experts expect the consultant to act his priestly role in a detached, uninvolved manner, and to be a superrational creature who is honor-bound as a member of an order of experts to consult sanctimoniously and assess the organization through his magic methods. Occasionally the consultant will appear to come close to revealing his secret practices, through discussions of his remarkable successes at other institutions and the ensuing and substantial problems of those institutions that failed to follow his recommendations.

A lack of involvement comes easily to most consultants, for they are only too aware of the organizational hierarchy through which their recommendations must pass, and the very low probability that anything they recommend will be enacted as policy. To someone who does not belong to an order of experts, that might seem discouraging.

However, there are compensating factors. Not only is the consultant very well paid, but the local experts and staff act as if they will carry out his recommendations. He in turn acts as if he believes them. In actuality, it is quite possible that neither believes the other and each is aware of it. But professional courtesies make the process pleasant and professionally self-enhancing.

A second major strategy to garner the consultant's time is the attempt by orders of local experts to establish private "professionals only" meetings with him. The important point is not the meeting itself, for rarely does anything worthwhile occur. Generally the participants relax, enjoying the camaraderie of practitioners of expertism. "Where's Jones now?" is replaced by "You're doing a wonderful job!" The strategic points of the meeting are the entrances and exits. Each local expert will plan his order of appearance to reflect his status and involvement in the meeting. And regardless of success or failure in entering and exiting, he benefits substantially from merely having been there. The assumption operating among those who were not invited will be that, again, certain local experts have been parties to private information about the institution.

The Departure. An almost religious ritual of meetings surrounds the departure of the consultant. First there is a closed meeting of local experts and the consultant much like that described above. Next there is the public meeting. All interested personnel can attend, which of course is virtually everyone who can free himself to be present. To be publicly defined as interested is socially desirable and can be stored for future bargaining purposes. The public meeting follows a predictable routine. The consultant delivers a relatively formal talk, mentioning the significant problems facing the hospital and briefly stating his opinion of the methods being used to solve these problems. With one or two reservations, he finds himself in considerable agreement with the local experts. Finally the real business of the public meeting emerges. The organizational consultant praises, or blesses, the local experts and the fine job they are doing under difficult circumstances. That substantially reinforces their prestige.

Occasionally the consultant may single out one discipline for particularly honorable mention. The real value of the compliment is determined by the degree to which the consultant and those staff members have interacted pleasantly. Usually they have enjoyed each other, and a public compliment from him in this final public meeting is an endorsement of the integrity of that professional group's policies. On the other hand, such a compliment can be quite problematical if the consultant and staff have been at odds with each other during his visit.

At the conclusion of that meeting the consultant is rushed to his Departure Committee, who then see him to the point of embarkation. Again, mystery shrouds his mode of travel, departure time, and destination. It is as if he rides away into the grayness of existential limbo, waiting there to be summoned by another institution needing help. At that point most of the staff, particularly the experts, are focusing on the membership of the Departure Committee. It may be revealing if there have been shifts from the composition of the Welcoming Committee. To have displaced someone is a significant victory for the new member, and an equally significant defeat for the replaced member.

As with the Welcoming Committee, the real value of membership is symbolic rather than actual. The members are the last to have a private audience with the departing shaman. Upon their return to the hospital, they may subtly imply that important things were said on the trip to the airport, matters that cannot be discussed at this time. If they are certain the consultant will not return to the hospital for some time, they may falsely hint that many portentous utterings occurred.

Following the consultant's departure the local experts renew their jockeying for position and power. The most noticeable game centers around the use of the consultant's name. Typically the frequency of using his name is directly related to the user's status, with high-status experts using the name more frequently. That continues for a minimum of four and a maximum of seven days. By then the low-status people have caught on to the game and use the consultant's name more frequently. A new game is thus called for, and predictably occurs: criticizing the consultant.

The new game is very risky, and is indulged in only by those who have thoroughly prepared themselves to play. Usually they are the same people who managed to get appointed to the Welcoming Committee. The game consists of two basic steps: one, point out small, insignificant, and esoteric deficiencies in the consultant's recommendations; two, admit the general correctness of his position.

If properly carried out, the game can substantially enhance the status of the local expert, for he becomes more expert than his colleagues had imagined. His expertise appears to transcend that of the consultant, at least in one area, however insignificant. The local expert is also displaying himself as one who is willing to speak out and deviate from the apparently prevailing norm, even though his deviance occurs well within informally defined tolerance limits.

The game of criticizing the consultant also has value only for a fixed time period—roughly one week following the end of the consultant's–name game. Again, many catch on, and skilled, esoteric criticism is increasingly replaced by personal hostility until very little is to be gained by being critical. Also, by then a few of the more enterprising experts will have reviewed the literature on the most prevalent or "in" criticisms, and will have a well-stocked repertoire of rebuttals.

After that final round, games involving the consultant rapidly cease, and professional life returns to its regularized institutional patterns. The old games return, and the never-ending, circular processes of attempts to influence continue.

From the patient's point of view, all the preceding creates hardly an interruption in his daily life pattern. The problems and pressures of Expertland have little bearing on his existence. Life in the mental hospital goes on.

18. Overcoming Cultural and Professional Myopia in Education for Human Service *

Robert Morris

The high degree of professionalization and specialization which has characterized staff of human service organizations has created, in the following author's words, a "professional myopia." One consequence of this problem in professional nearsightedness is that we have not been aware of important changes in communities served by human service organizations. Rather, we have continued to apply relatively unchanging programs to often rapidly changing communities.

As communities, agencies, and training centers have acted to both apply a corrective lens to professional vision and corrective action to organizational programs, the very complex nature of the problem of role and organizational change has become apparent. Creating another, updated, training program for more professionals is clearly not a viable solution to this problem. Rather, a training system which reflects the problems of related human systems must be generated if meaningful change is to occur. The following article suggests some approaches which might alter our presently myopic socio-organizational vision.

A few years ago the concept of international exchange for scholars and professional persons was premised on a rather simple belief that professional and scientific personnel would enrich their views of the world by a relatively brief opportunity to learn about the conditions, practices, approaches, behaviors, and organizational structures in other cultures. Despite the social upheavals of the twentieth century, it was assumed that conditions and behaviors in each nation were sufficiently stable for an outside observer to learn from, to understand about, and to benefit from observations

*This paper was originally presented at the U.S.-Italy Conference on Future Tasks for Educational Exchange in Social Welfare, held in Rome, Italy, from June 22 to July 5, 1969.

233

of one specialized aspect of a society. At a less scholarly level, the popularity of tourism represents a search not only for new experience but also for enrichment in the lives of ordinary citizens without great academic scholarly pretensions.

New Conditions for Educational Exchange

This concept of international exchange now seems wholly inadequate for a number of reasons. Perhaps first among these reasons is our increased awareness that each individual views an alien culture through the limited perceptions of his own culture. The capacity for an outsider to learn from an alien situation is determined by the observer's ability to perceive differences and to step outside of the value constraints of his own culture. Unfortunately, most of us carry with us a predetermined image of the world—the appropriate ways in which human relations and institutions should be patterned—and judge other patterns against this model. In a sense, much exchange provides only an opportunity for viewing the mirror image of one's self. The limitations can be overcome only by combining sensitive awareness with suitable preparation for cross-national comparative observation.

A second and more complex explanation for the obsolescence of this earlier view of exchange lies in the nature of the twentieth century itself. Today, nearly all cultures and societies are experiencing upheaval and great social change. The situation I came to observe in Italy four years ago is today so much in upheaval and in the processes of alteration and change that it is extraordinarily difficult to grasp what is occurring. This difficulty in perception is often as true for one who is immersed and embedded in his own culture as it is for an outsider.

These limitations are especially true for social work, and I use "social work" here to refer to that loose-knit body of persons concerned with the improvement or melioration of the human condition. At least the limitations are true for the American social worker. In the United States, we have not only seen our professional position and our social welfare institutions shaped by our particular history, values, and political relationships but, as a profession, we have also sought to establish or to create a homogeneous professional identity. Such a uniform professional identity, especially in the early years of formation, tends to be intolerant of aspirants competing to a similar professional identity.

In the United States, our past professional formation has been based so much upon the psychological explanation of human affairs and we have been so wedded to the medical-clinical model—especially to one sub-model, the Freudian or dynamic psychological approach—that it has been extraordinarily difficult to grasp the reality of other approaches. Such other approaches can be dimly perceived in the social administration of the United Kingdom, the philosophical-analytical initiatives in Italy, or the nurse-welfare or industrial-welfare approach in France.

However, the current dissatisfaction so widespread in the world should offer us hope rather than discouragement. Dissatisfaction with existing patterns in each culture or society—patterns of thought, education, or organization—encourages the intellectual effort to break out of the straitjacket of traditional ways of viewing the world. In an era of change, the world of national societies may constitute a vast laboratory in which the socially committed of any nation may observe—even study—varieties of experiments to improve the social condition. Each social experience, or experiment, dealing with the problems of society is still shaped by the variables of history, of intellectual tradition, habit, resources, and the like. Because of this, direct copying or borrowing is neither possible nor desirable. The defects as well as the successes of each national experience can be observed and can stimulate creative innovation in the thinking of the outside observer.

This optimistic view is encouraged by reading the CENSIS report, "The Social Situation of the Country."[1] To the American reader, it is both startling and reassuring to see that this report, with very little change in language, could be distributed in the United States as a description of the malaise and confusion which confronts the American society and American institutions. In many ways, the conceptual framework in which the CENSIS report is cast constitutes a better way of viewing the American scene than many more elaborate American reports of the same situation. The "tensions" described in the CENSIS report also present the nature of the American scene today. These tensions are derived from: (1) social mobility, (2) the demand for increasing participation, (3) the movement of population groups into marginal positions in society, and (4) the demands for efficiency and rationalization in social intervention.

If I am correct in believing that the existence of disaffection is widespread across national boundaries, then the socially committed and intellectually interested in every nation may have a common cause in which they can join, even across national boundaries. I

[1]*Report on the Social Situation of the Country* (Rome, Italy: distributed by The National Council for Economy and Labor, 1968).

approach this subject from the standpoint of the American scene in order to identify areas of mutuality and common interest on which to build a more satisfactory foundation for educational exchange in social welfare. In so doing, I hope it will soon be evident that I base my hopes on a broad conception of social welfare as a profession which is intolerant of narrow professional protections but rather is concerned with the common task of satifying human wants and needs in a complex and unsettled epoch.

THE CHALLENGE TO THE WELFARE STATE

The conception of the welfare state, which has governed so much of social work throughout this century, is under the most vigorous challenge. In the United States, for example, governmental expenditures for social welfare alone represent nearly fifteen percent of the Gross National Product, or nearly fifteen percent of all the goods and services produced in the United States.[2] This expenditure has resulted in the development of a very large number of public and voluntary health and welfare agencies with large professional staffs whose activities reach into all parts of the nation and touch on the lives of almost all citizens, directly or indirectly.

But, as in Italy, the dissatisfaction with the social conditions has increased, almost in direct ratio to the increasing investment in welfare. Social work has lead in the demand that more and more funds be invested in welfare, and social work education has encouraged this view. It is upsetting to schools of social work and to social work educators in the United States, as it is to other citizens, to realize that there is no clear correlation between such an expenditure of funds and human satisfaction or well being.

This overturning of our most basic conception derives from a sudden realization that our usual solution—an even more massive expenditure of funds—has most serious consequences for the state of society. What we begin to perceive is that a vastly increased rate of expenditure also requires a radical alteration in the political-social balance of the society. The wealthy are not the only group

[2] See "Social Welfare Expenditures, 1929-1967," *Social Security Bulletin*, Vol. 30, No. 12 (December, 1967), p. 11. In these tabulations, the term social welfare expenditures under grovernmental auspices includes payments for all forms of social insurance, public welfare, and health and medical programs not paid for by the individual consumer, verterans' programs, education, housing, rehabilitation, child welfare, and the like. This represents an increase of 700% from 1890, when the estimated expenditures were 2.4% of the Gross National Product, and 100% increase in the last twenty years alone when, in 1947, the estimated expenditures were 7.8% of the GNP.

who resists a mayor redistribution in society; even one segment of the working class resists a shift in favor of the most outcast.

We now know that there is nothing in our social work education which teaches us about either the consequences of, or even the approaches to, so radical a readjustment. On the contrary, social work education in the United States has build most of its intellectual enterprise upon the firm foundation of a network of established welfare and health institutions supported by ever-increasing expenditures. Social work education, as well as the social work profession, has taught the protection of these institutions against attack from unsympathetic sources. The result has been to bind and tie social work ever more closely to established forms and structures. With each gain, the prospect of serious reform in our social institutions has receded further into the background.

To nations where social work does not yet have this firmly established institutional and establishment base for its operations, our experience may be instructive. It may also be instructive for those of us in the United States to study alternative approaches to social work education used in nations where this establishment bias has not yet become a professional commonplace style of thought.

A second challenge, both to the welfare state concept and to social work education, is found in new ad hoc governmental attempts to deal with persisting social problems—problems which have persisted despite the remedial efforts of the past. The clearest example of innovations from our own government lies in the so-called "war on poverty." Although the dimensions of this federal program and its underlying conceptions differ substantially from the situation in Italy, I believe that the consequences may be compared with the Italian efforts in dealing with poverty in southern Italy through the *Cassa Per il Mezzogiorno*.

The pragmatic problem-solving approach in the United States omits adequate attention to goals and ideology, nevertheless, the war on poverty did have a relatively clear foundation in social analysis and an adequately linked program based upon a limited analysis. What was lacking was an explicit statement of the philosophical base, or the societal aims, which underlay the social analysis.

The war on poverty program set in motion actions designed: (1) to increase the bargaining power of the disadvantaged and the poor in the population and to make more visible their wants and demands and opinions at all decision-making centers of power; (2) to introduce a modest program of job development, job training, and child care on the assumption that only lack of skill and motivation stand between poverty and affluence; and (3) to search for a substitute for the social work-created institution of the past—namely, public assistance.

This series of federal initiatives, while not massive, has forced a substantial reconsideration of curriculum by all schools of social work. The voice of the disadvantaged did have some small place in former studies, although there was very little which prepared social workers for any significant transfer of authority from the elite in society to the underprivileged. The other remedies—a negative income tax, job development, training, and the like—have always been a peripheral interest in social work schools.

A third upset to conventional ways of thinking is found in the youth protest and student power movements in the American universities. Although the specific objectives and the initiating causes are different, it cannot be denied that expressions of student dissatisfaction have played an important part in the unfreezing of university activities in many countries—certainly in the United States. This is not to suggest that this thawing of the university environment has produced a satisfactory substitute for the old situation. On the contrary, we seem to be living in a period of uncertainty, anxiety, and chaos.

Students, however, in many universities now have moved into an effective position to modify the nature of the curriculum, the setting of qualification standards, and the selection of faculty. Faculty committees which design curriculum now have voting student members; the decision about what type of research in which a school engages is determined jointly by faculty and students; evaluation of faculty for promotion is shared by students. This alteration in the decision-making and governing structure of American universities is already having an effect on the response of schools of social work to these disturbing and upsetting events.

THE REACTION OF SOCIAL WORK EDUCATION IN THE UNITED STATES

The reaction of American educational institutions to these conditions is most easily perceived in a series of pragmatic case reports. However, I have attempted to derive some general tendencies which will, I hope, indicate whether change in a period of crisis in one nation lends itself to cross-national exchange and communication. This summation is not intended to serve as a new or revised philosphical foundation for American schools of social work. I doubt if any pattern has yet been fixed, although some competing ideological approaches may be discerned.

The Quest for Social Purpose

One result of the dissatisfaction has been a demand by students to turn the university's interest to the outer community. The university is being asked to use its resources to attack the social ills of society. This had already occurred for the technical and scientific faculties' work for the military, industrial, and medical worlds. The new demand is to reverse the priorities and concentrate on poverty, racism, and social alienation.

In some schools, individual faculty members and students already act as technical advocates for disadvantaged groups in designing plans to rebuild the centers of our cities, to improve the occupational structure of our society, to alter the income maintenance provisions, or to plan new housing. A few schools of social work are even operating small welfare service centers and placing students among political and clientele groups where this ferment is most active. But what is now demanded is much more than the curriculum *in toto* be turned to such concerns.

Unfortunately, active proponents of this direction are only able to ask the questions, to make the demands. We have not yet evolved the ways and means by which our curricula and universities should, in fact, proceed. We are at a turning point in which uncertainty reigns, while faculties and students—and both rich and poor citizens— try to create new institutions in answer to two questions: "What kind of world can we fashion" and "How shall we proceed?" The future cannot be predicted with confidence, for a reaction might return us all to former methods just as readily as reform may project us into new directions.

The Widening of Educational Horizons

The monolithic framework for social work education has, by and large, been replaced by a more complex approach, although this shift has not yet found reality in all institutions in all parts of the country.

We once relied upon a thorough grounding in dynamically oriented psychology for all social workers. This was expanded to a curriculum based on the foundation of human growth and development. However, the social and structural aspects of the subject continued to be overshadowed by the massive time devoted to psychological understanding. In such a curriculum, a scattering of peripheral courses were offered dealing with the community and group relationships and with sociological theory. Hardly any time was devoted to political or economic science.

Today, there is a great ferment in almost all schools to experiment with multiple paths of education. Some schools offer two or more paths of training; a few schools specialize, one concentrating on social policy, another on community organization, and a third on the individual psychological approaches. More schools experiment with ways to conceptualize a generic technical and scientific approach to social welfare, which will provide a foundation for all forms of practice. Other schools admit candidly that such uniformity is now no longer feasible and argue that the richness and range of human knowledge does not permit such simplification. In the latter schools, it is possible for candidates for the social work degree to spend their entire professional study learning about social policy making and planning and organization.

There are a number of signs of a shift in the direction of social work education:

1. A recent study reports that 26% of all full-time classroom instructors teach in the area of social policy (and social services) and another 20% teach in the area of community organization and administration.[3] These figures do not indicate how sophisticated or how extensive this teaching is, but the fact that so large a proportion of faculty are beginning to teach in these hitherto peripheral areas indicates the extensiveness of new interest in policy planning and organization.

At the same time, the tensions of American schools can be seen by the fact that 82% of all students are still concentrating in casework and only 5% of all students have yet selected community organization and administration.

2. The enrichment of the educational process is also seen by the fact that 43% of all full-time classroom instruction is now offered by persons holding a Ph.D. Only 30% of all of those teaching Ph.D.'s were earned in the field of social work. The balance were earned in the fields of law, education, the social sciences, medicine, economics, political science, and philosophy. This infusion of scholarship from a variety of backgrounds is undoubtedly a recognition by the schools of social work of the complex phenomena for which they are training their graduates. Unfortunately, this distribution is still unbalanced; only 3% of the Ph.D.'s teaching in American social work schools earned their degrees in philosophy, history, or political science.

[3]Richard Onken, *A Survey of Faculty in Graduate Schools of Social Work* (New York: Council on Social Work Education, 1968).

3. The Council on Social Work Education has recently completed an extensive study of the curriculum for community organization alone which has, in this single area of social work, identified and proposed alternate levels of practice and study. It hastens the development of a more complex and sophisticated curriculum.

4. To an increasing extent, field experience is now located at the center of social action and policy making. Students are assigned as assistants to senators, congressmen, city councilmen, and mayors. They develop data and propose alternative approaches for social problems which such legislators and public administrators confront. Students are also assigned to work with groups of the disadvantaged and the poor to help them organize themselves; other students are working actively to organize public support for the programs which such groups of the disadvantaged advance on their own behalf.

New Ideological Foundations

In the past, social work education frequently talked about social reform and action, but its major effort was to staff established institutions and to protect their purposes. In recent years, schools of social work have given a new interpretation to the concept of the social worker as the "change agent" at all levels of social organization—the individual, the family, the small group, and the community. It is now commonplace for social work education to stress that its product must be concerned with the transformation of agencies as well as the transformation of individuals and with the transformation of society in conjunction with others, as much as with the transformation of agency programs.

Unfortunately, and realistically, this renewed interest in the philosophical concept of change is still immature. School curricula give little attention to the nature of the society which is to be created. There is very little basic challenge to the underlying social, economic, and political structure which may be the object of change. As a matter of fact, the object of change is often very small and is assumed to take place without fundamental re-ordering of society.

A part of the student unrest is based on a demand that these larger considerations of social change become the major object of educational attention. Such students are no longer concerned primarily with the ethics of social work practice nor even about the place of social welfare in society. Rather, they are asking with increasing persistence "What is to be the nature of the society we wish to have about us?" The search for answers to this question are frequently worked out in a kind of "underground" fashion through discussions which take place among students and through informal colloquia involving students and faculty where general questions of value are discussed with limited didactic structure. In a more formal sense, students here and there are demanding courses in epistemology, logic, and the like. More students are demanding that teaching of social change include *all* approaches to reform and change, including the approaches of violent confrontation and rebellion.

It cannot yet be said with certainty what any school's response will be to this demand. Only one thing is certain—there will be renewed attention to the reform tradition of social work, coupled with an insistence that the reshaping of society be considered in a much wider analytical and philosophical context than has been the case in the past.

This represents one of the areas in which the Italian educational experience, with its attention to philosophical and analytical development, may have a very useful contribution to make to the American scene as a complement to the ad hoc problemsolving solutions to which we are so given.

An Interest in Structural Change

Although the educational response to the demand for radical change is as yet imperfect, the commitment to structural change as one form of social development is very clear. This can be seen in two developments. First, schools of social work now give substantial attention to new approaches to the redistribution of income through the negative income tax or a guaranteed wage as an advance over the past public welfare and social insurance schemes developed during the past century.

Of equal interest is the amount of attention now given to the attempts to alter the decision-making structure of American social work institutions. It is no longer possible to ignore the social policy consequences of several major governmental enactments. All public assistance programs are legally required to have citizen advisory boards. It is now required that at least a third of the members of these advisory boards be recipients themselves—the poor who are on relief. The Office of Economic Opportunity, with its wide network of local action programs, requires that a dominant voice be that of poor residents, whether or not they are on relief. The

Model Cities experiment, in which an attempt is made to reconstruct the character of poor ghetto neighborhoods, requires that the administrative agency take no action without the approval of residents affected. In some communities, this has gone so far that all major development programs are submitted to referendum vote.

This significant shift from a reliance on the elite to the consumer or recipient is only one minor illustration of the structural changes being fought over and fought about in America and in its universities. One university has provided the intellectual spearhead for a national welfare rights union of the agency clientele, while another has taught the techniques of "controlled hatred of injustice."

The Absence of Technological Competence

There is a growing recognition that these reforming, and even radicalizing, tendencies lack a technical or scientific underpinning which can translate general philosophical considerations into application. In other words, the American penchant for technical solution is also challenged, at least in the area of social relationships. There is now a burgeoning of interest in new kinds of technical and scientific tools which can be placed in the hands of social workers who will be concerned with social policy, administration planning, and community organization. These technical and scientific elements have several forms. One involves a reintroduction of political theory and political science analysis into the curriculum of schools of social work. Even more interesting, however, is the attempt to adapt more rigorous technical tools for evaluation and measurement.

A task force of the federal government, with the assistance of a major foundation, has begun a systematic analysis of social indicators in an attempt to ascertain whether indicators and measurements of social change can, in time, be as effective for policymaking as are economic indicators in the area of economic development and planning. Despite widespread general enthusiasm, these studies indicate that, as yet, there are no wholly satisfactory indicators applicable to the social welfare enterprise. We can describe certain social phenomena in a limited way: the population and income distribution, production of goods, employment, family structure, external religious observance, consumption patterns, illness prevalence, and educational achievement. Not only are these indicators crude and imprecise, we *cannot* give human significance and meaning to these indicators. And we cannot project the consequences of these facts into the future. They tell us at best where we have come from, not what we are heading toward. Until we can give human social and predictive meaning to such data, we are at the elementary stage of social renewal.

New approaches to the analysis of systems are being studied. It is now recognized that in most advanced societies, social institutions, agencies, and organizations constitute a rough system to deal with general social problems such as poverty, deviant behavior, and the like. From general systems theory and from engineering have evolved the means for establishing the boundaries of such systems, for studying how they function, for evaluating how agencies affect each other, and for following and tracing the course of consumers or clients through the maze of agency services.

The CENSIS Report, which refers to the inefficiency of the social structure for welfare, applies equally well to the United States. The complexity of agency regulations and relationships is frequently so great that not even the expert is aware of the interrelationships of one element with the rest of the system. We already need super-experts to give information to other information specialists. Here, the much abused and criticized computer has begun to appear as a valuable ally, not because it takes decisions out of the hands of human beings, but rather because it permits the rapid organization of an enormous amount of information about vast numbers of persons and thus permits human beings to make more intelligent judgments.

The techniques for systems analysis have an additional function. They assist professional personnel to generate more varied approaches to a common goal. Rather than teaching, as we once did, that a given problem has a given satisfactory programmatic solution, it is now recognized that each social problem may have a variety of possible and alternative approaches. These need to be identified and judged by welfare specialists so that any decision -making apparatus can choose the most satisfactory. Unfortunately, unless a variety of approaches are both developed and evaluated, policy and program decisions will still be made on the basis of prejudice and historical bias. New but poorly developed devices, such as the analysis of the ratio between costs and benefits, are now being tested out and are even taught in a few schools. Finally, the training of competent social research personnel has increased. Over 400 research-qualified Ph.D. degrees have been awarded. In many schools, complex methods of correleation and regression and matrix analysis are now taught in addition to the methods of field and survey research. Computer techniques are now available to many social work schools.

New Career Patterns

These events, which have been so briefly sketched, have resulted in a fundamental reordering of the whole career conception for social welfare. This has moved in two directions.

First, there is the demand that the content and quality of education at the professional degree level be improved. The professional degree serves two different ends. A significant part of professional education, although not all of it, needs to be directed towards the production of persons competent either to manage the large establishment already described, to plan systematically for the innovation of new programs, or to provide leadership in the construction of significant social changes. The professional degree is now concerned with personnel for these functions. The second direction is concerned with production of highly skilled clinical personnel capable of competing with physicians, psychiatrist, and psychologists.

There is also a move in social work today to open up more and more opportunities for subprofessional and paraprofessional workers trained at less than the professional degree level. The field of social welfare is now being flooded with evidence from experimental projects which indicate that many of the tasks previously performed solely by the professional social worker can be performed with equal and sometimes greater satisfaction by persons with only a baccalaureate degree or with a high school education. These subprofessional personnel can benefit from certain kinds of specialized study.

This devolution of professional skill to less skilled personnel has already proceeded far in the fields of medicine and nursing, where many functions, only a few years ago considered legally the responsibility of the M.D. and the registered nurse, are now being performed with great confidence and satisfaction by nurses' aides and medical assistants.

The adaptation in the field of social welfare to this kind of system is beginning to gather momentum for two reasons, First, many agencies find it impossible to carry out their functions with only professionally trained personnel who are in short supply, and they employ and train subprofessional workers. There is also greater pressure to employ persons from certain cultural and economic backgrounds so they might work among their friends and neighbors. The community mental health movement in the United States has found that, for many mental health purposes so-called indigenous workers recrited from the ranks of the target population—the poor or handicapped—are capable of performing functions which augment the talents of the psychiatrist, social worker, and psychiatric nurse.

These trends are beginning to take shape and are altering the membership standards of the professional association, although the final form of the career pattern is not yet evident. There is still hardly any provision for continuous movement up the career ladder from the lowest subprofessional category into the professional level of study and practice. It is also very difficult to arrange for the transfer of subprofessional personnel from one type of organization to another, since the credentialling and accrediting processes are not standarized.

It is also difficult to perceive exactly the role to be performed by schools of social work in providing for this more intricate career pattern. However, there are now 222 baccalaureate training centers for social work personnel, which are accredited by the Council on Social Work Education. It remains only for such schools to strengthen their educational component and to absorb certain tasks which have hitherto been reserved solely for the advanced professional school. Once this is achieved, it is quite likely that employing agencies will draw more and more upon this reserve of pre-professional personnel. A number of junior colleges are also experimenting with vocational-level training for social work.

Some agencies and some faculties of schools of social work also undertake in-service training programs of a substantial nature for employees with a high school degree or less. In Massachusetts, the Department of Public Health has a systematic training program which uses professional staff and faculties from schools of social work to accredit social work technicians who have a high school degree or less. These employees are now in substantial demand among a number of the large public agencies.

At least two universities have advanced plans for opening up the career ladder between various levels so that it will be possible for employees to enter at the lowest level and to move systematically up the ladder by successive leaves of absence for study. In one such plan, a housekeeper may, by steps, become a child welfare aide, a nursery school aide, a nursery school teacher, a social worker, and a supervisor.

Lest this conception seem far-fetched, attention might be directed to the class origins of many social workers in the United States. The recent survey of faculties of schools of social work notes that present social work school faculties are drawn from families where less than 10% of the parents were college graduates.[4] Over 50%

[4]Ibid.

of the fathers of present instructors in schools of social work were either farmers or semi-skilled workers. The possibility for upward mobility should not be denied a current generation simply because earlier generations made so rapid a transition from the blue collar to the middle class.

In this respect at least, the tendency in American education to provide high school, college, and university level opportunities for approximately 50% of the college-age population represents a difference from the more elitist educational systems in other countries. However, the fact remains that even within this system it has been necessary to draw upon manpower with less than a college education in order to man the human services agencies.

INTERNATIONAL STUDY IN SOCIAL WELFARE

Thus far I have considered some general developments in education. There have also been shifts of a different type in programs of international study.

The American professional schools have, for a long time, believed in the value of international studies, but serious and significant programs have not developed in the curricula. In part, this is due to a limitation of resources, in part to a parochial concentration on the welfare problems of the United States scene. It also is due to a confusion of aims. For some time the American schools have sought for an enlargement of international understanding and enlightenment, but the methods have been unbalanced—provision is made for foreign workers to *study* in the American schools while American faculty members go to *teach* at foreign universities.

A few attempts to evaluate this program indicate that the American education has not been transferable to either work or practice in another country, and it has had limited utility. Fortunately, the personal and professional relationships which have resulted from this exchange have laid the foundation for better exchange arrangements which are beginning to appear in a few American universities.

There are four tasks which the present crisis in U.S. social work places before us: (a) the need to renew and reinvigorate our professional foundation by comparative analysis with the experience in other cultures; (b) a better match between theoretical analysis and the pragmatic problemsolving which underlies professional preparation; (c) the development of a more varied professional foundation for the management of social welfare institutions in the modern society; and (d) the evolution of scientific and technological tools and concepts which have widely generalizable utility.

To all of these tasks, an international exchange program can contribute—but only if the following conditions are met: (1) that provision is made for long-term continuity between institutions in the two or more countries, (2) a concentration on professional and scientific enrichment among several disciplines in order that the gap which separates conceptual analysis and technological competence analysis and technological competence is closed, and (3) that faculties be exchanged in *both* directions for purposes of teaching rather than perpetuating the present situation in which American faculty goes abroad to teach whereas foreign faculty comes to the United States to study.

19. Purists and Politicians*

Don K. Price

The following article examines the roles of scientists and scientific organizations in public policy. As social institutions, scientific associations are faced with the same incompatible alternatives as all other organizations. They can remain removed from the rigors of politics and public policy, demonstrate enlightened self-interest, advocate broadly within their competence, or they can take a general political stance. At issue is the degree of compatibility among these various alternative roles. Can they retain credibility as a scientific organization and simultaneously extend themselves into political and policy issues beyond their professional competence? As the American Medical Association increasingly proclaimed its theories of economics, it simultaneously lost credibility to speak on medically specific issues.

As private citizens, as nonscientists in politically-oriented organizations, scientists or other specialists have rights equal to all others, but possess no special credence because of their technical competence.

Yet, can those substantially responsible for the exponential rate of technological change remain removed from the subsequent consequences of social changes? And, what do they have to contribute, individually or collectively, to the resolution of these problems? Can they assist in combatting the increasing impersonality, alienation, and dehumanization of the human spirit? Can they help to bring balance between the material and the humane?

The role of science in public policy is to offer an additional analytic technique to the already complicated existing panoply of solution mechanisms. It can offer the strategy of knowledge accumulation, the spirit of analysis, of synthesis, of reductionism to the sharper identification of alternatives and the implications of changing technology.

Thus Price poses some of the challenging issues of the day. Is science

---

*This is the text of the AAAS presidential address, delivered 28 December 1968 at the Dallas meeting.

249

to be the current fallen idol? Are there any new panaceas to which man can hitch his destiny? Scientists per se *have no magic to offer. Science does not offer political or policy insights.*

Sometimes the tone of a headline tells you more than the news. Last summer a New York *Times* headline read "Pure Physicists Stay That Way: Vote to Remain Out of Politics." The story was a straightforward account of the decision by the members of the American Physical Society that it would adopt no resolutions on political issues (1). The flavor of the headline suggested a great deal more: that the typical newspaper readers and perhaps even a good many scientists are still inclined to think that the moral obligation of a scientist is to remain aloof from policy issues and political controversy.

Since I applauded the tactical decision of the physicists but deplored the implications of the headline, it occurred to me that this apparent contradiction was worth some further thought. Perhaps it is the crux of the apparent dilemma which the entire scientific community shares with the physicists. The dilemma is ages old—the dilemma between truth and power, or, rather, between starving in the pursuit of truth and compromising truth to gain material support. But it takes its new form in the dilemma posed for the scientific community as it now comes under attack simultaneously from two sides—from a political reaction and from a new kind of rebellion.

This attack from the two extremes makes it hard for the scientific community to continue its traditional political strategy, especially since—as sometimes happens in politics—the two extremes may in effect be allies, even though superficially in conflict.

The traditional polticial strategy of scientists has been to keep their sights set firmly on the advancement of basic knowledge in the conviction that their mode of thinking is in the vanguard of political and economic progress, and at the same time to persuade politicians and philanthropists to support science for its indirect payoffs in power and wealth.

This strategy was based on a belief in automatic progress that had its origins in the same way of thinking that produced economic laissez-faire. Scientific knowledge, like economic initiative, could be relied on to produce progress if government could be persuaded not to interfere, except with the necessary subsidies.

The Two-Front Attack

But now, under attack on two fronts, scientists find this strategy harder to sustain.

On one side, the attack comes from a political reaction, which has three main purposes. Politicians want to cut down on the appropriations for research, to have more of the money spent on practical technology and less on academic theory, and to break down the degree of autonomy which the leaders of the scientific community gained a generation ago in the procedures by which research grants are distributed. On each of these points the reaction conforms to the best American tradition of the political pork barrel.

On the other side, the rebellion is a cosmopolitan, almost world-wide, movement. One is tempted to identify it with its violent and fantastic and adolescent fringe—flower power and student insurrec-tions. Obviously, the young are the ones who charge the cops in Chicago and barricade the buildings at Columbia or Berkeley. They have to be: my contemporaries no longer have the muscle and the wind for such exertions. Today's youth are indeed the student activists, just as today's youth are the infantry in Vietnam. But it would be as much a mistake to give the student leaders credit for the ideology of the rebellion as to give the G.I.'s credit for the war plans of the Joint Chiefs.

The ideology of the rebellion is confused; you can find in it little clarity or consistency of purpose. Its mood and temper reflect the ideas of many middel-aged intellectuals who are anything but violent revolutionaries. From the point of view of scientists, the most important theme in the rebellion is its hatred of what it sees as an impersonal technological society that dominates the individual and reduces his sense of freedom. In this complex system, science and technology, for from being considered beneficent instruments of progress, are identified as the intellectual processes that are at the roots of the blind forces of oppression.

For example, André Malraux, denying that the problem is one of conflict between the generations, says that "the most basic prob-lem of our civilization" is that it is a "a civilization of machines," and that "we, for the first time, have a knowledge of matter and a knowledge of the universe, which . . . suppresses man" (2).

Jacques Ellul, one of the heroes of alienated young Europeans, presents a more systematic indictment of scientists as sorcerers who are totally blind to the meaning of the human adventure, whose system of thought is bringing about "a dictatorship of test tubes rather than hobnailed boots" (3).

The theme was echoed by Erich Fromm in his support of Senator McCarthy's presidential candidacy, in a public protest against the type of society in which "technical progress becomes the source of all values" and we see as a consequence "the complete alienation and dehumanization of man" (4).

Herbert Marcuse, who is of course the favorite philosopher of the rebels, reduces the issue to its fundamental point (5): "the mathematical character of modern science determines the range and direction of its creativity, and leaves the nonquantifiable qualities of *humanitas* outside the domain of exact science . . . [which then] feels the need for redemption by coming to terms with the 'humanities.' "

In one sense, the challenge does indeed come from the humanities. The student rebels and their faculty sympathizers, at home and abroad, are found more conspicuously in the departments of humanities and in schools of theology than in the natural sciences or engineering (6). If the danger comes from the humanities, however, it comes not because they are politically powerful but, rather, because, as Mr. Marcuse suggests, they may have convinced scientists themselves that science is an inhuman discipline. The case for laissez-faire vanished when businessmen themselves became aware that unregulated initiative brought depressions and economic disaster. The potential effects of the power created by modern science and technology are so obviously dangerous to the modern world—whether in terms of the cataclysm of war or the slower but equally disastrous degradation of the environment—that it would not be surprising if even scientists should wonder whether we have been reduced to these dangers by the reductionism of their system of thought.

The Pressure from the Reaction

Most scientists try to avoid thinking about this basic problem very much because they are apt just now to worry more about the reaction than the rebellion. For the reaction touches sensitive budgetary nerves in anyone who is a laboratory director or a department chairman or even an aspirant to a fellowship.

I think this choice is a mistake. The reaction is a tolerable discomfort, the rebellion fundamental challenge—and a challenge that poses problems scientists should think about critically rather than dismiss with contempt.

It is easy and misleading to blame the reaction on the Vietnam war and therefore to sympathize with the antimilitary sentiments of the rebellion. But this view overlooks the facts that two earlier wars produced more money and autonomy, not less, for science, and that the civilian agencies of government (including those with some of the most generous and humane purposes) have been more likely than the military to insist that research funds be spent on practical problems, and that they be distributed more evenly among universities and regions.

Indeed, it seems to me that the reaction mainly uses the war as an excuse, and it is hard to see how the reaction could have been so long delayed. In slowing down the rise in appropriations, congressmen were reacting naturally to the projection of curves on the budgetary graphs that lumped basic science together with engineering development. In emphasizing application, they responded to the salesmanship of scientists who told them in congressional hearings a great deal about how science would make us healthy and wealthy and very little about how it would make us wise. And, in their avarice on behalf of thier own districts and institutions, congressmen differed only in degree from scientists themselves. In these practical ways, the reaction is in the highest tradition of the English-speaking scientific world, which has always assumed that science was justified in large part by its contribution to material welfare—the tradition of Francis Bacon, who caught cold and died while trying to learn how to refrigerate poultry, and of the Royal Society, with its initial interest in "Manufactures, Mechanick practices, Engynes, and Inventions," and of Ben Franklin's American Philosophical Society, "held at Philadelphia for promoting useful knowledge."

The Novelty of the Rebellion

But the rebellion is a different matter. It is the first international radical political movement for two or three centuries (I am tempted to say since Francis Bacon) that does not have material progress as its purpose. Far from proposing to use science and technology to improve the material welfare of the poor, it rejects technological progress as a political goal. Far from calling on government to distribute the fruits of technology more equitably, it denounces big organization in government and business indiscriminately. For three centuries science has worked on the comfortable assumption that it could pursue fundamental truth and at the same time contribute to human welfare and humane values. Since Bacon, revolutionary leaders have accepted this assumption and considered science to be in the vanguard of political progress. But now the rebels say that science, by its intrinsic nature, has reduced itself to an inhumane mode of thought, and our polity to an engine of oppression, and so they conclude that humane feelings demand the overthrow of the whole system, if necessary by an irrational rebellion.

Even though many of the young rebels call themselves Marxists, the guiding spirit of the rebellion is as much in conflict with Marxism-Leninism as with Western democracy—perhaps more so, because communism believes that science can provide the basis for political values, and the New Left considers the degree of scientific influence over our political system a disaster. Communism is a system of rigorous discipline and meticulous dogma; the New Left has neither. It is more like a religious heresy, renouncing a concern for power and wealth, than like a political movement, and even its emphasis on drugs and sex is reminiscent of the antinomian rebellions of the Middle Ages (7).

The rebels are right when they complain of the symptoms of sickness in modern society—symptoms that afflict the Communist as well as the capitalist world. We have not learned how to make our technological skills serve the purposes of humanity, or how to free men from servitude to the purposes of technological bureaucracies. But we would do well to think twice before agreeing that these symptoms are caused by reductionism in modern science, or that they would be cured by violence in the name of brotherhood or love.

As the first step toward a diagnosis of our problem, we must admit that, as scientists, we have not been very clear in the past as to the basic relation of science to politics. When the rebels charge science with destroying freedom by subverting moral values or controlling policy decisions, we cannot dismiss the charge by repeating the old principle that political authorities determine policies on the basis of philosophical or moral values, and that scientific knowledge only tells us how best to carry out these policies—that is, tells us the best means to those ends. This reply will no longer do. In Marxist countries official dogma holds that science determines the basic values, and in America many scientists have been hypocritical on the issue: they use the old formula as a defense for public relations, even though they realize that science has, and must have, a profound influence on values, and are inclined to believe that science could provide the answers to policy questions if politicians were not so stupid.

It is high time that we become more critical—instead of hypo-critical—in facing this fundamental issue. As we do so, we should remember that the relationship of science to politics has at least three aspects. They are knowledge, institutions, and policy.

Knowledge

Let us consider knowledge first. The way people think about politics is surely influenced by what they implicitly believe about what they know and how they know it—that is, about how they acquire knowledge, and why they believe it. In traditional political systems—a few still persist in the world— issues were decided on the basis of immemorial custom, religious tradition, or the divinely sanctioned will of a ruler. Before this could change to a system in which elected assemblies could consider facts—perhaps even on the basis of scientific evidence—and then deliberately enact policies, a revolution in the nature of knowledge had to take place. That long slow revolution went along with the progress of science, and the main line of progress has of course been that of *reduction*— the change from systems of thought that were concrete but complex and disorderly, and that often confused what *is* with what ought to be, to a system of more simple and general and provable concepts.

It is clear, as Mr. Marcuse points out, that this reduction of knowledge to its abstract and quantitative bases is a caluclating approach to reality that makes no allowance for humane sentiments or moral judgments. It is also clear that serious practical politicians who disapprove in theory of Mr. Marcuse may agree with him in practice, and may fear that reductionism will impair our political responsibility. For example, leading candidates for political office have charged that the Supreme Court's weakness for sociology and statistics is eroding the moral fiber of the nation, and congres-smen in committee hearings have expressed concern that the new mathematical techniques of systems analysis may dominate our strategic decisions.

But it is not all clear to me that reductionism is a threat to political freedom or responsibility. In their practical political behavior, scien-tists are not quite so consistent or doctrinaire. To say that science feels the need for redemption seems to me (if I may use a technical literary term in addressing a scientific audience) a pathetic fallacy. Science feels nothing. Scientists have feelings, and on political issues their feelings seem to me to be just as varied and moralistic as anyone else's.

On a more theoretical level, it seems to me that reductionism has not been pushing scientists generally toward a belief that science as such can solve the issues in which the average man is most interested, or can determine the nature of the political system. Although other branches of science admit their growing reliance on mathematics and physics, they seem no more likely than they were a century ago—perhaps less likely—to assume that they can solve all their problems by reducing their disciplines to atomic or subatomic bases.

The notion that scientific advance cuts down the freedom of the human spirit, and reduces the range of choice open to mankind, is an obsolete idea; on the contrary, every new grand simplification opens up a new range of complex questions for exploration. Man found it hard to change from the astronomical conception of a closed world to one of an infinite universe; the notion that scientific advance on reductionist principles will cut down our freedom, in either intellectual or political terms, seems to me the result of hanging onto an obsolete and narrowly mechanistic 19th-century conception of science.

Before we decide that the remedy for our present disorders is to put moral sentiments back into science, it may help us to remember that science is not the only mode of thought which has gone through a reductionist trend and then found that the simpler abstract concepts provided less specific guides to action than one might hope. If reduction is the change from complex and disorderly ideas that confuse what *is* with what men would like, to more simple and general (if not always provable) beliefs, the change in theology from polytheism to monotheism was reductionist, and so was the change from the Ten Commandments and the intricacies of the Talmud to the simpler commandment to love God and your neighbor as yourself. And in theology, as in science, reductionism brought a shocking denial that natural laws were in harmony with human righteousness: "for He makes His sun rise on the evil and on the good, and sends rain on the just and on the unjust."

If science can learn any lesson from theology on this point, it is that reductionism does not cause the political problem, nor can it solve it. For the simple law of love was taken, over the centuries, as the antinomians' justification for the abandonment of all moral laws as well as for the rigorous moralism of Calvinist Geneva and the Spanish Inquisition, for the anarchy of the hermits and the Ranters as well as for the ruthless tyranny of the Byzantine emperors.

The trouble with reductionism, as far as politics is concerned, is not that it gives *all* the answers to the important issues but that it gives hardly any. I suspect that the current attacks on science come less from those who have always feared it than from those who were frustrated when they tried to put too much faith in it. To them, it was another god that failed. Science is quite impartial in debunking idols—its proudest claim is that it is always debunking itself.

Institutions

If we are concerned with political freedom we cannot concern ourselves only with the theory of knowledge. Reductionism in science is not the real problem. We do harm not by reducing science to its mathematical bases but only by reducing men to a concern for nothing but science. As we ponder the political status of science it may help us to recall that freedom of religion resulted less directly from the reformation of theological thought than from the competition of dissenting churches and from changes in the political system itself. That brings us to the second aspect of the relation of science to politics—institutions. And so we must face the question whether a scientific and technological establishment, or the aggregate of scientific and technological institutions, is a threat to freedom, especially because of its intimate alliance with a bureaucracy managed on scientific principles.

At the same time that science has been reducing knowledge to fewer and simpler general concepts, society has been expanding the number and the variety of the institutions that develop and apply that knowledge. From the traditional community ruled by a priest-king, combining in one set of institutions political power and the preservation and transmission of traditional knowledge, has been evolved the complex structure of modern society. This process of *specialization* has separated from the center of political power various more or less autonomous institutions that are then permitted to operate according to their own functional requirements.

The fundamental basis for the freedom of specialized institutions is that the public recognizes that they can do their particular job better for society if they are not immediately controlled by those who hold ultimate political power. The business corporation can be more efficient, the scientific laboratory can be more innovative, if it is granted substantial autonomy. And the same principle works, within limits, within the formal structure of government itself; it is the justification not only for a nonpolitical judiciary but for a professional diplomatic or military service and for a civil service run on merit principles.

But the free institutions' role in serving society is not merely to be more efficient within their specific functions. It is also to serve as a source of independent criticism of those who hold power. It is, in short, to prevent centralization of authority. Scientific and technological competence is so necessary today for understanding the complex programs of government that scientists who are employed by institutions outside the immediate executive hierarchy have an important role to play in criticizing official policy and checking centralized power.

If they are to play that role, they must be close enough to the big issues to understand them, but they must have enough independence of action to speak without fear of damage to their status or careers. But how can they be closely enough involved without sacrificing their independence? Logically, the dilemma seems absolute. The judiciary cannot get into the fight over civil rights without being accused of usurping the power of the legislature. Churchmen cannot preach social justice without coming under political attack. And scientists cannot get involved as consultants to government, or universities accept contracts for applied research, without being accused of prostituting themselves to political power.

Obviously, an institution can be more surely free of political influence if it deals with pure science and shuns the competition for power. But absolute purity is a delusion. It is a delusion partly because every institution needs material support and cannot isolate itself from the society that supports it. Even more important, absolute purity is a delusion because it is a refusal to serve one of the essential purposes of an independent and nonpolitical institution, that of providing some independent standards of criticism of public policy.

You can resolve the dilemma in one of two ways. If your approach is doctrinaire, you can try to resolve it by forcing the competing elements together within a single institutional system. Politics and religion are obviously related, so church and state cannot be separated. Economic and political power are related, so the state must own the means of production. Political decisions must be made scientifically, so science must provide a theory of politics and a methodology for deciding public issues, and then must be controlled by the state. That way, of course, lies totalitarianism.

But if you are sensitive to the danger that any single doctrine or theory may be perverted in the interests of power, you will take a more pluralistic and more discriminating approach. You can distinguish between different types and degrees of political involvement on the part of nonpolitical institutions; even more important, you can distinguish between what it is prudent and effective for an institution to do and what that institution's members are free to do in their capactiy as private citizens or as participants in other institutions. (I hope it was this line of reasoning, more than any fundamental distaste for politics, that led the American Physical Society to abstain from political resolutions.) A member of a church may also be a member of a political party, and need not expect both institutions to play the same roles. A professor in the university may also be a consultant to a research corporation or a government agency and a member of a scientific society. His freedom to play different roles in these different institutions—and to defend the autonomy of each institution against the others—is one of the most important safeguards of freedom in modern society.

Independent institutions are not, of course, the fundamental basis of freedom. Their independence comes from their roots in the way people think and what people believe. You will not want to let a university or scientific society function free from governmental direction if you think its work will immediately determine the major political decisions of the day.

We believe in free academic and scientific institutions not because we consider them irrelevant to practical political concerns but because we tacitly understand that their type of knowledge does not directly and clearly provide the answer to any complex political issue. Does this contradict the power of the reductionist approach that has given science its great effectiveness in dealing with practical as well as theoretical problems? I think not. Reduction in knowledge and specialization in the definition of institutions and their roles go hand in hand. Just as the zoologist or botanist may admit the great contributions that biochemistry and biophysics have made to biology and still see that tremendous problems remain at the more complex levels of organization, to be dealt with by different modes of thought, so the politician (and his scientific adviser) may make full use of analytical science and yet be left with difficult problems of synthetic judgment in making his decision.

The type of thought that, in the style of the Marxist dialectic, rejects traditional dogma in favor of reductionist science, and then tries to make science the basis of a new dogma, is not reductionist, but only dogmatic. Reductionist knowledge provides no rationale, and no rationalization, for centralized authority. Like the specialized institutions in which it is developed, it tends to be a check on general political power, an impediment to sovereignty rather than a tool of tyranny. Reductionism and specialization have indeed biased our political system toward some of the practical abuses of power that rebels deplore, but they have done so not by creating a centralized system. On the contrary, they have so greatly strengthened the productivity and power of specialized concentrations of economic wealth and technological competence that our general constitutional system is incapable of controlling them.

Policy

This brings me to the third aspect of the relation of science to politics—policy, or the definition of public purpose by responsible authority.

As a complex civilization has developed its system of knowledge by *reduction*, and its institutions by *specialization*, its policy has moved over the centuries toward *generalization*. The purposes of politics have broadended from the tribe to the feudal community to the nation, and are beginning dimly to be perceived in terms of world interests; they have broken down the rigid lines of caste and class, and are beginning to transcend difference of race. With almost as much difficulty, the general purposes of responsible politics must now try to control the specialized functions and institutions of government in the general interest.

This movement toward political concern for all men, and toward the sharing of power with them, was perhaps made possible by the other two aspects of politics—the reduction of knowledge to a more effective scientific basis and the transfer of specialized social functions away from the general system of sovereignty to institutions less concerned with power and more with material welfare. Without new techniques of communication to let men share ideas from place to place, and new techniques of production to give them enough material goods to share, the broadening of political concern would have been impossible.

I am also inclined to believe that this broadening of public purpose was encouraged by that earlier form of reductionism, the theological reductionism that slowly and partially converted religion from a complex of local superstitions to a broader and simpler faith. As far as the general evolution of public policy is concerned, the processes of reduction toward simpler and more fundamental ideas in science and in religion have had similar effects.

But I must qualify this assertion of faith with a cynical concession.

Science has an intellectual advantage over religion: a reductionist science comes out with grand generalities in the form of mathematical equations that the layman reveres because he cannot understand them; a reductionist religion comes out with grand generalities in the form of platitudes that only embarrass the layman because he thinks he understands them all too well. For example, the tough-minded ghost writers for one of our leading politicians, I am told, were always annoyed at being required to put into each of his speeches a reference to what they called BOMFOG—their derisive acronym for the Brotherhood of Man and the Fatherhood of God.

As scientists we are apt to take pride in this distinction: even pious people, unless they are simpleminded, can laugh at BOMFOG, but nobody makes fun of $Ehmc^2$. But such pride is ill-founded. If we ridicule BOMFOG, it is not because we do not believe in God or human brotherhood; indeed, the more we believe, the more we are likely to see that such belief does not solve practical political problems, and that a politician who appeals to such abstractions for self-serving purposes is absurd. It seems obvious to us that $Ehmc^2$, while it may be the fundamental equation of atomic energy, does not tell us even how to make atomic bombs, much less how to get international agreement against their use; no politician would win votes by using a basic scientific formula as an incantation.

But this is a parochial idea. We may not make a political slogan out of a scientific concept, but others do. We find it hard to imagine the political quarrels that took place in Russia over the scientific philosophy of Mach or Einstein (8), or to understand how Societ scientists give credit for their discoveries to Marxist-Leninist doctrine, and Chinese scientists give credit to the thoughts of Mao. But, at least in Russia, the more sophisticated scientists react to the scientific dialectic the way we react to BOMFOG— with an appropriate mixture of reverence and ridicule.

If, as Americans, we have escaped the Communist habit of muddling scientific theory with political practice, we cannot claim too much credit. We had been inoculated, so to speak, by the English-speaking historical culture against the translation of the great simple truths into practical policy. We had tried that under Puritanism —under Oliver Cromwell and John Winthrop—and had had enough. So Jefferson, as clearly as Burke, was against the Worship of Reason in the French Revolution, and T. H. Huxley opposed Comte's conversion of science into a political dogma—the dogma (which Lenin later enforced) that diversity of opinion was no more to be tolerated in politics than in chemistry.

With respect to knowledge and institutions, politics becomes more civilized as it moves in the analytical direction—toward reduction and specialization. But policy is a synthetic prosess: generalization requires more than analytical skills. Indeed, it demands special care with respect to analysis and specialization, not to prevent but to control and use them, and not to be misled by thinking that any one type of basic knowledge or institutional skill will solve the problems of a complex political organization. Reduction is the prescription for basic knowledge, but reductionism—taken neat— can be poisonous for policy.

America is not entirely free of the idea that some specific formula will guarantee our political salvation. The president of the AAAS gets frequent letters outlining such schemes. If I were not too honest to steal such secrets from their authors, I could tell you how to provide unlimited energy without cost, and thus eliminate poverty, and how to remove all feelings of hatred and aggression, and thus guarantee universal peace. But it is typical, I think, that most of those American scientists whom their colleagues consider crackpots are interested, not in basic theory or ideology, but in gadgetry—in finding gimmicks to cure the world's ills.

Pragmatic Reductionism

This taste for the so-called "practical," of course, the crackpot shares with his fellow countrymen. In America, we are not dialetical materialists, only practical materialists. We do not convert our science into political faith—only our technology into business profits. We do not make our political theory into a revolutionary crusade; we only assume that technical assistance and more calories will make peasants contented, and that B-52's are cost-effective in pacifying jungle villages, and that welfare payments will remove racial hate in our urban ghettos.

The philosophers who blame such blunders on scientific reductionism—who believe that the mathematical and fundamental approach to knowledge is the basic flaw in modern politics—are themselves reducing the problem to a more abstract level than is useful. We get into political difficulties less because our method of knowing is wrong than because we put too much confidence in specialized programs and institutions and show too little concern for the processes of government that relate those specialities to general policy. It is true, of course, that many political controversies are over meaningless issues or insoluble problems, and new "technological fixes" [as Alvin Weinberg calls them (9)] are often useful ways out. But this approach will work best if it is tried by some responsible authority who is thinking about the problem as a whole, as a part of the general political system; it can be disastrous if it is peddled to politicians by a special interest in the business or bureaucratic world that is concerned only with increasing its own profits or professional influence.

To deal with any public issue of any consequence, we need to bring science and politics together in all their aspects. We need more precise knowledge. We need more effective institutions. And we need both the will and the competency required for the synthesis of general policy. Of these three, the most difficult is the policy aspect, for generalization cannot be reduced to precise techniques, or delegated to a specialized profession or institution.

But synthesis and analysis are not incompatible processes of thought, any more than facts and values are totally separated from each other. The new techniques for the analysis of complex systems developed by mathematicians, physicists, econimists, and other scientists have become the most powerful tools for the critical study of the components of policy, and hence for the development of general policies.

You cannot synthesize a sensible policy unless you have first analyzed the problem. Reductionism is not the enemy of humane political thought; it is the first practical step toward it. To take both steps is hard work, and requires the scientist to share the complexities and uncertainties that harass the politician, and to join in compromises that offend the purist in either science or morals.

From these uncertainties, the human mind is tempted to seek refuge in phony reductionism—the new rebels reducing the complexities of politics to the simplicities of moral feeling, the scientists taking shelter in the purity of research. Both these paths to purity are like BOMFOG—you feel obliged to respect them, but the trouble comes in putting them into effect.

The Alliance of Opposites

What is wrong with the purists, on both the moral and scientific sides, is not that their objectives are evil but that they tackle the problem at the wrong level of abstraction. In the United States we are in no danger of using science to deny political freedom, or of rejecting BOMFOG in favor of a theology that would support a caste system. But there is a real danger, it seems to me, that the two types of purists—the scientist and the moralist—will withdraw from public affairs and leave responsible political authority without support against the powerful combination of technological skill and special industrial and bureaucratic interests.

For example, take the Institute for Defense Analyses. IDA is a prime target for the new rebels; to them it symbolizes the corruption of the purity of scholarly institutions by military power. IDA is also not very popular among theoretical scientists; it represents the kind of applied work with government support that does little for pure science. Yet IDA was not created in the interest of irresponsible military power. On the contrary, it was a part of the effort to give responsible civilian political authority the ability to control the competing special military interests. The constitutional authority had always been there, but without the special knowledge or the special institutional controls needed to make that power real, and hence to make possible the synthesis of the independent missions of our Army, Navy, and Air Force into a general policy.

Even before 1961, IDA was one of the tools the Secretary of Defense used as an aid in the synthesis of general policy. There was no antithesis here, in either theory or practice, between, on the one hand, reductionist knowledge and specialized staff institutions and, on the other, an effort to make general policy supreme over special technological interests.

In opposition we saw officers from the most powerful and independent segment of American bureaucracy, the career military services, supported by industrial clients who disapproved on principle of any not-for-profit corporation, rise to denounce the whiz kids in the research corporations and the Office of the Secretary of Defense. The use of mathematical and scientific techniques to deal with military policies, such as strategic plans and weapons systems, was a cold and calculating and heartless approach, they said, to what ought to be an affair of the heart—a vocation to be followed on moral rather than quantitative principles. Or as Admiral Rickover put it (10), "The Greeks at Thermopylae and at Salamis would not have stood up to the Persians had they had cost effectiveness people to guide them."

I find much of Admiral Rickover's critique of our overemphasis on technology and bureaucracy refreshing—especially coming from an Admiral. What other Admiral would ask (11), "Does man exist for the economy or does the economy exist for man?" and charge that the "larger bureaucratically administered organizations" in which most Americans now work, as a result of the Industrial and

Scientific revolutions, "are in every respect the obverse of a free society"?

But I doubt that this rhetoric, which ought to endear the Admiral to the new rebels, really advances our understanding of the nature of freedom in modern society. Whenever a powerful special interest begins to appeal to basic moral or philosophical principles in an effort to escape subordination to general policy, we are entitled to be skeptical if not cynical. The new purists in morals and in science who join with rebellious segments of the Air Force and Navy in attacks on IDA and the Office of the Secretary of Defense are in much the same position as the contemporary religious fundamentalists who become allies of reactionary industrialists by seeing social security, the income tax, and the regulation of business as the work of Godless communism.

In the current state of the world the question whether scientific societies should pass political resolutions is a trivial tactical issue; the community of science needs to look to its broader strategy.

In this strategy the idea of scientific purity—of avoiding involvement in political compromise—was once a useful notion. It helped to free science from the teleology of the earlier philosophers, and scientific institutions from the obligation to work on practical problems as practical men defined them.

This reductionist strategy, while protecting the freedom of scientific institutions, did not slow down the practical application of science in political systems that had shaken off feudal or bureaucratic constraints in an era of optimism about material progress.

But the new rebels are right in thinking that that era of optimism—that blind faith in automatic progress—has ended.

That optimism misled Western thought in two ways for a century or two after the Enlightenment.

After the French Revolution there spread eastward through Europe and Asia the optimistic notion, stemming from the Enlightenment, that science, by perfecting our philosophy and our values, will teach us how to revolutionize society and eliminate the corruptions of politics; in its Marxist form, that notion proposed to let the State itself wither away.

After the American Revolution, the pragmatic West came to a less doctrinaire but almost equally optimistic conclusion: that the advancement of science would lead to the progress of technology and industry and an increase in material prosperity, and to a withering away of governmental interference with private initiative.

The rebels are right in being pessimistic about such notions. I do not think they are even pessimistic enough. To me it seems possible that the new amount of technological power let loose in an overcrowded world may overload any system we might devise for its control; the possibility of a complete and apocalyptic end of civilization cannot be dismissed as a morbid fantasy.

And the rebels are far too romantically optimistic in their remedy. Mere rebellion to destroy the existing order—mere purposeless violence to upset the establishment—assumes that those who gain power by violence will be nobler and more generous in purpose than those who now try to hold together the delicate web of civilized institutions.

If scientists wish to maintain the freedom of their science and, at the same time, play a rational and effective role in politics, they need to adopt a strategy that is more modest in its hopes for the perfectibility of mankind and more pessimistically alert to the dangers of power—not only power that is obviously political but the power—not only power that is obviously political but the power that calls itself private as well. They should start by acknowledging in theory what in the United States we have always taken for granted as a practical matter: that reductionism in scientific knowledge, while it may provide the fundamental advances in scientific theory, does not alone provide the answers in the realm of policy, or the basis for a political ideology.

If this point is clear, no one will need to take seriously the charge that the scientific mode of thought is a fundamental threat to humane values. The threat comes not from the theoretical reductionism of science but from the very pragmatic reductionism which assumes that applications of advanced technology are automatically beneficial, or that we are always justified in granting special concentrations of technological and industrial concentrations of technological and industrial power freedom from central political authority.

If everyone understands that science, as such, does not control policy decisions, scientists will then be free—and, in my view, will be morally obliged—to devote their synthetic as well as their analytic skills to the formulation and criticism of policies by which the nation may control technology and apply science in the public interest.

In an era which is beginning to be alert to the threats posed by modern technology to the human environment, the role of science in politics is no longer merely to destroy the irrational and superstitious beliefs which were once the foundation of oppressive authority. It is, rather, to help clarify our public values, define our policy options, and assist responsible political leaders in the guidance and control of the powerful forces which have been let loose on this troubled planet.

REFERENCES AND NOTES

1. New York *Times* (14 July 1968).
2. *Ibid.* (22 Oct. 1968), pp. 49 and 56.
3. J. Ellul, *The Technological Society*, (Knopf, New York, 1964), pp. 434 and 435.
4. Statement in campaign advertisement, New York *Times* (22 May 1968).
5. H. Marcuse, "The individual in the Great Society," in *A Great Society?*, B. M. Gross, Ed. (Basic Books, New York, 1968), p. 74.
6. For a confirmation of this impression, see D. W. Brogan, "The student revolt," *Encounter*, July 1968, p. 23; and S. M. Lipset, "Students and politics in comparative perspective," in *Dædalus*, Winter 1968, p. 1. A similar observation regarding the lack of participation in Germany by young scientists, technologists, and medical students may be found in M. Beloff, "Letter from Germany," *Encounter*, July 1968, p. 29. It seems likely that the difference in this respect among the disciplines is less important than that between the academic disciplines and the various types of professional training.
7. On the distinction between the new rebels and Communists, see P. Goodman, "The black flag of anarchism," New York *Times Magazine*, 14 July 1968; on its antinomian overtones, see D. P. Moynihan, "Nirvana," *Amer. Scholar*, Autumn 1967. For a fuller account of the medieval rebellions, see N. Cohn, *The Pursuit of the Millennium* (Essential Books, New York, 1957).
8. D. Joravsky, *Soviet Marxism and Natural Science* (Columbia Univ. Press, New York, 1961).
9. A. M. Weinberg, "Social problems and national socio-technical institutes," in *Applied Science and Technological Progress* (National Academy of Sciences, Washington, D.C., 1967) (available from the Government Printing Office, Washington, D.C.).
10. Testimony, 11 May 1966, on Department of Defense appropriations for 1967, before the House Committee on Appropriations Subcommittee on the Department of Defense, 89th Congress, 2nd Session, part 6. I do not argue here that the systems analysts have been right, only that they have been attacked for the wrong reasons.
11. H. G. Rickover, "Technology and the citizen," address before the Publishers' Lunch Club, New York, 7 January 1965.

Section B

Roles and Role Problems:
A Case in Point—
Innovative Roles in Mental Health

As strategic changes occur in social policies and priorities, concommitant changes occur in both the organizational properties and internal processes of human service organizations. These changes often set up pressures leading to various kinds of identity crises at both social-organizational and individual-psychological levels. As the time-honored and traditional anchor points of organizational structures, policies, and roles begin to shift, that which has been familiar begins to recede in the organization, and that which has been unfamiliar become more prominent. At this point the vicissitudes of participants' personalities interact both with the changing internal and external demands of intra- and inter-organizational relationships and professional standards to give rise to questions such as "Who and what were we?", "Who are we?", "Who and what shall we be?"

Major and significant changes have occurred in social policies, programming, and organizational development in mental health over the past 10 years. These changes have generally occurred in the direction of a greater involvement of mental health workers in communities and more awareness of community dynamics. Members of mental health organizations are likely to be found today spending greater amounts of time and energy away from their offices and clinical roles. The role descriptions and organizational sanctions which previously reinforced a relatively formalized office-centered, clinical-therapeutic approach to the problems of mental health, has begun to yield to a growing support for what might be described as a relatively informal, nonclinical, community involvement within the more general roles of mental health workers. The focus has switched from tertiary prevention (rehabilitative treatment), to secondary prevention (early case finding and treatment), with some experimentation in primary prevention. These changes have had profound effects upon the participants' public and private views of themselves and their roles.

Organizationally the traditional hierarchical authority system which has been so typical in the past of health and welfare organizations has begun to give way to relatively nontraditional, nonhierarchical, collateral organizational structures and interpersonal relationships. As this has occurred it has generated numerous social-psychological and organizational crises. The following articles provide perspectives on the roles of the traditional actors in the human service drama as they consider the nature of their roles, the consequences of remaining in their more traditional roles, and the possibilities and promises of moving in more nontraditional directions.

20. The Community Psychiatrist and Political Action*

Harvey M. Freed, M.D.

Should psychiatrists attempt to engage in effective political action? Is this a legitimate concern for both training institutions and practitioners? How should it be carried out? What are its limits? How should one prepare for this type of role? Alternatively, can the community mental health specialist avoid such roles and still claim to be interested in influencing those forces which negatively affect behavior?

In a larger sense, what are the manifest and latent consequences which might stem from increasingly politicized psychiatric roles? What kind of professional life-style might emerge for psychiatrists described by Freed, as contrasted with those engaging in the more traditional kinds of clinical involvement? Would this open up opportunities for more effective primary prevention programs? Or, does it create program risks and constraints?

More importantly, does the model of action described in the article have implications for other groups of mental health workers—professional and nonprofessional?

As the psychiatrist moves into the community, he is faced with many new challenges. While some of these are easily mastered, others prove to be more taxing. Even at this early phase in the development of community psychiatry, it is clear that certain tasks pose difficult ethical and practical problems.

It is important to develop a typology of the roles the community psychiatrist is expected to play. Beyond that it is helpful to record the difficulty encountered in the performance of each role. While personal idiosyncracies have considerable influence on the success

*From the Laboratory of Community Psychiatry of the Harvard Medical School.

of the role shift, they will, of course, be less significant to the profession than other factors which are more generalizable.

I am not aware of any papers which focus on this subject. Whatever dialogue has occurred has had to do with the move into community psychiatry in general (1,2). From recent personal experiences, I most certainly agree with Caplan (3) who feels that the crucial issue is one of identity. It is much easier to learn how to be a community pyschiatrist than to learn whether to be one. Once the identity crisis has been resolved, one begins to discover that the many facets of work in the community vary in appeal and in difficulty.

To highlight some of these problems I am going to present a vignette of the recent experiences of one psychiatrist as he endeavored to develop a mental health center in his community.

CASE HISTORY

Dr. Philip Lane has been interested in the mental health center concept for some time. After assuming the directorship of the Department of Psychiatry at Riverside Hospital, he began to work actively for the development of the center. He spoke with Dr. Morton, the Director of the State Department of Mental Health, and engaged his cooperation. The latter was anxious to dot the map with mental health centers and willingly lent his support. He also contacted the trustees and administrator of the hospital and found them quite responsive.

Finally, he approached the community. He spent some months finding out who the leaders were before venturing forth to meet them. When he finally did, he was well prepared. He contacted at least fifteen people individually, presented his early plans and his thinking, and sounded them out. In many instances their suggestions were incorporated into the planning. Ultimately a community advisory committee was formed which was chaired by Father Collins, a Jesuit Priest.

All of this was a new experience for Dr. Lane because heretofore he had never consulted the community in his program planning. He put a great deal of effort into his attempts to involve the community and was successful in wooing a number of influential Riverside leaders.

However, there was one man whom he was unable to win over or even to communicate with at all. That was Chick Morelli, the

State Representative from Riverside. Morelli was a politician of the "old school" with a spotty reputation. He kept in very close touch with his constituents, doing them favors in return for their loyalty. His concern was that his supporters were being driven out by urban renewal and by the expansion of the hospital. He saw the development of the mental health center as a part of this expansion and therefore as a threat to his political existence.

Lane knew that Morelli would be a problem. He had been forewarned by Father Collins, who knew Morelli well. When he phoned the Representative, the latter refused to meet with him. Morelli was also invited to the advisory committee but did not come. Attempts were made to reach Morelli through Father Collins, Dr. Morton, and other community leaders. All of these efforts went for naught. Morelli said that he did not want to be "brainwashed."

With this as background, the stage was set for the drama. Dr. Roswell, the hospital administrator, suggested that the center be built on land now owned by the hospital rather than on state-owned property as planned. In essence the hospital and the state would trade property. The rationale was that this plan would make the hospital a continuous run of buildings uninterrupted by the mental health center.

Dr. Lane was cool to the idea initially, because the land swap would have to be approved by the legislature and could jeopardize the development of the center. In the end he backed the proposal and became the prime mover in negotiating the swap. Again he enlisted the support of a great many people, including several legislators who attended a luncheon where the idea was discussed with them.

The bill came to the floor of the legislature somewhat earlier than had been planned and Morelli immediately introduced a motion to return it to committee, which would have killed it for a year. This motion carried, but was amended at the last minute at the suggestion of a lone legislator that there be 24 hours to reconsider.

During those 24 hours, Drs. Lane and Roswell worked very hard. A great deal of pressure was put on the legislature by influential people who had been contacted by them or their allies. Several legislators called Father Collins to find out what his position was.

When the bill came up again the following day, the discussion was heated. Morelli spoke convincingly, but the 24-hour interlude had proved fatal to his cause. The bill was passed by a large margin, clearing the way for the land swap and the mental health center.

DISCUSSION

While this short case history might touch on many aspects of a community psychiatrist's functioning, I am going to focus on his immersion in the political life of the community in order to implement his program. By the latter I simply mean the process of influencing those decisions and actions of professional politicians or governmental administrators which affect the community mental health program.

To begin with I think it is important to point out that even if we omit the question of participation in social action, community psychiatry cannot avoid such immersion. The very decision to open a mental health center is always a political one when public funds are sought. Beyond that, the medical profession is beginning to recognize that much of the dissatisfaction with medical care today has to do with inadequacies in its delivery rather than in its quality per se. And in order to improve the delivery system it is often necessary to obtain the approval and active support of local politicians and officials.

In the case above, it would not have been possible for Dr. Lane to have avoided political involvement. Even if he had not had the land exchange to worry about I am certain that he would have had to deal with Morelli at some point. Morelli correctly saw the expansion of the hospital as a threat to his political existence. The mental health center seemed to him to be vulnerable and he would simply have chosen another opportunity to try to block its development.

Some people argue that while political action in the sense of attempting to influence decisions is a necessary concomitant of the functioning of a community psychiatrist, political battles can be avoided. They might feel that in this situation Lane could have reached Morelli if he had approached him in an appropriate fashion early in the game. That is, if Lane had focused on the superordinate goal of the "good of the community," had been willing to "play the political game" of giving Morelli ample public credit in return for his help, he might have been successful.

This may be the case, but there is little evidence for it. In fact the evidence points in the opposite direction. It suggests that, if anything, Lane was slow to recognize the clearly oppositional character of Morelli's behavior. He tried personally and through intermediaries to reach Morelli, but to no avail. He failed to recognize how threatening the mental health center development was to Morelli politically and thus neglected to prepare adequately for the legislative contest. It came close to being a very costly oversight. But for the action of a friendly legislator, the bill would have been returned to committee for one year and thus probably defeated.

Looking at the situation for a moment, it is easy to see why Morelli felt threatened politically by the hospital expansion. Not only would his supporters be displaced. They would likely be supplanted by voters not sympathetic to his type of politics. High-rises which typically spring up around medical centers do not house the working class people who form Morelli's base of support. Further, the infusion of services and the interaction of professionals with the community would detract from another source of his power: his ability to get services for his constituents because of his political influence. The hospital's expansion provides Riverside's inhabitants with an alternative to supporting Morelli.

It is pertinent to ask why Dr. Lane was so reluctant to view Morelli as an opponent. The answer details some of the reasons why political action is fast developing the reputation of being the most difficult new role the psychiatrist must play as he goes through the transition into community psychiatry.

POLITICS AND THE INTELLECTUAL

There are constraints against political involvement in various social systems of which the psychiatrist is a member. To begin with, politics has long been a dirty word in the American intellectual community. While the likes of Wilson, Roosevelt, Stevenson, and Kennedy have occasionally wedded national affairs and the intellectuals, the marriages have been unstable. The present disenchantment with the Johnson Administration in many quarters is much more typical.

Local politics, of course, has a much sorrier record when it comes to attracting intellectuals. Town-gown battles are rampant in university communities. Until very recently, most intellectuals have limited their political action to occasional sarcastic "letters to the editor" of local papers.

Medical Ideology

Medical mores are very much in the same tradition. Glaser (4) spells out in considerable detail how the profession places little value, at best, on work done in the political arena. Cunningham (5) epitomizes the view of the medical world when he says, "The doctor's dilemma today emerges from the fact that politics is a dirty-hands business, and medicine has always been a clean-hands profession. Healing and heeling don't go together."

To get at the root of this it is necessary to look at the ideology of medicine. Ben-David (6) feels that "the conduct of the physician is regulated by two different norms: (a) service to the others, and (b) living up to scientific standards."

Parsons (7) agrees with him. He feels that the first obligation of the physician is the welfare of the patient. He argues that there are cogent reasons why a "service" orientation should be foremost. "The most obvious line of argument concerned the facts that on the one hand a major feature of illness is helplessness and therefore sick people are particularly open to exploitation. On the other hand the medical profession is characterized by a special technical competence which is not open to the layman, who is incompetent not only to perform medical functions but even to judge whether they are being properly performed."

He also emphasizes the scientific orientation of the physician. He contrasts "self-interest" with "scientifically-oriented rationality." Rational action is aided by three features of the physician's role. These he calls "universalism," "specificity of function," and "affective neutrality." The first refers to the "impartiality" necessary in treating "a sick patient as presenting a problem for applied science. The imperative of scientific objectivity required abstracting from considerations of personal relationship or group belongingness in favor of diagnosis and treatment as a 'case' of whatever the disease category happened to be." The second refers to limiting the scope of the physician's concern to "the health of the patient." Physicians have no claim to information irrelevant to this. The third refers to "a 'neutral' attitude in the sense that he (the physician) inhibits what would otherwise be 'normal' emotional reactions."

The significance of these arguments to us is that they help to explain a central feature of medical ideology; that is, the charge to the physician to be objective and impartial with his patients. Only by remaining somewhat aloof and uninvolved can he both further scientific knowledge and serve the patient. A common error of neophyte physicians is to overidentify with their patients. This is usually corrected by the end of the rigorous indoctrination period characteristic of medical training. The result is an attitude called "coldness" or "hardness" by some, but which ideally serves as protection for both patient and physician.

How does this mesh with the attitude of the politician? The very essence of politics is its partiality. One of the definitions of the word "political" is "of or pertaining to politicians in their *partisan* activities." Adlai Stevenson (8) never ceased to admire professional politicians for what he called "their single-minded devotion to the business of getting votes." He was amused by "their total lack of interest in the issues involved." Banfield (9) makes a similar point. He indicates that the outcome of political issues is a function of "influence" and its vicissitudes rather than the actual merits of the situation. Medical ideology, then, in respect to the features of impartiality and objectivity, is the very antithesis of political ideology.

Psychiatric Nonpartisanship

The psychiatric profession borrows heavily from medical ideology. (Parsons (7) notes that the point of the psychoanalyst's predilection for being a physician is that an important part of the work is already done by being in the role type adapted to the therapeutic function. Further, many elements of the medical etiquette have come to be used as technical tools of psychoanalysis, i.e., trust between doctor and patient, the handling of uncertainty, an insistence on the autonomy of the patient and his will to be cured.)

In addition, the psychiatrist's awareness of the concept of transference contributes to an attitude of impartiality and objectivity. He recognizes that the patient's behavior vis-a-vis him is often irrational and in the service of resistance. Confident that the therapeutic contract has established that he and the patient have the same goal of treatment in mind, he can interpret the resistance instead of reacting to it.

This is a crucial point. In medical or psychiatric practice the practitioner always has the therapeutic contract to fall back on. That is, he knows that despite all protestations to the contrary, the fact that the patient has come to him for treatment and that he has agreed to it means that both parties have the same goal in mind—treatment of the patient. Either party can break the contract at any time if dissatisfied. (Committed patients may be an exception but even there the therapist knows he can address himself to "the healthy side of the ego.")

In politics, again, things are very different. The goal of the politician is to win votes, and to be elected or re-elected. To think that he can be induced to overlook this and to enter into an agreement "for the good of the community" would be to apply the rules of psychotherapy inappropriately in place of the rules of politics. If he judges that another's activities may harm his chances for election, then nothing that person can do will make the politician an ally. His opposition will be conscious and calculating and viewing his behavior as unconscious resistance will be disastrous.

Comment

All of this should begin to explain why Dr. Lane was slow to view Representative Morelli's behavior as oppositional and why he was not prepared to deal with it as such. There are many forces against such clear vision. First there is the general distaste for anything political in the intellectual and medical communities. Second is the medical admonition to be impartial so as not to obtrude on scientific objectivity or service to the patients. Impartiality puts one at a distinct disadvantage when engaged in a contest. Third is the psychiatric awareness of the phenomenon of transference. Oppositional behavior is explained away as irrational within the safety of the therapeutic contract.

It behooves the psychiatrist whose program hinges on a political issue to recognize that he may have to cast aside the mantle of scientific objectivity and impartiality if he is to be successful. If he does not accept this thesis he may come to grief in his attempts to serve the community.

There may, however, be an alternative. Perhaps the psychiatrist can delegate the responsibility for political action necessary to his program. Dunham (10) argues that psychiatrists may lose their professional effectiveness by getting into the power structure. With vested interests they could no longer be useful as advisors or consultants. Parsons (7) points out that medicine is moving away from the private practice model towards specialization and differentiation of function. Perhaps therapeutic skills needed for a community oriented practice should be distinguished from the administrative and political skills needed to organize services. These latter could be left to lay administrators or community organizers. (Parsons (7) suggests that the physician's reluctance to give up certain tasks may be a vestige of the need for the private practitioner to perform all of them). By dissecting away these functions the psychiatrist would be saved some of the trouble of having to struggle with a hard-won professional identity. His therapeutic ideology would not have to be too strained.

My own view is that much would be lost by protecting the psychiatrist from such involvements. First is the contribution to the specific community with which the psychiatrist is involved. Aside from the application of scientific methodology to local issues and the knowledge of pertinent research findings, Wedge (11) points out that the clinician has something to contribute to an understanding of political behavior which is unique. The clinician catches what is unspoken as well as what is spoken. He can play the role of "enabler" in a very special way.

Second is the contribution he can make to the scientific community. Coles (12) recently stated that the difficulties involved in observing and participating in social issues is substantial but adds that research in this area is badly needed. If we are ever to make a serious attempt to do preventive psychiatry, we must come to understand how social systems affect human behavior. Psychiatrists are skilled at participant observation and can contribute much to an understanding of social issues from such a vantage point.

Third is the contribution to the psychiatric profession itself. Ben-David (13) feels that practice is invaluable in locating relevant problems not implied in existing scientific theory and methodology. In fact innovation occurs when people trained a certain way are faced with new tasks. He cites Freud as a prime example.

I do not think that the partisan behavior which is a political necessity will place too much of a strain on the psychiatric role. Again I feel that the crucial problem is one of acquiring a new professional identity. Once the security in this new identity develops it is possible to perform very different roles with very different ideological supports at different times without feeling stressed. Thus many psychiatric administrators continue to do psychotherapy.

Further, there is precedent within our own profession for such a role shift, that to administration. The struggles faced by a psychiatrist-administrator are quite similar to those of a community psychiatrist in many ways. Waldo (14) points out that whereas prior to 1930 administration and politics were thought to be quite separate, this is no longer the case. He characterized administration and politics as representing "fact" and "value," respectively, and adds that they are now thought to be intertwined.

Ben-David (6) has noted that when expectations of the professional clash with the institutionalized norms for his particular role, one of two things happen. The first possibility is that the norms change. The second is the elimination of the expectations. It is my expectation, and the contention of this paper, that societal forces today are such that the second alternative will not be open to community psychiatrists. That is, there will be no way for them to eliminate community pressures. The result is that we can anticipate changes in the role of the psychiatrist working in the community.

References

1. Trist, E. L., "The Need of the Social Psychiatrist to Influence Wider Social Networks and Their Environments," *Psychother Psychosom* 13, 229-237, 1965.
2. Duhl, L. J., "New Directions in Mental Health Planning", *Arch Gen Psychiat*, 13, 403-410, 1965.
3. Caplan, G., "An Approach to the Education of Community Mental Health Specialists," *Ment. Hyg.* (N.Y.), 43, 268-280, 1959.
4. Glaser, W. A., "Doctors and Politics," *Am J Sociol*, 66, 230-245, 1960.
5. Cunningham, R. M. Jr., "Can Political Means Gain Professional Ends?," *The Mod Hosp*, 77, 51-56, 1951.
6. Ben-David, J., "The Professional Role of the Physician in Bureaucratized Medicine: A Study in Role Conflict," *Hum. Relat*, 11, 255-274, 1958.
7. Parsons, T., "Some Theoretical Considerations Bearing on the Field of Medical Sociology," in *Social Structure and Personality*, Glencoe Free Press, New York, 1964. Chap 12, 325-358.
8. Ball, G. W., "Flaming Arrows to the Sky: A Memoir of Adlai Stevenson," *The Atlantic*, 217, 41-45, 1966.
9. Banfield, E. C., *Political Influence*, Glencoe Free Press, New York, 1961.
10. Dunham, H. W., "Community Psychiatry—the Newest Therapeutic Bandwagon," *Arch Gen Psychiat*, 12, 303-13, 1965.
11. Wedge, G., "Social Psychiatry and Political Behavior," *Bull Men Clin*, 28, 53-61, 1964.
12. Coles, R., "Observation or Participation: The Problem of Psychiatric Research on Social Issues," *J Ner and M Dis*, 141, 274-284, 1965.
13. Ben-David, J., "Roles and Innovations in Medicine," *Am J Sociol*, 65, 557-568, 1960.
14. Waldo, D., "The Value Problem in Administrative Study," *The Study of Public Administration*, Random House, Inc., N.Y., 1955, (Chap. six, 60-66).

21. Involving the Urban Poor in Health Services Through Accommodation–The Employment of Neighborhood Representatives*

James A. Kent, M.A.
C. Harvey Smith, M.P.H.

Perhaps the most visible change in the cast of human service organization characters in the late 1960's occurred with the addition and legitimizing of nonprofessionals.

As health and welfare programs increasingly intertwined with the problems of the communities they were designed to serve, the perceptual and behavioral limitations imposed by professional roles and identities became more and more evident. Two strategies for dealing with this problem emerged: 1) alter the selection and training of professionals; and 2) use indigenous nonprofessionals.

The former strategy provides a possible long-term solution to the problem, but one which has the potential for massive internal resistance from organizations concerned with improving professional statuses. The latter strategy not only holds promise for dealing with present problems, but, based on its effectiveness thus far, may have long-term viability if it can solve its own problems, such as continued training, promotion, and status. However, it may be that all present solutions are circular and that the indigenous nonprofessionals may follow the same path as all identifiable disciplines before them.

Public health practitioners are concerned with the difficulties of providing health services to persons in poverty and ethnic subgroups residing in urban "medical ghettos."[a] Although the concept

*This paper was presented before the Maternal and Child Health Section of the American Public Health Association at the Ninety-Fourth Annual Meeting in San Francisco, Calif., November 1, 1966.

a. The term "medical ghetto" is used to designate not only the complete isolation and alienation of a group from society, but also the isolation from medical care sponsored by the larger society. Generally the medical ghetto is coexistent with

281

of multiple etiology of disease has been formulated for some time and some awareness of the value system differences between the middle-class professional and the disadvantaged patient has been gained, the latter is still referred to as "hard-to-reach."[1]

The position of this paper is that the culturally and socially disadvantaged patient is not "hard-to-reach" when programs accommodate his motivational orientation. This paper will consider the following concepts:

1. Patient accommodation as a means whereby the disadvantaged individual is recruited to health care.
2. The urban "neighborhood" as the basic unit for organizing health care programs.
3. The employment of indigenous workers to involve the disadvantaged patient in the accommodation process.

The Ghetto and Accommodation

In the urban medical ghetto there are prevalent feelings of "we" and "they." The ghetto member sees persons operating outside his life space[2] as "they," while his fellow members are designated as "we." In the wide field of social welfare, the ghetto member sees the ADC worker, the probation officer, and the public health professional as the unwanted "they" group. The ghetto member feels unable to influence the welfare programs promoted in his behalf.[1] Although dependent upon them, he resists involvement and remains dependent.

Ghetto members lead crisis-ridden lives. Dealing with these crises creates a value system that gives highest priority to satisfaction of immediate needs. In this system, disease is a concern only when it is an emergency. A value for preventive health care cannot arise in such an environment.

In view of these two factors—the resistance to involvement and the crisis orientation of the poor—health programs must include a component of social action that transcends the mere provision of medical care. Immediate problems demand immediate solutions. In this regard, accommodation of immediate needs can become a vehicle for recruiting the disadvantaged client to health care.

the socioeconomic ghetto. However, it is conceivable to have a medical ghetto even without the accompanying socioeconomic alienation. See Miller, S. M. "The American Lower Classes: A Typological Approach." In: Reissman, Frank; Cohen, Jerome; and Pearl, Arthur (Eds.). Mental Health of the Poor: New Treatment Approaches for Low-Income People. New York: Free Press of Glencoe, 1964, pp. 139-154.

In this sense, a value for health develops as a latent consequence of a more general problem-solving process.

The Neighborhood[b].

In order to accommodate a patient group, the characteristics of that particular group must be identified and program methods tailored to specific needs. With this in mind, the disadvantaged urban neighborhood should be considered as the unit of public health programing. Because the neighborhood tends to be more homogeneous when contrasted to larger communities, programs can be designed to accomplish particular goals unique to the neighborhood.

Evidences of the existence of "neighborhoods" are as follows:

1. Large extended families within a specific area.
2. Isolation of specific areas by freeways, rivers, and industrial infiltration of residential areas.
3. Similar social and economic problems among residents of a given area.
4. An interaction pattern confined to a specific area.
5. Use of facilities, such as stores, close to their residences.
6. The isolation of ethnic groups (a form of ethnocentrism).[3]
7. An informal network of "caretakers"[4] both internal and external serving a residential area.

The actual development of technics, specific to a particular neighborhood group and conducive to the accommodation process, demands some significant departures from traditional public health practice. People cannot be helped if they cannot be reached. A wide variety of innovations must be considered. Among these are role changes of the professional staff and the addition of new members to the health task force.

Professionals have experienced difficulties in effectively communicating with, and ultimately involving, the disadvantaged client. Even the most thoughtful attempts by genuinely sensitive professionals to "go native" often go unrewarded.

Reiff and Reissman identify this problem and its potential solution.

b. This concept has been given new emphasis and a process orientation by the writers. Early classical theories on the neighborhood were formulized by: Cooley, Charles. Social Organization. New York: Scribner's Sons, 1915, and Park, Robert. The City: Suggestions for the Investigation of Human Behavior in the City Environment. Am. J. Sociol. 20:577-612 (Mar.), 1915. Studies concerned with empirically

"Even professionals who have excellent relationship skills are limited by the nature of their function as an 'expert'. This definition of role, which they and the poor both hold, prevent the development of a fully-rounded everyday relationship. Yet it is this very type of relationship that is the key to effective program participation on the part of the poor. And it is the very type of relationship that the indigenous nonprofessional can establish. He 'belongs', he is a significant other; he is 'one of us'. He can be invited to weddings, parties, funerals, and other gatherings—and he can go."[5]

The Neighborhood Representative

Departing from the concept of the indigenous nonprofessional,[c] the Maternity and Infant Care Project,[d] administered by Denver's Department of Health and Hospitals, has created a new role for indigenous people. Neighborhood representatives, as they are called, are hired specifically to represent their disadvantaged neighborhood. In this regard, the neighborhood representative, as a semi-independent worker, becomes a "link" representing community life and values to the professionals and health programs to the low-income client. Unlike the non-professionals, representatives are not closely supervised nor are subprofessional tasks imposed upon them. Emphasis is placed on the development of their unique style and relationships with the population being served. The natural skills of the representatives enable them to

investigating the boundaries of neighborhood are scarce. However, see Shenky, Eshrep, and Lewin, Molly. Your Neighborhood: A Social Profile of Los Angeles. The Hayes Foundation, 1949; Hacon, R. F. Neighborhoods or Neighborhood Units? Sociological Rev. 3:235-246 (Dec.), 1955.

c. The recent acceptance of the indigenous nonprofessional in social welfare programs has primarily occurred as a function of two issues. The first being the recognition that certain routine tasks heretofore performed by professionals could be transferred to persons with considerably less academic and professional training. Related to this was the realization that persons in poverty could be prepared to perform these routine tasks, and in so doing be provided an exit from poverty.

Potential problems of these nonprofessional careers is that the very nature of the subprofessional position suggests the involvement of persons who seek the job as a vehicle to escape from poverty—and in so doing begin to alienate themselves from the population they propose to serve. Furthermore, the training of the nonprofessional has tended to superimpose upon these persons certain professionally styled skills at the expense of the further development of natural skills. Oversupervision and the demand for loyalty to the agency further rob the indigenous worker of his potential effectiveness. He becomes, in essence, contaminated, and thereby loses his ability to be effective as an agent of accommodation.

d. Funded by the Children's Bureau, Department of Health, Education, and Welfare.

interpret the nature and extent of health services in a manner appropriate to the subculture. Newly learned skills in terms of knowledge of other social agencies, the services they offer, and methods of contact allow the neighborhood representative to solve other problems of a more immediate nature, which may act as barriers to the clients' use of health services. In this new role, the neighborhood representative can destroy the myth of the "hard-to-reach" patient.

Critical to the ultimate success of the neighborhood representative are: the criteria used in their selection and recruitment; the nature of their training; the style of supervision; and their specific role function.

Selection and Recruitment

After understandings of specific neighborhoods were developed, the following selection criteria were established. Neighborhood representatives were to:

1. Be identified with the subcultural group being served.
2. Possess subculturally oriented communication skills.
3. Be a resident of the particular neighborhood, preferably for some length of time.
4. Possess a value for work. [e]
5. Be accepted as a member of the neighborhood.
6. Be socially mobile within the neighborhood.
7. Possess an identifiable value for health care.
8. Not be a member of a group identifiably middle-class. [f]
9. Be over 35 years of age, and female. [g]

e. Emphasis was placed on recruiting persons from the working class for several reasons. Unlike the subprofessional who aspires to a professional position, the career path of the neighborhood representative exists only within the confines of this unique role. This factor demands the selection of persons who desire to remain within the neighborhood even though they may be economically able to move. The working-class person is a rather permanent member of the neighborhood and is likely to remain. Furthermore, although the working class has a high value for work, they share the life-style of the low-income group. This value for work is important because much of the neighborhood representatives' activities must be ultimately self-directed.

f. Extensive participation of the prospective neighborhood representative in middle-class organizations may represent their subtle rejection of the subculture and a striving for status—a factor which, if identified by the individual's peers, could cut him off from participation in the culture.

g. The decision to select women over 35 was based on several observations. Generally speaking, the mature woman tends to be more sensitive to the needs of peers

Recruitment of neighborhood representatives was particularly time-consuming. The uniqueness of the role and selection criteria eliminated certain traditional sources of manpower. Social agencies (community centers, tenant councils, neighborhood clubs, and the like), supposedly internal to the specific neighborhood provided minimal assistance.

Success came through informal acquaintance with neighborhood residents. Having developed these acquaintances, recruiters were able to proceed from friend to friend until an appropriate selection could be made.

Training

The training philosophy involved the development of the neighborhood representative as a secure semi-independent agent using her natural style and skills. Consistent with the action orientation of the indigenous worker, "doing" and not "talking" was the emphasis. Because of this, training is a dynamic two-way process. Formal classroom sessions and reading assignments were conspicuously absent in the training program. Essentially, training neighborhood representatives has been a continuous problem-oriented process and not a structured program terminated at a certain point.

After a two-day orientation concerned with project goals and philosophy, representatives were immediately involved in unstructured problem-oriented training. This occurred within the specific neighborhoods to be served.

Following several initial visits to stores and homes accompanied by a professional, representatives were sent out "on their own" and were encouraged to discuss the new clinic in a manner natural to themselves. Beyond informing residents of the new clinic, the main purpose of these first visits was to become acquainted with and known to neighborhood families. They were encouraged to spend as much time in a particular home as they desired, enabling them to interact at a meaningful level and to identify individual problems.

From this point the training process evolved from problem identification to problem analysis and finally to problem solving. This process cycle promoted movement from developing simple

than the younger woman. She is less isolated in terms of relationships with individuals and neighborhood groups: she has a greater understanding of "how to get things done," and particularly among Spanish-Americans, she tends to command greater respect.

problem-solving skills to solving of problems of greater complexity. Once one neighborhood representative was functioning, she became the trainer for other neighborhood representatives, thus minimizing the professional trainers' role.

Supervision

Given the unique natural skills of the neighborhood representative and the desire to accommodate the patient group, supervision in the traditional sense has been minimal. Since the representative is in many respects already an expert, supervision becomes a relationship of mutual respect where the representative works "with" the supervisor rather than "for" him. The relationship becomes one in which the representative (rather than the professional) identifies the "need," while the professional merely assists in resolving this need.

Supervision in the more traditional sense occurs at various times. The indigenous worker must be protected from certain middle-class tendencies and discouraged from overidentifying with the professional staff. This occurs in a positive manner by praising the representative for taking a patient's "side" in a case conference or negatively by criticizing the representative for communicating that subtle disdain for low-income patients so often typical of middle-class professionals. This protection is essential until neighborhood representatives become secure in their role and until other members of the professional team accept, and become sensitive to, this role.

Functions

As a relatively independent worker, the neighborhood representative has three functions: that of service expediter, neighborhood organizer, and patient representative.

In the role of service expediter, the neighborhood representative interprets to neighborhood residents the services of the Mother and Infant Care Center and, when appropriate, attempts to solve individual problems of a more immediate nature regardless of whether or not the individual is a prospective patient. Representatives not only become a "link" to needed services, but also demonstrate to the individual being served how to "get things done." In so doing, they enhance the ability of the disadvantaged person to influence and control his environment, a critical step in the accommodation process.

Neighborhood organization, as performed by the representative, occurs in the form of organization for action and for education. Organization for action is accomplished by seeking out neighborhood caretakers who might ultimately be involved in self-help social action projects based on mutually recognized neighborhood needs. As an organizer of persons who "help other people," the representative fosters an increased competence on the part of the socially and economically deprived to cope with neighborhood problems. In so doing, she encourages the development of leadership among the low-income group. A further neighborhood organization function is the establishment of a lay advisory council concerned in part with the operation of the neighborhood Maternity and Infant Care Center. Offered the opportunity to influence clinic practices in terms of appropriate clinic hours, suggesting additional needed services, or advising administrators on the suitability of clinic locations, a greater number of neighborhood residents are involved in and actually influence the accommodation process.

In organizing for education, the representative identifies specific concerns and develops informal gatherings designed to consider these concerns. As these groups develop solidarity and stability, neighborhood representatives are able to direct interest to matters more closely related to the educational goals of the Maternity and Infant Care Project.

As a patient representative, they help patients document their complaints regarding care received during clinic or hospital visits. These complaints in turn are relayed through the appropriate channels and necessary action is taken. This action has at times involved hospital administrators meeting with patients in the ghetto in an effort to resolve specific problems. In one instance pressure created by patient criticism contributed to the resignation of a clinic physician.

Outcomes

In terms of the representatives' ability to resolve some of the problems of traditional concern among public health practitioners, the following evidence is offered. Use of clinic services has shown 42 per cent higher attendance during the same period of time in neighborhoods served by representatives when contrasted with neighborhoods without representatives. Four months after the establishment of a Mother and Infant Care Clinic in one neighborhood, it was determined that in excess of 60 per cent of the patients had been referred by the representative. Clinics served by representatives reported an average of 20 per cent more unwed mothers than in comparable neighborhoods not served by representatives. Of further importance was their ability to recruit expectant mothers earlier in pregnancy. In neighborhoods where representatives have been employed for six months or more, 50 per cent of the patients are being seen in their first or second trimester. This contrasts with 32 per cent in unserved neighborhoods. Although the numbers are small, trends appear to be meaningful.

As an expediter of services to meet immediate needs, the representative has proved particularly effective. Securing food orders and clothing for needy families, accompanying a mentally ill mother during shopping tours, providing transportation to individuals in need of immediate medical attention, contacting immigration authorities concerning certain problems of a family new to the neighborhood, assisting in the appropriation of welfare grants for individuals and families unaware of available funds are examples of the neighborhood representatives' problem-solving functions.

In association with neighborhood "caretakers," neighborhood representatives have organized rummage sales and bake sales. Funds raised were used to resolve various types of financial emergencies arising in the neighborhood. Decisions regarding the specific use of these funds have been made exclusively by indigenous persons. These activities are particularly significant as meaningful examples of the poor actually helping the poor.

Professional staff are frequently involved on an informal basis in activities organized by the representative. In this regard, the professional becomes increasingly sensitive to the disadvantaged individual and begins to destroy the traditional "they" and "we" relationship.

To date, minimal success has been experienced in establishing lay advisory groups or councils specifically concerned with the operation of the Mother and Infant Care Clinics. It is believed that an interest in clinic policy will occur subsequent to the continued accommodation of more immediate neighborhood concerns.

Conclusion

It has been the contention of this paper that the accommodation of prospective patients, in terms of helping to solve immediate needs, must be a component of medical care programs designed to involve the hard-to-reach.

Furthermore, in order for accommodation to occur, public health programs must become "specific" to the particular cultural and economic groups being accommodated. The neighborhood has been suggested as the appropriate unit for programing the urban ghetto.

The ability of neighborhood representatives, through their unique role of effectively involving the disadvantaged client in accommodation process, has been documented.

A further consequence of the processes herein described transcends the effectiveness of recruiting the disadvantaged to health care. It is proposed that health care can become a "permeable area" [h] through which the urban poor can move toward participation in the dominant social order. The disadvantaged finds an opportunity, by involvement in health services, to identify and internalize patterns of behavior necessary to more effective participation in society.

Essential to the implementation of the concepts and proposal suggested in this paper, is the sponsoring agency's commitment to the total need of the patient group and a willingness to create programs that go beyond traditional public health practice.

References

1. James, George. Poverty as an Obstacle to Public Health Progress in Our Cities. A.J.P.H. 55,11: 1757-1771 (Nov.), 1965.
2. Lewin, Kurt. Field Theory in Social Science. New York: Harper and Brothers, 1951, p. 57.
3. Suchman, Edward. Social Factors in Medical Deprivation. A.J.P.H. 55,11:1725-1733 (Nov.), 1965.
4. Gans, Herbert. The Urban Villagers. New York: Free Press, 1962.
5. Reiff, Robert, and Reissman, Frank. The Indigenous Non-Professional. National Institute of Labor Education, Mental Health Program, Rep. No. 3, 1964, pp. 8-9.

h. This concept was originally investigated in a report published by the Training Center for Delinquency Control, University of Denver. (See Kent, James A.; Fliegler, Louis A.; and Ferguson, John R. The Impact of the Spanish-American Culture upon the Production of Juvenile Delinquency. University of Denver (July), 1965.) This was further expanded in a conceptual model called the "Linkman" in which a theory of marginal acculturation is proposed. (See Kent, James A., and Ferguson, John. Improving the Role Function of Disadvantaged Spanish-Americans through the Use of an Intervening Agent. Latin American Reseach and Service Association, Denver, Colo., 1966.)

Part V

**Management and Planning
Tactics and Strategies**

Introduction

Typically, theories of organizational behavior are elaborated by students of such behavior; only occasionally do the experts participate in the application of their hypotheses. The organizational manager, however, deals with organizational behavior pragmatically on a day-to-day basis, using a variety of managerial theories and tools. In the material which follows, selected components of the theory and practice of administration and planning, with special emphasis on strategies and tactics, are presented with the hope that it will be of help in generating more effective problem-solving strategies for the organizational manager.

As human service organizations have become increasingly complex and specialized, more sophisticated management and planning tools have evolved. However, old problems have not disappeared, and new sets of human problems have accompanied new social and technological inventions and interventions. As the ecology movement has made abundantly clear, change is not without its side effects. For example, one necessary organizational tool, information systems, has brought into sharp relief such issues as the protection of individual rights (privacy and confidentiality), and finding new ways to guarantee public participation in policy making. Public fear of the "establishment," of authority, technocrats, experts, professors, and do-gooders, all reflect a concern about loss of individual liberties.

Improvements in life style through programmatic intervention depend upon improving our decision-making capacity in order to respond effectively and quickly to identifiable problems. We must also be able to fix responsibility and accountability. At the same time problems of alienation have brought about a focus on process and on participation factors which must be built into the development of improved delivery systems. Developing mechanisms to accommodate to these and other forces are responsibilities of the manager and the planner.

In a world that is changing at an exponential rate, with its complex, pluralistic, and politicized forces, planning becomes more difficult and more necessary. As envisioned in this volume, planning is seen as both a management tool required of all organizations, and a basic activity generic to organizations dedicated exclusively to planning.

Administrative Requirements

Competence in money management, personnel policies, decision-making, coordination, planning, project management, evaluation, forecasting, and human relations are among the many requisite skills of modern managers. Presumably, it would also help to be familiar with the substance and technology of the chosen field. Since a man cannot possibly possess all of this knowledge and the many skills associated with it, it is somewhat surprising to note the low status assigned to administration in the health and welfare fields; especially health.

As noted earlier, the discrepancy between this neolithic attitude and the realities of our complex society almost defies explanation, and suggests that our clinical fields both draw from highly selected populations and reinforce this narrow perspective in their training programs. It is reasonable to expect change, however. Even the private medical practice solo-practitioner must develop nominal administrative and organizational skills.

In medicine even this elementary solo-practice model is disappearing, if not through formal group practice, then through informal collaborative arrangements in which laboratories, technicians, and other skills and facilities are shared. Even the private practitioner is not truly independent. Only in the relative isolation of the treatment process can the solo model be accommodated; research, education, planning, social action, and consultation all increasingly require a more formal organizational arrangement. Substantially dependent on pharmaceutical houses, the local drug store, the community hospital, organized laboratories, and third-party payers, this bastion of the independent entrepreneur does not exist except in mythology.

Complex societies are increasingly dependent upon complex organizations. Their organizational goals must be identified, including both those goals which are overt and those which are covert. In addition there must be a clear identification of the organization's primary and secondary missions, as well as the ways through which these are established, displaced, and changed. Clarification of organizational values, functions and dysfunctions, and superordinate and operating goals, all become legitimate and necessary areas of analysis.

For analytic purposes, it is helpful to view organizations intra-organizationally. Often, on the surface, it appears that intraorganizational decisions are centralized, while in fact this generalization depends very much on the structure and function of the organization. Organizations deriving their sanctions from coalitions or federated systems (e.g., The United Way of America) are very much dependent on their input organizations. Although it may not be necessary to touch base with each constituent organization, the attitudes and feelings of the constituents will be considered as a class or grouping before decisions are made which may affect constituents positively or negatively. Thus the administrator leads, if ever he truly does, by suasion.

Unitary or corporate organizations are relatively freer to take stands and make decisions, but even they are seldom free-standing (e.g., the federal government). In fact, it is unlikely that any complex organization is free of important and limiting constraints. They need continuing support, finances, labor, clients, and information. In our complex environment all organizations have a relatively high degree of interdependence with other organizations. Organizations, like men, seldom stand alone.

Thus, an effective administrator also needs interorganizational skills. If, for example, the goal is to maximize the effectiveness of a care-giving network, eliminate barriers and reduce gaps in the delivery of services, new interorganizational arrangements will be necessary. Alternatively, a single system could be posited, necessarily governmental. But the government is, by definition, a patchwork of compromise and conflicting issues and parties, superimposed by a central mechanism counterbalanced by the legislative and judicial branches and reporting to multiple interests and constituencies.

Politics and politicians are not only inseparable bedfellows for public administrators, they shape a legitimate public administrative role for him. Nor are private administrators, profit and nonprofit, far removed from comparable role requirements. The complex and increasing interrelationship between public and private domains is one of the striking features of American life. Political science skills are necessary for all administrators. Some of the necessary tools: political, communication, planning, decision-making, fiscal, co-alignment, coordination, and leadership, are described in the articles which follow.

Planning

Perhaps no greater problem presently confronts decision-makers in the human services than that of developing strategies for social and organizational change in this period of environmental turbulence.

Defined in several ways, planning can be perceived as a series of overlapping steps: (1) collect the information essential for the planning; (2) establish objectives; (3) assess the barriers and determine how they can be overcome; (4) appraise the apparent and potential resources, funds, and personnel and see how they fit together; and (5) develop the plan of operation including a definite mechanism for continuous evaluation.[1]

These steps can be subsumed under each of four separate categories of planning: (1) policy; (2) problem solving; (3) interorganizational; and (4) intraorganizational. These in turn can be focused on people (social planning) or things (facilities or physical planning).

While the above are conceptually helpful as specific and separate planning categories, they fail to indicate the subtleties and interdependency of their component parts. For example, physical planning at its early stages is necessarily subordinate to social decisions; the decision to build or renovate a building for public or voluntary nonprofit purposes should be demonstrated as serving a nonduplicative public purpose; a "simple" site location decision may be politically very complicated; a careful programming of the services to be offered and functions to be performed should be accomplished in detail before any decisions or discussion about organizational structure.

Ordinarily planning as an organized process develops only after some felt need becomes manifest; e.g., a hospital becomes overcrowded, a visiting nurse association cannot meet federal standards for reimbursement, the delinquency rate continues to rise, summer services to youth appear inadequate, or a community wishes to apply for a mental health or retardation staffing grant.

[1]World Health Organization. Suggested Outline for use by countries discussing Health Education of the Public. *A12 Technical Discussions*. March 31, 1958.

The visiting nurse association could try to reorganize itself to meet federal standards or the local health and welfare planning council may be invited in or invite itself in to assist the organization. But as is often the case, failing a large infusion of new funds, no way can be found to effectively reorganize a given agency except to link it to another agency either through a formal merger or by a contractual mechanism. Thus, an intraorganizational issue can easily become an interorganizational problem.

Following this example further, a major end result of becoming eligible for medicare funds is that over a period of time there has been a diversion of the energies and skills of visiting nurse associations into more and more work with the aged. An admirable and needed program by itself, this outcome has meant that other needed services, not supported by third-party fees, have begun to suffer and a new community-wide service problem becomes evident. At a policy level, can the administrator hope that third-party payers are likely to pay for preventive home visits?

Ordinarily, planning sponsorship is of two kinds: an organization plans for itself, or an organization with broader community interests consults with it upon request. In addition, as a community becomes larger and more complex, planning could become the principal function of a free-standing organization. But whatever the auspice, the tools and problems are basically the same. We would hope that the reader would see planning as an integral administrative tool to be used on an ongoing basis by any operating agency. They may plan to improve their services to solve their organizational problems, to relate their own agency to others, or to influence the larger policy or organizations which impinge upon them. In the latter case, their goals may be to directly enhance their own functioning or to promote the public good.

As human services are increasingly perceived as universal rights, independent of financial means, and as the human service systems become increasingly costly, the functions of planning will grow in scope and intensity.

As any reader knows, it is one decision to plan and another very different one to implement a plan. Five major sets of obstacles to effective planning can be identified: (1) the equating of planning with socialism, controls, and regimentation; (2) the view that planning is an overhead or product development cost thus limiting expenditures; (3) the implicit threat to boundary, domain, and organizational integrity; (4) the sheer complexity of many variables in our pluralistic society; and (5) the exponential rate of social and technological change.

The articles which follow have been chosen, in part, because they do not gloss over these many problems. How does planning reinforce innovation and alternative organizational means? How does one introduce the concept of systems and still avoid depersonalization? Ends and means must be continually clarified and delimited. Are centralization and decentralization antithetical? How is the plan to be implemented? Funded? Is consensus an effective decision-making tool? How do we protect the privacy and confidentiality of clients and at the same time build an adequate data base? Given many diverse authority sources, is planning really possible without either clout or carrot? Can low-income individuals be truly integrated into planning? How do we control the technician so that he does not make all the significant decisions? Who manipulates whom? And finally, to what degree are rational decisions possible?

Our dilemma is a very simple one to state: planning is increasingly necessary; planning is increasingly difficult. Successful planning merely raises the odds in your favor by reducing the risks. The further ahead one attempts to forecast or the more comprehensive the perspective, the more variables that are introduced and the less the likelihood of success.

One major policy shift may be worth more than 100 expanded agencies.

22. Policy Paper: A New Look at Public Planning for Human Services

Edward Newman
Harold W. Demone, Jr.

The human services which are delivered by a human service organization are only in part a function of the basic competence of the staff of that organization. Rather, if appropriate considerations have not been given to the planning of the delivery of services, the level of competence is not likely to make any meaningful difference in the lives of persons in need.

In the article to follow, planning trends in the human services are examined. The functional and dysfunctional consequences of these planning trends and strategies are analyzed, and placed in short-term and long-term perspectives. In addition, some of the more seductive, but dangerous, practices in planning, such as bypassing state delivery systems and encroaching on the domain of parallel or competitive organizations, are examined.

In this paper, we will consider seemingly divergent trends in human service fields on the simultaneous emphases of high impact and state planning, comprehensive and categorical planning and technology and participation.

As social planners, we have noted a widespread interest in new efforts directed at urban centers and have sensed an impatience by some health and social welfare professionals with the potential contribution of the state in the solution to urban problems.

As part of a separate trend over the past few years, an increasing cadre of planners in health related fields has been attempting to devise viable statewide systems for the delivery of services. Yet, the proliferation of statewide planning efforts has occasionally bred confusion and sometimes conflict over issues of service domains and jurisdictional prerogatives.

Amid these trends, new planning technologies have emerged which may themselves give rise to new power centers. We will attempt to analyze these trends, and then comment on some new directions in planning for human services, for we prefer the broader human services perspective even to the admittedly wide range of programs now subsumed under comprehensive health planning.

LOCAL AND STATE PLANNING APPROACHES

The Problems of the Local Jurisdiction.   While urban governments are criticized for their impotence, lack of creativity and inability to change, some suggest that the solution to their problems is in sharing their power. Unfortunately, for those advocating this power realignment, very few really significant decisions are left for the neighborhood, community and even large city.

How many city governments have the capacity to deal with such problems as mental illness, underemployment and unemployment, inadequate public education and transport, air and water pollution, and solid waste disposal? Few significant problems present a sufficiently limited territorial base, even assuming that local government possessed an adequate tax structure. This may explain why local governments, those closest to the people, even with outstanding leadership, often appear to be the least responsive to community needs (as compared to the more remote state and federal governments). Compounding the problem is the essential conservatism of local government which has traditionally directed its attention toward keeping the tax rate down. It sees its obligation as primarily directed toward those who contribute to the tax base, not to those who seemingly take from it.

What some people have called a new trend, namely, the federal to local axis (usually medium or large cities), for the provision of human services programs has bypassed traditional structures (i.e., federal to state to local) of traditional health and welfare services. Instead, new federally stimulated high impact programs, such as the Model Cities and Neighborhood Services Programs, have been designed for direct receipt of federal funds. These programs are expected to "coordinate with," "cooperate with" and in some instances "receive the approval of" relevant state authorities. Formally, they are instructed to include state authorities and their local counterparts in their planning. Informally, they are instructed not to antagonize the established interests.

The federal-to-local high impact programs are reflections of the relative urgency required for dealing with the problems and demands of the socio-economically deprived and politically limited sub-groups. The states in the past have responded (with variable commitments and effectiveness) through services usually dispensed on a case basis rather than to geographic pockets of poverty—especially those in central cities of states with rurally dominated legislatures.

Until very recently it has been the politically sophisticated middle class citizen, frequently suburbanite, who effectively lobbied for a service facility such as a psychiatric clinic for his community. We are beginning to see some stirring by previously nonpolitical disadvantaged residents of central cities. It is still too early to measure the latter's potential success in influencing major health and welfare decisions. We can predict that their success will be minimal if only the local government structure is influenced.

The bulk of the funds and program controls will still be supplied by state governments for the foreseeable future. The federal constitution fails to provide cities with an independent political existence. Constitutionally, local jurisdictions are creatures of their various states. Our unhappiness with ponderous and sometimes bureaucratically encrusted state programs for serving human needs should move us to strategies for reforming these systems. It would be a far more formidable task to bypass the state.[1]

The Central Role of the State. In planning for human services, it is important, first, to differentiate between services intended for the general population and services directed to geographic pockets of disadvantaged "high risk" populations.

In the public arena, the traditional route by which health and welfare services are funded and delivered has been federal-to-state-to-local government. The state, usually operating under general federal guidelines, has been the key level of government for determining the scope and the standards for these programs.

In the mental health field, for example, the state has historically had major responsibility for institutional programs for the mentally ill, although some states ceded the partial operation of these programs to county or other local jurisdictions. It has only been under the impetus of the federal mental health service acts of this decade that the federal government has begun to provide funds and set minimum standards for services, staffing and facilities. (Even today the federal proportion of service costs is very limited.)

Federal support for retardation services follows this pattern to a considerable extent. The public federal-state rehabilitation program requires that a state agency, under state statutes and regulations and state matching funds, run the program. The state rehabili-

[1]See Alexander Heard, State Legislatures in American Politics, pp. 30-36 for a summary analysis of the status of federal-state and state-local relations.

tation agency submits an annual state plan which allows some flexibility for state and local arrangements. The public welfare program, with huge federal financial backing and many federally imposed standards and regulations, still points to the state welfare agency as the officially designated authority for dispensing public welfare benefits and services.

The public health field, traditionally designed along categorical lines (until PL 89-749, the Partnership of Health Act), has similarly required the state to design an annual plan for program operation. Its funds, as in mental health and retardation, are principally derived from state and local taxes.

In all major health and social welfare programs, it is the state which is required to submit an annual plan making it eligible for federal formula or block grants. Counties, cities and towns are eligible only as they conform to the state plan.

The pattern, then, of substantial state authority in the supervision, and often operation, of health and welfare services has been established and solidified over the years. Powerful constituencies have been built up from citizens, professional groups and associations of bureaucrats in support of the central role of the state in the provision or overall supervision of health and welfare services.

STATE PLANNING IN A PLURALISTIC CONTEXT

In the last few years, some unique planning opportunities for reforming state human services programs have presented themselves in the form of comprehensive statewide planning in mental health, mental retardation and vocational rehabilitation. In each of these fields, through acts of Congress, the states and territories have been provided with the financial means to develop statewide plans for defining policy directions, proposing programs and for setting priorities for the phasing of recommended programs for mentally and physically disabled populations. Although the accomplishments of these state planning projects are just beginning to emerge, at least some states have successfully generated impressive new structural alignments, broad program directions, some continued planning capacity of their own, and even specific service gains. In other states, little substantive change is noted. The fact, though, that even some substantial movement can be attributed to the activity of the planning projects leads us to ask what were some of the essential preconditions to change.

Preconditions for Change. In the case of mental health and retardation, a penetrating charge by the late President Kennedy stimulated broad, articulate citizen movements, which combined at the national level with officials and professionals to produce national indictments and national directions to respond to the needs of these vulnerable groups.

Congress legitimated the activities of the Joint Commission on Mental Illness and the President's Panel on Mental Retardation by providing planning funds for all the states to be expended by state "authorities" designated by each governor. Federal conditions for each state's acceptance of the planning funds included the requirements that planning be comprehensive in scope, include all relevant public, private and consumer interests in the preparation of proposals and link these interests, programmatically, to provide coordinated services for affected populations.

To add some incentives, Congress created legislation which provided beginning federal support for construction and staffing of mental health and retardation facilities and which provided funds for "implementation" to follow planning in retardation.

These, then, were some of the supports to state planning provided by the federal government: A national platform; Congressional legitimation and planning grants; the convening authority of the governor; the promise of some tangible reward if the task were accomplished reasonably well; the stipulation that all relevant local interests must participate; and that all relevant service units should coordinate their programs on behalf of designated client groups. With this seemingly impressive array of "props" undergirding the planning, the probabilities of successful reform had risen sufficiently to provide the state planner and his allies with a fighting chance.

Massachusetts, like most states, suffers from serious fiscal problems. A host of proposals continually vie for limited resources. Those proposals which project themselves as widely supported will enhance their chances for consideration by the governor, legislature or by the administrator of a public agency.

A Case Illustration. In Massachusetts, considerable discontent was generated from citizens' associations for retarded children, which were dissatisfied with some of the programs and facilities for the retarded operated by the state Department of Mental Health. These associations and their influential state and federal legislative and bureaucratic allies seriously considered proposing the transfer of retardation programs from the Department of Mental Health to the Department of Public Health or the establishment of a separate state retardation agency. (This threat was not to be taken lightly;

separate state agencies for the retarded have recently been established in a number of states.)

A number of findings from the Mental Retardation Planning Project[2] converged to show that the proposal would not benefit retarded persons in Massachusetts. Among these findings was the fact that the Department of Public Health did not want these programs, nor was this department organized or staffed to run them. The Department of Mental Health did possess many of the requisite staff and had demonstrated in at least some of its programs the capacity to improve its services to the retarded. The Planning Project found that, in fact, seven major state agencies served retarded clients and their families in various ways (a fact generally unknown or unacknowledged). By definition, the choice of any single department presented serious organizational difficulties. Contrariwise, extracting retardation programs from this functional and bureaucratic maze to a new consolidated specialized agency presented equally unresolvable problems. Therefore, a coordinated interdepartmental approach to this problem was seen as most feasible if: (1) coordinated services to the retarded could be developed at the point of delivery, and (2) each agency could be monitored and made more accountable for performing its mandated tasks for this client group.

The Planning Project developed an organizational structure and a set of functions and responsibilities for a proposed new agency—an Office of Retardation, to be located within the governor's Executive Office for Administration and Finance. The new office would plan, monitor, coordinate, provide staff training, evaluate and stimulate programs and research in retardation among relevant state departments providing direct services. The proposal, developed by staff, was discussed, amended and refined by representatives of the major health, education and welfare agencies of the state, each carefully scrutinizing it to guard against major abridgments of autonomy.

Included on Project task forces were members of the legislature, the state association for retarded children and the state taxpayers association. The willingness of the bureaucrats to accept the proposal stemmed from a recognition (reinforced by Project staff) that the Office of Retardation was an acceptable alternative to either

[2]In Massachusetts the federal funds for mental retardation planning were assigned to the Department of Mental Health which contracted with a voluntary noncategorical health agency, the Medical Foundation, Inc., to conduct the study. The co-authors of this paper served as the Director (Demone) and Project Coordinator (Newman) of the Project.

transferring the retardation programs and facilities from one major
state department to another, or developing an entirely new agency.

The new Office appeared to satisfy or at least to pacify consumer
group demands. For the first time, retardation was legitimized and
programmed at the highest level of state government.[3] The federal
government adjudged the proposal to be innovative and provided
matching support for the next five years. The governor, in acknowledgment of the need and administrative complexity, and with an
eye to federal support, created the new Office with minimum time
lag. The Legislature agreed, after some difficulty.

The point of presenting this brief case example is not to illustrate
a planning "success," although those engaged in the process were
pleased with the outcome. What, after all, was accomplished? A
new Office was created which holds some promise of eventually
bettering the lives of retarded people. This structural innovation
represents one reasonable, yet limited, means toward meeting more
general objectives. It was not the only alternative, but appeared
on balance to satisfy both substantive and strategic considerations
at the present time in Massachusetts. A client group would receive
more planful and potentially more responsive services. The
bureaucratic machinery serving this group was rationalized and
opened to public scrutiny.

Toward a New Level of Comprehensiveness
in State Human Services Planning

Now that we have described one example of a planning "success"
in a special problem area (retardation) we would be less than candid
if we did not point up at least a major limitation of this kind of
planning. If we return to the federally stimulated comprehensive
state planning efforts in this decade—beginning with mental health,
and then mental retardation, vocational rehabilitation, now comprehensive health (and in part heart, cancer and stroke)—we have
witnessed a spiraling of federal attempts to stimulate the states
to plan for their human resource needs.

At first glance, one might think that an elaborate master plan
had been devised wherein the Administration and Congress, in
their wisdom, had recognized that the rationalization of several
fields of service could not be accomplished in one fell swoop and

[3]For a summary of the rationale and proposed functions of the new state unit
see Edward Newman and Allan Spiegel, "Massachusetts Plans For its Retarded,"
in Mental Hygiene, January 1969.

decided to stimulate the states to pace their efforts over a span of years.

On could argue that the intial passage of the Mental Health Act made it easier for those interested in planning in other fields to get Congressional support for their areas of interest. The fact remains that, like other products of the political process, these provisions for statewide comprehensive planning reflect the formulations and support of organizations and interests within and outside government which had commitments or stakes in the categorical field to which a particular planning project would address its efforts.

Each of the Congressional enactments for statewide comprehensive planning gave the governors the authority to designate the state agencies which were to have jurisdiction over the planning activities. In almost all instances, the governors chose, as their "authorities," those agencies with a primary responsibility for operating programs in mental health, retardation, vocational rehabilitation and public health.

Expansion of Domains.   To the people involved in these planning ventures—the newly appointed policy groups, the task force members and the staff—the efforts did appear to be sufficiently broad in scope to be labeled "comprehensive." Comprehensive planning, to these people, meant being involved in an enterprise which sought solutions to questions on a larger scale than they had ever before experienced and for an increasingly broader interpretation of relevant populations "at risk."

It has been our observation that some persons who have been in the state planning projects have seized upon the mandate for producing comprehensive plans as a means to extend their particular domains. The professionals, administrators and citizen backers in each of these planning efforts earnestly attempted to find pathways for responding to federal strictures for the improvement and extension of services and for the wide participation of relevant interests, including consumers, in both planning and service provisions. However, one of the significant findings from the Massachusetts experience has been that what was perceived by the planners and their backers as statesmanlike attempts to improve and extend services were, in turn, perceived by those whose domains were "invaded" as unstatesmanlike aggrandizement.

Specialization.   The increasing specialization of health and health-related services has produced individuals whose world views stem from their respective professional training and socialization. These specialists influence special interest groups and concerned citizens to their perspective. Their prestige values are peer-oriented. As they attempt to extend their domains, they confront others who are themselves rethinking responsibilities from their own and different vantage points.

In Massachusetts, for example, the mental health interests were surprised at the vehemence of the response from retardation interests to their "willingness" to subsume retardation programs under the mental health area of responsibility. The psychiatrists, for example, were surprised to hear of the claims of the pediatricians, the psychologists and the special educators.

The retardation interests and the vocational rehabilitation people argued about who should operate a vocational training facility for the retarded. The vocational rehabilitation agency was blamed for paying insufficient attention to chronic populations traditionally served by the public health system. The public welfare system reminded the others of the generic responsibilities of its domain.[4] The good intentions of each service system were either not appreciated or received rebuffs from other systems as it strived to become more "comprehensive" and succeeded in threatening other domains by its attempts to extend services.[5]

It is easy to fall into a number of traps which await the individual who attempts to "clean up" the untidiness which characterizes our pluralistic approaches to the delivery of human services programs. It is easier to delineate the concept of comprehensiveness than it is to impact the real world of multiple planning and service systems. Planners have frequently conceived comprehensive and rational systems—on *paper*. These same paper plans have been the products by which social and physical planners have been most closely identified in the public mind.

TECHNOLOGY AND PARTICIPATION

The public is now displaying an increasing impatience with mere paper plans for the allocation and distribution of public goods

[4]These conflicting domain concerns seldom reach the public arena. It might be considered "unsightly" to debate in public. This would happen, in the usual course of events, as a last resort (a serious threat to the integrity of an agency, with no alternative recourse).

[5]Cf. Sol Levine, "Organizational and Professional Barriers to Interagency Planning," (mimeographed paper) who suggests that a critical planning stage is reached when it is necessary to consider what rewards an organization may obtain as substitute for relinquishing a part of its domain.

and services. (Any large state agency worth its salt should be able to supply at least one of these studies per year.)

We might add to our earlier formulation that if the successive statewide planning acts were not part of an overall master plan, they still reflected a changing attitude toward planning—especially planning for implementation—and a felt need that something should be done.

Clearly, the executive branch, the Congress and the various interested constituencies perceived problems. The service maze was becoming increasingly difficult to negotiate. The specialists were becoming further specialized. The personal touch was lacking. Gaps and overlap appeared to occur simultaneously. The more money expended, the more was requested. Expected results were not achieved. Probably most important, increasing population, urbanization, congestion, mobility, sharpening of class and racial differences, and continued ethnic tensions helped to create a feeling of alienation from the decision-making and increasingly technically oriented care-giving systems.

Some effort to humanize, rationalize and economize was overdue. We have suggested some limitations to the form of planning which attempts to rationalize only a single domain or field of service. Do we have an alternative under our system of multiple centers of authority and influence?

The choice may be thrust upon us by a technological explosion whose very existence may threaten our ideas of democratic participation. American scholars of social and physical planning, and some of its practitioners, are now engaged in an effort to find an accommodation between an increasing tendency to use the findings of science and to simultaneously involve citizens at decision-making levels.

In principle, by means of large digital computers, we have the capacity to reduce large numbers of variables to manageable limits. We can control many of the variables, perform sophisticated analyses on large clusters of data and simulate social experiments. We possess meaningful fiscal control measures in cost effectiveness studies, and performance and program budgets. The theories of the economic, physical and social planners are beginning to converge. General systems theorists have extrapolated from biological models.

The technology and language of planning is, even at its present elementary stage, becoming increasingly complex. Escalating sophistication could estrange even the well educated non-planner, professional, businessman and community leader from decision making centers. One urgent need is a system of government with the competence and authority to do its job.

McGeorge Bundy (1968), president of the Ford Foundation, in his recent Godkin lectures, suggested that executive branches of government must be strengthened, not weakened, if we are to cope with our serious domestic issues. He says: "What is wrong . . . is the absence of the clearly concentrated authority and responsibility . . . But . . . executives need release also from other normal constraints: from laws so loaded with detail that discretionary responsibility is crushed; from patterns of power in which their normal subordinates are almost wholly autonomous from legislative oversight."

Obviously, if we want our government to share its influence, it must first be permitted authority and competence. It cannot share that which it does not possess.

Effective democratic participation, we believe, is dependent upon the development of strong, not weak governments. Then, and only then, will governments have something to share. To be effective, this participation must be at the level of policy superordinate to technological manipulations. The public must be given the opportunity to participate in the determination of policy objectives; even the most sophisticated technocrat can exercise only his individual wisdom here equally with all others.[6]

Increased rationality and a higher level of comprehensiveness in the development of human services programs will depend upon our ability to capitalize upon technological advances while finding new ways in which citizen participation can be built into the system.

A more sophisticated technology will give us the methods for answering complex questions. But who will pose the questions? We must experiment with new ways of using the great untapped reservoir of citizen knowledge and desire to become engaged in real problems confronting our public systems. We must seek ways to grant our chief executives and top administrators the requisite authority to carry out their responsibilities with minimal encumbrances. A starting point would be to develop new organizational forms which are capable of balancing the new technology with the citizen policy advisor—within and among service domains.

A Challenge to Professionals.   At some point, and we suggest it

[6]Cf. to E. E. Schattschneider's claim that "nobody knows enough to run the government. . . . Democracy is like nearly everything else we do; it is a form of collaboration of ignorant people and experts." From his book, The Semi-Sovereign People, he adds: "Even an expert is a person who chooses to be ignorant about many things so that he may know all about one." Pp. 136-137.

is now, program development procedures must be designed to focus on the needs of the consumer rather than on professions or service domains. This would mean that existing service systems would have to be effectively coordinated or merged into integrated programs at local points of service delivery.

Planners and administrative decisionmakers will continue to be confronted with choices which posit market place pressures with the values and myths of the professional disciplines and, increasingly, with the emerging findings of the new planning and management technologies.

Health and social science professionals, as part of this unfolding pattern, can take leadership by continually clarifying the needs of the consumer and pressing toward clarification of the responsibilities of all care-giving systems. Professionals should support efforts to give executives the requisite authority to make important administrative decisions; to extend technology, but balance its contribution with imaginative and relevant participation of the consumer and the citizen-at-large to stem the growth of alienation of people from professionals and their bureaucracies.

Finally, professionals can become leaders and statesmen for emerging directions in the delivery of human services, if they can look beyond their immediate domain concerns and continue to reassess their own roles from the vantage point of the myriad interests and fields associated with our expanding human services programs.

Conclusion

On the basis of our observations we have attempted to sketch in this paper some significant trends in planning for the provision of human services. Each trend has been posed as an opportunity for attacking a delimited aspect of human service problems—and as a potential danger if it were to be ceded undue emphasis. We began by recognizing the urgent need for direct federal intervention for high impact programs in urban centers; but pointed out the longer run dangers of bypassing delivery systems controlled by the state. We presented a brief summary of the creation of a state executive level planning instrumentality for the rationalization of services in a special problem area—retardation; but illustrated the need to negotiate through a maze of agencies and interests whose consent or neutralization were required. Comprehensive statewide planning projects were lauded for their efforts to improve and extend services. The dangers of their competing with or encroaching upon other service domains were also noted. Finally, we mentioned the potentials of technology for reducing complex problems to manageable limits; but voiced concern about the potential for relinquishing public policy decisions to the technocrat-planners. We have argued instead for greater executive authority which welcomes a strengthened citizen policy role.

REFERENCES

Bundy, McGeorge. 1968 Godkin Lectures. Cambridge, Massachusetts: Harvard University.

Heard, Alexander. 1966 State Legislatures in American Politics. Englewood Cliffs, New Jersey: Prentice Hall.

Levine, Sol. 1966 Organizational and Professional Barriers to Interagency Planning. Waltham, Massachusetts: Brandeis University.

Newman, E. and A. D. Spiegel. 1969 "Massachusetts plans for its retarded." Mental Hygiene 53 (January): 100-104.

Schattschneider, E. E. 1960 The Semi-Sovereign People. New York: Holt, Rinehart and Winston.

23. The Limits of Rationality in Planning

Harold W. Demone, Jr, Ph.D.

Although the author would like to build a case for rational decision-making in planning, the existential nature of many issues, the pluralism of forces, and the many existing commitments by power brokers make political accommodation inevitable. Human service networks and organizational relationships at a community level, having grown out of compromise and accommodation in planning, usually contain the conflicts and problems, rational and irrational, of the superordinate groups involved in the planning process.

These factors operate as parameters or definitive conditions within which plans must be developed. Seldom does the planner operate with tabula rasa, and rarely does he have the sanctions or knowledge to guarantee results. Paradoxically, he is often required to develop rational plans within an irrational framework.

Are there clearly defined parameters for the activities accepted as planning? Are there common methods of making decisions? Can a useful theory of planning evolve from a careful analysis of one case history or a series of case studies?

The World Health Organization (1958) suggests a planning model with the following steps:
1) Collect information essential for planning.
2) Establish your objective.
3) Assess the barriers to health education and show how they can be overcome.
4) Appraise the apparent and potential resources, funds, personnel and see how they fit together.
5) Develop the detailed educational plan of operation including a definite mechanism for continuous evaluation.

There are other procedures. Dr. Dean Roberts, Executive Director of the National Commission of Community Health Services,

This paper was read at the annual meeting of the American Psychological Association, Chicago, 1965.

Inc., cites seven different planning models. Essentially all are a means-end schema in which a course of action to achieve ends is selected. The pragmatist would say that good planning means choosing "that procedure which is most likely to achieve your ends."

For the purposes of this paper, experiences with two planning activities—the statewide Massachusetts Mental Health and Mental Retardation Planning Projects—will be used to illustrate various concepts. The Mental Health Planning Project is sponsored by the National Institute of Mental Health in its program of Grants-in-Aid for state mental health planning. The Massachusetts Mental Retardation Planning Project is supported by a Grant-in-Aid under the terms of the Mental Retardation Planning Amendment of the Maternal and Child Health Act of 1936 (Public Law 88-156). These projects were operated by the Massachusetts Department of Mental Health, in cooperation with The Medical Foundation, Inc., a voluntary health organization.

To what degree do the activities of these two projects fit the rational planning models described above? The answer to this question must reflect the fact that as mental health and retardation planners we are only one small part of a very large system, and our claim as planners to rationality is directly related to the coalescence of goals in the various subsystems. It is suggested that inherent limits of our role can be found in any planning endeavor.

CONCEPT OF RATIONAL CHOICE

An examination of the concept of rational choice is required before moving to some of the nonrational factors. Our planning procedures, steps, or techniques will not be described. Instead we will go directly into the theory of ideal types and reflect some of our experiences against the ideal type rational planning model, using it as a "straw man." The literature details the rational choice mechanism. In the ideal type model, one analyzes the situation, collects information, and establishes alternate courses of action.

To what extent do the resources, authority, skills, time, information, and legal rights of the Massachusetts Planning Projects or the Massachusetts Department of Mental Health inhibit or help in determining choices? Basically, efforts were directed toward end reduction and elaboration in establishing objectives, narrowing our goals, and moving toward them.

To what extent are our ends clear? Do we really have goal consensus in mental health, urban renewal, or highway construction? A function of planning is to sharpen the ends as well as the means.

But even ends must be delimited. The active must be separated from the contextual. An active goal was to secure authority for eminent domain proceedings to take land adjoining the Massachusetts Mental Health Center, to allow for program expansion. Contextual action resulted immediately. Community residents, whose houses were to be taken, were able to arouse opposition in the legislature. The residents and some of the legislators objected and were able, even though the legislature itself overrode them, to persuade the Executive Council to block the move. The Department of Mental Health states that alternate action courses were not available. The planner must ask, given the reality factors, what the relative value is of the consequence to the ends. Is the alienation of three or four legislators and some citizens worth the end? What will be the long range effect? These questions are fundamental to effective planning.

Continuing with the rational process of planning, one is told one must first design a general course of action, then specific courses within it. But, in fact, when designing a general course of action, one often, by definition, excludes certain specific courses. By emphasizing the general hospital as a focus of community mental health programs, it is possible that one may be precluded from developing a therapeutic community—a procedure which has low value to the general hospital, but high value in modern mental health practice. The consequences need continuing evaluation. Good planning must include unanticipated consequences. Banfield (1962) says, "the planner must somehow strike a balance between essentially unlike intangibles." This is not a simple balance sheet.

Concept of Nonrational Choice

How much rationality is there? Can we assume that various planning models have any relation to fact? Is there a tradition of rational planning in the mental health system, or in the social, health, and welfare system in general? Banfield suggests that most important decisions, "those constituting the development course of action, are the result of accident rather than design" (Banfield, 1962). With this caution in mind, some features of the rational planning model will be examined.

Range of Alternatives

To what extent do we really have a range of alternatives? The existentialists, who focus on man in the flesh, note the frequency of situations in which man is faced with impossible choices. There is often no sharp option between good and evil; no way of avoiding some unpleasantness. Or, slicing this differently, how often do we have alternatives? What are these limits? Can planners who are committed to implementation, realistically conceptualize the total range of alternatives available to deal with mental health problems? When the Congress, the Massachusetts General Court (the state legislature), the State Department of Mental Health, and the last four state administrations are already committed to development of community mental health centers primarily located in general hospitals, obviously our range of alternatives for this question is limited. Are there other options?

It has been suggested that state hospitals should be liquidated. We have to ask the basic question of whether, if this goal is appropriate, they can really be liquidated. Would it be realistic? What about the financial investment, personnel involved, and organized labor? Who is to give prolonged patient care should you remove the state hospital? Are the system maintenance requirements too great? In Massachusetts, we have decided that they should not be abolished but instead helped to become more viable, more community-directed, and better coordinated with other appropriate organizations. We are, therefore, trying to develop administrative mechanisms which will help toward this goal.

Within the range of alternatives, we look to various sanctioning authorities for direction. What about Massachusetts statutes? Does the law help us in determining our goals or our procedures? Actually, except for assigning specific responsibility to the State Commissioner of Mental Health, the statutes are quite general and meaningless insofar as determining direction. However, generality allows for flexibility and change, so in a sense it is a plus—it gives us some freedom. On the other hand, the state constitution does place some limitations on mental health programming. It forbids the Commonwealth or any political division from "maintaining or aiding" any private hospital in the same terms in which it separates the state and religion and the state and private education. Reasonable compensation for services rendered is however possible (Massachusetts Constitution). Ours is a government of laws which affects the social welfare system in a variety of significant ways. They cannot be ignored.

Although we are not directed by the constitutional provision, it is clear that certain models used elsewhere, such as grants-in-aid to private general hospitals, are excluded. In fact, we found it necessary to have a constitutional review by legal counsel in order to be clear as to our limits.

To what extent does the Massachusetts Department of Mental Health, which contracted with The Medical Foundation to do this planning, have consensus within itself; to what extent does any single institution, physical or social, have consensus within itself? In any system, public or private, profit or nonprofit, those in responsible positions usually have a commitment to their own domain. Others within the same system have commitments to other domains. In the Department of Mental Health, the state hospital superintendents have a goal—they want to develop effective state hospitals. The Division of Mental Hygiene, which operates certain outpatient facilities, wants to develop community centers and clinics; until recently its primary interest was in child guidance clinics. The state school superintendents (retardation) want to improve their programs and expand their sphere of influence. The Commissioner of Mental Health has the responsibility to strike a balance between these and other various interests.

Psychiatrists working in state mental hospitals are paid regular state salaries, while the Division of Mental Hygiene, which has a financial link with cities and towns through private mental health associations, had a different reimbursement system until recently. The Division of Legal Medicine, another part of the Department of Mental Health, uses consultants extensively. Thus inconsistent definitions and practices exist within one system, and conflict accordingly occurs.

Unintended Consequences

To what extent are decisions technical or political? A major financial investment in the health field in the last 10 years has been in nursing homes. Who made the decision and how did all of this happen? At best it appears that it was a simple decision. The government likes to have roughly two million housing starts a year. About 10 or 12 years ago the housing starts had gone down, and Congress was looking for ways to stimulate the building industry. This concern is most reasonable, since, preceding the 1929 depression, the construction industry was the first major business sector to feel the effect of the economic slump. Therefore, the Administration and Congress, always sensitive to economic indexes, combined this pressure with another, the increasing number of aged. Loans were made readily available for construction of profit and nonprofit nursing homes. This was an economic decision made primarily to counter a dip in the economic cycle. The result is a major new health resource. The other significant factor in this growth is public assistance medical care. More than half of the patients in nursing homes are receiving such aid. This shows how one institution influences another. The point for the health planner is that he should be sufficiently broad in perspective to have recognized the potential for change. It has been abundantly clear for some time that we were developing a major reservoir of aged people and that new institutional mechanisms would have to be developed to balance the ideal of a small nuclear, mobile family, and the fact of increasing numbers of aging parents and grandparents. To be of influence, we should participate in the planning phase, not merely the reacting phase as was the case in this illustration.

Who makes the decision regarding the location of a public clinic? Are these political decisions or technical decisions? Most state departments have a formally articulated policy which declares that they will respond to community needs in relation to the establishment of new programs. The philosophy is that the state does not impose its will on the people. But what really happens? The planner abdicates responsibility for looking at total needs and, in a sense, turns the decision over to those communities which are best organized to speak for themselves. It is certainly not the poverty-stricken areas which speak out—for they possess neither the capacity nor the power. The result is a system of programs established in those middle-class communities which believe, for example, in the concept of preventive medicine or mental health, which are somewhat dynamically oriented, and which know how to lobby. Even a "democratic" philosophy has to be looked at in terms of its consequences. References to the great process of democratic pluralism may be, in fact, rationalizations for evasion of principled leadership.

On the other hand, on drawing boards or close to construction, there are five community mental health centers. These are not small clinics but well-located all-purpose centers. One is on the edge of a section containing a large skid row bordering on our largest Negro community. This is a good location. It has a high priority by any criterion. We are very close to establishing programs, and the money has been allocated for construction, in other communities, including Fall River and Lowell. These are deprived areas where the mills have moved out. If you look at all five community mental health centers which preceded our arrival on the scene, they make sense. These decisions were made not at the local level but at the state level. They were made by the Department of Mental Health as it viewed total needs and resources. They accepted the difficult task of thinking in terms of justifiable priority among human needs.

318 HANDBOOK OF HUMAN SERVICE ORGANIZATIONS

There is considerable consensus in the field of mental retardation that the formal public educational system for the retarded should include the age range from 3 to 21. This recommendation can be supported on both technical and humanitarian grounds. It also has important social policy and political implications. Why should the retarded be singled out for an extended form of compulsory education? If the public educational system is to be expanded at both ends of the age scale, what will be the social, political, and economic costs? To what extent will this expansion compete with the private education system which in part fills this gap? Will the traditional age groups, from 6 to 18, suffer by this extension of the manpower and economic resources? Whatever the humanitarian or technical recommendation, the final decision will have political implications.

Consider the question of primary, secondary, and tertiary prevention—well known concepts in public health. Contemporary mental health programs are increasingly interested in the possibility of programs directed toward primary and secondary prevention. The modern general hospital, where we are going to direct many of our future activities, has yet to accept these fundamental public health precepts as equally legitimate, in action terms, as curative activities. Does this imply that the new mental health developments will suffer? Or is the reverse possible? Will the new developments in community public and mental health and medical care force a change in the general hospital? Whatever happens, the integration is certainly not going to be simple, and some accommodation is going to be necessary. Will the return to the general hospital (and it is a return, since the treatment of mental disorders was one of the prime purposes of the first American general hospitals) bring psychiatry closer to the traditional practice of medicine, or will psychiatry influence the other medical disciplines in their direction? What are the advantages and disadvantages of each? In a recent examination of psychiatric services in general hospitals, the ease by which psychiatric programs were integrated into the hospital appeared to correlate with the degree to which organic psychiatry was practiced. Apparently organic psychiatry has a much better "fit" with traditional medical practice than psychoanalytic or dynamically-oriented psychiatry.

When mental health services are finally accepted by the general hospital, what will happen to the psychologists and social workers? Will they still be allowed to practice psychotherapy as they do in many psychiatric clinics and psychiatric hospitals? More generally, what is going to happen to all of the allied disciplines who ordinarily have higher status in the psychiatric services than they do in the general hospital? All sorts of unintended consequences are possible. Grafts do not always succeed either in plant life or in human or social organisms. We must resist the tendency to make the new into something old and familiar, albeit with a new name.

Quality of Information

The quality of information must be considered. Remember the variables. Every good planning operation, every rational planning operation, should have data. How much hard data is available? What do we really know about key variables? Even the demographic data, on which we lean very heavily in public health, has shown some limitations. Demographers' predictions on population growth have not been exactly accurate over the last 20 years. Compensating for this, we can ask what difference it makes when the difference between ends and means is so gross. Since the size and the dimension of the mental health problem is so great and our resources are so limited, why concern ourselves with sophisticated demographic and ecological predictions? It is not really going to change anything. The goal will probably not be achieved in our lifetime. According to our best demographic data, 280 additional beds should meet the needs of Boston. Therefore, new community mental health centers will be built with this number of collective beds, attached to the Boston University Medical School, Tufts University Medical School, and the Massachusetts General Hospital, which is part of the Harvard Complex. However, we suspect that this is similar to the visible part of an iceberg. As soon as you open up a new facility, previously undiscovered patients come to the surface.

Rational and Nonrational Ends

The Boston University Program, now in the second phase of design, is to have 120 beds and be an all-purpose facility. It will be, no doubt, a very exciting and creative program. The facility is going to be right on the boundary of the South End and Roxbury. The South End contains a substantial skid row area, and Roxbury is our most densely populated Negro section. A mental health center in this kind of complex obviously is going to find itself in the middle of race relations, because race relations are a significant problem for half of the resident population. The center is also going to have to deal extensively with the socially isolated homeless man. They are planning for the latter, but they don't really know what to do about the race relations problem. What is the responsibility of a mental health program (which is in a neighborhood to serve that neighborhood) in race relations? How do we plan for this? How will this kind of development change our goals and programs?

Equally complex, having determined an appropriate role in a population committed to civil rights, how are the necessary adjustments made to keep pace with the rapid change in the Negro community? And too, the South End will likely change as the result of a major self-help program aided by a well-conceived and creative urban renewal and redevelopment program. The basic question is, how do we cope with constant change, and how do we plan for obsolescence? Many of the mistakes made in public health and mental health have been because we have not sufficiently anticipated obsolescence. We should expect and hope that whatever we do now is going to be obsolete tomorrow or soon after. Staff must be trained to value change.

Differing Views

Everybody has his own ideas on how best to do this job. What are the significant forces? We're hired by the state Department of Mental Health using federal funds, and that gives us immediately three sets of views. We chose as our target no single group but an ideology. We said we were going to attack the status quo. But there are many additional sets of forces. Medical schools, in many states, present a major force. Can a medical school, with its focus on training and research, be expected to develop a truly community-centered program? Should it be expected to? Should we try to compensate for its biases, and maximize its unique advantages? Can you expect a program which is a part of a major teaching hospital of a medical school to serve the total community irrespective of whether the patients meet the research and teaching needs of the institution?

General hospitals constitute another major force. It is reasonable to expect these hospitals to develop psychiatric services following the traditional models, and many are doing so. But is it reasonable to expect these hospitals to develop comprehensive mental health programs which go far beyond the traditional concept of psychiatric services? In either case, can they be developed without state financial aid?

Some private practicing psychiatrists are another group who are very concerned about this new development. The exact reasons for their concern, and, in some cases, opposition, are not entirely clear, but the specter of socialized medicine has been raised. How can the private practitioner be linked in an effective way to the newly developing system? How do we reverse a century of separation?

How will the development of consultation and mental health education programs, which we hope to build in as integral parts of these mental health centers, affect the roles of the voluntary mental health association? If the state develops mental health boards in relation to each of the community mental health centers, what will happen to the many volunteers whose attachment to the present voluntary health association is inseparably linked to their official relation to mental health clinics? What will happen if we clarify roles? Some participants are interested only in the treatment component—not community organization, political action, or mental health education. In what way will this affect the nature and type of volunteer now associated with the mental health association?

What about nonmedical personnel? Where do they stand in all of this? It was mentioned earlier that system changes require role and status adjustments in the actors, especially in the case of the psychologist, nurse, social worker, occupational therapist, and recreational therapist. They all have professional standing and legitimate interest. What are their views? One of the encouraging experiences was that every one of these groups wanted to be involved in the planning process.

Statement of Ends

Banfield (1962) said, "Serious reflection on the ends of the organization, and especially any attempt to state ends in precise and realistic terms, is likely to be destructive of that organization." He suggests that you play your ends a little loose. He is implying that there can be situations in which the goals should not be too specific. Health and welfare systems probably fall within that category. We often lack adequate knowledge in too many areas to be too precise. Banfield states:

"Rationality is less likely to be found in public than in private organizations . . . One reason for this is that the public agency's ends often reflect compromise among essentially incompatible interests. This is not an accident or occasional feature of public organization in democracy. When conflict exists and every conflicting element has to be given its due, it is almost inevitable that there be an end system which rides madly off in all directions."

If we can accept his theory, which appears to have substance to it, does this reflect on what we are doing? How can we be creative and yet realistic simultaneously? What ends are we going to sacrifice? Are we going to sacrifice our therapeutic community, our primary prevention? Any accommodation requires some loss of sovereignty.

CONCLUSION

Do decisions depend for their validity upon agreement of all those concerned? Do we have to persuade all of society to agree with us before we move ahead? Do we have to develop a nice, neat, tight, logical, and useful system? Can there be several logical systems? Can there be several logical alternatives of reasonably equal merit? Is goal-setting rational or is it also a value alternative?

In focusing so heavily on nonrational factors involved in planning—while adding that there is a willingness to accept another term for nonrational—there is no intention to decry reason, or to be negative or nihilistic, but rather to be frank and objective. This is the world we find ourselves in. In a sense, reality testing is being encouraged as is the suggestion that we can better cope with nonrational factors if we acknowledge their existence.

There are at least two basic factors which must be considered, the planner and his organization, and the systems with which he will interact. It is necessary first to settle on a general goal and then to view the stance of the various social systems which will be affected by and affect your choice of goals. What are their conscious or unconscious means-ends schemas? Even if you had the funds, sanctions, and authority, it is unlikely that you could superimpose your program. There can never be a blueprint.

To what degree are your goals incompatible? At the point where your level of knowledge about the goal variances is sufficiently adequate to make decisions about gains and losses, it is appropriate to make judgments about alternate courses of action. It may be necessary to accept incremental planning to achieve certain goals over a period of time. With this perspective, any decision consistent with your goal is rational, any decision inconsistent with your goal is nonrational.

REFERENCES

Banfield, E. C. Ends and means in planning. In S. Mailick & E. H. Van Ness (Eds.) *Concepts and issues in administrative behavior.* Englewood Cliffs, N.J.: Prentice-Hall, 1962. pp. 70-80.

Commonwealth of Massachusetts. *Constitution, Articles of Amendment.* No. 40: Section 2, Section 3.

World Health Organization. Suggested outline for use by countries in discussing health education of the public. A12/Technical Discussions/1, March 31, 1958.

24. Program Change Through Mental Health Planning*

Franklin Fogelson, LL.B., Ph.D.
Harold W. Demone, Jr., Ph.D.

The primary themes of the following article are those of organizational integrity or viability, and political adaptation. Both of these characteristics seem of critical importance if a planning organization, particularly a new organization, is to have significant impact on the organization and allocation of resources in the public sector.

In the case history described in this article, the problems of both organizational integrity and political adaptation are dealt with. The consequences of the development of these factors can be inferred as the outcomes of the project becomes evident.

Planning cannot occur in isolation; a planning body must have open and active information channels into those organizations with vested interests in the outcomes of the planning process. To the extent that this is not true, the planning body will be engaging itself in an expensive production of irrelevant trivia.

Neither can planning occur without clout; a planning body must have built into it those sanctions which give it legitimacy and direction. It must be validly seen as an organization which can affect the lives and interrelationships of human service organizations.

The last decade has been an era of planning in the fields of health and welfare. It has also been an era of innovative program change. Although innovation and planning are often part of the same endeavor, they are not necessarily synonymous either in intent or product. Planning may legitimately have as its objective the reordering or redistribution of resources or services toward a greater

---

* An earlier version of this paper was presented at the Northeastern Regional Institute of the National Association of Social Workers, Boston, Massachusetts, March 1, 1967.

degree of efficiency, equity, or coordination than had theretofore been achieved. Implicit in the concept of innovative program change on a large scale, however, is that although a sufficient objective of planning is efficiency and equity, a necessary objective of innovation is the introduction of new or substantially altered programs. Planning as a professional art may be carried out without innovational motives. However, innovation as a conscious effort should not be attempted without a planning component as an integral part of the process.[1]

A dramatic example of innovation through planning may be found in the statewide two-year Mental Health Planning Projects conducted throughout the country from July 1963 through June 1965.

Background

Although certain of the activities of this endeavor have been reported in the literature,[2] it will be helpful to place the project within a historical perspective.

The Massachusetts Mental Health Planning Project was one of the fifty-three two-year statewide, District of Columbia, and territorial comprehensive planning efforts funded by an annual $4.2 million grant from the National Institute of Mental Health. Although considerable latitude was given to the states, it was made clear in the invitation for proposals that the states' responsibility

[1]We obviously view planning as a progressive process. It is equally possible to plan to go backwards.

[2]Fogelson, Franklin, "Statewide Planning in Mental Health: An Early Report," *Social Work*, October, 1964, pp. 26–33.

Demone, Harold W., Jr., "The Limits of Rationality in Planning," *Community Mental Health Journal*, Winter, 1965, pp. 375–381.

Demone, Harold W., Jr., "Massachusetts—A Prototype for Mental Health Planning," *Psychiatric Opinion*, Vol. 3, No. 1, Winter, 1966, pp. 25–32.

Schulberg, Herbert C., and Demone, Harold W., Jr., "The Impact of Mental Health Planning," *Psychiatry Digest*, Vol. 27, Jan. 1966, pp. 33–41.

Schulberg, Herbert C., "Private Practice and Community Mental Health," *Hospital and Community Psychiatry*, Vol. 13, 1966, pp. 363–366.

Schulberg, Herbert C., and Wechsler, Henry, "The Uses and Misuses of Data in Assessing Mental Health Needs," *Community Mental Health Journal*, in press.

Demone, Harold W., Jr., Spivack, Mayer, and McGrath, Mark, "Decision Making Issues in the Development of Community Mental Health Centers," submitted for publication.

Spivack, Mayer, and Demone, Harold W., Jr., "Mental Health Facilities: A Model for Physical Planning," submitted for publication.

in this mutual venture included planning toward a comprehensive community mental health program for the entire state.[3]

The planning grants were but a link in a chain of increasing Federal commitment to the concept of mental health programs located in and developed as an integral part of the communities they served. Less than a decade after the establishment of The National Institute for Mental Health (NIMH) in 1946, the Congress enacted the Mental Health Study Act of 1955, which directed the Joint Commission on Mental Illness and Health to study existing resources and made recommendations for combating mental illness. The Commission's Report to Congress, published in 1961, under the title, *Action for Mental Health,* elicited a spirited response. In 1961, the Surgeon General's Ad Hoc Committee on Planning Mental Health Facilities recommended "that the governor of each state consider taking whatever steps are necessary to stimulate the development of a plan for mental health facilities."[4] In the following year both the Conference of State and Territorial Mental Health Authorities and The National Governors' Conference went on record as strongly recommending the allocation of Federal funds to make feasible the development of statewide planning efforts with the aim of implementing the developing community mental health concept. Responding in part to the urging of these prominent groups and in part to his own personal concern for the plight of the mentally ill, in February of 1963 the late President Kennedy issued his now famous mental health message to Congress. In this message he called for a "wholly new emphasis and approach to care for the mentally ill" in which treatment would be offered "in their own communities," and in which emphasis would be on quickly returning the mentally ill to a useful place in society. The Federal guidelines which followed very specifically called for active community and professional participation in a planning effort directed toward community-based programs in contrast to the classical custodial institutional model.

The Massachusetts Commitment to Community

It would, of course, be inaccurate to suggest that any movement in the direction of community mental health programs was a journey into virgin territory. In many states mental health programs of

[3]Public Health Service, National Institute of Mental Health, "*Digest, State Mental Health Planning Grant Proposals, 1963.*"

[4]Public Health Services, *Planning Facilities for Mental Health Services* (Washington, D. C.: U.S. Department of H.E.W., January, 1961) p. 3

a community nature had been in operation for many years. For the most part, however, these programs constituted appendages to the main body of mental health treatment programs, as measured by the proportions of funds expended for community programs in contrast to hospital programs. Massachusetts, due to the inspired leadership of such individuals as Dr. Harry C. Solomon and Dr. Jack Ewalt,[5] had progressed well along the road toward the development of mental health programs, primarily child guidance clinics, in which the community played an active role. Nevertheless, as measured by expenditures, the bulk of the mental health programs in the state and in the nation operated with nominal community participation and in settings which were psychologically (if no longer physically) isolated from the community. By accepting funds to plan for the development of a comprehensive system of community mental health programs, the states were making an implicit commitment to major program change.

Comprehensive Approach to Comprehensive Planning

Herman Field suggests that a basic characteristic of the planning method is a holistic or gestalt view.[6] When one plans for as extensive an entity as an entire state, the delineation of the components of the field is itself a comprehensive task. The system is an interacting complex of socio-economic, political, professional, technical, bureaucratic, and other considerations. In this paper examination will be limited to certain selected principles underlying the efforts of the Massachusetts Mental Health Planning Project as it attempted to both sharpen the direction of change and to accelerate its process. Some of the other dimensions are described in the references cited earlier.

Identification as an Autonomous Entity

Inherent in the type of planning discussed here is the vast array

[5]Dr. Solomon, during the period of the Mental Health Planning Project, was the Commissioner of Mental Health for the Commonwealth of Massachusetts, and was previously Superintendent of the Massachusetts Mental Health Center, considered by many to be a prototype of the community mental health center. Dr. Ewalt is currently Superintendent of the Massachusetts Mental Health Center; a former Commissioner of Mental Health for Massachusetts, he directed the previously mentioned national study of the Joint Commission on Mental Illness and Mental Health. Other significant Massachusetts community mental health innovators included Dr. Erich Lindemann and Dr. Gerald Caplan, both of Harvard.

[6]Field, Herman, "Organizing the Planning Process," *Annals of the New York Academy of Science*, September 27, 1965, p. 671.

of competing forces likely to be affected. Many will have a strong
vested interest in preserving a portion of the status quo, e.g., a
voluntary mental health group may be committed to the concept
of a coordinated state-wide program in community mental health;
they may, however, have strong reservations about surrendering
any of their perceived domain over local mental health programs;
the state mental health authority (official state agency) may
enthusiastically engage in interdepartmental planning for a particular target population (for instance, the retarded or the criminally
insane) so long as such planning does not clearly lead to the diminu-
tion of the departmental budget or authority or to the imposition
of unwanted responsibilities; the legislative leadership may appreciate the value of developing flexible intervention programs
but resist granting to community units the fiscal freedom necessary
for such flexibility. It must be understood that problems of the
type noted may be symptomatic of long standing positions, or
merely pertinent manifestations of recurring issues independent
of mental health. In any case, they represent the realities facing
all planners. Where they represent manifest or latent conflict
between competing parties they not only limit the planners' freedom, but impair the establishment of needed relationships with
influential competing camps within the system toward which the
innovative effort is being directed.

Two steps to effective planning are the need to acquire an intensive understanding of the inner workings of the system, and, lacking
power, the need to proceed under the umbrella of positive sanction.
These factors are closely related. In seeking to bring about major
change within a system as large as that in Massachusetts, a vast
amount of technical and political information, often of an historical
nature, is needed. Most cannot be found in written reports nor
even through sophisticated interviewing techniques. Often the
sense of this information can only be achieved through deep immersion into the workings of all aspects of the system, e.g., the problems
of the Department of Mental Health in delivering services and
working with the legislature, the problems of the statewide voluntary mental health association in securing adequate financing and
in their relationships with their constituent agencies; the difficulties
of the medical society (and other professional groups as well) as
they sought to frame an appropriate response to changes, some
of which were perceived as threatening. Such intelligence can often
only be obtained either through actual involvement in the problem-
solving process or through the confidence of those who view the
planners as collaborative fellow actors. The need for positive sanc-

tion goes not only to information gathering but to conceptualization of the direction of planned change and the implementation of plans as well. Unless sanction to alter the status quo comes from a wide range of actors both within and outside the system, effective innovation seems doomed to failure.

The course chosen by the Planning Project Director was organizational autonomy rooted within but not of the system. The Department of Mental Health contracted with The Medical Foundation, Inc., a Boston-based voluntary noncategorical health agency receiving support from United Funds, to do the planning. The Foundation later received similar contracts in mental retardation and rehabilitation. The Executive Director of the Foundation also served as Director of the Planning Project. The objective was to obtain a maximum of systemic sanction, access to "inside" information, freedom to improvise, and expectation of a mutual effort toward implementation.

The Commissioner of Mental Health, however, retained veto power over the selection of the planning staff and was chairman of the Planning Project Advisory Council. Key departmental persons also served on the Council and the various task forces. DMH leaders regularly attended and participated in Project staff and strategy meetings and several Project members did the same with the Department. A staff member of the Project religiously attended the meetings of the State Hospital Superintendents. The Project organized an interdepartmental meeting of commissioners and often staff members served as trouble-shooters for the Department in its relationship with other government departments, voluntary agencies, and the public at large. Thus a serious effort was made to be a part of the Department but not its creature, to be free enough to communicate effectively with Departmental critics, and to be sufficiently linked to be appropriately informed.

Attempts were made to involve key state legislators in the planning process. Although more than 30 were formal participants, these efforts were only partially successful. This may have been in part because the legislature saw this as a project funded through the executive branch. As such the Project was no doubt viewed with some suspicion and as a potential adversary. Additionally, the Massachusetts legislature, unlike any other in the country, must respond to free petition by both public hearings and a formal vote. Consequently they are almost always actively engaged in the legislative process, leaving little free time for voluntary activities. More success was had with the executive department, (the product would eventually be theirs) even with a change in administration and political party midway in the Project's life. Not only were high executive officials of the Commonwealth actively involved in planning, but staff professionals were used by both governors as consultants and "idea" men (i.e., the mental health and retardation component of both governors' annual messages to the legislature were the product of collaboration between the governors' staffs and Planning Project Personnel).

Equally complex was the establishment of an effective relationship with the nongovernmental portions of the mental health system. In addition to the inclusion of leaders from the various agency and professional associations as integral partners of the planning process, a regular system of feedback was employed. This included not only the formal exchange of ideas at both regular and specially called meetings, but also through many informal networks. To illustrate these processes special reference will be made to the State Medical Society and the statewide voluntary mental health association.

The Massachusetts Medical Society, following the lead of the American Medical Association, initially adopted a somewhat neutral 'wait and see' attitude toward our planning efforts. Of course, within the society, the spectrum of opinion ran from those who opposed the Project's goals (e.g., opposed to nonmedical participation in health matters; opposed to government; opposed to mental health; opposed to psychiatry; opposed to dynamic psychiatry; opposed to planning; and opposed to the concept of community mental health as an effective psychiatric tool) to those who wholly supported the goals. The Project's response to the medical society, as to all groups, was one of conciliatory firmness. Participation of all segments of medical and other professional opinion was sought although it was made clear that domination by any single group was in the interests of neither the medical nor nonmedical actors in the mental health system, the public, or the prospective patients. Suggestions for names of task force leaders and members were sought from and reviewed with the medical society leadership. The Project remained open to all suggestions regarding the most appropriate approaches to mental health, but made clear to the President of the Society and its Mental Health Committee that they felt that domination by any professional or special interest group of the Advisory Council and task forces would be inimical to true comprehensive planning (the support of the Society President at this time was most important). By the same token, it was made clear that there was appreciation of the special role and interest of the medical profession and that these views would be significantly represented in the decision-making process. Particular attention was given to the Mental Health Committee of the Society and, in a precedent-breaking move, they invited the Project Director (not a physician), following his introduction by the Commissioner of Mental Health, to sit in on their regular meetings during the course of the Project. The Project also conducted joint surveys with several psychiatric and nonpsychiatric medical specialty groups in order to delineate the nature of the mental health components of their private practice. The results of the surveys were shared with the groups involved.[7] With continuing communication, any possibility of adversary relationship between the Society and the Project was alleviated. This was of particular importance since relations between the state mental health authority and the Society were strained. Although areas of disagreement continued through the planning effort, avenues for accommodation were always kept open. Most important was that the great majority of the Society leadership accepted the Project as neither the captive of the Department, nor as members of an antimedical intrigue.

Another group with whom it was imperative the Project relate was the state voluntary mental health association. They were long at odds with the DMH policy to establish "mental health associations" as community partners in the child guidance clinic system. It was possible that they would perceive the Project as a further Governmental incursion into their domain. Given their understanding and expertise in the system and the constituency of citizen leaders they represented, the active opposition resulting from such a perception could have been very harmful to the planning effort. A new executive director from out of state arrived to assume leadership of the Association at about the time the Project began. Among his problems were familiarizing himself with the complexities of the state system and at the same time coping with internal dissension from the lay leadership of several of the constituent local agencies over the issue of their providing direct mental health services counter to national and state mental health association policy.

The Project staff immediately made available to the new executive as much information as it could regarding the state and its mental health system. Again suggestions were solicited for task force and advisory council membership and selections were reviewed with the leadership of the association. Many of those on task forces were, along with other qualifications, in some way identified with mental health associations. They included those who were in opposition to the state association's leadership and often the project provided the most neutral forum in which the opposing groups could

[7] For one illustration, see Schulberg, Herbert C., "Private Practice and Community Mental Health," *Hospital and Community Psychiatry*, 1966, Vol. 17, pp. 363-366.

meet. The Project by its long-range program orientation also provided topics for discussion between the Department of Mental Health and the local associations which were less inflammatory than those which had dominated many previous communications. In providing this forum the Project pointedly adopted a neutral stance and in so doing helped to establish its identity independent of either the state department or the voluntary association. One of the basic points of conflict which eventually emerged in the project was the appropriate role and degree of control which citizen volunteers were to have in connection with new programs. As might be anticipated, the Department of Mental Health and the voluntary association sometimes found themselves at opposite ends of the continuum. In the often hard-hitting conflict that followed, the independent role of the Project, which was accepted by both partisans, made it possible to work through compromises which were at least reasonably acceptable to most of those concerned.

Flexibility of Coalitions

The second basic principle adhered to was that coalitions and alliances formed at various stages of the planning process were necessarily flexible and subject to change. It was assumed that as the nature of the innovations became more specific, allies would become more discriminating in their support; e.g., as the likelihood of recommendations for optional selected nonmedical administration became apparent, (made by a task force with a physician chairman and a majority of physician members), the antiproject voices within the medical society became more prominent; as the Project's middle-of-the-road position on citizen control emerged, so did opposition within the state and local voluntary mental health association (and also from the state hospital superintendents, but for opposite reasons). Again, what emerged was the obvious fact that consensus seeking had substantial limits and unanimous approval of the innovations sought was impossible to achieve. While vigorously seeking consensus, expression of dissent was sanctioned throughout the process, and the Project published dissenting opinions in many task force reports and in the final project report itself.

The combination of strategies, consensus seeking within limits and sanctioned, formalized dissent led to an effort to delineate the nature of opposition to specifics so that objection to one segment of the recommendations need not be inconsistent with general support of the plan.

A prime example of this approach was seen in the Project's relationships with the Massachusetts Association for Mental Health. As has been mentioned earlier, the question of citizen control of programs proved to be a key point of dissension. The consistent position of the Association was that both fiscal and program control should be vested in local citizen community mental health boards. The Task Force on Administration, on legal, practical, political, historical, and philosophical grounds, proceeded from the position that such control had to be selectively exercised and limited. In many meetings, at all levels, the position of the Project was argued and attempts were made to convince both lay and professional people in the Association that their concept was not valid for Massachusetts. The result was that this series of issues was separated from the many other agreed upon issues. The difference was not allowed to become divisive. The broad commitment of the Association to innovation in mental health was thus preserved. The Association continued vigorously to put forth their position not only within the Project and their own group but among key legislative leaders. Things came to a head when, shortly before the final report was to be issued, a leading Boston newspaper brought the issue before the public with a front-page headlined article which indicated that the report would call for a centralized Department of Mental Health with only token representation by citizen volunteers in the community mental health program. This, of course, did not accurately reflect the tenor of the Project's recommendations, nor was this the Association's true appraisal of them, but was a reflection rather of the art of writing page-one headlines. Nevertheless, by bringing the question into the public domain in such a way as to suggest that the differences between the Project's report and the Association's position were qualitative rather than quantitative, the success of the whole could have been in jeopardy. When this possibility was discussed with the Association leadership, they quickly agreed and threw themselves wholeheartedly behind the Project report, contenting themselves with a pro forma dissent to a few minor points. When legislation based on this report was being considered, they continued in this vein.[8] Both in their active lobbying and testimony before several legislative committees, they enthusiastically supported the bill. They indicated that while they felt that the citizen participation sections were weak and should be reconsidered in future years, the bill itself was valid and deserved support. Even

[8]An important feature of the Massachusetts effort is that legislation was a major goal. This is not to imply that successful planning need be equated with legislation, but that legislation may sometimes be necessary.

when the legislature further cut the authority of citizen boards, the Association remained firmly behind the bill. The superordinate goal—to improve the quality of mental health services through a community mental health program—won out over jurisdictional issues.

A somewhat different situation prevailed in connection with the Medical Society. As previously mentioned, there was general reservation among some physicians about the role of nonmedical agents in the projected community program. Concern was also felt over the role of government as a competitor in a field which was perceived as the property of the private practitioner. These concerns and questions were not voiced in the context of active opposition to the Project, but rather in a wait-and-see attitude which allowed for full cooperation with the planning effort (although with far less commitment as to outcome than was found in the Association).

Within the Society, however, there was a small group who had strong feelings about these issues and who opposed the underlying concepts of community mental health. For a variety of reasons this group, prior to the beginning of the Project, had been constituted as the official spokesmen for the Society in questions of mental health. From this position of strength they could be in a position to persuade the Society to place itself on record as being opposed to the planning effort. Such an eventuality was viewed as a real possibility and one which could have been a mortal blow to the likelihood of a successful outcome for the Project. It became a task of the Project staff to establish mechanisms leading to a coalition with the medical society.

The Project staff actively reached out to the Mental Health Committee of the Medical Society and actively involved them in the planning process. Their most articulate spokesman, along with the President of the Medical Society, served on the Advisory Council. In addition, many other physicians were also on the Council. Other members of the Committee and many more not on the Committee participated as task force members. It is important to recognize that what went on was something more than a pro forma cooptation of a difficult group. They were truly a part of the project whose views were considered and who made a real impact in shaping the direction of the final recommendation of the project as a whole. The relationship was not an easy one, and basic value differences often led to stormy sessions. However, these disagreements were played out within the context of a coalition which sought to develop a worthwhile report. At no time was it presumed that this group would permanently ally itself to the Project and actively support uncritically the implementation of the final Project report in all of its details. However, the legitimation given to this group within the Project made it possible for the Medical Society to move from a neutral to a cooperative role. It is interesting that although the leader of the dissident group filed a forceful dissent to a few of the 170 Project recommendations, the Medical Society did not; although members of this group testified against selected features of the Mental Health Bill before the legislature, they supported its major elements. In fact, the majority of physicians taking a public position supported the general recommendations and the proposed legislation. By way of epilogue, clear testimony as to the fragility of alliances appeared in the form of a letter to the editor to all Boston papers shortly after the passage of the Community Mental Health-Retardation Act, which closely paralleled the Project's recommendations. In it the leader of the dissident group decried the bill passed in concept, in content, and in particular because the medical profession was not involved in its development.

Flexibility of Interventive Stances

The final underlying principle which will be examined here is the nature of the intervening stance played by the planner. The conceptualization of the stance taken by planners in itself merits a more complete explanation in a separate paper. For that reason it will be touched upon here only briefly. The literature abounds with thoughtful analyses and conceptualizations in this field of interest. Particularly noteworthy has been the work of Roland Warren, Robert Morris, and Martin Rein.[9]

The planner must have a clear understanding of the substance of the change he seeks to achieve. He must also avoid becoming the victim of his own rigidity as to the form of the change. The willingness to compromise, to assess and evaluate the realistic limits of the change which can be effected, is basic. For example, it was clear that a large measure of fiscal flexibility would be valuable in developing viable community programs. However, an assessment of the political situation in the Commonwealth made it clear that such a request to the legislature might result in the sabotaging of the entire program. Accordingly, the Planning Project Report called for very circumscribed fiscal independence (a simplified bud-

[9] Warren, Roland L., "Types of Purposive Social Change at the Community Level," *Brandeis University Papers in Social Welfare*, No. 11, Brandeis V. 1965.

Morris, Robert, and Rein, Martin, "Emerging Patterns in Community Planning," *Social Work Practice*, 1963 (New York, Columbia University Press, 1963).

get transfer procedure) which, although it did represent movement in the right direction, was far short of the ideal. However, this was a recommendation which had a reasonable chance of being implemented. (In fact, this measure remained in the bill until just before passage when it was eliminated by the Ways and Means Committee.)

Finally, the planner must see himself within a historical perspective. There is a tendency to equate innovation with dramatic change. Occasionally such a breakthrough can be made, but more often innovation is accomplished in modest steps. It is a continuing process but one in which successful implementation of only partly realized goals for change may have a major effect upon the system impacted upon.

Summary

Planning for an innovative program change, often discussed yet seldom analyzed, has here been examined through references to selected experiences of the Massachusetts Planning Project. We have used the concept innovative planning and have thus directed our inquiry to that process which seeks as its end product the introduction of new or substantially altered programs. Fundamental to an understanding of the dynamics of such a process is the capacity to see the parts as a whole.

The arena in which this project was conducted was extremely complex and populated by a vast array of divergent forces. The planning was carried out on the state-wide level and as part of the national effort. Affected were practically all the action systems in the community. Additionally, the planners became part of a field particularly subject to often bitter differences of opinion, e.g., the competition between the mental health and nonmental health systems for scarce resources; conflict between governmental and voluntary protagonists regarding their proper functions in the provision of mental health services; lack of mutual role expectations between the various mental health disciplines; and basic disagreements between those who supported community mental health as a viable approach to problem solving and those who discounted it. It was noted that in the absence of an existing entity accepted as a relatively neutral sanctioning body by the forces concerned, the planning organism itself as an organizational system must develop some autonomy and sanction of its own. It must possess credibility as a legitimate change system capable of precipitating action on the recommendations resulting from its deliberations.

However, such autonomy must not negate active participation in a cooperation with all key elements of the action system. Conscious mechanisms must be developed to insure interaction. To be stressed is the critical nature of open communication, two-way participation, flexibility, and a clear understanding of the nature of the desired change.

Dissent may be massive, nondirected, or aimed at specific elements of the innovative change. In such cases, strategies of neutralization of conflict are necessary. The planning body must engage in a series of ever-changing flexible coalitions. The nature of the coalition is directed by the particular problem at hand, rather than by over-all identification with the goals or aspirations of any particular segment within the action system. To the degree possible, it must preserve its neutrality throughout the planning process. Alliances must be calculated to strengthen the organization, not weaken it.

And finally, change is slow. Dramatic innovations are much sought, and seldom found.

25. Implementing Mental Health Planning Recommendations into Statutes: The Legislative Process in Massachusetts*

William J. Curran, LL.M., S.M. Hyg.
Harold W. Demone, Jr., Ph.D.

One problem constantly underlined by and for planners is implementation. It has often been noted that most plans lie on shelves, unimplemented and gathering dust. Although no data is available to confirm or deny this assertion, it is a widely held view. It may be that the plans deserve their fate, but for the morale of the planners, their colleagues, and supporters, not to mention the welfare of the general public, occasional successes are necessary.

One mechanism to identify and sanction planned change for public agencies is via the legislative route. For nonprofit voluntary organizations, corporate charter and by-law changes may be considered an equivalent route.

The Curran and Demone case history, which follows, describes such an effort in Massachusetts. Although amendments to existing statutes may have been adequate, it was felt that to gather support for a new approach to mental health, a new organizational enabling act should be written and introduced into the legislature. Passage would make clear to all that a new day in mental health was envisioned.

In fact, the recommendations which evolved out of two years of study and planning became the major issue in a political campaign.

The authors, acting as planner-scientist and legal counsel, found it difficult to remain aloof from the personal and party political struggles that ensued. In retrospect, they became identified as political warriors and in winning earned political respect, although not always friendship, from those taking the opposite side. In using contest social change strategies, the change agent may have to choose between love and respect.

---

*An earlier version of this paper was presented at the Annual Meeting of the American Public Health Association in Miami Beach, Florida, on October 23, 1967.

338

BACKGROUND

One of the most significant developments in American government in the mid-twentieth century is the growth of national leadership and action in areas traditionally left either totally or largely to the states and local communities. Civil rights protection may be the most prominent, but there are many more, from Medicare, to juvenile delinquency control, to secondary education.

One of the newest areas where national leadership and policy-making have been making a strong impact in the United States is that of mental health services. The U.S. Congress has traditionally been reluctant to enter directly into the mental health services area (beyond a grant-in-aid program of a limited nature). Not only is it a field historically occupied almost exclusively by the states, but it is also a very expensive responsibility, being the largest or one of the largest items in every state budget.

After the publication of the Report of the Joint Commission on Mental Illness and Health in 1961, however, it was only a matter of time and the appropriate issue before the national government would more vigorously support mental health services. It had become apparent that the excellent Federal programs of research and training could not alone provide a breakthrough in methods of caring for and treating mental illness. The huge state hospitals were still the focal point of the service system in nearly all parts of the country. Nearly all of them were chronic-care institutions run by the state governments with little or no local government involvement. Political and economic forces in the states supported the status quo in these large institutions and kept the budgets low and the professional staffs grossly inadequate.

FEDERAL ACTION IN COMMUNITY MENTAL HEALTH

The new Federal administration in 1960 and President Kennedy, with his personal and family interest in mental health programs, seized upon the just-beginning community mental health movement as the vehicle by which the status quo in mental health services could be altered. Through this movement, the national government could support promising new methods of treatment and delivery of services for the mentally ill; it could reach patient populations and types of pathology hardly touched at all by the state hospitals; and, very importantly, it could promote a governmental alternative to the state hospital system.

One of the major strategies of the Federal government designed to create this new system of mental health services in the states were the Planning Grants to each of the 50 states and territories from 1963 to 1965 under which, in compliance with Federal guidelines, the comprehensive community mental health movement would be installed.

IMPLEMENTATION IN MASSACHUSETTS

In this paper we would like to describe the implementation in Massachusetts legislation of a State-wide, Comprehensive Community Mental Health and Mental Retardation Program based upon this Federal program. The new Massachusetts law,[1] enacted in late 1966, provides for a total reorganization of mental health services in the State. It is a direct result of the Federally-supported Mental Health Planning Project and follows the Federal guidelines and objectives very closely.

The story of the preparation of this law, its incredibly stormy course as a bill through the State Legislature, and its final enactment in the last days of 1966 is a very exciting commentary on our political era. For the first time in Massachusetts history, and perhaps in the history of any state, a mental health bill became the most important issue in a state gubernatorial election. The campaign was fiercely contested on both sides with the Democratic Party controlling both Houses of the Legislature while the Republicans controlled the Executive offices. At stake was the State's first four-year term Governorship.

The Massachusetts Planning Project

In Massachusetts, the Federal funds for Mental Health Planning were assigned to the Department of Mental Health which contracted with a voluntary, noncategorical health agency, the Medical Foundation, Inc.,* to conduct the study. The Medical Foundation hired and directed a professional staff, established a series of 18 task forces, and reported its findings to a State-wide Advisory Council of 67 persons appointed by the Governor. The Advisory Council, with the Commissioner of Mental Health as Chairman, took final responsibility for the Report of the Planning Project. The two-year Project, from July, 1963, to June, 1965, was a massive effort formally involving over 400 people. Participants included, among others,

---

*An organization whose basic budget is provided by a number of United Funds in the Greater Boston area.

32 state legislators, 101 physicians, 47 social workers, 27 psychologists, and some 56 members of the staff of the State Department of Mental Health.

The Report of the Planning Project[2] contained detailed and extensive recommendations for the reorganization of Mental Health Services in Massachusetts. It proposed the establishment of a decentralized system organized in 37 community mental health areas. These areas would be groupings of cities and towns within population limits eligible for Federal aid to community mental health programs. The areas would also be grouped together into six regional subdivisions of the State. Neither the area nor the regional boundaries (with two exceptions) coincided with existing political divisions, such as counties, within the Massachusetts government. They were entirely new governmental entities proposed for the special purpose of operating mental health services. The areas and regions would each have boards representing citizens in the localities.

Another major recommendation of the Planning Project concerned financing. Unlike nearly all other states in the Union, the Project did not recommend basing the community mental health programs upon local tax support with a state matching-grant or other form of participating share of State support. It recommended retaining the existing system in Massachusetts under which nearly all support of all levels of mental health services are a State responsibility. The plan would allow local participation of public or private monies in support of local programs, but it was not required. The Massachusetts program would be a State Government structure with regional and area subdivisions, and, very importantly, it would completely integrate the State hospitals into the comprehensive system, rather than leave them fully or partially outside the system, as in most states. Considering the very limited tax revenues on the local level in Massachusetts, this was the only realistic approach that could be taken to provide community mental health services on an equitable basis throughout the State.

The Preparation of the Bill

The Planning Project Report did not contain proposed drafts or recommendations concerning legislation, though consideration was given to legislative matters during the study. This is explained on the basis that the Foundation did not consider the preparation of legislation a part of its mandate.[3]

The preparation of legislation, if any, was thus left to the Governor to whom the Report was presented publicly by the Commissioner of Mental Health on November 4, 1965. Matters were complicated by the fact that the Project had begun under another governor of the other political party, a man defeated by the then-incumbent Republican Governor John A. Volpe.

We were fortunate, however, in the fact that the Governor and his Lt. Governor took a keen interest in the Planning Project (as did the previous governor) and strongly supported its recommendations. Lt. Governor Richardson chaired a series of three public hearings on the Report in different parts of the State in mid-December.

The hearings went very well and further committed the Executive Branch to implement the Plan. An editorial in support of the Report in the *New England Journal of Medicine* mentioned the hearings, the participation of numerous members of the Massachusetts Medical Society in the study, and concluded that "a feeling of optimism pervades all who participated in the project."[4]

Following the public hearings the Governor asked the senior author of this paper, Legal Counsel for the Medical Foundation, to prepare any necessary legislation with the advice and participation of the other author, the Executive Director of the Foundation and Director of the Planning Project.

The first recommendation made by the legel draftsman, and the touchstone of all other drafting strategies, was to the effect that we prepare a single, comprehensive *Community Mental Health Act* for Massachusetts under that title and as a separate, new chapter in the laws of the Commonwealth. Separate pieces of legislation as amendments to current laws could have accomplished many if not all of the objectives of the Report at least from a technical, legal standpoint. This had been the traditional approach in Massachusetts in dealing with mental health law. The wave of Community Mental Health Acts adopted in various states in the late 1950's and early 1960's had passed Massachusetts by. The State had some community programs, mainly a set of child-guidance clinics operated cooperatively with voluntary, local Mental Health Associations and some court clinics, but no comprehensive legislation. In fact, we had very little legislative framework for the conduct of programs in mental health. It was what one might call the style of operation in Massachusetts to avoid legislative structuring of programs on a State-wide basis. Local groups were encouraged to go directly to the Legislature to lobby through special, local legislation for their own programs with no rational, State-wide consideration of priorities of need. This method of operation was made to work largely by the fact that nearly all programs were conducted under one large State agency with its own employees at all levels. Our county governments in Massachusetts are extremely weak. One of the few statutes we did have specifically barred cities, towns, and counties from setting up programs or paying for the care of any mental patients.

Abortive attempts were made in earlier years to gain consideration of a Community Mental Health Act in Massachusetts, but the efforts always foundered because of lack of support from the State Department of Mental Health. Why then did the Legal Counsel recommend, and the Director of the Planning Project enthusiastically support, the preparation of a comprehensive, single, and very large piece of legislation for Massachusetts?

The reasons were as much strategic as legal. Not only would this approach provide the best technical instrument for so widespread a reorganization, but it would provide a focal point for rallying public support for the enactment of the Project's recommendations. The citizen movements in mental health and in mental retardation were very active in the State. We needed them as allies in any legislative-action program. The leaders in these movements were aware of the fact that the passage of such Acts in numerous states had resulted in greatly increased public expenditures for community mental health services. Therefore, the very title of our legislation, its size and complexity, would suggest wider citizen participation in decision-making increased state expenditures for locally-based programs, and acceptance of Federal involvement in community mental health for Massachusetts. As a matter of law, this title also enabled us to identify the program broadly, rather than referring to it only as a reorganization, or reform, of the State Mental Health Department.

The next major strategic issue in the preparation of the bill which had to be decided was the degree of detail to be adopted in implementing each recommendation in the Report. Should we spell out everything in the law, or should we leave a great deal to the discretion of the administrators under broad, legislative guidelines? The tendency of most legislative draftsmen is toward the latter. Both of the authors of this paper are personally inclined this way. However, we were working under direction of the Governor who had asked us to implement the plan. We chose a middle ground. The bill went into considerable detail in formulating the structure of the new agencies and in determining responsibilities and authority, but it was broad in its description of program content.

Detail was necessary in the former areas because they involved an entirely new governmental structure for the State. There was no experience to guide administrators here as there was in program operation. Also, we were concerned that the more comfortable, traditional style of operation of mental health services in the State would not be moved toward change quickly enough, or comprehensively enough, with State-wide participation in decision-making on all levels, unless it was required and spelled out, with deadlines for action, in the legislation itself. We felt that the State Mental Health Department, upon whom so much new responsibility would rest, would be helped by fairly comprehensive guidance under the law. The Department did not have enough experience with citizen involvement, State-wide planning, or legal structures to function well under either too loose or too strict a legislative direction.

To understand fully the complexities of our position, reference to role theory is necessary. Much of the behavior of the important figures in the State can only be understood in relation to their positions in the government, the two political parties, and the community. Massachusetts was in the midst of a realignment of powers between the executive and legislative branches. Recent constitutional changes had increased the power of the executive and decreased the power of the legislative branch. Some of the key factors in the State political situation may be summarized as follows.

Our legislation was introduced in an election year. The Republican Governor was a candidate for reelection. The Democratic President of the Senate was first a gubernatorial candidate in the Democratic primaries and, failing to secure nomination, served as the campaign manager of the Democratic nominee. The Republican Lt. Governor was seen as a likely Republican candidate for Governor in 1970.

Federal grants are traditionally made to the executive branch of government, thus giving them resources not usually available to the Legislature. The planning-project grant was of this type.

The tenuous balance between the various mental health professionals would be altered by the proposed legislation. Many private practitioners of medicine saw the proposals as a further inroad of state medicine. The traditional autonomy and influence of the State Mental Hospital Superintendent would be altered by the legislation.

In summary, the traditional balance of power and the sovereignty of many significant actors on the political and professional scene were subject to change. Our bill therefore had many potential side effects completely independent of its merits. The legislative struggle which followed was significantly affected by these predetermined conditions essentially independent of the merits of the proposed legislation.

As planners we too had role difficulties. We were told, "state studies gather dust," "planners don't introduce legislation," and above all, "planners should avoid political conflict."

Presentation to the Governor

Our draft legislation was presented to Governor John A. Volpe early in January, 1966. It was a single piece of legislation designed to establish a system of regional and community mental health and mental retardation programs for the entire State of Massachusetts. It also included a reorganization of the central office of the Department under a Commissioner, a Deputy Commissioner, and five Assistant Commissioners.

The bill was reviewed by the Department of Mental Health, the State's voluntary mental health and mental retardation agencies, professional groups, labor organizations, and industrial and taxpayer groups before it was submitted, with some changes, to the State Legislature in a Special Message of the Governor on March 8, 1966 as House Bill 3167.

The Legislative Conference

The first public discussion of the bill, even before it received its first hearing in the Legislature, was before a Legislative Conference organized by the Massachusetts Association for Mental Health and its affiliated local chapters on March 10, 1966, just two days after the public release of the bill.

The featured dinner speaker was a senior official from the National Institute of Mental Health who was to talk on state legislation in the field of community mental health. This was to be preceded by an afternoon panel discussion on the new legislation for Massachusetts. The participants were the authors of this paper, the Republican Lt. Governor, and a high-ranking State Senator, a Democrat, who was Chairman of the Joint Legislative Committee to whom the bill would undoubtedly be referred in the Legislature.

At the end of this panel discussion, we were clearly in for some trouble. The Lt. Governor had endorsed the bill wholeheartedly. The State Senator, however, though he supported the bill in principle, attacked it for not giving more extensive power and authority to the local-level citizen boards. Since he was addressing an audience of local members of mental health associations who fully expected to be strongly represented on these new local boards, this message was keenly heard and appreciated.

That evening, the senior NIMH official complicated matters even further. He delivered a speech in which he described approvingly community mental health legislation in states all over the country where local agencies (almost all of them county governments) control programs and expenditures and receive state grants. The speech, though it was an excellent review, was all but totally irrelevant to Massachusetts conditions and was in many respects directly contradictory to our bill. He spoke about community mental health programs "authorized by law," and, without suggesting the possibility of alternatives, described these laws as providing for "locally administered state standards for personnel; (programs) jointly financed by the State and the community; and (programs which) are optional rather than mandatory."[5] Our legislation provided for none of these. Fortunately, the NIMH speaker concluded, "I am sure that if a Massachusetts Community Mental Health Services Act becomes law this year, your State's position of leadership in this area of mental health will be even more enhanced."[6]

The Legislative Process

A public hearing on the bill, House No. 3167, was held shortly afterward on April 17, 1966. The bill received basic endorsement by every witness in the day-long hearing. No complete opposition was heard. However, as might have been predicted from the meeting on March 10, the state and local mental health associations, though endorsing the bill strongly, advocated moving much of the decision-making on planning and budgets from the regional boards to the local community mental health boards. The State Medical Society also testified in favor of the bill in principle, but in contrast opposed any "lay involvement" in the administration of the program on the area level and opposed the regional plan and boards as "unwieldy and unnecessary" and recommended their elimination. As to who should run the program, the Medical Society made this very clear:

> "Full medical-psychiatric responsibility for the Community Mental Health program from patient to Commissioner should be in the hands of the medical profession as represented by psychiatrists. This would

require that the wording be changed in the act where necessary to bring this principle into effect."[7]

The Massachusetts Association for Retarded Children was the only group which endorsed our plan to give important authority to the regional-level boards. Retardation groups throughout the state were supporting our bill very strongly since we had incorporated the mental retardation programs into the total comprehensive plan. In this respect, we had gone beyond the report of the Mental Health Planning Project and we were anticipating the report of the Mental Retardation Planning Project which was also based in the Medical Foundation.

The Department of Mental Health was ambivalent at this stage. No departmental representative appeared to testify at the Public Hearing, either for or against the bill. The Department apparently did not want to give more power to the local citizen boards, but also many in the Department opposed the regional structure in the bill which would have affected more fundamentally the integration of the State hospitals into the new system.

Nevertheless, it became apparent quickly that the bill had great public appeal and it received widespread support in newspaper, radio, and television editorials throughout the state.

The Debate Heats Up

The bill quickly became the subject of a massive tug-of-war between the two major political parties, the Democrats, who controlled the Legislature, and the Republicans, who controlled the Executive Branch. In order to share credit for the bill with the administration, the Democrats took to "amending" it. Thus, the regional citizen boards were entirely eliminated from the bill and the power of approval of budgets and the annual plan of operations was placed at the local level and put into the hands of the 37 area boards, locally selected and locally self-perpetuating.

The bill was favorably reported out of the joint committee of the House and Senate, but with a new number, Senate 889. The renumbering was designed to make it the Democrats' own Mental Health bill. The authors of this paper were consulted by the committee in its redrafting. We cooperated in order to avoid radical surgery to other aspects of the bill. The committee chairman dealt quite fairly with us and respected the basic objectives of the program. We encouraged Governor Volpe to support the bill in its amended form. He accepted our recommendation and continued his public advocacy of the legislation.

The House of Representatives, controlled overwhelmingly by the Democrats, passed the amended version of the bill. As election time approached, however, the Senate Democratic leadership had a change of heart. They had not been able to divorce the bill from the Governor in the public eye. They turned to opposing their own version, Senate 889, and tried to substitute a new and hastily drafted bill prepared in the Senate Ways and Means Committee. The Senate Republicans still supported Senate 889.

The Senate Democratic leadership began to attack "the Mental Health Bill," publicly giving up all effort to identify Senate 889 as their own. They said that the 37 area boards would become "Republican spear carriers appointed by John Volpe" and would produce a new political force all over Massachusetts. This charge was easily rebutted by showing the restrictions in the bill on persons who could be appointed, and by the fact that the Commissioner of Mental Health, not the Governor, made most of the appointments, based on local nominations. Newspaper commentators and editorial writers severely criticized the Democrats for these remarks.

The opposition then took another tack, questioning the constitutionality of giving power to the local mental health boards over state budget monies. They even went to the extent of asking the State Supreme Court to give an advisory opinion on these issues. They seemed to have forgotten at this stage that it was the Democratically-controlled committee which had inserted these provisions in S. 889.

In early September, without waiting for an opinion from the Supreme Court, the Democrats in the Senate killed the Mental Health bill.

The Governor, in a very forceful statement, refused to accept the defeat on the alleged grounds of doubts of constitutionality. He returned the bill to the Legislature by Special Message, with a new so-called "severability clause" which would allow the bill to stand as law in all parts not found unconstitutional by court decision. He threatened the Legislative leadership that unless they passed the Mental Health bill, he would call them into Special Session after the election to enact the bill. This maneuver clearly put the Democrats on the spot. Now they could not retreat behind the question of constitutionality. They had either to amend the bill to eliminate this question, and thus return the bill to much of its original form and pass it as a victory for the Governor; or to defeat the bill outright. They chose the latter. In an atmosphere of angry, frustrated, political name-calling, they defeated the bill and ended the Legislative session for the year.

The Governor allowed the Legislature to adjourn (or "to prorogue," as it is called in Massachusetts) on September 7, but he admonished them severely for having killed the Mental Health bill. He said, "Apparently [the Senate President] has decided, for reasons best known to himself, that the people of Massachusetts will not have the benefits of this vital legislation this year."[8] The Senate President returned to his charge that the Mental Health bill was "a patronage grab"[9] on the part of the Republican administration. On the threat of the Governor to call the Legislature back after the election to enact the bill, he retorted that this was "strictly academic." He said, "After the general election Governor Volpe will have only 8 weeks left in office before he takes the long walk out of the State House—a good thing for all the people of the Commonwealth."[10]

Lt. Governor Richardson, now Republican candidate for Attorney General, charged that the Democrats had made "political prisoners" of the mentally ill and mentally retarded. He pointed out that the Democratic nominee for Governor had publicly endorsed the bill months before, "yet his own campaign manager, the President of the Massachusetts Senate, is negotiating its defeat."[11]

One of the leading political writers of the state, Robert Healy of the *Boston Globe,* in his column of the same day put it very aptly. His column was headed, "Fortune Pats Volpe on Head," and he wrote, "the frosting for Volpe's political cake comes from the Legislature, which gives him a can't lose situation on his mental health bill."[12] Two days later, the major political writer for another Boston newspaper wrote a similar column. Cornelius Dalton of the *Boston Traveler* wrote a story entitled "Volpe Given a Big Issue By Democrats."[13]

The political campaign went on in this manner until November. The Governor made the failure of the Legislature to pass the Mental Health bill the major issue in his fight to become the State's first four-year term Chief Executive. He kept the Democrats, usually the advocates of more programs for the mentally ill and other unfortunate groups, constantly on the defensive. He ran as much against the Senate leadership and the Legislature as against his actual opponent. There is no doubt but that the Governor was made to look good in the exchange. It was shades of Harry Truman in 1948 running against the "Do-Nothing" 80th Congress, with the threat of a Special Session and all.

The Republicans won a sweeping victory in Massachusetts in

350 HANDBOOK OF HUMAN SERVICE ORGANIZATIONS

the November election. Governor Volpe was reelected by a substantial margin. True to his promise, he ordered the legislature back into Special, Extraordinary Session on December 4, 1966 in order to pass the Mental Health bill.

At first, the Special Session went along smoothly. Some changes had been made in the bill to eliminate the questions raised by the Democrats earlier. The budget-approval powers given to the area boards under the earlier Democratic amendments were struck out, thus eliminating the question of unconstitutionality. A public hearing was held by the same joint committee of the House and Senate which had heard the original bill. All forces were reconciled behind the bill, though it eliminated budget approval on the local level, a power the Massachusetts Association for Mental Health had originally insisted upon and which we as draftsmen had not given them. The Senate President now supported the bill. The committee chairman said after this hearing that he expected the bill to be passed by both Houses within a few days. The Legislature, it seemed, would be home for Christmas. But this was not to be.

Further Problems

We suppose we should have expected trouble, considering the rocky course we had had all through the previous session. The new problems, however, came from a source which had up to now maintained a judicious, though at times ominous silence: the State Department of Mental Health. It will be recalled that the Department had not even offered testimony at the first hearing on the original bill the previous April. The same posture was taken at the hearing on the bill in the Special Session. High-level departmental representatives sat in the hearing room and listened, but no testimony, no support or opposition, no suggestions for any changes, came from the Department.

Now, however, as it looked as if the bill would be the law of the Commonwealth within a few days, repercussions began to be heard from the Department. Employee groups were thrown into a panic over what they were told could be massive changes and losses of jobs. Rumors of marches to the State House by job-holders were heard in every corridor. There was a provision in the bill guaranteeing continuation of all present employees and guaranteeing continued civil service protection, but this did not seem to satisfy some in the Department. Statements were even being made that if the bill passed, the hospitals would be forced to release all of their patients.

The Departmental opponents of the bill then brought forth another formidable objection. They produced a letter from the Federal Regional Director for the Public Health Service in answer to a letter from the Commissioner of Mental Health. The Commissioner had asked the Regional Office to review the bill in regard to any Federal problems with merit-system requirements. The answer from the Regional Director was a bombshell. It charged that in its present form the bill, by exempting physicians from the Massachusetts Civil Service laws, "would represent a serious deviation from the requirements of the Federal Standards . . ."[14] It was publicly asserted that this deficiency in the Mental Health bill could cost the State millions of dollars in Federal funds.

To us as draftsmen of the bill this was the unkindest cut of all. The provision exempting all physicians from Civil Service laws was not a part of the Community Mental Health Act at all. It was already the law in Massachusetts and had been on our statute books for many years. It was merely a provision in the bill reprinted from the current law because the entire chapter of the General Laws was repeated for purposes of clarity. This "serious deviation" had apparently caused no problems before. Physicians in the Department had never been subject to the Civil Service laws.

An emergency public hearing on the bill was called for the next day, December 13. The star witness at the hearing before a battery of TV cameras was the previously silent Commissioner of Mental Health.

The Commissioner expressed a number of fundamental objections to the bill. He also asserted that in any form, the program would be very, very expensive. When asked by a Republican member of the committee why he had not voiced these objections previously on a bill which had been before the Legislature since April, the Commissioner answered that he had not seen the bill until four days before. Apparently the Commissioner meant by this that he had not seen S.1029, the version which had been submitted to the Special Session. The objections he made, however, were unassociated with the newer version. They had been a part of the bill all along. The newspapers picked up the remark in headlines that afternoon. They said, "Mental Health Department in Dark" and "Commissioner Says Volpe Didn't Contact Him About Reorganization."

The Democrats now, for the first time, had the bill firmly in their hands. They proceeded to "amend" the bill to meet these various objections, this time doing a complete reordering of the provisions. We, as authors of the original bill, for the first time

lost all contact with the committee. We were very much afraid
that in their haste they would do further and further harm to
the fundamental objectives of the program. However, to our relief,
we found that when the bill was reported out again, with another
new number, S.1033, it was still substantially in accord with the
basic plan for reorganization of the Department. The committee
had rearranged the bill so that no section had its original place
in the bill. If one read the sections, however, they were not much
changed in actual language. However, the amendments did impose
a much stricter civil service system throughout the Department.
With an antiquated civil service system in Massachusetts containing
absolute veterans preference and denial of educational qualifications for most positions, we did not consider these changes
improvements.

The month of December was now passing rapidly. If the delays
continued, the year would end and we would be forced into a
new Legislative session. The Legislature would have defeated the
Governor's efforts to get a bill during 1966. Under the Massachusetts system, to go beyond the end of the year could delay
any action for months and months to come.

While the Senate was rewriting and renumbering the bill, the
House of Representatives was busy considering the financing of
the program. In a very strange maneuver the leadership tacked
a rider onto the bill to require that the program be paid for out
of the newly enacted State Sales Tax! If this provision remained,
it would scuttle the entire bill. The Sales Tax itself was not favored
by the Democrats. Its imposition some months before had been
a major victory for Governor Volpe. No one knew yet what the
revenues would be under the tax. Furthermore, it had been enacted
only as a temporary tax to be reviewed again a year later. Most
importantly, the revenues under the tax had been earmarked for
the local communities, not State programs. To make matters worse,
however, the House changed the Sales Tax itself under the rider
requiring that it be collected from certain previously exempt
sources. These included certain industrial purchases of heavy
machinery and purchases by communications media, including
newspapers.

The public unroar against this rider, led by the newspapers,
industry, and the cities and towns, reversed the situation again
overnight. The Democrats were again pictured as obstructionists
using petty political tricks to kill the Mental Health bill. The Democrats were forced to retreat. They had to take out the Sales-Tax
rider. After two nearly all-night sessions (there had been many

before on the bill), the Legislature finally passed S.1033 and sent it to the Governor on December 28, 1966. The Governor signed the Mental Health Act that same day in a public ceremony about one hour after he received it. The time of the signing was 6:35 p.m.

COMMENTS ON THE PROCESS OF POLITICAL CHANGE

In so complex a political story as the one just related, it is difficult for people such as the authors who were so deeply involved to reconstruct an analysis of the forces which made the events move as they did. We can, however, offer some comments which may be significant in an explanation of how the eventual result was achieved.

First of all, the climate in Massachusetts was favorable for change and improvement in mental health services. The people were very well disposed toward the new Federal programs for aid to the states in community mental health. This state was the home of President John F. Kennedy. His personal support and that of his Massachusetts family for better programs for the mentally ill and retarded were well known here. The Federal Community Mental Health Act was considered one of the major accomplishments of the late President. Republicans and Democrats alike in Massachusetts invoked his memory in nearly every statement of endorsement for our bill.

Many people in the State also thought that this kind of effort was connected with the violent death of the President. It was often alleged that Lee Harvey Oswald was a sociopath who might have been helped earlier in his life if more extensive community mental health services had been available. The death of the President might thus have been prevented.

Also, violence and senseless killing were close to home to the people of the Boston area in those years. We had just gone through nearly two years of public terror over "the Boston Strangler" who was alleged to have killed at least 11 women over this period under very horrible circumstances. Many women living alone in Boston and its suburbs were in constant fear over every knock on the door all during these months. The unknown Strangler or Stranglers were constantly referred to in the press as maniacs, as severely mentally ill.

The people in Massachusetts wanted more mental health services and they wanted them close to home. The Community Mental Health and Retardation Services Act promised just that. It was a fairly simple issue and could be simply stated in the press and at public meetings. We were definitely on the side of good; it was a "good cause" in the clearest of terms. City dwellers and suburbanites, all social classes, church leaders, professionals, all of the politically alienated who generally do not care very much who wins or loses in a local political campaign could band together to fight for this one.

The Democratic leadership found itself involved in a simplistic picture of good and bad in politics. By their apparent opposition to the fundamental objectives of the bill, and expressed partisan statements or maneuvers, they became "the bad guys."

We must give a vast amount of the credit for sustained support and interest in the bill to the state and local mental health associations. They not only lobbied with every individual legislator, but they kept the media supplied with copy and editorials in a constant stream. They quickly answered all of the charges made against the bill, providing facts and figures where needed. Also, they flushed out the political figures very early and had just about all of them on record as supporting the original bill. These early statements were most embarrassing later to the Democratic Senate President, the Democratic House Speaker, and the Democratic candidate for Governor, each of whom had provided a hearty personal endorsement.

In the later stages of the Legislative fight, the Associations for the Mentally Retarded, particularly the State Association, also were extremely valuable allies. They were somewhat later in "peaking" in their actions, because Mental Retardation Planning was itself later in getting started. In the Legislature, however, these groups were particularly effective.

It must be said also that the bill benefited from support by those groups that had become disenchanted with the established leadership in mental health services in the State. The bill was designed to "open up" the system: not only to citizen (or "lay") board involvement, but to more important roles for psychologists, social workers, educators, and other professionals who had been largely excluded from the mental decision-making process in Massachusetts. In this regard, the opposition to the bill of the Massachusetts Medical Society and its Mental Health Committee on the ground that we did not vest all authority in psychiatrists was a clear asset to us in rallying the other groups to our support.

The mass media were an extremely important factor. The newspapers, radio, and television were all with us. They kept up a constant barrage in favor of the bill. Organizations such as the Junior

Chamber of Commerce, and the State Labor Council, AFL-CIO, were solidly behind us and used their publications in support of the bill.

We would like to note that the authors, who were constantly involved, tried to avoid partisan appearance at all times. We always referred to the bill as bipartisan in nature and origin, which it was. We worked with the Democratically-controlled joint committee, whose chairman supported the basic objectives of the plan throughout, as well as with the Governor, even when the Democratic leadership was publicly attacking the bill, or amending it, or renumbering it.

The above paragraphs have identified some of the assets in this campaign. There were liabilities also. Our biggest problem was the partisan division between the Executive Branch and the Legislature. We had no choice but to make our Report to the Governor, as required by the Federal legislation. We tried to avoid all partisan coloring of our efforts, as indicated above. We believe we may have succeeded personally in remaining nonpartisan, but the bill did not.

There were other liabilities. The lack of firm support and participation in the process by the State Department of Mental Health was a serious problem. We who were involved in the legislative process were probably at fault in not trying other methods to achieve more effective cooperation. In these last few days, the efforts of some Departmental members, though perhaps not so intended, almost succeeded in defeating the bill.

Medical groups in general were of only limited help in obtaining passage of the legislation. We have already mentioned the role of the State Medical Society. The local branch of the Psychiatric Association also opposed our proposed structural changes in the Department and the involvement of "laymen" in decision-making. The child psychiatrists' group did, however, succeed in a bit of personal lobbying. They were able to convince the Legislature to write into the bill an additional Assistant Commissioner for Children's Services. This new position was not assigned line responsibility for program administration, however, a move which would have again split the Departmental programs into categorical fields.

Some Concluding Remarks

The battle is now over and the Massachusetts Community Mental Health and Retardation Services Act is law. The Department of

Mental Health is being reorganized and community services are being developed under the dynamic leadership of the new commissioner, Dr. Milton Greenblatt. The Act as passed may not be as good as the bill originally submitted, at least in our biased judgment, but with all of its faults and the compromises that had to be made, the basic structure of the Planning Project Report was maintained.

We believe that the key factor in the achievement was the fact that the people involved in the Report "stayed with it" through the implementation stages. They did not fold up their planning and research instruments and silently steal away, on to the next research job. They changed hats. They prepared the legislation. This forced them to make certain specific decisions left open or answered only vaguely in the consensus sought in most planning reports. It was also important that those involved in the Planning Project, and others like Lt. Governor Richardson, were experienced in governmental programs in health and welfare, in Massachusetts politics, and in the legislative process.

Jeremy Bentham, the first great legislative reformer of Public Health and Welfare laws, said over 150 years ago that successful public legislation is that which will do the most good for the most people. He was also the first legislative reformer to recognize and use the great power of the press. In the mid-1960's, we were able to improve very little on Jeremy Bentham's techniques.

REFERENCES AND NOTES

1. Chapter 735, Acts of 1966, Massachusetts Session Laws.
2. *Mental Health for Massachusetts*, Report of the Massachusetts Mental Health Planning Project, June 30, 1965.
3. Ibid., p. 72.
4. *New England Journal of Medicine*, V. 274, No. 7, p. 407 (January 17, 1966).
5. News Letter, *Massachusetts Association for Mental Health*, p. 2 (April, 1966).
6. Ibid.
7. Letter of Dr. William W. Babson, M.D., President, Massachusetts Medical Society, to all members of the Legislature, December 7, 1966.
8. *Boston Traveler*, p. 15, September 7, 1966.
9. Ibid.
10. Ibid.
11. *Boston Globe*, p. 24, September 7, 1966.
12. *Boston Globe*, p. 18, September 7, 1966.
13. *Boston Traveler*, p. 23, September 8, 1966.
14. Letter from Mabel Ross, M.D., to Dr. Harry C. Solomon, dated December 8, 1966.

26. The Health Syndicate: Washington's Noble Conspirators

Elizabeth Brenner Drew

Since World War II federal funding of health and welfare programs and research has grown to become a multi-billion dollar operation. By 1972 the health industry was the nation's fourth largest and growing rapidly. The dynamics of this growth in health programs are perceptively outlined in the following article. The article provides an interesting perspective on the origins, consequences, and possible future of federally-funded health programs in the United States.

In addition the article provides a framework within which one might begin to conceptually generate the factors which make up the political and socio-organizational contexts of human service organizations.

Since the end of World War II, the direct involvement of the U. S. government in trying to improve the health of its citizens has grown by enormous proportions. Federal agencies support research into the causes of disease, into development of cures and application of the most advanced medical findings. At the National Institutes of Health in Bethesda, Maryland, the government has built the greatest biomedical research institution in the world. In the eleven institutes on the Bethesda campus—each devoted to a specific problem such as heart disease, cancer, neurological diseases, mental illness—and through grants to researchers in clinics and medical schools, the NIH directly supports over 40 percent of the biomedical research in this country. It is, moreover, a government enterprise of exceptional quality which attracts many of the nation's outstanding scientists.

Yet even more interesting than the fact of the growth of the government's role is how it happened. For one thing, it probably represents a unique historical phenomenon. For another, the decisions behind it have been made, as they must be, in the political context. And while there is no question that it represents a great achievement, within that overall achievement, even because of it, there have arisen some distortions and questionable departures in federal health policy.

The extraordinary growth of the federal role in medical research had as its base a historical confluence of forces in the post-war period. First, the "payoffs" from research in the physical sciences during the war—radar, the Bomb—gave basic research new respectability in political circles. Second, the end of the war left the nation with unemployed scientists and more money. Third, the medical societies concerned with specific diseases such as polio and cancer were taken over from the doctors by civilians and turned toward promotion to raise money and educate the public. Finally there were three remarkable men in positions of great power in Washington whose consuming interest was medical research: Dr. James Shannon, for the last twelve years the director of NIH; the late Representative John E. Fogarty of Rhode Island, who died of a heart attack early this year; and Senator Lister Hill of Alabama.

But it was Mrs. Mary Lasker, a very wealthy public-spirited citizen of New York with a fierce interest in health, who spun the web that linked all of these factors together. She did it with the help of what is referred to as her "stable" of doctor-allies, including men from the great medical centers such as Dr. Sidney Farber of Harvard and Dr. Michael DeBakey, the famous heart surgeon of the Baylor Medical School and a doctor who guards the health of the President of the United States; of her longtime friend Mrs. Florence Mahoney, who entertains government figures in her elegant Georgetown home and pushes both her own and Mrs. Lasker's causes; of her able Washington lobbyist, Mike Gorman, a redhead who wears a Phi Beta Kappa key and talks like a rough, cynical impresario. She also did it with her own brains, charm, appetite for power, and unshakable belief in the efficacy of money. For the past twenty years Mrs. Lasker has been, in the words of one federal health official, "the most important single factor in the rise of·support for biomedical research." In the process, she has helped the NIH budget to explode from $2.5 million in 1945 to $1.4 billion this year, influenced Presidents, immobilized Secretaries of Health, Education, and Welfare, selected health policy makers, and pushed health policy in controversial directions.

Mrs. Lasker's network is probably unparalleled in the influence that a small group of private citizens has had over such a major area of national policy. One federal official refers to it as a 'noble conspiracy.' Gorman calls it a "high class kind of subversion, very high class. We're not second story burglars. We go right in the front door."

Speaking at the Lasker Medical Awards luncheon last year, Douglass Cater, President Johnson's White House assistant on health matters, told the audience: "President Johnson's last appointment before he left the White House for the hospital was with Mary Lasker. And he didn't get away, either, without two memoranda from her to study while he was recuperating." "Mary and her colleagues," said Cater, "have set a new fashion in lobbyists. The moving and shaking done by such womenfolk affects everybody, including the most obdurate of politicians. Be glad for them, for our children's children will reap the benefits."

A problem with health policy making in general, and the role of the health syndicate in particular, is the tendency to attempt to translate personal experience and concerns into national health policy. This leads to a good deal of flukiness. There is probably no more award-laden field—in which the $10,000 Lasker Awards are the most prestigious. Everyone who is for health is doing the Lord's work. This does not, however, preclude some questions about who has a direct line to heaven, or some fallings-out among the disciples.

The health movers and shakers found each other through a combination of accidents and word of mouth. When Albert D. Lasker, an advertising genius, married Mary Woodard Reinhardt in 1940, his bride, a cum laude graduate of Radcliffe and former graduate student of Oxford, was already a successful businesswoman and energetic devotee of public causes. Albert Lasker, meanwhile, amassed a fortune, which one associate estimates at close to $80 million by the 1940's.

In 1942 Lasker liquidated his advertising business and set up the Albert and Mary Lasker Foundation, to push for federal support for medical research, then a new and controversial idea. It was Albert Lasker's thought that the foundation should provide the "seed money" for research projects, then catalyze the federal government to follow on once the private efforts became established. Their primary interests were in mental health, birth control, and —after the Laskers' cook was stricken with cancer in the early 1940's—cancer research. (Albert Lasker died of cancer in 1952).

Albert Lasker used to vacation in Miami Beach, and there he introduced Mary to his friends Florence and Daniel Mahoney. Daniel Mahoney's late first wife had been the daughter of Ohio Governor James Cox, and Mr. Mahoney had inherited a substantial position in the Cox family newspaper chain, the largest Democratic chain in the country. Florence had always been interested in medicine to the point of taking pre-med courses. Now, through her husband's own interest in medicine, the Cox family's connections, the outlet of the newspapers, and her access to the congressional press galleries, she could push her causes.

Florence Mahoney read about the crusade to improve treatment of the mentally ill by an Oklahoma newspaperman named Mike Gorman. "I asked Mahoney," she recalls, "to get him to work on the paper in Miami. He came for two weeks and stayed for six weeks. He wrote a sensational series—headlines every day. Then Mike went to the state legislature to lobby them, and he got $6 million for mental health within six weeks."

In 1944 Senator Claude Pepper (Democrat, Florida) was persuaded by the Mahoneys (whose newspaper support he needed) and the Laskers (who contributed campaign funds) to hold hearings on federal support of health research. Mrs. Lasker supplied the senator with horrifying statistics about the mortality and morbidity rates of various diseases. She suggested that he read these off, have outside witnesses testify to the need for more research, and then ask federal officials how much they were spending to combat the diseases. The total being spent at the then modest National Institute of Health and its affiliated Cancer Institute was $2.5 million. The Lasker forces believe that the Pepper hearings, the first of their kind, were very influential. Historically, they were the beginning of what became the health syndicate's highly developed *modus operandi* in Congress.

Both Mrs. Lasker and Mrs. Mahoney were friendly with the Trumans (Mrs. Truman was helpful in passing on messages and memoranda to her busy husband), and during the Truman Administration there was White House support for building the NIH. The budget began to be increased, and the number of subsidiary institutes expanded. The great defeat of the Truman health insurance program taught Mrs. Lasker, who had devoted large amounts of money and energy to the fight, that head-on clashes with the AMA were to be avoided. But the AMA was so busy combating "socialized medicine" that it failed to notice the implications for medical practice and medical education of the growing federal budget for health research. This, in turn, provided health research as a platform from which congressmen could voice a concern for health without incurring the powerful wrath of the AMA.

Toward the end of the Truman Administration the President established, largely through the efforts of his medical adviser, Dr. Howard Rusk, the President's Commission on Health Needs of the Nation. Dr. Rusk has been a friend of Presidents through his pioneering work in vocational rehabilitation in his clinic at New

York University and his influential medical column in *The New York Times*. He has also been a friend of Mrs. Lasker's. The executive director of the President's commission and author of its report was Mike Gorman. The report called for higher levels of federal spending for medical research.

This was the first evidence of what was to become another piece of the health syndicate's pattern: what Gorman calls "the White Paper device." "Through this type of study," he explained in a recent speech, "you develop the facts, you involve a great number of organizations previously not interested, and you hopefully create a militant consensus in support of the findings of the Commission. The White Paper, or Commission report, is the foundation stone for legislation, and it provides an obvious answer to the familiar myriad of charges raised by hostile legislators—you didn't study the problem long enough, your conclusions were hastily drawn, you didn't consult a broad enough segment of professional groups or of the American people at large, and so on."

After his effective work on the commission, Mrs. Lasker asked Mike Gorman to run a Washington operation for the Lasker Foundation. Gorman, with his great interest in psychiatry and mental health, wanted a committee of his own to operate. "You want a committee?" he recalls Mrs. Lasker asking, and they thereupon set up what is now the National Committee Against Mental Illness—Mrs. Albert D. Lasker and Mrs. Florence Mahoney, co-chairmen; Mike Gorman, executive director. From the committee's offices on Connecticut Avenue, Gorman pushes Mrs. Lasker's interests in Washington.

In 1950, Mrs. Mahoney, having divorced her husband, moved to Washington and established what has become the utterly purposeful social side of the syndicate's operations. It is probable that there is no one who has been important to health policy in Washington who has not dined—on, among other things, assorted but tasty health foods—at Mrs. Mahoney's. They usually leave with an armload of reading matter. (At one point, Mrs. Mahoney sent material on birth control to the Pope.) When Kennedy White House aides played softball, Mrs. Mahoney showed up at the games and invited them back to her house for beer. She taught Jacqueline Kennedy about export porcelain, and when Luci Johnson was married gave her a set of rare china. Mrs. Mahoney will help officials' wives find maids, and she will send a tureen of soup to the officials at their offices.

Both Mrs. Lasker and Mrs. Mahoney are guests at the intimate dinners given by the Johnsons. Happily for Mrs. Lasker, she and

Mrs. Johnson now share an interest in planting shrubs and flowers all over the country. Mrs. Lasker is known for her parties at her Beekman Place townhouse in New York, where the worlds of politics and medicine meet, and when she comes to Washington she stays and entertains at Mrs. Mahoney's. Mrs. Lasker is admired; Mrs. Mahoney is liked. Mrs. Lasker has been considered an able woman who has done good things, but is too covetous of power, too insistent on her pursuits, too confident of her own expertise in the minutiae of medicine. Mrs. Mahoney is seen as gentler and warmer, and since she has never made the same claims, she has been easier to take.

When Mrs. Lasker comes to Washington, she puts in long and strenuous days in pursuit of health. She carried in her handbag a folded onionskin chart tracing the rise of NIH appropriations over the years. Mrs. Lasker is known to be one of the nation's more generous campaign contributors. "I'm on a first-name basis with one hundred fifty, one hundred seventy-five members of the House," says Gorman. "You know. A warm relationship." "We work on all the members of the Appropriations committees," he says. One year, the key vote was held by the late Senator Styles Bridges of New Hampshire, the ranking Republican on the Senate Appropriations Committee. Mrs. Lasker had been cultivating Bridges' friendship; she sent him the latest drugs and brought him special diet food for his hypertension. One day Mrs. Lasker waited over three hours to see Bridges. Once in his office she talked about his hypertension and discussed the importance of more research facilities. "General Motors can't work without equipment, styles," she told him. Bridges agreed to support an increased appropriation.

Early in 1967 Senate Majority Leader Mike Mansfield of Montana agreed to host a luncheon for his colleagues, at which Mrs. Lasker could press for more funds for heart research. Some thirty-six senators attended. Dr. DeBakey and other distinguished cardiologists told the senators about the million people who die of heart disease each year. "I order the food," says Gorman, "and see that the tables are bussed properly; Mansfield makes the opening remarks, and we go to work."

When Lyndon Johnson was running the Senate, Mrs. Lasker befriended him, too. In 1959, Mr. Johnson agreed to speak in support of a $200 million increase in the NIH budget over that requested by President Eisenhower. (Two years later Vice-President Johnson was the featured speaker at the Lasker Medical Awards luncheon.) The 1959 speech was his maiden speech on health research. It was written by Mike Gorman. It was a classic of sorts;

"In the childhood of many of us in this chamber, diphtheria, typhoid fever, smallpox, pneumonia, tuberculosis and a host of other diseases brought heartbreak to hundreds of thousands of American families. Few were the families in Texas, or in any part of the country for that matter, who did not lose at least one child to one of these major killers ... Over the past decade alone, cancer has claimed the lives of five members of this body ... Cancer has killed many of our military heroes whom enemy bullets failed to stop ... By another ironic twist of fate, the Senate Appropriations Committee hearings on the Budget for the National Cancer Institute for the coming year were held on the very day that our great Secretary of State, John Foster Dulles, was laid to rest ... Its deadly stranglehold upon the fiber of our democracy was nowhere better assessed than in a brief editorial which appeared several days after the death of John Foster Dulles in the *Machinist*, the official publication of the International Association of Machinists: 'For six years the Communists tried every trick in the book to get John Foster Dulles out of their hair. What the Commies couldn't do to our former Secretary of State, cancer did.' "

The technique of reminding the lawmakers of their mortality has been consistently effective in raising the ante for health research, and this accounts in good part for the astounding exponential growth of the NIH budget. So do the "fact books" produced by the National Health Education Committee, another Lasker organization in New York, showing how biomedical research has increased longevity, and the clear-cut definition of what the congressmen were being asked to vote for: to "cure" cancer, heart disease, and so on. "Cancer and heart disease have more money," says Mrs. Lasker, "because they are major causes of death, and the members of Congress can understand that." The story goes that in the days when one of the NIH branches was called the Institute of Microbiology, one congressman asked, "Whoever died of microbiology?" The name was changed to the Institute of Allergy and Infectious Diseases.

The growth of NIH can also be attributed to the concurrent appearance on the scene of Senator Hill, Representative Fogarty, and Dr. Shannon. John Fogarty was a brilliant rough-edged Irishman who entered Congress in 1941 at the age of twenty-eight with a high school education and ten years' experience as a bricklayer. In 1949 he became the chairman of the House Appropriations subcommittee that handled the funds for health, a post of great power. Until a couple of years ago, Fogarty underscored his own power by denying sufficient staff to the Secretary of HEW. Gorman claims that Mrs. Lasker "made" Fogarty, taught him everything he knew, but this is not quite the case. It understates Fogarty's independent, impressive mastery of the details of federal health programs. Moreover, though Mrs. Lasker and Fogarty were close allies, Fogarty was even closer to Dr. Shannon. Shannon, through an extraordinary combination of professional standards and political instincts, traits which in other men are frequently at cross-purposes, managed to build both a great research institution and political base for it in Congress. Mrs. Lasker was closer to Hill than to Fogarty. Hill, as it happens, had an innate interest in health policy; his father was a prominent surgeon, five cousins and two brothers-in-law were doctors, and Hill himself was named for the great surgeon Joseph Lister. Hill directed health policy from a dual position of power in the Senate, as chairman of the Labor and Public Welfare Committee, which authorizes health programs, and as chairman of the Appropriations subcommittee which provides the money.

In the raising of the budget, Fogarty, Hill, Shannon, and Lasker performed each year as a highly polished quartet. First, the Administration would submit a budget request. As with just about every government agency's request, it would be lower than the NIH had suggested to HEW and than HEW in turn had suggested to the Budget Bureau. Holding his hearings, Fogarty would castigate the White House for the "cutbacks" and elicit from the NIH officials, as if he didn't already know, the amount they had initially requested and the comment that they could do well with the full amount. Fogarty would say that he did not care what the bureaucrats in the Budget Bureau thought; he wanted to hear from the "experts." Then Gorman would field his "citizen witnesses," well-known physicians such as DeBakey, Farber, Paul Dudley White, Karl Menninger, who would state the case for more money.

Finding good medical witnesses, according to Gorman, is not easy. "Their language is extremely technical, jargonistic. I *forbid* doctors to use the term 'myocardial infarction.' I say, 'You call it heart attack or you leave the room.' That and 'no smoking.' Those are the two rules. It's hard to find the right combination. DeBakey is unique; he has the aura of a surgeon, he's articulate, enthusiastic. Most doctors are not enthusiastic, not used to the verbal give and take. The Rusks, Farbers, DeBakeys have the evangelistic pizzazz. Put a tambourine in their hands and they go to work."

Carefully assessing the mood within his own subcommittee, and the more conservative full Appropriations Committee, Fogarty would then raise the NIH budget and write a justifying report in which Gorman and Shannon usually had a hand. Such is the stature of the Appropriations subcommittee chairmen in general, and such was Fogarty's in particular, that he had his way when the bill came to the House floor.

The budget raises which Fogarty produced enabled Hill to take them still higher. Essentially the same routine would be followed in the Senate—"citizen witnesses" and all. During this time, Gorman and Mrs. Lasker would be making their rounds, doing what they could to assure the success of Fogarty's and Hill's budget-raising performances.

In 1959, after years of what Gorman calls "glorious adversity" during the Eisenhower Administration (the NIH budget went from $59 million to $400 million between 1953 and 1960), some Republicans began to propose a closer look at the runaway NIH budget. Senator Hill graciously offered to direct himself, and appointed a Committee of Consultants on Medical Research. Among its members were Michael DeBakey, Sidney Farber, and others who were in the health syndicate's inner circles. Gorman helped out with the report, which called for a substantial rise in federal support for medical research. The study, says Hill, was "very helpful."

In their view, one of the most satisfying successes of the health syndicate is the federally sponsored system of special centers for the treatment of heart disease, cancer, and stroke which is now being established throughout the country. In 1960 Mike Gorman succeeded in getting inserted into the Democratic platform a call for a special White House study of heart disease and cancer. In 1961, a specially appointed body produced a report now known as the "Bay of Pigs Report," both because it was presented to President Kennedy on the day of the invasion, and because it was so badly done that it was a bit of a disaster in its own right. The Lasker forces pushed for another commission, and it is said that it was suggested now that it be a commission on stroke as well as on cancer and heart disease, although strokes are considered a subspecies of heart disease, to appeal to President Kennedy, whose father had suffered a stroke. In any event, the President was considering a new commission before he was killed.

Behind the efforts for such a commission lay the Lasker group's growing impatience to get the results "off the shelf," as they say, and out into the country. They visualized a network of heart, cancer, and stroke institutes which would conduct research, training, and patient care. The idea appealed to Prsident Johnson. Beyond the fact that Mr. Johnson likes Mrs. Lasker and admires her achievements, her impatience to get practical application of the fruits of research was consistent with his own nature. In the spring of 1964, the President's Commission on Heart Disease, Cancer, and Stroke was established. Its chairman was Michael DeBakey. Among the members were Mrs. Florence Mahoney, Mrs. Harry Truman, Dr. Sydney Farber, Dr. Howard Rusk, Dr. Edward Dempsey, and a number of others close to the Lasker circle. "We had a quorum" says Gorman.

Included in that quorum was Dr. J. Willis Hurst of Emory University, the man who monitors President Johnson's heart. ("He's with us," says Gorman.) Being the President's doctor seems to be a promising route into a position of health policy making. Dr. James Cain of the Mayo Clinic is a longtime friend of Mr. Johnson's and has general responsibility for his health. Dr. Cain told the President over dinner one night that he was worried about the way that the Pentagon was drafting doctors, and this led to establishment of the National Advisory Commission on Health Manpower (its areas of concern were broadened at the insistence of other health officials). Dr. Cain, of course, served on the commission. Dr. Wilbur Gould, who operated on the President's larynx, has been suggested by the White House for a position on a health advisory council, and he is expected to be making health policy before the year is out. Even Luci Johnson Nugent's doctor's wife was named to a consumer advisory council not long ago.

In December, 1964, the President's Commission on Heart Disease, Cancer, and Stroke reported, calling for a national network of heart disease, cancer, and stroke centers which would conduct research training and patient care. So hurriedly was the legislation drafted for the forthcoming session of Congress that one man working with the White House who saw the bill zip by says that "in all my experience I never saw a piece of legislation leave the White House on which there was less clarity on what the federal government was going to do." Nevertheless, the President made it one of his priorities, and the bill was passed by Congress in 1965.

While the goals of the Lasker forces in pushing the heart disease, cancer, and stroke program may seem unexceptionable, others who are as in favor of health as they are, are disturbed by the decision to embark on this type of program. For it raises some of the most serious and difficult questions, moral as well as medical and financial, involved in defining the federal government's role in health care. The centers are to provide the most advanced treatment of these diseases, but in most cases even the most advanced treatment can only ameliorate them, not cure them, and can only postpone death. Is the government therefore assuming responsibility for the care of these patients for the rest of their lives? If the federal government is going to begin to provide centers for certain diseases, would it be better to provide them for diseases which can be cured or for those which cannot yet be cured? Similarly, if such a departure is to be made, should it focus on diseases which affect primarily the elderly, as these do, or on diseases which affect primarily the young? These kinds of policy considerations should have preceded a decision to initiate a program of centers for heart disease, cancer, and stroke, but they did not. The very name of the commission, and its membership, preordained its conclusions.

Moreover, the issues involved in producing the "payoffs" from research, in getting the findings "off the shelf," are not so simple as the Lasker forces make out—as President Johnson at great pain learned this past year.

The Lasker forces feel that the NIH directors must be pushed into more concern for faster "payoff" for the research dollar. "They should be paying more attention to helping human beings," says Mrs. Lasker, "who after all are the ones who are paying for research. I know you have to have basic research, but once you've spent $8.5 billion, I think you should do more to see how the dollars apply to human beings. The NIH people are not people with a sense of mission to reduce the death rate directly. I don't mean that they're not well motivated. Too many of them are without a sense of deep urgency." As Gorman puts it, "We figure they get the seven-year itch in eight years."

One of the ways that the Lasker group has pushed for "payoff" has been through getting themselves appointed to the NIH advisory councils, which approve all research grants and therefore have considerable voice in NIH policy. Mrs. Lasker has served on the councils more often than has anyone else, and way up there are Mrs. Mahoney, Dr. Farber, and Dr. DeBakey. Mrs. Lasker's sister, Alice W. Fordyce, is on the National Advisory Allergy and Infectious Disease Council. Their uses of these positions have often put them at odds with Dr. Shannon and the directors of specific institutes.

A few years ago, for instance, the National Advisory Heart Council stated that the highest priority should be given to a $100 million program to develop an artificial heart. Shannon resisted, on the grounds that there was not yet a sufficient scientific base on which to devleop an artificial heart. He knew, moreover, that development would be highly expensive, and once started, the demands for the product could end in consuming all of the funds for research on artificial hearts—at the cost of a better product in the longer run. The limits on medical and economic resources raise, again, difficult social as well as medical issues. When is it scientifically feasible to proceed with the development of such devices? Would the price, in deaths, of postponement be offset by the saving of more lives through a more effective instrument at some future time? Shannon initiated instead a smaller, highly directed program designed to learn a good deal more about what kinds of devices would be useful at what stages in what sorts of heart problems. Resisting the all-out artificial heart production program was not easy, particularly since it had the backing of Dr. DeBakey, a physician quite adept at publicizing his causes.

Another way that the Lasker group has pushed for earlier cures is through allies in Congress. Senator Hill has been especially helpful. "There is nothing more important," he says, "than getting the findings and getting them out to the patient's bedside." Dr. Farber has been a strong supporter of studying the effects of various drugs on cancer, and Senator Hill, through simply adding the money for it to its budget, pushed the NIH into a massive program of cancer chemotherapy. The program, which began in 1955 over the objections of a large number of scientists, has now cost about $250 million. Although there have been a few useful results, many question whether more progress would not have been purchased through a similar investment elsewhere. A special committee which studied the NIH in 1965 (this group contained no traces of the syndicate) said that the program had been begun on too large a scale, based on too little scientific data. "The availability of money," it said, "exceeded the availability of sound ideas." A second objection to the cancer chemotherapy program has been that it was a search for a cure when there was little knowledge about the cause, and that this seldom works. Finally, the availability of research money in a given medical field has circular defects: the money attracts the researchers who in turn request more money. There are always vogues in medicine. If the most enthusiastic supporters of a certain vogue have political access, the circular effect can be intensified. If the program doesn't show sufficient results, its backers can say that it is because it needs more money. This can cause some serious displacement. Cancer chemotherapy research for example, consistently received ever expanding funds, while those interested in viruses as a cause of cancer received little support. It now appears that the study of viruses might produce the most important knowledge yet about cancer.

In recent years, Mrs. Lasker has become increasingly insistent upon large-scale field trials of drugs. People who know her ascribe this to a combination of her general interest in health and her own limitations of mortality. This year, for example, her forces persuaded Senator Hill to add $4 million to the NIH budget, without asking NIH, for a test of an anticoagulant drug, to see if it will reduce heart attacks. NIH scientists say that the project is poorly conceived, and that it may take ten years and over $100 million to test just this one drug.

Still another way to push for "payoff" is to go straight to the President. One day last spring, during a White House meeting of doctors and hospital officials on Medicare, President Johnson made the slightly irrelevant announcement that he was "serving notice" on his Secretary of Health, Education, and Welfare to convene a meeting of the NIH directors, which the President would attend, to hear the plans, if any, they have of reducing deaths and disability, of expanding research." It pleases the Lasker group that this was the first that HEW officials heard about it. But no one was unclear about where the President got the idea. At the meeting which took place a few weeks later, the President asked the NIH directors a series of questions, drawn up by Mrs. Lasker and Gorman.

The President's initiative, as if he didn't have enough problems, caused an explosion among the scientists and in the universities. They took it to mean that the Lasker forces were in the saddle; that support for applied research and development was to be substituted for support for basic research by an anti-intellectual, unsophisticated President who could never understand such things. Many scientists feel that basic research in general gets shortchanged. (Officially, less than half of the federal health research budget is classified as going for basic research; in many other scientific fields, the balance is heavily on the side of application and development.) They know that premature application can lead to wasteful, or imbalanced, programs. They feel that national policy reflects this country's instinct for the practical, its assumption, as one leading scientist put it, "that it can buy research by the yard." This leads them to conclude that basic research must have the strongest possible advocacy in the public arena. Their opponents argue that too high a proportion of the biomedical research dollar has gone to basic research, and that unless the strongest possible advocacy is given to clinical testing and production of medical services, the fruits of the research will remain in the laboratories. Too much of what might help us, they say, is left to serendipity and Germanic journals.

While there is obviously some validity to what both sides say, the argument is not quite real because it implies far greater separa- .

tions and distinctions between basic and applied biomedical research than actually exist. There are many examples in the work at NIH. Through basic research in genetics more was learned about the origins of a number of diseases. Basic research on tissue culture led to a series of virus vaccines. The argument posits a clear-cut choice between one or the other. This is an issue which calls for sophisticated policy-making machinery, not to come up with a single policy, but to constantly weigh the priorities between alternatives, each of which is laudable. This is not an issue which should be decided on the basis of who happens to have the President's ear.

Sometime last spring Mrs. Lasker thought it was time for the President to prod the NIH directors again. This time, however, the President heard from some of his official advisers that the entire affair had done him no good. In a dramatic attempt to recoup, the President helicoptered to the NIH campus in Bethesda, nodded approvingly at the facilities, and made a speech which managed not to make either side mad. He bowed to basic research ("The government supports this creative exploration because we believe that all knowledge is precious; because we know that all progress would halt without it.") and to cures ("There is no use in opening someone up and saying, 'It is too far gone. I can't do anything about it' "). But most of all he made the men at NIH happy by calling their institution a "billion-dollar success story." In scientific circles, the President's trip is referred to as "the Pedernales solution."

There are a number of thoughtful people with a role in health policy who are apt to become highly exasperated with Mrs. Lasker. But then they remind themselves of the contribution that she and her group have made. In its buccaneering fashion, the health syndicate has done great good.

"People get so mad at her," says one government man, "that they say that Mary Lasker is almost always wrong. In fact, she has been almost always right. Her instincts are very correct—that biomedical research must be built up, that there must be more delivery of health services. The problems come when these get mixed up with her personal interests, her politicking, and her taste for power, and then she gets into trouble and causes trouble." The exasperation stems largely from the fact that Mrs. Lasker's group would not recognize the need for choices, but then do-gooders seldom do. It is questionable that the Lasker forces should be blamed for the fact that they were so successful or for the related fact that there were no equivalent forces pressing for other health priorities. It is not their fault that the U.S. Public Health Service, a quasi-military corps based on an eighteenth-century concept, has been so lacking in courage and imagination, so deferential, in dealing with everything from disease prevention to pollution control, to the status quo.

Nonetheless, the resulting distortions in federal health policy cannot be blinked aside. To be very hard about it, the prevention, or postponement of death among the aged may not be the most important priority in medicine, yet that is the decision that the politicians have made. The resources that go into the research and treatment of diseases which affect primarily the aged, in combination with Medicare and Medicaid and other health programs of benefit to the elderly, consume at least 50 percent of the federal health budget. While roughly one-eighth of the U.S. population is over 60, almost half of it is under 25. And for all of its medical prowess, the United States has an infant mortality rate that is worse than that in fourteen other countries. About 40 percent of those called up for the draft fail to pass its tests for mental, physical, or emotional health. It has been estimated that large percentages of the handicapping conditions which children now suffer—congenital malformations, vision or hearing defects, psychiatric problems, and others—could be prevented. This year, the federal government is spending only $167 million on child health services programs, and another $65 million on child health and mental retardation research at NIH's Institute of Child Health and Human Development, as against $165 million at the Heart Institute for research alone. There is much less federal support for research on trauma and accidents, which hopitalize more than 2 million people each year and kill another 100,000, than there is on diseases that kill or disable far fewer people at a far lower social cost. Moreover, distortions beget distortions. Physicians who go into research are attracted to the fields where there is a large amount of support for research.

Nor can some of the assumptions on which health policy has been sold be accepted on their face. Despite the claims of the Lasker group about how our investment in health research has produced longevity, this is not at all clear. Longevity in the United States has increased, but it has increased more in other nations, even those which started from a higher longevity base. The mortality rate is a crude indicator, in any event. It says nothing about the social, economic, or emotional consequences of diseases. It does not measure the effect of chronic diseases that are not primarily killers.

It is not at all clear either, that in buying health services we have bought health. HEW policymakers say that they have searched, but have not been able to find, documentation of the assumption that people who receive regular medical attention are healthier than those who do not. This may require an entirely new definition of the components of "health." A great many more deaths might be prevented, or diseases "cured," if smoking were reduced, if automobiles were safer, if the air were cleaner, than through post-facto, disease-oriented research and services. In the days when there were less social and military claims on the budget, and when these alternatives were less understood, such choices did not have to be faced. But now they do.

Even the "payoff" argument has somewhat missed the point. It is now widely believed that the great gap in the delivery of health services is not simply between the laboratory and the practitioner, but between the treatment received if one is lucky enough to have access to a great university medical complex and the treatment received in the small towns and rural areas, or between the treatment in the medical complexes and the ghetto. These gaps are less romantic, and they are more difficult to deal with.

There is increasing concern among health policy makers over the disorganization and inequities in medical services. There is a growing feeling that the categorical, disconnected, disease-oriented, specific-fee-for-specific-service approach is outmoded. (Even Medicare does not ensure comprehensive medical treatment; it ensures the payment of doctors' bills.) The comprehensive health clinics which the poverty program has begun to open in ghetto neighborhoods, using new approaches to health care, are seen as the first step in a new direction. This, the general awareness of the needs of the poor that came with the poverty program, the demands of the labor movement, the involvement of the insurance companies, the restiveness of the medical students—all are going to have an increasing voice in defining health policies.

This means that the voice of the health syndicate will be diminished. This comes at a time when its powers would inevitably fade. John Fogarty is dead. Lister Hill is seventy-two and in political trouble. Mary Lasker and Florence Mahoney are no longer young women. The political climate is changing. The health syndicate has been, therefore, a historical phenomenon, probably an unparalleled one, certainly an important one. There may never be anything like it again.

27. *Organizational and Professional Barriers to Interagency Planning*

Sol Levine, Ph.D.

The nonprofit, public and voluntary human service provider system, in its competitiveness, parallels the American corporate profit-making structure. In addition its hierarchical authority is unclear, operating goals and organizational domains may be in conflict, rewards and incentives are often secured intraorganizationally, rather than through service delivery, and policies are formulated to enhance the individual organization.

Organizational survival is dependent upon three types of resources: recipients to serve, resources (money, equipment, and knowledge), and the necessary services or personnel to husband the resources to the client subsystem. Since it is seldom that any given organization will contain sufficient of these resources, it must necessarily turn to its external organizational environment (fund-raising, recruitment of personnel and clients, etc.).

Some interorganizational cooperation may also be necessary if ends are to be achieved and organizational survival enhanced. An organization may reach out, or in turn be courted, or a third party may intervene. Effective planning may enhance these new relationships. Semiautonomous, pluralistic, and containing multiple authority systems, the practice of interagency planning requires skill and tenacity if the obstacles and impediments to cooperation are to be overcome.

Closely adhering to the American ideologies of rugged individualism, caveat emptor, *and survival of the fittest through competition, the underlying ideologies of many human service organizations may need reexamination if effective interagency cooperation is truly desired.*

I have set for myself the task of identifying some of the major factors that interfere with the ability of state departments of public welfare to assume leadership in community planning. My remarks stem from my own studies of organizational relationships within the health and welfare world and the role of professionals in that world. I believe that some general propositions about organizational and professional behavior tend to hold for all organizations, including those in the health and welfare field and for the state departments of welfare, as well. I will therefore try to draw attention to some major obstacles and impediments to cooperation and joint planning among health and welfare organizations and will leave to the members of this conference the task of suggesting specific means and mechanisms by which the planning functions of state welfare departments may be enhanced and implemented.

A Range of Different Types of Agencies

Social scientists have used the term "political pluralism" to describe the diverse and multiple sources of authority within the American scene—a concept that has relevance to the world of health and welfare agencies. The health and welfare system includes a range of different types of agencies, each of which is relatively autonomous with a separate locus of authority. There are, for example, different levels of government in the American community, such as a local health or welfare department, a district or regional health office, a state rehabilitation agency, and a U. S. Veterans Administration Hospital. Similar variations in authority are evident among voluntary organizations. On the one hand are what might be termed the "corporate" health agencies like the National Foundation and the American Cancer Society, where the authority is delegated downwards from the national or state level to the local chapter or affiliate. On the other hand, "federated" organizations like the Visiting Nurse Association and the Family Service Association of America are relatively autonomous in the local area but delegate some of the authority they possess upwards to the state or national level.

Given such diverse and multiple sources of authority, it is often difficult to achieve maximum cooperation and planning among agencies. It is safe to say that in most communities and within most states no single agency is charged with the responsibility of coordinating the activities of other health and welfare organizations. While the state welfare department, the state health department, or the community council may claim the responsibility of assuming leadership in interagency planning, and in fact may have some legal or other basis for this claim, it appears, in reality, that most agencies are not as yet prepared to invest in a single person or agency the responsibility of establishing priorities for other agencies. Along these lines, it will be of interest to this conference that in the few communities we have studied, we have found that other agency personnel are less willing to accept the welfare department as the coordinator or planner than they are to accept leadership from the health department and the community council, though the leadership role of these agencies is also far from established. Thus, while a number of agencies often decry the lack of planning and coordination, and express the need for greater interaction and cooperation with other agencies, they have been less prone to accept, in practice, the direction or even the active leadership of another agency that may infringe on their own jurisdictions.

No Clear Pattern for Hierarchical Authority

We have already referred to one major impediment to interagency planning—the fact that there is no clear pattern of hierarchical authority. Individual agencies are relatively autonomous, and unless there are compelling reasons the trend is to resist direction from others. A second and related obstacle is that organizations have varying goals and objectives that may conflict with one another; even though all of them may subscribe to the same ultimate values—such as the promotion of health, the prevention of disease, and the total well-being of the client. Since agencies may have divergent goals they may differ in their judgment as to what measures are necessary and, even more, as to how they would allocate the priorities that are, in fact, the heart of the planning process. A state rehabilitation agency, for example, whose task it is to return to employment persons who have suffered some serious illness, may have different standards in evaluating its success than will the state welfare department. The rehabilitation agency tends to view its success in terms of the actual numbers of persons who have been returned to self-sufficient roles in the community. Accordingly, the goals of the rehabilitation agency are seen as unfulfilled unless the agency is selective about the types of handicapped persons it accepts as clients. Other public and voluntary agencies, therefore, are often blocked in their efforts to get the rehabilitation agency to accept certain clients for rehabilitation. In the view of these frustrated agencies, the rehabilitation agency is failing to fulfill its responsibility. The state rehabilitation agency, however, is reluctant to commit its limited personnel and resources to the lengthy and time-consuming job of trying to rehabilitate what may seem to be very poor risks. While the state rehabilitation agency may share the general values of other official and voluntary agencies, and may indeed be concerned with the need to rehabilitate the more serious cases, it has to consider the standards that others, such as its parent organization and legislators, may use in judging its own success. It is clear, then, that although health and welfare organizations may subscribe to the same fundamental values and general goals, their specific goals and objectives may vary from one another and, in fact, on some cases actually conflict.

Domain Conflict

A third factor that impedes interagency cooperation and planning and is somewhat related to the problems of divergent organizational goals is the lack of domain consensus between organizations. By domain consensus between two agencies we mean the degree to which they agree and accept each other's claims with regard to the social or health problems covered, services offered, and type of recipient served. Unless two agencies achieve some minimal consensus they may fail to cooperate and may find themselves in active competition. We have all witnessed a number of instances testifying to the absence of domain consensus or, in more active terms, the existence of domain conflict between agencies. Vying for patients or clients, contesting the right or competence of another organization to provide particular services to certain classes of patients, and, at times, even questioning another organization's right to exist—these are some of the bitter fruits growing out of domain conflict.

With regard to the central concern of this conference—the leadership role of the state welfare department in the planning process—it is worth considering how other agencies may feel about this role residing within the legitimate domain of the welfare department. On the basis of some of our own findings we would guess that there is considerable reticence on the part of other agencies to assign planning functions to the welfare department. Professionals in other agencies are often critical of what they regard as the nonprofessional character of the welfare department personnel. In some of the communities studied, we found several instances of conflict between strong social work agencies whose personnel have graduate training in social work and welfare departments whose staff workers are often called social workers, although many of them lack special academic preparation in the general field of social work. Welfare departments are rarely assigned the same degree of prestige as, for example, family service agencies, visiting nurses associations, or such service agencies as the Red Cross and the Salvation Army.

Different Authority Systems

Nor is it to be assumed that the problem is automatically solved by staffing different agencies with the same kind of professionals. There is often lack of cooperation between the same kind of professionals when they are subject to different authority systems. Consider, for example, trained nurses who may be employed by the health department, the Visiting Nurses Association, and the school health department. While, from a professional point of view, these nurses may be in considerable agreement in their approach to the patient and his problems, the respective organizations for which they work may have divergent policies regarding ways of handling the patient and of referring him to other agencies. While professionals have norms and standards of behavior that transcend organizational boundaries, they are also subject to the demands and requirements of the organizations for which they work. It should also be pointed out that barriers to interorganizational cooperation and planning exist not only on the horizontal level—between different agencies on the state level—but are evident on the vertical level from the state to the community. We would posit that not only would a state welfare department encounter some difficulties in developing a planning relationship with a local community council, for example, but that a state welfare department may also encounter various problems in developing a planning program with other local welfare departments.

Decisions Made on A Group Basis

In trying to develop more interagency planning and cooperation, administrators in the health and welfare world have available two broad types of approaches. The first may be termed the group dynamics approach, which utilizes group discussion, conference methods, and a range of other techniques to produce greater involvement and commitment on the part of the participants. A few agency executives and supervisory personnel—the groups may range through the whole spectrum of health and welfare agencies to a few whose work is naturally related (e.g., agencies involved in home care of chronically ill)—meet together at regular intervals under the direction of a leader. Two agencies might discuss their mutual problems, the barriers to more effective cooperation between them, and why they do not work together more closely in referring clients, transmitting information, sharing transportation, lending each other personnel, working together on common administrative problems, and so on. In the process of these face-to-face discussions and in the presence of significant others, excuses might be exposed, past irritations might come to the fore, and real differences might be uncovered—all of which may hopefully lead to a more effective working relationship. It is expected, too, that more effective implementation will ensue when the decisions are made on a group basis than if they are made unilaterally or without the presence and participation of the group members. This is done in part, of course, in certain community council meetings and in routine interagency case conferences. The procedure may be an even more problem-centered and task-oriented approach and may respect less some of the formal amenities and platitudes that can cloud issues and impede solutions. This type of approach presumably may also be useful in helping to solve interprofessional differences.

Rewards and Incentives

The second approach, while not opposed to the group dynamics method, focuses on the development of appropriate administrative means and mechanisms whereby professional personnel and organizations, per se, are provided with rewards or incentives for furthering the objectives growing out of community-wide planning. Because the average health or welfare professional has internalized broad professional norms, he tends to act to safeguard and further the welfare of his clients, and, when necessary, to cooperate with other agencies to assure the welfare of the client. However, unless the worker's positive behavior to his client and his readiness to cooperate with other agencies is valued or approved by the individual agency by which he is employed, there is a limit to the degree to which his professional norms can sustain him. In short, it is not sufficient to plead with or exhort professionals to modify their behavior; incentives must be introduced within each agency to foster the activities that are required to fulfill the objectives emanating from the planning process. It is not only important to realize the needs and requirements of individual professionals as a prerequisite to community-wide planning; it is also necessary to consider the needs and requirements of organizations.

In order to appreciate why organizations may enter into or resist the planning process we must focus on the organizations themselves. Every organization has some kind of goal or objective toward which it directs or measures its activities. A health department may be concerned with the general promotion of health and the prevention of disease; a family service agency may have as its primary aim the development of psychologically healthy children and parents; and a tuberculosis association may have as its main goal the control of that disease. In order to achieve these goals an organization must have three main elements or resources. It must have recipients to serve (directly or indirectly); it must have resources in the form of funds, equipment, and specialized knowledge; and it must have the services or personnel to direct these resources to the recipients. Few, if any, organizations have access to enough of these resources to attain their objectives fully. Organizations, accordingly, select particular functions or services which permit them to achieve their ends as fully as possible.

Although scarcity may require that an organization restrict its activity to specific functions, it can seldom carry out even these more limited functions without some cooperation and interaction with other health and welfare agencies. It is in this manner that an organization is able to get additional precious resources in the form of clients, personnel and nonhuman resources. This need for various resources which other agencies may supply is an important and even salutary basis around which community-wide planning can be built. However, it would seem that it would also constitute a crucial requirement or precondition for planning—that the planning process be a mechanism by which organizations are to realize their objectives. In situations where the planning process requires an organization to relinquish a part of its domain and, consequently, its right to specific resources, it is necessary to consider what rewards an organization may obtain as a substitute for this loss. I would suggest that this is one of the critical stages in the planning process. Personnel and organizations are not motivated by ideology alone; they also respond in terms of some of the more pragmatic needs that we have mentioned. One of the great tasks challenging the ingenuity of the planner and the community organizer is how to make the needs and functions of agencies congruent with one another so that, in turn, they are congruent with the needs and problems of the recipient population.

Where Organizational Policies are Formulated

One final note: a number of problems cannot be solved on the organizational level alone. There are problems that can only be solved by turning to the state and even the federal political level. It is here where the conditions of the organizational game are established and it is here where much of the organizational reward system is determined. State agencies must fulfill minimal obligations to their parent or legitimizing bodies. There is a limit to which changes in policy can be effected by action or pressure on the organizational level. While there may be little point in investing time and energy in criticizing organizational activities, some headway may often be made by working on the state or national level where organizational policies are formulated.

28.   PPB or Not to Be?

Carl Martin

Budgeting must be viewed as one component in a series of analytic tools, including program auspice, program plan, accounting, auditing, program information system, and some form of cost-benefit analysis.

Independent of the other components is the need to develop a program plan for a given year or a series of years. Where is the organization going? What will it cost? How will it be financed?

How does the program (or client) information system relate expenditures to programs and personnel usage? What is the product? How much did it cost? With what results? For universities program outcomes might include student performance and faculty research or honors. For a family agency outcomes might be numbers of families seen, clients effectively treated, or number of consultations.

For human service organizations cost-benefit decisions are essentially human decisions, even though, from an economic benefit point of view, expenditures for children would have better cost-benefit ratio than expenditures for the aged. Our inadequate resources force difficult decisions—for example, who is to receive the kidney transplant—for the loser may die. Who makes these decisions, and how? How are cost factors integrated into this kind of decision-making? Finally, what is the role of moral and ethical values in programming and service delivery decisions?

Will PPB, systems analysis, comprehensive planning and operations research be incorporated into Fund and Council practices? Whatever the eventual answer, there are many who believe the continued success of Funds and Councils, perhaps a condition for their continued existence, depends on the adoption in whole or part of these sophisticated planning and management processes.

PPB (planning-programming-budgeting) is sweeping the federal bureaucracy). In August 1965, President Johnson directed major federal agencies to install a PPB system. The starting point of such a system is the identification of basic objectives, under which are grouped (regardless of the agency in which they are carried out) all activities which contribute toward the same objectives. All pertinent costs are considered for each activity. Then comes the cornerstone of PPB—program analysis. Major alternatives are identified, cost/benefit and cost/effectiveness estimations are considered for each, and the impact of proposed programs on other programs is anticipated and weighed. The aim of PPB is "best" resource allocation and "best" program selection.

Once I believed the complexity of these processes, and the costliness of the hardware needed, would eliminate them from practical Fund-Council application except in a few of the largest communities. However, I have come to realize that these processes, as concepts, can be carried on at many levels of refinement; even the less rigorous applications enjoy respectability.

Considerable illumination, for example, can come from contemplating program alternatives, uniting activities (regardless of organizational placement) under the objectives they serve, and seeking the best available estimates of cost and benefits. These steps are within the reach of smaller communities. Furthermore, an article in the July-August 1968 issue of COMMUNITY described how one United Fund in a medium-sized community (San Bernardino, Calif.) applied a systems analysis approach to develop a totally new concept for integrating local problem and goal identification, delivery of services, and funding. Finally, the more we become aware of time-sharing on computers the more hardware appears within the financial reach of many Funds and Councils.

Benefits or Penalties?

Having said all this, can I also say that these planning and management processes may bring more penalties than benefits? In doing so, I join a respectable (even growing) body of social scientists who question if these processes, when applied to public administration, achieve what is claimed for them; who go so far as to suggest that they have longrange, deleterious effects which we have been reluctant to face.

We are so accustomed to hearing the exhortation, "Be comprehensive," we have lost sight of the fact that goal achievement of a high order can and does occur within the pluralistic and fragmented character of the social welfare system as we have known it. In *The Politics of the Budgetary Process,* Professor Aaron Wildavsky of the University of California states, "I am prepared to argue that the partial-view-of-the-public-interest approach is preferable to the total-view-of-the-public-interest approach ... A partial adversary system in which various interests compete for control of policy seems more likely to result in reasonable decisions—that is, decisions which take account of the multiplicity of values involved—than one in which the best policy is assumed to be discoverable by a well-intentioned search for the public interest for all by everyone."

If what Wildavsky envisions is to have any meaning, all parties, *including the United Fund,* must become strong advocates of their own preferences for community goals, policies, and the desired distribution of shares. Unfortunately, what so often happens is that United Funds cop out, articulate no community goals of their own, and agencies in turn offer only warmed-over claims of their merit. For these reasons we fail to make a pluralistic system work as it might.

A budget committee is an example of what Wildavsky sees as one element in a "a partial adversary system." For a budget committee to say it feels "confused" is not a bad thing, if you reinterpret the meaning of this. Of course, confusion resulting from inadequate information or insufficient time for examination and deliberation is unfortunate. But so-called "confusion" may really mean that hard choices among competing claimants are to be made, and no absolutely or demonstrably right answer is at hand. The committee then is forced to exercise its collective value judgments and arrive at some majority decision.

Decisions emerging from the value judgments of a budget committee are not capricious; they spring from the style of life, the culture, the relevant issues, and the dynamic interplay of competing values in the community. Decisions made in this context, piecemeal though they may be, are as much valid planning as the products of the "better mousetrap"—PPB.

No matter how many "comprehensive" plans are produced, people do in fact muddle through. In a classic study, *A Strategy of Decision,* Braybrooke and Lindbloom call this process "disjointed incrementalism." (As soon as I encountered the term I felt an instant rapport.) They claim that in observation of actual behavior, even where the ideal of comprehensive planning is upheld, institutions and policies change only in incremental, ameliorative and marginal ways. They contend that the complexity of society and its pluralism require (in a democracy at least) that social planning be a series of reconciliatory moves. Change takes place because opposing camps offer only incrementally different policies in each policy area in which they wish to compete. Nobody moves too fast, too far or too many areas at once. (Contrast the demands of the black militants and the support they get from well-intentioned, nonincremental social planning.) Braybrooke and Lindbloom say that in the face of prodigious grand-scale planning, there is a tendency to evade or cheat on the radical change which is expected. With little thought of any "master-plan," change in the real order occurs by reconciliatory small moves and step-by-step adjustments.

Costly Standardization

They also ask, "Is comprehensive analysis always worth its cost?" Many of us have experiences indicating that quite often it is not. This costliness of analysis is a fundamental fact that planning strategies should face—and seldom do.

Comprehensive planning, PPB and the rest, seem to require in us a belief that as rational men we are driven to constant searching for the Best Possible Answer. Yet one of the most respected students of organizations, Herbert Simon, questions if we actually act this way. Quite to the contrary, he suggests that we follow a "satisficing process" in which we aim for a tolerable level of satisfaction rather than the maximum good or the best alternative, which have frustrated planners since the first comprehensive plan—the Creation.

Robert Boguslaw, an expert in system design, critically sees comprehensive planners and PPB poohbahs as the New Utopians (the title of his book). "The simple fact of the matter," he writes, "seems to be that classically designed computer-based systems, like classical utopias, resolve problems of conflict, consensus, and reality by simple fiat." From his own experience he finds this means insisting upon a uniformity of perspective, a standardization of language, and a consensus of values, all of which intensifies some unwanted characteristics of authoritarian, bureaucratic society.

Boguslaw is also concerned that the persons most affected by planning decisions will be denied the opportunity to participate and react, since they have not the knowledge, the technique, nor the position to program the computer or to challenge it. Although computer programmers are "unbiased," the limitations of their equipment introduce a set of restrictions on the decisions that can be made. Computerese is a bias only another technician can understand.

Flaws in Utopia

In *The Open Society and its Enemies,* Karl Popper, an early critic of attempts at large scale and comprehensive social reform, defends piecemeal social engineering on the basis that it can be adjusted more readily when it goes wrong. In a piecemeal or incremental approach, we are not architects of any utopia which weighs on us to be right in a great many interlocking decisions. Some of the most elaborate, comprehensive and computerized planning went into the production of the F-111 (TFX) fighter and the M-16 rifle. One critic of PPB, Dr. Victor Thompson, dryly observes that the plane crashes and the rifle jams.

Victor A. Thompson, chairman of the political science department at the University of Illinois, has made extensive studies of the general conditions that promote or inhibit innovation in organizations. Writing in *Trans-Action*, he states, "The style of administration in government (PPB dominated) is moving away from, not closer to, a climate that encourages innovation." Thompson finds that innovation is most apt to occur in organizations having a fairly loose organizational structure in which there is "slack"—or "the embarrassment of unused resources." He sees the scientific management approach, of which PPB is the leading example, as the opposite of the loose, overlapping structure with plenty of slack which is most conducive to innovation.

What all these writers seem to say is that planning is a political, human relations process and not a technological, intellectual operation. They seem to agree that planning is a series of incremental reconciliatory moves, which zig-zag ahead rather than taking quantum leaps into the future. Each of them places creativity and innovation, even at the cost of occasional waste of resources, as a higher goal than efficiency. All are suspicious of "Master Plan" approaches. Instead they believe that social planning calls for a flexible agency, which can help a community respond creatively to each challenge as it presents itself, rather than adherence to a grand design projected years ahead.

Lured by the hope of better things, some United Funds will follow the yellow brick road of PPB, systems analysis, comprehensive planning, operations research and the like. Many more probably will learn as a matter of necessity how to get more out of the existing non-system of fragmented agencies and associations. Briefly I can project four ways (and there are numerous others) in which we can make our present pluralistic system work better: (1) agency claimants for community support need to be put to stronger tests of relevancy and results; the dialogue between Fund and agencies on these subjects is of prime importance; (2) the United Fund needs to be a strong advocate of its own vision of community service goals and priorities, in spite of differences and impending conflict with agencies, (3) United Fund needs to foster greater diversity in problem-solving methods and agency structures (precisely what PPB cannot do); and above all (4) United Fund needs to set a climate rewarding innovation and provide training in the techniques that foster creativity.

The-partial-view-of-the-public interest, piecemeal social engineering, slack, disjointed incrementalism—who would have ever thought that these offer anything to our planning aspirations? Put in proper context, there may be more in our United Fund nonsystem system than we ever realized. We are somewhat like the farmer who rejects the opportunity to learn scientific farming on the ground that he isn't farming now as well as the knows how. But more than that, if we stop to look at "disjointed incrementalism," we have a good thing—even if it is embarrassingly closer to the naked ape than to General Motors.

29. Best Resource Allocation and Best Program Selection

(Response to Carl Martin)
Alan M. Cohen

Carl Martin's article entitled "PPB or Not to Be?" in my opinion does not accurately assess the issues; this is an attempt to place the subject in sharper focus.

The first issue that must be decided is the ultimate purpose of any organization using a Planning Programming Budgeting System (PPBS). Mr. Martin states, "The aim of PPB is 'best' resource allocation and 'best' program selection." Surely no one can argue with that aim. By itself it neither encourages nor denies flexibility, neither assumes nor demands a "grand plan." It simply means that all resources are used most efficiently, leaving open-ended the question of who determines this efficiency.

The obvious but all too often bypassed question is *how* to obtain the best resource allocation and best program selection for any organizational structure. The first step must be to determine what the organization is trying to do; the second, to decide what program to use to achieve these goals. In selecting a program or series of programs, the potential for success of the various alternatives must be considered; no agency has sufficient manpower and financial resources to do everything it wants to do. It is not sufficient to consider these alternatives over too short a time span because of the potential cumulative benefits of some programs, and because changing costs could inhibit or enhance the potential for meeting program goals effectively.

Once these alternatives have been assessed, it is possible to say that the attempt has been made to obtain the best resource allocation and best program selection. However, circumstances may change. The only way to insure the continuing validity of the program for meeting the goals is to reassess both program and goals periodically, to see that they are doing what is wanted at present.

This series of steps to arrive at the fundamental objective is the very process of PPBS; namely:

387

1. *Setting specific objectives:* Defining the "program" (broad project) in terms of the specific results (goals) or outputs desired.

2 *Identifying alternative methods.* Systematic identification of all possible alternative ways of meeting the specific objectives. This implies going beyond the particular agency program into the *total field* of relevant program activity.

3. *Comparing costs of methods.* Framing budgeting proposals in terms of programs directed toward achievement of the objectives (cost-benefit analysis). This analytical activity must employ consistency in defining components in quantitative terms for possible computerization.

4. *Projecting the costs of these programs in the future.* Five years usually is considered an appropriate time horizon.

5. *Formulating plans of achievement* year by year for each program.

6. *Establishing an information system for each program* to supply data for monitoring achievement of program goals and reassessment of program appropriateness and objectives.

The fundamental weakness in Carl Martin's argument is his focus on the individual components of PPBS rather than on the total *process.* He expresses concern about "grand-scale planning," "comprehensive plans" or "master plans," assuming that these will limit flexibility by eliminating the "pluralistic and fragmented character of the social welfare system."

If the reason for implementing PPBS were to achieve uniformity and eliminate flexiblity, I would be as concerned as Mr. Martin. However, he and others have missed the point by not approaching PPBS as a total *process;* a systematic and orderly (as opposed to intuitive) approach to the problem of how best to allocate scarce resources to achieve the goals for which the program was established.

Behind this process lies the crucial problem of who actually determines policy—who decides the goals and which programs will be adopted to achieve them. The boards of service agencies and fund organizations, which are vested with the ultimate decision-making authority, in many instances do not have sufficient information to make effective decisions. The result is that they all too often abdicate their decision-making function, allowing others with technological expertise to make the decisions (which they merely rubber-stamp), or maintaining a status quo in a mobile society.

How can a fund-raising organization give proportionally more money to one agency than another without some method of evaluating what the agency *actually* is doing as related to what it says it is doing (its goals)? How can a social agency board decide whether to expand a service, restrict its growth, or start an entirely new program, when it has almost no knowledge of the implications of the various alternatives?

Does evaluating mean that we no longer can be flexible? Must we assume that the decision-makers will be unable to appreciate the subtle benefits of alternatives, just because they may have more information upon which to base their decisions? It is true that if PPBS were taken to its extreme, a Grand Plan could be established by the federal government, in which every agency would have its "place." But just as a totalitarian regime *could* develop out of too much control and centralization, it also *could* develop out of the chaos of uncontrolled diversity.

The role of the non-governmental agencies traditionally has been to meet the social needs of people at the local level. Does fulfilling this function with the best resource allocation and best program selection mean that we have to cease being flexible and responsive to new needs? On the contrary, unless we have some way of assessing how to meet these new, more complex needs effectively, with the limited resources available, the entire system is in jeopardy. The fact that the legitimate policy-maker (in this case the agency board) would have more information on the actual results of the agency program in meeting its stated goals would seem to enhance flexibility, not inhibit it.

The misunderstandings probably arise from a misinterpretation of the role of program analysis in the total PPBS process. The official "Planning Programming Budgeting Guide" for senior government management, published by the government of Canada in July 1968, states: "It would be unfortunate if the emphasis necessarily given to techniques of analysis were to create the impression that analysis is being presented here as a substitute for managerial judgment and that the application of the techniques leads automatically to the 'right' decision. In a PPB System, analysis is expected only to promote better decisions since analysis is likely to bring forward a greater range of alternative courses of action for consideration by management and to make more apparent the probable effects of each course of action."

It is true that the potential exists for the policy-makers to abdicate their responsibility to the technical data men, but this is a perversion of the PPBS process. It also is true that computerized evaluative techniques are crude at the present time. However, since PPBS is official government policy in both the United States and Canada, it is essential that the nongovernmental agencies become familiar with both its benefits and serious handicaps, as a prerequisite to any attempt to guide and influence governmental or nongovernmental use of these processes.

To say that PPBS is the answer to all agency problems obviously is incorrect. The alternative—denying the benefits of a total process of evaluating programs in relation to their goals—in my estimation is equally fallacious.

Carl Martin's "four ways in which we can make our present pluralistic system work better" are almost meaningless generalizations unless they are related to an explanation of how they are to be implemented. In this context, they emphasize rather than deny the need for the *process* of PPBS:

1. "Agency claimants for community support need to be put to stronger tests of relevancy and results. . . ."

But how can we demand stronger tests of relevancy and results unless there is some better way of evaluating the agencies' program performance in relation to their stated goals?

2. "The United Fund needs to be a strong advocate of its own vision of community service goals and priorities. . . ."

But this, in effect, is establishing a comprehensive plan. How can this plan or goal be established without going into the process of PPBS?

3. "United Fund needs to foster greater diversity in problem-solving methods and agency structures (precisely what PPB cannot do)."

But this is precisely what PPB can do. How can the United Fund reallocate scarce resources unless it can justify new and greater diversity by showing the benefits of alternative methods over existing program activity?

4. "United Fund needs to set a climate rewarding innovation and provide training in the techniques that foster creativity."

But there is extreme pressure on financial resources just to meet existing program needs. Surely innovation and creativity cannot be fostered through their reallocation unless these new methods are shown to have a reasonable potential for improving the agency program as related to its goals. Some process such as PPBS is essential to weigh the alternatives and justify the direction of the innovation. The alternative Mr. Martin praises is to "muddle through."

It is not my intent to minimize the many achievements and benefits of the present system, but rather to state emphatically that our resources are not adequate to meet the increasingly complex needs of our society. New methods, which can reflect the advances in technology, must be implemented to insure for the United Way the best resource allocation and best program selection.

Part VI

*Assessing the Outcomes
of Administration and
Planning Strategies*

Introduction

After plans have been developed into programs, and programs have metamorphosed into reality, the human service organization and its members must live with that reality. The consequences of the planning process arrive, sometimes to greet and sometimes to haunt, planners and administrators.

There are those who would suggest that human beings have an inordinate capacity for avoiding the consequences of their actions. Similarly, many would suggest that, because of their more organized nature, complex organizations are even more effective in distorting and denying the reality that reflects the consequences of their actions. It was with this in mind that the present section was developed.

Whether through fault or default, organizations, and in particular human service organizations, most of whom lack the clear-cut criteria of a profit-making business, find it extremely difficult to assess the outcome and effectiveness of their efforts. We have attempted to provide two related points of view, each of which gives a perspective for examining the consequences of organizational policies and programs. These two perspectives, those of management, service delivery, and evaluative research, are commonly used, although not often interrelated or systematically employed. In our experience it has been a rare human service organization that has systematically and periodically taken stock of its progress through other than informal mechanisms or a very low level quantification of services. Although these methods might provide some rough indication of where the organization has been, and where it seems to be going, they lack the systematic feedback of more organized and periodically recurring approaches.

Human service organizations are in need of problem-oriented compasses and information processing instruments which might facilitate their development. It is our hope that this section will stimulate some of the thinking necessary to develop the best possible instrumentation for guiding these organizations.

Section A

Assessing the Outcomes
of Administration and Planning Strategies:
From the Point of View of Management

Administrators in human service organizations are consumers of their own operational strategies, and must live with the outcomes of their planning. While their concerns are often with the immediate realities of practical problem solving, the more sophisticated among them are constantly attempting to create some sense of long-range coherence in policies and planning. The articles in this section were selected to provide perspectives on these problems; i.e., the concerting of the practical considerations of immediate strategies and outcomes with the more abstract considerations of long-range planning.

Although both internal organizational changes and changes in the environmental field make perfection of this concerting process a practical impossibility, some workable alternatives are available which tend to minimize error.

A recurring theme in these articles, and one which has been referred to throughout this book, is the development among organizations, and their participants, of a reflective awareness of the consequences of their administrative and planning decisions. In addition to providing some thoughtful, reflective assessments of organizations in time and space, there is, in the following articles, one case study which details some of the dimensions of self-awareness in one kind of human service organization.

30. Can the Behavioral Sciences Contribute to Organizational Effectiveness?
A Case Study*

W. G. Bennis, M. F. Malone, N. H. Berkowitz, and M. W. Klein

Can administrators and planners in human service organizations make use of behavioral scientists in assessing the problems and dynamics of their organizations? Can the analyses and results of organizational dynamics be integrated into the internal milieu of an organization in a way that facilitates personal and organizational growth and development?

In the following article it is suggested that both these questions might be answered positively; however, important contingencies must be taken into consideration. These contingencies might be generally conceptualized as assuming the form of a series of emergent decisions regarding the direction of the research; decisions which are dependent upon findings at sequential points in time, and decisions which give the developmental flow of the research a sense of being organic to the emergent problems of the organization. Thus as findings assume some over-all structure near the end of a project, they are intimately related to the needs and problems of the organization.

To achieve this it would seem essential that there be periodic, systematic, and joint monitoring of research findings, as well as joint input into research planning, by selected organizational personnel and the research team. While this strategy contains certain risks of data contamination, these can be minimized through effective planning.

When Henry Adams returned to Boston after a long absence, he remarked on his surprise at finding the Unitarians, who dominated the Boston culture of that day, seemed to believe they had solved every great philosophical conundrum that had ever con-

*Paper read at the annual meeting of the American Public Health Association, October 22, 1959.

vulsed the human spirit.[1] At times, we fear, the behavioral scientist gets placed, unwittingly or not, by himself and his new lay clientele into positions of such false omniscience. It should be noted that it is only relatively recently that the behavioral scientist has had a willing lay-clientele, and that the newness of this relationship may produce utopian hopes on the part of the clients—usually practitioners—who believe that by receiving some magical amulet—i.e., nonunderstandable social science jargon—all their day-to-day organizational concerns will be extirpated. On the other hand, for their part, the behavioral scientists, with their zealous faith in the fruits of scientific method, can over-tout their wares and set up unreachable expectations. The danger here of course is that both parties get trapped in a false dream.

The relationship of the academic social researcher with a lay-clientele is only one of many merging problems which stem from this dramatically new development: the application of knowledge to concrete human affairs. Until very recently—Harry Alpert indicates that World War II was the catalyst—the social scientist was located in the laboratory or in the armchair. And when he took to the field he seemed more interested in the hobo and the prostitute, the Navahos and the whitehipster, prize-fighters and taxi-dancers, jazz musicians and other equally atypical groups who have been ink-blotted, sociogrammed, surveyed, depth-interviewed, and observed while the pressing problems of crucial institutions—such as hospitals—remain undescribed and unanalyzed. Even as late as 1940 the government's activities in the social sciences were confined largely to the collection and analysis of statistical information. Now, however, the situation has changed dramatically:

> "The events of the war on both the military and civilian fronts, and the problems of postwar readjustment as they affected the nation and the individual, provided the social sciences with dramatic opportunities to demonstrate their practical value and essential role in modern society. As a result, social science research firmly established its legitimacy as a fundamental contributor to national life."[2]

Today we see the evidence of pragmatic research marked by the birth of such disciplines as disaster research, medical sociology,

[1] Cited in L. Kubie, "Is Preventitive Psychiatry Possible?", *Daedalus*, (1959), 88: p. 647.

[2] H. Alpert, "The Growth of Social Research in the United States," in *The Human Meaning of the Social Sciences*, Ed. by D. Lerner, New York: Meridian Books, 1959: p. 79.

human engineering, industrial sociology and psychology, military psychology, propaganda and communications research, economic development, group dynamics, to mention only a few. The growth of such organizations as HUMRO, RAND, Air Forces Institute, Center for International Studies, and others indicates the rapid transition to a more honorific and powerful place for the applied social sciences.

This brings us headlong to the perplexing question which the title of this paper poses; a question, so shrewdly phrased by the program chairman and so innocently accepted by the authors; a question which generates so many derivative problems that no easy answer can be formulated—at least at this time. For the question itself implies: *value judgments* (What are, and how do we weight, the multifaceted criteria of organizational effectiveness? Can behavioral sciences provide conclusions which have a practical pay-off in the practical world? Is information about human behavior relevant for crucial decisions in complex organizations?); *scientific considerations* (Can systematic research succeed in applied settings where variables may not be controlled and measurement is often less precise, where specialists from a variety of disciplines have to work within an interdisciplinary framework? Where the role of the scientist-observer, scientist-interviewer may affect in an unpredictable manner, as in many other research settings, those very objects he wishes to study *au naturel?*); and *relationship questions* (What is the nature of the contract between researchers and their subjects in natural settings? What are the ethics with respect to anonymity of responses? Does the organization under study have the right to censor results? Is the behavioral scientist obliged to interpret his results and to what audience(s)?). The scope and time limitations of this paper quite naturally preclude definitive answers to these questions; and also, quite naturally, so does our available knowledge. But to return to the question which the title raises—can the behavioral sciences contribute to organizational effectiveness? —we can supply an answer to those who have a need for closure and for structure: Yes and no, or better yet, it depends.

In a more serious vein we can say that it is theoretically possible to alter organizational process and relationships on the basis of solid and systematic facts yielded by the application of scientific method to human relations; and in addition, that an alteration in these processes and relationships may lead to greater effectiveness in reaching the organization's goals—leaving aside for the moment the gnawing question of what is meant by organizational goals. Underlying this last statement are the premises that there is a discernible connection between the coordination of human resources and organizational goals and that valid knowledge about these human resources could lead to improved accomplishment. It is easier to recognize that something is wrong than to correct it. And although recognition is an essential prerequisite to future prevention, alterations in an organizational context have to be gingerly induced, delicately maneuvered, and intelligently implemented. Even then the ubiquitous fears of change create massive resistances—rational and irrational—right to the very roots of the organization. Putting this a little differently, we can say that the behavioral sciences can provide valid information, the application of which may lead to increased organizational effectiveness. But the application and infusion of the research results depends primarily on the usual decision processes of the organization under study.

Let us briefly state the essence of what has been said so far. The present state of applied research, given its novelty and hope for practical utility, has produced two sets of problems: The first has to do with the *role dilemmas* the social scientist finds himself embedded in with respect to his relationships to his various publics (fellow social scientists, the organizations under study, and intelligent lay audiences). The second has to do with his intellectual and scientific quest to identify and measure those factors which seem to be related to the organizational goals, even though the latter are not the primary goals of a purely scientific endeavor.[3] We should like to discuss both of these problems now, drawing on our experience, when appropriate, in conducting research on the role of the OPD nurse in eight Boston hospitals.

ROLE DILEMMAS OF THE APPLIED SOCIAL RESEARCHER

To dramatize this problem let us quote from a recent editorial in a social science journal:[4]

"A small upstate New York village has now been immortalized in anthropological literature under the name of "Springdale." The local newspaper reports that the experience has not been entirely a pleasing one. We pass on this account:

'The people of the Village waited quite a while to get even with

[3] For another discussion of this issue, see D. Levinson, "The Mental Hospital as a Research Setting: A Critical Appraisal," in *the Patient and the Mental Hospital,* ed. by M. Greenblatt, D. J. Levinson, and R. H. Williams. Free Press, Glencoe, Ill.: 1957: pp. 633-649.

[4] "Editorial," *Human Organization,* (1958) 17: p. 1.

(author), who wrote a *Peyton Place* type book about their town recently.

'The featured float of the annual Fourth of July parade followed an authentic copy of the jacket of the book, *Small Town in Mass Society*, done large scale by Mrs. Beverly Robinson. Following the book cover came residents of Springdale riding masked in cars labeled with the fictitious names given them in the book.

'But the pay-off was the final scene, a manure-spreader filled with very rich barnyard fertilizer, over which was bending an effigy of The Author.'

The account suggests that a good time was had by all—on this particular occasion. Nevertheless, local observers report that the disturbance caused by the book in the village has not been entirely compensated for by even such a ceremony carried out in the best anthropological traditions."

This editorial, which goes on to raise a number of important issues, indicates some of the present dilemmas of the applied social scientist. For one thing, he is no longer dealing with docile subjects like white rats, college sophomores, or preliterate people who can't talk back. It should be clear that the applied social scientist has some responsibility to his subjects, but he also has responsibility to report to his scientific colleagues the substantive findings of his research. The ethical balance between responsibility to the users of research—the subjects turned clients—and to fellow-producers of research is not an easy equilibrium to reach. And now that social scientists are studying more and more verbal and powerful organizations, this ethical problem has become more prominent.

The underlying issue here is: what is the nature of the contract between the researcher and the organization under study? Karl Menninger has diagrammed contractual relationships between a number of bargaining relationships: customer-vendor, barber-client, doctor-patient, and psychoanalyst-patient.[5] In all these cases, something was given for something obtained. Now what is the applied researcher giving for the opportunity he obtains to collect scientific data? Primarily, we can say, he is giving information which may be valuable to the client-organization. But this raises two other problems. First, can he *give* information away? After all, who really *owns* the information, the subjects who responded, the organization who cooperated with the research effort and made the subjects available, or the researchers? Second, if the issue of ownership were settled, an even stickier problem emerges. Let us suppose that the data are important and useful. If this is so, then undoubtedly in many cases the nature of the information may be unpalatable and even noxious to the recipient. Psychotherapy has developed

[5] *Theory of Psychoanalytic Technique*, New York: Basic Books, 1958: pp. 15-42.

a rich literature on the "analysis of the resistance" to interpretations. The only way data can be accepted as "valid" by the recipients is when there is a feeling of mutual trust and confidence between the researcher and the subject population. To develop this relationship, a good deal of time and effort must be invested. And even then, it appears to some that the goal of research—which is to understand—is antithetical to the goal of organization, which is to produce.

We cannot overemphasize this problem concerning the nature of the contract and mutual responsibilities of the researchers and their clients. One of the hospitals in our sample decided to withdraw from the study after almost three years of cooperation with us. The reasons for this termination are not even at this point clear. The reason given was that there was no explicit contract in the files which legitimized the research activity. This withdrawal came as a surprise to us as we had enjoyed a long tenure of what we had considered satisfactory relationships with this hospital. It may be no accident that this action followed almost immediately on our asking the physicians in the various OPD clinics to fill out a short questionnaire. Nurses may indeed be more docile than physicians; but our hunch is that when research activity touches on sensitive organizational nerves, resistances and balkiness become apparent. And if the applied researcher is properly doing his job, he cannot avoid symptoms which the organizations at times sacrifice considerable energy to ignore. And I suppose someday we will see the occasion where various organizations will riffle through a number of researchers until they find the one who will tell them what they want to hear.

Of course, the situation is exacerbated in the present situation where our research group had no formal organizational relationship to the hospitals under study. We were associated with a university and could establish a purely voluntary relationship with the hospitals. A formal relationship, while satisfactory on this issue, could become equally tenuous however, if the researchers' findings were deleterious to the organization's goals. (A research chemist told us recently that he was threatened with unemployment if he continued to do research on the rate of decay of his employer's products.)

The whole point of this discussion is that until some explicit contractual arrangement is developed, the applied researcher has no basis of power or authority to maintain the relationship. And unlike the analyst or even general practitioner, he does not have available the leverage of the transference.

Two other problems are worthy of mention before getting on to a discussion of some of our research results. One concerns the problem of secrecy; by this we mean that on some occasions the researcher cannot divulge the nature and purpose of a particular questionnaire or observation. Recently, for example, we wanted to observe the OPD nurse in her teaching capacity with patients. We recognized that if the nurse realized the purpose of the observations, it might affect her performance such that our results would not be reliable. Thus, we had to ask our cooperating hospitals to allow us to make certain observations without revealing the purposes. From the hospital's point of view this request was no small matter. It entailed complicated arrangements, making certain records available, communicating with certain hospital personnel, etc. We were also in a predicament. In order to persuade the hospitals of the ultimate utility of such observations, they quite obviously wanted to know why we wanted particular data. In this case we were not free to divulge the nautre of the data desired. The degree to which the relationship to our eight cooperating hospitals has been satisfactory can be indicated by the fact that all of the hospitals agreed to participate in this study without clearly understanding the reason for it, and at considerable risk and expense. We must also report, in all fairness, that our observers—all graduate nurses —were met with a wide range of reactions, from vacant stares to spiteful obedience, from suspicious glances to smiling acceptance. On a number of occasions, hospital personnel contorted themselves to get a look at the observational form—tucked well behind a clip-board. And in at least one case, a physician tried boldly to wrench away the clip-board from one of our nurse-observers. You may be interested to know that the nurse held fast, and curiosity and conscience were sacrificed on the alter of science.

One final point, concerning the nature of variables in applied social research. Paradoxically, behavioral scientists and hospital personnel view the other as having an excessive need to control and manipulate. The variables the scientist manipulates or controls in the laboratory are useful to the practitioner only insofar as he, the practitioner, can manipulate them, too. In other words, a high correlation or powerful effect of an independent variable provides utility only to the degree that the practitioner can use the variable to promote conditions in which individuals can change. What the practitioner views as strategic for change, say the number of physicians per clinic, may be impossible for the scientist to wield experimentally. We are not simply talking about measurement but about the manipulability of the particular variable as an experimental factor. In short, what the practitioner may view as significant in creating effective alterations may be inaccessible to scientific control. Conversely, what may register as an important scientific effect may not be manipulable by the practitioner.

Perhaps all this could be summarized by Adlai Stevenson's pithy remark that the road of the egg-head is not an easy one. And if we exaggerated his plight in this paper it is only out of deep subjective loyalty for the applied researcher who lives in perpetual fear of tenuous financing, negative—and worse—equivocal results; who is accused of not really understanding what he is studying and insensitive to the subtle nuances of "my situation"; whose research design undergoes searing attacks by those who claim little or no experience in research design; who hears that he is basically antihumanistic and overly-scientistic; upon whose effigy resentment is heaped for his secrecy and marginal position. Informants cozen him for inside dope; he is seen as pro-managerial and pro-worker simultaneously; his results are dismissed as too esoteric or too obvious; and who is seen—at least in some hospitals—as a *Look Magazine* reporter in disguise.

In point of fact this burlesque of the applied researchers' plight has some truth in it, but equally true is the fact that he is being granted more latitude and freedom and cooperation—if our own experience is any criterion—than ever before. The main problem between the researcher and the client organization was nicely phrased by Schopenhauer when he discussed how porcupines kept warm during the winter. They huddled together in order to keep warm, but when they got too close their sharp quills caused each other pain. Their problem was to reach that equilibration which maximized warmth and minimized pain.

Some Contributions to Organizational Effectiveness

Let us now turn to some of the research findings, uncovered over the past three years in our study of the role of the nurse in the OPD, and examine their relevance to organizational effectiveness. Primarily we were interested in those social psychological factors, organizational and interpersonal, which seemed to have a bearing on the nurses' performance and the clinics' functioning. Thus, our study quite naturally fell into two major compartments: the identification and measurement of the *strategic* social psychological variables; i.e., those manipulable variables that make a difference with respect to nurses' performance and clinic functioning. And second, we had to locate and measure acceptable criteria of nursing performance and clinic functioning. This latter problem—the definition and measurement of criteria of organizational effectiveness—cannot be discussed at length now. But a few words may be appropriate to demonstrate some of the complexities involved. First, it should be noted that before any manipulations of the social psychological matrix can or should be made, the question must be raised "for what?" What are the *goals?* By what *criteria* do organizations evaluate performance? Now in some settings this problem may be less complex; organizations, for example, where output is measured in terms of discrete numbers of products produced or profit rates or some discrete, operable unit. In service organizations, such as a hospital, criteria for evaluation are difficult to come by; first because of their vagueness (i.e., patient care), and second because the organizations typically require multiple criteria for performance evaluation. When we began our quest for the relevant criteria we were told by the best informed sources that "patient-care" was the pivotal focus for evaluation. We then went out and interviewed 24 administrative officials and nursing supervisors, individuals with long experience and with an overview of OPD functioning.[6] We asked these individuals to name the clinics which in all their experience they considered best and worst with respect to the quality of patient care. Then, we asked them to spell out the criteria they used in differentiating between good and bad clinics. Eighty different criteria were mentioned. When the 80 criteria were inspected for purposes of measurability, the number dropped drastically to about 20; and of these only 9 or so could be pinpointed as intrinsic aspects or causes of patient care—most were correlates of indices of good care with questionable causative function. Perhaps the most striking part of our findings, however, was the relatively low ranking given to patient teaching and understanding, usually cinsidered the foundation of nursing performance in the OPD; only 5 out of 24 respondents mentioned this factor. (Notwithstanding, because of the emphasis of the profession on this factor we later used patient teaching as a criterion, along with patient follow-through, which was high on the list.)

Another interesting and completely unanticipated finding from our criteria quest was the fact that those individuals who were asked to select good and bad clinics may have been implicitly utili-

    6 M. Klein, M. Malone, W. G. Bennis, and N. Berkowitz, "Technical Considerations in the Measurement of Patient Care in the Out Patient Department." In preparation.

zing another set of criteria; criteria which were never made explicit
or verbalized, but which appeared under statistical analysis. When
we examined the particular clinics that were mentioned and compared them with certain physicalistic elements ingrained in the
treatment, condition, and physical requirements of the clinic, we
discovered some remarkable relationships.[7] For example, one such
cluster of these physicalistic parameters, *difficulty of illness for the
patient,* is highly related to judgments of good patient-care; i.e.,
clinics treating illnesses which involve a higher degree of difficulty
for the patient are *judged* to give better care than those in which
the illness provides less difficulty for the patient. In other words,
the more chronic the condition, the more interference with life,
the higher the cost of treatment, the greater the need for ancillary
services, and the more visits required—all of these factors cluster
statistically—the more the clinic was judged to give good care.

Two other clusters of additional dimensions were also found
to be related to judgments of patient care. (All these relationships
mentioned are statistically significant.)

All the implications of these findings cannot be discussed here,
but aside from the remarkable substantive findings, three points
should be made. The first point is that these physicalistic phenomena—nature of the treatment, elements of the condition, and
physical accouterments—have an enormous, but typically implicit
effect on judgments of quality of patient care. If one wanted to
predict judgments of patient care, one could do so moderately
well from knowing the physical parameters of the clinics. Second,
it suggests criteria of measurement other than judgments alone;
this decreases the problem of subjectivity—so rampant in criteria
studies—and increases the prospect of attaining a validity estimate.
Finally, it should be noted that these physicalistic parameters must
be taken into account by behavorial scientists if they want to assess
the subtle effects of the social and psychological variables. We think
this last point is important enough to reiterate. If relevant parameters can be indentified *prior* to the selection of the units to be
studied, an element of control and refinement can be introduced
which is often lacking in organizational studies. A great deal of
time and effort can be saved, and the potential for supporting
hypothesized relationships considerably increased. Behavioral scientists should not be disenchanted about carrying on research in
order to find the effect of "their" variables on performance in

7 M. Klein, N. Berkowitz, and M. Malone, "Qualitative Judgments and the
Physicalistic and Task Parameters of the Judged Phenomena—An Instance From
a Medical Setting." In preparation.

a complex hospital setting where obviously many other non-social-pyschological variables have important effects. Rather, they should consider them and measure the effects of these variables within certain physicalistic conditions.

Earlier we mentioned some difficulties in observing nurses in the process of teaching patients. Most authoritative studies on the OPD regard patient-teaching as a pivotal function of the nursing role. We decided that this factor was a reasonable criterion for a measure of nursing performance. After interviewing 39 graduate nurses in OPD's out of our sample range, we constructed an observational form which included nine areas: treatments, tests, general information, follow-through, complications, orientation to the clinic, referral, explanation of examinations and procedures, and adjustment to living. While complete findings cannot be presented at this time, it is very clear that patient-teaching, as observed by graduate nurses using a valid observational instrument, is performed with remarkable infrequency. (These measurements were quantitative; we measured *amount* of teaching, not *quality* of teaching.) For example, there was scarcely any teaching concerning adjustment to living and complications. (The G.I., Gyn, G.U., and Medical clinics had the lowest scores, while Diabetes and Rectal clinics had the highest scores.) Of the percentage distribution by teaching areas, the frequency of teaching went from tests, which was the highest, to follow-through, explanation of procedures and examinations, treatment, referral, general information, adjustment to living, orientation to clinic, and complications, which was the lowest.

In additional to these data on patient teaching, we are also analyzing data on patient follow-through which the physicians are estimating.

To summarize work on the organizational effectiveness criteria, let us say that these are multiple and may vary for particular groups within the organization OPD nurses undoubtedly have different criteria from research physicians or administrators and possibly different from the ward nurses; that criteria measures should be compared with each other in order to establish whether or not they operate in the same direction. Mounting empirical evidence from industrial studies indicates that worker satisfaction and productivity are not positively related; striking examples have been shown where these two variables operate in negative directions and in most studies, have zero correlation.

In the brief time remaining, let us consider one area of our research finding which falls under the general social psychological rubric and which we believe, but cannot as yet prove, has relevance for organizational effectiveness. In a nutshell, the bulk of our findings from the first two years of our research, indicate that the professional nurse is turning into Organization Woman, that she is under enormous organizational pressure which tinctures and perforce, violates her standard of what nursing—legitimate nursing—is. Given the professional training of the nurse, the reasons why she entered nursing, and her strongly ingrained service orientation, she enters a social system where she finds herself stripped of precisely these role elements which she expected. When the nurse with an image of nursing as being bedside care of patients approaches the actual OPD job, she is in for a severe jolt. She was not prepared—psychologically or technically—for the myriad of other duties that she has to perform, and she is not really sure she likes it this way. In short, there is a sharp discrepancy between her image of the nursing profession and the actualities of work life.[8] It is our contention that this problem, as observed from the OPD study, is important enough to conceptualize in the following terms: where a role either violates or fails to meet (in practice) the role occupants' conception of that role, *role deprivation* exists.[9],[10] And we have found that this phenomenon—a surrendering of professional values and goals to organizational demands—exists to a surprising degree among the 90 nurses in our study sample. "No man, not even a doctor," as Florence Nightingale has often been quoted, "ever gives any other definition of what a nurse should be than this—'devoted and obedient.' This definition would do just as well for a porter. It might even do for a horse. It will not do for a nurse." And yet, today the nurse finds herself obedient and devoted—not to the patients—but to the records, to the administrative and organizational demands, to the red-tape. To make matters worse, it appears, though the evidence is not conclusive, that nursing supervision rewards and reinforces this tendency toward administrative and organizational functioning. Another part of our study showed that, in general, OPD nurses were not rewarded in a manner they thought appropriate. Moreover, the rewards they would have liked were virtually impossi-

[8] K. D. Benne and W. G. Bennis, "Role Confusion and Conflict in Nursing" Part I. "The Role of the Professional Nurse," *Am. J. Nursing,* Vol. 59, Feb. 1959. Part II. "What is Real Nursing," *Am. J. Nursing,* Vol. 59, March 1959.

[9] M. Malone, "A Study of Some Effects of Role Deprivation on Selected Aspects of the Behavior, Attitudes, and Values of Nurses in the Out Patient Department." Unpublished M. A. thesis. Boston University School of Nursing.

[10] N. Berkowitz, M. Malone, and J. Berkowitz, "The Professional in Formal Organizations: Cases of Role Deprivation in Hospital Settings." In preparation.

ble for the supervisor to control. Here we have a striking situation where supervision appears to lack the clear perception of what is an appropriate reward, or the usual ability to reward or deprive.[11]

For the past year or so we have been attempting to construct a questionnaire which would include a number of conflict situations where the nurse would have to choose between professional or organizational demands or some compromise position between these two poles. An example may help to illustrate this:

> You have a class at 3:00 that you want very much to attend. You'd have to leave now to get there, but there are a number of records to be filed, appointment slips to be handled, etc. Ordinarily the clinic clerk could do this, but today you are "breaking in" a new clerk. What are you most likely to do?

The code system would dictate that going to the class would confirm the professional value while remaining to finish the clinic work would indicate an organizational response. We had hoped to set up a number of situations in which the organizational and professional demands would have equal valence for the nurses. Yet our pretesting of this questionnaire has suggested that the nurse has such a strong disinclination to choose the professional response that we had to successively revise the conflict situations in order to get a decent distribution of professional and organizational responses. Before we could obtain in our pretesting sufficient variance in response we had to revise the question above to the following:

> You have a class outside the hospital at 3:00 that you want very much to attend. You and another person are scheduled to lead a discussion about the healing professions. You'd have to leave now to get there, but there are a number of records to be filed, appointment slips to be handled, etc. Ordinarily the clinic clerk would do this, but today you are "breaking in" a new clerk. You called the supervisor who has been unable to find anyone to help the clerk. What are you most likely to do?

Naturally no professional group working within organizational constraints can satisfy all their professional aspirations and realize all their internal standards. This is as true for the research scientist working with industry or the economist working for the government or the psychologist working for industry as it is for the nurse in

[11] W. G. Bennis, N. Berkowitz, M. Affinito, and M. Malone, "Authority, Power, and the Ability to Influence," *Hum. Rel.* Vol. 11, No. 2, 1958.

the OPD. Yet our impression is that OPD nurses are in more danger of professional erosion due to organizational demands than many other professional groups.

Data from another part of our study, collected for other purposes, dramatizes this conflict and suggests some ways for ameliorating its effect.[12] We had devised a set of cartoons portraying the OPD nurse in a variety of conflict situations. The nurses were asked to identify with the nurse in the cartoon and to fill in the empty bubble with what she would say in that particular situation. Most of the cartoons employed a "thought" bubble wherein the nurse would write in what she was thinking as well. The particular cartoon under discussion shows the nurse apparently tidying up the clinic area. A sign on the wall says that the clinic hours are from 10 A.M.—1 P.M. A clock on the wall indicates that the time is 1:30 P.M. A patient is shown coming into the clinic saying that she feels miserable. The nurse has two places to fill in answers; one, an overt statement in response to the patient; and the other, a covert thought. The nurse can resolve the situation in favor of the patient by attempting to have her seen by a physician (professional resolution) or could resolve it in favor of the organization by refusing to have the patient seen. The nurse can also compromise between both sets of forces by somehow ensuring that organizational factors are safeguarded while at the same time seeing that the patient receives care. This might be done by sending her to the emergency ward.

In the analysis of the data the responses were coded with respect to the resolution of the conflict and the amount of hostility expressed. (This latter category was difficult to code, so the findings with respect to it have to be interpreted with caution.) The modes of resolution could be in terms of favoring patient-care, or the organizational demands, or a compromise between the two. Our results show that if the nurse makes a compromise solution there is significantly less hostility expressed.

This finding, supported with some consistency elsewhere in our study, indicates that the mode of resolution will determine the extent to which the hostility will be directed toward the agents perceived as placing the nurse in the conflict situation (in the previous case, the patient or the clinic organization). A practical application might be to attempt to itemize the important conflict situations and establish institutional modes of resolution to reduce the dif-

[12] W. G. Bennis, N. Berkowitz, M. Malone, and M. Klein, "The Role of the Nurse in the Out Patient Department: A Preliminary Report." Monograph in preparation.

ficulties of the nurse in such situations. We found the compromise solution provided the optimum choice in terms of low expression of hostility. However, before compromise choices can in fact be made, organizational facilitation has to be provided. For example, in our cartoon data a compromise solution frequently mentioned was sending the patient to the emergency ward. Now if there is no emergency ward, no compromise alternative may be open to the "conflicted" nurse. Another possibility is to provide some cognitive and intellectual mastery of the forces involved in the representative conflict situations that may help nurses in making better decisions with a reduction of tension. It is sometimes surprising to learn that individuals enmeshed in conflict situations very rarely recognize them as such; the "recognition" goes on usually at some state of unconsciousness and is typically expressed in oblique ways, such as expression of hostility or self-deprecation. We feel that some steps should be taken—perhaps in the form of in-service training—to develop a "conflict inventory," and for the discussion of the major forces involved to form the basis of training.

Of course, while awareness of the forces involved probably equips the individual with improved basis for choice, it does not reduce the conflict completely. Thus, there are at least two methods for dealing with role conflict. One is a training approach; providing some cognitive mastery over the conflict situations. The other approach is directly tied in with the organization's responsibility for creating some legitimized compromise alternatives. Both of these approaches are probably necessary for the optimal reduction of conflict forces.

In summary we can say that our discussion has attempted to underline three aspects of the applied social science research process: the relationship between the researcher and his client-organizations; the research process and some substantive findings; and the utilization of research. As to the first, we have stressed the need for mutual trust and confidence on the part of the researcher and the organization; they need to tolerate the others' whims to some degree. Furthermore, we underlined the need for specifying the nature of the contract and the need for a more legitimized and protected role for the applied researcher; this would reduce his own conflict between organizational and professional demands which become extremely powerful in these settings.

This paper has not attempted to develop in great detail the strategy of change. But we should stress that it would be naive to imagine that changes can come easily—no matter how solid or sophisticated the scientific findings. It should also be said that as behavioral scientists we feel that our threshold is reached when we provide valid data on which certain practical decisions can be made. It is up to administration to determine how to promote conditions where performance can be improved.

When all these considerations are presented and all cautions are taken, it is very possible that the behavioral sciences can contribute to organizational effectiveness. But as we said earlier, it depends. Our vision for the future, although it may well be far off, is that the behavioral sciences will play a role somewhat equivalent to the role of preventive medicine. Behavioral scientists, both from within and from without organizations, may be able to diagnose and even prescribe certain alternatives for improving organizational effectiveness. The organization frequently provides a magnificent crucible where this kind of research may be carried on to the advantage of the organization as well as to scientific knowledge.

But for the time being let us end with a quote taken from an article on another perplexing American institution, the government:

> "Not everything is soluble. Not everything can be controlled. Some things have to be lived with. Some have to be taken on faith. Such choice as we have is to decide which risk is the lesser one."[13]

---

[13] S. Hyman, "The Issue of Presidential Disability," *New York Times Magazine*, 26 Feb. 1956.

31. Health Care Reforms: The Myths and Realities*

Walter J. McNerney, F.A.P.H.A.

If we are to accurately assess outcomes, and in turn use these data to improve patterns of health service delivery, it is important that we have a mature, fully-developed notion of what we are about as service providers. The following article examines many of the facets of health care from the perspective of both our myths about it, and its realities. To be sure, the two are often logically incompatible.

There are health care systems. The systems are not imaginary abstractions; they are real (as McNerney notes, if you don't believe it, try to change one). Their capacity, effectiveness, and perhaps their operational assumptions may be critically questioned. However, there remains the task of reliably defining the behavioral realities of these organizations and systematically using these data as the basis for change. McNerney's article will help accomplish this end.

Perhaps no field is more captive to myths, false images, and shibboleths than health. They now seriously jeopardize our ability to identify or resolve issues and to move forward, and the economic and emotional price of unfilled expectations is too high. It is critically important to test the validity of long-cherished beliefs and to accept seriously the importance of an ecological perspective.

In honoring the recipients of the Bronfman Prizes** and in response to the purpose of the awards, i.e., to recognize current achievements leading directly to improved health for large numbers of people, I should like to evaluate the current and prospective

*This Bronfman Lecture (the tenth in the series) was delivered at a General Session of the American Public Health Association at the Ninety-Eighth Annual Meeting in Houston, Tex., October 29, 1970.

**Karl Evang, M.D., Director-General, The Health Services of Norway; Alan F. Guttmacher, M.D., President, Planned Parenthood-World Population, New York; and The Honorable Edmund S. Muskie, United States Senator from Maine.

roles of public health in improving the effectiveness of our health system.

In essence, public health as a discipline has better conceptual equipment than most fields with which to address the issue of positive health but has fallen significantly below its potential in keeping this target in focus. To become more effective, it must: (1) help break false images; (2) start to practice community medicine as energetically as it is preached; and (3) help broaden our definition of health and relevant services. Otherwise, positive health will remain a fond hope and our health system will remain hopelessly captured in a mold of expensive, unproductive crisis medicine.

Today, the situation is more amenable to refocus than it has been in years. In 1961, for example, when the first Bronfman Public Health Prize was given, rising costs were of less concern, gaps in service were less visible, the enormity of access problems was less clearly defined, and the scale of dissatisfaction and unrest among members of the community was less widely appreciated than at present. Only relatively few persons saw significant weaknesses in the health system. Perhaps the majority could be forgiven for seeking a gradual, evolutionary path, feeling that weaknesses would be corrected in due course.

Since then, health care costs have out-stripped the rise in wages and earnings beyond the limits of public tolerance; inner city riots have highlighted the despair of the poor, and better reporting has made it impossible to ignore the problems inherent in health care goals, priorities, capital investment, distribution of resources and productivity. Now, by contrast, there is encouragingly widespread acceptance of the need to accelerate improvements in the health system.

Some of the flavor of current feeling is in the Report of the Task Force on Medicaid and Related Programs* which was reported to Secretary Richardson in June. The Task Force's membership was broadly representative from the standpoint of geography, age, sex, economic, and professional groups. Some of its recommendations have been or are being weighed seriously, others are not. But, at least, its findings are indicative of a mood and a new understanding that extends well beyond professional leadership. I should like to point out a few.

The Task Force felt that "the country is well into a transition from considering that health is largely an individual affair to under-

*Report of the Task Force on Medicaid and Related Programs. U.S. Department of Health, Education, and Welfare (June 29), 1970.

standing that health is a community affair as well. Personal transactions, no matter how well intentioned and effectively carried out, can no longer provide the answers to what have become essentially public policy and management problems."

In effect, the Task Force felt that the design of health care, with its heavy emphasis on sophisticated technical care of disease, has been influenced excessively by the vested professional and monetary interests of the physician and the crisis orientation of the patient who has been motivated to seek and pay for care more when his life or comfort has been threatened than when he has been reasonably well.

Also, it was aware that the current health system is complex and variegated and that effective intervention will require heroic and sophisticated measures to match the size and complexity of the problems. One hardly needs proof of this. The spate of legislative and scientific changes introduced into the system in the last decade has not been incorporated easily or consistently. In fact, there has been widespread public cynicism about oversold promises.

Three major themes emerged from the work of the Task Force.

First, it was felt that health must remain high on the scale of social, political, and economic priorities. Many misgivings were expressed about the growing tendency to become preoccupied excessively with cost at the expense of community goals. Whereas Medicaid legislation promised access to health care for the poor and near poor, the promise had, in fact, "vanished into the obscurity of State determinations of eligibility and the limitations of State resources and priorities." How completely this has happened is seen in the fact that in 1971, it is estimated that Medicaid will cover only 13 million of the 30 to 40 million poor and near poor, and currently only one of three children in the poor or near poor families is under Maternal and Child Health or Medicaid programs. Despite the concern expressed about costs, it was felt strongly that such gaps could not be tolerated, even if the expenditure of new funds added initially to an already severe problem of inflation in the health field. Task Force recommendations on short-run and long-run financing programs followed, keyed to the need for a new national policy permitting variety and adaptability, "not precluding the fitting together of various approaches into a consistent whole"—in effect, unified but not unitary.

Second, the Task Force concluded that new money alone would "not guarantee either capacity of effectiveness of the health system." "In fact, if a benevolent government were to begin to pay for all the basic health care needed by all those who cannot pay for it themselves, but no other change were introduced into the existing system, the result would be a disastrous rise in the cost of services that are already scarce," with, potentially, the higher income groups benefiting in some areas at the expense of low income groups.

"For two decades, programs financing medical care, whether public or private, have been reinforcing traditional ways of providing service." In recent years, only about 35 per cent of new money invested in the system resulted in new service. The rest was absorbed by inflation and, to a lesser extent, added population.

The Task Force had no prescription for a brand new health care delivery system. It felt that the concept "that any single formulation of resources could solve all the Nation's health care problems was as witless as the notion that a single remedy could cure all kinds of ailments."

In terms of specific recommendations, no simplistic solutions were seen, but the Department of Health, Education, and Welfare was urged to use dollars more effectively to improve delivery of services. For example, under Medicaid, the secretary would use up to 5 per cent of expenditures as front-end money to promote changes in the delivery system. A reorganization of HEW was called for to make it less politically reactive and more administratively assertive, and underscored was a need for a broader concept of health care, without which the public would pay a larger price with a proportionately diminishing yield; in effect, a plea was made to view health in context of the total life style.

Third, the report stated that health care is too often delivered at a time and place and in the way convenient to the provider rather than the consumer. "The day is past when doctors and hospital administrators and trustees and their associates may rely only on their own judgments on how they best distribute all the skills and resources at their disposal to what they see as the greatest advantage for the people they think they should be serving." The report states the consumer must play a stronger role and, incidentally, be provided with a greater range of choices among alternative forms of delivery together with the information to make the purchase decision a meaningful one.

Importantly, these and similar matters are not now the concern of the public health field alone. They concern, among others, government and the parties involved in collective bargaining, as labor and management seek to improve fringe benefits or to slow the deterioration of their worth. Those of us in prepayment must respond to such concern in all facets of our operations.

Some of the debate over change ahead inevitably will pivot around favorite ideas or personal ideologies. Some of it will be deeply rooted in politics. However, public health has the potential to confront many issues on their merits, and this influence must be forcibly felt; it is important to the dignity of human life.

But, the road from communicable disease control and environmental sanitation to the realm of public policy has been difficult. Some new or renewed commitments will help validate public health's stake in the action.

MYTHS

Challenging myths is risky. Folklore is part of every tradition, and, undoubtedly, it serves useful purposes. It serves, in fact, to make various stresses bearable (while it is impossible to get a cab in midtown New York between 3:00 and 6:00 p.m., it is important to think they are available). Possibly, images or myths are perpetuated to moderate change according to conventional social attitudes in a way we do not fully understand.

Regardless, we must try to differentiate between the folklore that ultimately enhances public satisfactions and that which adds primarily to the material well-being and status of those serving the public or is inimical to its interest.

Let me cite a few myths which impede progress.

A. *Most health services make a big difference in the health of the population—thus, with enough money, health can be purchased.*

In part, this public expectation is encouraged by the mass media. It also is encouraged by the professionals who make exaggerated claims, consciously or unconsciously promote undue optimism, or fail to disclaim overstatements.

This is a complex subject, but we know that in countries where infectious diseases are no longer among the predominant causes of death it is often difficult to demonstrate a strong relationship between longevity and the amount spent on health services. The amount spent on health resources can vary as much as 100 per cent and morbidity and mortality rates will vary on the order of 5 per cent.

This is not to deny that morbidity and mortality can be improved in the United States. They can, by attacking along a broad front reaching beyond health services, per se; but, certainly, personal health services do not have an impact near the level of public expectation.

Too many in preventive medicine have sat on the sidelines and watched the game too long, seemingly complacent that some day preventive medicine would provide the answers when the right opening presented itself. Without the test, who was to say yes or no?

As recently as 1968, a foundation started in New York introduced its Statement of Purpose with the following: "The ultimate answer to the problem of disease is prevention. In simple truth, a majority of the chronic illnesses and accidents which kill and afflict Americans can be considered preventable."

With broadening of benefits and new delivery systems being tested, preventive medicine will have more and more opportunities to test its worth. It will, if nothing else, because economic payoff is often cited as a major reason to act. The opportunities may prove to be a bit sobering.

Does early detection of diabetes or breast cancer alter the course of events that much? Do annual screenings improve the health of the population? Does early presymptomatic treatment of such conditions as hypertension,* defects of vision and hearing, and mild anemia improve the prognosis? I am not in a position to know the answers, but I know enough to say that the questions are valid, and should be answered.

There seems to be a conviction that existing health problems for the general population reflect essentially a lack of application of present knowledge rather than a lack of knowledge. One out of one person dies even if he receives all-American, multispecialty, group, prepaid, comprehensive health care. The surprising thing is the growing similarity (despite marked differences currently seen in several areas) of average length of life and causes of death in the best and least well-cared for populations in our country.

We may be nearer to having achieved the maximum response from disease care than we wish to admit—witness heart, cancer, and stroke programs. We are making regional cooperative arrangements, and we are applying new knowledge, but we do not seem to be influencing morbidity or mortality dramatically the way we did with immunization, nutrition, sanitation, and similar public health programs or with application of antibiotics to infectious disease. Perhaps, the over-all gap between what we know and its application is not that great.

Of course, the importance of any gap should not be minimized. Among the poor where it is often unconscionably great, it must

*In regard to hypertension, some evidence is beginning to lend credibility to presymptomatic treatment: Part II, Results in Patients with Diastolic Blood Pressure Averaging 90 Through 114 mm Hg, Veterans Administration Cooperative Study Group on Antihypertensive Agents, Effects of Treatment on Morbidity in Hypertension. J.A.M.A. 213:1143-1152 (Aug. 17), 1970.

be attacked on all possible fronts, and preventive and curative measures must be energetically pursued for all population groups, if suffering or pain can be lessened or life expectancy improved. But, at the same time, we should be realistic about our expectations and set our priorities accordingly.

B. *A major determinant of use is accessibility.*

Access is important, but the point is not that simple. The reverse is not true, i.e., creating access does not necessarily elicit use.

Poor people feel less healthy than the rest of America, and they place a higher priority on trying to achieve a healthy status than most others. Good health to the poor is viewed as a life-line to all else, and they have a growing appreciation of what constitutes good versus bad care.* But, among the poor, motivations differ; for example, Spanish-speaking people as opposed to other poor, and, importantly, motivations and how care is sought or services are used varies by economic classification. Transpose the poor and middle classes and access characteristics will soon shift in response. Who in the health establishment concerns himself with making access effective as well as available?

C. *The greater the technology, the better the health care.*

Today's specialist-oriented medicine holds that the medical care with the most extensive technical resources is the best, that first-level medical care is given best by specialists in a health center or hospital ambulatory care center.

The truth is that the great majority of ailments for which persons seek medical care can be competently diagnosed (separated from serious problems) and not only faithfully and adequately managed, but managed better in a simple than in a complex setting. Major needs in primary care are for understanding causes of a particular patient's problem and motivating and educating the patient to relieve these. Continuity and personalization of patient-health professional association is necessary for the understanding, support, and trust that are basic to primary care.

How many expensive, elaborate, impersonal facilities for ambulatory care are we going to build in the name of good health care? Probably as many as the giant high schools and colleges that we build in the name of good education.

D. *The proper center of health is the health department—the most democratic and accountable instrument close to the operational problems.*

Well and good, except the center will be a hospital, medical center, public health department, or something else—based on which pro-

*Sources, Blue Cross Association, Chicago, Ill., 1968.

duces—with as little preaching as possible. And, it is a wise man who thinks in pragmatic terms (e.g., J. Geiger, M.D., in Mount Bayou, Mississippi).

E. *An increase in the number of physicians will lower unit prices and improve distribution of key health services through the interacting forces of supply and demand.*

In the present health system the concept of a free market is so weakened by an inherent lack of competitive forces, by the ambivalence of need versus demand and the consumer's lack of real choice, that changing the number of doctors up or down 25 per cent (assuming it could be done immediately, instead of, more realistically, over ten years) would have little, if any, effect on unit price or distribution. The present "system" must be restructured before manpower productivity and access can be improved.

Structure per se is surrounded by myths. Contrary to popular notion, large structures, with all their weight, are inherently conservative rather than innovative, especially in a political environment where health rarely achieves high priority. Our evidence to date, in most fields, is that official structure, as deeply ingrained with the spirit of social justice as it may be, must be stimulated to be effective by adversary relations and private as well as community transactions. The utopia of a cohesive government or private system producing imaginative results needs to be examined.

F. *In the millenium, all care must be coordinated by the system.*

Attempts to educate the population to a limited degree on how to use health services have been humbling—the consumer can be remarkably unconcerned or cavalier about his health. And, of course, motivating anybody to do anything is difficult.

But, the opposite extreme, now being held out as the way to go will not work either. We cannot produce a foolproof maze, even in poor areas, where we can start from scratch. Despite all the design genius in the world, the consumer must meet the system halfway.

Thus, while we make the way easier, we must identify key people whom others will follow and train them how to utilize the system properly. To overlook this is to ask for a lowering return on an expanding investment.

G. *Areawide planning is a forceful and effective way to distribute programs and resources.*

Areawide planning has had little demonstrable effect in the United States since it began. In a sense, the situation, after considerable legislation and infusion of funds, has never been worse. We have the illusion of planning, which can be used as a rationalization with little payoff.

The problems are complex. Multiple authorities (Community Health Programs, Regional Medical Programs, Hill-Burton, and the like) do not help. Also, there is lack of consensus on objectives, format, and discipline. Is planning essentially facilitative or authoritarian? Does it derive its strength from sharing facts, getting individual institutions to project needs and focus on results, or from an intellectual force imposed on the field from above?

With one exception, past presidents of the Association of Areawide Health Planning Agencies are no longer in the planning field. Some agencies have been captured by the health professionals, others by the institutions they embrace. In the face of facts, exceptions are made blatantly, "for the good of the community."

H. *Whereas our current delivery system leaves much to be desired, the production data from it are useful for projecting needs.*

Doctors are not utilized well, all of us admit, but shortages are estimated on extrapolations of doctor/patient ratios.

Congress wrings its hands over the shortage of nurses, while the ratio of nurses to population is one-fourth in Arkansas of what it is in Connecticut.

Hospital bed need in the future (new and renovative) is confidently set forth while bed use varies on a scale of 2:1 across the country and even within regions. The myth is that there is something right about large numbers and averages. We have not yet figured out how to build temples to the norm while drastically changing the religion.

I. *Under large financing programs, there will be no interference in the doctor-patient relationships or the practice of medicine.*

Such a statement was put in Medicare and Medicaid legislation up front, but nobody meant it and the rule cannot be observed. Incentive reimbursement, utilization review, and licensure all obviously affect the way medicine is practiced. The key question is how, not whether, intervention takes place. Everyone should know this, or a lot of time and money will be spent allowing unproductive practices or stipulations to continue untouched, such as the outlawing of prepaid group practice as an eligible alternative in the public or private market.

What medicine fears is that the interference will be extensive, and it can be. In Canada, when the Province of British Columbia took over the financing of medical and hospital benefits and costs continued to climb, the province passed a law empowering the government to appoint hospital administrators and the majority of hospital trustees and to govern expenditures tightly through budgets.

It is a wise professional who helps to design the intervention and allied determination of priorities, not always to fight them. An it is important that he battle well. The crisis medicine and technical sophistication we have seen to date are not the best determinants of health services, but neither is low cost.

J. *Put enough money behind experiments and evaluation and new productive delivery methods will emerge.*

Everything is right about this except the record. For example, extensive money has been available under Medicare to help develop new incentive reimbursement methods. Everyone in the public and private sectors agreed that the need for improved methods was of near top priority. In the first year the money was available, only five decent proposals were made, a fewer number were funded. After two years, there have been few, if any, usable results.

Change in delivery of care takes leadership, imagination, and an understanding of how community forces operate, and it takes a sense of risk on the part of the grantor.

Most innovations arise in the field in response to operating problems, and these take time; for example, Permanente, and many skillful adjustments along the way. Is there reason to believe that an HEW grant will shorten the process?

The dramatic stroke is a rarity and most of our "experts" are on the move and not available for the long pull.

K. *People in the health field are not human, i.e., they will act the way they ought to.*

They do not and, as a result, our health system *is* tangential to many health problems. The reasons include the fact that they seem to become goal-directed and program-directed within special interests and special authorities instead of being problem-oriented. Also, within their interests, they tend to become preoccupied with status, trappings, and ceremonies, instead of results. When the threats of other special interests become severe enough, they protect themselves by licensure in the name of quality or by greater specialization in the name of science.

Perhaps such disorientation is inherent in human service with all of its uncertainties and stresses. It goes deep. For example, one sees a persistent resistance to organizing medical records around problems as opposed to function. It is resisted as lacking a flair and art, a classic confusion between freedom and discipline. Or, we see resistance to prepaid group practice on ethical grounds when the problem is essentially economic.

Admittedly, the establishment of priorities is, inherently, less than rational. In the absence of fact, some subjectivity is surely involved.

Also, how does one balance short and long run? Even with facts, it is hard enough. Would a comprehensive renal dialysis and kidney transplant program be worth $2.5 billion over the next 10 to 15 years?

In talking about bridging the gap, too few appreciate the cost. It is possible for a society to overcommit its resources for traditional services at the expense of environmental factors that determine health or well-being.

L. *Our current health system is badly fragmented, a bag of concessions, an institutional salad. It is, in fact, no system at all.*

Comment (as one way has put it): If you do not think there is a system, just try to change it.

The United States has a health system, and it is viable; however, it is not logical. Many public health people have been trained to improve it through a series of steps that, in the light of events, are cogent but not always wise. Perhaps a game plan tying the lower echelons to the upper and the various parts together, primarily under official auspices, should be reexamined in terms of feasibility, as alluded to before. Possibly, the trade-off mechanisms for centralization versus decentralization, uniformity versus diversity, and so forth, respond better (not exclusively) to gritty inputs like money and the exercise of options. At least, we should think about it.

Whether people in the system determine the shape of the system or reflect it, we detect unmistakable signs for institutional rigidity and old age. Similar problems are evident in education and welfare where youth is similarly frustrated.

In the last analysis, the consumers will have to break the bonds, assisted by some idoloclasts from within. We cannot live with a situation where it is possible to expand or contract so many health care efforts with so little effect on health.

The above and other legends must be dissected. The voices of public health will be needed. It is difficult enough to design and implement effective health and welfare programs; the last thing we need is the false reference points. In our continual efforts to humanize health, we should guard against backing into anti-intellectualism.

PUBLIC HEALTH AND COMMUNITY MEDICINE

A second major role for public health to play is in testing both pet theories and legends against experience to a greater extent than in the past.

I do not mean that this should be done only in a burst of humanitarian energy, such as establishing primary care and other clinical services where they are absent. Leave patient care per se to the clinicians. Clinical medicine equals clinical medicine wherever you find it, the setting does not change it.

What I do mean is a testing of the theories you have nurtured so long; theories that have become neater and neater, more polished over the years, without the test of an end point. You have valuable skills in epidemiology, statistics, and evolution of group phenomena. What you need are institutional patients where input and output can be related, where you can examine the maneuvers that make people well or keep them well. This is where you can help destroy the idols.

In some programs, you have been at the drawing board too long. What institutional arrangements get at improvements in emphysema beyond the realization that it is linked to smoking, or, how do you build on the wisdom of therapies to get less hypertension?

As the country moves toward serious debate on national health insurance and other major issues, we need the community insights you can help provide.

Some of the young men are *off* the bench participating in drug addiction programs and similar efforts, learning how to shield against biting criticism, how to take or understand the other side of an argument, how to mobilize social, political, and economic resources to reach a goal *and,* where having succeeded, how to rationalize being part of the establishment when confronted.

Needless to say, the going will not be easy. Public health will need to arm itself with new skills, such as hard-hitting administrative techniques, and with people who can get things done—once pointed in the right direction.

Results should be published and defended. At the moment, Congress and HEW have too few reliable sources to which to turn, and none of us relishes the prospect of having legislation formulated by technicians inexperienced in the strategems of health.

Yet another reason to move more energetically into the field is to guard against the undervaluing of health—an ever-present danger although perhaps hard to realize or appreciate in today's high expenditure market. Only Congress and other legislative or governing bodies can decide ultimately what trade-offs should be effected with alternate goods and services, but the price in well-being or satisfaction should be clear.

A Broader Definition of Health

Of all health groups, APHA members know better than to act as if health is determined by health care as now defined and practiced. But this is exactly what too many have done. With your present overpreoccupation on delivery of health care, you have essentially advocated making more of the same available to everybody but at a lower unit cost. This could be called playing the other fellow's game.

The public health game has taken the ecological view of health. The World Health Organization's definition of health is a "state of complete physical, mental and social well-being and not merely the absence of disease." While it has not been easy to use, it remains the best definition of health that I know.

We live in a nation where most of the traditional indexes of health (morbidity and mortality rates) are improving, while all around us are the signs of serious illness. The human species is in the midst of an epidemic—a pandemic—of dissatisfaction and maladaptation. The anger, frustration, fear and ennui, and the escape mechanisms they generate, are as function-impairing and discomfort-producing as any physical illness. And homicide, suicide, accidents, alcoholism, narcotics addiction, and war have moved to the front as causes of death in the productive years of our lives. I do not think that, from our ecological perspective, we really believe that even such critical mechanisms as prepaid group practice, national health insurance in any form, and training of physician's assistants will bring our nation back to health. I do not think we believe that national health (in the full WHO sense) will be restored through air pollution and pesticide control.

If we know better than our actions suggest we do, why have we had difficulty putting knowledge into action? First of all, we actually have done some things. We have had some successes. Comprehensive health planning and regional medical programs are, at least, noble efforts designed to pull disease care services together and to point them toward better health. They are steps in the right direction even though they may not yet have succeeded. One of our most exciting past successes was the Tennessee Valley Authority where a whole region was turned around through a coordinated attack on agricultural, industrial, educational, health, and environmental problems. Here we hit the target reasonably well. There are deep lessons in the TVA concept for our sick core cities.

One of the problems in putting our knowledge into action has been the constriction which our professional biases and institutional forms have placed on the generation of responses to new knowledge. As professionals within bureaus and departments with fixed program responsibilities and categorically allocated resources, we limit the number of alternatives we generate and consider as appropriate responses to problems. If you do not believe so, ask yourself how you would spend the nation's $70 billion annual health budget to improve its health. I suspect the way you would spend it is influenced heavily by your professional and institutional identities and that the differences would be great between yourselves and even greater between you and industrialists, economists, politicians, engineers, and others.

These differences need to be narrowed if an effective assault on health problems is to be undertaken—narrowed and focused through a more vital concept of public health. Moving more people in and out of hospital beds and ambulatory programs and starting primary care units in the slums or establishing utilization review mechanisms are not the ways to improve the welfare of despairing, unproductive people living in a sick society. They can be important parts of the logistics, but they cannot be the major strategy.

OTHER CONSIDERATIONS

How will we move to this higher level? How will we put it all together (our knowledge of determinants of health) as effective action? Let me identify a few over-all considerations.

One indispensable element is the consumer. The rise of consumer power in the sixties has revealed its great force as a determiner of national programs. Housewives, grape pickers, nature lovers, and war protestors—among others—have challenged sacred powers and behaviors. Consumers and users of service must be represented on key health policy boards in and out of government. Their special concern with satisfaction and effectiveness must have its day against the entrenched concern of professionals. And, as I mentioned previously, health consumers also must have a choice so that innovation is a function of both science and the process of selection.

Public health leadership must help to train consumers for their role, for they are not all accustomed to institutional essentials. The changing values of the current generation give hope that we will be willing to make some short-term sacrifices for long-term accomplishments.

Another force is money. For years, we have leaned heavily on law, regulation, and professional standards to shape change. Money was used essentially as the wherewithal that made the design work. Medicare, Medicaid, Hill-Burton, and other programs have been criticized for supporting, but only supporting, the present system of disease services. Gradually, we are accepting the fact that money can be used to change systems. We have a society which is able to channel its energies to accomplish socially accepted goals—war, space exploration, highway construction—and goals which reflect values of citizens, such as recreation. The driving force of these is economic reward for the participants. Can we (a) identify national priorities for health, (b) have them validated and endorsed by the people, and (c) accomplish them within the framework of our present society?

Yes, money has demonstrated awesome power in determining the priorities of medical school deans and in making it easier, unfortunately, to get sick care than well care. Administrative and professional people have shown a strong tendency to jump where the carrot is—despite the potential evil or promiscuity involved. On the other hand, money can be used to accomplish worthy ends. For example, it might be wise to condition grants in the biomedical area on a parallel effort along the broader front of ecology. One is tempted to suggest a considerable tightening of money except for demonstration projects exploring new paths. The challenge to the politicians will be not to use the interests of small groups to determine their priorities.

Neither consumer involvement nor money will work without goals or objectives. Once they are made clear, and there is consensus among the electorate as to what are problems and acceptable solutions, they can be translated, through the political process, into national commitment and accomplishment. There is dispute about whether the role of government extends effectively to operations on a broad scale, but there should be no doubt about government's responsibility to point the way in such a vital human service as health.

CONCLUSION

My purpose has not been to downgrade valuable clinical service or to mock popular notions about public health. However, in the light of demoralizing problems of society which should be, but too frequently are not, encompassed by health services, there is an imperative need to redress our priorities and to become more realistic about the relation of input to output. Our current health system is not endlessly inefficient or malintentioned; it simply is not geared sufficiently to positive health, and the inadequacy is becoming too expensive to bear in emotional *and* economic terms.

ACKNOWLEDGMENT—Just as every individual needs a clinician, every health administrator needs a community physician. Mine is Kenneth Rogers, M.D., professor and chairman, Department of Preventive and Social Medicine, University of Pittsburgh School of Medicine, whose assaults on the health establishment for which I labor are reflected in this paper. I am indebted to his help and his candor.

Section B

Assessing the Outcomes
of Administration and Planning Strategies:
Through Evaluative Research

Although this section deals primarily with the problems of evaluative research in mental health organizations and programs, many of the principles and strategies involved are adaptable to a variety of human service organizations.

In the following articles two focal concerns emerge as having considerable significance for methods of evaluative research and program development: 1) the development of research strategies and technology; and 2) the uses of research data in program development and evaluation.

We are concerned that a lack of sufficient attention to these factors has often resulted in: 1) rigorous research which cannot be translated into action; 2) action programs which are based on unreliable or biased research data; 3) inappropriate, and relatively indiscriminate, adoption and application of apparently successful programs (e.g., the indiscriminate development of "storefront" operations).

The skillful development and use of evaluative research will not ensure the development of effective programs. But, it will act as a stimulus to the emergence of programs and organizational structures which are relatively consonant with community needs.

429

32. The Uses and Misuses of Data in Assessing Mental Health Needs

Herbert C. Schulberg, Ph.D., M.S.
Henry Wechsler, Ph.D.

Social planners and researchers are increasingly joining their efforts in order to facilitate programming which meets community needs. While the next article focuses specifically on mental health needs, the problems which are alluded to are rapidly becoming characteristic of most areas of comprehensive health and educational programming. Central to these problems is the development of indices which validly reflect a community's human service needs.

At the same time there must be a conceptualizing of community social, political, and economic parameters or constraints around the development of programs designed to meet these needs.

In this article Schulberg and Wechsler emphasize broadening the definitions and criteria of community needs. We would add that as this occurs, planners and researchers in multiple, relatively independent areas of human service programming will begin to realize their own community of interests, and begin to generate what will become truly community based and oriented programs.

The growth of new community mental health programs has become the subject of considerable nationwide attention in recent years. Although much of the impetus has stemmed from the 1963 Community Mental Health Centers Act and the 1964 Federal Regulations (HEW 1964), this growth is the result of long-standing efforts to develop coherent, systematic services for the mentally ill.

Amidst the public enthusiasm for federal financial support in constructing new mental health centers, relatively little attention has been directed to the federally imposed need-assessment and priority-setting procedures that must precede this local construction. The Federal Regulations call upon each state seeking federal construction funds to spell out the specific steps through which it has assessed a community's mental health needs.

430

The following procedures must be undertaken in such an assessment:

A. Division of the state into geographical areas with a population base of not less than 75,000 and not more than 200,000.

B. Ranking of these areas according to their relative need for mental health services. The Federal Regulations indicate that need shall be determined on the basis of the extent of mental illness and emotional disorder, considering both the proportion of the population involved and the total number of people affected, taking into account such related indices as:

1. The existence of low per capita income, chronic unemployment, and substandard housing.
2. The extent of problems related to mental health, such as alcoholism and drug abuse, crime and delinquency.
3. The special needs of certain groups within the area, especially the physically and mentally handicapped, the aged, and children.

The validity of this relatively rational approach to mental health program planning and its utility are issues requiring careful analysis. Planners are confronted with demands of the biostatisticians and epidemiologists that objective, quantifiable data be given crucial consideration if stated program goals are effectively to be achieved. The ways in which statistical findings can be valuably utilized for planning are highlighted in recent papers by Kramer (1965) and Andrew (1965). In considering the variable of marital status, as an example, many studies repeatedly have emphasized the high risk associated with the never married, separated, widowed, and divorced groups in their utilization of psychiatric facilities. Nevertheless, Kramer laments that the implications of these findings have not yet been adequately considered in developing programs of community care.

Any experienced program planner, however, is aware of the many practical and political considerations constantly forcing him to disregard temporarily, or even abandon, an optimal rational approach and to resort instead to more expedient and feasible alternatives. As an example, although the greatest professional priority may be for a program serving the alcoholic, a legislature's interest in geriatric services can force the redefinition of immediate and possibly even overall program objectives. After considering the limits of rationality in planning a mental health program, Demone (1965) concluded that "In focusing so heavily on nonrational factors involved in planning . . . there is no intention to decry reason, or to be negative or nihilistic, but rather to be frank and objective. . . . Reality testing is being encouraged as is the suggestion that we can better cope with nonrational factors if we acknowledge their existence."

The purpose of this paper is to examine some of the implications of the 1964 Federal Regulations, both in terms of the assumptions made about mental illness and its treatment as well as about the planning process itself. The first step is to examine the assumptions underlying the specific Regulations; the second is to examine alternative means available to planners for complying with them. The discussion presented in this paper is based upon experiences gained through participation in the Massachusetts Mental Health Planning Project, one of 53 such projects conducted in the United States between 1963 and 1965. Although unique issues arose in Massachusetts, its planners were still confronted by many of the same conceptual and methodological problems in the use of data as faced planners throughout the country so that these comments are thought to have widespread applicability.

SIZE OF CATCHMENT AREA

A fundamental guideline in the Federal Regulations is the creation of programs designed to serve geographic catchment areas with populations between 75,000 and 200,000 people. A question immediately arises as to the rationale for this population range. Has it been arrived at on the basis of national hospitalization rates for psychiatric disorders, thus assuring sufficiently small inpatient populations for effective treatment? Is the range based on some conception of administrative efficiency in the management of the psychiatric needs of a population? Or is the range perhaps based upon a sociological-political conception of the optimal size of a community with which a mental health program can work most effectively? In the absence of any clearly formulated health program can work most effectively? In the absence of any clearly formulated rationale from NIMH, planners must carefully consider whether the 75,000 to 200,000 population base should be indiscriminately applied to both high population density and low population density areas. It would appear that, given catchment areas of this range, differences in population density will produce qualitative variations among community mental health centers with respect to both programs and populations serviced.

In the case of Massachusetts, the state was divided by planners after much consideration into 37 catchment areas, most having total populations within the federally prescribed range. To accommodate variations between rural and urban parts of the state, the density of population served by a single program ranges from only 78 people per square mile in rural areas to almost 20,000 in cities.

A major paradox in the development of community mental health programs now has been created by recent NIMH insistence that planned catchment areas not exceed a population of 200,000 even though the Surgeon General is empowered to modify this requirement in special circumstances. It has forced an arbitrary exclusion or division of towns and neighborhoods that traditionally have worked together to form the community base upon which comprehensive programs could be established. Arbitrary adherence to a given population range for administrative rather than conceptual reasons can be particularly frustrating when the goal is community-focused programs.

PSYCHIATRIC INDICES OF NEED

Need is to be assessed, according to the Federal Regulations, on the basis of prevalence of mental illness and emotional disorders, both in terms of rate and absolute number of persons affected. Epidemiologists in the field of mental illness, however, have repeatedly encountered difficulty in measuring the extent of actual disorder in a population because of the lack of clear-cut definitions of mental illness and because of the broad range of available methods for obtaining a "true count" (Scott, 1958). Is need to be measured on the basis of only the number of currently hospitalized patients? Should it include patients treated in outpatient or private facilities? Or should it even include persons not seeking treatment but who are, in the opinion of a professional, considered to be mentally ill or emotionally disturbed? The prevalence of mental disorder inferred only from hospitalization rates is lower than rates based on all treated cases. Both give lower prevalence rates than the surveys conducted on random samples of the general population (Dohrenwend & Dohrenwend, 1965).

These differences relate not only to the overall prevalence rate for a given geographic area but also pertain in terms of diagnostic composition and type of impaired functioning. In addition, under different methods of estimating mental illness, the social class and other background characteristics of the mentally ill population will differ. Judging by results of the "Midtown" study (Srole et al., 1962), if hospitalization rates are used to estimate prevalence, low socioeconomic areas of a state would be viewed as having the highest need. If, on the other hand, private treatment in the community is included, the relationship to socioeconomic status would be diminished. Finally, if some absolute standard is applied to a sample of the general population, the relationship to social class should change further, depending, of course, upon how related the selected standard is to social class values.

Approached from another perspective, planning for community mental health centers on the basis of admission rates to current mental hospitals or to other existing programs may perpetuate current patterns. Thus, an area having low rates of hospitalization or other treatment would be viewed as having low need. Quite the opposite may be true. The area may have low utilization rates because it has few facilities or because currently existing facilities are not designed to meet the needs of the population. The converse of this issue is just as complex. Planning strictly on the basis of the population's present high illness rates may disregard the question of the general population's willingness to utilize newly designed mental health facilities. It is one thing to diagnose a person as mentally ill and quite another to have him seek treatment.

A further difficulty in the use of first-admission rates for assessing mental health needs is the fact that recent experimentation with alternatives to hospitalization has shown that such rates may be readily altered. Zwerling & Wilder (1964) have demonstrated that the number of inpatient admissions may be reduced by as much as 50 per cent if a day hospital is available. Given this rapidly changing pattern of utilization of inpatient and outpatient resources, the interpretation of hospital admission rates becomes increasingly complex and even possibly misleading. It highlights sharply the value of a psychiatric case register in providing planners with an overview of the entire psychiatric scene (Miles & Gardner, 1966) rather than the restricted perspective of hospitalization rates.

Having made this strong theoretical case against the use of hospitalization rates for assessing need, one must then consider the practical methodoligical problems involved in collecting data on a variety of needed indices. The planner immediately finds that the necessary information is lacking. Given a time-limited deadline for assessing need, he must still resort to such restricted but accessible material as hospitalization rates. In Massachusetts, planners utilized the findings of a three-year analysis of first admissions from every city and town to state, private, and VA hospitals.

Statistical data regarding the mental health needs of children in every city and town of a state are even more difficult to assemble than the sparse information available for adults. The often cited contention that 10 per cent of children require professional treatment is often used for planning, but the deviation of this estimate is open to question. Professional services to children are provided under a wide variety of auspices, both psychiatrically and non-psychiatrically sponsored. Many problems remain untreated as the result of either lengthy waiting lists or because of parents' failure to turn to a mental health facility in the first place. The service statistics of existing children's facilities are of limited value for statewide planning, since these resources generally are located only in urban areas and considerable selectivity is exercised with regard to admissions. In the absence of studies specifically directed at this problem, which most planning projects could not undertake in their timelimited existence, it has been impossible to determine the true prevalence of childhood emotional disorders, and the blanket estimate of 10 percent was applied to all parts of a state. Future studies of the Joint Commission on Mental Health of Children should have a particularly illuminating value in this respect.

INDICES RELATED TO NEED
FOR MENTAL HEALTH SERVICES

Three specific indices have been spelled out in the Federal Regulations as being related to need for mental health services: poverty, social pathology, and population subgroups with special needs.

Poverty

The customary indices of poverty, i.e., low per capita income, chronic unemployment, and substandard housing, may be viewed as related to mental health need in two different ways. It may be assumed either that poverty prevents one from seeking help for mental disorders because of the inability to pay for treatment or that poverty is a factor in the etiology of mental and emotional disorders. The first assumption views poverty as an impediment to the accessibility of public and private community mental health resources rather than as an index related to need. The second assumption involving poverty as a causal factor is consistent with recent studies that have reported higher rates of mental disorders among individuals from lower social classes.

It is generally agreed (Mishler & Scotch, 1963) that the prevalence of mental disorders is higher in this subgroup of the population.

However, the unanswered question remains whether incidence is similarly higher among this group. Do slum areas have higher numbers of mentally ill individuals because slums produce mental illness or because the mentally ill drift to such areas because of an inability to successfully compete in the economic sphere? For purposes of planning secondary and tertiary prevention facilities, this problem need not be resolved. However, when the mental health center undertakes primary prevention, this issue is a crucial one.

In assessing mental health needs in Massachusetts, the federal concern with poverty was interpreted in the broadest sense to mean general socioeconomic status. In terms of each of the traditional components (occupation, income, education, and housing) planning interest was focused primarily on the extremes of socioeconomic deprivation, e.g., low income, poor housing, unemployment, and low education. However, other indicators also were used to ascertain the general occupational and educational standing of the community. Thus, a total of seven socioeconomic indices were included:

1. Median income per family
2. Number of families having an income of less than $3,000
3. Unemployment in the civilian labor force
4. Median value of one-unit housing
5. Percentage of total housing units considered deteriorating or dilapidated
6. Median years of education completed by people over 25
7. Number of people over 25 with less than 5 years' education

Although analysis of seven varying socioeconomic indicators provides the planner with a broad perspective, questions comparable to those raised about the validity of mental illness indices are relevant here as well. Even when the indicators are used, the planner still must consider whether each index is of equal or differential significance in affecting a community's level of emotional disorder. Since this problem could not be answered in any definitive manner, each of the seven indices was given equal weight by the Planning Project's Advisory Council. A local area's rank order on every specific index then totaled to produce a measure of relative overall socioeconomic need.

In addition to general population indices of poverty, welfare statistics can be used to provide additional information about mental health need. The number of welfare recipients in a given area will affect the nature of a local community mental health program in various direct and indirect ways. In view of the inability of most welfare recipients to arrange for private treatment (Schulberg, 1966), publicly supported programs have accepted the responsibility of providing these individuals with necessary services. Since rates of local welfare assistance are significantly related to an area's socioeconomic level, extensive public mental health programs will be required in these areas. A variety of new services are being established to cope more effectively with the needs of this group (Peck, Kaplan, & Roman, 1965) and further departures from traditional programs may be expected. A mental health center located in an area of high welfare need will be expected to direct a major segment of its resources toward social pathology as well as toward traditionally defined psychiatric illness, since high welfare rates are significantly related to high rates of social pathology (see Table 1).

Data regarding five types of welfare categories generally can be obtained for every local area of a state. These include:

1. Number of recipients of old-age assistance
2. Number of recipients of medical aid to aged
3. Number of recipients of disability assistance
4. Number of recipients of aid to dependent children
5. Number of recipients of general relief

With the clear understanding that these data are not absolutely perfect and again subject to careful scrutiny, each of the five types was given equal weight in Massachusetts, and an area's rank on each measure was totaled to produce an indication of overall level of welfare need.

Social Pathology

Specifically mentioned in the Federal Regulations as indices of the extent of mental illness are alcoholism, drug addiction, crime, and delinquency. These problems of social pathology will assume increased importance as the programs of mental health centers become integral components in the local network of community health and welfare services. Rather than being permitted to delimit its focus to traditionally defined psychiatric illness, a mental health program will be called upon increasingly to provide services to a wider variety of caseloads than was true several decades ago.

The mental health center, thus, will become a major resource in the community's effort to reduce social pathology. Alcoholics already constitute approximately 25 per cent of all admissions to mental hospitals.

In considering the level of present social pathology as it contributes to the total need of an area, four types of data were available to planners for every community in Massachusetts:

1. Total number of arrests by local and state police
2. Number of commitments to Youth Service Board facilities
3. Number of arrests for drunkenness
4. Number of arrests for violation of 1963 Narcotics Law

Again, each of the four types of data is open to scrutiny and each was given equal weight by the Planning Project's Advisory Council. A local area's rank on each measure was totaled to produce an overall relative measure of social pathology.

Population Subgroups with Special Needs

Need can also be measured through the presence of certain subgroups in the general population. Specifically mentioned in the Federal Regulations are physically and mentally retarded individuals, the aged, and children. The rationale for establishing mental health priorities on the basis of the presence of mentally retarded in the population is clearer than presence of physically handicapped individuals. In the case of the mentally retarded, certain direct services will be obtained by them at the mental health center. In the case of the physically handicapped, however, it must be assumed that inclusion of this group in the regulations is based on the assumption that such individuals are at greater risk for the development of mental and emotional disorders than the general population. Similarly, the inclusion of the aged and children in this list appears to be based on the assumption of high risk.

The frequently cited figure of 3 per cent is generally used to estimate the prevalence of mental retardation among the total population, but more precise statistical data usually are unavailable on an area-by-area basis. Many states, however, do maintain information concerning the specific number of children enrolled in special classes for the retarded. In Massachusetts, each local school system with at least five retarded youngsters is required by law to establish special classes for these children. Enrollment figures from the State Department of Education give a fairly reliable estimate of the number of identified retarded children in metropolitan areas. However, many small school systems, particularly in poorer towns, are known to avoid the identification of five retarded youngsters within their jurisdiction so as to obviate the necessity of establishing costly special classes. Planners must realize, therefore, that school enrollment data alone as an index of an area's identified mentally retarded may be contaminated by the area's economic ability.

Accurate prevalence statistics on the number of physically handicapped are not generally available for all communities in a state. Statistics reporting the number of children in special classes for the physically handicapped could be obtained, though, in Massachusetts from the Division of Special Education in the State Department of Education, and these rates were used instead in estimating the size of this group.

OVERALL COMMUNITY NEED

The final matter to be considered regarding the use of data in assessing mental health needs is the degree to which the different types of indices used by planners relate to each other. Since the Federal Regulations required each state to engage in a vast data collection program for assembling information about numerous indices, how diverse or similar are they? How different a conclusion does the planner reach about an area's mental health needs through use of multiple indices in contrast to use of a single index like hospitalization rates?

It is possible to answer this question at least partially by reducing the 19 individual indices (a table of intercorrelations among each of the 19 indices is available from the authors) considered by planners in Massachusetts into four major categories: Socioeconomic Indicators, Mental and Physical Illness, Social Pathology, and Welfare Indices. By correlating a catchment area's rank order on one category with its rank on each of the other three categories (Table 1), it was found that illness rates are independent, while the other three categories are significantly interrelated. As might be expected, an area's number of welfare recipients is highly related to its socioeconomic condition. There is also a significant relationship between an area's socioeconomic condition and rate of social pathology. There is not, however, a significant relationship between an area's socioeconomic condition and its rate of mental and physical illness (as defined by our indices). Nor is there any significant relationship between the number of welfare recipients in a given area and that area's rate of mental and physical illness. Since social pathology problems are receiving increasing attention in mental health programs, it is vital to note that there is a significant relationship between social pathology and mental illness rates.

Although the four categories of data considered here are interrelated to varying degrees, there is still sufficient uniqueness in each of them to require that all be given consideration in assessing an area's needs for broad, multifaceted mental health programs. This approach is even more imperative if we assume that new centers ultimately will provide primary as well as secondary and tertiary prevention.

Thus, in spite of the various theoretical and methodological questions raised about the present Federal Regulations, it is thought that their ultimate significance will stem from the manner in which they have broadened the planners' definition of community need. Consideration in the future will be given to an expanded array of environmental factors which together with individual-oriented indices will help to define the need for service in freshly conceptualized mental health centers.

REFERENCES

Andrew, G. Uses of data in planning community psychiatric services. *Amer. J. pub. Hlth,* 1965, 55, 1925-1935.

Demone, H. W. The limits of rationality in planning. *Comm. ment. Hlth J.,* 1965, 1, 375-381.

Dohrenwend, B., & Dohrenwend, Barbara. The problem of validity in field studies of psychological disorder. *J. abnorm. Psychol.,* 1965, 70, 52-69.

Kramer, M. Some implications of trends in the usage of psychiatric facilities for community mental health programs and related research. Paper presented at Annual Meeting of American College of Neuropsychopharmacology, December 13–15, 1965, San Juan, Puerto Rico. (mimeo)

Miles, H. C., & Gardner, E. A. A psychiatric case register: the use of a psychiatric case register in planning community mental health services. *Arch. gen. Psychiat.,* 1966, 14, 571-580.

Mishler, E. G., & Scotch, N. A. Sociocultural factors in the epidemiology of schizophrenia: a review. *Psychiat.,* 1963, 26, 315-343.

Peck, H. B., Kaplan, S., & Roman, M. Prevention, treatment, and social action: a strategy of intervention in a disadvantaged urban area. Paper read at Annual Meeting of American Orthopsychiatric Association, New York, March 1965. (mimeo)

Schulberg, H. C. Private practice and community mental health. *Hosp. & comm. Psychiat.,* 1966, 17, 363-366.

Scott, W. A. Research definitions of mental health and mental illness. *Psychol. Bull.*, 1958, 55, 29-45.

Srole, L., Langner, T. S., Michael, S. T., Opler, M. K., & Rennie, T. A. C. Mental health in the metropolis: the Midtown Manhattan study. New York: McGraw-Hill, 1962.

U.S. Department of Health, Education, and Welfare. Regulations: Community Mental Health Centers Act 1963. *Federal Register,* May 6, 1964.

Zwerling, I., & Wilder, J. F. An evaluation of the applicability of the day-hospital in treatment of acutely disturbed patients. *Israel Ann. Psychiat.,* 1964, 2, 162-185.

33. The Living Human Service Organization: Application of General Systems Theory and Research*

Frank Baker, Ph.D.

The notion of human service organizations as relatively unique forms of social organizations, differing significantly from production organizations, is further developed in the following article by Frank Baker. Moreover, Baker suggests that general system theory can provide a conceptually integrative and productive framework for reviewing these organizations. Baker also specifies some of the more relevant dimensions for the application of general system theory of human service organizations, and gives examples of this applicability.

The ideas developed in the article should be of value in providing a common ground on which researchers, theorists, and practitioners can engage in thought and action.

This paper will review applications of general systems theory and research to formal complex organizations, with particular emphasis on the human service type of organization. An allied goal will be to describe the usefulness, as well as some of the limitations, of this analogical approach which emphasizes the congruence of social organizations with other living systems.

Throughout the development of the social sciences the use of organic analogy in trying to understand complex social phenomena (Smelzer, 1967; Buckley, 1967) has been very appealing. However, many of the early theories of organization leaned more heavily on analogies drawn from physics than from biology. The work of the theoretical biologist, Ludwig von Bertalanffy (1950), focusing on the contrast of biological and physical phenomena, greatly

*Preparation of this paper was supported by NIMH Grant #18382-03. The author would like to acknowledge the helpful comments of Anthony Broskowski and the editorial assistance of Mrs. Joyce Olesen.

442

influenced the development among organizational theorists of a school of thought which holds that social systems .have important similarities to other living systems.

The major thrust of the view that living systems are essentially "open systems," as opposed to "closed systems," comes from an article in *Science* published by Bertalanffy in 1950. Bertalanffy had been a pioneer in the promotion of an organismic view in biology and first developed his "general system theory" in the thirties. However, he did not publish his general system ideas until the conclusion of World War II, later explaining that he waited until biology was more receptive to theory and model building (1968, p. 90). Bertalanffy is responsible for both introducing the term "general systems theory" and for initiating the intellectual movement for a unified science known by that name.

Over the past two decades general systems theory has taken what James G. Miller (1971) has called the "daring and controversial position that—though every living system is obviously unique—there are important formal identities of large generality across levels." Thus, one of the main thrusts of general systems theory as originally conceived by Bertalanffy and subsequently developed by scientists from many disciplines is the search for analogies and isomorphisms across the levels of living systems, including organism, group, and organization.

The widespread acceptance of general systems theory was initially hindered by the absence of experimentally derived data and the consequent forced dependence of its exponents on anecdotal illustrations. However, the usefulness of systems thinking as a way of looking at phenomena from biological systems to social systems has resulted in the adoption of general systems concepts and models in a wide variety of fields in recent years. Thus in a recent book, Klir (1972) was prompted to assert:

> After nearly two decades of development, general systems theory has sufficiently matured to be taken seriously. Once a new and radical movement in science, well motivated but ill defined, it has overcome many obstacles and has developed into a more moderate but by now a better defined and sophisticated area of human activities. Primarily, it offers scholars, educators, engineers, and artists newly harmonious ways of looking at tne world (p. v.).

WHAT IS A LIVING SYSTEM?

Basically, the difference between a living system and a nonliving system described by Bertalanffy and other general systems thinkers is in the nature of the relationship existing between the system and its environment. Living systems are open systems, i.e., they engage in an exchange with their environment in which they receive various inputs, transforming these inputs in some way and exporting outputs back to the environment. By taking in inputs of material, energy, and information which are of higher complexity of organization than the system's outputs, an open system offsets the process of entropy—a chaotic, random state in which there is no further potential for work or energy transformation (Miller, 1965). Unlike closed systems which tend to move *toward* entropy, open systems move *against* the tendency toward entropy and attempt to acquire a steady state of "negentropy," or negative entropy. Of course some entropic changes occur in living systems as they do everywhere else and living systems do experience deterioration, death, and decay. However, by operating in such a manner as to import resources of greater complexity than those which are exported as output to the environment, open systems are able to restore their own energy and repair breakdowns in their own organization and thus to offset, at least for a time, the processes of entropy.

A living system is made up of units or components of which at least some are composed of protoplasm and contain genetic material made up of deoxyribonucleic acid (Miller, 1971). The components of a living system are actively interrelated and operate together to produce some characteristic total effects (Hall & Fagen, 1956; Boguslaw, 1965). The set of interacting components composing this type of system function to take in the necessary inputs from the environment, and to transform or process them in such a way as to produce outputs.

The selection of kinds of inputs and outputs to and from the system, as well as their rate of flow, is determined by the system's boundary—the region separating one system's components from those of another system (Berrien, 1968). The concept of boundaries is helpful in attempting to understand the distinction between open and closed systems. An open system has boundaries which are at least partially permeable, permitting sizeable amounts of at least certain types of matter, energy, and information to pass to and from the environment. Closed systems have relatively impermeable boundaries which separate this type of system from its external environment.

These attributes of living systems characterize not only organic systems such as man and other animals, but may also be seen to apply in the description and study of social systems such as groups and organizations. Social systems whose components are also living systems may thus be viewed as systemic entities sharing with other levels of living systems the key system properties of being comprised of interdependent components, and of being greatly affected by a relatively large degree of openness to the external environment (Miller, 1971).

MODELS OF THE ORGANIZATION AS A LIVING SYSTEM

Influenced by the growth of general systems theory, the introduction of organic concepts emphasizing a language of process and growth rather than of mechanics into the field of organization theory and research has led to a major reorientation in thinking about human organizations. Rather than considering organizations as relatively self-contained structures acting independently of external forces, as had been the case with classical approaches, modern organization theorists and researchers tend to conceive of organizations as open systems sharing with biological organisms the key property of being acutely dependent on their external environments (Scott, 1961; Katz & Kahn, 1966; Baker, 1973).

Although there is as yet no single comprehensive theory conceptualizing organizations as open systems which is accepted by a majority of workers in the field, two limited theoretical approaches have stimulated extensive research on the relationship of organizations to their environments: (1) the socio-technical systems model, and (2) organization-environment contingency theory. Two additional conceptualizations which view the organization as characterized by systems openness are also significant: (3) the open systems model of organization of Katz and Kahn, and (4) James Miller's general systems behavior theory. This paper will review each of these open system approaches to the study of complex organizations, and in particular the extent of their application to human service organizations. First, however, it is necessary to clarify what is meant by the concept of the human service organization.

Human Service Organizations

It has become common usage to designate a community's variety of health, educational, and social welfare service enterprises as "human service organizations." Included in this category are public health, medical care, mental health, rehabilitation, social welfare, legal, correctional, and educational organizations. Grouping such a variety of organizations as hospitals, mental health centers, social service agencies, and schools in a single general category implies recognition of some common characteristics of this type of social structure which distinguishes it from other organizations, particularly business and industrial organizations. For example, in contrast with business concerns, whose prime beneficiaries are expected to be their owners, the prime beneficiaries of the human service organization are the clients it serves (Blau & Scott, 1962). Current broad usage of the term "human service organization" also reflects an appreciation of the generic quality integral to the helping actions of professional caregivers, the common problems in organizing effective human resources, and the growing effort by the government and associations of professionals and consumers to make these public organizations actively responsive to the needs of the populations they are intended to serve (Schulberg, Baker, & Roen, 1973).

Though the four models of organizations as living systems which will now be examined did not develop from the specific consideration of this type of organization, these models have important implications for human service organizations. Empirical examples of a model's application to this type of organization will be reviewed where available following discussion of each open system model and its development.

Socio-Technical Systems Model

Perhaps the most extensive body of theoretical and empirical work applying the systems perspective at the level of internal organizational processes is the socio-technical systems theory developed over the past two decades by behavioral scientists at the Tavistock Institute of Human Relations in London. Originally influenced by Bertalanffy's delineation of open systems, the concept of a socio-technical system was developed particularly by E. Trist, F. E. Emery, A. K. Rice, and E. Miller, from consideration of production systems and recognition that such systems require technological components (e.g., machinery, raw materials, and plant layout), as well as social components which structure the work relationship relating the human operators both to the technology and to each other (Emery & Trist, 1960). Whereas human relationists and behavioral scientists had focused on the psychosocial subsystem and management scientists had emphasized technical and economic subsystems, the socio-technical system model, focusing on a systemic approach to work organizations, emphasized consideration of both the technological and the social components of a productive organization since technology and social systems mutually influence one another.

The concept of a production system as a socio-technical system was first introduced by Trist and Bamforth (1951) in their study of British coal mines. Rice (1958) extended the model of a productive organization as a socio-technical system in a book based on his studies of calico mills in India. In this early publication, Rice first introduced the concept of "primary task" to discriminate between the varied goals of industrial enterprises, defining it as the task an organization had been created to perform. In a later book, Rice (1963) recognized the difficulty of treating the organization as if it had a *single* goal or task, citing the teaching hospital, the prison, and mental health services in particular as examples of institutions which carry out many tasks at the same time. He redefined primary task as the task an organization must perform to survive and observes that all enterprises perform many tasks simultaneously, noting that some organizations have not one primary task but many, each of which may be primary at a given time.

Essentially, Rice conceives of the enterprise as an open system defined by its dominant import-conversion-export processes. He describes the organization as differentiated into two major types of subsystems: (1) the operating systems which perform the primary task of the enterprise, and (2) the managing subsystem which is external to the operating systems and is required to control and service them. Rice subdivides operating subsystems into three types: (a) the import subsystem, which is concerned with the acquisition of raw materials; (b) the conversion subsystem, which is concerned with the transformation of imports into exports; and (c) the export subsystem, which is concerned with the disposal of the results of import and conversion. The second major type of subsystem according to Rice, the management subsystem, may be further differentiated according to service and control functions.

Eric Miller (1959) elaborates the Rice model of a socio-technical system and asserts that any production system may be defined along three dimensions—territory, technology, and time—which he views as intrinsic to the structure of the system task. He sees any large complex production system as divided into progressively smaller subsystems along these three dimensions and argues that task performance is impaired if the subsystems are differentiated along dimensions other than these.

In summarizing his system model of the organization, Rice (1969) observes that an organization containing more than one operating subsystem must also have a differentiated managing subsystem in order to control, coordinate, and service the activities of the different operating subsystems. This management subsystem will, in turn, have responsibilities for managing the total system, each operating system, and also those nonoperating subsystems which do not directly perform any part of the primary task of the total system but which provide controls over and services to the operating systems. Rice sees management as being responsible for regulating task system boundaries, sentient system boundaries, and the relations between task and sentient systems.

In his attempt to outline a theory of organizations applicable to both industrial and nonindustrial enterprises, Rice (1963) makes explicit use of organic analogy and describes his purpose as seeking "to establish a series of concepts and a theory of organization that treats enterprises as ... living systems [p. 179]." In a later book he co-authored with Eric Miller, the assertion is made that, "Any enterprise may be seen as an open system which has characteristics in common with the biological organism. . . . An open system exists, and can only exist by exchanging materials with its environment" (Miller & Rice, 1967, p. 3).

The socio-technical system model has been developed and applied for the most part in dealing with industrial and business organizations. The initial application of this model to human service organizations has been limited to a few studies dealing with hospitals. In 1957, the Tavistock group was approached by Banstead Hospital to conduct an appraisal of this mental hospital's structure and function. Two papers by Hutton (1962a, 1962b) report an application of the Tavistock socio-technical systems model to this human service organization as the hospital was in the process of transforming itself from an isolated custodial treatment institution to an active residential treatment unit with increased connections to its surrounding community and catchment area.

Conducting an analysis of the primary task of this organizational system, Hutton found it useful to apply the approach of treating the range of possible goals of an enterprise as a hierarchy in which one goal will gain primacy according to the balance of forces operating at a given time. The dominant goal was defined as the "primary task of the enterprise." The technology at the hospital was changing with the introduction of newer treatment methods and consequent shifts in the task hierarchy. In accord with this change, Hutton identified the primary task of the hospital as the "treatment of acutely disturbed patients received from the community and returned to the community as soon as practicable, using criteria of social capability, not 'cure'." A secondary task was identified as "the retention of chronic patients," and a tertiary task was to "provide a residential center for sick and senile old people."

At a fourth level on the task hierarchy, Hutton identified an additional task which, although less obvious and demanding than the three already mentioned, did not derive from them. This fourth task of the hospital was to train staff to occupy roles outside the hospital and emphasize the relationship between a hospital and its external environment. This fourth task raises the possibility of conflict between (1) the needs of the patients and the hospital in meeting them and (2) the needs of staff to meet the external criteria of training professionals advanced in their careers. Specifically, the hospital trained nurses to become qualified according to the general nursing council's requirements and also trained medical officers for their diploma in psychological medicine and their next career step.

Looking at the problem of defining the primary task in another way, it is possible to group the primary, secondary, and tertiary tasks all as subtasks of a single over-all primary task of "caring for patients." However, even if this is done, the hospital system remains a multiple task organization since the task of training remains as an important goal with regard to important environmental demands and constraints for this hospital. Hutton agrees that the structure of a socio-technical system and the allocation of responsibility within it should be derived from the primary task and should support it. He found, however, that the "hospital does not have unrestrained autonomy to determine its own structure and function, but is affiliated by environmental demands and constraints" (Hutton, 1962b, p. 311).

Another member of the Tavistock group, Sofer (1961), has shown that the organization required for one task may not fit easily with that required for other tasks of a hospital. Sofer focused on the conversion subsystems necessary for research purposes in a mental hospital and demonstrated that internal organization based on the assumption that the primary imports are "problems" and the exports "solutions" may not sufficiently take account of the patients who accompany the "problems."

Organization-Environment Contingency Model

Moving beyond the socio-technical system model focusing on organizations in the context of environmental influences, Emery

and Trist (1965) opened up the consideration of organizational
environments for their own sake in a paper entitled "The Causal
Texture of Organizational Environments." They used the concept
of "causal texture" to refer to those processes and interdependencies occurring within the environment itself. Describing and
classifying the range and type of system environments, Emery and
Trist proposed four ideal types which vary in the degree to which
environmental components are connected as a system.

Each of these four ideal types of environments differ in terms
of the degree of behavioral predictability available to the focal
organization regarding other organizations and groups in its
environment. Emery and Trist point out that each type of environment calls for a different organizational strategy. In the first, the
"placid, randomized environment," organizational adaptation is
easiest and an organization may proceed by trial and error and
still survive. However, in the second type, the "placid clustered"
environment, intelligence about the environment for the development of organizational strategy becomes crucial for survival, and
location within the environmental field becomes very important.
In the third type, the "disturbed-reactive" environment, overlapping effects of the action of other organizations become important
because of the existence of similar organizations, and an organization must calculate the actions and reactions of the other systems.
The fourth type, referred to as "the turbulent field," is still more
complicated, and environmental effects are uncertain because
dynamic processes arise from the field itself and not simply from
the interaction of the organizations and groups which comprise
the environment.

Recognizing the importance of different types of environments,
several empirical and theoretical studies have shown that different
organizational structures and patterns of system behavior are
required for organizational effectiveness in organizations relating
to different kinds of environments (Burns & Stalker, 1961; Harvey,
1968; Perrow, 1967; Lawrence & Lorsch, 1967, 1969; Thompson,
1967). In addition, Garbarro (1973) has pointed out that if an
environment changes, the patterns of organization necessary for
its continuing effectiveness must also change, and that an organizational pattern which initially may have been well suited to its
nvironment would not continue to be so if the environment has
undergone major changes.

Lawrence and Lorsch (1969) have described the group of studies
taking this approach as subscribing to a "contingency theory," since
they share the view that differences in internal system states and

processes of effective organizations are contingent on differences in their external environments. In their own work, Lawrence and Lorsch have advanced this approach and have stimulated the research and theoretical efforts of others along these lines. Conceptually, Lawrence and Lorsch view organizations as open systems capable of internal differentiation in response to environmental conditions. In their research on industrial organization (1967), they found empirical evidence of a relationship among such external environmental variables as certainty and diversity of the environment, and internal system states of differentiation, integration, and the processes of conflict resolution. In general, the Lawrence and Lorsch findings emphasize the importance of organization-environment "fit," i.e., if an organization's internal system states and processes are consistent with external environmental demands, the system will be more effective in dealing with its environment.

Differentiation and integration are reciprocal interdependent system processes viewed as having central importance in the interaction of an organization with its external environment. Differentiation may be defined as a process of evolutionary change in which components of a system develop specialized attributes responsive to the requirements of particular parts of the external environment. While differentiation refers to the elaboration of an organizational system into subsystems, integration may be defined as a process of unification of differing subsystems. Integration is a major defining characteristic of a system, for without a sufficient degree of integration among the parts, only a collection of isolated, individual elements exists, rather than a unified totality or "system."

Integration and differentiation processes in organization have mutually exclusive properties. For example, it has been shown that it is not possible to have both a high degree of differentiation and extremely precise integration (Lawrence & Lorsch, 1967, Ch. 4).

Recently a few exploratory studies have attempted to apply the differentiation-integration model of Lawrence and Lorsch to nonindustrial organizational systems. Gabarro (1973) conducted a comparative case study of two small urban schools which were attempting to adapt to the needs of increased minority enrollments. Utilizing several performance indicators, Gabarro identified one school system as more adaptive than the other. A major finding of this study was that the needs of increased minority enrollments required both differentiation and integration and the school system which had displayed more sustained performance over a decade of increasing minority enrollments had also attained higher states of differentiation and integration than the less adaptive school system.

Gabarro also found evidence that effective adaptation by the two school systems required increased integration of effort among the principals, pupil services, and central office support services in order to meet the increased needs of schoolhouse for these services. These three subsystems apparently related to essentially the same internal and external groups and organizations, although differentiation was required if the total system was to adequately deal with changing environmental situations. Without adequate differentiation, the total organization tended to engage in short-term reactive coping with the result that the system was not developing the specialized long-term functions necessary for adaptations to environmental turbulence.

In another study which focused on differentiation and integration of an urban school department, Derr (1971) postulated that any organization has three major subsystems which are to deal with somewhat different aspects of the external environment. These three major subsystems include: (a) the research and development subsystem, which functions to keep an organization apprised of knowledge and developments that help it to be more effective; (b) an externally oriented subsystem, which functions to relate the organization to the external world; and (c) a production subsystem which is necessary for the development of the major products of the organization and the accomplishment of goals. Analyzing data obtained from administrators from each of these three subsystems, Deer found that each subsystem related to different external subenvironments.

Although his analysis of a city's school department's environment suggested that there was a high need for differentiation, Derr's data showed that a relatively low state of actual differentiation existed. He concluded that the school system was not adequately adapting to the external environment's demands for diversity and that possibly this was due to the staff inbreeding and related lack of emotional and cognitive differentiation which existed in the school system.

Further analysis of his data indicated that administrators perceived a high degree of integration between organizational subunits, although Derr concluded that relatively little actual interaction between administrators in the system occurred. Derr explained the dysfunction of "perceived collaboration," related to the actual level of integration, as resulting from a situation in which such weak interdependencies obtained between subunits that no basis for subunits to disagree existed. Derr labeled this situation, in which collaboration was perceived to be high but actually low work-related interaction obtained, as "friendship systems"; and he cautioned that while friendship may be important for achieving integration, care must be taken not to assume that friendly relations mean that a high degree of work-related collaboration is taking place. This assumption was described by Derr as stemming from the inadequacy of applying the Lawrence and Lorsch method for operationalizing integration in a setting such as a school system.

Both of these differentiation-integration studies pose problems in terms of their definitions of environment. Derr's definition, which is close to that used by Lawrence and Lorsch, suffers certain limitations in its dependence on internal perceptions of information emanating from external groups. It is thus largely dependent on how perceptive the organization itself is of its environment. Gabarro used the concept of task domain (Levine & White, 1961), which defines the environment as including the services, clients, groups, and technologies an organization or its subunits assumes as its area of operation. Gabarro included uncertainty of information as well as other aspects of information coming from the environment in his definition of task domain, together with the issues posed by both external and internal groups relevant to the organization. Thus Gabarro does not distinguish between the internal and external environment of an organizational system.

Further work is clearly needed to refine definitions of organizational system environment. Most organization theorists and researchers have tended to define the nature of the external environment in terms of the information obtained from within the organization rather than on the basis of some external "objective" criteria. Although is is difficult to obtain operational measures of the "real" attributes of the environment which are distinct from the "perceptions" of this environment by organizational members, future theoretical and empirical efforts in this area may benefit from separating out variables descriptive of the internal environment, the external environment, and those aspects of the external environment which the organization perceives and to which it reacts.

Katz and Kahn: Open System Model

The Tavistock group and the contingency theorists have derived their open system models from empirical research as well as from abstract concepts of living systems theory. The open system model of Katz and Kahn and the general systems behavior model of James

Miller which we will now consider both make extensive use of open systems theory in integrating a wide variety of organizational research, but do not develop their models from research generated by this conceptual point of view. Although these two models may well stimulate much open systems organizational research, they did not primarily evolve from empirical work as did the models we have thus far discussed.

The shift in recent years in American organizational psychology from an emphasis on traditional concepts of individual psychology and interpersonal relations to open systems concepts is in large measure related to the major impact on the field of organization theory and research of Katz and Kahn's work, *The Social Psychology of Organizations*, published in 1966. Katz and Kahn had been involved with major empirical research in testing the human relations approach, and after encountering the general systems theory of Bertalanffy and his followers and the socio-technical systems approach of the Tavistock group, they adopted an open systems approach to organizations. Their book provides a convincing description of the advantages of an open system perspective for examining the important relations of an organization with its environment and the ways in which feedback processes enable an organization to survive in a changing environment.

Katz and Kahn (1966) display their endorsement of organic analogy by listing and discussing nine characteristics which they suggest characterize and define *all* open systems, including organizations. The common characteristics of open systems proposed by Katz and Kahn are: (1) importation of energy; (2) throughput; (3) output; (4) systems as cycles of events; (5) negative entropy; (6) information input, negative feedback, and the coding process; (7) the steady state and dynamic homeostasis; (8) differentiation; and (9) equifinality. They continue discussion of their acceptance of organic analogy by describing the open-system model as a "meta-theory" or general framework which may be used to comprehend all levels of living systems:

> Open-system theory is an approach and a conceptual language for understanding and describing many kinds and levels of phenomena. It is used to describe and explain the behavior of living organisms and combinations of organisms, but is applicable to any dynamic, recurring process, any patterned sequence of events (Katz & Kahn, 1966, p. 452).

Katz and Kahn identify five basic subsystems of an organizational system: (1) production subsystems concerned with getting the work of the organization done; (2) supportive subsystems for procurement, disposal, and institutional relations; (3) maintenance subsystems such as personnel administration which tie people into their functional roles; (4) adaptive subsystems concerned with organizational change; and (5) managerial subsystems for the direction, adjudication, and control of the various subsystems and activities of the organization.

Miller: General Systems Behavior Theory

Miller (1971) labels his version of general systems theory "general systems behavior theory," which is concerned with a special subset of systems, the living. He describes living systems as having the following characteristics: being open and complex; repairing and restoring their structure through the use of inputs; containing genetic material composed of DNA; and being composed of protein and other organic components. He also asserts that all living systems have certain specific critical subsystems which are "integrated together to form actively self-regulating, developing, reproducing unitary systems with purposes and goals" (Miller, 1971, p. 282). Finally, he asserts that living systems can exist only in a limited range of environments.

Miller divides the critical subsystems necessary for organizational survival into three major groupings. The first grouping, subsystems which process both matter-energy and information, includes the reproducer and boundary subsystems. The second major category consists of those subsystems which are concerned with matter-energy processing and includes the adjustor, distributor, converter, producer, matter-energy storage subsystem, extruder, motor, and supporter subsystem. The third category proposed by Miller includes those subsystems which have to do with information processing. This third group consists of the input transducer, internal transducer, channel and net, decoder, associator, memory, decider, inputter, and output transducer. Of all these critical subsystems, Miller viewed only the decider as essential in that a system cannot be dependent on another system for its deciding.

In applying these critical subsystem models to the organization, Miller (1972) is able to list specific structures which make up all the critical subsystems, except for the associator and supporter. He recognizes, however, that organizations are not explicitly subdivided into departments and other units according to his set of subsystems. He does assert that all living systems require the life functions associated with the nineteen subsystems which he hypothesizes and have either a complement of the critical subsystems or have an intimate association and effective interaction with systems which carry out the missing life functions for them.

Miller has published a series of articles in the journal *Behavioral Science* discussing different systems levels, including the cell, the organ, the organism, the group, and the organization. Each of these articles corresponds to a chapter in a book in preparation for some years; these articles and chapters follow the same outline, which emphasizes the cross-level formal identity among the different levels of living systems. In the nearly 200-page article on the organization, Miller lists some fifty-five hypotheses, many of which he has shown in other articles to be relevant to other levels of living systems as well. He asserts that these propositions concern cross level formal identities which can be demonstrated empirically. Many of the hypotheses, he admits, were suggested by the work of others, but usually were considered to relate to one level only and were not advanced originally as general systems hypotheses.

Through his compilation of systems concepts, review of relevant organizational literature, and proposal of explicit hypotheses, Miller offers the potential of stimulating much useful empirical work in this field which will not only test the similarities between organizations and other living systems but will also help develop a truly comprehensive and general theory of the organizational level of phenomena. Like Katz and Kahn, however, the model offered by Miller neither is derived from primary consideration of human service organizations nor has it directly stimulated much explicit empirical research with this type of organizational system.

LIMITS OF ORGANIC ANALOGY

In the search for a general systems theory comprised of concepts and propositions which may be employed across a variety of system levels, there is a danger that the special characteristics of phenomena at a particular level of analysis will be neglected in the search for general characteristics. Some general system theorists have recognized this danger and warned of its consequences. For example, Katz and Kahn (1966) note the limits of organic analogy and point out the importance of remaining aware of the differences between organization and organism:

> Our discussion of the common characteristics of all open systems should not blind us to the differences that exist between biological

and social systems. The stuff of which a system is constituted—the cells of a biological organism or the human beings in the social system—needs careful study. Otherwise we could know all there is to know about the political state from the science of cytology (Katz & Kahn, 1966, p. 30).

Miller (1965), while placing a heavy emphasis on the search for the isomorphies which are generalizable across all levels of living systems, notes nevertheless that "all systems at each level have certain common characteristics which differentiate them from systems at other levels [p. 216]."

One of the specific areas in which organizations differ from organisms is with regard to their boundaries (Katz & Kahn, 1966; Miller, 1972). Although physical structures such as buildings and fences are important components of boundaries in many types of organizations, in general various parts of an organization's boundaries do not necessarily have any immediate physical continuity. Thus organizations differ from organisms in the clarity with which their boundaries can be defined, since social structures are not bounded by the physical and psychological invariances of biological structures.

Organizations also differ from the organism with regard to the looseness of relationship between their parts. The organization, like the small group, is made up of a number of components which are actually individual organisms. Systems at the organism level are made up of components which have much less mobility in relationship to each other than the components of an organization. In like manner, the subsystems of an organism also have more fixed spatial relationships than the components of an organization, the latter being capable of moving about and coming together at a later time. Miller comments that it may be this striking difference between the mobility of the components of a social system and a biological system which is responsible for the difficulty experienced by many scientists in recognizing isomorphies which exist across these levels of system (1965, p. 216).

Unlike organisms, social systems are not born but are essentially contrived systems held together by psychological rather than biological bonds. Katz and Kahn (1966) observe that social systems have a structure of events rather than of physical parts and that the structure may therefore be separated from the functioning of the system. Katz and Kahn conclude that the quality of event structure of organizations and their essentially contrived nature implies a variability which has three major implications:

1) Organizations may be designed for a wide variety of objectives and may change functions during the course of their life history.
2) Since the components of an organization are not held together in the required interdependent fashion for their continued functioning as a total system by biological bonds, much organizational energy must be invested in special control mechanisms to keep the organization together and to reduce human variability, and to produce stability in activity patterns.
3) Organizations do not follow the growth curves typical of the life of biological organisms and thus are both more vulnerable to destruction and, paradoxically, may also exist for a much longer time than the biological organisms which originally created them.

Katx and Kahn (1966) point out that one of the implications of the organization's lack of the built-in stability of biological systems is that organizations resort to a multiplication of mechanisms to maintain themselves and tend to overdetermine behavior which is necessary to preserve their existence. They describe the counterpart of dynamic homeostasis in biological organisms, or the maintenance of equilibrium by a constant adjustment and anticipation, as the "system dynamic" in an organization which "moves a given structure toward becoming more like what it basically is" (Katz & Kahn, 1966, p. 67). An example of this system dynamic in a human service organization is the complex of motivational forces which moves a mental hospital originally organized as a custodial institution to become even more custodial over time unless significant new inputs come in from the environment. Even when major inputs do impinge upon such an organization, there is a tendency for the system dynamic to resist movement from the homeostatic position of custodialism which had earlier characterized the organization.

AN INTEGRATIVE SYSTEM MODEL OF THE LIVING HUMAN SERVICE ORGANIZATION

Although the open-system models of Katz and Kahn and James Miller have not emerged from specific systems-oriented research programs, each model does bring together in an open systems framework earlier research data not generated specifically on the basis of a systems perspective. Not only do they point the way to future research by integrating earlier research into a common comprehensive framework, but they also point the way for another kind of integration which is helpful in generating empirical work specifically with regard to the human service organization and the integration of open systems models. Each of the four major open systems models reviewed in this paper provides particular insights into how to most usefully conceptualize the human service organization.

For a number of years, the author and his colleagues at the Program Research Unit, Laboratory of Community Psychiatry, Harvard Medical School have been applying general systems concepts to the planning, management, and evaluation of human service organizations. Each of the four major theoretical models reviewed above, in combination with other statements of general systems theory, has been the source of useful concepts and propositions in this work. In this connection, however, the Katz and Kahn model, the socio-technical systems model, and the approach of the contingency theorists have posed problems in being applied to human service organizations because of their primary focus on industrial and business production types of organizational systems. This limitation, however, has not been specifically a problem with the use of James Miller's contribution to the development of living systems theory because of the cross-system orientation of his approach.

At the organizational system level of analysis, experience indicates that one can find useful analogies across types of organizations as was possible across systems at different levels. However, just as there are disidentities across systems levels, there are also important differences across types of organizations, and these limitations to generalizability are important to consider in their own right. The human service organization (HSO) is similar to other types of organizations in carrying on an input-throughput-output-feedback transaction cycle with its external environment. However, as contrasted with an industrial production system whose essential operating processes are concerned with the conversion of material resources, a human service organization tends to be primarily concerned with the processing of human resources. As a people-processing system, an HSO has important characteristics which differentiate it from an organization which produces specific tangible physical end products. A manufacturing enterprise which buys raw materials, converts these raw materials into products, and sells the products to its customers is inherently different from a community mental health center, which accepts clients for treatment, provides professional services, and then releases these clients back to the community.

People are a basic component of any organizational system. The

Tavistock group emphasized this in the "socio" part of their concept of the socio-technical system; "socio" for them meant the socio-psychological or the people dimension of the system (Trist, *et al.*, 1963). In the industrial production organization the people of concern are primarily the organizational members who are employed by the organization. The distinction between consumer and organization member, however, is less distinct in the human service organization. This was emphasized by research conducted in the 1950s which examined such custodial institutions as the mental hospital in terms of the importance of considering the patients or clients of the treatment organization as an important part of the system as well as the professional staff who worked in that type of human service organization (Caudill, 1958; Goffman, 1961; Stanton & Schwartz, 1954). People are not only important components of the human service organizational system but they are important because they are also that which is processed by this type of system. In an industrial production organization, the customers are outside the system, while in a human service organization the clients may be considered to be part of the human components which comprise the system. Through interaction with the staff of the HSO the client will not only be changed by the system but may in turn influence the system. The effects of students on colleges and universities during the decade of the 1960s offer a dramatic illustration of this last point.

The "technical" part of the concept "socio-technical system" indicated the degree to which the technological demands of industrial production organizations determined the structures and processes of that type of organizational system. While technology is certainly important in the human service organization, many types of HSOs—and this is perhaps particularly true with mental health and social service organizations—lack a clear base of demonstrably effective technology. They consequently tend to depend more on the attitudes, values, beliefs, and ideologies of the professional staff concerning the ideal patterns of conduct and ideal goal states.

A number of studies have shown the importance of belief systems for the professionals who work in human service organizations. Wessen (1958) showed that a general hospital is characterized by a set of disparate institutional ideologies which set limits upon the degree to which the members of the organization's various professional groups can be integrated. Levinson and his colleagues (Gilbert & Levinson, 1957; Sharaf & Levinson, 1957) found evidence that the psychiatric ideological positions of the 1950s related to the degree of custodial care offered in the mental hospital.

Strauss, *et al.* (1964), studying the psychotherapeutic, soma-
totherapeutic, and sociotherapeutic orientations in several psychiatric organizations concluded:

> Ideology makes a difference in the organization of treatment: in what
> is done to and for patients and in the accompanying division of labor
> (p. 361).

Several studies of community mental health ideology have shown
that this new belief system has broad implications for the pattern
of services offered in the contemporary community mental health
organization (Baker & Schulberg, 1967; Schulberg & Baker, in
press; Langston, 1970). Thus there is evidence that professional
beliefs play a significant role in the human service type of organizational system in determining what types of service are offered and
how patients or clients are treated.

Until recently the beliefs and values of professionals have tended
to prevail to the exclusion of consumer values in the pattern of
structuring and functioning of HSOs. Although in some sense
HSOs have always been responsible to the public interest and the
needs of a larger community, they have lacked the direct feedback
linkages available to profitmaking organizations by virtue of the
latters' relationships to the marketplace. Although human service
organizations are increasingly held accountable by their actual or
potential clients, there is still a strong tendency for the goals and
performance criteria of HSOs to be determined on the basis of
professional rather than consumer value judgments.

In addition to people and their beliefs, another major category
of elements integral to a human service organization includes the
nonhuman resources such as buildings, equipments, materials, and
financial assets. Gross (1966) has pointed out that such nonhuman
resources do not exist as resources apart from people. He observes
that "physical objects can become resources only when two conditions are met: (1) when there are people with certain interests
to be satisfied, and (2) when there are people with the knowledge
and technological know-how required to use such physical objects
to the satisfaction of such interests" (Gross, 1966, p. 192). While
the people-processing HSO lacks the well-developed machine
technology associated with the production of commercial products
in an industrial organization, nonhuman resources do play a significant role in this type of organizational system, particularly as they
relate to professional values.

In summary, a human service organization (HSO) may be conceptualized as an open *people-belief-resource* (PBR) *system*. The HSO is a living system expressive of the prevailing beliefs, ideology, and values which guide the actions of the people comprising this system as well as indicative of the way they utilize various nonhuman resources. The major dimensions of the human service organization are defined by the beliefs and capacities of the people who work in the organization in interaction with the available nonhuman resources, both being influenced by environmental conditions. Conceptualizing a human service organization in this manner as an open people-belief-resource system suggests a general area of study concerned with the interrelationships of people, beliefs, and resources in this type of organization as affected by the external environment.

Applications of the Integrative System Model of HSOs

The integrative model outlined above has been useful in guiding two major longitudinal studies of changing human service organizations. The first study, to be discussed shortly, focused on the complex changes occurring within a state mental hospital over a five-year period as it attempted to become more community oriented (Schulberg & Baker, in press).

Like other living systems, the human service organization is open to its environment and its input, throughput, output, and feedback structures and processes are largely influenced by the nature of its relationships with this external environment. In responding to various external subenvironments, the human service organizational system is subjected to the opposing forces of differentiation and integration which were described by the contingency theorists as characterizing all open organizational systems.

As an open system, the HSO faces considerable external uncertainty, both because of the diversity and change in its external environment and the difficulty of predicting the consequences of its own actions. In addition, the human service organization is a part of larger suprasystems of varying size and level of complexity. For example, a state mental hospital is a part of the state department of mental health, but also can be considered as part of a human service network of agencies serving a particular geographically-based community.

Human service organizations are criss-crossed by a number of overlapping systems as well. For example, its members may be active members of professional societies, some may be teachers in university-based training programs, some may be members of the boards of voluntary agencies, and so on. Because of their membership in other systems, the individual members of a human service organization may vary in degree of commitment to the organization. For example, a professional may display less allegiance to his organizational membership group than to an external professional reference group.

Because of the looseness of components which make up the system, and the processes of subsystem differentiation as different subsystems respond to various parts of the external environment, the HSO faces considerable internal uncertainty and experiences difficult problems in control and integration. Typically, the parts of the human service organization are imperfectly coordinated, partially autonomous, and only partially controllable. In responding to different subenvironments, different parts of the organization develop different goals, and human service organizations are characterized by multiple and sometimes conflicting goals.

Our case study of a mental hospital highlights some of the built-in conflicts for a modern human service organization experiencing problems of differentiation and integration and seeking to achieve multiple goals (Baker, et al., 1970). Like most state mental hospitals, the organization we studied was originally hierarchically structured according to professional disciplines and had departments of psychiatry, psychology, nursing, and social work. The staff were also secondarily organized into multidisciplinary subsystems related to major phases of traditional patterns for treating patients.

Environmental changes in professional belief systems began to differentially impinge upon the hospital's staff. Community mental health ideology, which was gaining wide acceptance across the nation, emphasized a geographical community focus and the development of generalist skills across professional disciplines. At the same time, some national professional groups, and particularly nursing, were emphasizing the development of specialist professional skills and a struggle for professional status. Acceptance by staff of one or the other of these different belief systems implied different goals and the development of different patterns of structure for a hospital organization.

In response to environmental trends emphasizing community approaches to mental health services, geographical decentralization and the development of cross-disciplinary generalist skills, the hospital changed its clinical structure into geographically-based treatment units staffed by multi-disciplinary teams. This restructuring was justified as a better way of organizing organizational resources to achieve the goals of treating acute patients, returning chronic patients to the community, and providing other community-oriented services. However, one centralized professional department was retained—the nursing department. This subsystem continued to pursue the opposing goal of providing specialized professional training emphasizing long-term individual patient-focused treatment rather than short-term population or community-oriented treatment. Responding to external developments in professional nursing which emphasized the growth of specialized roles for psychiatric nurses, the nursing department resisted the emphasis of geographic units on a generalist pattern of staff functioning.

Subsystem conflict developed as the nursing department and the geographic units continued to respond differentially to forces from the environment. Eventually, the management subsystem acted to integrate the subsystem parts. A new superintendent of the hospital brought together representatives from competing parts of the organization, emphasizing their interdependence, and decisions were developed and implemented which were clearly oriented to superordinate hospital goals. Despite forces toward fragmentation and disintegration, the hospital began to achieve new states of dynamic equilibrium.

In another phase of our research on the changing mental hospital we focused on boundary-spanning functions (Baker, *et al.*, 1969). Consistent with the view of a human service organization as an open people-belief-resource system, we predicted that the interactions between an occupant of a boundary-spanning role and other professional and nonprofessional people in the community would be affected by the role occupant's perceptions of them. Similarities and differences in the perception of the hospital's functioning by hospital staff and external agency personnel were predicted to be reflected in the ways people view the "people-channeling," or referral patterns between these different subsystems.

Identifying social workers at the hospital as a professional group whose role definitions included elements of boundary-spanning functions, an interview survey was conducted to assess this group's perceptions of the hospital, its role in providing essential community mental health services to its catchment area, the interaction patterns of social workers with other agencies, and their views of hospital-community referral practices. This data was compared with interviews with key staff of agency systems and the community served by the hospital.

In comparing the social workers' perceptions of the hospital's community image with the image of the hospital as expressed by health and welfare agency personnel, it was found that the image held by external community caregivers appeared to be slightly more positive than the image as perceived by the hospital's own social service staff. These beliefs were reflected in the patient resource exchanges between the hospital and external systems—referral patterns seem to be affected by both the actual negative attitudes among agency staff outside the hospital as well as beliefs of the hospital staff about these other systems. Perceiving their hospital as having a negative image, and anticipating rejection of offers of cooperation, hospital social workers hesitated to fully utilize the local agencies.

In the course of attempting to evaluate the complex changes occurring in the state mental hospital, we began to consider the broad implications of our system model for program evaluation (Baker, 1969; Schulberg, Sheldon, & Baker, 1969). The general issue of evaluation will be discussed in the next section of this paper, but at this point an insight which emerged from the consideration of problems of implementing research evaluation findings will be presented which relates to the previous discussion of boundary roles in an HSO.

Boundary-spanning personnel also have an important function in the operation of adequate feedback of evaluation of a human service organization. Baker and Schulberg (1969) have pointed out that the researcher conducting a program evaluation who is external to the organizational system in which the human service program is embedded must consider with the program administrator the problems of implementing program evaluation research findings. Boundary roles may occur at all levels of the organization but are usually found at the top and bottom of the administrative structure. The program administrator at the top of a structure may act in two distinct ways with regard to evaluation information: (1) he may act as a communication channel of research results because of his strong commitment to and participation in the implementation of new programs; or (2) he may act as a censor if negative evaluation of a program's effectiveness reflects adversely on his decision to back the program, and in such a situation, research findings may not be properly utilized. On the other hand, those occupying boundary roles low on the organization hierarchy often cannot make effective use of evaluation results because they do not have the formal authority to influence individuals at levels higher than themselves. Consequently, a lower-level boundary-role incumbent may pass on only that information which he thinks his superiors want to hear.

Another study conducted by the author and his colleagues was a three-year open systems analysis of a large, urban health and welfare planning council. One of the key organizational subsystems examined in this study was the Information and Referral Department (Broskowski & Baker, 1972). Potentially, the Information and Referral Department of this community planning organization could perform an important feedback function for other subsystems of the council by providing them with information about changing conditions in the organization's environment. In addition, the Information and Referral subsystem performed other important functions for the planning council. One of these, its boundary "filter" function, was in some ways opposed to the feedback function. For example, by intercepting the numerous demands for direct service from various environmental constituents, the Information and Referral Department shortcircuited these demands before they went directly to other council personnel who were primarily devoted to long-term planning and agency consultation. This filtering process represented a cost savings in time and distraction for the other operational planning subsystems. At the same time, however, this filtering process may have prevented feedback from entering the planning process in ways which would have enhanced its goals. Health and human service organizations do not usually maintain boundaries permeable enough to allow *all* information to pass into their internal subsystems without some regulation. This long-range planning organization which we studied exercised boundary regulation and information restriction so that the majority of its resources were not continuously subjected to short-term environmental demands for service. As a result, however, the environmental monitoring and feedback functions of this specialized boundary subsystem tended not to be fully utilized.

The above example is a manifestation of a major system dilemma for a health and welfare council in terms of its transactions with a complicated external environment. The dilemma of "boundary control versus boundary permeability" revolves around the difficulty in maintaining enough boundary regulation to provide adequate system stability, continuity, and pursuit of goals while the organizational system is being buffeted from all sides by environmentally-based disturbances or demands. On the one hand, a human service organization needs to maintain feedback functions, which permit openness to new information and to legitimate demands. On the other hand, if the organization becomes too open or permeable, it can lose its sense of control or direction. The council we have studied has experienced this dilemma, not only in terms of managing the appropriate integration of the Information and Referral subsystem into the system's total organizational functions, but in managing a number of day-to-day operations. It has attempted to concentrate sufficient resources to do long-range planning and broad policy promotion while simultaneously maintaining sufficiently open boundaries to allow for the input of necessary information, people, material resources, money, and legitimation.

Our open systems analysis of a health and welfare council has identified four additional "dilemmas" (Baker, Broskowski, & Brandwein, 1973). The first of these, "integration versus differentiation," was discussed earlier in terms of the problems faced by a changing mental hospital. These two major interdependent system processes of integration and differentiation, which emerge within any human service organization, have particular salience in terms of the total environment confronting most human service organizations today. The environments faced by contemporary human service organizations display the characteristics of "turbulence" which were described by Emery and Trist (1965). Maintenance of system properties therefore requires interdependent action or collaboration among subsystems. Otherwise, lacking sufficient action among subparts, the human service organizational system tends to break down and is unable to accomplish organizational tasks.

A third, related dilemma faced by a human service organization is the problem of maintaining sufficient "variety versus homogeneity." In order to be able to adapt to a particular environment, a certain degree of variety is required in terms of what is brought into the organizational system. While a sufficient degree of heterogeneity is necessary in terms of internal resources as well as new inputs, a high degree of heterogeneity, whether in feedback, information, or characteristics of organizational members, makes adequate system management and coordination difficult.

A fourth dilemma identified in the study of a changing health and welfare council relates to a distinction provided by Warren (1967) in his analysis of the relationships between large community organizations and their environments. Warren described two major types of constituencies: (1) an input constituency consisting of organizations or actors from which a human service organization receives necessary inputs and to which it in turn acknowledges a responsibility in helping to determine its policy in programs; (2) an output constituency consisting of those organizations or actors in any environment which an agency acknowledges as appropriate targets of activity and to which it directs its production of outputs.

In adapting to a complex total environment, a contemporary health and welfare organization is forced to adapt to conditions of conflicting demands, not only from different output constituencies, but also from highly diverse input constituencies. Our research indicated that in attempting to satisfy either input or output constituents, the human service organization risks alienation of one or the other. This dilemma is further complicated by the strong influence which certain organizations or individuals have by virtue of representing both types of constituencies simultaneously.

The fifth major type of dilemma faced by a human service organizational system is revealed in the attempt to achieve a balance between "proactivity versus reactivity." Systems differ in the nature of their action with regard to areas of their external environment along a dimension which may be described as proactivity versus reactivity. A system adopting a primarily *pro*active stance with regard to its environment tends to act in anticipation of future environmental conditions rather than *re*acting in a rather passive fashion to current environmental forces. A human service organizational system characterized by a proactive stance also tends to respond primarily to the task demands generated internally, while an organization in a reactive stance tends to respond to task demands from the external environment, including coercive pressures and positive inducements. The health and welfare council that we have studied (Baker, Broskowski, & Brandwein, 1973) moved from a pattern of action characterized largely by system maintenance toward a behavior pattern of policy promotion (Head & Drover, 1971). In doing so, the council tended to shift the balance of its action from short-term reactivity in response to environmental stimuli to a pattern of proactivity. Our research indicated, however, that a minimum degree of reactivity is required if a human service organization is to maintain its sanctioned position within the larger network of health and welfare organizations serving the community.

Evaluation of HSOs

An area in which an open systems model of the human service organization can be particularly useful is in the evaluation of this type of organization. Traditional models of evaluation have stressed a conception of evaluation as measurement of the degree of success or failure of an organization to reach predetermined objectives. This goal-attainment model of evaluation stresses the importance of the establishment of measurable outcome criteria. However, as has already been pointed out, the human service type of organization is not primarily concerned with easily quantifiable material products.

Two other problems occur in employing the goal-attainment models: (1) evaluations employing this model are prone to accept the "public" goals of the organization, i.e., the official statements of organizational leaders and/or the idealized statements of the organizational charter or other official documents—written or spoken pronouncements not really meant to be realized; and (2) the model does not adequately consider the multifunctional character of organizations—especially human service organizations—and does not recognize that organizations have multiple goals, which are not necessarily compatible, and that an organization invests its resources in nongoal activities as well as goal functions.

A system model approach to evaluation does not start with the goal itself (Schulberg, Sheldon, & Baker, 1969). Instead, it is concerned with establishing a working model of a social unit capable of achieving a goal (Etzioni, 1960). In addition to the achievement of goals and subgoals, Baker and Schulberg (1973) have observed that evaluation based on an open system model of the human service organization should be concerned with: (1) the effective integration and coordination of organizational subunits; (2) the acquisition and maintenance of necessary resources; and (3) the adaptation of the organization to the environment and to its own internal demands. This model assumes that some of the human service organization's means may necessarily be devoted to such nonobvious functions as maintenance activities. From the viewpoint of the system model, such activities are functional and may actually increase organizational effectiveness.

In contrast to the goal-attainment model of evaluation, which is concerned with degree of success in reaching a specific objective, a system model establishes a degree to which an organization realizes its goals under a given set of internal and external conditions. The key question is: Under the given conditions, how close does the organizational allocation of resources approach an optimum distribution? Optimum is the key word, and what becomes crucial is a balanced distribution of resources among all organizational objectives, not maximal satisfaction of any one goal (Etzioni, 1960). From this perspective, just as a lack of resources for any one goal may be dysfunctional, an excess of resources for the goal may be equally dysfunctional. In the latter instance, superfluous attention to one goal leads to depressed concern for the others, causing problems of coordination and competition.

In applying an open systems model of evaluation to the assessment of a human service organization, the evaluator moves from the more or less exclusive emphasis on output in the goal-attainment model to a concern for throughput as well as input processes (Baker & Schulberg, 1973). In addition to developing indicators of certain outcome characteristics, it is important to study the processes by which the human service organization reconciles the often conflicting beliefs and goals of its organizational members.

SUMMARY

In this article we have reviewed the development of the perspective that organizations as living systems share properties in common with other levels of living systems. Several models of the organization as a living system which have developed out of consideration of production organizations have been reviewed, and the applications of these models for conceptualizing the human service organization have been discussed. While it has been noted that there are limitations to the organic analogy implicit in treating organizations as having properties in common with other living systems, one of the purposes of this paper has been to show how examination of general systems may be useful in improving or understanding of social systems as well as biological systems. Finally, a derived integrative model of the human service organization as an open people-belief-resource system has been presented, as well as a review of some applications of this approach.

REFERENCES

Baker, F. An open systems approach to the study of mental hospitals in transition. *Community Mental Health Journal,* 1969, *5,* 403-412.

Baker, F. Organizations as open systems. In Baker, F. (Ed.), *Organizational systems: General systems approaches to complex organizations.* Homewood, Illinois: Richard D. Irwin, 1973.

Baker, F., Broskowski, A., & Brandwein, R. System dilemmas of a health and welfare council. *Social Service Review,* March, 1973.

Baker, F., & Schulberg, H. C. Development of a community mental health ideology scale. *Community Mental Health Journal,* 1967, *3,* 216-225.

Baker, F., & Schulberg, H. C. A system model for evaluating the changing mental hospital. In Baker, F. (Ed.), *Organizational systems: General systems approaches to complex organizational systems.* Homewood, Illinois: Richard D. Irwin, 1973.

Baker, F., Schulberg, H., & O'Brien, G. The changing mental hospital:

Its perceived image and contact with the community. *Mental Hygiene,* 1969, *53,* 237-244.

Baker, F., Schulberg, H., Yager, J., & O'Brien, G. Problems of a centralized department in a decentralized mental hospital. *Social Science and Medicine,* 1970, *4,* 239-252.

Berrien, F. K. *General and social systems.* New Brunswick, New Jersey: Rutgers University Press, 1968.

Bertalanffy, L. von. *General systems theory.* New York: George Braziller, 1968.

Blau, P. M., & Scott, W. R. *Formal organizations: A comparative approach.* San Francisco: Chandler, 1962.

Boguslaw, W. *The new utopians.* Englewood Cliffs, New Jersey: Prentice-Hall, 1965.

Broskowski, A., & Baker, F. The functions of an information and referral subsystem in a community planning organization. Laboratory of Community Psychiatry, Harvard Medical School, 1972 (unpublished paper).

Buckley, W. *Sociology and modern systems theory.* Englewood Cliffs, New Jersey: Prentice-Hall, 1967.

Burns, T., & Stalker, G. M. *The management of innovation.* London: Tavistock, 1961.

Caudill, W. *The psychiatric hospital as a small society.* Cambridge: Harvard University Press & Commonwealth Fund, 1958.

Derr, C. B. An organizational analysis of the Boston School Department. Unpublished doctoral dissertation. The Harvard Graduate School of Education, 1971.

Emery, F. E., & Trist, E. L. Socio-technical systems. In West-Churchman, C. W., & Verhulst, M. (Eds.), *Management sciences: Models and techniques.* Vol. II. New York: Pergamon Press, 1960.

Emery, F. E., & Trist, E. L. The causal texture of organizational environments. *Human Relations,* 1965, *18,* 21-32.

Etzioni, A. Two approaches to organizational analysis: A critique and a suggestion. *Administrative Science Quarterly,* 1960, *5,* 257-278.

Gabarro, J. J. Organizational adaptation to environmental change. In Baker, F. (Ed.), *Organizational systems: General systems approaches to complex organizations.* Homewood, Illinois: Richard D. Irwin, 1973.

Gilbert, D. C., & Levinson, D. J. "Custodialism" and "humanism" in staff ideology. In Greenblatt, M., Levinson, D. J., & Williams, R. H. (Eds.), *The patient and the mental hospital.* Glencoe, Illinois: The Free Press, 1957.

Goffman, I. *Asylums: Essays on the social situation of mental patients and other inmates.* Garden City, New Jersey: Doubleday Anchor, 1961.

Gross, B. The state of the nation: Social systems accounting. In Bauer, R. A., *Social indicators.* Cambridge, Massachusetts: MIT Press, 1966.

Hall, A. D., & Fagen, R. E. Definition of a system. *General Systems,* 1956, *1,* 18-29.

Harvey, E. Technology and the structure of organization. *American Sociological Review,* 1968, *33,* 247-259.

Head, W., & Drover, G. Social planning and the councils. *Canadian Welfare*, 1970, *46*, 12-17.

Hutton, G. J. Management in a changing mental hospital. *Human Relations*, 1962, *15*, 283-310. (a)

Hutton, G. J. Managing systems in hospitals. *Human Relations*, 1962, *15*, 311-333. (b)

Katz, D., & Kahn, R. L. *The social psychology of organizations*. New York: Wiley, 1966.

Klir, G. J. *Trends in general systems theory*. New York: Wiley, 1972.

Langston, R. D. Community mental health centers and community mental health ideology. *Community Mental Health Journal*, 1970, *6*, 387-392.

Lawrence, P. R., & Lorsch, J. W. Differentiation and integration in complex organizations. *Administrative Science Quarterly*, 1967, *12*, 1-47.

Lawrence, P. R., & Lorsch, J. W. *Organization and environment*. Homewood, Illinois: Richard D. Irwin, 1969.

Levine, S., & White, P. E. Exchange as a conceptual framework for the study of interorganizational relationships. *Administrative Science Quarterly*, 1961, *5*, 583-601.

Miller, E. J. Technology, territory, and time: The internal differentiation of complex production systems. *Human Relations*, 1959, *12*, 243-272.

Miller, E. J., & Rice, A. K. *Systems of organization*. London: Tavistock, 1967.

Miller, J. G. Living systems: Basic concepts. *Behavioral Science*, 1965, *10*, 193-237.

Miller, J. G. The nature of living systems. *Behavioral Science*, July, 1971, *16*, 278-301.

Miller, J. G. Living systems: The organization. *Behavioral Science*, 1972, *17*, 1-182.

Perrow, C. A framework for the comparative analysis of organizations. *American Sociological Review*, 1967, *32*, 194-208.

Rice, A. K. *Productivity and social organization: The Ahmedabad experiment*. London: Tavistock, 1958.

Rice, A. K. *The enterprise and its environment*. London: Tavistock, 1963.

Rice, A. K. Individual, group and intergroup processes. *Human Relations*, 1969, *22*, 565-584.

Schulberg, H., & Baker, F. Program evaluation models and the implementation of research findings. *American Journal of Public Health*, 1968, *58*, 1248-1255.

Schulberg, H. C., & Baker, F. Community mental health: Belief system of the 1960's. *Psychiatric Opinion*, 1969, *6*, 14-26.

Schulberg, H., & Baker, F. *The mental hospital and human services*. New York: Behavioral Publications, in preparation.

Schulberg, H. C., Baker, F., & Roen, S. (Eds.), *Developments in human services*, Vol. I. New York: Behavioral Publications, 1973.

Schulberg, H. C., Sheldon, A. S., & Baker, F. (Eds.), *Program evaluation in the health fields*. New York: Behavioral Publications, 1969.

Scott, W. G. Organization theory: An overview and an appraisal. *Journal of the Academy of Management*, 1961, *4*, 2-26.

Sharaf, M. R., & Levinson, D. J. Patterns of ideology and role differentiation among psychiatric residents. In Greenblatt, M., Levinson, D. J., & Williams, R. H. (Eds.), *The patient and the mental hospital.* Glencoe, Illinois: The Free Press, 1957.

Smelzer, N. J. Sociology and the other social sciences. In Lazarsfeld, P. F., Sewell, W. H., & Wilensky, H. L. (Eds.), *The uses of sociology.* New York: Basic Books, 1967.

Sofer, C. *The organization from within.* London: Tavistock Publications, 1961.

Stanton, A. H., & Schwartz, M. S. *The mental hospital.* New York: Basic Books, 1954.

Strauss, A., Schatzman, L., Bucher, R., Ehrlich, D., & Sabshin, M. *Psychiatric ideologies and institutions.* New York: The Free Press of Glencoe, 1964.

Thompson, J. D. *Organizations in action.* New York: McGraw-Hill, 1967.

Trist, E. L., & Bamforth, K. W. Some social and psychological consequences of the long-wall method of coal-getting. *Human Relations,* 1951, *4,* 3-38.

Trist, E. L. Higgin, G. W., Murray, H., & Pollack, A. B. *Organizational choice.* London: Tavistock, 1963.

Warren, R. The interorganizational field as a focus for investigation. *Administrative Science Quarterly,* 1967, *12,* 396-419.

Wessen, A. F. Hospital ideology and communication between ward personnel. In Jaco, E. G., *Patients, physicians and illness.* Glencoe, Illinois: The Free Press, 1958.

Part VII

Perspectives for the Future

Introduction

In the near future, major and pervasive advances in technology, combined with substantial alterations in population distribution, will create unprecedented demands upon the resources and problem-solving skills of human service organizations. If these organizations are to adequately meet these demands, it will be necessary to both anticipate the nature of the demands, and develop organizational alternatives which appear functional in a changing society.

This section was not designed to provide any definitive treatment of the future; rather, it is aimed at providing a future-oriented perspective on intelligent decisions regarding more adaptable, workable organizational alternatives.

Perhaps our greatest concern is that human service organizations will, virtually default, continue to design and implement relatively uncoordinated programs within what are, too often, dysfunctional models of human service organizations. The hierarchical, "pine tree" type organizational structures have become well known to all of us, and so much a part of our thinking and our work environment, that we often accept this as a condition of our professional existence. Like air, marriage, urban congestion, etc., it simply becomes a condition one takes for granted.

But, like most of the basic assumptions we make in life, we are often unaware that we have been making certain basic assumptions until an environment is positively experienced in which these assumptions are not operating. The last part of this section is directed toward that end.

Although it is our contention that human service organizations which are organized along the dimensions indicated in the last two articles will become more prevalent, it is only a guess. However, we do feel fairly certain that, on a nationwide scale, human service organizations which operate with traditional hierarchical internal organizations in changing, turbulent environments will become increasingly costly, inefficient, and dysfunctional.

The critical problem is that of actively exploring sensible, potentially workable alternatives. The cost of this exploration might, for a period of time, be high. But its potential long-term payoffs in terms of greater services at lowered unit costs, would, over time, make these temporarily elevated costs a good investment.

Section A

Perspectives for the Future:
Futurism

Although we often criticize our ability to know the future, some things are reasonably predictable. Barring a national catastrophe, our large and complex institutions, such as schools and general hospitals, are likely to continue operating and to consume large shares of human service expenditures. Public mental hospitals, in contrast, could well be eliminated in the next two decades if the political problems can be solved. *How* these organizations will be operating is another question. Significant and far-reaching decisions have yet to be made regarding the extent to which human service organizations will adopt strategies of active intervention aimed at altering human ecosystems, or, adopt more passive strategies of reactive responses to their client and community environments.

Major shifts in population distribution, and changes in life-style and approaches towards political activism have brought important pressures to bear on many human service organizations. It has become difficult for these organizations to both gain the resources necessary for organizational survival and to deliver effective services in rapidly changing environments. This has led to human service organizations' beginning to explore new forms of internal organizational structure and external interorganizational relationships.

We would suggest that, as a first step in solving the problem of delivering services, it is important for organizations to reduce the environmental turbulence affecting them. While the sources of turbulence stemming from such environmental factors as population shifts are not likely to be dealt with directly, the organizational uncertainty stemming from turbulence in interorganizational relationships can be reduced. To the extent that this is possible, structure and reliability can be developed in interorganizational communication and decision-making, thus improving the capacity for the rationalization of internal changes in organizational structure and programs among related human service organization.

479

34. A Funny Thing Happened on the Way to the Future*

Warren G. Bennis, Ph.D.

If, as we hope, comprehensive human service planning departs from traditional models of programming, it would seem to follow that it will also depart from traditional organizational processes and structures. Not to do so would seriously threaten the viability of most of these programs and plans.

In planning organizational structures, planners at all levels are likely to think in terms of those organizations that they know best. Only occasionally does their knowledge depart from the relatively centralized, pyramidal, "pine tree" structures which have become so common in both the public and private sectors in the U.S. The human service organization which is not organized along these lines is truly an exception.

In the following article Warren Bennis provocatively offers some organizational alternatives for the future, as well as some thinking on the problems of alternative organizational structures and styles.

Analysis of the "future," or, more precisely, inventing relevant futures, has become in recent years as respectable for the scientist as the shaman. Inspired by Bertrand de Jouvenal, Daniel Bell, Olaf Helmer, and others, there seems to be growing evidence and recognition for the need of legitimate base of operations for the "futurologist." Writing in a recent issue of the *Antioch Review*, groping for a definition of the future I wrote:

*This paper is a combination and revision of two papers given at professional meetings in early September 1969: an invited address to the Division of Personality and Social Psychology, American Psychological Association, September 2, Washington, D. C., and a speech for a panel on "Political Science and the Study of the Future," given before the American Political Science Association, September 4, New York. Reprinted from F. F. Korten, S. W. Cook, & J. I. Lacey (Eds.), *Psychology and the Problems of Society.* Copyrighted 1970 by the American Psychological Association.

For me, the "future" is a portmanteau word. It embraces several notions. It is an exercise of imagination which allows us to compete with and try to outwit future events. Controlling the anticipated future is, in addition, a social invention that legitimizes the process of forward planning. There is no other way I know of to resist the "tyranny of blind forces" than by looking facts in the face (as we experience them in the present) and extrapolating to the future—nor is there any other sure way to detect compromise. Most importantly, the future is a conscious dream, a set of imaginative hypotheses groping toward whatever vivid utopias lie at the heart of our consciousness. "In dreams begin responsibilities," said Yeats, and it is to our future responsibilities as educators, researchers, and practitioners that these dreams are dedicated [Bennis, 1968, p. 277].

Most students of the future would argue with that definition, claiming that it is "poetic" or possibly even "prescientific." The argument has validity, I believe, though it is difficult to define "futurology," let alone distinguish between and among terms such as "inventing relevant futures," scenarios, forecasts, self-fulfilling prophecies, predictions, goals, normative theories, evolutionary hypothesis, prescriptions, and so on. Philosophers and sociologists, for example, are still arguing over whether Weber's theory of bureaucracy was in fact a theory, a poignant and scholarly admonition, an evolutionary hypothesis, or a descriptive statement.

However difficult it may be to identify a truly scientific study of the future, most scholars would agree that it should include a number of objectives:

1. It should provide a survey of possible futures in terms of a spectrum of major potential alternatives.

2. It should ascribe to the occurrence of these alternatives some estimates of relative a priori probabilities.

3. It should, for given basic policies, identify preferred alternatives.

4. It should identify those decisions which are subject to control, as well as those developments which are not, whose occurrence would be likely to have a major effect on the probabilities of these alternatives [Helmer, 1969].

With these objectives only dimly in mind, I wrote a paper on the future of organizations (five years ago to the day that this paper was delivered to the American Political Science Association) which was called "Organizational Developments and the Fate of Bureaucracy" (Bennis, 1964). Essentially, it was based on an evolutionary hypothesis which asserted that every age develops a form or organization most appropriate to its genius. I then went on to forecast certain changes in a "postbureaucratic world" and how these changes would affect the structure and environment of human orgnizations, their leadership and motivational patterns, and their cultural and ecological values. A number of things have occurred since that first excursion into the future in September 1964 which are worth mentioning at this point, for they have served to reorient and revise substantially some of the earlier forecasts.

Perhaps only a Homer or Herodotus, or a first-rate folk-rock composer, could capture the tumult and tragedy of the five years since that paper was written and measure their impact on our lives. The bitter agony of Vietnam, the convulsive stirrings of black America, the assassinations, the bloody streets of Chicago have all left their marks. What appears is a panorama that goes in and out of focus as it is expressed through the new, less familiar media, the strikes, injunctions, disruptions, bombings, occupations, the heart attacks of the old, and the heartaches of the young. Strolling in late August 1969 through my own campus, lush, quiet, and sensual, I was almost lulled into thinking that nothing fundamental has happened to America in the past five years. Only the residual graffiti from last spring's demonstrations ("Keep the Pigs Out!" "Be Realistic—Demand the Impossible!"), hanging all but unnoticed in the student union, remind us that something has—though what it is, as the song says, "ain't exactly clear." One continually wonders if what has happened is unique and new ("Are we in France, 1788?" as one student asked), whether what is happening at the universities will spread to other, possibly less fragile institutions, and, finally, whether the university is simply the anvil upon which the awesome problems of our entire society are being hammered out. No one really knows. Despite the proliferation of analyses attributing campus unrest to everything from Oedipal conflicts (the most comforting explanation) to the failure of the Protestant Ethic, the crises continue relentlessly.

In his *Report to Greco,* Nikos Kazantzakis tells us of an ancient Chinese imprecation: "I curse you; may you live in an important age." Thus, we are all damned, encumbered, and burdened, as well as charmed, exhilarated, and fascinated by this curse.

In the rueful words of Bob Dylan:

> Come writers and critics
> Who prophesize with your pen
> And keep your eyes wide
> The chance won't come again.

And don't speak too soon
For the wheel's still in spin
And there's no tellin' who
That it's namin'
For the loser now
Will be later to win
For the times are a-changin'.

Reactions to our spastic times vary. There are at least seven definable types:

1. First and most serious of all are the *militants*, composed for the most part of impotent and dependent populations who have been victimized and infantilized, and who see no way out but to mutilate and destroy the system which has decimated its group identity and pride. Excluded populations rarely define their price for belated inclusion in intellectual terms, which confuses and terrifies the incumbents who take participation for granted.

The *apocalyptics*, who with verbal ferocity burn everything in sight. So, in *Supergrow*, Benjamin DeMott (1969) assumes the persona of a future historian and casts a saddened eye on everyone from the Beatles to James Baldwin, from the *Berkeley Barb* to Alfred Kazin, while contemplating the age of megaweapons. DeMott writes:

> By the end of the sixties the entire articulate Anglo-American community... was transformed into a monster-chorus of damnation dealers, its single voice pitched ever at hysterical level, its prime aim to transform every form of discourse into a blast.

These voices are hot as flamethrowers, searing all that get in their way and usually fired from a vantage point several terrain features away.

3. The *regressors*, who see their world disintegrating and engage in fruitless exercises in nostalgia, keening the present and weeping for a past: orderly, humane, free, civilized, and nonexistent. Someone recently recommended that the university insulate itself from outside pollutants—I suppose he meant students and the community—and set up, medieval Oxford style, a chantry for scholars which he warmly referred to as a "speculatorium."

4. There are the *retreaters*, apathetic, withdrawn, inwardly emigrating and outwardly drugged, avoiding all environments except, at most, a communal "roll your own" or a weekend bash at Esalen, longing for a "peak experience," instant nirvana, hoping to beat out reality and consequence.

5. The *historians,* who are always capable of lulling us to sleep by returning to a virtuous past, demonstrating that the "good old days" were either far better or worse. "The good old days, the good old days," said a Negro comedienne of the *30s,* "I was there; where were they?" I learned recently, for example, that the university, as a quiet place devoted to the pursuit of learning and unaffected by the turbulence of the outside world, is of comparatively recent date, that the experience of the medieval university made the turbulence of recent years seem like a spring zephyr. It was pointed out that a student at the University of Prague cut the throat of a Friar Bishop and was merely expelled, an expedient that may have had something to do with the fact that in dealing with student morals, university officials were constrained to write in Latin.

6. The *technocrats,* who plow heroically ahead, embracing the future and in the process usually forgetting to turn around to see if anybody is following or listening, cutting through waves of ideology like agile surfers.

7. And, finally, the rest of us, "we happy few," the *liberal-democratic reformers,* optimists believing in the perfectibility of man and his institutions, waiting for a solid scientific victory over ideology and irrationality, accepting the inevitability of technology and humanism without thoroughly examining *that* relationship as we do all others, and reckoning that the only way to preserve a democratic and scientific humanism is through inspiriting our institutions with continuous, incremental reform.

The 1964 paper I mentioned earlier was written within the liberal-democratic framework, and it contained many of the inherent problems and advantages of that perspective. The main strategy of this paper and its focus of convenience are to review briefly the main points of that paper, to indicate its shortcomings and lacunae in light of five years' experience (not the least of which has been serving as an administrator in a large, complex public bureaucracy), and then proceed to develop some new perspectives relevant to the future of public bureaucracies. I might add, parenthetically, that I feel far less certainty and closure at this time than I did five years ago. The importance of inventing relevant futures and directions is never more crucial than in a revolutionary period, exactly and paradoxically at the point in time when the radical transition blurs the shape and direction of the present. This is the dilemma of our time and most certainly the dilemma of this paper.

THE FUTURE: 1964 VERSION

Bureaucracy, I argued, was an elegant social invention, ingeniously capable of organizing and coordinating the productive processes of the Industrial Revolution, but hopelessly out-of-joint with contemporary realities. There would be new shapes, patterns, and models emerging which promised drastic changes in the conduct of the organization and of managerial practices in general. In the next 25–50 years, I argued, we should witness and participate in the end of bureaucracy as we know it and the rise of the new social systems better suited to twentieth-century demands of industrialization.

This argument was based on a number of factors:

1. The exponential growth of science, the growth of intellectual technology, and the growth of research and development activities.

2. The growing confluence between men of knowledge and men of power or, as I put it then, "a growing affinity between those who make history and those who write it [Bennis, 1964].

3. A fundamental change in the basic philosophy which underlies managerial behavior, reflected most of all in the following three areas: (a) a new concept of man, based on increased knowledge of his complex and shifting needs, which replaces the oversimplified, innocent push-button concept of man; (b) a new concept of power, based on collaboration and reason, which replaces a model of power based on coercion and fear; and (c) a new concept of organizational values, based on humanistic-democratic ideals, which replaces the depersonalized mechanistic value system of bureaucracy.

4. A turbulent environment which would hold relative uncertainty due to the increase of research and development activities. The environment would become increasingly differentiated, interdependent, and more salient to the organization. There would be greater interpenetration of the legal policy and economic features of an oligopolistic and government-business-controlled economy. Three main features of the environment would be interdependence rather than competition, turbulence rather than a steady, predictable state, and large rather than small enterprises.

5. A population characterized by a younger, more mobile, and better educated work force.

These conditions, I believed, would lead to some significant changes:

The increased level of education and rate of mobility would bring about certain changes in values held toward work. People would tend to *(a)* be more rational, be intellectually committed, and rely more heavily on forms of social influence which correspond to their value system; *(b)* be more "other-directed" and rely on their temporary neighbors and workmates for companionships, in other words, have relationships, not relatives; and *(c)* require more involvement, participation, and autonomy in their work.

As far as organizational structure goes, given the population characteristics and features of environmental turbulence, the social structure in organizations of the future would take on some unique characteristics. I will quote from the original paper.

> First of all, the key word will be temporary: Organizations will become adaptive, rapidly changing temporary systems. Second, they will be organized around problems-to-be-solved. Third, these problems will be solved by relative groups of strangers who represent a diverse set of professional skills. Fourth, given the requirements of coordinating the various projects, articulating points or "linking pin" personnel will be necessary who can speak the diverse languages of research and who can relay and mediate between various project groups. Fifth, the groups will be conducted on organic rather than on mechanical lines; they will emerge and adapt to the problems, and leadership and influence will fall to those who seem most able to solve the problems rather than to programmed role expectations. People will be differentiated, not according to rank or roles, but according to skills and training.
>
> Adaptive, temporary systems of diverse specialists solving problems, coordinated organically via articulating points, will gradually replace the theory and practice of bureaucracy. Though no catchy phrase comes to mind, it might be called an organic-adaptive structure.
>
> (As an aside: what will happen to the rest of society, to the manual laborers, to the poorly educated, to those who desire to work in conditions of dependency, and so forth? Many such jobs will disappear; automatic jobs will be automated. However, there will a corresponding growth in the service-type of occupation, such as organizations like the Peace Corps and AID. There will also be jobs, now being seeded, to aid in the enormous challenge of coordinating activities between groups and organizations. For certainly, consortia of various kinds are growing in number and scope and they will require careful attention. In times of change, where there is a wide discrepancy between cultures and generations, an increase in industrialization, and especially urbanization, society becomes the client for skills in human resources. Let us hypothesize that approximately 40% of the population would be involved in jobs of this nature, 40% in technological jobs, making an organic-adaptive majority with, say, a 20% bureaucratic minority) [Bennis, 1964].

Toward the end of the paper, I wrote that

> The need for instinctual renunciation decreases as man achieves
> rational mastery over nature. In short, organizations of the future
> will require fewer restrictions and repressive techniques because of
> the legitimization of play and fantasy, accelerated through the rise
> of science and intellectual achievements [Bennis, 1964].

To summarize the changes in emphasis of social patterns in the
"postbureaucratic world" I was then describing (using Trist's, 1968,
framework), the following paradigm may be useful:

From	*Toward*
Cultural Values	
Achievement	Self-actualization
Self-control	Self-expression
Independence	Interdependence
Endurance of stress	Capacity for joy
Full employment	Full lives
Organizational Values	
Mechanistic forms	Organic forms
Competitive relations	Collaborative relations
Separate objectives	Linked objectives
Own resources regarded as owned absolutely	Own resources regarded also as society's resources

I hope I have summarized the paper without boring you in the
process. One thing is clear; looking backward, reexamining one's
own work five years later is a useful exercise. Aside from the pro-
tracted decathexis from the original ideas, new experiences and
other emergent factors all help to provide a new perspective which
casts some doubt on a number of assumptions, only half implied
in the earlier statement. For example:

1. The organizations I had in mind then were of a single class:
instrumental, large-scale, science-based, international bureaucracies, operating under rapid growth conditions. Service industries
and public bureaucracies, as well as nonsalaried employees, were
excluded from analysis.

2. Practically no attention was paid to the boundary transactions
of the firm or to interinstitutional linkages.

3. The management of conflict was emphasized, while the strategy of conflict was ignored.

4. Power of all types was underplayed, while the role of the leader as facilitator—"linking pin"— using an "agricultural model" of nurturance and climate building was stressed. Put in Gamson's (1968) terms, I utilized a domesticated version of power, emphasizing the process by which the authorities attempt to achieve collective goals and to maintain legitimacy and compliance with their decisions, rather than the perspective of "potential partisans," which involves diversity of interest groups attempting to influence the choices of authorities.

5. A theory of change was implied, based on gentle nudges from the environment coupled with a truth-love strategy; that is, with sufficient trust and collaboration along with valid data, organizations would progress monotonically along a democratic continuum.

In short, the organizations of the future I envisaged would most certainly be, along with a Bach Chorale and Chartres Cathedral, the epiphany to Western civilization.

The striking thing about truth and love is that whereas I once held them up as the answer to our institution's predicaments, they have now become the problem. And, to make matters worse, the world I envisaged as emergent in 1964 becomes, not necessarily inaccurate, but overwhelmingly problematical. It might be useful to review some of the main organizational dilemmas before going any further, both as a check on the previous forecast, as well as a preface to some new and tentative ideas about contemporary human organizations.

Some New Dilemmas

The Problem of Legitimacy

The key difference between the Berkeley riots of 1964 and the Columbia crisis in May 1969 is that in the pre-Columbian case the major impetus for unrest stemmed from the perceived abuse or misuse of authority ("Do not bend, fold, or mutilate"), whereas the later protest denied the legitimacy of authority. The breakdown of legitimacy in our country has many reasons and explanations, not the least of which is the increasing difficulty of converting political questions into technical-managerial ones. Or, put differently, questions of legitimacy arise whenever "expert power" becomes ineffective. Thus, black militants, drug users, draft resisters, student protestors, and liberated women all deny the legitimacy of those authorities who are not black, drug experienced, pacifists, students, or women.

The university is in an excruciating predicament with respect to the breakdown of legitimacy. Questions about admissions, grades, curriculum, and police involvement—even questions concerning rejection of journal articles—stand the chance of being converted into political-legal issues. This jeopardizes the use of universalistic-achievement criteria, upon which the very moral imperatives of our institutions are based. The problem is related, of course, to the inclusion of those minority groups in our society which have been excluded from participation in American life and tend to define their goals in particularistic and political terms.

Kelman (1969) cites three major reasons for the crisis in legitimacy: *(a)* serious failings of the system in living up to its basic values and in maintaining a proper relationship between means and ends, *(b)* decreasing trust in leadership, and *(c)* dispositions of our current youth. On this last point, Flacks (1969)

> suggests the existence of an increasingly distinct "humanist" subculture in the middle class, consisting primarily of highly educated and urbanized families, based in professional occupations, who encourage humanist orientations in their offspring as well as questioning attitudes to traditional middle class values and to arbitary authority and conventional politics.... Although this humanist subculture represents a small minority of the population, many of its attributes are more widely distributed, and the great increase in the number of college graduates suggests that the ranks of this subculture will rapidly grow.

In short, as the gap between shared and new moralities and authoritative norms (i.e., the law) widens, questions of legitimacy inevitably arise.

Populist versus Elite Functions?

Can American institutions continue to fulfill the possibly incompatible goals of their elitist and populist functions? Again, the American university is an example of this dilemma, for the same institution tries to balance both its autonomous-elite function of disinterested inquiry and criticism and an increasingly service-populist-oriented function. This has been accomplished by insulating the elite (autonomous) functions of liberal education, basic research, and scholarship from the direct impact of the larger society, whose demands for vocational training, certification, service, and the like are reflected and met in the popular functions of the university. As Trow (1969) puts it:

> These insulations take various forms of a division of labor within the university. There is a division of labor between departments, as for example, between a department of English or Classics, and a department of Education. There is a division of labor in the relatively unselective universities between the undergraduate and graduate schools, the former given over largely to mass higher education in the service of social mobility and occupational placement, entertainment, and custodial care, while the graduate departments in the same institutions are often able to maintain a climate in which scholarship and scientific research can be done to the highest standards. There is a familiar division of labor, though far from clear-cut, between graduate departments and professional schools. Among the faculty there is a division of labor, within many departments, between scientists and consultants, scholars and journalists, teachers and entertainers. More dangerously, there is a division of labor between regular faculty and a variety of fringe or marginal teachers—teaching assistants, visitors and lecturers—who in some schools carry a disproportionate load of the mass teaching. Within the administration there is a division of labor between the Dean of Faculty and Graduate Dean, and the Dean of Students. And among students there is a marked separation between the "collegiate" and "vocational" subcultures, on the one hand, and academically or intellectually oriented subcultures on the other [p. 2].

To a certain extent, the genius of American higher education is that it *has* fulfilled both of these functions, to the wonder of all, and especially to observers from European universities. But with the enormous expansion of American universities, proportional strains are being placed on their insulating mechanisms.

Interdependence or Complicity in the Environment

The environment I talked about in 1964, its interdependence and turbulence, is flourishing today. Buy my optimism must now be tempered, for what appeared then to be a "correlation of fates" turns out to have blocked the view of some serious problems. The university is a good example of this tension.

The relationship between the university and its environment has never been defined in more than an overly abstract way. For some, the university is a citadel, aloof, occasionally lobbing in on society the shells of social criticism. Both the radical left and the conservative right seem to agree on this model, maintaining that to yield to the claims of society will fragment and ultimately destroy the university. Others, for different reasons, prefer a somewhat similar model, that of the "speculatorium," where scholars protected by garden walls, meditate away from society's pollutants. Still others envisage the university as an "agent of change," a catalytic institution capable of revolutionizing the nation's organizations and professions. In fact, a recent sociological study listed almost 50 viable goals for the university (Gross, 1968) (a reflection of our ambivalence and confusions as much as anything), and university catalogs usually list them all.

The role of the university in society might be easier to define if it were not for one unpalatable fact. Though it is not usually recognized, the truth is that the university is not self-supporting. The amount available for our educational expenditures (including funds necessary to support autonomous functions) relates directly to the valuation of the university by the general community. The extent to which the university's men, ideas, and research are valued is commensurate with the amount of economic support it receives. (Parsons, 1968). This has always been true. During the Great Awakening, universities educated ministers; during the agricultural and industrial revolutions, the landgrant colleges and engineering schools flourished; during the rise of the service professions, the universities set up schools of social welfare, nursing, public health, and so on. And during the past 30 years or so, the universities have been increasingly geared to educate individuals to man the Galbraithean "technostructure."

Thus, the charge of "complicity" of the universities with the power structure is both valid and absurd; without this alleged complicity, there would be no universities, or only terribly poor ones. In the late 60s, the same attack comes from the New Left. The paradox can be blinding, and often leads to one of two pseudosolutions, total involvement or total withdrawal—pseudosolutions familiar enough on other fronts, for example, in foreign policy.

If I am right that the university must be valued by society in order to be supported, the question is not should the university be involved with society, but what should be the *quality* of this involvement and *with whom?* For years, there has been tacit acceptance of the idea that the univeristy must supply industry, the professions, defense, and the technostructure with the brains necessary to carry on their work. Now there are emerging constituencies, new dependent populations, new problems, many without technical solutions, that are demanding that attention of the university. We are being called upon to direct our limited and already scattered resources to newly defined areas of concern—the quality of life, the shape and nature of human institutions, the staggering problems of the city, legislative processes, and the management of human resources. Will it be possible for the modern university to involve itself with these problems and at the same time avoid the politicization that will threaten its autonomous functions? One thing is clear, we will never find answers to these problems if we allow rational thought to be replaced by a search for villains. To blame the establishment, or Wall Street, or the New Left for our problems is lazy, thoughtless, and frivolous. It would be comforting if we *could* isolate and personalize the problems facing the university, but we cannot.

The last two dilemmas that I have just mentioned, elitist *versus* populist strains vying within a single institution and the shifting, uncertain symbiosis between university and society, contain many of the unclear problems we face today, and I suspect that they account for much of the existential groaning we hear in practically all of our institutions, not just the university.

The Search for the Correct Metaphor

Metaphors have tremendous power to establish new social realities, to give life and meaning to what was formerly perceived only dimly and imprecisely. What *did* students experience before Erikson's "identity crisis"? Greer (1969) wrote recently:

> [But] much of our individual experience is symbolized in vague and unstandardized ways. There is, as we say, no word for it. One of the great contributions of creative scientists and artists is to make communicable what was previously moot, to sense new meanings possible in the emerging nature of human experience, giving them a form which makes communication possible. The phrase-maker is not to be despised, he may be creating the grounds for new social reality. (On the other hand, he may merely be repackaging an old product.) [p. 46]

Most of us have internalized a metaphor about organizational life, however crude that model or vivid that utopia is—or how conscious or unconscious—which governs our perceptions of our social systems. How these metaphors evolve is not clear, although I do not think Freud was far off the mark with his focus on the family, the military, and the church as the germinating institutions.

Reviewing organizational metaphors somewhat biographically, I find that my first collegiate experience, at Antioch College, emphasized a "community democracy" metaphor, obviously valid for a small, town-meeting type of political life. In strong contrast to this was the Massachusetts Institute of Technology, which employed the metaphor (not consciously, of course) of "The Club," controlled tacitly and quite democratically, but without the formal governing apparatus of political democracies, by an "old-boy network," composed of the senior tenured faculty and administration. The State University of New York at Buffalo comes close, in my view, to a "labor-relations" metaphor, where conflicts and decisions are negotiated through a series of interest groups bargaining as partisans. There are many other usable metaphors: Clark Kerr's "City," Mark Hopkins' "student and teacher on opposite ends of a log," "General Systems Analysis," "Therapeutic Community," "Scientific Management," and my own "temporary systems," and so on, that compete with the pure form of bureaucracy, but few of them seem singularly equipped to cope with the current problems facing large-scale institutions.

Macrosystems versus Microsystems

One of the crude discoveries painfully learned during the course of recent administrative experience in a large public bureaucracy turns on the discontinuities between microsystems and macrosystems. For quite a while, I have had more than a passing *theoretical* interest in this problem, which undoubtedly many of you share, but my interest now, due to a sometimes eroding despair, has gone well beyond the purely theoretical problems involved.

My own intellectual "upbringing," to use an old-fashioned term, was steeped in the Lewinian tradition of small-group behavior, processes of social influence, and "action-research." This is not terribly exceptional, I suppose, for a social psychologist. In fact, I suppose that the major methodological and theoretical influences in the social sciences for the last two decades have concentrated on more microscopic, "manageable" topics. Also, it is not easy to define precisely where a microsocial science begins or where a macrosocial science ends. Formally, I suppose, microsystems consist of roles and actors, while macrosystems have as their constituent parts other subsystems, subcultures, and parts of society. In any case, my intellectual heritage has resulted in an erratic batting average in transferring concepts from microsystems into the macrosystem of a university.

An example of this dilemma can be seen in a letter Leonard Duhl wrote in response to an article by Carl Rogers which stressed an increased concern with human relationships as a necessary prerequisite for managing society's institutions. Duhl (1969) wrote:

> Though I agree with [Rogers] heartily, I have some very strong questions about whether, indeed, this kind of future is in the cards for us. I raise this primarily because out of my experiences working in the U.S. Department of Housing and Urban Development and out of experiences working in and with cities, it is clear that in the basic decision making that takes place, the values Dr. Rogers and I hold so dear have an extremely low priority. Indeed, the old-fashioned concerns with power, prestige, money and profit so far outdistance the concerns for human warmth and love and concern that many people consider the latter extremely irrelevant in the basic decision making. Sadly, it is my feeling that they will continue to do so.

The following examples from my own recent experience tend to confirm Duhl's gloomy outlook.

The theory of consensus falters under those conditions where competing groups bring to the conference table vested interests based on group membership, what Mannhein referred to as "perspectivistic orientation." Where goals are competitive and group (or subsystem) oriented, despite the fact that a consensus might rationally create a new situation where all parties may benefit—that is, move closer to the Paretian optimal frontier—a negotiated position may be the only practical solution. There was a time when I believed that consensus was a valid operating procedure. I no longer think this is realistic, given the scale and diversity of organizations. In fact, I have come to think that the quest for consensus, except for some microsystems where it may be feasible, is a misplaced nostalgia for a folk society as chimerical, incidentally, as the American search for "identity."

The collaborative relationship between superiors and subordinates falters as well under those conditions where "subordinates"—if that word is appropriate—are *delegates* of certain subsystems. Under this condition, collaboration may be perceived by constituents as a threat because of perceived cooption or encroachment on their formal, legal right.

Or, to take another example, in the area of leadership, my colleagues at the State University of New York at Buffalo, Hollander and Julian (1969), have written for *Psychological Bulletin* one of the most thoughtful and penetrating articles on the leadership process. In one of their own studies (Julian & Hollander, 1966), reported in this article, they found that aside from the significance of task competence, the "leader's interest in group members and interest in group activity" were significantly related to the group acceptance of the leader. Yet, in macropower situtations, the leader is almost always involved in boundary exchanges with salient interorganizational activities which inescapably reduce, not necessarily interest in group members or activities, but the amount of interaction he can maintain with group members. This may have more the overtones of a rationalization than an explanation, but I know of few organizations where the top leadership's commitment to internal programs and needs fully meets constituent expectations.

In short, interorganizational role set of the leader, the scale, diversity, and formal relations that ensue in a pluralistic system place heavy burdens on those managers and leaders who expect an easy transferability between the cozy gemütlichkeit of a Theory Y orientation and the realities of macropower.

Current Sources for the Adoption or Rejection of Democratic Ideals

I wrote (Bennis, 1966b), not long ago, that

> While more research will help us understand the conditions under which democratic and other forms of governance will be adopted, the issue will never be fully resolved.... I. A. Richards once said that "language has succeeded until recently in hiding from us almost all things we talk about." This is singularly true when men start to talk of complex and wondrous things like democracy and the like.[1] For these are issues anchored in an existential core of personality [p. 35]

Today I am even more confused about the presence or absence of conditions which could lead to more democratic functioning. Somedays I wake up feeling "nasty, brutish, and short," and, other times, feeling benign, generous, and short. This may be true of the general population, for the national mood is erratic, labile, depending on repression or anarchy for the "short" solution to long problems.

Let us consider Lane's (1962) "democraticness scale," consisting of five items: (a) willingness or reluctance to deny the franchise to the "ignorant or careless"; (b) patience or impatience with the delays and confusions of democratic processes; (c) willingness or reluctance to give absolute authority to a single leader in times of threat; *(d)* where democratic forms are followed, degree of emphasis (and often disguised approval) of underlying oligarchical methods; *(e)* belief that the future of democracy in the United States is reasonably secure.

Unfortunately, there has been relatively little research on the "democratic personality," which makes it risky to forecast whether conditions today will facilitate or detract from its effective functioning. On the one hand, there is interesting evidence that would lead one to forecast an increased commitment to democratic ideals. Earlier I mentioned Flacks' (1969) work on the "transformation of the American middle-class family," which would involve increased equality between husband and wife, declining distinctiveness of sex roles in the family, increased opportunity for self-expression on the part of the children, fewer parental demands for self-discipline, and more parental support for autonomous behavior on the part of the children. In addition, the increase in educated persons, whose status is less dependent on property, will likely increase the investment of individuals in having autonomy and a voice in decision making.

On the other hand, it is not difficult to detect some formidable threats to the democratic process which make me extremely apprehensive about an optimistic prediction. Two are basically psychological, one derived from some previous assumptions about the environment, the other derived from some recent personal experience. The third is a venerable structural weakness which at this time takes on a new urgency.

1. Given the turbulent and dynamic texture of the environment, we can observe a growing uncertainty about the deepest human concerns: jobs, neighborhoods, regulation of social norms, life styles, child rearing, law and order; in short, the only basic questions, according to Tolstoi, that interest human beings are How to live? and What to live for? The ambiguities and changes in American life that occupy discussion in university seminars and annual meetings and policy debates in Washington, and that form the backbone of contemporary popular psychology and sociology, become increasingly the conditions of trauma and frustration in the lower middle class. Suddenly the rules are changing—all the rules.

A clashy dissensus of values is already clearly foreshadowed that will tax to the utmost two of the previously mentioned democraticness scale items: "impatience or patience with the delays and confusions of democratic processes" and the "belief that the future of democracy in the United States is reasonably secure."

The inability to tolerate ambiguity and the consequent frustration plus the mood of dissensus may lead to the emergence of a proliferation of "minisocieties" and relatively impermeable subcultures, from George Wallace's blue-collar strongholds to rigidly circumscribed communal ventures. Because of their rejection of incremental reform and the establishment, and their impatience with bureaucratic-pragmatic leadership, their movements and leadership will likely resemble a "revolutionary-charismatic" style (Kissinger, 1966).

2. The personal observation has to do with experience over the past two years as an academic administrator, experience obtained during a particularly spastic period for all of us in the academy.[2] I can report that we, at Buffalo, have been trying to express our governance through a thorough and complete democratic process, with as much participation as anyone can bear. There are many difficulties in building this process, as all of you are undoubtedly aware: the tensions between collegiality and the bureaucratic-pragmatic style of administrators, the difficulty in arousing faculty and students to participate, etc. I might add, parenthetically, that Buffalo, as is true of many state universities, had long cherished a tradition of strong faculty autonomy and academic control. Our intention was to facilitate this direction, as well as encourage more student participation.

When trouble erupted last spring, I was disturbed to discover—to the surprise of many of my colleagues, particularly historians and political scientists—that the democratic process we were building seemed so fragile and certainly weakened in comparison to the aphrodisia of direct action, mass meetings, and frankly autocratic maneuverings. The quiet workings of the bureaucratic-democratic style seemed bland, too complex and prismatic for easy comprehension, and even banal, contrasted to the headlines of the disruptions. Even those of us who were attempting to infuse and reinforce democratic functioning found ourselves caught up in the excitement and chilling risks involved.

Erich Fromm (1941) said it all, I reflected later on, in his *Escape from Freedom*, but what was missing for me in his formulation was the psychic equivalent for democratic participants.

During this same period, I came across a paper by Argyris (1969) which reinforced my doubts about the psychological attractiveness of democracy. Using a 36-category group observational system on nearly 30 groups, in 400 separate meetings, amounting to almost 46,000 behavioral units, he found that only 6 of the 36 categories were used over 75% of the time, and these 6 were "task" items such as "gives information, asks for information," etc. Almost 60% of the groups showed no affect or interpersonal feelings at all, and 24% expressed only 1% affect or feelings. These groups represented a wide cross-section of bureaucratic organizations, research and development labs, universities, and service and business industries.

Argyris' data, along with my own personal experience, have made me wonder if democratic functioning can ever develop the deep emotional commitments and satisfactions that other forms of governance evoke, as for example, revolutionary-charismatic or ideological movements? The question which I leave with you at this time is not the one from the original paper ("Is democracy inevitable?"), but, "Is democracy sexy?"

3. The structural weakness in present-day democracy, using that term in the broadest possible political sense, is the 200-year-old idea first popularized by Adam Smith (1776) in *The Wealth of the Nations.* This was "the idea that an individual who intends only his own gain is led by an invisible hand to promote the public interest." The American Revolution brought about a deep concern for the constitutional guarantees of personal rights and a passionate interest in individuals' emotions and growth, but without a concomitant concern for the community.

In a recent issue of *Science,* Hardin (1968), the biologist, discusses this in an important article, "The Tragedy of the Commons." Herdsmen who keep their cattle on the commons ask themselves: "What is the utility to me to adding one more animal to my herd [p. 1244]?" Being rational, each herdsman seeks to maximize his gain. It becomes clear that by adding even one animal, as he receves all the proceeds from the sale of the additional increment, the positive utility is nearly +1, whereas the negative utility is only a fraction of −1 because the effects of overgrazing are shared by all herdsmen. Thus, "the rational herdsman concludes that the only sensible course for him to pursue is to add another animal to his herd. And another, and another . . . [p. 1244]," until

> Each man is locked into a system that compels him to increase his herd without limit . . . Ruin is the destination toward which all men rush . . . Freedom in a commons brings ruin to all [p. 1244].

A recent, less elegant example along these lines occurred at my own campus where there is a rather strong commitment against institutional racism. A recent form this commitment has taken is the admission of at least double the number of black students ever before admitted. However, more disadvantaged students could have been accepted if the students had chosen to vote for "tripling" in the dormitories. It was voted down overwhelmingly, and it was interesting to observe the editor of the student newspaper supporting increased admission for black students and at the same time opposing tripling.

The democratic process as we know it, expressed through majority vote, contains many built-in guarantees for individual freedom without equivalent mechanisms for the "public interest," as Gans' (1969) recent article in the Sunday Magazine section of *The New York Times* argues.

A character in Balchin's (1949) *A Sort of Traitors* expresses this structural problem with some force:

> You think that people want democracy and justice and peace. You're right. They do. But what you forget is that they want them on their own terms. And their own terms don't add up. They want decency and justice without interference with their liberty to do as they like.

These are the dilemmas as I see them now: the threat to legitimacy of authority, the tensions between populist and elitist functions and interdependence and complicity in the environment, the need for fresh metaphors, the discontinuities between microsystems and macrosystems, and the baffling competition between forces that support and those that suppress the adoption of democratic ideology. All together, they curb my optimism and blur the vision, but most certainly force a new perspective upon us.

A New Perspective

These profound changes lead me to suggest that any forecast one makes about trends in human institutions must take into account the following:

- The need for fundamental reform in the purpose and organization of our institutions to enable them to adapt responsively in an exponentially changing social, cultural, political, and economic environment.
- The need to develop such institutions on a human scale which permit the individual to retain his identity and integrity in a society increasingly characterized by massive, urban, highly centralized governmental, business, educational, mass media, and other institutions.
- The significant movement of young persons who are posing basic challenges to existing values and institutions and who are attempt-

ing to create radical new life styles in an attempt to preserve individual identity or to opt out of society.

• The increasing demands placed upon all American institutions to participate more actively in social, cultural, and political programs designed to improve the quality of American life.

• The accelerating technical changes which require the development of a scientific humanism: a world view of the social and humanistic implications of such changes.

• The necessity of a world movement to bring man in better harmony with his physical environment.

• The need for change toward a sensitive and flexible planning capability on the part of the management of major institutions.

• The rising demand for social and political justice and freedom, particularly from the American black community and other deprived sectors of society.

• The compelling need for world order which gives greater attention to the maintenance of peace without violence between nations, groups, or individuals.

A NEW FORECAST FOR PUBLIC BUREAUCRACY

The imponderables are youth, and tradition, and change. Where these predicaments, dilemmas, and second thoughts take us, I am not exactly sure. However, by way of a summary and conclusion—and at the risk of another five-year backlash, there are a number of trends and emphases worth considering.

The Organization's Response to the Environment Will Continue to Be the Crucial Determinant for Its Effectiveness

Economists and political scientists have been telling us this for years, but only recently have sociologists and social psychologists, like Terreberry (1968), Emery and Trist (1965), Levine and White (1961), Litwak and Hylton (1962), and Evan (1966), done so. To quote Benson Snyder,[3] concerning a recent trip to California universities:

> There is another consequence of this limited response to rapid change. The climate of society becomes suffused and distrait, positions ossified, and one hears expressions of helplessness increase, like dinosaurs on the plains of mud. Each in his own way frantically puts on more weight and thinks this form of strength will serve him. He doesn't know he has lost touch until the mud reaches the level of his eyes.

Three derivatives of this protean environment can be anticipated: First, we will witness new ecological strategies that are capable of anticipating crisis instead of responding to crisis, that require participation instead of consent, that confront conflict instead of dampening conflict, that include comprehensive measures instead of specific measures, and that include a long planning horizon instead of a short planning horizon.

Second, we will identify new roles for linking and correlating interorganizational transactions—"interstitial men."

Third, and most problematical, I anticipate an erratic environment where various organizations coexist at different stages of evolution. Rather than neat, linear, and uniform evolutionary developments, I expect that we will see both more centralization (in large-scale instrumental bureaucracies) and more decentralization (in delivery of health, education, and welfare services); both the increase of bureaucratic-pragmatic and of revolutionary-charismatic leadership; both the increase in size and centralization of many municipal and governmental units and the proliferation of self-contained minisocieties,[4] from the "status-spheres" that Tom Wolfe writes about like Ken Kesey's "electric kool-aid acid-heads" and the pump-house gang of La Jolla surfers to various citizen groups. Ethnic groups organize to "get theirs," and so do the police, firemen, small property owners, and "mothers fighting sex education and bussing," and so on.

Large-Scale Public and Private Bureaucracies Will Become More Vulnerable Than Ever Before to the Infusion of Legislative and Juridical Organs

These probably will become formalized, much like the Inspector General's office in the Army. In one day's issue of a recent *New York Times,* three front-page stories featured: *(a)* the "young Turks" within the State Department who are planning to ask the Department to recognize the Foreign Service Association as the exclusive agent with which the Department would bargain on a wide scale of personnel matters, *(b)* antipoverty lawyers within the Office of Equal Opportunity who have organized for a greater voice in setting policy, and *(c)* the informal caucus of civil rights lawyers in the Justice Department to draft a protest against what they consider a recent softening of enforcement of the civil rights laws.

I have always been fascinated by Harold Lasswell's famous analogy between the Freudian trinity of personality and the tripartite division of the federal government. Most bureaucracies today contain only one formal mechanism, that is, the executive or ego functions. The legislative (id) and the judicial (superego) have long been under-represented; this will likely change.[5]

There Will Be More Legitimization for "Leave-Taking" and
Shorter Tenure at the Highest Levels of Leadership

One aspect of "temporary systems" that was underplayed in my 1964 paper was the human cost of task efficiency. Recently, James Reston observed that the reason it is difficult to find good men for the most responsible jobs in government is that the good men have burnt out, or as my old infantry company commander once said, "In this company, the good guys get killed." Perhaps this creates the appearance of the Peter Principle, that is, that people advance to the level of their greatest incompetence. What is more likely is that people get burnt out, psychologically killed. Many industries are now experimenting with variations on sabbaticals for their executives, and I think it is about time that universities woke up to the fact that a seven-year period, for a legalized moratorium, is simply out of joint with the recurring need for self- and professional renewal.[6]

It may also be that leaders with shorter time horizons will be more effective in the same way that interregnum Popes have proven to be the most competent.

New Organizational Roles Will Develop Emphasizing
Different Loci and Commitments of Colleagueiality

Aside from consultants and external advisory groups, organizations tend to arrogate the full working time and commitments of their memberships. One works for Ford, or the Department of Health, Education and Welfare, or Macy's, or Yale. Moonlighting is permitted, sometimes reluctantly, but there is usually no doubt about the primary organization or where there might be a possible "conflict of interest." This idea of the mono-organizational commitment will likely erode in the future where more and more people will create pluralistic commitments to a number of organizations.

To use my own university as an example once again, we have set up one new experimental department which includes three different kinds of professors, different in terms of their relatedness and loci to the department. There is a core group of faculty with full-time membership in the department. There is an associated faculty with part-time commitments to the department, but whose appointment is in another department. And finally, there is a "network faculty," who spend varying periods of time in the department, but whose principal affiliation is with another university or organization. Similar plans are now being drawn up for students.

Similarly, a number of people have talked about "invisible colleges" of true colleagues, located throughout the world, who convene on special occasions, but who communicate mainly by telephone, the mail, and during hasty meetings at airports. I would wager that these "floating crap-games" will increase, and that we will see at least three distinct sets of roles emerge within organizations: those that are *pivotal* and more or less permanent; those that are *relevant*, but not necessarily permanent; and those that are *peripheral*. A person who is pivotal and permanent to one organization may have a variety of relevant and peripheral roles in others.

There are many reasons for this development. First and most obvious is the fact that we live in a jet age where air travel is cheap and very accessible. (A good friend of mine living in Boston commutes daily to New York City for his analytic hour and manages to get back to his office by about 10:30 A.M.) Second, the scarcity of talent and the number of institutions "on the make" will very likely lead more of the top talent to start dividing their time among a number of institutions. Third, the genuine motivational satisfaction gained from working within a variety of comparable institutions seems to be important not for all, but among an increasingly growing fraction of the general population.

We must educate our leaders in at least two competencies: *(a)* to cope efficiently, imaginatively, and perceptively with information overload. Marxist power was property. Today, power is based on control of relevant information. *(b)* As Michael (1968) says in his *The Unprepared Society:*

> We must educate for empathy, compassion, trust, nonexploitiveness, nonmanipulativeness, for self-growth and self-esteem, for tolerance of ambiguity, for acknowledgement of error, for patience, for suffering.

Without affective competence, and the strength that comes with it, it is difficult to see how the leader can confront the important ethical and political decisions without succumbing to compromise or to "petite Eichmannism."

We will observe in America a society which has experienced the consequences of unpreparedness and which has become more sanguine about the effects of planning—more planning not to restrict choice or prohibit serendipity, but to structure possibilities and practical visions.

Whether or not these forecasts are desirable, assuming their validity for the moment, really depends on one's status, values, and normative biases. One man's agony is another's ecstasy. It does appear as if we will have to reckon with a number of contradictory and confusing tendencies, however, which can quickly be summarized:

1. More self- and social consciousness with respect to the governance of public bureaucracies.

2. More participation in this governance by the clients who are served, as well as those doing the service, including lower levels of the hierarchy.

3. More formal, quasi-legal processes of conflict resolution.

4. More direct confrontations when negotiation and bargaining processes fail.

5. More attention to moral-ethical issues relative to technical efficiency imperatives.

6. More rapid turnover and varying relationships within institutions.

I think it would be appropriate if I concluded this paper with a quote from the earlier 1964 paper which still seems valid and especially pertinent in light of the new perspectives gained over the past five years. I was writing about the educational requirements necessary for coping with a turbulent environment (Bennis, 1964):

> Our educational system should (1) help us to identify with the adaptive process without fear of losing our identity, (2) increase tolerance of ambiguity without fear of losing intellectual mastery, (3) increase our ability to collaborate without fear of losing our individuality, and (4) develop a willingness to participate in social evolution while recognizing implacable forces. In short, we need an educational system that can help make a virtue out of contingency rather than one which induces hesitancy or its reckless companion, expedience.

REFERENCES

Argyris, C. The incompleteness of social-psychological theory: Examples from small group, cognitive consistency, and attribution research. *American Psychologist*, 1969, **24**, 893-908.

Balchin, N. *A sort of traitors*. New York: Collins, 1949.

Bennis, W. G. Organizational developments and the fate of bureaucracy.

Paper presented at the annual meeting of the American Psychological Association, Los Angeles, September 4, 1964.

Bennis, W. G. Organizational developments and the fate of bureaucracy. *Industrial Management Review*, 1966, **7**, 41-55. (a)

Bennis, W. G. When democracy works. *Trans-action*, 1966, **3**, 35. (b)

Bennis, W. G. Future of the social sciences. *Antioch Review*, 1968, **28**, 227.

DeMott, B. *Supergrow*. New York: Dutton, 1969.

Duhl, L. Letter to the editor. *Journal of Applied Behavioral Science*, 1969, **5**, 279-280.

Emery, F. E., & Trist, E. L. The causal texture of organizational environments. *Human Relations*, 1965, **18**, 1-10.

Evan, W. M. The organization-set: Toward a theory of interorganizational relationships. In J. D. Thompson (Ed.), *Approaches to organizational design*. Pittsburgh: University of Pittsburgh Press, 1966.

Flacks, R. Protest or conform: Some social psychological perspectives on legitimacy. *Journal of Applied Behavioral Science*, 1969, **5**, 127-150.

Fromm, E. *Escape from freedom*. New York: Farrer & Rinehart, 1941.

Gamson, W. A. *Power and discontent*. Homewood, Ill.: Dorsey Press, 1968.

Gans, H. J. We won't end the urban crisis until we end majority rule. *New York Times Magazine*, 1969, **119** (August 3), Section 6.

Greer, S. *The logic of social inquiry*. Chicago: Aldine, 1969.

Gross, E. Universities as organizations: A research approach. *American Sociological Review*, 1968, **33**, 518-544.

Hardin, G. The tragedy of the commons. *Science*, 1968, **162**, 1243-1248.

Helmer, O. Political analysis of the future. Paper presented at the annual meeting of the American Political Science Association, New York, September 4, 1969.

Hollander, E. P., & Julian, J. W. Contemporary trends in the analysis of leadership processes. *Psychological Bulletin*, 1969, **71**, 387-397.

Julian, J. W., & Hollander, E. P. A study of some role dimensions of leader-follower relations. (Tech. Rep. No. 3, Office of Naval Research Contract No. 4679) State University of New York at Buffalo, Department of Psychology, April 1966.

Kelman, H. C. In search of new bases for legitimacy: Some social psychological dimensions of the black power and student movements. Paper presented at the Richard M. Elliott Lecture, University of Michigan, April 21, 1969.

Kissinger, H. A. Domestic structures and foreign policy. *Daedalus*, 1966, **96**, 503-529.

Lane, R. E. *Political ideology*. New York: Free Press, 1962.

Levine, S., & White, P. E. Exchange as a conceptual framework for the study of interorganizational relationships. *Administrative Science Quarterly*, 1961, **6**, 583-601.

Litwak, E., & Hylton, L. Interorganizational analysis: A hypothesis on coordinating agencies. *Administrative Science Quarterly*, 1962, **6**, 395-420.

Michael, D. *The unprepared society*. New York: Basic Books, 1968.

Parsons, T. The academic system: A sociologist's view. *The Public Interest*, 1968, **13**, 179-197.

Sartori, G. Democracy. In E. R. A. Seligman (Ed.), *Encyclopedia of Social Sciences*. New York: Macmillan, 1957.

Terreberry, S. The evolution of organizational environments. *Administrative Science Quarterly*, 1968, **12**, 590-613.

Trist, E. *The relation of welfare and development in the transition to, post-industrialism*. Los Angeles: Western Management Science Institute, University of California, 1968.

Trow, M. Urban problems and university problems. Paper presented at the 24th All-University Conference, University of California at Riverside, March 23-25, 1969.

NOTES

[1] See Sartori (1957). "No wonder, therefore, that the more 'democracy' has become to be a universally accepted honorific term, the more it has undergone verbal stretching and has become the loosest lable of its kind [p. 112]."

[2] I am reminded here of Edward Holyoke's remark, written over 200 years ago on the basis of his personal experience: "If any man wishes to be humbled or mortified, let him become President of Harvard College."

[3] B. Snyder, personal communication, 1969.

[4] Sometimes it is difficult to distinguish the reform groups from the reaction groups, except that the affluent, particularly the young, uncommitted affluent, have already begun to invent and manage environments, cutting across class and ethnic lines, that reflect unique life styles. And these begin and end as rapidly as boutiques on Madison Avenue, which in many ways they resemble, rather than the massive, more familiar conglomerates of yesteryear.

[5] The labor unions have been relatively unsuccessful in organizing either top levels of management or professionals. They have failed to do so, in my view, because they have operated at the lowest level of the Maslow hierarchy of needs, economic, physiological, safety, failing to understand the inducements of most professionals: achievement, recognition, intrinsic quality of work, and professional development. Ironically, this has provided more "due process" and, in some cases, more legitimate participation to nonsalaried employees than to higher level personnel. It is no coincidence that the cutting edge of last year's French revolution, in addition to the students, were middle-class professional employees and technicians.

According to William Evan (1966), the lack of "due process" for the high-ranking managerial and professional personnel has led to or reinforced the "organization man."

[6] At Buffalo, we have tried to develop a policy whereby all administrators would hold an academic appointment as well as an administrative post. They would be expected to return to their academic calling after no longer than 5, possibly 10, years. The response to this formulation was less than positive, and I suspect that the basic reason for its unpopularity was the psychological blow to the self-concept which equates role-leaving (without manifest promotion) to failure.

35. Urban Renewal in 2000

Marion Clawson

The following article focuses on those reinforcing agents and policies which guide our behavior in the physical development of communities. Of specific concern in the article are the existing tax laws which reward owners for allowing their property to depreciate. Clawson suggests some alterations in these laws. In addition, some rather controversial suggestions are made, such as extending the power of eminent domain, under limited conditions, to private developers.

The article is thoughtful and provocative. It broadens the range of alternative intervention strategies. Moreover, it deals with problems which are becoming a major concern to those persons who are venturing out of their traditionally defined professional roles, and attempting to truly deal with the many interrelated facets of "community."

The Future Urban Renewal Problem

How great will the urban renewal problem of the future be? Considering how most cities have grown recently, and how comparatively young the buildings are in large parts of most cities, one intuitively feels that the problems of replacement and renewal have never been so great as the size of the cities would normally lead one to expect. That is, most cities have grown, providing new housing and new commercial districts at the margin, allowing the older sections to "filter down" to lower income occupants and users. The filtering down process, however, must some day come to an end—filtering down can slide into literally breaking down, as structures ultimately become unusable. Age of structure is not the only factor affecting the value and usability of a dwelling unit or of a commercial property, but it is almost certainly, in practice, an important factor. Good maintenance of the individual property, and, far more important, good maintenance of the *community*, in

507

the social as well as in the physical sense, may forestall depreciation and decay for relatively long periods. Good maintenance postpones the day of renewal, and this may be extremely important to racial and income groups dependent upon aged housing. But even the best maintenance will not obviate the need of eventual rebuilding, at least for most dwellings. In housing, as in automobiles and most durable consumer goods, American productive efficiency is vastly greater for the building of new ones than for the repair and rebuilding of older ones. It is at least arguable that it is good economics to count on a relatively rapid rate of building clearance and rebuilding, rather than to seek more extensive rehabilitation of existing buildings. Technological change and change in tastes have also operated to make much housing seriously outdated while yet physically capable of restoration.

Age of Present Housing

If age of structure is an important factor in value and usability of housing, then it is readily possible to estimate how much "old" housing there will be at any future date and where it will be. For what will be "old" a few decades from now is certainly middle aged today. This is what might be called a housing demographic approach. Not only is the demographic approach used to estimate total population and working force, but it has been used to estimate age distribution of autos at future dates and to estimate fruit and nut production at future periods.[1] The house that will be 70 years old 30 years from now is 40 years old now, obviously; but, of course, not all houses now 40 years old may still be here in 30 years. This approach to estimating future housing and its age can be relatively simple or more sophisticated, depending largely upon the data available.

Table 1 provides one estimate of housing unit age, from 1890 to 1960; the method for deriving this estimate is described in the Appendix.[2] Somewhat different methods, using alternative assumptions or estimates at various points in the estimating process,

[1]Marion Clawson, Carl P. Heisig, and Edgar B. Hurd, "Longterm Forecasting of Fruit and Nut Production," *Journal of Farm Economics*, 23, No. 3 (August 1941).

[2]This was written originally before Harry B. Wolfe's research note, "Models for Condition Aging of Residential Structures," appeared in the May 1967 issue of the *Journal*. His approach is more elegant than mine; it applies to one city and uses data not available for all cities; but considerable similarity exists between our results.

Table 1
Estimated Total Housing Units at Each Census,
1890 to 1960, by Decade Originally Built [a]

Period built	Housing units (millions)							
	1890	1900	1910	1920	1930	1940	1950	1960
Before 1890	(13.5)[b]	(9.6)	(7.4)	(6.2)	(3.4)	(3.9)	(4.7)	(2.9)
1890–1899	..	(6.9)	(6.7)	(6.5)	(6.2)	(5.8)	(5.4)	(4.9)
1900–1909	..	..	(6.9)	(6.7)	(6.5)	(6.2)	(5.8)	(5.4)
1910–1919	..	..	..	(6.6)	(6.4)	(6.2)	(5.9)	(5.6)
1920–1929	..	..	..	..	(9.5)	9.2	(8.9)	(8.6)
1930–1939	..	..	..	..	..	6.0	(5.8)	(5.6)
1940–1949	..	..	..	..	..	..	9.6	(9.3)
1950–1959	..	..	..	..	..	..	..	16.0
Total	(13.5)	(16.5)	(21.0)	(26.0)	(32.0)	37.3	46.1	58.3

[a] For derivation of this table, see Appendix.

[b] ( ) = estimates, derived as follows:

1. Totals for 1890 to 1930, reported occupied dwelling units, as shown in Table 2, adjusted upward to total housing units;

2. For all lines except the top one, census to census period declines based upon Figure 1; and

3. Top line calculated as difference between other items and total.

would have produced somewhat different results, but the essential features of the present housing stock, as far as age is concerned, would have remained roughly the same under any reasonable alternative estimates. These estimates might be improved, in the future, in one or more of several ways. For instance, this estimate is for housing on a national basis. The same sort of analysis might be made for individual cities or metropolitan areas, to see how well it would apply to them, and how closely the curves for one city conformed to those for others. In addition to this statistical manipulation, some date might be collected as to the age of residential structures demolished, although available data on demolishment are particularly scanty. Some research might be undertaken to ascertain why buildings of different ages were replaced, while others of the same age were not. It is obvious that factors other than age affect the need to demolish and/or replace residential structures; buildings of a given age cohort are not all replaced during the same decade. It would be most helpful if we had a frequency distribution of actual building demolishment, and of the reasons for it.

Table 1 presents a reasonable estimate of *past* practice in demolishment and replacement of residential structures. But it was not inevitable, I think, that demolishment and replacement should have followed this pattern; some other pattern might have been possible in the past. Still less do I regard it as inevitable that this pattern be followed in the future; other programs might be adopted, given the desire to do so.

Projected Housing Age and Housing Removals

On the assumption that future practice of residential demolishment will follow the general pattern of the past, and on the basis of the methodology developed in the Appendix, it is possible to construct Table 2, showing at each Census period up to 2000 the

Table 2
Housing Units Removed and Remaining by Decades

		(NUMBERS IN MILLIONS)							
	Actual	*Estimated*				*Estimated to be removed*			
Period built	*in 1960*	*remaining in*				*in decade of*			
		1970	*1980*	*1990*	*2000*	*1960's*	*1970's*	*1980's*	*1990's*
Before 1890	2.9	1.6	.5	.1	0	1.3	1.1	.4	.1
1890–1899	4.9	4.0	2.3	.6	.1	.9	1.7	1.7	.5
1900–1909	5.4	4.9	4.0	2.3	.6	.5	.9	1.7	1.7
1910–1919	5.6	5.2	4.7	3.8	2.2	.4	.5	.9	1.6
1920–1929	8.6	8.1	7.5	6.8	5.5	.5	.6	.7	1.3
1930–1939	5.6	5.4	5.1	4.7	4.3	.2	.3	.4	.4
1940–1949	9.3	9.0	8.6	8.2	7.6	.3	.4	.4	.6
1950–1959	16.0	15.5	15.0	14.4	13.6	.5	.5	.6	.8
Total	58.3	53.7	47.7	40.9	33.9	4.6	6.0	6.8	7.0

estimated numbers of housing units remaining from the 1960 stock and the estimated number to be removed in each decade. Although nearly all of the housing units constructed before World War I would be gone by 2000 according to these estimates, the fact that so much of the housing stock in 1960 had been constructed in comparatively recent years means that almost 60 percent of it would still be more or less livable in 2000; more than half of this would be post World War II housing. Nearly 13 million housing units in 2000, however, would be more than 60 years of age. Some may question how livable these will be, particularly in view of the high income society most economists envisage for the year 2000.

The number of housing units to be removed by decades climbs steadily, on the basis of these estimates, from 4½ million in the 1960's to 7 million in the 1990's. A small proportion of these, in each decade, will succumb to fire, other natural disasters, or to bulldozers clearing the site for conversion to other uses. The great majority of them, however, would be removed for renewal of the site for further housing usage. It may greatly be doubted that "natural" economic forces will lead to any such residential urban renewal. By the 1990's this residential renewal would cost something in the magnitude of $10 billion annually—a sum wholly within the economy's capacity to bear at that time, but still greatly out of line with any expenditure for this purpose up to now. Moreover, I think the estimate of the size of the residential renewal task in 2000 is on the moderate or low side. As noted, many of the housing units listed for continued occupancy in 2000 would be old and probably outdated; and, to the estent that renewal in the intervening years lagged, a backlog of existing but unusable, or barely usable, housing units from an earlier day would still remain.

Renewal in the 1990's, on this basis, still would be nearly half the rate of new house construction during the 1950's. To the extent that residential renewal did not occur at this scale, the amount of new housing construction on the suburban fringe would have to be larger, with consequent effects upon the areal extent and shape of cities.

This projection of probable future removals of residential units, based upon estimated average past experience, might consciously be modified to produce different results. For instance, governments at all levels and many private organizations might try to stimulate renovation of older residences, to keep them in tolerable-to-good condition a few more years. Even to add one decade, on the average, to the life of a housing unit before it was pulled down would add considerably to the supply of older housing. This would be especially important to low-income tenants who are highly dependent upon very old housing. Assuming that the new housing that could be built on this site was in fact built elsewhere, so that a longer retention of the old housing meant an added total supply of housing, this might help reduce rents for these older structures. A program of this kind, to the extent it were successful, would yield different estimates for each decade as to the probable number of housing units to be pulled down. But the problem of removing older housing units, and of replacing them with newer ones, would still remain; the precise structures and areas involved in a decade would be different, as might be the total numbers.

It would be possible in any city to estimate the general location of the renewal areas by decades, using this general approach. One could either map them solely on the basis of date of original construction of the housing units, or this could be modified by any available evidence as to the trend in maintenance of buildings and of the community. We have not tried to do this, partly to avoid unduly lengthening this article; but it does not present any specially difficult methodological or data problems. It might be objected that future events would make such projections inaccurate. For instance, a neighborhood which saw that it was slated for renewal in 20 or 40 years might be moved to provide better maintenance and thus postpone the renewal date. This would, of course, be a highly desirable outcome. The opposite possibility also exists, however: seeing that fairly early renewal seemed probable, people might flee the area or neglect the exising buildings, certainly an undesirable outcome. Changes of this sort, however, would not constitute evidence of the inaccuracy of the projections.

Stimulation of Private Urban Renewal

How can urban renewal, especially renewal for residential purposes, be accomplished in the future on anything like the required scale? A continuation of public urban renewal programs is probable, and, from my point of view, desirable. Such programs are likely to lead to some public benefits that would be lacking under wholly private renewal activities. But it seems completely unrealistic to expect public urban renewal activities of sufficient magnitude to meet the need unaided. The most probable alternatives are accumulated backlogs of decayed and uninhabitable or nearly uninhabitable housing, or else some stimulation of private efforts at urban renewal.

There seem to be at least three major obstacles to private urban renewal for residential purposes: cost of clearing sites, difficulties of land assembly into economic units, and a number of public policies which positively encourage retention of old buildings and discourage construction of new buildings. To these must be added, of course, the fact that many low-income families cannot pay the cost of new housing; but the foregoing obstacles arise even for the construction of housing for middle- and higher-income people. Even if one assumed that lower-income people would get enough filtered-down housing from the present stock, or that rent supplements were adopted on a large scale, or that economic progress eliminated the poor, the obstacles to urban renewal still would remain serious.

Public Programs to Assist Private Site Clearance

Demolition of existing structures and clearing of the site for the building of new housing are minor parts of the total cost of the new housing, yet they are costs, and sometimes may be the deciding factor between building new housing on a site now used for housing, as compared with building it on a site now vacant. If a site has an unusable housing unit on it, the value of that unit is less than zero. It may pay to clear the site for a parking lot or some other unimproved or temporary use, but this is usually true only for sites relatively close to commercial or industrial areas; it is unlikely to be true for most large areas of present housing that should be cleared over the next few decades.

It would be perfectly possible to develop a program which would make the clearance of old housing sites costless or even profitable. For instance, if a surcharge of 0.1 percent interest were added to each loan based on housing, the sum to be paid into an escrow account which would always stay with the property, and which could be used only for site clearance, the time would come in the life of every housing unit when it would pay to clear the site. This proposal is illustrated in Figure 1, where the original cost of the building is estimated at $10,000 and the use value of the structure is assumed to decline steadily to zero at 80 years. If the housing property originally carried a 90 percent loan, then 0.1 percent added to the interest would produce $9 a year. Even without allowing any interest on this escrow account, its accumulated amount would exceed the use value of the housing unit before the latter's value fell to zero; if interest were allowed, the date at which the sum in the escrow account would exceed the use value would be earlier, the exact time depending upon the interest rate. The matter of no interest versus accumulated interest on the escrow account will be considered later. The figures used, of course, are only for purposes of illustration.

If a program of this kind were required of all lending institutions whose operations were in any way supervised by federal agencies or whose depositors were in any way insured by the federal government, a substantial proportion of all housing units would accumulate a site clearance sum. For housing units built after such a program were initiated, or for older ones not more than perhaps

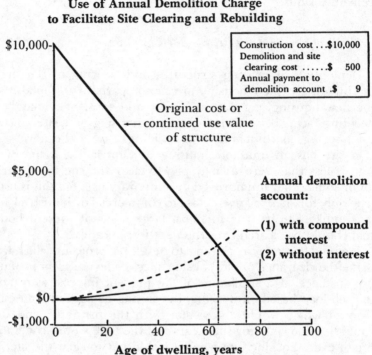

FIGURE 1
Use of Annual Demolition Charge
to Facilitate Site Clearing and Rebuilding

20 years old, a site clearance surcharge of 0.1 percent would generally provide enough money to clear the site by the time the structure
was no longer livable. For older structures, the site clearance account
would meet only part of the costs unless the federal government
supplemented it by payments to cover the years before the program
goes fully into effect.

It can be argued that, if a demolition account for each housing
unit is desirable, it should be established as a special tax on all
housing units rather than as part of loans. There are, however,
at least two arguments, one of administrative efficiency and the
other of political acceptability, in favor of using the loan approach.
Since most residential properties are under loan during a considerable part of their lives, and since escrow arrangements for real
estate taxes and fire insurance are typical for such loans, the addition
of a special demolition account could be accomplished easily and
relatively inexpensively. Since the federal government now exercises major influence or supervision over all institutions lending
upon private housing, the addition of a demolition account would

involve less break with the past than the establishment of a new demolition tax. It could also be argued that all demolition payments should be paid into a single fund, and that payments out of it should be made upon application and upon the need to assist in site clearance. I think, however, there are important advantages in a fund specifically tied to a particular piece of property, and to an account usable by any owner of that property whenever, in his judgment, the cleared site is worth more than the declining structure. These are all details, arguable and subject to compromise; but a site clearance account, however established, that provided funds to a property owner specifically for site clearance, would be a major help in getting sites cleared of housing no longer usable.

Public Programs to Assist Private Land Assembly

The land assembly problem is serious for urban renewal—indeed, as we have noted, one of the major contributions of the public urban renewal programs of the past has been land assembly. Even if all the housing units in an area are equally old and equally in need of replacement, it does not follow that their owners are all equally willing to sell. There are often great gains in being the last holdout in a land assembly scheme; the assembler, having already spent a lot, and in desperate need of the remaining tract, may be forced to a premium price. Even when this problem does not arise, the time and skill that must go into land assembly for a new housing project are usually costly.

Typically, the landownership units in a decadent housing area are much smaller than the landownership units must be in an economically viable new housing development on the same site. This is obvious when the conversion is from single family dwellings to apartments. But it is no less true when the conversion is from old single family dwellings to new single family dwellings. If a builder is to have an economic operation today or in the future, he must control a large area—not necessarily every tract, but most of them, and preferably all of them within his area of building.

Moreover, for some of the oldest housing which will have to be replaced, the age of housing units in a locality may differ considerably. Before World War II, generally one or a few houses were built in a particular location, often among older housing. In such neighborhoods, an economical renewal of housing may require scrapping some houses before the very last years of livability have been used up. In most recent years, house builders have typically built larger subdivisions. But the unit of housing construction in a few decades may well be a still larger neighborhood, requiring much larger areas of land.

The land assembly problem for private urban renewal could be largely resolved if states would give private developers the power of eminent domain under carefully controlled conditions. To those who may think this is radical or dangerous, let us point out again that the program of public urban renewal has operated to do just this. The process might be simplified if the private developer were permitted to do it directly, without public agencies serving as "middlemen." The developer should then be held to the following conditions:

1. He should own or have under option by far the greater part of the total area he sought—perhaps as much as 80 percent; his power to use eminent domain would be limited thereby to only a small proportion of the total area.

2. The area within which he could exercise this power should be naturally bounded, that is, delimited by water bodies, streets, highways, city boundaries, or other major landmarks. An alternative might be to extend the power of eminent domain only to tracts enclaved by land which the developer owned or for which he had options. What we are trying to avoid is voluntary acquisition of a larger area as a base from which to reach out, by use of eminent domain, for a separate and rather different kind of area.

3. The area and its proposed new use should conform to the general plans of the relevant public planning body, and the developer should be required to post bond or otherwise guarantee development in accordance with such plans. We would not limit this power to renewal for residential purposes only, but a developer should not be allowed to acquire an area under a proposal to develop it for residences and then in fact do something else with it; or to acquire it for one kind of housing and in fact build some other kind.

The power of eminent domain is not a magic wand for solving all land assembly problems. Anyone who has had experience with its use knows that one still pays high for the land he gets—in time and trouble as well as in cash. Its main advantage, perhaps, is that it makes serious bargaining between present owner and possible developer purposeful, and places some limits on obstructionism by the last holdouts.

One might, with reason, doubt that states would give the power of eminent domain to private builders. The argument that this might be essential for private residential renewal might indeed be insufficient to sway legislatures, even legislatures no longer rural-dominated. It is here that the difference between a no-interest and a compound-accumulated-interest site clearance account, such as was illustrated in Figure 1, could be decisive. The federal government might limit the granting of compound-accumulated interest to site developers in states which extended to them the power of eminent domain; elsewhere, developers would only be entitled to the no-interest clearance fund. The promise of added federal or quasi-federal funds would be a strong lever against state recalcitrance, and might give builders and developers more incentive to fight for this power.

Federal and Local Tax Policy to Stimulate Private Urban Renewal

Federal income tax policy and local real estate tax policy now combine to make profitable the retention of old buildings and to discourage the construction of new buildings, especially for rental housing but to some extent for owner-occupancy housing. Although tax policy can be changed only with difficulty, taxes are such a powerful weapon influencing private business action that their use for this purpose should be carefully explored.

Federal income tax law permits the owner of a business or income property to deduct depreciation on the price he paid for structures, regardless of how much any former owner may have claimed as depreciation on them. The law might be changed to permit the owner of rental housing to deduct depreciation on buildings at any rate he chose, within the limits of his net income from that property, but might stipulate that whatever fraction of the value was deducted by one owner could not be claimed as depreciation by later owners. The purchaser of an apartment house, under this arrangement, could use all the net income as depreciation, paying no income taxes, until the value of the structure was fully depreciated; but then neither he nor any subsequent owner could claim any further depreciation. Such an arrangement presumably would apply to existing ownerships at the time the law was passed, as well as to new ones. To the extent that one owner did not completely depreciate the value of the buildings for tax purposes, successive owners would be permitted to take over the remaining balance. Under this arrangement, the book value of a housing structure would ordinarily fall quickly. A subsequent owner could not obtain a large net income by depreciation on the price he paid. Owners or potential owners consequently would find it profitable to replace such buildings much more quickly than they do now.

Local real estate taxes apply to both buildings and land and, if a property is rebuilt or improved, the taxes are raised. Advocates of the single tax, from Henry George on down, have argued for a tax on land only, based upon its potential use and value, and no tax on improvements. A shift of this kind would almost certainly mean vastly higher taxes on land, as such, than now; the loss in assessed value of the buildings would have to be made up, at least in large part, by increases in taxes on the land. But it might mean no more and possibly less, taxes on the land and buildings together, for any particular property owner. To the extent that any significant part of the present tax on housing, especially on rental housing, could be shifted away from buildings and onto land, the incentive for residential renewal would be vastly greater. If the owner would be required to pay no more taxes for a property with a relatively new and well-kept housing unit than he would have to pay for an old and rundown one, there would be considerable incentive to build a new house or apartment house and thereby obtain a higher rental.

Proposals for shifting some real estate taxes away from improvements and onto land have been made many times but have gotten nowhere. In most states, a constitutional change would be necessary, and there is substantial local political opposition. As far as we know, there has never been a proposal for a federal incentive to such revision of local tax policy, but it would be readily possible to devise a significant federal financial incentive. The federal tax policy on income-residential property, suggested above, and the federal tax allowance in individual income tax returns for real estate taxes paid on homes owned and occupied by the taxpayer, could be made conditional on state law which required twice as high, or a higher rate of assessment in relation to market value for land as it required for improvements. This might be described as one step toward a single land tax. Improvements would still be taxed, but at a relatively reduced rate, and land would be taxed comparatively more. There is nothing magical in the twice as high or higher ratio of land to improvement assessments; I simply thought this might be politically possible when full single taxes would not, and that it would be sufficient to provide a real incentive. The significant aspect of my suggestion is that federal legislation could be made a powerful instrument affecting local policy on real estate taxes.

In Summary

The urban renewal problem in 2000 will be vastly greater than it is today. While public urban renewal programs are desirable, it seems highly unlikely that they will be adequate in scope. Unless the structure and form of present cities are to be seriously distorted, private urban renewal programs should be stimulated. The three major obstacles to private urban renewal are site clearance costs, land assembly problems, and federal and local tax policies which encourage holding of old buildings and discourage the building of new ones. Definite proposals for overcoming these obstacles are made—proposals which could be effective individually but would be more effective together. These proposals would by no means solve all housing problems, especially those for lower income people, but they should help promote a greater participation by private developers in the rebuilding of decadent residential areas.

Appendix: Derivation of Estimates of Housing by Age Groups

Unfortunately, available data on age of housing units leave much to be desired, both as to detail and accuracy. Censuses of housing obtain information on the dates when the structures were first built. However, in a great many cases neither the present owner nor the occupant knows when a structure was originally built; this is likely to be especially true for older structures, often occupied by low-income and perhaps not well educated tenants. Each census has rightly focused attention on the number of dwelling units built within the previous decade; information about these is almost certainly more accurate than for older structures, and there is often a great deal of interest in new housing.

The best available information as to age of all housing units in the United States is summarized in Table 3, in a form that permits a time comparison of the data. "Housing units" include houses, apartments, trailers, and even boats if lived in as the main housing place, and include second as well as first homes, vacant as well as occupied places, but include only habitable places. In each census, information was sought as to the date the structure was originally built, irrespective of later remodeling or additions. With the passage of time, some older structures may be converted into more housing units, especially by subdivision of large old houses into smaller apartments, thus making it possible to have more housing units in later rather than in earlier years. However, in some cases the opposite occurs—there is a *reduction* in housing units caused by the conversion of dwellings into commercial or industrial or service functions. Although we have little data on conversions,

TABLE 3

Number of Housing Units in the United States
By Period in Which Originally Built [a]

1940 Census[b]		1950 Census		1960 Census	
Period built	Housing units (1,000)	Period built	Housing units (1,000)	Period built	Housing units (1,000)
1909 and earlier	15,264	1919 and earlier		1929 and earlier	
1910–1919	6,940		21,104		27,121
1920–1929	9,169	1920–1929	9,280		
1930–1939	5,952	1930–1939	6,162	1930–1939	6,512
		1940–1949	9,591	1940–1949	8,640
				1950–1959	16,046
Total reported 37,325		Total reported 46,137		Total reported 58,318	

[a] Based upon data in Table M, p. xxxiv, United States Census of Housing 1960—United States Summary, States and Small Areas, Final Report HC (1)–1.
[b] Omits Alaska and Hawaii.

it is doubtful that they result in much net gain in housing units. Furthermore, every year some structures of each age class are destroyed by fire, flood, or other natural disasters, or are torn down so that the site may be used for other purposes; these forces always operate to reduce the number of structures of a given age-of-origin class. Thus, one would expect to find the total number of housing units in each age-of-origin class declining from census to census—slowly at first, more rapidly later.

A quick inspection of Table 3 shows some of the inaccuracies in the data mentioned above. In the 1940 census, nearly 6 million housing units were reported to have been built in the ten preceding years; since these would have been relatively new, presumably their occupants and owners were rather accurately informed about when they were built. In the 1950 census, more than 200,000 additional housing units in this cohort were reported, and in the 1960 census more than half a million units had been added. These latter two figures seem impossible; there almost certainly was some net decrease in the number of housing units originally built in the 1930's, during the years up to 1960. A probable explanation is that a good many people along the way simply upgraded their housing by stating that it was built later than it in fact was. This same phenomenon is readily apparent in a comparison of the 1940 census figures with those of the 1950 census regarding structures originally built in the 1920's. On the other hand, the decline in the number of units originally built in the 1940's, which is indicated in a comparison of the 1950 and 1960 censuses, is far greater than seems reasonable. It is most unlikely that the number of units declined by more than 10 percent, even if one assumes that some of these were temporary war housing demolished after the war.

Table 4 provides data on the numbers of occupied dwelling units at each census period from 1890 to date; presumably, these figures are relatively accurate at each date, because they rest on a simple count or interviewing, and do not involve possible memory biases

TABLE 4

Occupied Dwelling Units in the United States, 1890–1960 [a]

(Units in thousands)			
Year	*Total*	*Nonfarm*	*Farm*
1890	12,690	7,923	4,767
1900	15,964	10,274	5,690
1910	20,256	14,132	6,124
1920	24,352	17,600	6,751
1930	29,905	23,300	6,605
1940	34,855	27,748	7,107
1950	42,826	37,105	5,721
1960	53,024	49,458	3,566

[a] Series N 139, Historical Statistics of the United States.

as to age of buildings. The numbers here are somewhat lower than in Table 3 for the years which overlap because vacant buildings and housing units other than dwellings, such as trailers, are not included. The greatest difference, about 10 percent, is in 1960; one would expect the difference to have been less in earlier censuses because the miscellaneous forms of housing were then less common.

Based in part upon the data in Table 3, and in part upon intuition, a projection of the number of existing housing units of each age-of-origin class, at future dates is shown in Figure 2. A rough test of the accuracy of this estimate is provided later. For each 100 housing units constructed in any year, 97 would still be habitable ten years later, 94 habitable twenty years later, and so on. The rate of decline is relatively low but slightly accelerating, for the

FIGURE 2
Housing Units Still Habitable, by Age

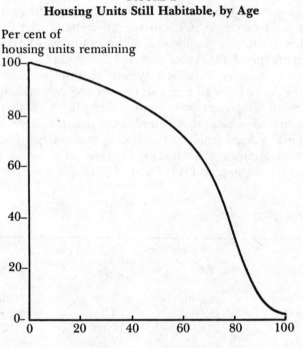

Years since original construction

first fifty years; at that point, it is assumed that 79 of the original 100 units would still be habitable. Thereafter, the rate of decline accelerates and is particularly rapid from 60 to 90 years of age; at the later date, 9 percent of the original units would still be habitable. We assume that 1 percent would be habitable after 100 years, and do not pursue the estimates beyond this date.

These estimates apply only in general and to large numbers of housing units. Few trailers will last fifty years, I judge; and certainly many housing units older than 100 years are still lived in—and some few of them are still good housing. These estimates are roughly analogous to a life expectancy table used for life insurance; that does not tell when any individual is going to die, but does provide the basis for a very large life insurance industry. Hopefully, these estimates of housing unit life may prove equally useful.

The cumulative disappearance of old dwelling units, shown in Figure 2, can be converted readily into proportions of all units which disappear by decades. The rate is low during the first decades, but rises gradually and at an accelerating pace, to reach a peak during the eighth decade. This one decade accounts for 25 percent of all the clearances or disappearances, and the next decade includes almost as many. Thereafter, the rate falls sharply, in large part because there are very few of the original structures left. The distribution of numbers of structures disappearing by decades is highly skewed.

On the basis of all the foregoing data, Table 1 was constructed. Numbers of reported occupied dwellings in 1930 and earlier were converted, by modest upward revisions to an approximate total number of housing units. Generally speaking, estimates of numbers of housing units most recently built, at the date of each census, were accepted as the most accurate basis for estimating, and then numbers at later censuses for each age-of-origin class were estimated by the relationship shown in Figure 2. However, the number of housing units in 1930 from the 1920's cohort was estimated by proceeding in the opposite direction, from data available for the 1940 census but not available in the 1930 census. For the 1920, 1910, and 1900 censuses, the number of housing units built in the preceding 10 years was estimated from the number of permanent dwellings started in the preceding decade, for which data are available in published sources.

The test of reasonableness of this procedure is found in the data in the top line of Table 1. At each census, this number was estimated by the difference between the itemized data, derived as described above, and the estimated total number of housing units, also estimated as described above. The total number of housing units reported in 1890 declines in reasonable fashion at each census through 1930; both the level and the trend of these figures are close to what one would expect. For 1940 and 1950, the estimated number of these older housing units rises considerably—an impossible relationship. Something is obviously wrong with some of the estimates. We decided not to go back and revise the estimating process, but to let this test of reasonableness stand as it came out. Moreover, the differences in absolute terms are not very great, compared with total numbers of all housing units, although they are considerable compared with probable true numbers in that age class for those census periods. By 1960, this oldest age class had begun to decline again, but it probably was above the true figure.

Section B

Perspectives for the Future: Innovation

The relationships between education, technology, and social planning are explored in the following section. Of particular concern are the extant, dysfunctional consequences of these relationships in the past, and the development of procedures to alter and improve these relations in the future.

Organizing, forecasting, and mapping the future has never gained widespread legitimacy as a practice in complex organizations. Planning has been traditionally treated as an overhead expense, operating largely on the periphery of organizational structures. In prophet-making organizations the focus has been on product development. Yet, as Alfred Sloan has noted, planning is of immense importance to an organization if that organization is to effectively adapt to a changing environmental field. And, systematically, those organizations which have developed effective, anticipatory, change-oriented internal mechanisms have, to large extent, been the organizations which have adapted and prospered.

Human service organizations, because they rely largely on tax dollars, and are often hard-pressed to fund needed basic services, have not found themselves able to develop organizational structures for planning and future development to nearly the same extent that these have operated in the private sector of the economy. However, if human service organizations are to grow and adapt in a future environment, the priorities and allocations for planning will need to be altered.

36. Education for Management and Technology in the 1970's*

Howard W. Johnson

Most newly developing organizations and programs contain innovative people and policies, although these innovative qualities vanish all too rapidly as organizations develop structures and interactional patterns over a span of time. The consequences and problems which are created by this loss are two of the themes articulated by Johnson in the following article.

Of greater importance, however, is Johnson's focus on how organizations can become aware of the losses inherent in institutional rigidity, and some possible strategies which might act to conserve and develop innovative potential within organizations.

The problems of facilitating social and socio-technical changes, which in organizations parallel technological innovation in the large society, are problems of the first magnitude. It is likely that these problems will be most effectively solved if we are able to take a radically different and highly critical look at what we have considered "givens" in our past concepts of organized socio-technical systems.

Any time in human history is one, I suppose, of paradox—of contradiction, of extreme and opposite conditions side by side. Wealth and poverty, beauty and squalor, genius and ignorance—the human condition tolerates, seems even to foster their coexistence. Dickens captured the mood of an earlier era when he wrote in *A Tale of Two Cities:*

> *"It was the best of times, it was the worst of times, it was the age of wisdom, it was the age of foolishness, it was the epoch of belief, it was the epoch of incredulity, it was the season of Light, it was the season of Darkness, it was the spring of hope, it was the winter of despair."*

*This article is adapted from an address delivered in London on March 13, 1968 before the British Institute of Management's 1968 national conference.

But perhaps more than ever before in our lifetimes, such extremes exist now: the paradox of hope and despair, the contrast of the potential and the reality—extremes of which technology at times seems the common cause. For technology is at once our blessing and our bane, the wellspring of our aspirations, yet the threat to our well-being. Technology is both social benefactor and social calamity. It offers us nuclear power and the specter of thermonuclear destruction, personal transportation and urban pollution, computers which multiply our creative power and threaten our privacy, mass communication and mass propaganda, an affluent but alienated youth. Technology offers the potential of the good life, but seems unable to lessen the poverty around us. A magnificent Lincoln Center exists side by side with the slums of Harlem. There are rich nations and poor nations, and the gulf steadily widens. Huxley may well have been right to ask: "What are you going to do with all these new things?"

Clearly science is not enough. But there is no turning back. The hope, I believe, lies in a partnership of technology and management (both industrial and social), intensely responsive to human need, to so order the distribution of technology's products and our national priorities as to resolve the paradox.

Remarkably, only concerning the advantage of effective management is there reasonable agreement for the moment. Management is regarded as a positive virtue from all points of view: American, British, Russian—perhaps even Chinese. The focus is thus strongly on the improvement of management—on education for management—and especially on the symbiotic relationship existing between management and technology. Societies will be strong economically in proportion to the strength of their management systems, their ability to harness technology in the service of the market, a term that here includes both the individual's and society's needs—for education, transportation, housing, health, adequate food, clean air and water.

The leadership of this management system demands rare and imaginative men, and I am persuaded that the corporate task of the 1970's will be to provide the climate in which such men are nurtured and in which their abilities are brought to full flower within the corporate frame. The world is changing with such speed that only the adaptive and innovative can keep the pace. We are in the process of a social, economic, and political evolution in which clearly only the fittest of enterprises will survive.

Robert Oppenheimer characterized our time in this way (1):

"One thing that is new is the prevalence of newness, the changing scale and scope of change itself, so that the world alters as we walk on it, so that the years of man's life measure not some small growth or rearrangement or moderation of what he learned in childhood, but a great upheaval."

And so I strongly believe that the managerial need of the 1970's will be for men who have entrepreneurial spirit and energy; who are innovative; who have the capacity for translating ideas and discoveries into action; who are both receptive to change and initiators of change; who have a high tolerance for ambiguity and uncertainty; who have the will to take risks.

These qualities are not a property of any class of men, the product of a particular education or background. They are widely, not narrowly, distributed in the population and will flower if properly cultivated. And so we need a broad range of human resources: men who are skilled analysts, trained to quantify the quantifiable in alternative courses of action; men adept at engineering and producing the product; men with a flair for presenting the product in the marketplace. Especially will we need imaginative men with trained scientific and technical minds who will apply the cutting edge of technology to the flinty problems in the understanding and mastery of our environment. The managerial leadership of the 1970's may emerge from among men with any of these competences, but, as leaders of enterprises caught up in a changing world, these men must above all be adaptive and innovative, themselves agents of change if they and their firms are to survive. And, in fact, the collective business leadership must be distinguished by an entrepreneurial spirit if the nation's economy is to flourish. The American historian Elting Morison, in his book, *Men, Machines and Modern Times* (2), made the point in this way:

"Change has always been a constant in human affairs; today, indeed, it is one of the determining characteristics of our civilization. In our relatively shapeless social organization, the shifts from station to station are fast and easy. More important for our immediate purpose. America is fundamentally an industrial society in a time of tremendous technological development. We are thus constantly presented with new devices or new forms of power that in their refinement and extension continually bombard the thick structure of our habits of mind and behavior. Under such conditions, our salvation, or at least our peace of mind, appears to depend on how sucessfully we can in the future become what has been called, in an excellent phrase, a completely "adaptive" society."

The Route-128 Phenomenon

Let me illustrate my emphasis on the demand for entrepreneurial qualities in our managers by describing a remarkable development in the Boston-Cambridge area. Within the past 15 years there has been created by private entrepreneurial enterprise what *The New York Times* (3) has called "The Golden Semicircle," bounded by a broad highway that sweeps in a great arc around the Boston-Cambridge heartland, meeting the sea on the north and south. Bordering this highway, prosaically, called Route 128, are the head-quarters or branches of some 700 companies. Many of these companies are new and are the product of a remarkably fertile interplay between entrepreneurship and technology, plus, I must add, an adequate supply of fertilizing capital provided by prescient Boston bankers.

The highway itself has come to symbolize a striking innovative process ("the Route-128 phenomenon") involving scientists and engineers, bankers and venture capitalists. The corporate names tell the story: Baird Atomic, High Voltage Engineering, Cryonetics, Itek, Microwave Associates, Bio-Dynamics, Maser Optics, Parametrics, Aerospace Research. These new companies have largely been formed by young men typically in their thirties, development-rather than research-oriented, entrepreneurially-minded, and with an idea they were determined to convert into a product or service and offer to the market. Many came from academic or government laboratories; others, from corporate laboratories. An important effect, in addition to the commercial and economic impact, of this flow of entrepreneurs from advanced technological organizations into businesses of their own is a significant transfer of technological knowledge. This is one of the primary mechanisms by which the basic and mission-oriented research of our space, defense, and health programs is transmuted from laboratory discoveries to marketable products and processes.

While the Boston-Cambridge area heads the list of American cities which have generated these new technologically-based companies, there are others. The essential ingredients for this explosively innovative mixture, according to a U.S. Commerce Department Report (4), are:

> a. Institutional and individual venture capital sources that are (i) "at home" with technologically oriented innovators and (ii) have the rare business appraisal capabilities necessary to diagnose the prospects of translating a technical idea into a profitable business.

b. Technologically oriented universities, located in an area with a business climate that encourages staff, faculty, and students to study and themselves generate technological ventures.

c. Entrepreneurs, who have been influenced by examples of entrepreneurship (for it is our contention that entrepreneurship breeds entrepreneurship).

d. Close, frequent consultations among technical people, entrepreneurs, universities, venture capital sources and others essential to the innovative process.

The Entrepreneurs and the Nature of Their Companies

While many aspects of this process of creation of new technological enterprises merit examination, I want to focus principally on the entrepreneurs themselves and the nature of their companies.

A study directed by Edward Roberts of Massachusetts Institute of Technology (5) explored the interplay between entrepreneurship and technology in the growth of over 200 companies founded by former employees of academic and government laboratories, a not-for-profit corporation, and an industrial electronics systems contractor. The companies studied were 4 to 5 years old, on the average, and though they are still small, they are growing rapidly. Their sales well exceeded that of the parent organizations. Most of these companies started in business as suppliers to the defense and space markets, but they have steadily moved in the direction of the commercial market and commercial applications of their products. For example, after only 4 or 5 years of life, an average of 40 percent of the business of companies formed by individuals formerly employed or trained in MIT laboratories came from the commercial market.

It may be useful to cite some of the characteristics of this technical entrepreneur. It is an interesting fact, one not a priori obvious, that 50 percent of the entrepreneurs studied have come from homes in which the father was self-employed. Second, since the study concerned technical entrepreneurs, it is not surprising that the group is composed of, on the whole, well-educated people with average education slightly beyond the requirements for the master of science degree. Of significance as well is the fact that the typical founder of a new company is in his early thirties. Very few of the men who move out to found their own companies are over forty. Also of interest is the fact that these men tend to be development-oriented rather than research-oriented; this suggests that those men whose primary interest is in the application of technical knowledge are the ones most stimulated to carry these skills into the marketplace.

The study went on to discriminate between the companies with higher performance and those with lower performance, and between the personal characteristics of the respective founders. The successful technical entrepreneur recognizes the importance of management skills and has typically involved in his company someone with those skills. He also manifests a concern for the people in the organization and gives careful attention to their needs and interests. It is clear, as well, that a high need for achievement characterizes the more successful entrepreneurs. The study concludes that "the difference between mere technical invention and successful innovation is largely attributable to the personal role of the entrepreneur. Better understanding and management of him and of a personally-based technical innovation process will lead to more rapid technically-based corporate and economic growth."

I have indicated that the sources of new-company formation have been university and government laboratories and industrial corporations. We understand and can encourage this flow of entrepreneurial initiative from the universities and government as representing an expression of their primary purposes of extension and application of knowledge. From the standpoint of the individual corporation, however—and I want to stress this point—such a flow presents a serious problem, since "those scientists and engineers who are committed to an action orientation and to the use of their knowledge are the ones who usually depart in this flow of entrepreneurship" (5). For the corporation, this entrepreneurial brain drain can be a serious problem, and it is important to recognize the causes if these technical entrepreneurs who are wellsprings of vitality in the firm are to remain—or are to remain vital.

In some fundamental respects this drain of technological entrepreneurs is a more serious national loss than the technology transfer which results from international migration of scientists and engineers. For it weakens the corporation and discloses its rigidities. It poses a higher risk for the flowering of a new idea than would exist if the originator remained within the corporate environment, sustained by its resources. Of still more serious concern, to me, is the brain drain between fields of inquiry—and especially the drawing down of national pools of scientists. Discovery in any field is certainly not directly proportional to the manpower applied. Still, a first-rate mind lost to science marginally reduces the nation's capacity for scientific inquiry. I argue, of course, for a balance appropriate to the needs of the time in a nation's mix of educated men. The contribution of the humanists and social scientists are equally vital to the nation's well-being and equally relevant to today's problems.

I am disturbed, however, when either the quality or the quantity of entrants in any field begins to lag. Thus, I was struck by the recent report from the British Council for Scientific Policy that, for at least the next several years, the annual increase in the supply of science graduates will be less than half the present rate of growth. This fact deserves both widespread notice and concern as a sign that the nation's heartbeat of scientific talent is faltering. As with the flow of entrepreneurs from their companies, this ebb from science to other fields reflects in part a weighing of opportunity alternatives, by individuals in their own interests and, collectively, counter to the national interest. And as with the potential entrepreneurs, so with the potential scientists, means must be found to redress the balance. We know enough about human motivation now to know that money is not the prime mover, but still it is an important incentive if it is used imaginatively and if the tax system permits it to have a high leverage.

To return briefly to the technical entrepreneur, we have found that even those companies which seek to challenge men with the offer of opportunities to develop within the corporate framework are not wholly successful, for the policies and attitudes in the large corporation often work to defeat entrepreneurial efforts. There is evidence that entrepreneurship is characterized by youth or at least by youthful energies. Yet there appears to be a definite bias against young men taking on venture responsibility within the firm. The MIT study showed that in a large electronics firm where 16 new product ventures were begun, the younger men were given less latitude for independent action, had less influence on criteria for judging their venture, experienced more trouble in securing company capital, and found less support for their project.

It is hardly surprising that many would-be entrepreneurs leave their organizations to set up their own businesses. The number who leave and their success suggest some of the potential gains to the corporation that can learn how to motivate and retain its entrepreneurially minded men within the company.

I have discussed these studies at some length, first because they shed light on one of the mechanisms in the United States by which laboratory discoveries are converted into marketable products and processes; second, because they identify some of the characteristics of that enterprising individual who should be the target of our management development energies; and third, because they suggest some of the influences within the corporation which force men of this caliber to seek outlets for their ideas outside the corporation.

I have stressed the corporation's need in the decade ahead for adaptive and innovative managers. I stress these qualities, not as the sole attributes of the manager of the 1970's, but, in a sense, as transcending qualities. There remains a requirement that the manager seek a mastery of the growing body of professional knowledge about management; that he be politically and economically educated, with a sensitivity to the environment in which his firm will exist; that he have a social awareness of the firm's responsibility in a modern society.

Expanding Knowledge about the Managerial Process

Let me review these points, with some initial comments about the way in which knowledge about the managerial process is expanding. This "knowledge explosion" is, of course, requiring the continued education of the manager and is, itself, a reason why the manager must be receptive to new ideas and to change. I had occasion recently to examine the changes in MIT's Sloan Fellowship Program in the past dozen years. (That program, I am happy to say, will have a British counterpart soon when the London-Sloan Program gets under way at the London Business School.) In 1955 the whole field of organizational behavior had only a slim foothold in the curriculum. The late Douglas McGregor and his colleague Alex Bavelas were groping for ways to couple the theories of the behavioral sciences to the problems of management and teach them effectively to the Sloan Fellows. While we are still a long way from applying in practice all that we know from behavioral science theory, the body of knowledge about the human side of enterprise has expanded enormously in the past decade.

In the field of finance, the instruction rested largely on assessment of the firm's requirements for funds and optimum means of obtaining them. The rigorous analytical approach to risk, uncertainty, and capital cost measurement in the management of corporate assets had not yet found its way into the classroom.

Application of the computer to the problems and processes of the firm was then vaguely foreshadowed, but in the short intervening years a great new field of management information systems has developed, in parallel with the new computer and communication technology.

Marketing as a field was long on practice, short on theory and analysis. Today increasingly the uncertainties of the marketplace are giving away—or, at any rate, being narrowed—through application of statistics and the methods of operations research.

The management of research and development as a subject of inquiry hardly existed a dozen years ago. Now there is a growing body of literature and organized instruction illuminating the special problems of organization for discovery.

I might add one other observation of interest—namely, that in the mid-1950's the Sloan Fellows, as young businessmen, were outraged by the tenets of Keynesian economics. The intervening years have made the theory intellectually acceptable even though the application turns out to be politically difficult.

This is by no means a complete catalog of changes in the content of a body of knowledge available to, and appropriate to be taught to, a group of young American managers. But let me only add one more entry, which is not so much an addition to the body of knowledge as it is an important reflection of our changing times. The Sloan Fellows are themselves deeply interested in what I would call the social responsibility of the businessman. They are concerned about the condition of our cities, about the quality of our environment, about the causes of poverty and the effects of discrimination. They are concerned that their companies should be concerned about these matters, and I sense a resolution that, when their opportunity for senior leadership comes, their companies will be in the forefront of the campaign to effect change in these areas.

By the foregoing discussion of changes in the curriculum of the MIT School of Management, I do not want to imply undue innovation on our part in bringing about these changes. They are a manifestation of a wide search for means to understand and improve the business process, a search greatly facilitated by the close coupling in America between the university and the business community, which exhibits itself only in part in the schools of business and in great measure between the scientific and technological arms of our universities and American industry. My primary point, of course, has been that the body of knowledge available to improve the practice of management has been growing and will grow more rapidly; that each managerial generation no longer has to learn primarily through experience and that this changes what the manager can do and what is demanded of him. The processes of management development of the 1970's must take cognizance of the needs of potential managers to acquire this body of knowledge—and skill in its application—but, more than that, must recognize that the acceleration of research on management and the rising accumulation of knowledge will very quickly make obsolete the manager who switches off his formal learning apparatus the day he leaves the university.

Changing Structure of the Firm

It is clear that the manager must be aware of changes taking place within the firm itself. The American labor force is increasingly better educated, with all this implies for a higher level of aspiration and a need for management to tap the creative capacities of this group and to motivate them effectively. For example, by 1975, six out of ten American workers over 25 years of age will be high school graduates, and one out of four will have had some university education. Professional, managerial, clerical, and sales personnel will make up nearly half the American labor force. Professional and technical personnel will outnumber skilled craftsmen in our economy. With vast sums being spent on reseach and development, men engaged in such work are thus an increasing proportion of the American work force, in great demand and therefore highly mobile. New approaches to organizing and directing their work are demanded, to achieve maximum effectiveness of their efforts. Computation and communication technology are having a profound effect on the internal structure of the firm, an effect which we are really only beginning to see and whose full implications we cannot yet perceive. There seems little question that the computer is becoming an indispensable and all-pervasive element in the modern corporation. By 1975 there are expected to be 85,000 computers in operation in the United States, representing an investment of more than $30 billion. The potentials of this kind of capacity for the control of processes, for the employment of information in the firm, for the handling of routine and increasingly sophisticated decisions, is certain to have a powerful effect upon the nature of managerial work, shifting it in the direction of unstructured, nonprogrammed work and away from more routine analysis, allocation, and evaluation. Goal setting, strategy formulation, and policy questions will occupy more of the manager's time, and he will be aided in his thinking by the information system at his fingertips. He will be more involved in understanding the environment and in defining the system in which he makes his decisions.

No less will the computer change education for technology and the application of technology. Its effect is already being felt in the classroom as it shows the potential for speeding the learning process through interaction of student and computer, and for quick transfer and retrieval of information within the university library system. And, of course, the computer has enormous power as the intellectual servant of the scientist or engineer in his research or design.

A third major area of change which influences the range of knowledge, the values, and the abilities of the manager of the 1970's is the increasing demand which the American society makes on the responsibility. I referred above to the Sloan Fellows' growing awareness in this area. Our society is clearly charging the corporation with responsibility for making its products safe and effective, and for raising the quality of the community through an active role as a corporate citizen and the application of its resources to find new solutions. It is becoming increasingly clear that the manager must understand politics and economics, in order to be sensitive to the political consequences of his actions and the consequences of politics for his enterprise, and in order to have the economic insight needed for adapting to a changing economic environment.

Changes in Economic Environment

The evidences of this change are many. The public uproar over automobile safety is an illustration, and I anticipate that the automotive industry will be increasingly challenged to take a leading role in the solution of the problems to which the automobile has contributed in our society—problems such as congestion of the cities and pollution of the air. American business is being challenged directly to take the initiative and leadership in providing job training and job opportunities for the hardcore unemployed. The opportunities for business enterprise to be innovative in solving the problems of education, of housing, of transportation, of rebuilding our cities into a viable and enriching social environment are manifold.

There is a final dimension: American business has become international in character as never before. The British have a long history and experience in the management of international ventures. We are comparative newcomers, at least on the scale of our present international involvement in Europe. Therein lies a need to acquire new political and economic insights and cross-cultural sensitivities which were not demanded of American managers in the past.

In sum, whether we will it or not, the world is being transformed, and the business enterprise with it. This enterprise is changing internally—in products and processes, in organizational form, in the employment of information technology to speed and refine its decisions. It is growing larger through merger and acquisition and as its market grows. Externally the firm is forced to be more responsive to government, to society, to its customers, to its employees and their unions. These are both challenges and opportunities for the American business enterprise in the next decade. It is this challenge and opportunity that led me to assert at the outset that the managerial leaders of enterprises caught up in this changing world must be adaptive and innovative, themselves agents of change if they and their firms are to survive.

Alfred P. Sloan (6), writing from the unique vantage point of his years with General Motors, stated the point succinctly:

> "The circumstances of an ever-changing market and an ever-changing product are capable of breaking any business organization if that organization is unprepared for change—indeed, in my opinion, if it has not provided procedures for anticipating change."

Role of the University

The universities clearly have a role in aiding the individual to develop the knowledge, skills, motivation, and attitudes which characterize this adaptive and innovative spirit. At the undergraduate level, MIT has been examining its programs carefully with the aim of increasing the student's independence and freedom of choice, giving him an opportunity to range more broadly over the curriculum, devising laboratory opportunities for the undergraduate to design and carry out his own projects. A particular experiment in the undergraduate program of the School of Management has attracted wide interest within MIT and elsewhere by providing a selected group of students in their final 2 years the opportunity essentially to take responsibility for their own education—to define their needs and interests, organize their program, and involve the faculty and segments of the business community as resources in their educational process. The outcome has clearly been a more confident, more venturesome spirit among the men who have taken part in that program.

I see increasing concern in the graduate schools of business, as well, for the development of an entrepreneurial outlook and attitude on the part of their students. I do not suggest that the schools are turning their backs on the enhancement of analytical knowledge and capacity or of organizational skills on the part of their students. Rather, they are looking for ways to identify those students who have the entrepreneurial spark, and to reinforce rather than inhibit these qualities through the educational process.

The university's role in contributing to an individual's development by no means ends with his graduation. Education must be continuous. The successful companies will be in partnership with the universities in this process of human capital formation. Not all continuing education will have to take place within the university framework, but the university has a responsibility for setting standards and for innovation. Again, for example, MIT's new Center for Advanced Engineering Study is seeking to develop new self-study materials and to train company officials at MIT who will themselves be trainers and guides in aiding others to self-renewal within the corporate frame.

This Center is a significant forward step in enabling experienced engineers and applied scientists to refresh their knowledge of the many developments in their professional fields. It is directly concerned with the problems of the engineer who finds all too often that his ability to create and exploit his experience fades because he has not had the opportunity to assimilate technological advances.

Before I leave this examination of the role of education in human development, let me speak to the issue of educational method. In this article I have not, up to this point, taken a stand in this unending debate, essentially because I am persuaded that methods are secondary to *concepts* of education. If the environment is right and the opportunities exist, the institutions will develop. In short, education is an individual rather than an institution-centered process, important as the institutions' role must be. A clear sign of progress is the rise of intellectual centers for management developments in Great Britain, and I see a critically constructive purpose for them.

I have discussed the managerial needs of the future in terms of the changing body of professional knowledge in the area of management, the changing structure of the firm and of the work force, and the challenges of the firm's envirnoment. I have tried to suggest that the managers of the next decade will require a mastery of this growing body of professional knowledge; a sensitivity to the aspirations of a better educated, more affluent, and more mobile work force; a satisfaction in the challenges of the less routine, less structured work situtation; and a sense of social responsibility. But I have urged that, above all, we seek out and nurture qualities of mind and spirit which lead men to be challenged by new ideas

and eager to test them. I have suggested the role of the university
in this process. Now let me deal explicitly with the enterprise itself
and the influence it brings to bear on the individual, which determines how he is molded—whether his ideas and initiative are sup-
pressed or encouraged—and which in the long run will determine
whether the organization retains its vitality.

Role of the Corporation

There may be some corporate leaders who will say, "Don't worry
about us. We're all right." Perhaps, but let me ask a few questions,
borrowed from Frederick Kappel (7) of AT&T, to measure the
vitality of your enterprise.
1) Do your people cling to old ways of working after they have
been confronted with new situations?
2) Are your older managers adhering rigidly to the ideas, methods,
and approaches of the past and passing this kind of thinking along
to young managers?
3) Is management failing to define new goals that are meaningful
and challenging?
4) Has your business developed a low tolerance for criticism?
5) Has there been a decline in reflective thinking about the adequacy
of current operations and the needs of the future?
6) Has institutionalism begun to set in? That is, has the business
come to be something apart from the people who comprise it?
7) Does the business have a reputation as a secure and stable outfit,
but not a venturesome one?
Parenthetically, perhaps the test of these questions applies as
well to other institutions, including governments, as to corporations.
And if the answer to all these questions is a strong "No," a chief
executive has reason for satisfaction and pride. If any must be
answered "unfortunately, yes," then the danger signals of loss of
vitality are flying. And since, as Kappel says, "vitality is an attribute
of people, not of things," it follows that, "a vital business is one
with vital people." The problem for the firm, then, is to challenge
such people, to give them opportunities for responsibility and the
exercise of initiative. And this brings us directly to the role of
the corporation and the influence it exerts over the individual by
its policies, its organization, and its leadership.
The first critical point in a person's development within the firm
is the point of entry, and it is precisely at this point that many
firms fail.

I was talking recently with a group of young men about to complete their business school studies. They were looking forward enthusiastically to their first jobs, interviewing company representatives, visiting plants, making what they believed to be careful career choices. I had neither the heart nor the desire to disillusion them, but the record shows that within 5 years 75 percent of those men will have left their carefully chosen companies and gone on to other jobs. This is real waste for their companies and for the men, and it points up the real problems in the process by which men are brought into the firm and educated to its values and norms. The psychologists have a word for this—*organizational socialization;* by this they mean learning the ropes, being indoctrinated and trained, being told what is important in the organization. The new recruit gets his guidelines from a variety of sources: from the official literature of the organization; from examples set by senior people; from instructions given him directly by his superior; from the example of his peers who have been around longer; and from the rewards and punishments which flow from his own efforts, the response to his ideas, the degree of challenge in the assignments he receives.

The question is, What does he come to believe the company considers important? Whom you know? How you dress? What clubs you belong to? Where you live? What kind of car you drive? What political party you belong to? What your college was? Or does the company consider these matters irrelevant? Is it primarily interested in values which are pivotal or central to the enterprise, and in your intelligent and creative adherence to them?

The new employee will have spent most of his life in an educational environment—an environment that puts a premium on personal and intellectual attainment, on the creative contribution of his mind. He comes to his first company eager to apply his knowledge to its processes and problems. If he finds his values in conflict with those of the organization, he may, according to Edgar Schein (8), respond in one of three ways. First, he may rebel, rejecting all the values and norms of the organization, and either be expelled from it or turn his energies to defeating its goals. Second, he may settle for conformity and accept all the norms and values. We know some firms which appear to demand so much conformity that their people all seem to have been stamped out by a company cookie cutter. Unfortunately, the conforming individual curbs his creativity and thereby moves the organization toward the sterile form of bureaucracy.

The third response has been labeled creative individualism—an acceptance of the pivotal and a rejection of the peripheral values and norms. It is for this response that companies should seek. They have an obligation first to understand their own organizational socialization or indoctrination practices and to select or devise those which focus on the pivotal values only. Second, companies have an obligation to give careful training to the men who will be the first supervisors of new management recruits in the organization, for it is they who really have the power to create the climate which will lead to rebellion, conformity, or creative individualism. Too many of those first supervisors concentrate on teaching the peripheral values of "how to get ahead in this outfit" and thus undermine the possibilities for creative individualism and improvement of the organization.

There is much evidence of the effects of the quality of supervision on motivation and creativity as the individual moves through the organization. Consider, for example, a study (9) made at the Texas Instruments Company, a company built on new technology. This investigation of the attitudes of nearly 1400 managers at all levels of the company showed that "highly motivated managers rather consistently characterized *their supervisors* as persons who are approachable and open-minded, maintain high expectations, provide ready access to company information, *encourage initiative and risk taking, help them learn from mistakes,* and give credit for top performance" (italics added). Poorly motivated managers often indentified their supervisors as authority-oriented, not usually receptive to conflicting ideas from subordinates, oversupervising, tending to discourage initiative and risk-taking, intolerant of mistakes, inclined to look for someone to blame for mistakes, and tending to overlook success and stress failure.

Clearly one of the management development tasks ahead, if the entrepreneurial qualities we prize are to be encouraged and young managers are to be motivated toward "creative individualism," is identification and reward of managerial performance which encourages such individuality and simultaneously discourages, through training and in other ways, supervisory styles which inhibit it.

Another matter of concern is the kind of work to which the man with entrepreneurial qualities is assigned. Several years ago A.T.M. Wilson (10) made this point in a paper entitled "The manager and his world." He asserted what he provocatively called "an elite principle in the early development of those intended for senior positions at a later date," recalling the cliche of the British regular officer between the two wars, "Never let your potential officer get into the sergeant's mess." Although admitting that the statement contained an expression of social prejudice, he suggested that it contained some managerial insight as well. He contrasted the functions in the "commercial" areas of the firm, classifying them as routine and clerical in nature at the lowest levels; as centering, at the middle range, on the *safeguarding* of assets; but as focusing, at the top level, on the *increase* of assets, and involving the judgments and decision-sharing about risks which make up such an important proportion of top-management work. He went on to say, "There is good reason to believe that a man who may well have considerable potential for this high-level work ... may be seriously damaged if he spends more than a short period of his career in the 'asset safeguarding' lower levels where the primary responsibilities are of a quite different character."

Organizational Forms, Existing and Proposed

Let me turn now to a brief discussion of the organizational characteristics which influence the young manager's development—that is, those which bear on the scope of his authority and his opportunity for exercise of independent initiative.

I believe there is reasonable agreement by now that a centralized organization structure with rigid functional lines and many levels limits the manager's chances for assuming responsibility, trying out new ideas, exercising judgment. In those companies where top-management decision-making is focused on strategic planning as opposed to close control of operations, there tends to be a dispersed distribution of authority within the firm and more opportunity for innovation and creative decision-making.

Some companies have been inventive about creating opportunities for younger men to try out their entrepreneurial energies in the development of new products. These approaches have included creating product or project teams—men working together within the framework of the company but having, as a group, a sense of independence and the freedom to be wholly responsible for developing and bringing a new product to the market (that is, responsible for its design, packaging, pricing, and promotion), seeking advice within the company and using the company's resources but taking the responsibility themselves.

Harold Guetzkow (11) has pointed out that such freedom to innovate requires a capacity and willingness on the part of the organization to absorb risk, for creativity and innovation push into unexplored areas where there is high potential for error. To determine whether new ideas are real contributions usually requires investigation and experiment—time and resources are required, to avoid premature judgment. If the organization is too tightly run, the climate is usually unfavorable for innovation. There must also be an ethos in the organization that is conducive to change. Risk-taking must be legitimate. Managers in such firms continually ask themselves, "How can this be done better?"

These observations are relevant to organizations as we know them today. It is quite clear, however, that dissatisfaction with existing structures is growing, and first-rate theorists are turning their attention to a development of alternatives to the existing pyramidal structures in which authority flows downward from the top. For example, Jay W. Forrester (12) argues that "new thinking in the social sciences indicates that moving away from authoritarian control in an organization can greatly increase motivation, innovation and individual human growth and satisfaction." He urges the abandonment of the authoritarian hierarchy as the central organizational structure, and replacement of the superior-subordinate pair as the fundamental building block of the organization. In the new corporate form Forrester proposes, the individual would not work under the supervision of a superior. "Instead, he would negotiate, as a free individual, a continually changing structure of relationships with those with whom he exchanges goods and services. He would accept specific obligations as agreements of limited duration. As these are discharged, he would establish a new pattern of relationships as he finds more satisfying and rewarding situations." Similarly, Warren G. Bennis (13) believes that in the social structure of the organizations of the future there will be adaptive, rapidly changing "temporary systems." These will be organized around "problems to be solved." The problems will be solved by groups of relative strangers who represent a set of diverse professional skills. The function of the executive thus becomes that of a coordinator or linking pin between the various project groups. "People will be differentiated not vertically according to rank and role but flexible according to skill and professional training. . . . In these new organizations, participants will be called on to use their minds more than (at) any other time in history."

These are evolving ideas from fertile and creative minds. They may or may not forecast the shape of the future. However, they do reflect a dissatisfaction with our existing corporate and organizational forms and a desire to give greater scope to the innovative and creative spirit of the individual. Clearly management development in the decade ahead will be powerfully concerned with the way in which these ideas develop.

Summary

In summary, then, let me restate my conviction that the most critical needs of management in the next decade will be met by the identification and cultivation of the innovative, creative, adaptable individual who sets as his goal the translation of technology for society's needs. He will require a command of the growing body of managerial knowledge. He will need a continual refreshment of that knowledge through contact with the university as he seeks to deal with a world in change. If his firm is to encourage and use his creative capacity, it will be careful about his entry into the organization and his movement up the ladder, stressing only the values that count, that are pivotal, and taking care not to drive him into rebellion or conformity. The firm will be inventive about ways to give him opportunities to test his ideas. It will experiment with organizational forms which promote creativity. It will encourage adventure and accept risk. And in its success, it will be serving the needs of our societies in ways that will make our greatest hopes for technology a full and human reality.

REFERENCES AND NOTES

1. J. R. Oppenheimer, "Prospects in the arts and sciences," *Perspectives U.S.A.* 1955, 10 (spring 1955).
2. E. E. Morison, *Men, Machines and Modern Times* (M.I.T. Press, Cambridge, Mass., 1966), p. 18.
3. H. R. Lieberman, "Technology: Alchemist of Route 128," *New York Times* 1968, 139 (8 Jan. 1968).
4. "Technological Innovation: Its Environment and Management," a report of the U.S. Department of Commerce, January 1967, by the Panel on Invention and Innovation, Robert A. Charpie, chairman.
5. E. B. Roberts, "Entrepreneurship and technology," in *The Human Factor in the Transfer of Technology*, W. H. Gruber and D. G. Marquis, Eds. (M.I.T. Press, Cambridge, Mass., in press).
6. A. P. Sloan, *My Years with General Motors* (Doubleday, New York, 1964), p. 438.
7. F. Kappel, *Vitality in a Business Enterprise* (McGraw-Hill, New York, 1960).
8. E. H. Schein, "Organizational Socialization and the Profession of Management," Douglas M. McGregor Memorial Lecture, Alfred P. Sloan School of Management, Cambridge, Mass., 1967.
9. M. S. Myers, *Harvard Business Rev.* 44, 58 (Jan.-Feb. 1966).
10. A. T. M. Wilson, *Ind. Management Rev.* 3, No. 1, 13 (1961).
11. H. Guetzkow, "The creative person in organizations," in *The Creative*

Organization, G. A. Steiner, Ed. (Univ. of Chicago Press, Chicago, 1965), p. 39.
12. J. W. Forrester, *Ind. Management Rev.* 7, No. 1, 5 (1965).
13. W. G. Bennis, *Changing Organizations* (McGraw-Hill, New York, 1966), p. 14.

37. Planning for Human Services: The Role of the Community Council

Harold W. Demone, Jr., Ph.D.

Herbert C. Schulberg, Ph.D.

Major forces of social change require that new interorganizational linkages and strategies of interorganizational policy-making be developed. The following article addresses itself in part to the forces of social change which affect human service organizations, as well as to problems of interorganizational relationships.

The Community Health and Welfare Planning Council, as an overlay on human service organizations supported by the United Way network, is proposed as one organizational strategy for generating stability and strength in interorganizational functioning. The responsibilities, problems, and perspectives for this policy-making body are examined, and some consequences for the future are projected.

Futurists, futurism, and long-term planning are becoming increasingly common concepts. Some futurists plan for the next decade, others are focusing on the year 2,000. In either case, efforts are being made to look ahead. A blending of systems theory, technocracy, and political sophistication underlies these planning efforts which have assumed a new saliency as the winds of seemingly exponential change affect us on all sides. It is the rare day which doesn't bring news of yet another venerable institution being challenged to revamp its societal functions and to play a new role in fulfilling community needs. The traditional categorical health and welfare agencies have been more formidable in withstanding the pressures of the 1960's; but they, too, are now yielding to the demands of consumers. Comprehensive human services are rapidly emerging as the organizational concept for providing one-stop or linked social welfare and health services on the basis of the individual's needs rather than categorical professional definitions, and this new delivery system is expected to grow during the 1970's (Demone, 1973).

A related societal institution also faced with the challenge of demonstrating its viability and contemporary relevance is the community health and welfare planning council. As federations of local voluntary health and welfare agencies supported in turn by federated fund-raising, community health and welfare councils were principally interested in bringing about coordinated and more efficient organizational functioning. In recent years, the focus of council interest has shifted to planning activities directed toward resolution of our massive social problems. Less distinction is being made about the auspices of those resources that can contribute to the solution of these problems, and community organization is still the tactic of choice. Further evolution of the council's planning thrust has led to a principal concern with social policy, both public and private, and the council is viewed as one of many local and regional planning instruments. Traditional concern with agency efficiency and coordination has been integrated into a more comprehensive framework for providing human services. Needs and resources are highlighted and existing agency programs are viewed as one of many alternative intervention possibilities.

This paper will review a series of national domestic trends which have implications for the development and operation of human services, and relate these to the community council's planning role, by suggesting unique contributions which it can make to the solution of outstanding problems.

NATIONAL TRENDS

Any knowledgeable observer of the American scene is aware of the myriad of interrelated influences affecting and constraining program planning and development in the field of human services. For purposes of this analysis, we have limited ourselves to the following four: population growth, citizen roles, technological advances, and changes in human service networks.

Population Growth

The ever-increasing size of our population and the concomitant trend to urbanization is critical and may represent even the major international problem. America's capacity to feed, clothe, and shelter its people at a standard approximating 1973 expectations is being increasingly diminished. And even if this problem is resolvable on a national scale, what about the billion or more living on a subsistence level throughout the rest of the world? Furthermore, the living patterns of a mass society create additional problems endemic to sheer density. Privacy and silence, even for the affluent, are increasingly difficult to obtain. Another aspect of this problem is that our large-city cores are experiencing major population shifts as their ethnic and social class composition changes to predominantly poor whites, blacks, and Spanish-speaking peoples. As the political balance of power adjusts to compensate for these urban transitions in racial and economic class, domain tensions will substantially increase. Our society has previously adjusted to waves of ethnics pouring into our large cities and successful experiences abound, but the adjustments were not easily achieved and resolution of the present challenges will produce similarly stressful encounters.

The national focus previously had been upon generating more employment opportunities, improved housing, desegregated education facilities, expanded public transportation, etc., but prominent recognition is now being given to the fact that population pressures also require modifications of health and welfare services. Inequalities in the services provided by the health system have been highlighted by minority groups and the welfare nonsystem is under attack from its increased number of clients, taxpayers, politicians, and even its administrators. The expanded populations being cared for have produced the need for a totally new approach to meeting human needs, and piecemeal solutions are no longer adequate.

Citizen Roles in Planning

A concomitant trend that has gained momentum in the face of societal problems is the intensive and widespread participation of citizens in community planning. The usual division between citizen and staff roles is becoming blurred, and maximum feasible participation and consumer control are now clearly in the public domain. Since our nation is dedicated to a democratic base, recently-designed federal human service programs, e.g., Model Cities, OEO, and Comprehensive Health Planning, all insist upon effective citizen participation in their planning, and all stress consensual decision-making.

A rather different manifestation of the citizen's role in planning is evident in the trend toward the use by some community groups of confrontation and conflict as the social change mechanism of choice. Aggressive dissent has escalated in relation to both domestic concerns, e.g., civil rights, and international issues, e.g., Vietnam. Violent political movements are, of course, very much a part of American history, with the three decades from the 1930's to the mid-1960's being perhaps the longest period relatively free of political violence. Nevertheless, this period of relative internal placidity and the advent of television, which generated an intense form of vicarious participation, have once again highlighted the issue of appropriate and inappropriate citizen participation as a social change mechanism in the field of human services. Every era demands the right to design its own procedures for muddling through crises and the problem of the 1970's is to contain the muddle within manageable limits.

Although citizen interest and concerns have recently become incorporated in local (community) decision-making, the stark facts suggest that a counter-trend is also very much on the scene in the form of increased state and federal determination of human service program directions. As a result, there is a simultaneous trend toward recognizing community-based concerns while also engaging in centralized decision-making. Can we, however, centralize and decentralize simultaneously? The surface incompatibility of this dual trend produces confusion, and can perhaps even lead to conflict; however, we are inclined to believe that both developments are legitimate, necessary, and accommodatible (Newman & Demone, 1969).

We are realistic enough, however, to recognize that the resolution will not be a simple one. The magnitude of concern is evident in the frequent discussions that appear in the nation's press and journals about both regionalization and local decision-making (community control). People are increasingly alienated from and disenchanted by the decision-making centers; in part, because the imputed power groups in fact lack the very power they are accused of not sharing. Power and influence have become so diffuse in our mass society with its complex multi-organizations, that few can readily make decisions. As a result, neither credit nor blame can be accurately assigned.

The government is now entering the human services planning field with energy and vigor, but obviously this is not without its problems. Edward Banfield (1962), an eminent Harvard political scientist, points out: "Rationality is less likely to be found in public than in private organizations . . . one reason for this is that the public agency's ends often reflect compromises among essentially incompatible interests. This is not an accidental or occasional feature of public organization in democracy. When conflict exists and every conflicting element has to be given its due, it is almost inevitable that there be an end system which rides madly off in all directions."

Particularly troublesome is the fact that very few really significant decisions about the scope and operation of human services are left for the neighborhood, community, or even large city to make since very few problems can be resolved at this limited territorial base. What will be the consequences of this powerlessness even if measures can be designed to permit and assure citizen participation? We foresee the necessity of citizens determining with clarity and specificity those human service programs of sufficient local concern to warrant "bucking the system" and then consistently striving for their implementation. Governments are essentially conservative, and most easily influenced by those community leaders whose attention is directed toward keeping the tax-rate down, and toward limiting rather than increasing services to the "undesirables" (Newman & Demone, 1969). Strenuous counter-pressures must be exerted by socially-conscious citizens concerned with human services if government, particularly at the state and federal level, is to remember that its obligations include social as well as fiscal responsibility.

Technological Advances

While contemporary American social planning is characterized by efforts to involve citizens and their humanistic concerns at all decision-making levels, this planning simultaneously is becoming increasingly dependent upon impersonal scientific developments. For example, the expanding use and influence of the computer must be recognized as a highly significant technological advance which permits the development of sophisticated information systems from which health and welfare indicators can be refined. A number of related projects are now occurring at the local and national levels and the possibility of technologically-determined rationality looms on the horizon. In principle, we have for the first time the means to control many of the significant variables and to simulate complex social experiments. Through this magnificent extension of our intellect and memory, we can manipulate innumerable variables and perform meaningful analyses on huge clusters of data. Our faith can be reinforced in the rationality of machines as against the infinite potential perfidy of man.

Increased sophistication in the application of technologically-derived data is also evident. Planners are utilizing pragmatic tools such as performance and program budgets to arrive at necessary decisions, and other controlled data collection techniques and analytic frameworks are providing new guidelines to problem-solving. Indeed, we rapidly are approaching a period in which the planners' major problem will not be the lack of data but rather that of acquiring the skills to effectively cope with a surfeit of information. Expert opinion can be called upon to distinguish between the basic and surplus variables; but this approach often is insufficient, particularly if citizen opinion is not given the same value as professional judgment.

In the face of the many advantages posited for an age of technological planning, it is crucial that we also come to grips with its associated perils. The technology and language of planning are becoming increasingly complex even at its present elementary stage. The escalating sophistication of this technology is going to make it increasingly complicated for even the well-educated nonplanner, be he professional, businessman, or community leader, to effectively participate in decision-making. Will this make such people secure or insecure as objectively-determined indexes and solutions controvert politically-reached solutions? If insecurity is fostered by the revision of priorities, the appropriateness of technological contributions will be increasingly questioned and perhaps even circumscribed.

Human Service Networks

Experimentation has again become popular in the field of human services, and it is being encouraged by public and private bureaucracies alike. It is true that our funding capacity and organizational structures have not caught up with these new visions, but ideas usually precede resources and behavior. The presumed division of labor and financing between the public and private sectors is increasingly being blurred. Under the influence of former Secretary of Defense Robert McNamara, there was an increasing trend on the part of federal agencies to contract services. General hospitals, VNA's, rehabilitation facilities, and even settlement houses are now receiving federal funds on a contract or fee-for-service basis. Private universities, whose gross budget may be two-thirds federally-supported, are another important bellwether of change. Some private universities are now even receiving routine grants-in-aid from state governments. Many state agencies are exploring program alternatives and new Community Mental Health, Mental Retardation, and Public Welfare Acts have sanctioned and encouraged mixed funding experiments. For voluntary agencies, this shift to a quasi-public status may very well be the most important influence upon their functions during the coming decade.

Simultaneous with the reduction in fiscal and programmatic autonomy among existing voluntary agencies is the Federal Government's encouragement of a series of new quasi-public agencies to organize and provide human services. Principally dependent on the whims of Congress, these organizations have had to make major programmatic shifts as funds are adjusted and usually made more categorical in nature. These new quasi-public bodies were initially suspicious of the "establishment," but they have themselves soon become perceived as establishment-oriented and, thus, subjected to the same suspicions by the even newer organizations which have been fostered by later federal legislation. One positive result of this cycle is a fresh awareness that it is easy to start new agencies when funds are available, but the fundamental problem is that of keeping them viable, open, and responsive to changing human needs.

A further influence upon the evolving human services network is the rapidly growing self-help movement, usually manifesting itself in small, aggressively autonomous units. In recent years, more new nonprofit groups have been spawned by people suffering from the focal problem than by any other means. The public has been dramatically made aware, for example, of the drug programs initiated and staffed by former drug-users and has expressed an unusual willingness to fund these ventures. The degree to which self-help groups can be effectively linked to the larger human services system and still remain viable is a major concern. Another crucial issue is that of continued funding, and this problem's severity varies with the methods of programming. For example, if Alcoholics Anonymous continues the strategies and program design of its founders, the financial problems are limited and controllable. However, if Alcoholics Anonymous members branch out to operate withdrawal centers or halfway houses, they enter the competitive marketplace for limited funds and inevitably encounter the same fiscal problems as do all other caregiving organizations. A related characteristic of the self-help movement is its general hostility toward and suspicion of the human services professional and his established caregiving mechanisms. Since clients, however, use a variety of helping systems, ways must be found to enhance their movement across organizational boundaries, self-help and professional, so that they are guaranteed those services deemed most beneficial regardless of organizational auspices.

Thus, the human services system is confronted with simultaneous but contradictory trends: movement toward both larger and more comprehensive organizations and toward smaller, more categorical agencies. The professionals, the business community, and government press for the former although they place maximum limits on size, while the patients and their families strive toward the latter, i.e., formation of their own smaller autonomous organizations.

THE ROLE OF THE COMMUNITY COUNCIL

The fund and council movement, at one time a federation of varied human service organizations, now is evolving into bodies of citizens rather than agencies. Even during this transitional stage, it already represents the greatest concentration of citizen participation in health and welfare services. The question arises, however, as to whether the voluntary social planning movement can adapt to increasingly sophisticated planning technology while simultaneously developing a strong, dynamic, and creative citizen's leadership broadly representative of interest groups in the community. We submit that the strongly entrenched citizen orientation of the council movement gives it a base firm enough to accommodate experiments in computer simulation and other technological innovations. Criticism of the community health and welfare councils has usually focused upon their overly elaborate, "process" oriented decision-making model. Impatience has grown with gentlemen who discuss, work through problems, and ultimately reach compromise solutions. However, given the nature of technology's rapid diffusion, this "process" base can serve as an important foundation on which to devise experimental human service programs.

Each system, by definition, has its own constraints and in some respects, the council movement suffers from constraints similar to those imposed upon government. The council's constituency, because of its close links to the United Fund, may be third in size only to the government and organized religions. As a consequence, some action alternatives are limited if not impossible. Nevertheless, the council's individual volunteers are likely to have an active social conscience and are usually influentials in the community so that other advantages are gained. Council members need not seek periodic election even though funds are raised annually. The council's flexibility is furthered by the fact that it does not

operate programs, and patronage is unnecessary. The council field
can deal differently, not necessarily better, with irrational issues
and controversy. Courage, imagination, and skill are required, but
opportunities do exist. If properly utilized, the council's resources
and participants provide comprehensive alternatives to governmental action.

It is clear that no single organization possesses the sanctions and
competence to deal with all issues, but many of the problems defined
as key to the inner city legitimately fall within the interests and
concern of community councils. There is no doubt that councils
must direct themselves to these ends, but it is less clear with what
means. As a starting point, what can we offer to, or learn from,
the politics of confrontation? We suggest that conflict and controversy may be functionally necessary and even the means of choice
in certain instances if we are to make significant progress. It often
is necessary to choose credibility rather than love. However, confrontation may not always be the means of choice and in our pluralistic society, it probably should be used very selectively and even
then principally in arenas designed for its use, e.g., the political
and legal systems. In considering alternative options, councils possess experience with many other techniques of social change, for
example, research, budgeting and cost analysis, general systems
theory, committees, consensus, coordination, information systems,
forums, conferences, seminars, community organization, consultation, and participation. Not all intervention strategies are equally
available to all organizations nor are they equally appropriate in
all situations, but the many council experiences are of extraordinary
value in choosing an optimal strategy.

Another significant factor affecting the council's role in developing human services is the trend toward closer relations between
the executive branch of government and the voluntary planning
council. A similar linking to the legislative bodies is in the testing
stage. The productiveness of this relationship is principally dependent upon the council's understanding of governmental processes
and its ability to develop techniques for impacting upon government
in knowledgeable and sophisticated ways. Councils cannot be
amateurs dabbling in government if they are to be accepted as
respected partners. It is our impression that the changing background and composition of council staff will facilitate acceptance
in this new linking role. From an organization of social workers
principally directed to "enabling" and "middle-men" functions, we
now see a variety of professional disciplines staffing planning councils—public health being the largest addition but also including

law, social and behavioral sciences, sociology, political science and social psychology, and public administration and physical planning. This multi-disciplinary group is increasingly assuming active, task-oriented leadership roles and is relating as equals to governmental human service specialists. As we sharpen our tools to do problem-solving planning, it is inevitable that councils will move toward increasing involvement in policy formulation. For example, if the problem is a lack of low-cost housing for the aged, it may be necessary to seek changes in the construction and financing policy of federal, state, and local governments in order both to increase the number of available units as well as their quality. Similarly, we may attempt to modify building restrictions to accommodate the special needs of the physically handicapped or aged.

The reorganizing of our existing human services system so that it is contemporarily relevant is a key responsibility and concern of the community council. The welfare nonsystem, malnutrition, family planning, and housing are instances of pressing social concerns that are within the functional competency of council planners. For example, they can assume a dual approach to organized public welfare, i.e., maximizing the present system's effectiveness while aiming toward major national modifications, i.e., adequate social security, national health insurance, and a guaranteed annual income. The issues concerning residents of our inner cities, i.e., economic viability, adequate jobs and housing, a decent education, effective public transport, the general administration of justice, credit reform, drug and alcohol abuse, are but some of the additional challenges to and opportunities for the community council. Perhaps formal education is not yet within the council's unique competence, but the quality of counseling services, special education, recreation programs, and opportunities to use the school physical plant as a base for a variety of local activities are legitimate and sanctioned concerns for community councils designing human service networks. Intrinsic to many of these efforts is the goal of clarifying dispersed responsibility and achieving consensus for its redistribution on functional bases.

UNANSWERED QUESTIONS

Community councils are confronting a series of major problems as they strive to assert their role in the planning of human services. The troublesome issues pertain to both the ambiguous nature of the planning function in the field of human services, and the transitional character of the council's constituency and sanctioned scope of functions. In a sense, some of the dilemmas are being resolved for the council movement by the trends cited earlier in this paper. Nevertheless, each council must determine for itself how national trends will uniquely manifest themselves in its particular community and then achieve an appropriate format for the future.

Planning for Human Serivces

Our country's society in general, and its human service system in particular, is characterized by a commitment to pluralism and an aversion to unifaceted solutions of critical problems. Accepting the benefits of this ethos, it is also necessary to remember that it generates various constraints upon program development. The field of human services has grown through the multiple inputs of public, private, and independently financed organizations. However, it has also occasionally wandered aimlessly and impulsively in misguided directions because of the absence of any central planning body which could serve as a guiding beacon through perilous straits. The pattern of program development in the field of drug abuse amply demonstrates the ability of a pluralistic society to mount a multiple-pronged attack upon a critical community problem. We can also observe, however, through this example the wasteful duplication and significant service gaps tolerated by a society unwilling to impose central planning directions upon rapidly developing human service efforts. The cultural value of pluralism is likely to continue, and community councils will have to actively seek an equitable and fruitful role alongside governmental and other interests if they wish to participate in determining the shape of human service programs of the 1970's.

The Council's Constituency and Functions

The council's ability to surge forward as a major force in the planning of human services is, to some extent, impeded by the internal transitions through which it still is passing. The council is struggling to clarify the explicit and subtle implications of a changed constituency as it shifts from its previous role as a body of agencies to its current structure as a citizen's spokesman. Among the issues to be resolved is the relationship between the community council, with its increased planning orientation, and the United Fund, with its money-raising perspective. Although the concerns

of the two groups are largely congruent, they also diverge in significant instances. The community council's credibility as a spokesman
for human service interests would in many ways be enhanced by
assuming an advocacy position on controversial issues. However,
such a stance might also antagonize key contributors and so the
council must cautiously determine which role would produce optimal benefits at the lowest cost. An outcome of this dilemma is
that councils are reassessing traditional funding patterns and turning toward a greater mixture of voluntary, public, and private funds
rather than relying as heavily on voluntary funds alone. These
new sources of fiscal support provide the council with greater flexibility and permit it to venture into areas that previously had been
beyond its ken.

CONCLUSION

We are clearly in a period of transition and adaptation in providing human services more responsive to massive social problems.
These changes are not occurring in a vacuum but are the direct
result of new planning structures which have been stimulated and
supported by federal, state, and local governments. Community
councils are required to extend their functions and to concentrate
on broad social problems if they are to relate effectively to the
contemporary issues and to the wide variety of new service and
planning organizations. This requires both a short- and long-range
perspective and fresh conceptions of an effective pattern of public
and private human services.

The task will not be easy. The planning process in a pluralistic,
democratic society has few clear characteristics, but it nevertheless
is the object of widely-held suspicions. Americans generally have
viewed planning as somewhat subversive and particularly so when
it pertains to human services. Planning is equated with the "planned
society" which in turn is equated with socialism. Program planning
by the voluntary sector's community council has some limited positive sanctions although even this approach is often carefully monitored. The curious paradox in this public ambivalence toward
planning is that it most often is expressed by highly successful
entrepreneurs, those very individuals who regularly and un-
abashedly plan for the future of their own private enterprises.

The community council's movement from institutional tinkering
to macro-change in the field of human services, from intraagency
management studies to influencing social and public policy, will
not come easily but the opportunities are there. Significant national

trends clearly permit an enlarged and more active role for the voluntary community health and welfare planning organization if its leadership will sanction such a development and its staff capitalizes upon the opportunities.

REFERENCES

Banfield, E. C. Ends and means in planning. Page 70 in S. Malik and E. H. Van Ness (Eds.), *Concepts and issues in administrative behavior.* Englewood Cliffs: Prentice Hall, 1962.

Demone, H. W., Jr. Human services at state and local levels and the integration of mental health. In G. Caplan (Ed.), *American Handbook of Psychiatry,* Vol. III. New York: Basic Books, 1973.

Newman, E., and Demone, H. W., Jr. Policy paper: A new look at public planning for human services. *Journal of Health and Social Behavior,* 1969, 10 (June), 142–149.

Section C

Perspectives for the Future:
An Example in Future Planning—Health

As already noted in this volume, at the present time the health needs of the nation are grave, costly, and often unmet. Vast numbers of bio-social problems remain unnoticed by persons who do not live in "the other America." Among those persons who live in a more affluent America, and who can afford the costs of health services, the largest part of their health dollar is being spent for hospitalization, a form of treatment practice which is being increasingly questioned.

If we are to deal with these problems in the near future in a manner which improves upon our past performance, it will be essential that we alter our traditional perceptions and behaviors regarding both the problems themselves and our means of dealing with these problems. The articles in this section has been selected because they have a clear and present bearing upon our future.

38. The Health Agenda for the Future

James P. Dixon

What are the practical problems and decisions which comprehensive health plans must incorporate? What are viable organizational alternatives for human service organizations? Where will additional needed manpower come from? These are but a few of the questions health planners must answer in the immediate future. And, they are problems which Dixon deals with in the following article.

While the reader may not find himself in complete agreement with all of Dixon's proposals, the suggested alternatives give a sense of immediacy and reality to what often becomes a purely academic set of issues.

Whether or not Dixon's proposals are adopted, the problems and questions will remain, and they will have to be dealt with. The question is how.

Two clear ideological lines seem to run through discussions concerning public policy with regard to health and welfare. These arguments are based on assumptions that are broader and more general than those that pertain only to the health field. The old moral order consisted of a major concern with integrity and wholeness. Now, however, one can see a new morality developing, in which the concern is with honesty and antihypocrisy. But much public policy still reflects the old morality, based on compassion and on a concern for quality in the evolution of public policy regarding health and social insurance.

More and more, society is being exhorted to adapt to the new morality, with its great emphasis on not promising what cannot be delivered, and on developing programs to meet broad-based demands rather than just professionally drawn goals. In a sense, a new type of politician has become the prophet of the new morality, and the "true church" tends to be bedded in a public policy. While the old values—the old morality—have been the justification for the development of social policy in the past, it is doubtful that they can continue to be the basis for future policy in the face of the new wave of public insistence.

Dealing with that problem would seem to call for something that sounds as odd as "the constructive manipulation of hypocrisy." It will not be possible to implement public policy without a full professional commitment of support, and to get that kind of support the behavior of the politicians must be such as to attract it.

The second ideological line relates to the productive qualities in human organization. As a culture, the United States is moving into a situation where group autonomy is considered to be essential to the effective productivity of a societal unit. The reason why this is so is not fully understood, but it is clear that up and down the line a massive attack is being mounted on conventional hierarchical organization. Perhaps, having rejected a conventional Satan, society has seized on human organization as a substitute. The feeling is that an orderly establishment creates a premature closure on creativity—that it necessarily thwarts the individual. Progress must be antiauthoritarian; responsibility must be exercised in role, not in rule.

Both of these ideological lines—the new morality overturning the old and the growing disaffection with orderly organization—are crucial in considering the politics and practice in the delivery of health services in society. To use New York City as an example (and reasons may be found not to), evidence is plain of the public concern for meeting people's immediate needs in an honest straightforward way, rather than worrying about organizational integrity and hypothetical standards of quality.

A central development that has received too little attention is that of new technologies that complement the new morality. One can ask whether radical social change can be accomplished through new technologies. The evidence is that not very much technology of any kind has been introduced into the delivery of health services. That refers mainly to "hardware" developments such as educational television and the computer. On the other hand, such "hardware" may have a much more profound effect than is expected on how people decide to get their health care. It has been demonstrated, for example, that commercial television has profoundly altered the way in which young children develop vocabulary recognition, so how about concept recognition? It seems entirely likely that a generation is growing up with thought processes that are quite different from those developed in a culture limited to the spoken and written language for communications.

An outgrowth of the new morality is the growing conviction that the availability of services to the community is more important than the quality of those services. It is a public imperative and if it is recognized, strategy considerations become simplified. The

maintenance of quality standards in the health field will continue
to be important, of course, and will continue to be tended to in
quasipublic ways. But the demands for broad availability, coupled
with the drive for group autonomy in social units and in production
units, will inevitably produce a large toleration of variances in quality
for some time to come.

Major unresolved dilemmas are encountered in the matter of
maintaining quality standards. For example, the question of conflicts of interest should be examined, as when professionals who
are engaged to provide one kind of service in fact spend their
energies in other kinds of activity. One could cite teachers or
administrators who spend their time in consulting, clinicians who
spend their time in research and so on.

By and large, the American system has delegated to private
agencies the responsibility of minimizing conflicts of interest and
of maximizing quality. In the immediate years to come it will continue to be the public policy to assume that the private sector is
maintaining quality and that governmental agencies will be concentrated upon assuring wider accessibility and availability of services.

It is deplorable that this nation really has no coherent and systematic public policy on health and social services. It is all the
more deplorable since substantial movement is taking place in the
form of new and altered programs without substantial guidelines
based on public policy. (The one exception to this generalization
is the seemingly consistent policy regarding the economic impact
of government spending as it relates to fiscal and monetary results.)

Turning to pla.ining, regionalization and the development of
leadership, it is clear that much needs to be done. Currently the
situation could be described as a vacuum. The United States Public
Health Service seems to be the most likely agency in which substantial changes can take place and where forthright action can be
stimulated to fill this vacuum. The Public Health Service has the
logical role to play in taking the leadership in planning and
regionalization.

The United States is not without experience in regionalized health
planning. In New York state, for example, hospital and health
planning has been tied to governmental approval of hospital capital
proposals, which affect the hospitals through dynamic "selective
deprivation." That is, of course, based on the old morality and
therefore must be considered dead. This approach is one of making
austerity a virtue in the presence of affluence, similar to community
chests around the country, which are consistently dispensing
philanthropic funds on criteria drawn up without any reasonable

concern for social priorities. (Leading, for example, to support for suburban Boy Scout troops in communities with problems of squalor and poverty.)

It also seems doubtful that the "house of intellect" will be able to provide effective leadership in regionalization and health planning. Most medical schools and universities have nothing more than an intellectual interest in the delivery of health services. The medical schools actually have specific educational and research purposes that are quite inconsistent with the recommendations of the Coggeshall Report. Besides, even if one were to charge the educational establishment with a leadership role, the fact is that the medical schools and universities move with glacial speed. The medical school—indeed the institution of higher learning—is designed for stability and for slow adaptation. As such, it simply cannot be expected to serve as a central source of leadership in this fast-moving era of social change.

The potentialities of leadership developing through the political organization of consumers is a new enough social phenomenon to seem to have momentum at present. The current apparatus of the phenomenon may be too fragile to have a national impact at this time, but regionally, and in New York City in particular, it could be most useful.

In any event, with leadership unlikely to come from the medical schools or from the organized consumer, it is up to the federal government to develop its capacities. What is needed now is a new and innovative drive within the United States Public Health Service itself.

Much discussion has centered on the meaning of leadership. It may be defined as a means of inventing ways for innovative ideas to become public practice, to connect people with change, to let conservative strictures be relaxed so that the doers in the field can do. Specifically, leadership will require the imagination to give away money with very few strings attached regarding program, though without abandoning strict scrupulousness about malfeasance in spending.

The Public Health Service must make continuing attempts to enunciate public policy in health care, but in doing so it must draw heavily on the collective informed intellect of the professional health field. It must do so, however, without developing a dependence upon them for participation. The federal government is the logical candidate for the leadership role because the problems and challenges are too immense for any smaller entity to grasp.

It is appropriate to digress for a moment to discuss patronage as a tool of progress. Patronage is the substitute for violence in a humane society and is needed if a program is to work. It is difficult for the new morality to cope with the necessity for patronage—it can cope best when the political power is being wielded in a sheltered situation by a trusted institution such as the Public Health Service.

The professional field must protect the Public Health Service from gross errors in professional judgment. The Public Health Service can return the favor by building institutional protections for the field from patronage traps. In that sense the federal government can at once support and protect localized regional planning bodies.

America has established a clear pattern of delegating, for better or worse, the main responsibility for delivering health services to provider institutions and especially to hospitals. Unfortunately, it may be pure fantasy to think of today's hospital as having the capacity to be a community health center. But in any event, it certainly has an extraordinarily important role and is the key asset in the organization of services.

The central challenge is now to connect the hospitals with their new social setting. Would it be practical or feasible to create a new institution to be responsible for the delivery of health services? Not a health center in the conventional sense of the term, but a new institution with heavy local representation to take primary responsibilities in assuring the population of the delivery of services. The new institution might have to include a facility, but not necessarily so. It could well be a kind of referral system without its own care resources. Certainly improved delivery systems are needed, and some of the country's most inventive people must be put to work in developing proposals along that line.

The health institutions should be heavily consumer dominated for several reasons, but at least because it is becoming necessary politically. If its clientele are not satisfied with the delivery of services, the institution will be in a continuing crisis. "Quality" is too elusive to use as a criterion. In the political sense it is accessibility and availability that count. In any event, the old notions about the nature of quality in medical care are changing. Although nostalgic memories and some solid virtues remain in the idea of the personal physician, he represents an obsolete idea for the urban community.

The health care system must be organized on a basis broader than individual hospitals. The assumption must be removed that the individual in the community should adapt to the hospital-based delivery system. Instead, satisfactory health care must be produced with random contacts between people and the system.

On the subject of manpower, since the availability of health services has become a matter of public commitment, it becomes the responsibility of the federal establishment to see that sufficient manpower is made available to produce on the promise. A formal responsibility for the development of health manpower can no longer be avoided.

As to the form of the federal commitment to manpower development, the military model seems promising. Professional health academies should be created that are related to the needed deployment of manpower and to the employment system. A great deal of flexibility should be permitted in the organizational relationships of the national academies and they should be made strong and autonomous centers.

There is little hope that the existing educational institutions will be able to adapt to the health manpower demands of the country. Certainly it is inappropriate to ask a medical school, for example, to train health planners. New educational forms are needed, and are needed rapidly. As a part of that the national manpower commitment will logically lead toward systems of national licensure for health personnel. If severe handicaps of distribution are to be overcome, health personnel must be universally interchangeable. Moreover, ways must be explored to solve manpower shortages that do not require the training of new personnel. People with existing skills may be hired without training them anew. An example would be the feldschers who are functional in other countries.

On the subject of community development, the power of novelty is strong in social change. As function is at least partly the result of structure, and as structure is often accidental in its final form, an atmosphere is needed in which novel structures can be devised and implemented. In short, if a community shows sufficient agreement that health care has a high priority, the government should be willing to support innovative ideas simply because they are there.

It all depends on whether people really are concerned about health care, and that is doubtful at times. It is worth looking at carefully, for the health producers may be trapped in a fantasy about the high priority of health services in people's minds. The available evidence would seem to indicate that health ranks below such other community concerns as jobs, votes and perhaps even education. But if evidence can be adduced that health has a high priority in the community, that health care provides a key motivating force, then let us lay hold of this and capitalize on it.

In conclusion, a thought on the value of capitalizing on the initiative power of minority groups within the society. Society is well past the notion that consensus produces sound policy. The challenge is to learn to use minority positions creatively to improve public policy. It is the passion of minority concerns that can provoke rational solutions. Society must learn how to manipulate minority interests creatively for the sake of the majority. Action, finally, is where change is. If the change can be identified, progress has been made toward developing public policy.

39. Principles and Criteria for National Health Insurance

Committee on Public Policy of the Medical Sociology Section,
American Sociological Association

It is impossible to forecast what health care systems of the future will look like, other than to conservatively predict that they will bear some resemblance to what we now have (for better or worse). To be sure, a pluralism of organizational models and system linkages will emerge.

However, it will be very possible to accurately forecast the functional criteria against which programmatic and organizational innovation in health care systems will be assessed; criteria which may guide the development of future health delivery systems. They may well be those of the following article.

The Committee on Public Policy* of the Medical Sociology Section, American Sociological Association, proposes a framework and criteria by which interested parties may assess plans advanced for any program of National Health Insurance. This statement is not intended to represent support for any specific proposal, since it is clear that during the next year or two specific proposals will be steadily changing in the light of political and professional developments. The position of the Medical Sociology Section is based on both professional judgment and commitment to certain humanitarian democratic principles:

—that the people of the nation have a right to comprehensive health care;

—that such health care should be effective and of high quality;

*Members of the Committee on Public Policy are: Harold W. Demone, Jr., Ph.D., Chairman; Ray H. Elling, Ph.D. (Ex-officio); Nancy N. Anderson, Ph.D.; Mr. Kent R. Autor; Roger M. Battistella, Ph.D.; Mr. D. Brian Heller; Louisa P. Howe, Ph.D.; Mr. Herman D. James; Howard Kelman, Ph.D.; Bernard M. Kramer, Ph.D.; Monroe Lerner, Ph.D. The statement in its present form was written by Demone, Howe, and Kramer.

568 HANDBOOK OF HUMAN SERVICE ORGANIZATIONS

—that it should be provided at times and places that render
it accessible;

—that it should be coordinated with other programs relating
to health and the prevention of disease;

—that it should offer continuity of care for individuals and
families;

—that health care, including the production and distribution
of drugs and medical supplies should be regarded as service
to the community and to the nation, rather than as profit-
making enterprises;

—that the people have the right and responsibility to participate
in shaping health policies and programs; and

—that the government has the duty to assure that these health
rights are fulfilled.

Since the present health industry has not adequately provided
these necessary components to the total population of the United
States, and since health is so heavily vested with the public interest,
we believe that a major reorganization of the health care apparatus
in accordance with the principles stated above is both desirable
and necessary. We believe this is what National Health Insurance
could be. This objective will not be achieved, however, unless
national health proposals are evaluated for their impact on the
organization as well as the financing of health care.

Such existing public efforts are Medicare-Medicaid, although useful and vital experiments, have also proved to be deficient in certain
respects. Although succeeding in reducing the economic barriers
that prevented or hampered the aged and poor from obtaining
health care, these programs have contributed to the inflation of
health costs in recent years. These programs, however, are initial
and incomplete efforts of the government to assume its proper
responsibility in securing adequate health care. It is imperative
that the deficiencies of these preliminary efforts be overcome. The
government's responsibility today calls for assuring that improved
health care is extended to all.

Current debate over National Health Insurance shows far greater
concern with cost and financing than with health care objectives
and means of achieving them. A National Health Insurance Program may require substantial increases in the allocation of national
resources to meet health needs. But these needs should be met
economically; more effective use of existing resources might well
obviate major increases.

As an acceptable means of meeting health needs, National Health
Insurance should respond affirmatively to the following questions:

1. *Does it provide universal coverage to all residents of the United States?*

Such inclusive coverage will (1) minimize existing inequities in the availability of health care to different population groups; and (2) allow greater precision in the actuarial prediction of risk within the population, which in turn will permit more precise budgeting and allocating of health resources.

2. *Are financial barriers removed so that health care is available to all?*

Requirements such as co-insurance or deductible payments should be eliminated since they penalize the needy for their very need of care.

3. *Does it immediately seek to correct outstanding deficiencies in providing desirable health care to all?*

The development of a basic level of comprehensive care for the total population will need to be accomplished through successive phases. In moving toward such comprehensive care, priority should be given to health care for people heretofore disadvantaged by relative exclusion from access to health resources, in order to move as quickly as possible toward achieving equitable care of high quality for all Americans. These are:

a. the young
b. the poor
c. blacks and other minority groups
d. the aged
e. the permanently and totally disabled and their dependents
f. women of child-bearing age
g. residents of core cities and remote rural areas

4. *Does it assure comprehensive, high quality, continuous, coordinated health care to all citizens and residents of the nation?*

To be comprehensive, benefits should include not only diagnosis and treatment, but also services to promote health, prevent illness, and rehabilitate the casualties of sickness and injury. Continuity of services within this complex system is of crucial importance.

Comprehensive health care also includes primary, secondary, and tertiary preventive efforts, such as mass screening, nutrition, health education, and training of the handicapped. It includes such responsibilities as those for mental health, dental health, family planning, and genetic counseling.

5. *Does it provide means for maximizing consumer satisfaction, preserving individual dignity, and permitting choice among available subsystems of health care?*

In emphasizing the consumer, we do not ignore the necessity for meeting technical and professional standards; rather we wish to point out that assuring choice to the consumer encourages providers of care to be concerned with meeting the consumer's expressed needs and according him dignity and respect. Quality of care must be defined by consumer satisfaction as well as by professional acceptability.

6. *Does it reward economies and penalize wastefulness in the delivery of services?*

Without impairing quality and the capacity for innovation, compensation should aim at encouraging economy and minimizing wasted effort and resources in the organization of health services.

7. *Does it assure a balance of service, manpower development, facilities construction, and advancement of knowledge?*

The program should take a long view of growing needs of a growing population as well as changing technical and social conditions. It should include an over-all support system to deal with requirements in manpower, research, and facilities.

8. *Does it provide a fair basis for sharing the program's costs and take income level into account?*

General tax revenues should form the financial base of the program in order to assure an equitable distribution of the burden of costs.

9. *Is the program designed to meet public purposes and the public good? Is it open to scrutiny, and held accountable to the public?*

The imperative for public accountability justifies participation of consumers in setting policy and evaluating health programs. If there is to be a public-private partnership in the establishement and operation of National Health Insurance, then the principle of public accountability must be applied to health care providers. Continued public reporting of aggregate data about benefits, beneficiaries, and providers will enhance public accountability.

10. *Is the program an instrument of positive change to improve the existing health care system? Does the program itself have change capacity as well as built-in provisions for the assessment and control of quality?*

Both financial and regulatory mechanisms should be used to induce improvement in the organization, delivery, and quality of health services. The program should have a capacity for rational planning that can focus both on internal organizational dynamics and on larger system issues.

In order to assure continuing improvements in the quality of health care, it is important to provide for program monitoring in addition to permitting choice on the part of consumers or consumer groups.

11. *Are consumers and health workers included as legitimate partners in the planning of health policies and programs?*

Participation of consumers and subprofessional health workers in the decision-making processes will make policies and programs more responsive to public needs. Such participation will promote accountability and responsibility on the part of the system, and will tend to strengthen informed use of the health system.

12. *Does it promote linkages to the larger human service network?*

The program should encourage formal linkage of the health subsystem to the larger human services network. Policy, planning, and delivery efforts which support separation from, rather than integration with, this network should be discouraged.

Concluding Note

It is possible for a National Health Insurance Program to contribute significantly to improving the organization of health care. A number of alternative structural means are available. Existing health-related services could be linked by various sanctioning procedures. Existing voluntary associations or communities might contract with providers or groups of providers for the comprehensive services their members require. Or private and voluntary health service organizations serving specified populations residing in regions could be unified under a single line of authority and support.

Alternatively there could be a national network of regional administrative organizations, within each of which would be centralized certain administrative functions. Other integrating models have also been suggested.

Whatever organizational model is eventually chosen, it should be designed to meet the criteria included in this statement and simultaneously reflect sociological realities such as occupational, ethnic, and social class differences, neighborhood attachments, and community affiliations.

Index

Kahn, R. L., *see* Katz
Kaiser-Permanente Health Plan, 171
Kantor, David, "The Concept of Coordination by a State-Sponsored Alcoholism Program," 196-207
Kappel, Frederick, 539
Katz, D., and R. L. Kahn, 22, 24, 445, 453-59
The Social Psychology of Organizations, 454
on systems limitations, 456-58
Kelman, Howard C., 489, 567n
Kennedy, John F., 208-9, 275, 303, 339, 365
assassination of, 353
mental-health message of, 326
Kent, James A., "Involving the Urban Poor in Health Services Through Accommodation—The Employment of Neighborhood Representatives, 281-90
Kentucky, 170, 178-84
Kimberly-Clark Corp., 87
Kirkbride building projects, 48
Kirschner Associates study (1966), 136-37, 139-44, 146-48, 150-51
number of centers studied, 156
Kissinger, Henry A., 497
Klein, M. W., "Can the Behavioral Sciences Contribute to Organizational Effectiveness?: A Case Study," 396-411
on judgments of patient care, 405
Klir, G. J., 443
Knowles, Dr. John H., 169
Kramer, Bernard M., "Principles and Criteria for National Health Insurance," 567-71
Kramer, M., 431
Kravitz, Sanford, 134
Kristol, Irving, "Decentralization for What?" 208-18

Labor and Public Welfare Committee, Senate, 364

"Labor-relations" organization, 493
LaGuardia Hospital (New York), 86
Land assembly, 515-17
Lane, Dr. Philip, 272-75, 278
Lane, R. E., 495-96
Lasker, Albert D., 359-60
Lasker, Mary, 177, 358-72
influence exerted by, 358
Lasker Medical Awards, 358-59, 362
Lasswell, Harold, 501
Lawrence, P. R., 450-51, 453
Leadership, 310, 494-95
among the poor, 288
community, access to, 112
forecast for, 501-503, 562-63
in health field, 68, 562-63
See also Authority; Charisma
Leaves of absence, 502
Legitimacy, crisis in, 488-89
Levin, M., 77
Levine, Sol, 453, 500
"Organizational and Professionnal Barriers to Interagency Planning," 307n, 373-80
Levinson, D. J., 460
Lewin, Kurt, 19, 96, 493
Liberal-democratic reformers, 484
Life-cycle stages, 56-57
Life-expectancy (longevity) statistics, 170, 371
London, Samuel, 85-86
London-Sloan Program, 533
Long, David F., 12
"Information-Referral: The Nucleus of a Human-Needs Program," 128-32
Long, Norton E., 102, 122
Lorsch, J. W., 450-51, 453
Lowell, Mass., 317

McGregor, Douglas, 533
Machinist (publication), 363
McNamara, Robert S., 551
McNerney, Walter J., "Health Care Reforms: The Myths and Realities," 412-27

Organizational consultants, 227-
32
Organizational criteria, list of
four, 4
Organizational effectiveness, *see*
Effectiveness criterion
Organizational ends, *see* Goals
—organizational
Organizational metaphors, 492-93
Organizational networks, *see* Networks
Organizational socialization, 540-
41
Organizational theory, 22-25
applications of, 445-58
organization-environment
system, 449-53
organizational structure,
457-58
private vs. public organizations,
91-93
Oswald, Lee Harvey, 353
Outreach operations, neighborhood, 139
Overcrowding, pathological, 57-
58

Parks, 60
Parsons, Talcott, 276-86, 491
Partial adversary system, 382-83
Participation, citizen, 19, 489, 504,
568
on community councils, 548-50
decentralization affording, 208,
210-11
demand for, 235
in mental-health programs, 343
citizen control, 332-34, 346-
47
in neighborhood centers, 145,
152
technological threat to, 307-10
See also Community action; Personnel—subprofessional;
Political action; Social action; Volunteers
Partnership of Health Act (PL 89-
749) (1966), 67, 74, 302
Patient-teaching criterion, 404,
406
Patients, *see* Clients
Patronage, 563-64

Peattie, L. R., 9
Pennsylvania, regional programs
of, 78
People-belief-resource (PBR) system, 462, 464
People-processing system, 459-61
Pepper, Claude, 360
Perceived collaboration, 452-53
Percy, Charles H., 38-39, 49-52
Performance criteria, *see* Program
evaluation
Perkins, Carl, 180-82
Perlman, Robert, and David Jones,
15-16
on neighborhood centers, 136,
137, 139-41, 143, 145, 147-
49
number of centers studied by,
156
on social action, 148, 149, 151
"Permeable areas," 290
Personnel, service, 462-65, 486
administrative, 113, 152, 279,
309-10
bureaucratic forecast, 485
shifting power, 112
see also Management tools
—administrative
business vs. service, 27, 92, 460
civil-service, 350-52
communication problems of,
203-4
community-council, 554-55
health-care, 110-14, 419-22,
565, 570
increasing specialization,
106, 110, 306-7
labor walkouts, 111
new occupations, 106, 245-
46, 253, 281-90
OPD nurse behavior, 401-
404, 406-10
planning problems, 316, 321
politically active, 114
shortages, 165, 166, 175, 420
see also Physicians; Visiting
nurse associations
para-professional, 129, 245
subprofessional (nonprofessional), 571
indigenous, 137, 139, 141,
145, 147, 153

behavior, *see* Behavior psychology
organizational, 454
as professional sub-mode, 234-35, 239-40
Public building projects, 40-42, 48-50, 68, 296
design quality of, 41-42
groups isolated by, 58-59
sculptural criteria for, 41
Public health, 112
environmental health planning, 62-69
reform of, 412-27
community medicine and, 413, 422-25
See also Health care; Neighborhood representatives
Public Health Service, U.S., 167, 371, 562-64
Regional Director of, 351
Public Law 88-156, *see* PL 88-156
Public Law 89-749 (Partnership of Health Act) (1966), 67, 74, 302
Public policy, *see* Policy
Public Works and Development Act (1965), 77
Pyramiding (pine-tree structure), 477, 480, 543
of agencies, 7-8

Race, *see* Blacks; Ethnic groups
Racial heterogeneity, 215
Rainwater, Lee, 150
Reasoning ability as power base, 103
Rebellion, radical (revolution), 251-55, 264-66, 483, 491
ideology of, 251, 497-98
Reciprocity as power base, 105
Recreation, 45, 426, 555
neighborhood center providing, 135
play-space allocation, 40, 47
Reductionism, 255-66
pragmatic, 262-63, 266
Referral, *see* Alcoholism treatment programs—clinical-referral program; Information and referral services
Referral patterns, 464-65

Reform-school rehabilitation, 191-92
Regional delivery systems, 70-81, 424
development of, 77-80
purposes of, 75-77
Regional health planning, 116, 118-121, 168, 420
environmental planning, 74-75, 77-79
future, 562-64, 571
major impact of, 103
regional mental-health boards, 346-47
Regional Medical Care Program, 113, 115
Regressors, 483
Rehabilitation agency goals, 375-76
Reiff, Robert, 283-84
Rein, Martin, 150, 335
Reissman, Frank, 283-84
Relevant uncertainty, 94-95, 485
Renewal programs, *see* Urban renewal
Report to Greco (Kazantzakis), 482
Republican Party, 344, 347-51, 353
Research, 485, 489-90, 530-35, 570
on alcoholism, 188-89, 202
behavior, 396-411
motivation, 541
research-produced problems, 399-403
secrecy of purpose, 402
evaluative, 404, 421, 429-73
mental-health data, *see* Community mental-health services—interpreting the data for
neighborhood studies reviewed, 138-52
periodic monitoring, 396
research-development subsystem, 452
systems applications, 442-73
traditional evaluation model, 468-70
funding of, *see* Finance—scientific research funds

experimental approaches, 239-41
health administrators, 120-21
in-service, 246, 410
learning social roles, 449
medical schools, 113, 320, 563
national health academies, 565
nonprofessionals, 245-46, 286-87
planning barrier, 376-77
status base, 226
see also Social workers—training of
See also Alcohol education programs; Schools
Trans-Action (periodical), 385
Transference, therapeutic, 277-78
Transportation, 46, 59, 61, 73
Trist, E. L., 93-95, 446-47, 460, 467, 487, 500
"The Causal Texture of Organizational Environments," 450
Trow, M., 491
Truman, Bess, 360, 366
Truman, Harry S, 349, 360
Turbulent environment, *see* Environmental turbulence
TVA (Tennessee Valley Authority), 424

Uncertainty, 94-95, 485
United Community Services of Metropolitan Boston, 128-29
United Funds, 80, 553, 556-57
budgeting tactics of, 381-83, 385-86, 390
financial support from, 13, 329
United Kingdom (Great Britain), 446-47, 526n, 532, 536
management training in 533, 538
social administration of, 235
See also Royal Society; Tavistock Institute of Human Relations
Universalism, 276
Urban complexity, 60
"Urban regions," 77

Urban renewal, 207, 507-23
given housing age, 507-12
dwelling conversion, 519-20, 523
projected age and removals, 510-12
by private developers, 511-19
obstacles, 512-13, 519
public programs of, 511, 513-19
housing unit's size, 515-16
See also Central-city decay; Model Cities Program

Values, 266, 307, 310, 425
business vs. service, 27
human needs vs. economic, 64-66
future analysis of, 485-87, 491, 494, 504
conformity, 540, 544
cultural values, 556
dissensus, 496-97
health as, 118, 282-83, 285, 423
politics deemphasized in, 275-76
turbulence affecting, 95-97
value conflicts, 18
value judgments, 398
See also Ideology; Morality
Variety vs. homogeneity, 467
Vietnam War, 251, 253, 482, 549
Violence, 353, 549, 564
as power base, 105, 266
"Visible government," 210
Visiting nurse associations, 297, 374, 376-77
regional program of, 75-76
Vocational rehabilitation, 302, 306-7, 569
Volpe, John A., 342, 345, 347-53
special-session clout used by, 348-50, 357-59
Voluntary human services, 321, 552-54, 557-58, 571
domain of, 328, 331-32
growth of, 106
regionalization of, 78, 80
See also Community councils; United Funds
Volunteers, staff, 75, 130; *see also* Personnel—subprofessional
Voter registration, sponsorship of, 149